P9-CQS-664

VALENCIA AND MURCIA
Pages 232–253

ARAGÓN
Pages 216–231

CATALONIA
Pages 196–215

Donostia
(San Sebastián)

Iruña
(Pamplona)

0 kilometres   100

0 miles   100

Zaragoza   Lleida

Barcelona

EASTERN SPAIN

BARCELONA
Pages 132–185

THE BALEARIC ISLANDS

Cuenca

Palma de
Mallorca

Albacete

Valencia

Alacant
(Alicante)

Murcia

THE BALEARIC ISLANDS
Pages 482–503

mería

THE CANARY ISLANDS

THE CANARY ISLANDS
Pages 504–527

ANDALUSIA
Pages 434–477

Santa Cruz
de Tenerife

Las Palmas
de Gran Canaria

EYEWITNESS TRAVEL GUIDES

SPAIN

EYEWITNESS TRAVEL GUIDES

SPAIN

DK

DK PUBLISHING

LONDON • NEW YORK • MUNICH
MELBOURNE • DELHI

PROJECT EDITOR Nick Inman
US EDITORS Mary Sutherland, Michael Wise
ART EDITORS Jaki Grosvenor, Janis Utton
EDITORS Catherine Day, Lesley McCave, Seán O'Connell
DESIGNERS Susan Blackburn, Dawn Davies-Cook,
Joy Fitzsimmons, Helen Westwood

MAIN CONTRIBUTORS
John Ardagh, David Baird, Vicky Hayward, Adam Hopkins,
Lindsay Hunt, Nick Inman, Paul Richardson, Martin Symington,
Nigel Tisdall, Roger Williams

PHOTOGRAPHERS
Max Alexander, Joe Cornish, Neil Lukas, Neil Mersh,
John Miller, Kim Sayer, Linda Whitwam, Peter Wilson

ILLUSTRATORS
Stephen Conlin, Gary Cross, Richard Draper,
Isidoro González-Adalid Cabezas (Acanto Arquitectura y
Urbanismo S.L.), Claire Littlejohn, Maltings Partnership,
Chris Orr & Assocs, John Woodcock

Reproduced by Colourscan (Singapore)
Printed and bound by South China Printing Co. Ltd, China

First American Edition, 1996
8 10 9 7
Published in the United States by
DK Publishing, Inc., 375 Hudson Street,
New York, New York 10014
**Reprinted with revisions 1996, 1997, 1999, 2000, 2001,
2002, 2003**

Copyright 1996, 2003 © Dorling Kindersley Limited, London
A Penguin Company

Published in Great Britain by Dorling Kindersley Limited.

A CATALOGING IN PUBLICATION RECORD IS AVAILABLE FROM
THE LIBRARY OF CONGRESS.

ISBN 0 7894 9388 8

THROUGHOUT THIS BOOK, FLOORS ARE REFERRED TO IN ACCORDANCE
WITH EUROPEAN USAGE, I.E. "FIRST FLOOR" IS ONE FLOOR UP.

See our complete product line at
www.dk.com

**The information in this
Dorling Kindersley Travel Guide is checked annually.**
Every effort has been made to ensure that this book is as up-to-date
as possible at the time of going to press. Some details, however,
such as telephone numbers, opening hours, prices, gallery hanging
arrangements and travel information, are liable to change. The
publishers cannot accept responsibility for any consequences arising
from the use of this book, nor for any material on third-party
websites, and cannot guarantee that any website address in this
book will be a suitable source of travel information. We value the
views and suggestions of our readers highly. Please write to:
Publisher, DK Eyewitness Travel Guides,
Dorling Kindersley, 80 Strand, London, Great Britain WC2R 0RL.

CONTENTS

HOW TO USE
THIS GUIDE 6

King Alfonso X the Learned

INTRODUCING
SPAIN

NORTHERN SPAIN

BARCELONA

Previous pages: Pilgrimage of the Virgin of the Bridges, Belalcázar, near Córdoba in Andalusia

Grapes growing in La Mancha, the world's largest expanse of vineyards

Statue of Alfonso XII, Madrid

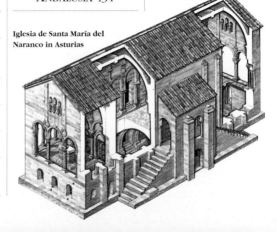
Iglesia de Santa María del
Naranco in Asturias

HOW TO USE THIS GUIDE

THIS GUIDE helps you to get the most from your visit to Spain. It provides detailed practical information and expert recommendations. *Introducing Spain* maps the country and sets it in its historical and cultural context. The five regional sections, plus *Barcelona* and *Madrid,* describe important sights, using maps, photographs and illustrations. Features cover topics from food and wine to fiestas and beaches. Restaurant and hotel recommendations can be found in *Travellers' Needs.* The *Survival Guide* has tips on everything from transport to using the telephone system.

BARCELONA, MADRID AND SEVILLE

These cities are divided into areas, each with its own chapter. A last chapter, *Further Afield,* covers peripheral sights. Madrid Province, surrounding the capital, has its own chapter. All sights are numbered and plotted on the chapter's area map. Information on each sight is easy to locate as it follows the numerical order on the map.

Sights at a Glance lists the chapter's sights by category: Churches and Cathedrals, Museums and Galleries, Streets and Squares, Historic Buildings, Parks and Gardens.

All pages relating to Madrid have green thumb tabs. Barcelona's are pink and Seville's are red.

A locator map shows where you are in relation to other areas of the city centre.

1 Area Map
For easy reference, sights are numbered and located on a map. City centre sights are also marked on Street Finders: Barcelona *(pages 175–81);* Madrid *(pages 297–303);* Seville *(pages 429–33).*

2 Street-by-Street Map
This gives a bird's-eye view of the key areas in each chapter.

Stars indicate the sights that no visitor should miss.

A suggested route for a walk is shown in red.

3 Detailed information
The sights in the three main cities are described individually. Addresses, telephone numbers, opening hours, admission charges, tours, photography and wheelchair access are also provided, as well as public transport links.

1 Introduction
The landscape, history and character of each region is outlined here, showing how the area has developed over the centuries and what it has to offer to the visitor today.

SPAIN AREA BY AREA
Apart from Barcelona, Madrid and Seville, the country has been divided into 12 regions, each of which has a separate chapter. The most interesting cities, towns and villages, and other places to visit are numbered on a *Pictorial Map*.

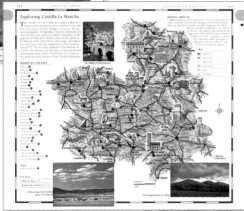

2 Pictorial Map
This shows the road network and gives an illustrated overview of the whole region. All interesting places to visit are numbered and there are also useful tips on getting to, and around, the region by car and public transport.

Fiesta boxes highlight the best traditional fiestas in the region.

Each area of Spain can be quickly identified by its colour coding, shown on the inside front cover.

3 Detailed information
All the important towns and other places to visit are described individually. They are listed in order, following the numbering on the Pictorial Map. *Within each town or city, there is detailed information on important buildings and other sights.*

For all top sights, a Visitors' Checklist provides the practical information you will need to plan your visit.

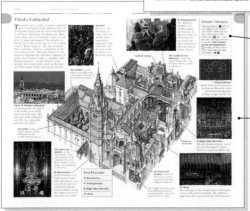

4 Spain's top sights
These are given two or more full pages. Historic buildings are dissected to reveal their interiors. The most interesting towns or city centres are shown in a bird's-eye view, with sights picked out and described.

INTRODUCING
SPAIN

Putting Spain on the Map

S PAIN, IN SOUTHWESTERN Europe, covers the greater part
of the Iberian Peninsula. The third largest country in
Europe, it includes two island groups: the Canaries in the
Atlantic and the Balearics in the Mediterranean, and two
small territories in North Africa. Its southernmost point
faces Morocco across a strait,
making Spain a
bridge between
continents.

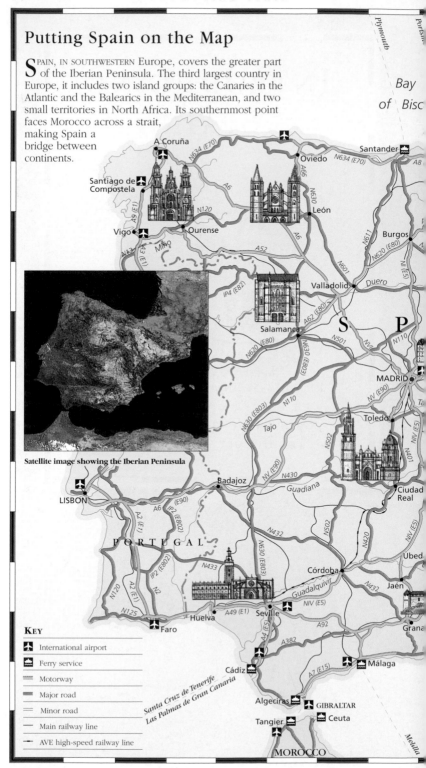

Satellite image showing the Iberian Peninsula

KEY

✈	International airport
⛴	Ferry service
▬	Motorway
▬	Major road
═	Minor road
—	Main railway line
→	AVE high-speed railway line

◁ *Rooftops, Fortna Lux, Mallorca* (1969) by Frederick Gore

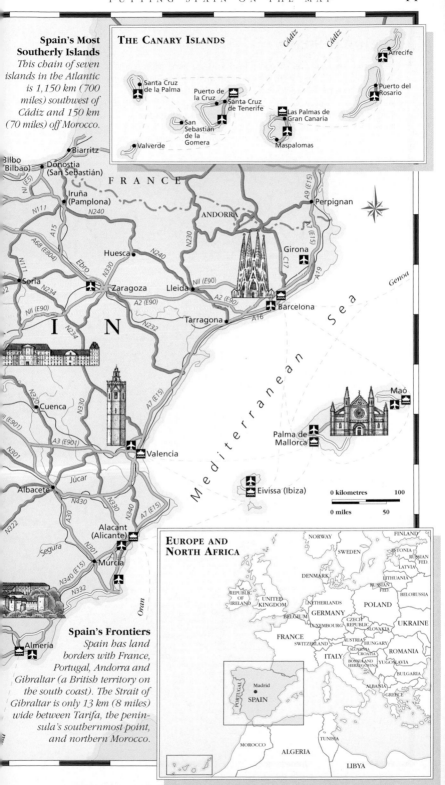

THE CANARY ISLANDS

Cádiz   Cádiz

Arrecife

Santa Cruz de la Palma

Puerto de la Cruz

Santa Cruz de Tenerife

Puerto del Rosario

San Sebastián de la Gomera

Las Palmas de Gran Canaria

Valverde

Maspalomas

Spain's Most Southerly Islands
This chain of seven islands in the Atlantic is 1,150 km (700 miles) southwest of Cádiz and 150 km (70 miles) off Morocco.

Biarritz

Bilbo (Bilbao)

Donostia (San Sebastián)

N I (E5)

F R A N C E

Iruña (Pamplona)

N111

N240

ANDORRA

Perpignan

A9 (E15)

A15

A68 (E804)

Huesca

N240

N330

N II (E90)

Girona

A9

C17

Soria

N111

N234

Ebro

Zaragoza

Lleida

N II (E90)

Barcelona

Genoa

N234

A2 (E90)

A2 (E90)

Tarragona

A16

I   N

N232

Maó

M e d i t e r r a n e a n   S e a

Cuenca

N320

N330

A7 (E15)

Palma de Mallorca

N320 (E901)

A3 (E901)

Valencia

Júcar

Albacete

N301

N340

A7 (E15)

Eivissa (Ibiza)

0 kilometres   100

0 miles   50

N322

N30

Segura

Alacant (Alicante)

N301

Murcia

N340 (E15)

N332

Oran

Almería

EUROPE AND NORTH AFRICA

Spain's Frontiers
Spain has land borders with France, Portugal, Andorra and Gibraltar (a British territory on the south coast). The Strait of Gibraltar is only 13 km (8 miles) wide between Tarifa, the peninsula's southernmost point, and northern Morocco.

NORWAY

SWEDEN

FINLAND

DENMARK

ESTONIA

RUSSIAN FED.

LATVIA

LITHUANIA

REPUBLIC OF IRELAND

UNITED KINGDOM

RUSSIAN FED.

BELORUSSIA

NETHERLANDS

GERMANY

POLAND

BELGIUM

LUXEMBOURG

CZECH REPUBLIC

UKRAINE

FRANCE

SWITZERLAND

AUSTRIA

HUNGARY

SLOVAKIA

SLOVENIA

ROMANIA

ITALY

CROATIA

BOSNIA AND HERZEGOVINA

YUGOSLAVIA

BULGARIA

PORTUGAL

Madrid

SPAIN

ALBANIA

GREECE

MOROCCO

ALGERIA

TUNISIA

LIBYA

Regional Spain

Spain has a population of 39 million and receives more than 57 million visitors a year. It covers an area of 504,780 sq km (194,900 sq miles). Madrid is the largest city, followed by Barcelona and Valencia. The country is dominated by a central plateau drained by the Duero, Tagus (Tajo) and Guadiana rivers. This book divides Spain into 15 areas, but officially it has 17 independent regions called *comunidades autónomas*.

GETTING AROUND

Spain's regional capitals and islands are linked by regular flights and there is a shuttle service between Madrid and Barcelona. The TALGO and AVE high-speed trains provide fast rail services between many provincial cities and are backed up by regional and local rail networks. Some motorways have expensive tolls, but are fast. Other roads range from rapid, modern highways to scenic, but often rough, byways. The Balearic and Canary islands are served by regular ferries from the mainland.

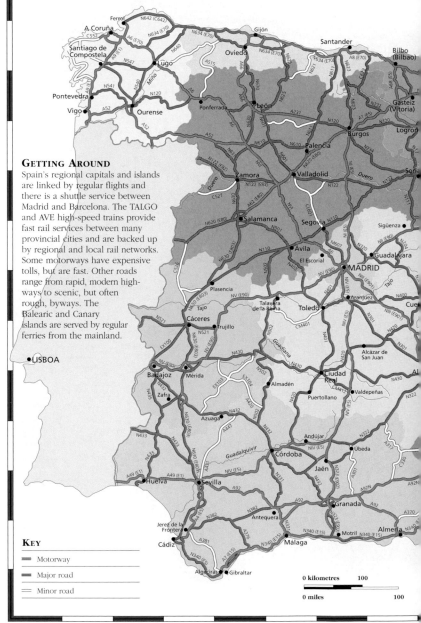

KEY

— Motorway

— Major road

— Minor road

0 kilometres   100

0 miles   100

Eyewitness Spain Regions

Each of the chapters in this guide has a colour code. The chapters are grouped into five sections: Northern, Eastern, Central and Southern Spain and Spain's Islands; and two cities: Madrid and Barcelona.

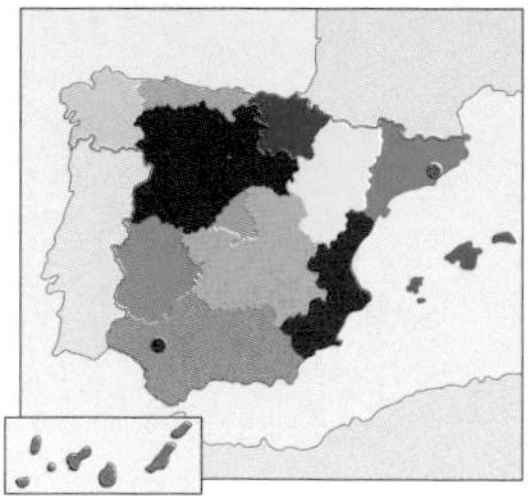

stiá
(Sebastián)

Iruña
(Pamplona)

N135

N240

NA125

N330(E7)

A127

N134

Tudel

Zaragoza

NII (E90)

N232

A2(E90)

Huesca

N123

N240

N330

N260

N330

N230

N260

N152

La Seu
d'Urgell

N260

C26

Figueres

Vic

C17

A7 (E15)

Girona

Manresa

C16 (E9)

Lleida

A2(E90)

NII

A7 (E15)

Barcelona

N211

N420

Reus

Tarragona

N234

Ebro

Tortosa

N232

Teruel

N330

CV15

CV190

N34

Castelló de la Plana

CV35

A3 (E901)

Turia

Sagunt

N340

Valencia

N330

A7 (E15)

Imansa

N330

Alcoi

Benidorm

N344

A7 (E15)

Alacant
(Alicante)

Elx

N301

Murcia

Cartagena

THE BALEARIC ISLANDS

Ciutadella

Menorca

Maó

Mallorca

Palma de
Mallorca

PM27 (E25)

Manacor

Cabrera

Ibiza

C731

Eivissa (Ibiza)

Formentera

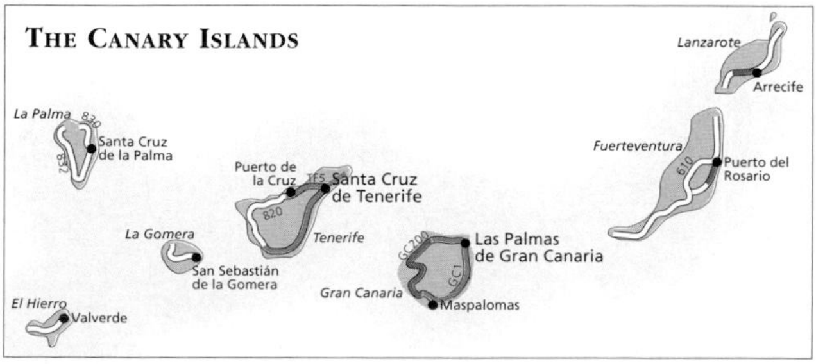

THE CANARY ISLANDS

Lanzarote

Arrecife

La Palma

B20

Santa Cruz
de la Palma

Fuerteventura

Puerto del
Rosario

Puerto de
la Cruz

TF5

Santa Cruz
de Tenerife

La Gomera

B20

Tenerife

GC2

Las Palmas
de Gran Canaria

San Sebastián
de la Gomera

Gran Canaria

GC1

El Hierro

Valverde

Maspalomas

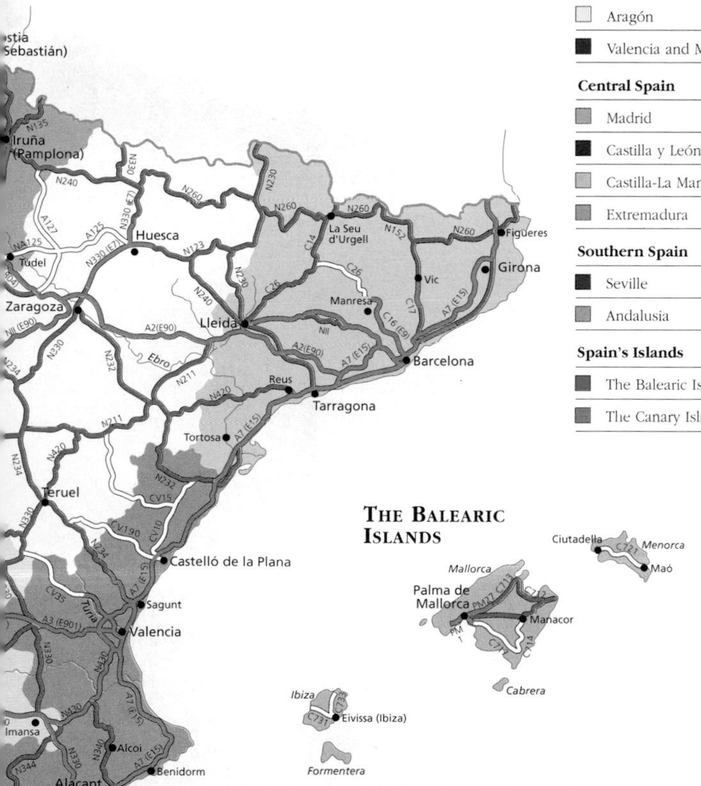

Spain's Atlantic Territories

The Canary Islands, in the Atlantic Ocean off the coast of Africa, are an integral part of Spain. They are one hour behind the rest of the country.

A PORTRAIT OF SPAIN

THE FAMILIAR IMAGES OF SPAIN – *flamenco dancing, bullfighting, tapas bars and solemn Easter processions – do no more than hint at the diversity of the country. Spain has four official languages, two major cities of almost equal importance and a greater range of landscapes than any other European country. These remarkable contrasts make Spain an endlessly fascinating country to visit.*

Separated from the rest of Europe by the Pyrenees, Spain reaches south to the coast of North Africa. It has both Atlantic and Mediterranean coastlines, and includes two archipelagos – the Balearics and the Canary Islands.

The climate and landscape vary from snow-capped peaks in the Pyrenees, through the green meadows of Galicia and the orange groves of Valencia, to the desert of Almería. Madrid is the highest capital in Europe, and Spain its most mountainous country after Switzerland and Austria. The innumerable sierras have always hindered communications. Until railways were built it was easier to move goods from Barcelona to South America than to Madrid.

In early times, Spain was a coveted prize for foreign conquerors including the Phoenicians and the Romans. During the Middle Ages, much of it was ruled by the Moors, who arrived from North Africa in the 8th century. It was reconquered by Christian forces, and unified at the end of the 15th century. A succession of rulers tried to impose a common culture, but Spain remains as culturally diverse as ever. Several regions have maintained a strong sense of their own independent identities. Many Basques and Catalans, in particular, do not consider themselves

Statue of Don Quixote and Sancho Panza, Madrid

Landscape with a solitary cork tree near Albacete in Castilla-La Mancha

◁ **The outlandishly dressed *Peliqueiros* who take to the streets during Carnival in Laza, Galicia**

Peñafiel castle in the Duero valley (Castilla y León), built between the 10th and 13th centuries

to be Spanish. Madrid may be the nominal capital but it is closely rivalled in commerce, the arts and sport by Barcelona, the main city of Catalonia.

THE SPANISH WAY OF LIFE

The inhabitants of this very varied country have few things in common except for a natural sociability and a zest for living. Spaniards commonly put as much energy into enjoying life as they do into their work. The stereotypical *"mañana"* (leave everything until tomorrow) is a myth, but time is flexible in Spain and many people bend their work to fit the demands

"Vinegar Face" in Pamplona's Los Sanfermines fiesta

of their social life, rather than let themselves be ruled by the clock. The day is long in Spain and Spanish has a word, *madrugada*, for the time between midnight and dawn, when city streets are often still lively.

Spaniards are highly gregarious. In many places people still go out in the evening for the *paseo*, when the streets are crowded with strollers. Eating is invariably communal and big groups often meet up for tapas or dinner. Not surprisingly, Spain has more bars and restaurants per head than any other country.

Underpinning Spanish society is the extended family. Traditionally, the state in Spain has been very inefficient at providing public services – although this has improved in the last 20 years. The Spanish have therefore always relied on their families and personal connections, rather than institutions, to find work or seek assistance in a crisis. This attitude has sometimes led to a disregard for general interests – such as the environment – when they have conflicted with private ones.

Most Spaniards place their family at the centre of their lives. Three generations may live together under one roof, or at least see each other often. Even

Tables outside a café in Madrid's Plaza Mayor

lifelong city-dwellers refer fondly to their *pueblo* – the town or village where their family comes from and where they return whenever they can. Children are adored in Spain and, consequently, great importance is attached to education. The family in Spain, however, is under strain as couples increasingly opt for a higher income and better lifestyle rather than a large family. One of the most striking transformations in modern Spain has been in the birth rate, from one of the highest in Europe, at 2.72 children for every woman in 1975, to one of the lowest in the world, only 1.07 in 1999.

The windmills and castle above Consuegra, La Mancha

Virgin of Guadalupe in Extremadura

Catholicism is still a pervasive influence over Spanish society, although church attendance among those under 35 has declined in recent years to below 25 per cent. The images of saints watch over some shops, bars and lorry drivers' cabs. Church feast days are marked by countless traditional fiestas which are enthusiastically maintained in modern Spain.

SPORT AND THE ARTS

Spanish cultural life has been reinvigorated in recent years. Spanish-made films – notably those of cult directors Pedro Almodóvar and Bigas Luna – have been able to compete effectively with Hollywood for audiences. The overall level of reading has risen (though only one in ten buy a daily newspaper), and contemporary literature has steadily gained a wider readership. The performing arts have been restricted by a lack of facilities, but recent major investments have provided new venues, regional arts centres and new symphony orchestras. The country has

A matador plays a bull in the Plaza de Toros de la Maestranza, Seville

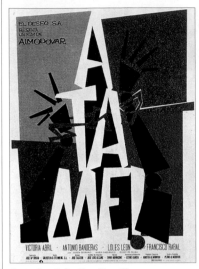

Poster for a Pedro Almodóvar film

the mainstays of TV programming. Spanish sportsmen and women have been very successful – for example, tennis players Conchita Martínez, Juan Carlos Ferrero, and Arantxa Sánchez Vicario, cyclists Miguel Induráin and Oscar Freire. Such role models have encouraged participation in sport and new facilities have been provided to meet this demand. Most popular are basketball and, above all, soccer.

Bullfighting has enjoyed renewed popularity since the late 1980s. For aficionados, a *corrida* is a unique occasion that provides a link to Spain's roots, and the noise, colour and argumentative attitude of the crowd are as much of an attraction as the bullfight itself.

produced many remarkable opera singers including Montserrat Caballé, Plácido Domingo and José Carreras. Spain has also excelled in design, particularly evident in the interior furnishings shops of Barcelona.

Spaniards are the most avid TV-watchers in Europe after the British. There are now 16 state-owned TV channels in Spain, as well as the various independent channels and many regional TV stations. Sports are one of

SPAIN TODAY

In the last 40 years Spain has undergone more social change than anywhere else in western Europe. Until the 1950s, Spain was predominantly a poor, rural country, in which only 37 per cent of the population lived in towns of over 10,000 people. By the 1990s, the figure was 65 per cent. As people flooded into towns and cities many rural areas became depopulated. The 1960s saw the beginning of

A farmer with his crop of maize hanging to dry on the outside of his house in the hills of Alicante

Beach near Tossa de Mar on the Costa Brava

The Basque terrorist group ETA is a constant thorn in the side of Spanish democracy.

During the 1980s Spain enjoyed an economic boom as service industries and manufacturing expanded. Even so, GDP remains below the European Union average and growth has been very unevenly spread around the country. Agriculture is an important industry but while it is highly developed in some regions, it is inefficient in others. Tourism provides approximately ten per cent of the country's earnings. Most tourists still come for beaches. But increasingly, foreign visitors are drawn by Spain's rich cultural heritage and spectacular countryside. Anyone who knows this country, however, will tell you that it is the Spanish people's capacity to enjoy life to the full that is Spain's biggest attraction.

spectacular economic growth, partly due to a burgeoning tourist industry. In that decade, car ownership increased from 1 in 100 to 1 in 10.

After the death of dictator General Franco in 1975 Spain became a constitutional monarchy under King Juan Carlos I. The post-Franco era, up until the mid-1990s, was dominated by the Socialist Prime Minister Felipe González. As

King Juan Carlos I and Queen Sofía

well as presiding over major improvements in roads, education and health services, the Socialists increased Spain's international standing. The PSOE could not continue forever, however, and in 1996 revelations of a series of scandals lost the PSOE the election. Spain joined the European Community in 1986, triggering a spectacular increase in the country's prosperity. The country's fortunes seemed to peak in the extraordinary year of 1992, when Barcelona staged the Olympic Games and Seville hosted a world fair, Expo '92.

With the establishment of democracy, the 17 autonomous regions of Spain have acquired considerable powers. Several have their own languages which are officially given equal importance to Spanish (strictly called Castilian). A significant number of Basques favour independence for the Basque Country.

Demonstration for Catalan independence

Architecture in Spain

SPAIN HAS ALWAYS IMPORTED its styles of architecture: Moorish from North Africa, Romanesque and Gothic from France and Renaissance from Italy. Each style, however, was interpreted in a distinctively Spanish way, with sudden and strong contrasts between light and shady areas; façades alternating between austerity and extravagant decoration; and thick walls pierced by few windows to lessen the impact of heat and sunlight. Styles vary from region to region, reflecting the division of Spain before unification. The key design of a central patio surrounded by arcades has been a strong feature of civil buildings since Moorish times.

The 15th-century Casa de Conchas in Salamanca *(see p343)*

ROMANESQUE AND EARLIER (8TH–13TH CENTURIES)

Romanesque churches were mainly built in Catalonia and along the pilgrim route to Santiago *(see p79)*. Their distinctive features include round arches, massive walls and few windows. Earlier churches were built in Pre-Romanesque *(see 102)* or Mozarabic *(see p335)* style.

Round arch   **Multiple apses**

The Romanesque Sant Climent, Taüll *(p201)*

MOORISH (8TH–15TH CENTURIES)

The Moors *(see pp48–9)* reserved the most lavish decoration for the interior of buildings, where ornate designs based on geometry, calligraphy and plant motifs were created in *azulejos* (tiles) or stucco. They made extensive use of the horseshoe arch, a feature inherited from the Visigoths *(see pp46–7)*. The greatest surviving works of Moorish architecture *(see pp404–5)* are in Southern Spain.

The Salón de Embajadores in the Alhambra (see p466) *has exquisite Moorish decoration.*

GOTHIC (12TH–16TH CENTURIES)

Gothic was imported from France in the late 12th century. The round arch was replaced by the pointed arch which, because of its greater strength, allowed for higher vaults and taller windows. External buttresses were added to prevent the walls of the nave from **Gothic arched** leaning outwards. Carved decoration **window** was at its most opulent in the Flamboyant Gothic style of the 15th century. After the fall of Granada, Isabelline, a late Gothic style, developed. Meanwhile, Moorish craftsmen working in reconquered areas created the highly decorative hybrid Christian-Islamic style Mudéjar *(see p51)*.

Rose window   **Tracery**

Pointed arch   **Flying buttress**

The nave of León Cathedral (see pp336–7), *built in the 13th century, is supported by rib vaulting and is illuminated by the finest display of stained glass in Spain.*

Sculptural decoration above the doorways of León cathedral's south front depicted biblical stories for the benefit of the largely illiterate populace.

RENAISSANCE (16TH CENTURY)

Around 1500 a new style was introduced to Spain by Italian craftsmen and Spanish artists who had studied in Italy. The Renaissance was a revival of the style of Ancient Rome. It is distinguished by its sense of symmetry and the use of the round arch, and Doric, Ionic and Corinthian columns. Early Spanish Renaissance architecture is known as Plateresque because its fine detail resembles ornate silverwork (*platero* means silversmith).

The Palacio de las Cadenas in Úbeda (see p473) has a severely Classical façade.

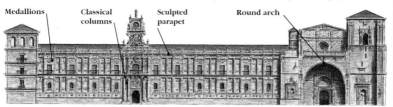

Medallions   Classical columns   Sculpted parapet   Round arch

The Hostal de San Marcos in León (see p335), one of Spain's finest Plateresque buildings

BAROQUE (17TH–18TH CENTURIES)

Baroque was driven by a desire for drama and movement. Decoration became extravagant, with exuberant sculpture and twisting columns. Although the excessive Baroque style of Churrigueresque is named after the Churriguera family of architects, it was their successors who were its main exponents.

The ornamentation on the Baroque façade of Valladolid University (see p348) is concentrated above the doorway.

Finials   Statues on parapet

The façade of the Museo Municipal in Madrid (pp294–5)

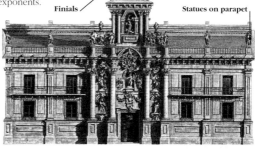

MODERN (LATE 19TH CENTURY ONWARDS)

Modernisme (see pp136–7), a Catalan interpretation of Art Nouveau, is seen at its best in Barcelona. Its architects experimented with a highly original language of ornament. In recent decades, Spain has seen an explosion of bold, functionalist architecture in which the form of a building reflects its use and decoration is sparingly used.

Torre de Picasso in Madrid

Curving parapet   Spiral chimney   Decorative ironwork

Casa Milà, in Barcelona (see p161), was built in 1910 by Modernisme's most famous and best-loved architect, Antoni Gaudí, who drew much of his inspiration from nature.

Vernacular Architecture

A<small>S WELL AS ITS CATHEDRALS</small> and palaces, Spain has a great variety of charming vernacular buildings. These have been constructed by local craftsmen to meet the practical needs of rural communities and to take account of local climate conditions, with little reference to formal architectural styles. Due to the high expense involved in transporting raw materials, builders used whatever stone or timber lay closest to hand. The three houses illustrated below incorporate the most common characteristics of village architecture seen in different parts of Spain.

Window in Navarra

A cave church in Artenara *(see p521)*, on Gran Canaria

STONE HOUSE

The climate is wet in the north and houses like this one in Carmona *(see p107)*, in Cantabria, are built with overhanging eaves to shed the rain. Wooden balconies catch the sun.

Detail of stonework

Family and farm often share rural houses. The ground floor is used to stable animals, or store tools and firewood.

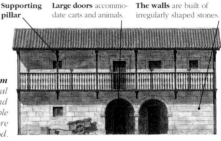

Supporting pillar

Large doors accommodate carts and animals.

The walls are built of irregularly shaped stones.

TIMBER-FRAMED HOUSE

Spain, in general, has few large trees and wood is in short supply. Castilla y León is one of the few regions where timber-framed houses, such as this one in Covarrubias *(see p352)*, can be found. These houses are quick and cheap to build. The timber frame is filled in with a coarse plaster mixed from lime and sand, or adobe (bricks dried in the sun).

Half-timbered wall

The ends of the beams supporting the floorboards are visible.

Stone plinths below upright timbers provide protection from damp.

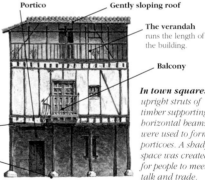

Portico

Gently sloping roof

The verandah runs the length of the building.

Balcony

In town squares, upright struts of timber supporting horizontal beams were used to form porticoes. A shady space was created for people to meet, talk and trade.

WHITEWASHED HOUSE

Houses in the south of Spain – often built of baked clay – are regularly whitewashed to deflect the sun's intense rays. Andalusia's famous white towns *(see p444)* exemplify this attractive form of architecture.

Clay-tiled roof

Windows are small and few in number, and deeply recessed, in order to keep the interior cool.

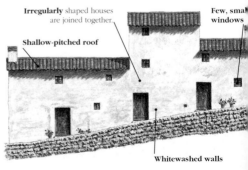

Irregularly shaped houses are joined together.

Shallow-pitched roof

Few, small windows

Whitewashed walls

THE PLAZA MAYOR

Almost every town in Spain centres on a main square, the *plaza mayor*, like this one in Pedraza de la Sierra *(see p347)*, near Segovia. More than a market square, it acts as a focus for local life. It is usually overlooked by the church, the town hall, shops and bars and the mansions of aristocratic families.

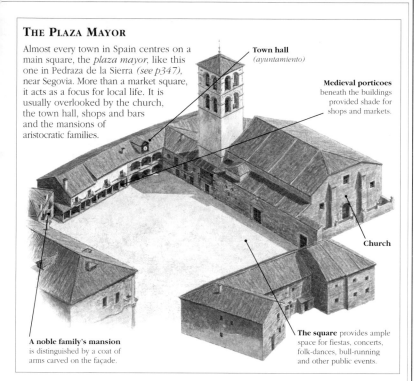

Town hall
(ayuntamiento)

Medieval porticoes beneath the buildings provided shade for shops and markets.

Church

A noble family's mansion is distinguished by a coat of arms carved on the façade.

The square provides ample space for fiestas, concerts, folk-dances, bull-running and other public events.

RURAL ARCHITECTURE

A variety of distinctive buildings dots the countryside.

Where the rock is soft and the climate hot, subterranean dwellings have been excavated. Insulated from extremes of temperature, they provide a comfortable place to live.

Hórreos, granaries raised on stone stilts to prevent rats climbing up into the grain, are a common sight in Galicia (where they are stone-built) and Asturias (where they are made of wood). In fields you will often see shelters for livestock or for storing crops, such as the *teitos* of Asturias.

Windmills provided power in parts of Spain where there was little running water but plentiful wind, like La Mancha and the Balearic Islands.

Almost everywhere in the Spanish countryside you will come across *ermitas*, isolated chapels or shrines dedicated to a local saint. An *ermita* may be opened only on the patron saint's feast day.

Cave houses in Guadix near Granada *(see p469)*

Teito **in Valle de Teverga in Asturias** *(see p101)*

Hórreo, **a granary, on the Rías Baixas** *(see p91)* **in Galicia**

Windmill above Consuegra *(see p376)* **in La Mancha**

Farming in Spain

SPAIN'S VARIED geography and climate have created a mosaic of farming patterns ranging from lush dairylands to stony hillsides where goats graze. Land can be broadly divided into *secano*, or dry cultivation (used for olives, wheat and vines), and much smaller areas of *regadío*, irrigated land (planted with citrus trees, rice and vegetables). Farming in many parts is a family affair relying on traditional, labour-intensive methods but it is becoming increasingly mechanized.

Donkey in Extremadura

***Plains of cereals** make up much of the farmland of the central meseta of Spain. Wheat is grown in better-watered, more fertile western areas; barley is grown in the drier south.*

Cork oaks thrive in Extremadura and western Andalusia.

MADRID

SEVILLA

0 kilometres	20
0 miles	100

***Sheep** grazed on the rough pastures of Central Spain are milked to make cheese, especially* manchego, *which is produced in La Mancha (see p321).*

THE AGRICULTURAL YEAR

| | **Jul–Aug** Wheat harvested in Central Spain | **Sep** Rice harvest in Eastern Spain. Grape harvest at its height | **Oct** Maize harvested in Northern Spain

Oct–Nov Table olives picked | **Dec–Mar** Olives for making oil picked |
|---|---|---|---|---|
| **Spring** | **Summer** | **Autumn** | | **Winter** |
| **Mar–Apr** Orange trees in blossom on Mediterranean coast | | **Nov–Dec** Oranges picked | | **Feb** Almond trees in blossom |
| **Jun–Aug** Haymaking in Northern Spain | **Sep** Start of wild mushroom season | **Dec** Pigs are slaughtered when cold weather arrives | | |

The high rainfall and mild summers of Northern Spain make it suitable for dairy farming. Farms are often small, especially in Galicia, one of the country's most underdeveloped regions. Crops such as maize and wheat are grown in small quantities.

Wine is produced in many parts of Spain *(see pp576–7)*. The country's best sparkling wine grapes are grown in Catalonia.

Rice is grown in the Ebro delta, in the Marismas del Guadalquivir, around L'Albufera near Valencia and also at Calasparra in Murcia.

BARCELONA

Oranges, lemons and clementines are grown on the irrigated coastal plains beside the Mediterranean. The region of Valencia is the prime producer of oranges.

Olive trees are planted in long, straight lines across large swaths of Andalusia, especially in the province of Jaén. Spain is the world's leading producer of olive oil.

Cork oaks stripped of their bark every ten years

CROPS FROM TREES

The almond, orange and olive create the three most characteristic landscapes of rural Spain but several other trees provide important crops. Wine corks are made from the bark of the cork oak. Tropical species, such as avocado and cherimoya, a delicious creamy fruit little known outside Spain, have been introduced to the so-called Costa Tropical of Andalusia *(see p459)*; and bananas are a major crop of the Canary Islands. Elsewhere, peaches and loquats are also grown commercially. Figs and carobs – whose fruit is used for fodder and as a substitute for chocolate – grow semi-wild.

Almonds grow on dry hillsides in many parts of Spain. The spring blossom can be spectacular. The nut, enclosed by a fleshy green skin, is used in a variety of sweetmeats including the Christmas treat turrón (see p191).

Olive trees grow slowly and often live to a great age. The fruit is harvested in winter and either pickled in brine for eating as a tapa or pressed to extract the oil which is widely used in Spanish cuisine.

Sweet oranges are grown in dense, well-irrigated groves near the frost free coasts. The sweet smell of orange blossom in springtime is unmistakeable. Trees of the bitter orange are often planted for shade and decoration in parks and gardens.

Spain's National Parks

F EW OTHER COUNTRIES in western Europe have such unspoiled scenery as Spain, or can boast tracts of wilderness where brown bears live and wolves hunt. More than 200 nature reserves protect a broad range of ecosystems. The most important areas are the 12 national parks, the first of which was established in 1918. Natural parks *(parques naturales)*, regulated by regional governments, are also vital to the task of conservation.

Giant orchid

Clear mountain river, Ordesa

MOUNTAINS
Much of Spain's finest scenery is found in the mountains. Rivers have carved gorges between the peaks of the Picos de Europa. Ordesa and Aigüestortes share some of the most dramatic landscapes of the Pyrenees, while the Sierra Nevada has an impressive range of indigenous wildlife.

Rough terrain in the Picos de Europa

Eagle owls are Europe's largest owl, easily identified by their large ear tufts. At night they hunt small mammals and birds.

Chamois are well adapted to climbing across slopes covered in scree. They live in small groups, always alert to predators, and feed on grass and flowers.

WETLANDS
Wetlands, including coastal strips and freshwater marshes, are ever-changing environments. Seasonal floods rejuvenate the water providing nutrients for animal and plant growth. These areas are rich feeding grounds for birds. Spain's best-known wetland is Doñana. Tablas de Daimiel, in La Mancha, is much smaller.

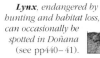

Lynx, endangered by hunting and habitat loss, can occasionally be spotted in Doñana (see pp440–41).

Black-winged stilts, with their long, straight legs, are adept at stalking tiny freshwater crustaceans.

Laguna del Acebuche, Parque Nacional de Doñana

ISLANDS
Cabrera, off Mallorca, is home to rare plants, reptiles and seabirds, such as Eleonara's falcon. The surrounding waters are important for their marine life.

Lizards are often found in rocky terrain and on cliff faces.

Cabrera archipelago, Balearic Islands

NATIONAL PARKS

① Mountains

⑤ Wetlands

⑦ Islands

⑧ Woods and Forests

⑩ Volcanic Landscapes

MOUNTAINS

① Picos de Europa *pp104–5*
② Ordesa y Monte Perdido *pp222–3*
③ Aigüestortes y Estany de Sant Maurici *p201*
④ Sierra Nevada *p461*

WETLANDS

⑤ Tablas de Daimiel *p381*
⑥ Doñana *pp440–41*

ISLANDS

⑦ Archipiélago de Cabrera *p493*

WOODS AND FORESTS

⑧ Cabañeros *p369*
⑨ Garajonay *p509*

VOLCANIC LANDSCAPES

⑩ Caldera de Taburiente *p508*
⑪ Teide *pp514–15*
⑫ Timanfaya *pp524–5*

VISITORS' CHECKLIST

All but one of the national parks are managed by the Ministerio de Medio Ambiente. 91 597 55 47. *Parque Nacional d'Aigüestortes y Estany de Sant Maurici is administered by Catalonia's Department of Agriculture.* 973 62 40 36. *Most, but not all, of Spain's national parks have visitors' centres.*

WOODS AND FORESTS

Deciduous broad-leaved forests grow in the northwest of Spain, and stands of Aleppo and Scots pine cover many mountainous areas. On the central plateau there are stretches of open woodland of evergreen holm oak and cork oak in the Parque Nacional de Cabañeros. Dense, lush *laurasilva* woodland grows in the Parque Nacional de Garajonay, on La Gomera, one of the smaller Canary Islands.

Parque Nacional de Garajonay

Black vultures *are the largest birds of prey in Europe, with an enormous wingspan of over 2.5 m (8 ft).*

Hedgehogs, *common in woodlands, root among fallen leaves and grass to find worms and slugs.*

VOLCANIC LANDSCAPES

Three very different parks protect parts of the Canary Islands' amazing volcanic scenery. Caldera de Taburiente on La Palma is a volcanic crater surrounded by woods. Mount Teide in Tenerife has unique alpine flora, and Lanzarote's Timanfaya is composed of barren but atmospheric lava fields.

Rabbits *are highly opportunistic, quickly colonizing areas in which they can burrow. In the absence of predators, populations may increase, damaging fragile ecosystems.*

Canaries *belong to the finch family of songbirds. The popular canary has been bred from the wild serin, native to the Canaries.*

Colonizing plant species, Mount Teide (Tenerife)

Spanish Art

THREE SPANISH PAINTERS stand out as milestones in the history of Western art. Diego de Velázquez was a 17th-century court portrait painter and his *Las Meninas* is a seminal work. Francisco de Goya depicted Spanish life during one of its most violent periods. The prolific 20th-century master, Pablo Picasso, is recognized as the founder of modern art. To these names must be added that of El Greco – who was born in Crete but who lived in Spain, where he painted religious scenes in an individualistic style. The work of these and Spain's many other great artists can be seen in world-renowned galleries, especially the Prado *(see pp282–5).*

***In his series,* Las Meninas** *(1957), Picasso interprets the frozen gesture of the five-year-old Infanta Margarita. Altogether, Picasso produced 44 paintings based on Velázquez's canvas. They can be seen in Barcelona's Museu de Picasso (see p149).*

RELIGIOUS ART IN SPAIN

The influence of the Catholic Church on Spanish art through the ages is reflected in the predominance of religious imagery. Many churches and museums have Romanesque altarpieces or earlier icons. El Greco *(see p373)* painted from a highly personal religious vision. Baroque religious art of the 17th century, when the Inquisition *(see p264)* was at its height, often graphically depicts physical suffering and spiritual torment.

The Burial of the Count of Orgaz* by El Greco *(see p372)

Self-portrait of Velázquez

The king and queen, reflected in a mirror behind the painter, may be posing for their portrait

LAS MENINAS *(1656)*

In Velázquez's painting of the Infanta Margarita and her courtiers, in the Prado *(see pp282–5),* the eye is drawn into the distance where the artist's patron, Felipe IV, is reflected in a mirror.

TIMELINE OF GREAT SPANISH ARTISTS

The Saviour by José de Ribera

1285–1348 Ferrer Bassà	**1390–1410** Pere Nicolau				**1598–1664** Francisco de Zurbarán
	1363–95 Jaume Serra	**1428–1460** Luis Daimau			**1591–1652** José de Ribera
1300		**1400**		**1500**	
	1388–1424 Luis Borrassa		**1474–95** Bartolomé Bermejo		**1565–1628** Francisco Ribalta
			1450–1504 Pedro Berruguete		**1599–1660**
Virgin and Child *by Ferrer Bassà*		**1427–52** Bernat Martorell		**1541–1614** El Greco	Diego de Velázquez

José Nieto, the queen's chamberlain, stands in the doorway in the background of the painting.

Court jester

MODERN ART

The early 20th-century artists Joan Miró *(see p168)*, Salvador Dalí *(see p205)* and Pablo Picasso *(see p148)* all belonged to the Paris School. More recent artists of note include Antonio Saura and Antoni Tàpies *(see p160)*. Among many great Spanish art collections, the Centro de Reina Sofia in Madrid *(see pp288–9)* specializes in modern art. Contemporary artists are accorded great prestige in Spain. Their work is to be seen in town halls, banks and public squares, and many towns have a museum dedicated to a local painter.

Salvador Dalí's painting of the *Colossus of Rhodes* (1954)

Collage (1934) by Joan Miró

The Family of King Charles IV *was painted in 1800 by Francisco de Goya (see p229), nearly 150 years after* Las Meninas. *Its debt to Velázquez's painting is evident in its frontal composition, compact grouping of figures and in the inclusion of a self-portrait.*

The Holy Children
with the Shell
by Murillo

1893–1983 Joan Miró

1904–89
Salvador Dalí

1881–1973 Pablo Picasso

1746–1828
Francisco de Goya

1863–1923
Joaquín Sorolla

1923–
Antoni
Tàpies

| 1700 | 1800 | 1900 |

1642–93 Claudio Coello

1618–82 Bartolomé
Esteban Murillo

Jug and Glass
(1916) by Juan Gris

1887–1927
Juan Gris

1930–1998
Antonio Saura

Literary Spain

The 14th-century *El Libro de Buen Amor*

DON QUIXOTE, considered the first modern novel, is the best-known work of Spanish literature. However, Spain has produced many major works over the last 2,000 years. The Roman writers Seneca, Lucan and Martial were born in Spain. Later, the Moors developed a flourishing, but now little-known, literary culture. Although Spanish (Castilian) is the national tongue, many enduring works have been written in the Galician and Catalan regional languages. Basque literature, hitherto an oral culture, is a more recent development. Many foreign writers, such as Alexandre Dumas, Ernest Hemingway and Karel Capek, have written accounts of their travels in Spain.

MIDDLE AGES

AS THE ROMAN EMPIRE fell, Latin evolved into several Romance languages. The earliest non-Latin literature in Spain derives from an oral tradition that arose before the 10th century. It is in the form of *jarchas*, snatches of love poetry written in Mozarab, the Romance language that was spoken by Christians living under the Moors.

In the 12th century, the first poems appeared in Castilian. During the next 300 years, two separate schools of poetry developed. The best-known example of troubadour verse is the anonymous epic, *El Cantar del Mío Cid*, which tells of the heroic exploits of El Cid *(see p352)* during the Reconquest. Works of clerical poetry – for example, Gonzalo de Berceo's *Milagros de Nuestra Señora*, relating the life of the Virgin – convey a moral message.

Spanish literature evolved in the 13th century after Alfonso X the Learned *(see p51)* replaced Latin with Castilian

Romance (later called Spanish) as the official language. Under his supervision a team of Jews, Christians and Arabs wrote scholarly treatises. The king himself was a poet, writing in Galician Romance.

The first great prose works in Spanish appeared in the 14th and 15th centuries. *El Libro de Buen Amor*, by an ecclesiastic, Juan Ruiz, is a tale of the love affairs of a priest,

Alfonso X the Learned (1221–84)

interleaved with other stories. Fernando de Rojas uses skilful characterization in *La Celestina* to tell a tragic love story about two nobles and a scheming go-between. This was an age in which tales of chivalry were also popular.

GOLDEN AGE

The prolific Golden Age dramatist, Félix Lope de Vega

THE 16TH CENTURY hailed the start of Spain's Golden Age of literature. But it was also a period of domestic strife. This found expression in the picaresque novel, a Spanish genre originating with the anonymous *El Lazarillo de Tormes*, a bitter reflection on the misfortunes of a blind man's guide.

Spiritual writers flourished under the austere climate of the Counter-Reformation. St John of the Cross's *Cántico Espiritual* was influenced by oriental erotic poetry and the Bible's *Song of Songs*.

The 17th century saw the emergence of more great talents. The life and work of Miguel de Cervantes *(see p315)* straddles the two centuries of the Golden Age. He published his masterpiece, *Don Quixote*, in 1615. Other important writers of the time include Francisco de Quevedo and Luis de Góngora.

Corrales (public theatres) appeared in the 17th century, opening the way for Lope de Vega *(see p280)*, Calderón de la Barca and other dramatists.

Don Quixote's adventures portrayed by José Moreno Carbonero

18TH AND 19TH CENTURIES

INFLUENCED BY the French Enlightenment, literature in the 18th century was seen as a way to educate the people. Such was the aim, for instance, of Leandro Fernández de Moratín's comedy *El Sí de las Niñas*. This period saw the development of journalism as well as the emergence of the essay as a literary form. Romanticism had a short and late life in Spain. *Don Juan Tenorio*, a tale of the legendary irrepressible Latin lover by José Zorrilla, is the best-known Romantic play.

The satirical essayist Larra stands out from his contemporaries at the beginning of the 19th century. Towards the end of the century, the novel became a vehicle for realistic portrayals of Spanish society. Benito Pérez Galdós, regarded by many to be Spain's greatest novelist after Cervantes,

studied the human condition in his *Episodios Nacionales*. The heroine in Clarín's *La Regenta* is undone by the reactionary prejudices of provincial town society.

20TH CENTURY

WRITERS AT THE turn of the century, including Pío Baroja *(see p60)*, Miguel de Unamuno and Antonio Machado, described a Spain falling behind the rest of Europe. Exploring the grotesque, the only way he could describe society, led Ramón María del Valle-Inclán to lay the foundations for modern Spanish theatre. In poetry, the Nobel Prize winner, Juan Ramón Jiménez, strived for pureness of form.

José Zorrilla (1817–93)

The so-called "Generation of 27" combined European experimental art with Spain's traditional literary subjects and forms. The best known of them is the poet and playwright Federico García Lorca

who was executed by a Fascist firing squad in 1936 *(see p63)*. He drew on the legends and stereotypes of his native Andalusia to make universal statements in his poems and plays, such as *Yerma*.

In the aftermath of the Civil War, many intellectuals who had backed the Republic were forced into exile. The Franco regime tried to create its own propagandist culture. Yet the finest literature of the period was written in spite of the prevailing political climate. Camilo José Cela's *La Colmena*, a description of everyday life in the hungry, postwar city of Madrid, set a mood of social realism that inspired other writers.

Poster for a Lorca play

The novel has had a rebirth in Spain since the 1960s, with the emergence of writers like Juan Goytisolo, Joan Benet, Julio Llamazares, Antonio Muñoz Molina, José Manuel Caballero Bonald and Juan Marsé.

The 20th century has also witnessed a surge of great Spanish literature from Latin America. Prominent authors include Jorge Luis Borges and Gabriel García Márquez.

Camilo José Cela, Nobel Prize-winning novelist, by Alvaro Delgado

The Art of Bullfighting

**Poster for a
bullfight**

BULLFIGHTING is a sacrificial ritual in which men (and also a few women) pit themselves against an animal bred for the ring. In this "authentic religious drama", as poet García Lorca described it, the spectator experiences vicariously the fear and exaltation felt by the matador. Although some Spaniards oppose it on grounds of its cruelty, nowadays it is as popular as ever. Many Spaniards see talk of banning bullfighting as striking at the essence of their being, for they regard the *toreo*, the art of bullfighting, as a noble part of their heritage. Bullfights today, however, are often debased by practices which weaken the bull, especially shaving its horns to reduce its aim.

Plaza de Toros de la Maestranza,
*Seville. This ring is regarded, with Las
Ventas in Madrid, as one of the top
venues for bullfighting in Spain.*

The matador wears a *traje de
luces* (suit of lights), a colourful
silk outfit embroidered with
gold sequins.

The passes are made with
a *muleta*, a scarlet cape
stiffened along one side.

Well treated at the ranch, *the
toro bravo (fighting bull) is
specially bred for qualities of
aggressiveness and courage. As
aficionados of bullfighting point
out in its defence, the young bull
enjoys a full life while it is being
prepared for its 15 minutes in
the ring. Bulls must be at least
four years old before they fight.*

THE BULLFIGHT

The *corrida* (bullfight) has three stages, called *tercios*. In the first one, the *tercio de varas*, the matador and *picadores* (horsemen with lances) are aided by *peones* (assistants). In the *tercio de banderillas*, *banderilleros* stick pairs of darts in the bull's back. In the *tercio de muleta* the matador makes a series of passes at the bull with a *muleta* (cape). He then executes the kill, the *estocada*, with a sword.

The matador *plays the bull with
a capa (red cape) in the tercio de
varas. Peones will then draw the
bull towards the picadores.*

Horses are now
padded.

Picadores *goad the bull with
steel-pointed lances, testing its
bravery. The lances weaken the
animal's shoulder muscles.*

THE BULLRING

The *corrida* audience is seated in the *tendidos* (stalls) or in the *palcos* (balcony), where the *presidencia* (president's box) is situated. Opposite are the *puerta de cuadrillas*, through which the matador and team arrive, and the *arrastre de toros* (exit for bulls). Before entering the ring, the matadors wait in a corridor *(callejón)* behind *barreras* and *burladeros* (barriers). Horses are kept in the *patio de caballos* and the bulls in the *corrales*.

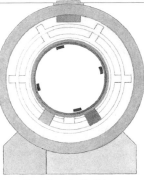

Plan of a typical bullring

KEY

- ☐ Tendidos
- Palcos
- Presidencia
- Puerta de cuadrillas
- Arrastre de toros
- Callejón
- Barreras
- Burladeros
- ☐ Patio de caballos
- ☐ Corrales

Banderillas, barbed darts, are thrust into the bull's already weakened back muscles.

Manolete is regarded by most followers of bullfighting as one of the greatest matadors ever. He was eventually gored to death by the bull Islero at Linares, Jaén, in 1947.

The bull may go free if it shows courage – spectators wave white handkerchiefs, asking the *corrida* president to let it leave the ring alive.

Joselito is one of Spain's leading matadors today. He is famous for his purist approach and for his flair and technical skill with both the capa and the muleta.

The bull weighs about 500 kg (1,100 lb).

***Banderilleros** enter to provoke the wounded bull in the* tercio de banderillas, *sticking pairs of* banderillas *in its back.*

***The matador** makes passes with the cape in the* tercio de muleta, *then lowers it and thrusts in the sword for the kill.*

***The estocada recibiendo** is a difficult kill, rarely seen. The matador awaits the bull's charge rather than moving to meet it.*

The Fiestas of Spain

ON ANY DAY of the year there is a fiesta happening somewhere in Spain – usually more than one. There isn't a village, town or city in the country which doesn't honour its patron saint, the Virgin or the changing seasons with processions, bull-running, fireworks, re-enacted battles, some ancestral rite or a *romería* – a mass pilgrimage to a rural shrine. Whatever the pretext, a fiesta is a chance for everyone to take a break from normal life (most shops and offices close) and let off steam, with celebrations sometimes going on around the clock.

The Passion, Semana Santa

Many *romerías* wind through the countryside during the year

SPRING FIESTAS

THE END OF WINTER and the start of spring are marked by Valencia's great fire festival, Las Fallas *(see p245)*, in which huge papier-mâché sculptures are set alight in a symbolic act of burning the old in order to make way for the new.

Alcoi's noisy mock battles between costumed armies of Moors and Christians in April *(see p245)* are the most spectacular of the countless fiestas which commemorate the battles of the Reconquest.

Seville's great April Fair *(see p413)*, is the biggest celebration held in Andalusia.

During Los Mayos, on 30 April and the following days, crosses are decorated with flowers in parts of Spain.

EASTER

EASTER IS SPAIN'S main fiesta. Almost every community observes it in some form with pomp and solemnity.

It is heralded by the processions of Palm Sunday. The most impressive of these is in Elx, where intricate sculptures are woven from blanched leaves cropped from the most extensive forest of palm trees in Europe *(see p251)*.

The best Semana Santa (Easter Week) processions are those held in Seville *(see p413)*, Málaga, Murcia and Valladolid. Brotherhoods of robed men carry *pasos*, huge sculptures depicting the Virgin, Christ or scenes of the Passion, through the streets. They are accompanied by people dressed as biblical characters or penitents, in tall conical hats. In some towns passion plays are acted out. In others, people carry heavy crosses. Sometimes the centuries-old ritual of self-flagellation can be witnessed.

SUMMER FIESTAS

THE FIRST MAJOR fiesta of the summer is Pentecost (also known as Whitsun), in May or June, and its most famous celebration is at El Rocío *(see p439)*, where many thousands of people gather in a frenzy of religious devotion.

At Corpus Christi (in May or June) the consecrated host is carried in procession through many cities in an ornate silver monstrance. The route of the procession is often covered with a carpet of flowers. The main Corpus Christi celebrations take place in Valencia, Toledo and Granada.

On Midsummer's Eve, bonfires are lit all over Spain, especially in the areas along the Mediterranean coast, to

The Brotherhood of Candlemas, Semana Santa (Easter Week) in Seville

herald the celebration of St John the Baptist on 24 June.

During Los Sanfermines *(see p128)* in Pamplona in July, young people run through the streets in front of six bulls.

The Virgin of Carmen, who is revered as the patron of fishermen, is honoured in many ports on 16 July.

The important Catholic holiday of Assumption Day, 15 August, is marked by a huge number and variety of fiestas.

AUTUMN FIESTAS

THERE ARE FEW FIESTAS in autumn, but in most wine regions the grape harvest is fêted. The annual pig slaughter has become a jubilant public event in some villages, especially in Extremadura. In Galicia it is traditional to roast chestnuts on street bonfires.

On All Saints' Day, 1 November, people remember the dead by visiting cemeteries to lay flowers, especially chrysanthemums, on graves.

CHRISTMAS AND NEW YEAR

NOCHEBUENA (Christmas Eve) is the main Christmas celebration, when families gather for an evening meal before attending Midnight Mass, known as *misa del gallo* (Mass of the rooster). During the Christmas period, *belenes* (crib scenes) of painted figurines abound. You may also see a "living crib", peopled by costumed actors.

The losers end up in the harbour in Denia's July fiesta *(see p245)*

Spain's "April Fools' Day" is 28 December, the Day of the Holy Innocents, when people play practical jokes on each other. Clown-like characters may act out the role of mayor and make fun of passers-by.

To celebrate New Year's Eve *(Noche Vieja)*, crowds gather beneath the clock in Madrid's central square, the Puerta del Sol *(see p262)*. Traditionally people eat 12 grapes, one on each chime of midnight, to bring good luck for the year.

Spanish children do not receive their Christmas presents until Epiphany, on 6 January.

WINTER FIESTAS

ANIMALS HOLD centre stage in a variety of fiestas on 17 January, the Day of St Anthony, patron saint of animals, when pets and livestock are blessed by priests.

St Agatha, the patron saint of married women, is honoured on 5 February when women, for once, are the protagonists of many fiestas. In Zamarramala (Segovia), for example, women take over the mayor's privileges and powers for this particular day *(see p350)*.

St Anthony's Day in Villanueva de Alcolea (Castellón province)

CARNIVAL

CARNIVAL, in February or early March (depending on the date of Easter), brings a chance for a street party as winter comes to an end and before Lent begins. The biggest celebrations are held in Santa Cruz de Tenerife *(see p512)* – comparable with those of Rio de Janeiro – and in Cádiz *(see p439)*. Carnival was prohibited by the Franco regime because of its licentiousness and frivolity. It ends on or after Ash Wednesday with the Burial of the Sardine, a "funeral" in which a mock sardine, representing winter, is ritually burned or buried.

A spectacularly costumed choir singing during Carnival in Cádiz

SPAIN THROUGH THE YEAR

ESTIVALS, cultural events and sports competitions crowd the calendar in Spain. Even small villages have at least one traditional fiesta, lasting a week or more, when parades, bullfights and fireworks displays replace work (see pp34–5). Many rural and coastal towns celebrate the harvest or fishing catch with a gastronomic fair at which you can sample local produce.

Matador with a cape playing a bull

Music, dance, drama and film festivals are held in Spain's major cities throughout the year. Meanwhile, the country's favourite outdoor sports – football, basketball, cycling, sailing, golf and tennis – culminate in several national and international championships.

It is a good idea to confirm specific dates of events with the local tourist board as some vary from year to year.

SPRING

L IFE IN SPAIN moves outdoors with the arrival of spring, and terrace-cafés begin to fill with people. The countryside is at its best as wild flowers bloom before the onset of the summer heat, and irrigation channels flow to bring water to the newly sown crops. The important Easter holiday is a time of solemn processions throughout the country.

Feria del Caballo (Festival of the Horses) in Jerez de la Frontera

MARCH

International Vintage Car Rally (first Sun), from Barcelona to Sitges.
Las Fallas (around 19 Mar), Valencia (see p245). A spectacular fiesta which also marks the start of the bullfighting (see pp32–3) season.
Religious Music Week (Mar), Cuenca.

APRIL

Trofeo Conde de Godó (mid-Apr), Barcelona. Spain's

premier international tennis championship.
Moors and Christians (third week), Alcoi (see p249). Costumed celebration of the Christian victory over the Moors in 1276.
April Fair (two weeks after Easter), Seville. Exuberant Andalusian fiesta (see p413).
Feria Nacional del Queso (late Apr/early May), Trujillo (Cáceres). A week-long festival celebrating Spanish cheese (see p389).

MAY

Feria del Caballo (first week), Jerez de la Frontera. Horse fair showing Andalusia at its most traditional, with fine horses, and beautiful women in flamenco dresses.
Spanish Motorcycle Grand Prix (May), Jerez de la Frontera race track.
Fiestas de San Isidro (8–15 May), Madrid (see p280). Bullfights at Las Ventas bullring are the highlights of the taurine year.
National Flamenco Competition (mid-May, every third year: 1998, 2001), Córdoba.
Peugeot Open de España (mid-May), Club de Campo, Madrid. Golf tournament.
Spanish Formula One Grand Prix (May/Jun), Montmeló circuit, Barcelona. International motor race.
A Rapa das Bestas (May and Jun), Pontevedra (Galicia). Wild horses are rounded up so that their manes and tails can be cut (see p94).

Onlookers lining the street during the Vuelta Ciclista a España

San Sebastián, one of the most popular resorts on the north coast

SUMMER

AUGUST is Spain's big holiday season. The cities empty as Spaniards flock to the coast or to their second homes in the hills. Their numbers are swelled by millions of foreign tourists, and beaches and camp sites are often full to bursting. As the heat starts in the centre and south, entertainment often takes place only in the evening, when the temperature has dropped. In late summer the harvest begins and there are gastronomic fiestas everywhere to celebrate food and drink, from the fishing catches of the north coast to the sausages of the Balearic Islands.

JUNE

International Festival of Music and Dance *(mid-Jun–early Jul)*, Granada. Classical music and ballet staged in the Alhambra and the Generalife.
Grec Arts Festival *(Jun–Aug)*, Barcelona. Both Spanish and international theatre, music and dance.
Copa del Rey *(Apr–Jun)* Football cup final.

JULY

Classical Theatre Festival *(Jul–Aug)*, Mérida. Staged in the Roman theatre and amphitheatre *(see p392)*.
Guitar Festival *(first two weeks)*, Córdoba. Performances range from classical to flamenco *(see pp406–7)*.
International Classical Theatre Festival of Almagro *(4–28 Jul)*. Spanish and classical repertoire performed in one of the oldest theatres in Europe *(see p381)*.

The pouring and tasting of cider in Asturias's Cider Festival

Cider Festival *(second Sat, even years only)*, Nava (Asturias). Includes traditional cider-pouring competitions.
International Festival of Santander *(Jul–Aug)*. Celebration of music, dance and theatre.
Pyrenean Folklore Festival *(late Jul/early Aug, odd years only)*, Jaca (Aragón). Display of folk costumes, music and dance.
International Jazz Festivals in San Sebastián *(third week)*, Getxo *(first week)* and Vitoria *(mid-Jul)*.

AUGUST

Certamen Internacional de Habaneras y Polifonía *(late Jul–early Aug)*, Torrevieja (Alicante). Musical competition of 19th-century seafarers' songs.
HM the King's International Cup *(first week)*, Palma de Mallorca. Sailing competition in which Juan Carlos I participates.
Descent of the Río Sella *(first Sat)*. Canoe race in Asturias from Arriondas to Ribadesella *(see p103)*.
Assumption Day *(15 Aug)* The Assumption is celebrated throughout the country.

Participants in the Descent of the Río Sella canoe race

Semanas Grandes *(early–mid-Aug)*, Bilbao and San Sebastián. "Great Weeks" of sporting and cultural events.
Misteri d'Elx *(14–15 Aug)*, Elx *(see p251)*. Unique liturgical drama performed in a church and featuring spectacular special effects.

Vines and the village of Larouco in the Valdeorras wine region of Galicia *(see p74)* in autumn

AUTUMN

AUTUMN USUALLY brings rain after the heat of summer, and with the high tourist season over, a large number of resorts practically close down. Harvest festivities continue, however, and the most important celebrations are in honour of the grape. The first pressings are blessed and, in some places, wine is served for free.

Wild mushrooms

In woodland areas, freshly picked wild mushrooms start to appear in various dishes on local restaurant menus. The hunting season begins in the middle of October and runs until February. Autumn is also the start of the new drama and classical music seasons in the major cities of Spain.

SEPTEMBER

Vuelta Ciclista a España *(Sep)*. Annual bicycle race around Spain.
International Folklore Gala *(late Aug/early Sep)*, Ronda (Málaga). Music and dancing.
Grape Harvest *(first week)*, Jerez de la Frontera. Celebration of the new crop in the country's sherry capital.
Madrid Autumn Festival *(mid-Sep–mid-Nov)*. Drama, dance and music by national and foreign companies.
San Sebastián Film Festival *(last two weeks)*. Gathering of film-makers *(see p119)*.
Bienal de Arte Flamenco *(last two weeks, even years only)*, Seville. Top flamenco artists perform.

OCTOBER

Día de la Hispanidad *(12 Oct)*. Spain's national holiday marks Columbus's discovery of America in 1492. The biggest celebration in the country is the exuberant fiesta of Día del Pilar in Zaragoza *(see p229)*, which marks the end of the bullfighting year.

Driving down the fairway in the Volvo Masters Golf Championship

IBERFLORA *(mid-Oct)*, Valencia. Flower show.
Saffron Festival *(late Oct)*, Consuegra (Toledo).
Volvo Masters Golf Championship *(late Oct)*, Valderrama (Cádiz).

NOVEMBER

All Saints' Day *(1 Nov)*. The traditional start of the *matanza* (pig slaughter) in rural areas of Spain.
Os Magostos *(11 Nov)*. Various towns in Galicia hold chestnut-harvest fairs.
Latin American Film Festival *(last two weeks)*, Huelva *(see p438)*.

Lana Turner on centre-stage at the San Sebastián Film Festival

PUBLIC HOLIDAYS

Besides marking the national holidays below, each region *(comunidad autónoma)* celebrates its own holiday and every town and village has at least one other fiesta each year. If a holiday falls on a Tuesday or a Thursday shops, offices and monuments may also be closed on the intervening Monday or Friday, making a long weekend called a *puente* ("bridge").

Año Nuevo *(New Year's Day)* (1 Jan)
Día de los Reyes *(Epiphany)* (6 Jan)
Jueves Santo *(Maundy Thursday)* (Mar/Apr)
Viernes Santo *(Good Friday)* (Mar/Apr)
Día de Pascua *(Easter Sunday)* (Mar/Apr)
Día del Trabajo *(Labour Day)* (1 May)
Asunción *(Assumption Day)* (15 Aug)
Día de la Hispanidad *(National Day)* (12 Oct)
Todos los Santos *(All Saints' Day)* (1 Nov)
Día de la Constitución *(Constitution Day)* (6 Dec)
Inmaculada Concepción *(Immaculate Conception)* (8 Dec)
Navidad *(Christmas Day)* (25 Dec)

Assumption Day in La Alberca (Salamanca)

WINTER

WINTER VARIES greatly from region to region. In the mountains, snowfalls bring skiers to the slopes; while in lower areas, olive and orange picking are in full swing. The higher parts of Central Spain can become very cold. Andalusia, the east coast and the Balearic Islands have cool nights but often sunny days. The winter warmth of the Canary Islands brings the high tourist season. Christmas is a special time of celebration – an occasion for families to reunite, share food and attend religious celebrations.

Skiers in the Sierra de Guadarrama, north of Madrid *(see p311)*

"El Gordo", the largest Spanish lottery prize, being drawn

DECEMBER

El Gordo *(22 Dec).* Spain's largest lottery prize, "the Fat One", is drawn *(see p622).*
Noche Buena *(24 Dec)* is a family Christmas Eve, followed by Midnight Mass for the devout *(see p35).*
Santos Inocentes *(28 Dec),* Spain's version of April Fools' Day, when people play tricks.
Noche Vieja *(31 Dec).* New Year's Eve is most celebrated in Madrid's Puerta del Sol.

JANUARY

Canary Islands International Music Festival *(Jan–Feb).* Classical concerts are held on La Palma and Tenerife.
Opera Season *(Jan–Apr),* Teatro Coliseo, Bilbao.

Vigo Video Festival *(last week).* Screenings and other events exploring all aspects of video film-making.

FEBRUARY

Festival of Ancient Music *(Feb–Mar),* Seville. Early music is played on period instruments.
ARCO *(mid-Feb),* Madrid. International contemporary art fair attracting galleries from across the world.
Pasarela Cibeles (Fashion Week) *(mid-Feb),* Madrid. Women's and men's fashion shows in the capital.
Carnival *(Feb/Mar).* Final fiesta before Lent, with colourful costumes. Those in Santa Cruz de Tenerife and Cádiz are among the best.

The Climate of Spain

SPAIN'S LARGE LANDMASS, with its extensive high plateaus and mountain ranges, and the influences of the Mediterranean and Atlantic produce a wide range of climatic variation, especially in winter. The north is wettest year round, the eastern and southern coasts and the islands have mild winters, while winter temperatures in the interior are often below freezing. Summers everywhere are hot, except in upland areas.

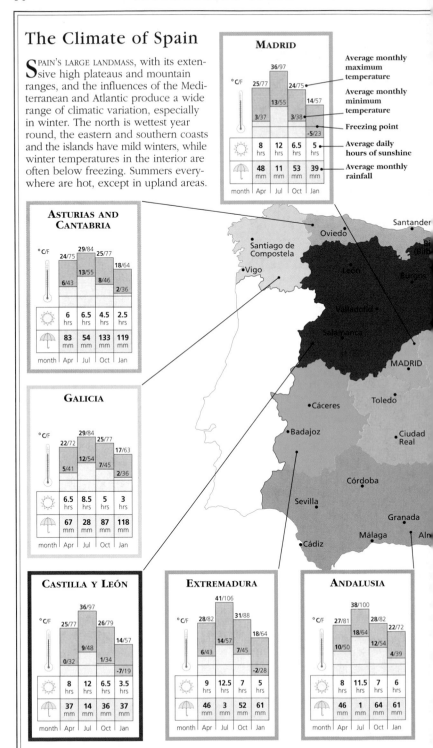

MADRID

Average monthly maximum temperature

Average monthly minimum temperature

Freezing point

Average daily hours of sunshine

Average monthly rainfall

°C/F				
	36/97			
25/77		24/75		
	13/55		14/57	
3/37		3/38		
			-5/23	
8 hrs	12 hrs	6.5 hrs	5 hrs	
48 mm	11 mm	53 mm	39 mm	
month	Apr	Jul	Oct	Jan

ASTURIAS AND CANTABRIA

°C/F				
	29/84			
24/75		25/77		
	13/55		18/64	
6/43		8/46		
			2/36	
6 hrs	6.5 hrs	4.5 hrs	2.5 hrs	
83 mm	54 mm	133 mm	119 mm	
month	Apr	Jul	Oct	Jan

GALICIA

°C/F				
	29/84			
22/72		25/77		
	12/54		17/63	
5/41		7/45		
			2/36	
6.5 hrs	8.5 hrs	5 hrs	3 hrs	
67 mm	28 mm	87 mm	118 mm	
month	Apr	Jul	Oct	Jan

CASTILLA Y LEÓN

°C/F				
	36/97			
25/77		26/79		
	9/48		14/57	
0/32		1/34		
			-7/19	
8 hrs	12 hrs	6.5 hrs	3.5 hrs	
37 mm	14 mm	36 mm	37 mm	
month	Apr	Jul	Oct	Jan

EXTREMADURA

°C/F				
	41/106			
28/82		31/88		
	14/57		18/64	
6/43		7/45		
			-2/28	
9 hrs	12.5 hrs	7 hrs	5 hrs	
46 mm	3 mm	52 mm	61 mm	
month	Apr	Jul	Oct	Jan

ANDALUSIA

°C/F				
	38/100			
27/81		28/82		
	18/64		22/72	
10/50		12/54		
			4/39	
8 hrs	11.5 hrs	7 hrs	6 hrs	
46 mm	1 mm	64 mm	61 mm	
month	Apr	Jul	Oct	Jan

Santander

Oviedo

Santiago de Compostela

Vigo

León

Bi (Bil

Burgos

Valladolid

Salamanca

MADRID

Cáceres

Toledo

Badajoz

Ciudad Real

Córdoba

Sevilla

Granada

Málaga

Aln

Cádiz

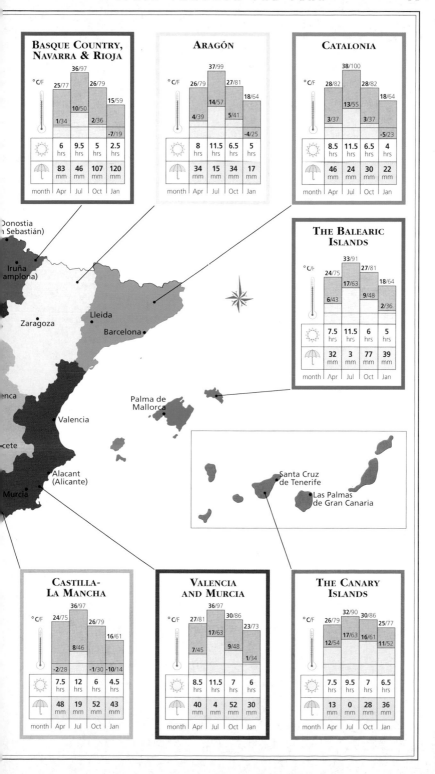

BASQUE COUNTRY, NAVARRA & RIOJA

°C/F		36/97		
	25/77		26/79	15/59
		10/50		
	1/34		2/36	
				-7/19
☼	6 hrs	9.5 hrs	5 hrs	2.5 hrs
☂	83 mm	46 mm	107 mm	120 mm
month	Apr	Jul	Oct	Jan

ARAGÓN

°C/F		37/99		
	26/79		27/81	18/64
		14/57		
	4/39		5/41	
				-4/25
☼	8 hrs	11.5 hrs	6.5 hrs	5 hrs
☂	34 mm	15 mm	34 mm	17 mm
month	Apr	Jul	Oct	Jan

CATALONIA

°C/F		38/100		
	28/82		28/82	18/64
		13/55		
	3/37		3/37	
				-5/23
☼	8.5 hrs	11.5 hrs	6.5 hrs	4 hrs
☂	46 mm	24 mm	30 mm	22 mm
month	Apr	Jul	Oct	Jan

THE BALEARIC ISLANDS

°C/F		33/91		
	24/75		27/81	18/64
		17/63		
	6/43		9/48	
				2/36
☼	7.5 hrs	11.5 hrs	6 hrs	5 hrs
☂	32 mm	3 mm	77 mm	39 mm
month	Apr	Jul	Oct	Jan

Donostia (San Sebastián)

Iruña (Pamplona)

Zaragoza

Lleida

Barcelona

enca

Palma de Mallorca

Valencia

cete

Alacant (Alicante)

Murcia

Santa Cruz de Tenerife

Las Palmas de Gran Canaria

CASTILLA-LA MANCHA

°C/F		36/97		
	24/75		26/79	16/61
		8/46		
	-2/28		-1/30	-10/14
☼	7.5 hrs	12 hrs	6 hrs	4.5 hrs
☂	48 mm	19 mm	52 mm	43 mm
month	Apr	Jul	Oct	Jan

VALENCIA AND MURCIA

°C/F		36/97		
	27/81		30/86	23/73
		17/63		
	7/45		9/48	1/34
☼	8.5 hrs	11.5 hrs	7 hrs	6 hrs
☂	40 mm	4 mm	52 mm	30 mm
month	Apr	Jul	Oct	Jan

THE CANARY ISLANDS

°C/F		32/90	30/86	
	26/79			25/77
		17/63	16/61	11/52
	12/54			
☼	7.5 hrs	9.5 hrs	7 hrs	6.5 hrs
☂	13 mm	0 mm	28 mm	36 mm
month	Apr	Jul	Oct	Jan

THE HISTORY OF SPAIN

THE IBERIAN PENINSULA, first inhabited around 800,000 BC, has long been subject to foreign influences. From the 11th century BC it was colonized by sophisticated eastern Mediterranean civilizations, starting with the Phoenicians, then the Greeks and Carthaginians.

The Romans arrived in 218 BC to fight the Carthaginians, thus sparking off the Second Punic War. They harvested the peninsula's agricultural and mineral wealth and established cities with aqueducts, temples and theatres.

Gold Aztec statue from America

With the fall of the Roman Empire in the early 5th century AD, Visigothic invaders from the north assumed power. Their poor political organization, however, made them easy prey to the Moors from North Africa. In the 8th century, the peninsula came almost entirely under Moorish rule. Europe's only major Muslim territory, the civilization of Al Andalus excelled in mathematics, geography, astronomy and poetry. In the 9th and 10th centuries Córdoba was Europe's leading city.

From the 11th century, northern Christian kingdoms initiated a military reconquest of Al Andalus. The marriage, in 1469, of Fernando of Aragón and Isabel of Castile, the so-called Catholic Monarchs, led to Spanish unity. They took Granada, the last Moorish kingdom, in 1492. Columbus discovered the Americas in the same year, opening the way for the Spanish conquistadors, who plundered the civilizations of the New World.

The succeeding Habsburg dynasty spent the riches from the New World in endless foreign wars. Spain's decline was exacerbated by high inflation and religious oppression. Although the Enlightenment in the late 18th century created a climate of learning, Spain's misfortunes continued into the next century with an invasion by Napoleon's troops and the loss of her American colonies. A new radicalism began to emerge, creating a strong Anarchist movement. The political instability of the late 19th and early 20th centuries led to dictatorship in the 1920s and a republic in the 1930s, which was destroyed by the Spanish Civil War. Victorious General Franco ruled by repression until his death in 1975. Since then Spain has been a democratic state.

Bullfighting in Madrid's Plaza Mayor in the 17th century

◁ Moors paying homage to Fernando and Isabel, the 15th-century Catholic Monarchs

Prehistoric Spain

Helmet of Celt-Iberian warrior

THE IBERIAN PENINSULA was first inhabited by hunter-gatherers around 800,000 BC. They were eclipsed by a Neolithic farming population from 5000 BC. First in a wave of settlers from over the Mediterranean, the Phoenicians landed in 1100 BC, to be followed by the Greeks and Carthaginians. Invading Celts mixed with native Iberian tribes (forming the Celtiberians). They proved a formidable force against the Romans, the next conquerors of Spain.

SPAIN IN 5000 BC

☐ *Neolithic farming settlements*

Iron Dagger *(6th century BC)*
Weapons, like this dagger from Burgos, represent the later Iron Age, in contrast to earlier metal objects which were for domestic use.

Stone Age Man
This skull belongs to a Palaeolithic man, who hunted deer and bison with tools made of wood and stone.

The 28 bracelets have perforations and moulded decorations.

Small silver bottle

Incised geometric pattern

La Dama de Elche
Dating from the 4th century BC, this stone statue is a fine example of Iberian art. Her austere beauty reveals traces of Greek influence.

THE VILLENA TREASURE
Discovered in 1963 during works in Villena, near Alicante, this Bronze Age find consists of 66 dazzling objects mostly of gold, including bowls, bottles and jewellery *(see p250)*. The treasure dates from around 1000 BC.

TIMELINE

800,000 BC *Homo erectus* arrives in Iberian Peninsula	**35,000 BC** Cro-Magnon man evolves in Spain	**2500 BC** Los Millares *(p477)* is inhabited by early metalworkers with belief in the afterlife	**1800–1100 BC** Civilization of El Argar, an advanced agrarian society, flourishes in southeast Spain
300,000 BC Tribes of *Homo erectus* live in hunting camps in Soria and Madrid			

800,000 BC		**2500**	**2000**
500,000 BC Stones used as tools by hominids (probably *Homo erectus*)	**100,000–40,000 BC** Neanderthal man in Gibraltar	**5000 BC** Farming begins in Iberian Peninsula	
Bison cave drawing, Altamira		**18,000–14,000 BC** Drawings by cave dwellers at Altamira (Cantabria), near Ribadesella (Asturias) and at Nerja (Andalusia)	

Greek Ceramic Vase
*The Greek colonizers
brought new technology,
including the potter's wheel,
as well as refined
artistic ideals.
Ceramics, such as this
6th-century BC vase
depicting the Labours of
Hercules, provided
sophisticated models.*

The largest of the
treasure's five bottles,
made of silver, stands
22.5 cm (9 in) high.

**Bowls of beaten
gold** may have
originated in
southwest Spain.

**Brooches
with separate
clasps**

**The smaller
pieces** are of
unknown use.

Astarte *(8th century BC)
Worship of Phoenician deities was
incorporated into local religions.
One of the most popular was the
fertility goddess Astarte, shown on this
bronze from the kingdom of Tartessus.*

WHERE TO SEE PREHISTORIC SPAIN

The most famous cave paintings
in Spain are at Altamira *(see
p108).* There are dolmens in
many parts of the country; among
the largest are those at Antequera
(see p451). The Guanches – the
indigenous inhabitants of the
Canary Islands – left behind
more recent remains *(see p523).*

*La Naveta d'es Tudons is one
of the many prehistoric stone
monuments scattered across the
island of Menorca* (see p503).

*An excavated Celtic village, with
its round huts, can be seen near A
Guarda in Pontevedra* (see p92).

Phoenician gold ornament

1500	1000	500

1100 BC
Phoenicians
believed to have
founded modern-
day Cádiz

600 BC Greek
colonists settle
on northeast
coast of Spain

228 BC
Carthaginians
occupy south-
east Spain

1200 BC The "talaiotic"
people of Menorca erect
three unique types of
stone building: *taulas,
talaiots* and *navetas*

Taula in Menorca

775 BC
Phoenicians
establish colonies
along the coast
near Málaga

300 BC *La Dama de
Elche* is carved *(p286)*

700 BC Semi-mythical
kingdom of Tartessus
thought to be at its height

*Carthaginian
glass necklace*

Romans and Visigoths

Roman vase

THE ROMANS CAME TO SPAIN to fight the Carthaginians and take possession of the Iberian Peninsula's huge mineral wealth. Later, Hispania's wheat and olive oil became mainstays of the empire. It took 200 years to subdue the peninsula, which was divided in three provinces: Tarraconensis, Lusitania and Baetica. In time, cities with Roman infrastructure developed. The fall of the empire in the 5th century left Spain in the hands of the Visigoths, invaders from the north. Politically disorganized, they fell victim to the Moors in 711.

SPAIN (HISPANIA) IN 5 BC

☐ *Tarraconensis*

☐ *Lusitania*

■ *Baetica*

Trajan *(AD 53–117)*
Trajan was the first Hispanic Roman emperor (AD 98–117). He improved public administration and expanded the empire.

Portico overlooking the gardens

Good acoustics at every level

A Classical façade served as a backdrop for tragedies. Additional scenery was used for comedies.

Seneca *(4 BC–AD 65)*
Born in Córdoba, the Stoic philosopher Seneca lived in Rome as Nero's adviser.

The *orchestra,* a semicircular open space for the choir

Visigothic Relief
This crude Visigothic stone carving, based on a Roman relief, is in the 7th-century church of Quintanilla de las Viñas, near Burgos (p352).

The auditorium seated over 5,000. The audience was placed according to social status.

TIMELINE

218 BC Scipio the Elder lands with a Roman army at Emporion *(p206).* The Second Punic War begins

c.200 BC Romans reach Gadir (modern Cádiz) after driving Carthaginians out of Hispania

155 BC Lusitanian Wars begin. Romans invade Portugal

26 BC Emerita Augusta (Mérida) is founded and soon becomes capital of Lusitania

19 BC Augustus takes Cantabria and Asturias, ending 200 years of war

200 BC	100	AD 1	AD 100

219 BC Hannibal takes Saguntum *(p239)* for Carthaginians

Hannibal

133 BC Celt-Iberian Wars culminate in destruction of Numantia, Soria *(p359)*

61 BC Julius Caesar, governor of Hispania Ulterior, begins final conquest of northern Portugal and Galicia

82–72 BC Roman Civil War. Pompey founds Pompaelo (Pamplona) in 75 BC

AD 74 Emperor Vespasian grants Latin status to all towns in Hispania, completing process of Romanization

Gladiator Mosaic
Mosaics were used as decoration both indoors and out. Themes range from mythical episodes to portrayals of daily life. This 4th-century AD mosaic shows gladiators in action and has helpful labels to name the fighters and show who is dead or alive.

WHERE TO SEE ROMAN SPAIN

Like Mérida, Tarragona *(see p214)* has extensive Roman ruins and Itálica *(see p452)* is an excavated town. A magnificent Roman wall rings Lugo in Galicia *(see p95)*. Built in Trajan's rule, the bridge over the Tagus at Alcántara *(see p392)* has a temple on it.

***Emporion**, a Roman town, was built next to a former Greek colony in the 3rd century BC. The ruins include grand villas and a forum (see p206).*

Segovia's Roman aqueduct *(see p347), a huge monument with 163 arches, dates from the end of the 1st century AD.*

The gardens were used as a foyer during intervals by the Hispanic nobility, dressed in elegant togas.

Stage building in granite and marble

***Scaena**, the platform on which the actors performed*

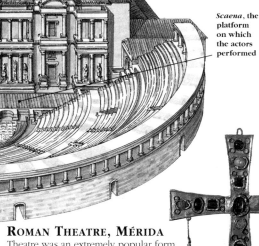

ROMAN THEATRE, MÉRIDA
Theatre was an extremely popular form of entertainment in Hispania. This reconstruction shows the theatre at Mérida *(see p392)*, built in 16–15 BC.

Visigothic Cross
Although Visigothic kings seldom ruled long enough to make an impact on society, the early Christian Church grew powerful. Fortunes were spent on churches and religious art.

Mosaic from Mérida

415 Visigoths establish their court at Barcelona

409 Vandals and their allies cross Pyrenees into Tarraconensis

446 Romans attempt to win back rest of Hispania

476 Overthrow of the last Roman emperor leads to end of Western Roman Empire

200	300	400	500

258 Franks cross Pyrenees into Tarraconensis and sack Tarragona

312 Christianity officially recognized as religion under rule of Constantine, the first Christian emperor

The Codex Vigilianus, a Christian manuscript

589 Visigothic King Reccared converts from Arianism to Catholicism at Third Council of Toledo

Al Andalus: Muslim Spain

THE ARRIVAL OF ARAB and Berber invaders from North Africa, and their defeat of the Visigoths, gave rise to the most brilliant civilization of early medieval Europe. These Muslim settlers, often known as the Moors, called Spain "Al Andalus". A rich and powerful caliphate was established in Córdoba and mathematics, science, architecture and the decorative arts flourished. The caliphate eventually broke up into small kingdoms or *taifas*. Meanwhile small Christian enclaves expanded in the north.

Alhambra Vase
(see p467)

SPAIN IN 750

☐ *Extent of Moorish domination*

Water Wheel
Moorish irrigation techniques, such as the water wheel, revolutionized agriculture. New crops, including oranges and rice, were introduced.

The palace, dating from the 11th century, was surrounded by patios, pools and gardens.

Astrolabe
Perfected by the Moors around AD 800, the astrolabe was used by navigators and astronomers.

Remains of a Roman amphitheatre

Silver Casket of Hisham II
In the Caliphate of Córdoba, luxury objects of brilliant craftsmanship were worked in ivory, silver and bronze.

Fortified entrance gate

Curtain walls with watchtowers

TIMELINE

711 Moors, led by Tariq, invade Spain and defeat Visigoths at battle of Guadalete

732 Moors' advance into France is halted by Charles Martel at Poitiers

778 Charlemagne's rearguard defeated by Basques at Roncesvalles *(p130)*

785 Building of great mosque at Córdoba begins

Charlemagne (742–814)

750	800	850

722 Led by Pelayo, Christians defeat Moors at Covadonga *(p105)*

756 Abd al Rahman I proclaims independent emirate in Córdoba

744 Christians under Alfonso I of Asturias take León

Pelayo (718–37)

822 Abd al Rahman II begins 30-year rule marked by patronage of the arts and culture

c.800 Tomb of St James (Santiago) is supposedly discovered at Santiago de Compostela

Puerta de Sabbath in Córdoba's Mezquita
Wealth and artistic brilliance were lavished on mosques, especially in Córdoba (see pp456–7). Calligraphy was a major element in decoration.

WHERE TO SEE MOORISH SPAIN

The finest Moorish buildings are found in Andalusia, especially in the cities of Córdoba *(see pp454–7)* and Granada *(see pp462–8)*. Almería *(see p477)* has a large, ruined *alcazaba* (castle). In Jaén *(see p469)* there are Moorish baths. Further north, in Zaragoza, is the castle-palace of La Aljafería *(see p227).*

***Medina Azahara** (see p453), sacked in the 11th century but partly restored, was the final residence of Córdoba's caliphs.*

Torre del Homenaje, the keep, was built by Abd al Rahman I (756–88).

Baths

Patio with Moorish decoration

ALCAZABA AT MÁLAGA

An *alcazaba* was a castle built into the ramparts of a Moorish city, often protected by massive concentric walls. In Málaga *(see p450)* – the principal port of the Moorish kingdom of Granada – the vast Alcazaba was built in the 8–11th centuries on the site of a Roman fortress, and incorporated massive curtain walls and fortified gates.

Moorish Sword
A fine example of late Moorish craftsman-ship, this sword has a golden pommel. The blade is inscribed with Arabic writing.

Warrior Helmet
Practical as well as ornate, this Islamic nobleman's helmet, made of iron, gold and silver, incorporates inscriptions, a coat of arms and chain mail.

905 Emergent Navarra becomes Christian kingdom under Sancho I

976 Al Mansur, military dictator, usurps caliphal powers and sacks Barcelona. Córdoba Mezquita finished

1010 Medina Azahara sacked by Berbers

900

950

1000

913 Christian capital is established at León

936 Building of Medina Azahara palace starts near Córdoba

Bronze stag from Medina Azahara

1013 Caliphate of Córdoba breaks up. Emergence of *taifas*: small, independent Moorish kingdoms

The Reconquest

THE INFANT CHRISTIAN KINGDOMS in the north – León, Castile, Navarra, Aragón and Catalonia – advanced south gradually in the 11th century, fighting in the name of Christianity to regain land from the Moors. After the fall of Toledo in 1085, the struggle became increasingly a holy war. Militant North African Muslims – Almoravids and Almohads – rallied to the Moorish cause and ultimately took over Al Andalus in the 12th century. As the Christians pushed further south, soon only Granada remained under Moorish control.

Cross of the Knights of St James

SPAIN IN 1173

☐ *Christian kingdoms*

◻ *Al Andalus*

Golden Goblet
The exquisite goblet (1063) of Doña Urraca, daughter of Alfonso VI, shows the quality of medieval Christian craftsmanship.

Fernando I
Fernando formed the first Christian power bloc in 1037 by uniting Léon with Castile, which was emerging as a major military force.

Armies of Castile, Aragón and Navarra

The Almohads
fight until the bitter end, although many comrades lay slain.

Alhambra, Palace of the Nasrids
Moorish art and architecture of singular beauty continued to be produced in the Nasrid kingdom of Granada. Its apogee is the exquisite Alhambra (see pp466–7).

LAS NAVAS DE TOLOSA

The Christian victory over the Almohads in the Battle of Las Navas de Tolosa (1212) led to Moorish Spain's decline. The army of Muhammad II al Nasir was no match for the forces of Sancho VII of Navarra, Pedro II of Aragón and Alfonso VIII of Castile. A stained-glass window in Roncesvalles *(see p130)* depicts the battle.

TIMELINE

Uniforms of military orders

1037 León and Castile united for first time under Fernando I

1065 Death of Fernando I precipitates fratricidal civil war between his sons

1086 Almoravids respond to pleas for help from Moorish emirs by taking over *taifas* (splinter states)

1158 Establishment of the Order of Calatrava, the first military order of knights in Spain

1050

1100

1150

12

1085 Toledo falls to Christians under Alfonso VI of Castile

1094 The legendary El Cid *(see p352)* captures Valencia

El Cid

1137 Ramón Berenguer IV of Catalonia marries Petronila of Aragón uniting the two kingdoms under their son, Alfonso II

1147 Almohads arrive in Al Andalus and make Seville their capital

1143 Portugal becomes separate kingdom

1212 Combined Christian forces defeat Almohads at battle of Las Navas de Tolosa

Cantigas of Alfonso X *(1252–84)*
*This detail of a manuscript by Alfonxo X portrays the
confrontation between Moorish and Christian cavalry.
Alfonso the Learned encouraged his scholars to
master Arab culture and translate ancient
Greek manuscripts brought by the Moors.*

WHERE TO SEE MUDÉJAR SPAIN

The Mudéjares – Muslims who
remained in territories under
Christian occupation – created
a distinctive architectural style
distinguished by its ornamental work in brick, plaster and
ceramics. Aragón, particularly
Zaragoza *(see pp226–7)* and
Teruel *(see pp230–31)*, boasts
some of the finest Mudéjar
buildings. Seville's Reales
Alcázares is an exquisitely
harmonious collection of
patios and halls built under
Pedro I *(see pp422–3)*.

The Mudéjar tower of Teruel
*cathedral combines both brick
and colourful ceramics to
highly decorative effect.*

Sancho VII of
Navarra leads the
Christian forces.

Santa María la Blanca (see
p373), *a former synagogue
and church, shows the fusion
of cultures in medieval Toledo.*

St James (Santiago)
*Known as the Moor-
slayer, St James is said
to have miraculously
intervened at the
Battle of Clavijo in
844. This powerful
figurehead is the
patron saint of Spain.*

?15 Foundation of
?lamanca University

1230 Fernando III
reunites Castile
and León

*Crest of Castile
and León*

1385 Portuguese defeat Castilians at
Aljubarrota, crushing King Juan's
aspirations to throne of Portugal

1388–9
Treaties end
Spanish
phase of
Hundred
Years War

1250	1300	1350	1400

1250 Toledo at its height as a centre
of translation and learning, influenced
by Alfonso X, the Learned

1386 Invasion of Galicia
by the English, ended
by Bayonne Treaty

1232 Granada becomes capital
of future Nasrid kingdom.
Building of the Alhambra begins

Alfonso X

1401 Work starts in Seville
on what was then the world's
largest Gothic cathedral

The Catholic Monarchs

Fernando of Aragón

THE FOUNDATION of the Spanish nation-state was laid by Isabel I of Castile and Fernando II of Aragón *(see p66)*. Uniting their lands in military, diplomatic and religious matters, the "Catholic Monarchs", as they are known, won back Granada, the last Moorish kingdom, from Boabdil. The Inquisition gave Spain a reputation for intolerance, yet in art and architecture brilliant progress was made and the voyages of Columbus opened up the New World.

SPAIN'S EXPLORATION OF THE NEW WORLD

— *Route of Columbus's first voyage*

Tomb of El Doncel *(15th century)*
This effigy of a page who died in the fight for Granada combines ideals of military glory and learning (see p364).

Boabdil, the grief-stricken king, moves forward to hand over the keys to Granada.

Alhambra

The Inquisition
Active from 1478, the Inquisition (see p264) persecuted those suspected of heresy with increasing vigour. This member of the Brotherhood of Death took victims to the stake.

Baptizing Jews
After the Christian reconquest of Granada, Jews were forced to convert or leave Spain. The conversos (converted Jews) were often treated badly.

THE FALL OF GRANADA *(1492)*
This romantic interpretation by Francisco Pradilla (1846–1921) reflects the chivalry of Boabdil, ruler of Granada, as he surrenders the keys of the last Moorish kingdom to the Catholic Monarchs, Fernando and Isabel, following ten long years of war.

TIMELINE

1454 Enrique IV, Isabel's half-brother, accedes to throne of Castile

1465 Civil war erupts in Castile

1478 Papal bull authorizes Castilian Inquisition with Tomás de Torquemada as Inquisitor General

Torquemada

1450	1460	1470	1480

1451 Birth of Isabel of Castile

Fernando and Isabel on 15th-century gold coin

1469 Marriage of Fernando and Isabel in Valladolid unites Castile and Aragón

1474 Death of Enrique IV leads to civil war; Isabel triumphs over Juana la Beltraneja, Enrique's supposed daughter, to become queen

1479 Fernando becomes Fernando II of Aragón

Columbus Arriving in the Americas
The Catholic Monarchs financed Columbus's daring first voyage partly because they hoped for riches in return, but also because they expected him to convert infidels.

Boabdil
As the forlorn king left Granada, his mother reputedly said, "Don't cry as a child over what you could not defend as a man".

ernando f Aragón

Isabel, queen of Castile, witnesses the surrender of Granada, surrounded by a glittering entourage.

WHERE TO SEE GOTHIC ARCHITECTURE IN SPAIN

Spain has many great Gothic cathedrals, especially in Seville *(pp418–19)*, Burgos *(pp354–5)*, Barcelona *(pp144–5)*, Toledo *(pp374–5)* and Palma de Mallorca *(pp496–7)*. Secular buildings from this era include commodity exchanges like La Lonja in Valencia *(p241)* and castles *(pp326–7)*.

León cathedral (pp336–7) has a west front covered in statuary. Here Christ is seen presiding over the Last Judgment.

Crown of Isabel
Worn at the surrender, Isabel's crown is now in her final resting place, the Capilla Real in Granada (see p462).

1494 Treaty of Tordesillas divides the New World territories between Portugal and Spain		**1509** Cardinal Cisneros' troops attack Oran in Algeria and temporarily occupy it	*Cardinal Cisneros*
	1496 Foundation of Santo Domingo, on Hispaniola, first Spanish city in the Americas		

1490	1500	1510
1492 Fall of Granada after ten-year war. Columbus reaches America. Expulsion of Jews from Spain	**1502** Unconverted Moors expelled from Spain *Columbus's ship, the Santa María* **1504** Following death of Isabel, her daughter Juana la Loca becomes queen of Castile with Fernando as regent	**1516** Death of Fernando **1512** Annexation of Navarra, leading to full unification of Spain

The Age of Discovery

FOLLOWING COLUMBUS'S ARRIVAL in the Bahamas in 1492, the conquistadors went into Central and South America, conquering Mexico (1519), Peru (1532) and Chile (1541). In doing so, they destroyed Indian civilizations. In the 16th century, vast quantities of gold and silver flowed across the Atlantic to Spain. Carlos I and his son Felipe II spent some of it on battles to halt the spread of Protestantism in Europe, and in the Holy War against the Turks.

Aztec god (c.1540)

SPANISH EMPIRE IN 1580
☐ *Dominions of Felipe II*

Mapping the World
This 16th-century German map reflects a new world, largely unknown to Europe before the era of conquistadors.

Galleons were armed with cannons as a defence against pirates and rival conquerors.

Aztec Mask
In their great greed and ignorance, the Spanish destroyed the empires and civilizations of the Aztecs in Mexico and the Incas in Peru.

The lookout was essential for spotting enemies and making landfall.

Forecastle

Seville
Granted the trading monopoly with the Americas, Seville, on the banks of the Guadalquivir, was Europe's richest port in the early 16th century.

TIMELINE

1519 Magellan, Portuguese explorer, leaves Seville under Spanish patronage to circumnavigate the globe

1520-21 Revolt by Castilian towns when Carlos I appoints foreigner, Adrian of Utrecht, as regent

1532 Pizarro takes Peru with 180 men and destroys Inca empire

1554 International Catholic alliance created by marriage of future king Felipe II with Mary Tudor of England

Pizarro

| 1520 | 1530 | 1540 | 1550 |

1519 Conquest of Mexico by Cortés. Carlos I crowned Holy Roman Emperor Charles V

1540 Father Bartolomé de las Casas writes book denouncing the oppression of Indians

Conquistador Hernán Cortés

Bartolomé de las Casas

Defeat of the Spanish Armada
Spain's self-esteem suffered a hard blow when its "invincible" 133-ship fleet was destroyed in an attempt to invade Protestant England in 1588.

NEW WORLD CROPS

Not only did Spain profit from the gold and silver brought across the ocean from the Americas, but also from an amazing range of new crops. Some, including potatoes and maize, were introduced for cultivation in Spain while others, such as tobacco and cacao, were mainly grown in native soil. Cocoa, from cacao beans, gained favour as a drink.

Cacao plant

Peruvian with exotic New World fruit

Armour of Felipe II
Felipe II (1556–98) was a cunning administrator, who claimed to rule the world with paper rather than military might.

Flag of Spain (until 1785)

Storage space for New World treasures

SPANISH GALLEON

Although sturdily built to carry New World treasure back to Spain, these ships were hard to manoeuvre except with the wind behind. They were often no match for smaller, swifter pirate vessels.

Carlos I *(1516–56)*
During his tumultuous 40-year reign, Carlos I (Holy Roman Emperor Charles V) often led his troops on the battlefield.

1557 First of a series of partial bankruptcies of Spain

1561 Building of El Escorial, near Madrid, begins

El Escorial (see pp312–3)

1588 Spanish Armada fails in attack on Britain

1560	1570	1580	1590

1561 Madrid becomes capital of Spain

1571 Spanish victory over Turks in naval battle of Lepanto

1580 Portugal unites with Spain for the next 60 years

1568 Moriscos (converted Moors) in the Alpujarras (Granada) rebel against high taxes and persecution

1569 Bible published for first time in Castilian

The Golden Age

SPAIN'S GOLDEN AGE was a time of great artistic and literary achievement led by the painters – El Greco and Velázquez *(see pp28–9)* – and writers *(see pp30–31)*, especially Cervantes and the prolific dramatists, Lope de Vega and Calderón de la Barca. This brilliance occurred, however, against a background of economic deterioration and ruinous wars with the Low Countries and France. Spain was gradually losing its influence in Europe and the reigning house of Habsburg entered irreversible decline.

THE SPANISH EMPIRE IN EUROPE IN 1647

☐ *Spanish territories*

Don Quixote and Sancho Panza
Cervantes' satire on chivalrous romance, Don Quixote, *contrasts the fantasy of the main character with his servant's realism.*

A clock is a reminder of the inevitable passage of time.

The knight is dressed in mid-17th-century fashion.

Money represents worldly wealth.

Duke of Lerma
This bronze statue depicts the Duke of Lerma (c.1550–1625), a favourite of King Felipe III.

THE KNIGHT'S DREAM *(1650)*
This painting, attributed to Antonio de Pereda, is on a familiar Golden Age theme: human vanity. A young gentleman sits asleep beside a table piled with objects symbolizing power, wealth and mortality. The pleasures of life, we are told, are no more real than a dream.

TIMELINE

Felipe III

1600 Capital temporarily moves to Valladolid

1609 Felipe III orders the expulsion of the Moriscos

1619 Construction of Plaza Mayor, Madrid

1621 Low Countries war resumes after 12-year truce

1625 Capture of Breda, Netherlands, after one-year siege

1643 Fall of Count-Duke Olivares. Spain heavily defeated by France at battle of Rocroi

1600	1610	1620	1630	1640

1605 Publication of first of two parts of Cervantes' *Don Quixote*

1609 Lope de Vega publishes poem on the art of comic drama

1622 Velázquez moves from Seville to Madrid to become court painter the following year

Lope de Vega (1562–1635)

1640 Secession of Portugal, amalgamated with Spain since 1580

Fiesta in the Plaza Mayor in Madrid
This famous square (see p263) *became the scene for pageants, royal celebrations, bullfights and executions, all overlooked from the balconies.*

SEVILLE SCHOOL OF ART

Seville's wealth, together with the patronage of the Church, made it a centre of the arts, second only to the royal court. Velázquez, who was born in Seville, trained under the painter Pacheco. Sculptor Juan Martínez Montañés and painters Zurbarán and Murillo created great works which are displayed in the Museo de Bellas Artes *(see p412).*

San Diego de Alcalá Giving Food to the Poor (c.1646) by Murillo

An angel warns that death is near.

The banner says, "It (death) pierces perpetually, flies quickly and kills".

A mask symbolizes the Arts.

Expulsion of the Moriscos
Although they had converted to Christianity, the last Moors were still expelled in 1609.

Weapons represent power.

The skull on the book shows death triumphant over learning.

Surrender of Breda
Spain took the Dutch city of Breda on 5 June 1625 after a year-long siege. The event was later painted by Velázquez.

1652 Spanish troops regain Catalonia, following 12-year war with France

Calderón de la Barca

1669 Calderón de la Barca's last work, *La Estátua de Prometeo,* is published

1683–4 Louis XIV attacks Catalonia and Spanish Netherlands

1650	1660	1670	1680	1690	1700

1648 Holland achieves independence from Spain by Treaty of Westphalia, ending Thirty Years War

1659 Peace of the Pyrenees signed with France. Louis XIV marries Felipe IV's daughter María Teresa, leading to Bourbon succession in Spain

Coin from the reign of Felipe IV

1700 Death of Carlos II brings Habsburg line to an end. Felipe V, the first Bourbon king, ascends the throne

Bourbons to First Republic

THE WAR OF THE SPANISH SUCCESSION ended in triumph for the Bourbons, who made Spain a centralized nation. Their power was at its height during the reign of the enlightened despot, Carlos III. But the 19th century was a troubled time. An invasion by revolutionary France led to the War of Independence (Peninsular War). Later came the Carlist Wars – caused by another dispute over the succession – liberal revolts and the short-lived First Republic.

Isabel II

SPAIN IN 1714

☐ *Domain after Treaty of Utrecht*

The Enlightenment

The Enlightenment brought new learning and novel projects. On 5 July 1784 this Montgolfier balloon rose above Madrid.

A Franciscan friar is among the innocent victims.

Queen María Luisa

The dominating María Luisa of Parma, portrayed by Goya, forced her husband Carlos IV to appoint her lover, Manuel Godoy, prime minister in 1792.

Spanish rebel faces death in a gesture of crucifixion.

Hundreds of lives were taken in the executions, which lasted several days.

Battle of Trafalgar

The defeat of the Franco-Spanish fleet by the British admiral, Lord Nelson, off Cape Trafalgar in 1805 was the end of Spanish sea power.

TIMELINE

1702–14 War of the Spanish Succession. Spain loses Netherlands and Gibraltar by Treaty of Utrecht

1724 Luis I (son of Felipe V) gains throne when his father abdicates, but dies within a year; Felipe V reinstated

1767 Carlos III expels Jesuits from Spain and Spanish colonies

| 1700 | 1720 | 1740 | 1760 | 17 |

1714 Siege and reduction of Barcelona by Felipe V

Felipe V, the first Bourbon king (1700–24)

Count of Floridablanca (1728–1808)

1762–3 English government declares war on Spanish over colonies in America

1782 Count of Floridablanca helps to recover Menorca from England

Carlos III Leaving Naples
When Fernando VI died without an heir in 1759, his half-brother Carlos VII of Naples was put on the Spanish throne as Carlos III. His enlightened reign saw the foundation of academies of science and art and the beginning of free trade.

French soldiers, operating on orders from Marshal Murat, execute Spanish patriots.

General Prim *(1814–70)*
General Prim was one of 19th-century Spain's most influential figures. He forced the abdication of Isabel II, and pursued liberal policies until assassinated in Madrid.

French infantry helmet

THE 3RD OF MAY BY GOYA *(1814)*
On 2 May 1808, in reaction to Napoleon's occupation of Spain, the people of Madrid rose in vain against the occupying French forces. The next day the French army took its revenge by executing hundreds of people, both rebels and bystanders. These events sparked off the War of Independence.

Baroque Magnificence
The sacristy of the Monasterio de la Cartuja in Granada is typical of Spanish Baroque, more sumptuous than anywhere else in Europe.

1805 Battle of Trafalgar. Nelson defeats French and Spanish at sea	**1809** Wellington's troops join with Spanish to triumph over French at Talavera		**1841–3** María Cristina, followed by General Espartero, acts as regent for Isabel II
	Duke of Wellington		**1868** Revolution under General Prim forces Isabel II into exile. Amadeo I is king for three years from 1870
1800	**1820**	**1840**	**1860**
1808–14 Joseph Bonaparte on throne. War of Independence	**1824** Peru is the last South American country to gain independence	**1833–9** First Carlist War	**1836** Mendizábal seizes monastic property for the Spanish state
1812 Promulgation of liberal constitution in Cádiz leads to military uprising			**1847–9** Second Carlist War

Carlist soldiers

Republicans and Anarchists

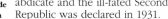

SPAIN'S FIRST REPUBLIC lasted only a year (1873) and consumed four presidents. The late 19th century was a time of national decline, with Anarchism developing in reaction to rampant political corruption. The loss of Cuba, in 1898, was a low point for Spain, although there was a flurry of literary and artistic activity in the following years. The country's increasing instability was briefly checked by the dictatorship of Primo de Rivera. Spanish politics, however, were becoming polarized. Alfonso XIII was forced to abdicate and the ill-fated Second Republic was declared in 1931.

Primo de Rivera

THE LEGACY OF SPANISH COLONIZATION IN 1900

☐ *Spanish-speaking territories*

Anarchist Propaganda
Anarchism was idealistic, though often violent. This poster states, "Anarchist books are weapons against Fascism".

Workers unite, calling for radical social reform.

Pío Baroja
Baroja (1872–1956) was one of the most gifted novelists of his day. He was too original to be grouped with the writers of the Generation of 1898, who tried to create a national renaissance after the loss of Spain's colonies.

POWER TO THE PEOPLE
Political protest was rife under the Second Republic, as shown by this Communist demonstration in the Basque Country in 1932. Industrial workers banded together, forming trade unions to demand better pay and working conditions, and staging strikes. The Spanish Communist Party developed later than the Anarchists, but eventually gained more support.

TIMELINE

1873 Declaration of First Republic, lasting only one year

First Republic's last president, Emilio Castelar (1832–99)

1888 Universal Exhibition in Barcelona creates new buildings and parks, such as the Parc de la Ciutadella

1897 Prime Minister Cánovas del Castillo assassinated by an Italian Anarchist

1870 — 1880 — 1890 — 1900

1875 Second Bourbon restoration puts Alfonso XII on throne

1870–75 Third Carlist War

Alfonso XII and Queen María

1893 Anarchists bomb opera-goers in the Barcelona Liceu

1898 Cuba and Philippines gain independence from Spain following the Spanish-American War

Tragic Week
Led by Anarchists and Republicans, workers in Barcelona took to the streets in 1909 to resist a military call-up. The reprisals were brutal.

Universal Exhibitions
In 1929, Seville and Barcelona were transformed by exhibitions promoting art and industry. The fairs brought international recognition.

The banner appeals for working-class solidarity.

Picasso
Born in Málaga in 1881, the artist Pablo Picasso spent his formative years as a painter in the city of Barcelona (see p148) before moving to Paris in the 1930s.

Cuban War of Independence
Cuba began its fight for freedom in 1895, led by local patriots such as Antonio Maceo. In the disastrous campaign, Spain lost 50,000 soldiers and most of its navy.

The Garrotte
Convicted Anarchists were executed by the garrotte – an iron collar that brutally strangled the victim while crushing the neck.

	Second Republic election poster		
1912 Prime Minister José Canalejas murdered by Anarchists in Madrid	**1921** Crushing defeat of Spanish army at Anual, Morocco	**1931** Proclamation of Second Republic with a two-year coalition between Socialists and Republicans	**1933** General election returns right-wing government
1910	**1920**	**1930**	
1909 Semana Trágica (Tragic Week) in Barcelona. Workers' revolt against conscription for Moroccan Wars quashed by Government troops	**1923** Primo de Rivera stages victorious coup to become military dictator under Alfonso XIII	**1930** Primo de Rivera resigns after losing military support	**1934** Revolution of Asturian miners suppressed by army under General Franco
		1931 Republicans win local elections, causing Alfonso XIII to abdicate	

Civil War and the Franco Era

SPAIN ON 31 JULY 1936
☐ *Republican-held areas*
■ *Nationalist-held areas*

NATIONALIST GENERALS rose against the government in 1936, starting the Spanish Civil War. The Nationalists, under General Franco, were halted by the Republicans outside Madrid, but with support from Hitler and Mussolini they inched their way to victory in the north and east. Madrid finally fell in early 1939. After the war, thousands of Republicans were executed in reprisals. Spain was internationally isolated until the 1950s, when the United States brought her into the western military alliance.

Franco

Franco's Ideal World
Under Franco, Church and State were united. This poster shows the strong influence of religion on education.

Anguished mother with dead child

Composition reflecting total chaos

GUERNICA *(1937)*
On behalf of advancing Nationalists, the Nazi Condor Legion bombed the Basque town of Gernika *(see p114)* on 26 April 1937 – a busy market day. This was Europe's first air raid on civilians, and it inspired Picasso's shocking *Guernica (see p289)*. Painted for a Republican Government exhibition in Paris, it is full of symbols of disaster.

POR LAS ARMAS
La Patria el Pan y la Justicia

Nationalist Poster
A Nationalist poster adorned with Fascist arrows reads "Fight for the Fatherland, Bread and Justice".

TIMELINE

1936 Republican Popular Front wins the general election on 16 January. On 17 July, Nationalist generals rise against Republicans	**1938** On 8 January, Republicans lose battle for Teruel in bitter cold	**1945** By end of World War II, Spain is diplomatically and politically isolated
	1939 In March, Madrid, Valencia and Alicante fall in quick succession to Franco's troops	**1947** Spain declared monarchy with Franco as regent
1935	**1940**	**1945**	**1950**
1936 Nationalists declare Franco head of state on 29 September	**1939** Franco declares end of war on 1 April and demands unconditional surrender from Republicans	**1953** Deal with US permits American bases on Spanish soil in exchange for aid
1937 On 26 April, Nazi planes bomb Basque town of Guernika (Gernika-Lumo)	**1938** On 23 December, Nationalists bomb Barcelona	*Soldiers surrendering to Nationalist troops*

GARCÍA LORCA

Federico García Lorca (1898–1936) was Spain's most brilliant dramatist and lyric poet of the 1920s and '30s. His homosexuality and association with the left, however, made him a target for Nationalist assassins. He was shot by an ad hoc firing squad near his home town of Granada.

Scene from his play _Blood Wedding_

A wounded horse representing the Spanish people

Witnesses to the massacre stare in wonder and disbelief.

Anarchist Poster
Anarchists fought for the Republic, forming agricultural collectives behind the lines. Their influence waned when they were discredited by the Communist Party.

Crucifixion gesture

The flower is a symbol of hope in the midst of despair.

The Hungry Years
Ration cards illustrate the postwar period when Spain nearly starved. Shunned by other nations, she received aid from the US in 1953 in return for accepting military bases.

Spanish Refugees
As the Nationalists came closer to victory, thousands of artists, writers, intellectuals and other Republican supporters fled Spain into indefinite exile.

1962 Tourism on the Mediterranean coast is boosted by official go-ahead

Sunbathers

1969 Franco declares Prince Juan Carlos his successor

1973 ETA assassinates Admiral Carrero Blanco, Franco's hard-line prime minister

1955	1960	1965	1970	1975

1959 Founding of ETA, Basque separatist group

1970 "Burgos trials" of the regime's opponents outrage world opinion

1955 Spain joins United Nations

Franco's funeral, 23 November 1975

1975 Death of Franco results in third Bourbon restoration as Juan Carlos is proclaimed king

Modern Spain

FRANCO'S DEATH left Spain's political future hanging in the balance. But few people wanted to preserve the old regime and the transition from dictatorship to democracy proved surprisingly swift and painless. The previously-outlawed Socialist Workers' Party, under Felipe González, won the general election in 1982 and set about modernizing Spain. Considerable power has since been devolved to the regions. A major threat facing central government has been the persistent violence of ETA, the Basque separatist organization. Spain's international relations have been strengthened by her membership of NATO and the European Union.

Contemporary Spanish fashion

SPAIN TODAY

☐ *Spain*

■ *Other European Union states*

Castilla and León's modern pavilion was one of EXPO's 150 pavilions built to innovative designs.

Hi-tech floodlight

Coup d'Etat, 23 February 1981
Civil Guard colonel, Antonio Tejero, held parliament at gunpoint for several hours. Democracy survived because King Juan Carlos refused to support the rebels.

Anti-NATO Protest Rally
When Spain joined NATO in 1982, some saw it as a reversal of Socialist ideals. To others it represented an improvement in Spain's international standing.

EXPO '92
Over 100 countries were represented at the Universal Exposition which focused world attention on Seville in 1992. The many pavilions displayed scientific, technological and cultural exhibits.

TIMELINE

1977 First free elections return centrist government under Adolfo Suárez. Political parties, including Communists, are legalized

1981 Military officers stage attempted coup d'etat to overthrow democracy

1982 World Cup held in Spain. Spain joins NATO

Felipe González

1980

1985

Spanish royal family

1982 Landslide electoral victory brings Socialist Workers' Party (PSOE), under Felipe González, to power

1983 Semi-autonomous regional governments are established to appease Basque Country and Catalonia

1986 Spain joins EC (now EU)

1989 Spain holds presidency of European Community

Tourism
From 1959–73 the number of annual visitors to Spain grew from 3 million to 34 million, transforming the once-quiet coasts and islands.

Felipe González Elected
In 1982 the Spanish Socialist Workers' Party (PSOE) leader was elected prime minister. González transformed Spain during his 13 years in power.

Leaning blue tower
rises above Andalusia's pavilion.

Ana Belén
Spanish women have enjoyed ever greater freedom and opportunity since the advent of democracy. In a 1980s opinion poll, they voted the singer and actress, Ana Belén, the woman they most admired.

El País
Founded in Madrid in 1976, the liberal daily El País *is the best-selling newspaper in Spain. During the transition to democracy it had a great influence on public opinion.*

A monorail
carried visitors around the site.

Barcelona Olympic Games
The opening ceremony of the Barcelona Olympics included stunning displays of music, dance and colourful costumes.

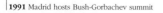

| 1992 Spain celebrates quincentenary of Columbus's voyage to America | 1993 González wins third term in office | 1994/5 Corruption scandals rock the long-serving government | 1996 In the general election on 3 March, González loses to a coalition led by Aznar |
| | | | 1998 ETA, the Basque separatist terrorist group, announces a ceasefire |

990	1995	2000

1992 Barcelona Olympics and Seville Expo '92 place Spain firmly within community of modern European nations

2000 Religious celebrations for the Millennium year in Spain's churches

1991 Madrid hosts Bush-Gorbachev summit

Cobi, Barcelona Olympic Mascot

Rulers of Spain

Spain BECAME A NATION-STATE under Isabel and Fernando, whose marriage eventually united Castile and Aragón. With their daughter Juana's marriage, the kingdom was delivered into Habsburg hands. Carlos I and Felipe II were both capable rulers, but in 1700 Carlos II died without leaving an heir. After the War of the Spanish Succession, Spain came under the French Bourbons, who have ruled ever since – apart from an interregnum, two republics and Franco's dictatorship. The current Bourbon king, Juan Carlos I, a constitutional monarch, is respected for his support of democracy.

1665–1700 Carlos II

1516–56 Carlos I of Spain (Holy Roman Emperor Charles V)

1479–1516 Fernando, King of Aragón

1598–1621 Felipe III

1474–1504 Isabel, Queen of Castile

1400	1450	1500	1550	1600	1650
INDEPENDENT KINGDOMS			**HABSBURG DYNASTY**		
1400	1450	1500	1550	1600	1650

1469 Marriage of Isabel and Fernando leads to unification of Spain

1504–16 Juana la Loca (with Fernando as regent)

1621–65 Felipe IV

Fernando and Isabel, the Catholic Monarchs

UNIFICATION OF SPAIN

In the late 15th century the two largest kingdoms in developing Christian Spain – Castile, with its military might, and Aragón (including Barcelona and a Mediterranean empire) – were united. The marriage of Isabel of Castile and Fernando of Aragón in 1469 joined these powerful kingdoms. Together the so-called Catholic Monarchs defeated the Nasrid Kingdom of Granada, the last stronghold of the Moors *(see pp52–3)*. With the addition of Navarra in 1512, Spain was finally unified.

1556–98 Felipe II

1843–68 Isabel II reigns following the regency of her mother María Cristina (1833–41) and Espartero (1841–3)

1814–33 First Bourbon restoration, following French rule: Fernando VII

1871–3 Break in Bourbon rule: Amadeo I of Savoy

1939–75 General Franco Head of State

1724 Luis I reigns after Felipe V's abdication, but dies within a year

1759–88 Carlos III

1931–9 Second Republic

1875–85 Second Bourbon restoration: Alfonso XII

1700	1750	1800	1850	1900	1950

BOURBON DYNASTY   **BOURBON**   **BOURBON**

1700	1750	1800	1850	1900	1950

1808–13 Break in Bourbon rule: Napoleon's brother, Joseph Bonaparte, rules as José I

1746–59 Fernando VI

1788–1808 Carlos IV

1724–46 Felipe V reinstated as king upon the death of his son, Luis I

1902–31 Alfonso XIII

1886–1902 María-Cristina of Habsburg-Lorraine as regent for Alfonso XIII

1873–4 First Republic

1700–24 Felipe V

1868–70 The Septembrina Revolution

1975 Third Bourbon restoration: Juan Carlos I

NORTHERN SPAIN

Introducing Northern Spain

INCREASING NUMBERS of visitors are discovering the quiet, sandy beaches and deep green landscapes of Northern Spain. The Atlantic coast, from the Pyrenees to the Portuguese border, is often scenic but at its most attractive in the cliffs and rias of Galicia. Inland, the mild, wet climate has created lush meadows and broad-leaved forests, making this area ideal for a peaceful, rural holiday. The famous medieval pilgrimage route to the city of Santiago de Compostela crosses Northern Spain, its way marked by magnificent examples of Romanesque architecture. Plentiful seafood and dairy produce, and the outstanding red wines of La Rioja, add to the pleasure of a tour through this part of Spain.

Oviedo (see p102) *has a number of Pre-Romanesque churches, most notably the graceful Santa María del Naranco, and a fine Gothic cathedral.*

Lugo

A Coruña

GALICIA
(see pp80–95)

Asturias

ASTURIAS AND CANTABRIA
(see pp96–109)

Ourense

Pontevedra

The Rías Baixas (see p91) *is one of Spain's prettiest coastlines. Scattered around its pretty towns and villages are many quaint* hórreos, *grain stores, raised on stone stilts.*

Santiago de Compostela (see pp86–9) *attracts thousands of pilgrims and tourists each year. Its majestic cathedral was one of the most important shrines in medieval Christendom.*

The Picos de Europa *mountain range* (see pp104–105) *dominates the landscape of Asturias and Cantabria. Rivers have carved deep gorges through the mountains and there are many footpaths through a variety of spectacular scenery.*

| 0 kilometres | 50 |
| 0 miles | 25 |

Santillana del Mar (see p108), *with its well-preserved medieval streets, is one of the most picturesque towns in Spain. The Convento de Regina Coeli houses a small museum containing a collection of painted wooden figures and other works of religious art.*

San Sebastián (see p118), *the most elegant holiday resort in the Basque Country, is sited around a beautiful horseshoe bay of golden sandy beaches. The city hosts international arts events, including Spain's premier film festival.*

Cantabria

Vizcaya

Guipúzcoa

Álava

Navarra

THE BASQUE COUNTRY, NAVARRA AND LA RIOJA
(see pp110–31)

La Rioja

Pamplona (see pp128–9), *the capital of Navarra since the 9th century, is best known for its annual fiesta, Los Sanfermines. The highlight of each day of riotous celebration is the* Encierro, *in which bulls stampede through the streets of the city.*

The Monasterio de Leyre (see p131), *founded in the early 11th century, was built in a lonely but attractive landscape. The monastery was once the burial place of the kings of Navarra and its crypt is among the finest examples of early Romanesque art in Spain.*

Regional Food: Northern Spain

THE CUISINE of Northern Spain is distinguished by abundant fish and seafood from the Atlantic. The region is also Spain's dairy and the source of some of the country's finest cheeses. Year-round rainfall yields a variety of fresh vegetables, particularly potatoes, cabbages and sweetcorn. Vast mountain ranges mean plentiful game, hams and cured sausages, which are combined with beans to form hearty stews. The Basques, with their famous gastronomical societies and New Basque Cuisine, are said to produce the most sophisticated and varied food in Spain: intriguing sauces boost even salted cod to gourmet heights. Asturias is recognized for its plentiful fish, vegetables and the production of dry cider from apples; while inland Navarra is famed for its locally grown white asparagus, which it cans for the whole of Spain, as well as supplying the country with the essential, spicy, pointed pepper *pimiento piquillo*.

White asparagus

Txangurro relleno *is a Basque dish made with spider crab. The meat is cleaned, stuffed into the shell and cooked au gratin.*

Beans are an essential element of northern cooking, and there are many specially cultivated varieties. The best, and the most expensive, are La Granja beans from Asturias. Costing double the price of lamb, they are probably the best beans in the world. Tolosa, in the Basque Country, is famous for its red and black beans.

Revuelto, *creamy scrambled egg, is served all along the north coast. It is tastiest accompanied by prawns and wild asparagus.*

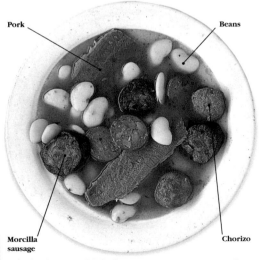

Pork

Beans

Morcilla sausage

Chorizo

Fabada, *the regional dish of Asturias, is a savoury stew combining pork and beans. Fat buttery* fava beans are simmered with tocino *(salt pork), morcilla (black sausage), smoky chorizo sausage and ham. Beef is also included sometimes. The beans take on the rich flavour of the meat, especially the* tocino.

Empanada, *the Galician flat pie, is stuffed with salted cod or tuna. Shellfish and pork are alternative fillings.*

Angulas *(elvers), a winter luxury in the Basque dining clubs, are cooked lightly with oil, garlic and chilli.*

Pimientos rellenos, *from Navarra, are the local spicy pointed red pepper stuffed with fish, seafood or meat.*

Truchas a la Navarra *are cleaned and deboned mountain trout which are stuffed with serrano ham and fried or grilled.*

Vieras de Santiago *are scallops (the symbol of St James) in the shell, covered in a tomato and brandy sauce and grilled.*

Lacón con grelos *is the Galician national dish of cured pork shoulder with turnip tops and sausage.*

Chilindrón de cordero, *a rich dish of spicy lamb stewed with local dried or fresh peppers, is a speciality of Navarra.*

Casadielles   Carajitos

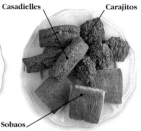

Sobaos

Cakes and biscuits *include* sobaos *(a Cantabrian breakfast sponge),* hazelnut *carajitos and* walnut-stuffed *casadielles.*

CHEESES

From the Asturian mountains come the famous pungent blue Cabrales and Picón. Galicia is noted for soft cheeses, especially *tetilla*. Pear-shaped San Simón, smoked Basque Idiazábal and Roncal are also recommended.

Idiazábal

Cabrales

Tetilla

Bacalao   **Anchovies**   **Canned tuna**   **Scallops**   **Mussels**   **Spider crab**

FISH AND SEAFOOD

Some of the most delicious seafood in Europe comes from the Atlantic coast of Spain. Specialities include mussels, scallops, lobsters, octopus, and unusual tall, black barnacles known as *percebes*. The north coast also supplies spider crabs, fat anchovies, and top quality tuna, much of which is canned. The Basques fish for cod off the coasts of Iceland and Norway. Most of the catch is salted, dried and sold throughout Spain as the ever popular *bacalao*.

Wines of Northern Spain

S PAIN'S MOST PRESTIGIOUS wine region, Rioja is best known for its red wines, matured to a distinctive vanilla mellowness. Some of the most prestigious bodegas were founded by émigrés from Bordeaux, and Rioja reds are similar to claret. Rioja also produces good white and rosé wines. Navarra reds and some whites have improved dramatically, thanks to a government research programme. The Basque region produces a tiny amount of the prickly, tart *txacoli* (*chacolí*). Larger quantities of a similar wine are made further west in Galicia, whose best wines are full-bodied whites.

Repairing barrels in Haro, Rioja

Ribeiro, the popular everyday wine of Galicia, is slightly fizzy. It is often served in white porcelain cups (tazas).

KEY

- Rías Baixas
- Ribeiro
- Valdeorras
- Txacoli de Guetaria
- Rioja
- Navarra

0 kilometres   50

0 miles   25

Lagar de Cervera is from Rías Baixas, where Spain's most fashionable whites are made from the Albariño grape.

WINE REGIONS

The wine regions of Northern Spain are widely dispersed. Cradled between the Pyrenees and the Atlantic are the important regions of Rioja and Navarra. Rioja is divided into the sub-regions of Rioja Alavesa, Rioja Alta and Rioja Baja, divided by the Río Ebro. The river also cuts through the wine region of Navarra. To the north are some of the vineyards of the Basque country: the miniscule Txacoli de Guetaria region. In the far west lie the four wine regions of rugged, wet Galicia: Rías Baixas, Ribeiro, Valdeorras, and the newly created Ribera Sacra.

Wine village of El Villar de Álava in Rioja Alta

Gathering the grape harvest in the traditional way in Navarra

Remelluri, one of
the new single-
estate "Château"
Riojas, from the
vineyards of Rioja
Alavesa, is soft and
not too oaky.

Chivite, from a family
bodega in Navarra, is
made entirely from
Tempranillo and aged in
the barrel, resulting in a
style similar to Rioja.

Viña Ardanza is
blended, as are most red
Riojas. The best, like this
reserva, are aged for
two or more years in
American oak casks.

N634 SANTANDER A8
N635 N621 N611 N629
BILBO (BILBAO) Zumaia Getaria DONOSTIA (SAN SEBASTIÁN)
A8 A68 N240 N130 N135
GASTEIZ (VITORIA) N1 A15
IRUÑA (PAMPLONA) N240
Haro Lizarra (Estella)
A68 Logroño Tafalla A15
Nájera Olite
Calahorra Ebro
Arnedo Alfaro
Corella
Tudela N13 A68

Key Facts about Wines of Northern Spain

Location and Climate
Rioja and Navarra are influenced by both Mediterranean
and Atlantic weather systems.
The hillier, northwestern parts receive some
Atlantic rain while the hot Ebro plain has a
Mediterranean climate. The Basque region
and Galicia are both cool, Atlantic regions
with high rainfall. Soils everywhere are stony
and poor, except in the Ebro plain.

Grape Varieties
The great red grape of Rioja and
Navarra is Tempranillo. In Rioja it
is blended with smaller quantities
of Garnacha, Graciano and Mazuelo, while
in Navarra Cabernet Sauvignon is permitted
and blends excitingly with Tempranillo.
Garnacha, also important in Navarra, is used

for the excellent *rosados* (rosés). Whites of
Navarra and Rioja are made mainly from the
Viura grape. Galicia has many local varieties,
of which the most important are Albariño,
Loureira and Treixadura, which is now
taking over from the inferior Palomino.

Good Producers
Rías Baixas: Fillaboa, Lagar de
Fornelos, Morgadío, Santiago Ruiz.
Ribeiro: Cooperativa Vinícola del
Ribeiro. **Rioja:** Bodegas Riojanas
(Canchales, Monte Real), CVNE (Imperial,
Viña Real Oro), Faustino Martínez, Federico
Paternina, Marqués de Cáceres, Marqués de
Murrieta, Martínez Bujanda, Remelluri, La
Rioja Alta (Viña Ardanza). **Navarra:** Bodega
de Sarría, Guelbenzu, Julián Chivite (Gran
Feudo), Magaña, Ochoa, Príncipe de Viana.

Forses of the North

Forest in Northern Spain in autumn

MUCH OF SPAIN was once blanketed by a mantle of trees. Today, just ten per cent of the original cover remains, mostly in the mountainous north, where rainfall is high and slopes too steep for cultivation. Large areas of mixed deciduous forest – mainly beech, Pyrenean oak and chestnut, with some ash and lime – dominate the landscape, particularly in Cantabria and the Basque Country. The undergrowth of shrubs and flowering plants provides habitats for many insects, mammals and birds. The forests are also the refuge of Spain's last brown bears *(see p100)*.

Purple emperor butterfly

REGENERATION OF THE FOREST

Dead materials – leaves, twigs and the excrement and bodies of animals – are broken down by various organisms on the forest floor, especially fungi, bacteria and ants. This process releases nutrients which are absorbed by trees and other plants, enabling them to grow.

Fly agaric mushrooms

Lichens *grow slowly and are sensitive to pollution. Their presence in a forest often indicates that it is in good health.*

The stag beetle *takes its name from the huge antler-like mandibles of the male. Despite their ferocious appearance, these beetles are harmless to humans.*

Millipede and fungus on a woodland floor

BEECH FOREST

Beech, the dominant species in the Cantabrian mountains and Pyrenees, grows on well-drained soils. Some trees retain their distinctive copper-red leaves through the winter. Beech mast (nuts) are collected to feed to pigs.

Beech leaf and mast

The thick crown shuts out light, inhibiting undergrowth.

Long, thin orange buds

Male golden orioles, *among the most colourful European birds, are hard to spot because they spend much of their time in the thick cover provided by old woodlands. Females and juveniles are a duller yellow-green with a brownish tail.*

Beech martens *are nocturnal. By day, they sleep in a hollow tree or another animal's abandoned nest. At night they feed on fruit, birds and small mammals.*

DISTRIBUTION OF BROAD-LEAVED FORESTS

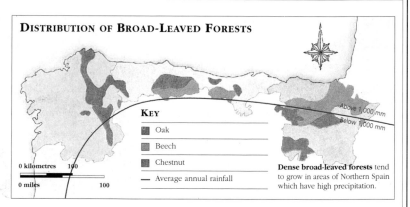

KEY

- Oak
- Beech
- Chestnut
- — Average annual rainfall

0 kilometres 100

0 miles 100

Above 1,000 mm

Below 1,000 mm

Dense broad-leaved forests tend to grow in areas of Northern Spain which have high precipitation.

CHESTNUT FOREST

Chestnut trees grow on well-drained acidic soils. They have slender yellow flowers and in summer produce their fruit, which is eaten by wild boar, dormice, squirrels and mice. The wood is hard and durable but splits easily.

Leaf and chestnut

OAK FOREST

Three main species of oak tree – pedunculate, Pyrenean and the evergreen holm oak – dominate the ancient woodlands of the north. Over 300 species of animal, such as wild boar, squirrels and nuthatches, feed off oaks.

Oak leaf and acorn

Large leaves have sharp, serrated edges.

Few massive, spreading branches

Grey twigs ending in numerous buds

Deep spiral ridges on trunk

The pipistrelle bat is a nocturnal species common in woodlands. It catches and eats small insects in flight. Larger insects are taken to a perch. The bat hibernates in winter in a hollow tree or cave.

The jay, a member of the crow family, is a common but somewhat shy woodland bird with a distinctively raucous cry. It can be identified in flight by its white rump, black tail and above all by its bright blue wing patch.

Blue tits feed mainly in the tree canopy of broad-leaved woods and rarely come down to the ground. The male and female have similar, distinctive plumage. They may raise the back feathers of the crown if alarmed.

Red squirrels bury large numbers of acorns during autumn to last through winter, since these diurnal creatures do not hibernate. Many of the acorns are left to sprout into seedlings.

The Road to Santiago

St James on horseback

ACCORDING TO LEGEND, the body of Christ's apostle James was brought to Galicia. In 813 the relics were supposedly discovered at Santiago de Compostela, where a cathedral was built in his honour *(see pp88–9)*. In the Middle Ages half a million pilgrims a year flocked there from all over Europe, crossing the Pyrenees at Roncesvalles *(see p130)* or via the Somport Pass *(see p220)*. They often donned the traditional garb of cape, long staff and curling felt hat adorned with scallop shells, the symbol of the saint. The various routes, marked by the cathedrals, churches and hospitals built along them, are still used by travellers today.

19th-century painting of the Pórtico da Gloria of Santiago cathedral

A certificate is given to pilgrims covering 100 km (62 miles) of the route on foot, or 200 km (125 miles) on horseback.

Astorga *(see p334), once a Roman city, was an important halt on the pilgrim route in the Middle Ages. The museum within its cathedral has a collection of gold and silver plate including a 13th-century gold filigree cross.*

O Cebreiro *(see p95)* has a 9th-century church and some of the ancient *pallozas* the pilgrims often used for shelter.

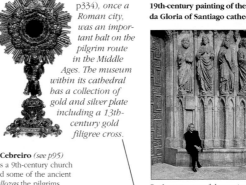

León *was one of the main pilgrim stops. Its cathedral (see pp336–7) contains one of Spain's finest collections of stained glass.*

Ribadeo

Oviedo

A Coruña

SANTIAGO DE COMPOSTELA

Maritime Route

Vilar de Donas

Ligonde

Portuguese Route

PORTO ↓ LISBOA

O Cebreiro

Villafranca del Bierzo

Ponferrada huge Templar castle stands close to the town centre *(see p334).*

Ponferrada

Astorga

Hospital de Órbigo

Sahagún

LEÓN

Vigo

Silver Route

Scallop shells, staffs and gourds to carry water are symbols of the pilgrimage.

0 kilometres   50

0 miles   50

SALAMANCA

ROMANESQUE CHURCH ARCHITECTURE

The Romanesque style of architecture *(see p20)* was brought to Spain from France during the 10th and 11th centuries. As the pilgrimage to Santiago became more popular, many glorious religious buildings were constructed along its main routes. Massive walls, few windows, round heavy arches and barrel vaulting are typical features of Romanesque architecture.

Carved capital

Octagonal lantern

Twin round towers

Barrel vault

Thick walls

Round arch

Façade

Cross-section

San Martín de Frómista (see p350), *built in the 11th century, is the only complete example of the "pilgrimage" style of Romanesque. The nave and aisles are almost the same height and there are three parallel apses.*

Parallel apses   **Aisle**   **Nave**

Floorplan

Pamplona's *(see p128) Gothic cathedral was one of the pilgrims' first stops after crossing the Pyrenees at Roncesvalles.*

Santo Domingo de la Calzada's *(see p124)* pilgrim hospital is now a parador.

Puente la Reina *(see p127) takes its name from the 11th-century humpbacked bridge (puente), built for pilgrims and still used by pedestrians.*

Santander

Northern Route

Donostia (San Sebastián)   ↗ PARIS

Bilbo (Bilbao)

LE PUY VEZELAY

Valcarlos

↑ ARLES

Frómista preserves one of the finest Romanesque churches on the French route.

Orreaga (Roncesvalles)

Iruña (Pamplona)

Lizarra (Estella)

San Juan de Ortega

Santo Domingo de la Calzada

Puente la Reina

French Route

Sangüesa

Aragonese Route

Jaca

San Juan de la Peña

Nájera   **Logroño**

rómista

BURGOS

ROUTES TO SANTIAGO

Several traditional pilgrimage roads converge on Santiago de Compostela. The main road from the Pyrenees is known as the French Route, with the Aragonese Route as a variation.

Burgos has a magnificent Gothic cathedral *(see pp354–5).*

GALICIA

··

LUGO · A CORUÑA · PONTEVEDRA · OURENSE

REMOTE IN THE NORTHWEST CORNER *of the peninsula, Galicia is the country's greenest region. In its hilly interior, smallholdings are farmed by traditional methods. Galicia is Spain's main seafaring region – three of its four provinces have an Atlantic coastline, and its cuisine is based on superb seafood. The Galicians, whose origins are Celtic, are fiercely proud of their culture and language.*

Much of Galicia still has a medieval quality. Some inland farms are divided into plots too tiny or steep for tractors to work, so oxen and horses are used for ploughing. Grain is stored in quaint, pillared granaries called *hórreos*. The misty, emerald countryside abounds with old granite villages and is dotted with *pazos* – traditional stone manor houses.

The discovery of the supposed tomb of St James the Apostle, in the 9th century, confirmed medieval Santiago de Compostela as Europe's most important religious shrine after St Peter's in Rome. Pilgrims and tourists still follow this ancient route of pilgrimage across Northern Spain. The Galician coast is incised by many fjord-like rias; the loveliest of these are the Rías Baixas in the west. Elsewhere it juts defiantly into the Atlantic in rocky headlands, such as Cabo Fisterra, Spain's most westerly point. Many people still make a living from the sea. Vigo in Pontevedra is the most important fishing port in Spain.

Galicia's official language, used on most signs, is *gallego*. It has similarities to the language of Portugal, which borders Galicia to the south. The Celtic character of this haunting land is still evident in the Galicians' favourite traditional instrument, the bagpipes.

Staple crops – maize, cabbages and potatoes – growing on the harsh land around Cabo Fisterra

◁ **The west façade of Santiago de Compostela's cathedral, overlooking the Praza do Obradoiro**

Exploring Galicia

Santiago de Compostela is Galicia's major tourist attraction. This beautiful city is the centrepiece of a region with many fine old towns, especially Betanzos, Mondoñedo, Lugo and Pontevedra. The resorts along the coastline of the wild Rías Altas, with their backdrop of forest-covered hills, offer good bathing. The Rías Baixas, the southern part of Galicia's west coast, has sheltered coves and sandy beaches, and excellent seafood in abundance. Travelling through the interior, where life seems to have changed little in centuries, is an ideal way to spend a peaceful, rural holiday.

Students in traditional dress playing music in Pontevedra

SIGHTS AT A GLANCE

Baiona ⑪
Betanzos ③
O Cebreiro ㉑
Celanova ⑭
A Coruña ④
Costa da Morte ⑤
A Guarda ⑫
Lugo ⑳
Monasterio de Oseira ⑱
Monasterio de Ribas de Sil ⑰
Mondoñedo ②
Ourense ⑯
Padrón ⑦
Pontevedra ⑨
Rías Altas ①
Santiago de Compostela
    pp86–7 ⑥
A Toxa ⑧
Tui ⑬
Verín ⑮
Vigo ⑩
Vilar de Donas ⑲

The isolated monastery at Ribas de Sil

SEE ALSO

• *Where to Stay* pp536–8

• *Restaurants and Bars* pp578–9

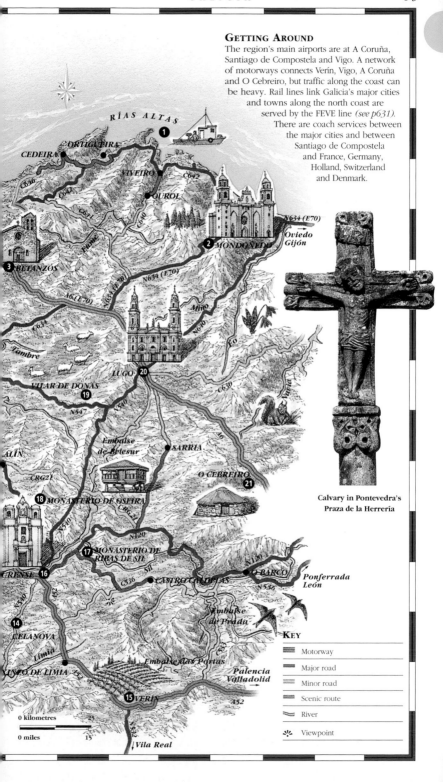

GETTING AROUND

The region's main airports are at A Coruña, Santiago de Compostela and Vigo. A network of motorways connects Verín, Vigo, A Coruña and O Cebreiro, but traffic along the coast can be heavy. Rail lines link Galicia's major cities and towns along the north coast are served by the FEVE line *(see p631)*. There are coach services between the major cities and between Santiago de Compostela and France, Germany, Holland, Switzerland and Denmark.

Calvary in Pontevedra's Praza de la Herrería

KEY

▬	Motorway
▬	Major road
▬	Minor road
▬	Scenic route
∿	River
☀	Viewpoint

0 kilometres　25

0 miles　　　15

Carved coat of arms on a house-front in Mondoñedo

Rías Altas ❶

Lugo & A Coruña. 🚂 Ribadeo.
🚌 Viveiro. 🛈 Foz, 982 14 06 75.
🚍 Tue.

DEEP RIAS are interspersed with coves and headlands along the beautiful north coast from Ribadeo to A Coruña. Inland are hills covered with forests of pine and eucalyptus. Many of the small resorts and fishing villages are charming.

The lovely, winding **Ría de Ribadeo** forms the border with Asturias. To the west of it is the small fishing port of **Foz**, which has two good beaches. Nearby, the 10th-century Iglesia de San Martín de Mondoñedo, standing alone on a hill, contains carvings of biblical scenes on its transept capitals – note the story of Lazarus. **Viveiro**, a summer holiday resort, is a handsome old town surrounded by Renaissance walls and gateways, typically Galician glassed-in balconies or *galerías*, and a Romanesque church. Near the pretty fishing village of O Barqueiro is the headland of Estaca de Bares, with its lighthouse and wind turbines.

Westward along the coast, the lovely **Ría de Ortigueira** leads to the fishing port of the same name, characterized by neat white houses. Around this area there are also many wild and unspoiled beaches.

High cliffs rise out of the sea near the village of **San Andrés de Teixido**, whose church is the focal point for pilgrims every 8 September.

According to local legend, all those who fail to visit the church in their own lifetime will come back to it as an animal in the afterlife. The village of **Cedeira**, which sits on a quiet bay, is a prosperous summer resort with neat lawns, modern houses with *galerías*, and a long, curving beach.

Mondoñedo ❷

Lugo. 🏠 5,100. 🚌 🛈 Praza do Concello 1, 982 52 40 03 (Apr–Sep: 982 50 71 77). 🚍 Thu & Sun. 🎭 San Lucas (18 Oct).

THIS DELIGHTFUL TOWN, an old provincial capital, is set in a fertile inland valley. There are stately houses with carved coats of arms and *galerías* in the main square. This is dominated by the **cathedral**, a building of golden stone in an unusual mix of styles. It has 18th-century Baroque towers, a Romanesque portal with a 16th-century stained-glass rose window and 17th-century cloisters. A statue in the south ambulatory, Nuestra Señora la Inglesa, was rescued from St Paul's cathedral in London. The **Museo Diocesano** contains statues, altarpieces and works by Zurbarán and El Greco.

🏛 Museo Diocesano
Plaza de la Catedral. 📞 982 52 19 48. 🕐 All year round. 🎟

Betanzos ❸

A Coruña. 🏠 14,000. 🚌 🚂
🛈 Plaza Constitución 1, 981 77 29 08. 🚍 Tue, Thu & Sat. 🎭 San Roque (14–25 Aug).

THE HANDSOME TOWN of Betanzos lies in a fertile valley slightly inland. Its broad main square has a replica of the Fountain of Diana at Versailles. In its steep narrow streets are fine old houses and Gothic churches. The **Iglesia de Santiago**, built in the 15th century by the tailors' guild, has a statue of St James on horseback above the door. The **Iglesia de San Francisco**, dated 1387, has statues of wild boars and a heraldic emblem of Count Fernán Pérez de Andrade, whose 15th-century tomb is inside the church. For centuries his family were the overlords of the region.

Ornate tomb in the Iglesia de San Francisco in Betanzos

ENVIRONS: 15 km (9 miles) north is the large, though pretty, fishing village of **Pontedeume**, with its narrow, hilly streets. Its medieval bridge still carries the main road to the large industrial town of **Ferrol**, to the north. This port became an important naval base and dockyard town in the 18th century, and its Neo-Classical buildings survive from that time. General Franco *(see pp62–3)* was born in Ferrol in 1892, and an imposing equestrian statue of him stands in the Praza de España.

Pavement cafés in Betanzos' Plaza de García Hermanos

Stone cross standing above the perilous waters of the Costa da Morte

A Coruña **4**

A Coruña. 👥 200,000. ✈ 🚆 🚌
ℹ Dársena de la Marina, 981 22
18 22. 🎭 Fiestas de María Pita (Aug).
🌐 www.turismocoruna.com

THIS PROUD CITY and busy
port has played a sizeable
role in Spanish maritime
history. Felipe II's doomed
Armada sailed from here to
England in 1588 (see p55).
Today, the sprawling industrial
suburbs contrast with the
elegant town centre, which is
laid out on an isthmus leading
to a headland. The **Torre de
Hércules**, Europe's oldest
working lighthouse, is a
famous local landmark. Built
by the Romans and rebuilt
in the 18th century, it still flashes
across the deep. Climb its 242
steps for a wide ocean view.
On the large, arcaded Praza
María Pita, the city's main
square, is the handsome town
hall. The sea promenade of
La Marina is lined with tiers
of glass-enclosed balconies or
galerías. Built as protection
against the strong winds, they
explain why A Coruña is often
referred to as the City of Glass.
The peaceful, tiny Praza de
Santa Bárbara is enchanting.
A Coruña has several fine
Romanesque churches such as
the **Iglesia de Santiago**, with
a carving of its saint on horse
back situated beneath the

tympanum, and the **Iglesia de
Santa María**. This church, featuring a tympanum carved with
the Adoration of the Magi, is
one of the best-preserved 12th-
century buildings in Galicia.
The quiet Jardín de San
Carlos contains the tomb of the
English general Sir John Moore,
killed by the French in battle.
This old part of town is still
somewhat military, and army
jeeps are a common sight in
its narrow streets.

The lofty Torre de Hércules
lighthouse at A Coruña

Costa da Morte **5**

A Coruña. 🚌 A Coruña, Malpica,
Santiago de Compostela. ℹ A Coruña,
981 22 18 22.

FROM MALPICA to Fisterra the
coast is wild and remote. It
is called the "Coast of Death"
because of the many ships
lost in storms or smashed on
the rocks by gales over the
centuries. But the headlands
are majestic and the sunsets
beautiful. Inland, the countryside is breezy and open. There
are no coastal towns, only simple villages, where fishermen
gather gastronomic percebes
(barnacles), destined for the
region's restaurants.
One of the most northerly
points of the Costa da Morte,
Malpica, has a seabird sanctuary. Laxe has good beaches
and safe bathing. **Camariñas**,
one of the most appealing
places on this coast, is a fishing
village where women make
bobbin-lace in the streets.
Beside the lighthouse on
nearby Cabo Vilán, a group
of futuristic wind turbines, tall
and slender, swirl in graceful
unison – a haunting sight.
To the south is Corcubión,
exuding a faded elegance,
and lastly, **Cabo Fisterra**
"where the land ends". This
cape, with its lighthouse, is a
good place to watch the sun
go down over the Atlantic.

Street-by-Street: Santiago de Compostela **❻**

Vegetable stall in Santiago market

IN THE MIDDLE AGES Santiago de Compostela was Christendom's third most important place of pilgrimage (see pp78–9), after Jerusalem and Rome. Around the Praza do Obradoiro is an ensemble of historic buildings that has few equals in Europe. The local granite gives a harmonious unity to the mixture of architectural styles. With its narrow streets and old squares, the city centre is compact enough to explore on foot. Two other monuments worth seeing are the Convento de Santo Domingo de Bonaval, to the east of the centre, housing a Galician folk museum, and the Colegiata del Sar, a 12th-century Romanesque church, located to the east of the city.

★ **Convento de San Martiño Pinario**
The Baroque church of this monastery has a huge double altar and an ornate Plateresque façade with carved figures of saints and bishops.

Pazo de Xelmírez

RÚA

RÚA DA TROIA

RUELA DO VAL DE DEUS

PRAZA DA INMACULADA

RÚA DE SAN FRANCISCO

PRAZA DO OBRADOIRO

★ **Hostal de los Reyes Católicos**
Built by the Catholic Monarchs as an inn and hospital for sick pilgrims, and now a parador (see p537), this magnificent building has an elaborate Plateresque doorway.

Praza do Obradoiro
This majestic square is one of the world's finest and the focal point for pilgrims arriving in the city. The cathedral's Baroque façade dominates the square.

The Pazo de Raxoi, with its Classical façade, was built in 1772 and houses the town hall.

Convento de San Paio de Antealtares
This is one of the oldest monasteries in Santiago. It was founded in the 9th century to house the tomb of St James, now in the cathedral.

VISITORS' CHECKLIST

A Coruña. 🏠 100,000. ✈ 10 km (6 miles) north. 🚌 Calle Hórreo 75a, 902 24 02 02. 🚉 Avenida Rodríguez de Viguri, 981 58 77 00. 🛈 Calle Rúa do Villar 43, 981 58 40 81. 🗓 Sat. 🎭 Semana Santa (Easter Week). 🖧 www.santiagodecompostela.org

Praza da Quintana, under the cathedral clock tower, is one of the city's most elegant squares.

Praza das Praterias
The Goldsmiths' Doorway of the cathedral opens on to this charming square with a 17th-century fountain in the centre.

KEY

— — — Suggested route

– – – Pilgrims' route

Rúa Nova is a handsome arcaded old street leading from the cathedral to the newer part of the city.

To tourist information

0 metres 100

0 yards 100

Colegio de San Jerónimo

STAR SIGHTS

★ **Convento de San Martiño Pinario**

★ **Hotel de los Reyes Católicos**

★ **Cathedral**

★ **Cathedral**
This grand towering spectacle has welcomed pilgrims to Santiago for centuries. Though the exterior has been remodelled over the years, the core of the building has remained virtually unchanged since the 11th century.

Santiago Cathedral

WITH ITS TWIN BAROQUE TOWERS soaring high over the Praza do Obradoiro, this monument to St James is a majestic sight, as befits one of the great shrines of Christendom *(see pp78–9)*. The present building dates from the 11th–13th centuries and stands on the site of the 9th-century basilica built by Alfonso II. Through the famous Pórtico da Gloria is the same interior that met pilgrims in medieval times. The choir, designed by Maestro Mateo, has been completely restored.

The gigantic botafumeiro

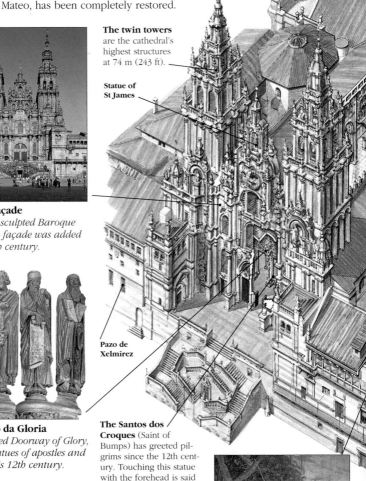

"Passport" – proof of a pilgrim's journey

The twin towers are the cathedral's highest structures at 74 m (243 ft).

Statue of St James

Pazo de Xelmírez

★ **West Façade**
The richly sculpted Baroque Obradoiro façade was added in the 18th century.

★ **Pórtico da Gloria**
The sculpted Doorway of Glory, with its statues of apostles and prophets, is 12th century.

The Santos dos Croques (Saint of Bumps) has greeted pilgrims since the 12th century. Touching this statue with the forehead is said to impart luck and wisdom.

Tapestry Museum
A new addition to this collection of antique tapestries is an exhibition of Oriental medieval cloths dating as far back as the 13th century.

STAR FEATURES

★ West Façade

★ Pórtico da Gloria

★ Porta das Praterias

The *botafumeiro*, a giant censer, is swung high above the altar by eight men during important services.

Mondragon Chapel (1521) contains fine wrought-iron grilles and vaulting.

VISITORS' CHECKLIST

Praza do Obradoiro. 📞 981 58 35 48. ⏰ 7am–9pm daily. ✝ 9:30 am, noon, 7:30 pm Mon–Fri. ♿ **Museum** 📞 981 56 05 27. ⏰ Jun–Sep: 10:30am–1:30pm & 4–6:30pm daily; Oct–May: 11am–1pm & 4–6pm daily. 🖼

Clock Tower

High Altar
Visitors can pass behind the ornate high altar to embrace the silver mantle of the 13th-century statue of St James.

Cloisters

★ **Porta das Praterias**
The 12th-century Gold-smiths' Doorway is rich in bas-relief sculptures of biblical scenes.

Crypt
The relics of St James and two disciples are said to lie in a tomb in the crypt, under the altar, in the original 9th-century foundations.

Chapterhouse

Padrón ❼

A Coruña. 🔢 10,700. 🚉 🚌 ℹ️
Avenida Compostela 27, 981 81 13
29. 🚢 *Sun.* 🎆 *Santiago (24–5 Jul).*

THIS QUIET TOWN on the Río
Ulla, known for its piquant
green peppers, was a major
seaport until it silted up. Legend has it the boat carrying
the body of St James to Galicia
(see p78) arrived here. The
supposed mooring stone, or
padrón, lies below the altar
of the church by the bridge.

The leafy avenue beside the
church features in the poems of
one of Galicia's greatest writers,
Rosalia de Castro (1837–85).
Her creeper-covered home on
the edge of town, where she
spent her final years, has been
converted into a museum.

ENVIRONS: The estuary town
of Noia (Noya) lies on the
coast 20 km (12 miles) west.
Its Gothic church has a finely
carved portal. East of Padrón is
Pazo de Oca, a manor house,
with a crenellated tower, idyllic
gardens and a lake.

🏛 **Museo Rosalia de Castro**
La Matanza. 📞 981 81 12 04.
⏹ *Tue –Sat.* 🎟 ♿

The picturesque gardens and lake of Pazo de Oca

A Toxa ❽

Near O Grove. 🚌 ℹ️ *Ayuntamiento,*
O Grove, 986 73 14 15. 🚢 *Fri.*

A TINY pine-covered island
joined to the mainland by
a bridge, A Toxa (La Toja) is
one of the most stylish resorts
in Galicia. The *belle époque*
palace-hotel *(see p537)* and
luxury villas add to the island's
elegant atmosphere. A Toxa's
best-known landmark is the
small church covered with
scallop shells. Across the bridge
is O Grove (El Grove), a
thriving family resort and fishing port on a peninsula, with
holiday hotels and flats alongside glorious beaches.

Scallop-covered roof of the church on A Toxa island

Pontevedra ❾

Pontevedra. 🔢 65,000. 🚉 🚌
ℹ️ *Calle General Mola 1, 986 85*
08 14. 🚢 *Sat.* 🎆 *Fiestas de la*
Peregrina (second week in Aug).

PONTEVEDRA lies inland, at the
head of a long ria that is
backed by green hills. The
delightful old town is typically
Galician and has a network of
cobbled alleys and tiny graceful squares with granite calvaries, arcades, flower-filled balconies and excellent tapas bars.
On the south side of the old
town is the Gothic **Convento
de Santo Domingo**. It is now
a museum containing Roman
steles and Galician coats of
arms and tombs. To the west,
the 16th-century **Iglesia de
Santa María la Mayor** contains a magnificent Plateresque
(see p21) façade that includes
richly carved figures of oars-
men and fishermen at the top.

On the **Praza de la Leña**,
two 18th-century mansions
form the **Museo de
Pontevedra**, one of the best
museums in Galicia. The Celtic
Bronze Age treasures found
locally are superb. Among the
paintings on display are 15th-
century Spanish primitives, and
canvases by Zurbarán and
Goya. The top floor holds a
collection of drawings and
paintings by Alfonso Castelao, a
Galician artist, writer and
nationalist, who forcefully
depicted the misery endured
by his people during the
Spanish Civil War.

🏛 **Museo de Pontevedra**
Calle Pasanteria 10. 📞 986 85 14 55.
⏹ *10am–2:15pm, 5–8:45pm (Oct–*
May: 10am–1:30pm, 4:30–8pm) Tue–
Sat, 11am–2pm Sun. 🎟 *for non-EU.*

Rías Baixas

THIS SOUTHERN PART of Galicia's west coast consists of four large rias or inlets between pine-covered hills. The beaches are good, the scenery is lovely, the bathing safe and the climate much milder than on the wilder coast to the north. Though areas such as Vilagarcía de Arousa and Panxón have become popular holiday resorts, much of the Rías Baixas (Rías Bajas) coastline is unspoiled, such as the quiet stretch from Muros to Noia. This part of the coastline provides some of Spain's most fertile fishing grounds. Mussel-breeding platforms are positioned in neat rows along the rias, looking like half-submerged submarines; and in November, the women harvest clams.

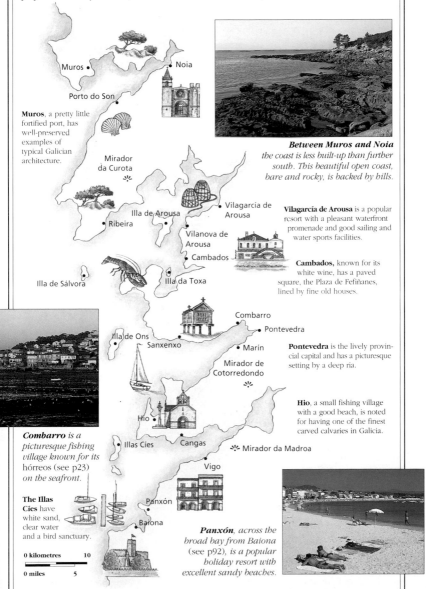

Muros, a pretty little fortified port, has well-preserved examples of typical Galician architecture.

Between Muros and Noia the coast is less built-up than further south. This beautiful open coast, bare and rocky, is backed by hills.

Vilagarcía de Arousa is a popular resort with a pleasant waterfront promenade and good sailing and water sports facilities.

Cambados, known for its white wine, has a paved square, the Plaza de Fefiñanes, lined by fine old houses.

Pontevedra is the lively provincial capital and has a picturesque setting by a deep ria.

Hío, a small fishing village with a good beach, is noted for having one of the finest carved calvaries in Galicia.

Combarro is a picturesque fishing village known for its hórreos (see p23) *on the seafront.*

The Illas Cíes have white sand, clear water and a bird sanctuary.

0 kilometres 10

0 miles 5

Panxón, across the broad bay from Baiona (see p92), *is a popular holiday resort with excellent sandy beaches.*

Cannons on the battlements of Monterreal fortress, Baiona

Vigo ⓾

Pontevedra. 🏠 *300,000.* ✈ 🚃
🚌 ℹ *Cánovas del Castillo 22, 986
43 05 77.* 🚌 *Sun.* 🎭 *Cristo de los
Afligidos (Jul).*

GALICIA'S LARGEST TOWN is
also the biggest fishing
port in Spain. It is situated in
an attractive setting near the
mouth of a deep ría spanned
by a high suspension bridge,
and is surrounded by wooded
hills. Vigo isn't noted for its
old buildings but does have
striking modern
sculptures such as
local artist Juan José
Oliveira's horses
statue in the Praza
de España. The
oldest part of the
town, Barrio del Berbes,
is near the port and
used to be the
sailors' quarter.
Its cobbled alleys
are teeming with
bars, and here
you can find
some of the
finest

Bronze sculpture by Oliveira in
Vigo's Praza de España

tapas bars, which serve mainly
seafood. The Mercado de la
Piedra, near the port, sells
reasonably priced fish and
shellfish – particularly oysters.

Baiona ⓫

Pontevedra. 🏠 *10,000.* 🚃
ℹ *Calle Ventura Misa 17, 986
38 50 55.* 🚌 *Mon.* 🎭 *Santa
Marina (18 Jul).*

THE PINTA, one of the cara-
vels from the fleet of
Christopher Columbus, arrived
at this small port on 10 March
1493, bringing the first news
of the discovery of the New
World. Today Baiona (Bayona),
which is sited on a broad bay,
is a popular summer resort,
its harbour a mix of pleasure
and fishing boats. The 12th-
century **collegiate church** is
Romanesque and Gothic. Symbols carved on the arches,
indicate the local guilds that
helped build the church.
A royal fortress once stood
on Monterreal promontory, to
the north of town. Its huge
defensive walls remain, but the
interior has been converted
into a smart parador *(see
p536)*. The cannons used as
protection against pirates can
still be seen. A walk around
the battlements offers superb
views of the coast.
On the coast about 3 km
(2 miles) further south is a
huge granite statue of the
Virgen de la Roca. During
important religious festivals,
visitors climb up inside and
on to the ship she holds.

A Guarda ⓬

Pontevedra. 🏃 *10,000.* 🚌
ℹ *Praza do Reló, 986 61 00 00.* 🚢
Sat. 🎭 *Monte de Santa Tecla
(second week of Aug).*

THE LITTLE FISHING PORT of A
Guarda (La Guardia) has a
reputation for good seafood
and is particularly well known
for the quality of its lobsters.
On the slopes of Monte de
Santa Tecla are the remains of
a Celtic settlement of some
100 round stone dwellings
which are dated around
600–200 BC. The **Museo de
Monte de Santa Tecla** is
situated on a nearby hilltop.

ENVIRONS: About 10 km
(6 miles) north, the tiny
Baroque **Monasterio de Santa
María** stands by the beach at
Oia. Semi-wild horses roam
the surrounding hills and, in
May and June, are rounded
up for branding in a series of
day-long fiestas *(see p94).*

🏛 Museo de Monte de
Santa Tecla

A Guarda. 🎟 *986 61 00 00.*
🕐 *Mar–Dec: daily.*

Circular foundations of Celtic
dwellings at A Guarda

Tui ⓭

Pontevedra. 🏃 *16,400.* 🚃 🚌
ℹ *Calle Colon, 986 60 17 89.*
🚌 *Thu.* 🎭 *San Telmo (week after
Easter; Descent of the Río Miño (Aug).*

SPAIN'S main frontier town
with Portugal, Tui (Tuy)
stands on a hillside above the
Río Miño. Its graceful old
streets curve up to an old quarter and the 13th-century hilltop
cathedral. The two countries
were often at war during the
Middle Ages, and as a result
the church is built in the style

Unloading the catch in Spain's largest fishing port, Vigo

FISHING IN SPAIN

The Spanish eat more seafood per head of population than any other European nation except Portugal. Half of this is caught by Galician fishing fleets. Some 90,000 fishermen and 20,000 boats land over a million tonnes of fish and shellfish a year, much of this caught offshore where sardines, tuna, lobster and clams are plentiful. In recent years, the stocks in the seas around Spain have become depleted by overfishing, forcing deep-sea trawlers to travel as far as Canada and Iceland.

ornate altarpiece and Gothic choir stalls. In the garden is the 10th-century Mozarabic **Iglesia de San Miguel**.

ENVIRONS: At **Santa Comba de Bande**, 26 km (16 miles) to the south, is an even older little church. The features of this Visigothic (see pp46–7) church, which is thought to be 7th century, include a lantern turret and a horseshoe arch that has carved marble pillars.

Verín ⓯

Ourense. 🏠 11,500. 🚉 🚌 Avenida San Lazaro 26–8, 988 41 16 14. 🚌 3rd, 11th & 23rd of month. 🎭 Santa María la Mayor (15 Aug)

THOUGH IT STANDS amid vineyards, Verín produces more than wine. Its thermal springs have given it a thriving bottled water industry. The town has a number of 17th-century houses with arcades and glass balconies, or *galerías*. The **Castillo de Monterrei**, built during the wars with Portugal, is 4 km (2 miles) to the west. Inside its three rings of walls are a square 15th-century keep, an arcaded courtyard, and a 13th-century church with a delicately carved portal. The castle once housed a monastery and hospital.

of a fortress, with towers and battlements. It has a cloister and choir stalls and a richly decorated west porch.

Nearby is the **Iglesia de San Telmo**, dedicated to the patron saint of fishermen, whose Baroque ornamentation shows a Portuguese influence. Below the cathedral is an iron bridge, the **Puente Internacional**, built by Gustave Eiffel in 1884 to stretch across the river to Valença do Minho in Portugal.

The Gothic **Iglesia de Santo Domingo**, situated beside the Parque de la Alameda, contains ivy-covered cloisters and tombs with delicately carved effigies. The church overlooks the river, which is filled with boats in August for the Descent of the Río Miño, a canoe race and fiesta.

Celanova ⓮

Ourense. 🏠 6,200. 🚉 🚌 Plaza Mayor 1, 988 43 22 01. 🚌 Thu. 🎭 San Roque (15 Aug).

ON THE MAIN SQUARE of this little town is the massive **Monasterio de San Salvador**, which was formerly one of the most important monasteries in Spain. Founded during the 10th century and later rebuilt, it is mainly Baroque, though one of its two lovely cloisters is Renaissance. The enormous church of this Benedictine monastery has an

Ceramic tiled floor of the Iglesia de San Miguel

The Castillo de Monterrei, standing high above the town of Verín

GALICIA'S FIESTAS

Os Peliqueiros
(Carnival, Feb/Mar), Laza (Ourense). Dressed up in grinning masks and outlandish costumes, with cowbells tied to their belts and brandishing sticks, *Os Peliqueiros* take to the streets on Carnival Sunday. They are licensed to lash out at onlookers, who are forbidden to retaliate. On Carnival Monday morning a battle takes place, with flour, water and live ants used as ammunition. Laza's carnival comes to on end on the Tuesday with a reading of the satirical "Donkey's Will" and the burning of an effigy.

The outrageous costumes of *Os Peliqueiros* in Laza

A Rapa das Bestas
(May and Jun), Oia (Pontevedra). Semi-wild horses are rounded up by local farmers for their manes and tails to be cut. What was once a chore is now a popular fiesta.
Flower pavements
(Corpus Christi, May/Jun), Ponteareas (Pontevedra). The streets of the town along which the Corpus Christi procession passes are carpeted with intricate designs made from brightly coloured flower petals.
St James's Day *(25 Jul)*, Santiago de Compostela. On the night before, there is a firework display in the Praza do Obradoiro. The celebrations are especially wild when 25 July falls on a Sunday.

Ourense ⑯

Ourense. 🏘 *100,000.* 🚆 🚌
ℹ *Rua do Progreso, 988 37 20 20.*
📅 *7th & 17th of each month.* 🎉
Os Maios (3 May); San Martín (11 Nov).

THE OLD QUARTER of Ourense was built around the city's well-known thermal springs, Fonte as Burgas. Even today, these spout water at a temperature of 65°C (150°F) from three fountains.

This old part of the town is the most interesting, particularly the small area around the arcaded Plaza Mayor. Here the **cathedral**, founded in 572 and rebuilt in the 12th–13th centuries, has a vast gilded reredos by Cornelis de Holanda. On the triple-arched doorway are carved multicoloured figures reminiscent of the Pórtico da Gloria at Santiago *(see p88)*. Nearby is the elegant 14th-century cloister, the **Claustro de San Francisco**.

One of the city's landmarks is the 13th-century **Puente Romano**, a seven-arched bridge which crosses the Río Miño, north of the town. It is built on Roman foundations and still used by traffic.

ENVIRONS: Allariz, 25 km (16 miles) south, and Ribadavia, to the west, have old Jewish quarters with narrow streets and Romanesque churches. Ribadavia is also noted for its Ribeiro wines – a dry white and a port-like red *(see p74)* – and has a wine museum.

Ornate Gothic reredos in the cathedral at Ourense

Monasterio de Ribas de Sil ⑰

Ribas de Sil. 🚆 *San Esteban de Sil.*
🚌 *from Ourense.* ☎ *988 20 11 27 (town hall).* 🕐 *Wed–Sun.*

NEAR ITS CONFLUENCE with the Miño, the Río Sil carves a deep curving gorge in which dams form two reservoirs of dark green water. A hairpin road winds to the top of the gorge, where the Romanesque-Gothic Monasterio de Ribas de Sil is situated high on a crag above the chasm. Partly dilapidated, partly over-restored – it has an enormous glass wall in one of the three cloisters – it nevertheless has a certain ghostly grandeur.

The Río Sil winding its way through the gorge

The grandiose Monasterio de Oseira surrounded by the forests of the Valle de Arenteiro

Monasterio de Oseira ⑱

Oseira. 🚉 🚌 *from Ourense.* 🄲 *988 28 20 04.* ◯ *9:30–noon Mon–Sat, 3:30–5:30pm daily.* 🈂

THIS MONASTERY stands on its own in a wooded valley near the village of Oseira, named after the bears *(osos)* that once lived in this region. It is a grey building with a Baroque façade dating from 1708. On the doorway is a statue of the Virgin as nurse, with St Bernard kneeling at her feet. The interior of the 12th–13th-century church is typically Cistercian in its simplicity. The vaulted chapterhouse is particularly impressive.

Fresco of a *dona* in the monastery at Vilar de Donas

Vilar de Donas ⑲

Lugo. 🏠 *80.* 🛈 *Ctra de Santiago 28, 982 38 00 01.* 🎭 *San Antonio (13 Jun), San Salvador (6 Aug).*

THIS HAMLET on the Road to Santiago *(see pp78–9)* has a small church, just off the main road. Inside are tombs of some of the Knights of the Order of Santiago, and 15th-century frescoes of the nuns who lived here until the 15th

century. The church is closed except during mass times, though visits can be arranged by calling 982 37 41 31.

The Cistercian **Monasterio Sobrado de los Monjes**, to the northwest, has a medieval kitchen and chapterhouse, and a church with attractive domes.

Lugo ⑳

Lugo. 🏠 *80,000.* 🚉 🚌 🛈 *Praza de España 27–9, 982 23 13 61.* 🎪 *Tue & Fri.* 🎭 *San Froilán (4–12 Oct).*

CAPITAL of Galicia's largest province, Lugo was also an important centre under the Romans. Attracted to the town by its thermal springs, they constructed what is now the finest surviving **Roman wall** in Spain. The wall, which encircles the city, is about 6 m (20 ft) thick and 10 m (33 ft) high with ten gateways. Six of these have stairways to the top of the wall, from where there is a good view of the city.

Inside the wall, the old town is lively though dignified, with pretty squares. In the **Praza de Santo Domingo** is a black statue of a Roman eagle, built to commemorate Augustus' capture of Lugo from the Celts in the 1st century BC. The Romanesque **cathedral** is large and rambling, and modelled on that of Santiago. It features an elegant Baroque cloister, and a chapel containing the alabaster statue of Nuestra Señora de los Ojos Grandes (Virgin of the Big Eyes). The **Museo Provincial** exhibits Celtic gold

torcs, local Roman finds, a life-size model of a farm kitchen, modern Galician paintings and a curious statue of a kneeling peasant woman holding a miniature priest.

ENVIRONS: The stone hamlet of **Santa Eulalia**, situated in lovely open country to the west, conceals a curious building excavated in 1924: a tiny temple, with lively, bright frescoes of birds and leaves. Though its exact purpose is unknown, it is thought to be an early Christian church and has been dated at around the 3rd century AD.

🏛 **Museo Provincial**
Plaza de la Soledad. 🄲 *982 24 21 12.* ◯ *daily.* ● *Sun in Aug.* ♿

O Cebreiro ㉑

Lugo. 🏠 *16.* 🚌 🛈 *982 36 70 25.* 🎭 *Santo Milagro (8 Sep).*

UP IN THE HILLS in the east of Galicia, close to the border with León, is one of the most unusual villages on the Road to Santiago. Its 9th-century church was supposedly the scene of a miracle in 1300 when the wine was turned into blood and the bread into flesh. Near the church there are several *pallozas*, round thatched stone huts of a Celtic design. Some of these ancient dwellings, which often had annexes for livestock and grain, have been restored. One of them is now a folk museum.

Painted gourd in O Cebreiro's museum

🏛 **Museo Etnográfico**
O Cebreiro. ◯ *Wed–Sun.*

ASTURIAS AND CANTABRIA

ASTURIAS · CANTABRIA

THE SPECTACULAR PICOS DE EUROPA *massif sits astride the border between Asturias and Cantabria. In this rural region cottage crafts are kept alive in villages in remote mountain valleys and forested foothills. There are many ancient towns and churches, and pretty fishing ports on the coasts. Cave paintings, such as those at Altamira, were made by people living here over 10,000 years ago.*

Asturias is proud that it resisted invasion by the Moors. The Reconquest of Spain is held to have begun in 718 when a Moorish force was defeated by Christians at Covadonga in the Picos de Europa.

The Christian kingdom of Asturias was founded in the 8th century, and in the brilliant, brief artistic period that followed many churches were built around the capital, Oviedo. Some of these pre-Romanesque churches still stand. Today, Asturias is a province and a principality under the patronage of the heir to the Spanish throne. In the charming, unspoiled Asturian countryside cider is produced and a quaint dialect, *bable,* is spoken.

Cantabria centres on Santander, its capital, a port and an elegant resort. It is a mountainous province with a legacy of Romanesque churches in isolated spots. It also has well-preserved towns and villages such as Santillana del Mar, Carmona and Bárcena Mayor.

Mountains cover more than half of both provinces, so mountain sports are a major attraction. Expanses of deciduous forests remain in many parts, some sheltering Spain's last wild bears. Along the coasts are pretty fishing ports and resorts, such as Castro Urdiales, Ribadesella and Comillas, and sandy coves for bathing. Both the coastal plains and uplands are ideal for quiet rural holidays.

Peaceful meadow around Lago de la Ercina in the Picos de Europa massif

◁ One of the pretty cobbled streets of Santillana del Mar, Cantabria

Exploring Asturias and Cantabria

THE MOST OBVIOUS ATTRACTION in this area is the group of mountains that straddles the two provinces – the Picos de Europa. These jagged peaks offer excellent rock climbing and rough hiking, and in certain parts can be explored by car or bicycle. These and several other nature reserves in the area are home to rare species of flora and fauna, including the capercaillie and brown bear. The coast offers many sandy coves for bathing. Santander and Oviedo are lively university cities with a rich cultural life. There are innumerable unspoiled villages to explore, especially the ancient town of Santillana del Mar. Some of the earliest examples of art exist in Cantabria, most notably at Altamira, where the cave drawings and engravings are among the oldest to be found in Europe.

Typical flower-covered balcony in the village of Bárcena Mayor

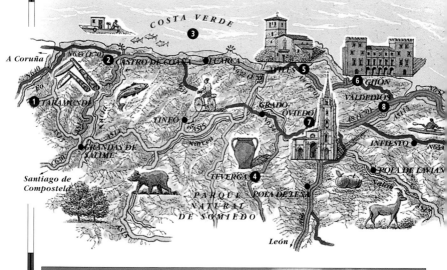

A Coruña

COSTA VERDE

CASTRO DE COAÑA

LUARCA

VILLES

GIJÓN

TARAMUNDI

GRADO

OVIEDO

VALDEDIÓS

TINEO

GRANDAS DE SALIME

NAVIA

INFIESTO

Santiago de Compostela

TEVERGA

POLA DE SIERO

POLA DE LAVIÁN

PARQUE NATURAL DE SOMIEDO

León

A view along the crowded beach of Playa del Camello, Santander

SIGHTS AT A GLANCE

Alto Campoo **15**
Avilés **5**
Cangas de Onís **10**
Castro de Coaña **2**
Castro Urdiales **21**
Comillas **13**
Costa Verde **3**
Cuevas de Altamira **16**
Gijón **6**
Laredo **20**
Oviedo **7**
Parque Nacional de los Picos de Europa pp104–5 **11**
Potes **12**
Puente Viesgo **18**
Ribadesella **9**
Santander **19**
Santillana del Mar **17**
Taramundi **1**
Teverga **4**
Valdediós **8**
Valle de Cabuérniga **14**

Cantabrian dairy farmers loading hay on to their cart

GETTING AROUND

The main road through the region is the N634, which is still narrow and hilly in places, and often suffers from heavy lorry traffic. Most other major roads follow the directions of the valleys and run north to south. Minor roads are generally good but can be slow and winding. The private FEVE railway, which follows the coast from Bilbao to Ferrol in Galicia, is both useful and extremely scenic. A twice-weekly Brittany Ferries service links Santander with Plymouth. Asturias has a small international airport near Avilés. Parts of Cantabria are closer to Bilbao airport.

Carved figure in the Convento de Regina Coeli, Santillana del Mar

SEE ALSO

• *Where to Stay* pp538–40

• *Restaurants and Bars* pp580–81

KEY

▬ Motorway

▬ Major road

▬ Minor road

▬ Scenic route

≈ River

☼ Viewpoint

Craftsman making knife blades in a forge at Taramundi

Taramundi ❶

Asturias. 🏠 1,000. 🚉 Plaza del Poyo, 985 64 67 02 (weekends: 985 64 68 77). 📅 Día del Turista (last Sun of Jul). 🌐 www.taramundi.net

SITUATED in the remote Los Oscos region, this small village houses a rural tourism centre which organizes forest tours in four-wheel drive vehicles and has several hotels and holiday cottages to rent. Taramundi has a tradition of wrought-iron craftsmanship. Iron ore was first mined in the area by the Romans. There are approximately 24 forges in and around the village, where craftsmen can still be seen making traditional knives with decorated wooden handles.

ENVIRONS: About 20 km (12 miles) to the east, at **San Martín de Oscos**, there is an 18th-century palace. At **Grandas de Salime**, 10 km (6 miles) further southeast, the Museo Etnográfico has displays showing local crafts, traditional life and farming.

🏛 **Museo Etnográfico**
Calle el Ferreiro 17. 📞 98 562 72 43. 🕐 Tue–Sun. 📷 ♿

Castro de Coaña ❷

Asturias. 🚉 5km from Navia. 📞 985 97 84 01. 🕐 Tue–Sun. 📷

ONE OF the most important Celtic settlements in Spain, Castro de Coaña was established in the Iron Age and later occupied by the Romans. Set on a hillside in the Navia valley are the well-preserved remains of its fortifications and the stone foundations of circular dwellings, some of which stand head high. Inside can be found hollowed-out stones which may once have been used as funerary urns or for crushing corn.

The museum on the site displays many of the finds that have been unearthed at Castro de Coaña. Among the interesting remains on display are pottery, tools and Roman coins.

Circular stone foundations of dwellings at Castro de Coaña

Costa Verde ❸

Asturias. 🚉 Avilés. ✈ Oviedo, Gijón. 🛈 Plaza del Ayuntamiento, Aviles, Calle Ruiz Gomez 21, 985 54 43 25.

THE APTLY NAMED "green coast" is a succession of attractive sandy coves and dramatic cliffs, punctuated by deep estuaries and numerous fishing villages. Inland, there are lush meadows, and pine and eucalyptus forests, backed by mountains. This stretch of coastline has been less spoiled than most in Spain; the resorts tend to be modest in size, like the hotels.

Two pretty fishing ports, **Castropol** and **Figueras**, stand by the eastern shore of the Ría de Ribadeo, forming the border with Galicia. To the east are other picturesque villages such as Tapia de Casariego and Ortiguera, in a small rocky cove. Following the coast, **Luarca** lies below a church and a quiet cemetery on a headland, and has a neat little harbour packed with red, blue and white boats. The village of **Cudillero** is even more delightful – outdoor cafés and excellent seafood restaurants crowd the tiny plaza beside the port, all of which are squeezed into a narrow cove. Behind, white cottages are scattered over the steep hillsides.

Further along the coast is the rocky headland of Cabo de Peñas where, in the fishing village of **Candas**, bullfights are sometimes held on the sand at low tide. East of Gijón, **Lastres** is impressively located below a cliff, and **Isla** has a broad open beach. Beyond Ribadesella is the

THE BROWN BEAR

The population of Spain's brown bears *(Ursus arctos)* has dwindled from about 1,000 at the beginning of the 20th century to less than 100. Hunting by man and the destruction of the bear's natural forest habitat have caused the decline. But now, protected by nature reserves such as Somiedo, where most of the bears in Asturias are found, together with new conservation laws, it is hoped this magnificent omnivore will thrive again.

One of the few remaining bears in the forests of Asturias

Church and cemetery overlooking the sea from the headland at Luarca

lively town of **Llanes**. Among the attractions of this old fortified seaport, with its dramatic mountain backdrop, are ruined ramparts and good beaches.

Teverga ❹

Asturias. 🚌 *La Plaza.* 🛈 *Plaza del Ayuntamiento La Plaza, 985 76 42 02.*

THIS AREA, southwest of Oviedo, is rich in scenery, wildlife and ancient churches. Near the southern end of the narrow Teverga gorge is **La Plaza**. Its 12th-century church, the Iglesia de San Pedro, is a beautiful example of Romanesque architecture.

Just to the west of La Plaza is **Villanueva**, with its Romanesque Iglesia de Santa María. To the east, the Quirós valley, with hamlets dotted around its hillsides, is picturesque.

ENVIRONS: The large **Parque Natural de Somiedo** straddles the mountains bordering León. Its high meadows and forests of chestnut, beech and oak are a sanctuary for wolves, brown bears and capercaillies, as well as a number of rare species of wild flowers.

The park has 18 glacial lakes, and is peppered with herdsmen's traditional thatched huts, known as *teitos (see p23)*.

Avilés ❺

Asturias. 🚹 *88,000.* ✈ 🚌 🚃 🛈 *Calle Ruiz Gomez 21, 985 54 43 25.* 🚌 *Mon.* 🎉 *San Agustín (28 Aug).*

AVILÉS BECAME the capital of Asturias' steel industry during the 19th century, and is still ringed by big factories. Even though it is sometimes criticized for having little to offer

the visitor, the town hides a medieval heart of some character, especially around the Plaza de España. The **Iglesia de San Francisco** is decorated with ancient frescoes and has a Renaissance cloister. The **Iglesia de San Nicolás** contains a fine 14th-century chapel and holds the tomb of the first Governor of the US state of Florida. All around are arcaded streets with lively bars. The international airport outside Avilés serves all Asturias.

Gijón ❻

Asturias. 🚹 *260,000.* 🚃 🚌 🛈 *Calle Marqués de San Esteban 1, 985 34 60 46.* 🚌 *Sun.* 🎉 *San Antonio (13 Jun); La Virgen de Begoña (15 Aug).*

THE PROVINCE'S largest city, this industrial port has been much rebuilt since the Civil War when it was bombarded by the Nationalist navy. The city's most famous son is Gaspar Melchor de Jovellanos, an eminent 18th-century author, reformer and diplomat.

Gijón's old town is on a small isthmus and headland. It centres on the arcaded Plaza Mayor and the 18th-century **Palacio de Revillagigedo**, a Neo-Renaissance folly with towers and battlements. The long sandy beach, near the city centre, is popular in summer.

🏛 **Palacio de Revillagigedo**
Plaza del Marqués. 📞 *985 34 69 21.* 🔲 *for exhibitions.* ⬤ *public hols.* ♿

The pretty 12th-century Iglesia de San Pedro at La Plaza

Oviedo ❼

Alfonso II El Casto, 6. 🏛 *180,000.* 🚉
🚌 ℹ *Plaza de Alfonso II el Casto 6,*
985 21 33 85. 🛒 *Thu & Sun.*
🎪 *San Mateo (21 Sep).*

OVIEDO, A UNIVERSITY city and the cultural and commercial capital of Asturias, stands on a raised site on a fertile plain. The nearby coal mines have made it an important industrial centre since the 19th century. It retains some of the atmosphere of that time, as described by Leopoldo Alas ("Clarín") in his great novel *La Regenta (see p31).*

In and around Oviedo are many Pre-Romanesque buildings. This style flourished in the 8th–10th centuries and was confined to a small area of the kingdom of Asturias, one of the few enclaves of Spain not invaded by the Moors.

The nucleus of the medieval city is the stately Plaza Alfonso II, bordered by a number of handsome old palaces. On this square is situated the Flamboyant Gothic **cathedral** *(see p20)* with its high tower and asymmetrical west façade. Inside are tombs of Asturian kings and a majestic 16th-century gilded reredos. The cathedral's supreme treasure is the Cámara Santa, a restored 9th-century chapel containing statues of Christ and the apostles. The

Cross of Angels in the treasury of Oviedo cathedral

chapel also houses many works of 9th-century Asturian art including two crosses and a reliquary – all made of gold, silver and precious stones.

Also situated in the Plaza Alfonso II is the **Iglesia de San Tirso**. This church was originally constructed in the 9th century, but subsequent restorations have left the east window as the only surviving Pre-Romanesque feature.

Sited immediately behind the cathedral is the **Museo Arqueológico**, which is housed in an old monastery with fine cloisters. It contains local prehistoric, Roman and Romanesque treasures.

The **Museo de Bellas Artes**, in the handsome 18th-century Velarde Palace, has a good range of Asturian and Spanish paintings, such as Carreño's portrait of Carlos II *(see p66).*

Two of the most magnificent Pre-Romanesque churches are on Mount Naranco, to the north.

SANTA MARÍA DEL NARANCO

This church, on Mount Naranco, was originally built as a summer palace for Ramiro I in the 9th century. It is one of the finest examples of Pre-Romanesque or Asturian architecture, a style characterized by the slender proportions of its buildings and their original and graceful ornamentation.

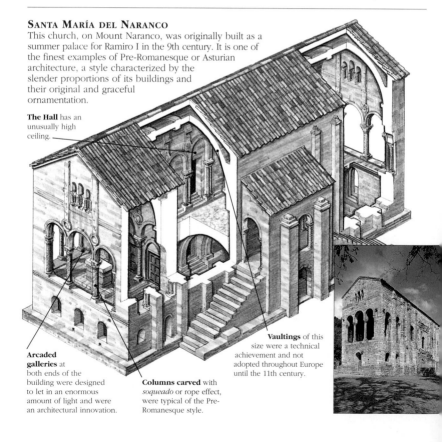

The Hall has an unusually high ceiling.

Arcaded galleries at both ends of the building were designed to let in an enormous amount of light and were an architectural innovation.

Columns carved with *soqueado* or rope effect, were typical of the Pre-Romanesque style.

Vaultings of this size were a technical achievement and not adopted throughout Europe until the 11th century.

Church overlooking the sea at Ribadesella

Santa María del Naranco has a large barrel-vaulted hall on the main floor and arcaded galleries at either end. Some of the intricate reliefs on the door jambs of the nearby **San Miguel de Lillo** show acrobats and animal tamers in a circus.

The early 9th-century church of **San Julián de los Prados** stands on the road leading northeast out of Oviedo. It is the largest of all the Pre-Romanesque churches and is particularly noted for the frescoes which once covered the whole of its interior.

🏛 **Museo Arqueológico**
Calle San Vicente 5. 〖 985 21 54 05. ◯ Tue–Sun.

🏛 **Museo de Bellas Artes**
Calle Santa Ana 1. 〖 985 21 30 61. ◯ Tue–Sun.

Valdediós ❽

Asturias. 👥 150. ℹ Villaviciosa, 985 89 23 24.

SET ALONE in a field near this hamlet, the tiny 9th-century **Iglesia de San Salvador** is a jewel of Pre-Romanesque art. Its ceiling has vivid Asturian frescoes, and by the portal are stone recesses where pilgrims slept. The church in the monastery next door is 13th-century Cistercian, with cloisters dating from the 15th century.

ENVIRONS: To the north, the graceful little resort town of **Villaviciosa** lies amid apple orchards and glorious hilly scenery, and has glass-fronted mansions in its narrow streets. In nearby **Amandi**, the hilltop Iglesia de San Juan has a 13th-century portal and delicate carvings and friezes.

Iglesia de San Salvador de Valdediós in its idyllic setting

Ribadesella ❾

Asturias. 👥 6,400. 🚃 🚌 ℹ Plaza Reina María Cristina 1, 985 86 00 38. 🛒 Wed. 🎉 Descent of the Río Sella (first Sat of Aug).

THIS ENCHANTING little seaside town bestrides a broad estuary. On one side is the lively old seaport full of tapas bars below a clifftop church. Across the estuary is a holiday resort. A multicoloured flotilla of kayaks arrives here from Arriondas (upstream) in an international regatta that is held every year on the first Saturday in August.

On the edge of town is the **Cueva de Tito Bustillo**. This cave is rich in stalactites but is best known for its many prehistoric drawings, which were discovered in 1968, some dating from around 18,000 BC. These include red and black pictures of stags and horses. To protect the paintings, only 390 visitors are allowed in per day; numbered tickets are given out from 9:30am every day. A museum on the site includes an artist's impressions of prehistoric living conditions.

🏛 **Cueva de Tito Bustillo**
Ribadesella. 〖 985 86 11 20. ◯ Wed–Sun. ● caves: Oct–Apr. 🎟

Cangas de Onís ❿

Asturias. 👥 3,300. 🚌 ℹ Calle Cárcel 5, 985 84 80 05. 🛒 Sun. 🎉 Fiesta del Pastor (25 Jul).

CANGAS DE ONÍS, one of the gateways to the Picos de Europa *(see pp104–5)*, is where Pelayo, the 8th-century Visigothic nobleman and early hero of the Reconquest, set up his court. The town has a Romanesque bridge and the 15th-century chapel of Santa Cruz built on an old dolmen.

ENVIRONS: About 5 km (3 miles) east is the **Cueva del Buxu**, which has engravings and rock-drawings over 10,000 years old. Only 25 visitors, in groups of five, are allowed in to see the caves each day.

🏛 **Cueva del Buxu**
〖 985 94 00 54. ◯ Wed–Sun. 🎟

Parque Nacional de los Picos de Europa ⓫

Lefebvre's Ringlet

Tʜᴇsᴇ ʙᴇᴀᴜᴛɪғᴜʟ mountains were reputedly christened the "Peaks of Europe" by returning sailors for whom this was often the first sight of their homeland. The range, now Europe's biggest national park, straddles three regions – Asturias, Cantabria and Castilla y León – and has diverse terrain. In some parts, deep winding gorges cut through craggy rocks while elsewhere verdant valleys support orchards and dairy farming. The celebrated creamy blue cheese, Cabrales (see p73), is made here. The Picos offer rock climbing and upland hiking as well as a profusion of flora and fauna. Tourism is well organized, with good roads and many hotels and refuges.

Covadonga
The Neo-Romanesque basilica, built between 1886 and 1901, stands on the site of Pelayo's historic victory.

Lago de la Ercina
Together with the nearby Lago Enol, this lake lies on a wild limestone plateau above Covadonga and below the peak of Peña Santa.

Desfiladero de los Beyos
This deep, narrow gorge with its high limestone cliffs winds spectacularly for 10 km (6 miles) through the mountains. Tracing the route of the Río Sella below, it carries the main road from Cangas de Onís to Riaño.

KEY

═══	Major road
═══	Minor road
▪ ▪	Footpath
▬▬	National park boundary
🛈	Tourist information
�☆	Viewpoint

Desfiladero del Río Cares
The River Cares forms a deep gorge in the heart of the Picos. A dramatic footpath follows the gorge, passing through tunnels and across high bridges up to 1,000 m (3,280 ft) above the river.

a dramatic view of the mountains of the Picos de Europa

VISITORS' CHECKLIST

Cangas de Onís, 985 84 80 05. *Oviedo to Cangas de Onís.* **Fuente Dé cable car** *942 73 66 10.* *Jul–Sep: 9am–8pm daily, Oct–Jun: 10am–6pm daily.* *25 Dec–Feb.*

PELAYO THE WARRIOR

A statue of this Visigothic nobleman who became king of Asturias guards the basilica at Covadonga. It was close to this site, in 722, that Pelayo and a band of men – though vastly outnumbered – are said to have defeated a Moorish army. The victory inspired Christians in the north of Spain to reconquer the peninsula *(see pp48–51)*. The tomb of the warrior is in a cave which has become a shrine, also containing a painted image of the Virgin.

Pelayo's statue

Naranjo de Bulnes, with its tooth-like crest, is in the heart of the massif. At 2,519 m (8,264 ft) it is one of the highest summits in the Picos de Europa.

Fuente Dé Cable Car
The 900-m (2950-ft) ascent from Fuente Dé takes visitors up to a wild rocky plateau pitted with craters. From here there is a spectacular panorama of the Picos' peaks and valleys.

Statue of the Virgin, San Vicente de la Barquera

ASTURIAS AND CANTABRIA'S FIESTAS

La Folía *(Apr)*, San Vicente de la Barquera (Cantabria). The statue of the Virgen de la Barquera is said to have arrived at San Vicente in a boat with no sails, oars or crew. Once a year, it is put in a fishing boat decorated with flags and flowers, which sails at the head of a procession to bless the sea. Groups of young girls, called *picayos*, stand on the shore singing traditional songs of the region in honour of the Virgin. La Folía usually falls at the end of April, but its date is dependent on the local tides.

Fiesta del Pastor *(25 Jul)*, near Cangas de Onís (Asturias). Regional songs and dances are performed at the annual Shepherds' Festival beside the shores of Lake Enol in the Picos de Europa National Park.

Battle of the Flowers *(last Fri of Aug)*, Laredo (Cantabria). Floats adorned with flowers are paraded through this small resort. A flower-throwing free-for-all follows the procession.

Nuestra Señora de Covadonga *(8 Sep)*, Picos de Europa (Asturias). Huge crowds converge on the shrine of Covadonga *(see p104)* to pay homage to the patron saint of Asturias.

Potes **⓬**

Cantabria. 🏠 *1,500.* ℹ *Calle de la Independencia 12, 942 73 07 87.* 🚌 *Mon.* 🎉 *Santisima Cruz (15 Sep).*

A SMALL ANCIENT TOWN, with old balconied houses lining the river, Potes is the main centre of the eastern Picos de Europa. It is situated in the broad Valle de Liébana, whose fertile soil yields prime crops of walnuts, cherries and grapes. A potent spirit called *orujo* is made in the town. The **Torre del Infantado**, in the main square, is a defensive tower built in the 15th century.

ENVIRONS: Between Potes and the coast runs a gorge, the **Desfiladero de la Hermida**. Halfway up it is **Santa María de Lebeña**, a 10th-century Mozarabic *(see p335)* church with horseshoe arches.

West of Potes is the monastery church of **Santo Toribio de Liébana**, one of the most revered spots in the Picos de Europa. Founded during the 7th century, it became known throughout Spain a century later when it received reputedly the largest fragment of the True Cross, kept in a silver reliquary. An 8th-century monk, St Beatus of Liébana, wrote the *Commentary on the Apocalypse*, later much copied and illuminated. The restored Romanesque buildings of the monastery, which was rebuilt in the 13th century, are now occupied by Franciscan monks.

Comillas **⓭**

Cantabria. 🏠 *2,500.* ℹ *Calle la Aldea 6, 942 72 07 68.* 🚌 *Fri.* 🎉 *El Cristo (16 Jul).* **Palacio** 🕐 *Jun–Sep: daily; Sep–Jun: Wed– Sun.* **Universidad** 🕐 *daily.*

T HIS PRETTY RESORT is known for its unusual buildings by Catalan Modernista architects *(see pp136–7)*. Antonio López y López, the first Marquis of Comillas, hired Joan Martorell to design the **Palacio Sobrellano** (1881), a huge Neo-

Stone bridge and houses in the ancient town of Potes

Surviving Classical columns among the ruins of the Roman town of Juliobriga, near Reinosa

Gothic edifice. Comilla's best-known monument is Gaudí's *(see p160)* **El Capricho**, now a restaurant *(see p580)*. It was designed for a rich business-man from 1883–9 and is a Mudéjar-inspired fantasy with a minaret-like tower covered in green and yellow tiles. Another of the town's Modernista buildings is the **Universidad Pontificia**, which overlooks the sea from a hilltop. It was designed by Joan Martorell to plans by Domènech i Montaner *(see p136)*.

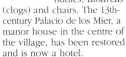

Wall tile on the façade of El Capricho

ENVIRONS: The fishing port of **San Vicente de la Barquera** has arcaded streets, ramparts and the Gothic Romanesque church of Nuestra Señora de los Ángeles.

Valle de Cabuérniga ⓮

Cantabria. 🚌 *Bárcena Mayor.*
ℹ *Ayuntamiento, Ruente, 942 70 91 04 (summer only).*

TWO EXCEPTIONALLY picturesque towns, notable for their superb examples of rural architecture, draw visitors to the Cabuérniga Valley. A good road takes you to the once-remote **Bárcena Mayor**. Its cobbled streets are furnished with old lamps and filled with boutiques, and restaurants serving a range of regional dishes. The pretty houses have flower-covered balconies, and cattle byres on the ground floor.

Carmona is an old, unspoiled village approximately 20 km (12 miles) to the northwest of Bárcena Mayor. Its solid stone houses, with pantiled roofs and wooden balconies, are typically Cantabrian *(see p22)*. Woodcarving, the traditional craft of the region, is still practised in this village, where men work outside their houses on a variety of artifacts including bowls, fiddles, *albarcas* (clogs) and chairs. The 13th-century Palacio de los Mier, a manor house in the centre of the village, has been restored and is now a hotel.

The extensive, wild beech woods near **Saja** have been designated a nature reserve.

Traditional balconied houses in Bárcena Mayor

Alto Campoo ⓯

Cantabria. 🏠 *1,900.* 🚌 🚋
ℹ *Estación de Montaña, 942 77 92 22 (am only).* 🎿 *Nuestra Señora de las Nieves (5 Aug), San Roque (16 Aug).*

SITED HIGH in the Cantabrian mountains, this winter resort lies below the Pico de Tres Mares (2,175 m/7,000 ft), the "Peak of the Three Seas", so called because the rivers rising near it flow into the Mediterranean, the Atlantic and the Bay of Biscay. The Río Ebro, one of Spain's longest rivers, rises in this area and its source, at Fontibre, is a beauty spot. A road and a chair lift reach the summit of Tres Mares for a breathtaking panorama of the Picos de Europa and other mountain chains. The resort is small, with ten pistes totalling 17 km (10 miles) in length, and has few facilities for après-ski.

ENVIRONS: Reinosa, some 26 km (16 miles) to the east of Alto Campoo, is a handsome market town with old stone houses. Further southeast is Retortillo, a hamlet where the remains of **Juliobriga**, a town built by the Romans as a bastion against the wild tribes of Cantabria, can be seen.

The main road south out of Reinosa leads to **Cervatos**, where the former collegiate church has erotic carvings on its façade. This novel device was meant to deter the villagers from pleasures of the flesh.

At **Arroyuelo** and **Cadalso**, to the southeast, are two churches built into rock faces in the 9th and 10th centuries.

One of the many paintings of bison at Altamira

Cuevas de Altamira 🔟

Cantabria. ☎ *942 81 80 05* 🖳
Santillana del Mar. **Caves** ○ *by appt;
see below.* 📷 **Museum** ○ *Tue–
Sun.* ● *24, 25, 31 Dec & 1 Jan.*

THESE CAVES contain some of
the world's finest examples
of prehistoric art. The earliest
engravings and draw-
ings, discovered in 1879,
date back to around
18,000 BC *(see p44)*.
Entry to the caves is
limited to 25 people per
day; there is a 3-year
waiting list. To
apply, contact the
on-site museum,
which contains a
replica of the
caves open to all.   **Carved figure of Christ in**
Alternatively, the   **the Convento de Regina Coeli**
first 15 visitors outside the
museum at 9:30am are put on
a waiting list; for each person
with an appointment that does
not arrive by noon, one person
from this list is admitted.

Santillana del Mar 🔟

Cantabria. 🏠 *4,000.* 🚉 🚌 *Calle
Jesus Otero 22, 942 81 88 12.*
📷 *Santa Juliana (28 Jun).*

SET JUST INLAND, belying its
name, this town is one the
prettiest in Spain. Its ensemble
of 15th- to 17th-century golden

stone houses survives largely
intact despite the many tourists and souvenir shops.
    The town grew up around
a monastery, which was an
important pilgrimage centre,
the Romanesque **La Colegiata**.
The church houses the tomb
of the local early-medieval
martyr St Juliana, and contains
a 17th-century painted reredos
and a carved south door. In its
lovely cloisters, vivid biblical scenes have been
sculpted on the capitals.
On the town's two main
cobbled streets there are
houses built by local
noblemen. These
have either fine
wooden galleries
or iron balconies,
and coats of arms
inlaid into their
stone façades. In
the past, farmers
used the open ground floors as
byres for stabling their cattle.
    In the enchanting **Plaza
Mayor**, in the centre of town,
is a mansion-turned-parador

(see p540). The **Museo
Diocesano** is housed in the
restored Convento de Regina
Coeli, east of the town centre,
and has a collection of painted
carvings of religious figures.

🏛 **Museo Diocesano**
Avenida Le Dorat 2. ☎ *942 81 80 04.*
○ *Thu–Tue.* ● *Feb.* 📷

Puente Viesgo 🔟

Cantabria. 🏠 *2,500.* 🚉 🚌 *Calle
Manuel Pérez Mazo 2, 942 31 07 08.*
📷 *San Miguel (28–9 Sep).*

THE SPA of Puente Viesgo is
best known for the caves
– especially **Cueva de El
Castillo** – dotted around the
limestone hills above the town,
which were decorated by prehistoric man. It is thought the
late Palaeolithic cave dwellers
used the deep interior as a
kind of sanctuary. They left
drawings of horses, bison and
other animals there, and some
50 hand prints – almost always
the left hand. The ochre and
other colours used to create
the images were extracted
from minerals in the cave.

ENVIRONS: The lush Pas valley,
to the southeast, is home to
transhumant dairy farmers, the
Pasiegos. In the main town of
Vega de Pas, you can buy two
Pasiego specialities – *sobaos*,
or sponge cakes *(see p73)*,
and *quesadas*, a sweet which
is made from milk, butter and
eggs. In **Villacarriedo** there
is a handsome 18th-century
mansion, with two Baroque
façades of carved stone hiding
a medieval tower.

🐾 **Cueva de El Castillo**
Puente Viesgo. ☎ *942 59 84 25.*
● *Mon.*

Main façade of La Colegiata in Santillana del Mar

The Palacio de la Magdalena in El Sardinero

Santander ⑲

Cantabria. 🏘 200,000. ✈ 🚆 🚌 ⛴
ℹ Plaza de Velarde 5, 942 31 07 08.
🏛 Thu–Tue. 🎉 Santiago (25 Jul).
🌐 www.ayto-santander.es

CANTABRIA'S CAPITAL, a busy port, enjoys a splendid site near the mouth of a deep bay. The town centre is modern – after being ravaged by fire in 1941 it was reconstructed.
The **cathedral** was rebuilt in Gothic style, but retains its 12th-century crypt. The **Museo de Bellas Artes** houses works by Goya, Zurbarán and Mengs, as well as regional artists. The town's **Museo de Prehistoria y Arqueología** displays finds from caves in Cantabria, such as Neolithic axe heads, and Roman coins, pottery and figurines. The **Museo Marítimo** has rare whale skeletons and 350 species of local fish. It re-opens mid-2002 so call to check opening times.

The town extends along the coast around the Península de la Magdalena, a headland on which there is a park, a zoo and the **Palacio de la Magdalena** – a summer palace built for Alfonso XIII in 1912, reflecting the resort's popularity at the time with the Royal Family.

The seaside suburb of **El Sardinero**, north of the headland, is a smart resort with a long graceful beach, backed by gardens, elegant cafés and a majestic white casino. A cultured, self-confident place, in July and August El Sardinero plays host to a major theatre and music festival.

🏛 **Museo de Bellas Artes**
Calle Rubio 6. 📞 942 23 94 85.
🏛 Mon–Sat.
🏛 **Museo de Prehistoria y Arqueología**
Calle Casimiro Saenz 4. 📞 942 20 71 05. 🏛 Tue–Sun.
🏛 **Museo Marítimo**
Promontorio de San Martin. 📞 942 27 49 62. 🌑 until mid-2003.

Laredo ⑳

Cantabria. 🏘 14,000. 🚌 ℹ Calle Lopez Seña, 942 61 10 96.
🎉 Batalla de Flores (last Fri of Aug), San Martín (11 Nov).

THE EXCELLENT long, sandy beach of this small town has made it one of Cantabria's most popular bathing resorts. The old part of the town is attractive: narrow streets with balconied houses lead up to the 13th-century **Iglesia de la Asunción**, with its Flemish altar and enormous bronze lecterns. One of the highlights of the year in Laredo is the colourful fiesta of the Battle of the Flowers *(see p106).*

Castro Urdiales ㉑

Cantabria. 🏘 15,500. 🚌
ℹ Avenida de la Constitución 1, 942 87 15 12. 🏛 Thu. 🎉 Coso Blanco (27 Jun), Santa Ana (26 Jul).
Iglesia 🏛 4–6pm daily.

CASTRO URDIALES, a busy fishing town and popular holiday resort, is built around a picturesque natural harbour. Above the port, on a high promontory, stands the pinkish Gothic **Iglesia de Santa María**, as big as a cathedral. Beside it there is a half-ruined castle built by the Knights Templar, which has been converted into a lighthouse. Handsome glass-fronted houses, or *galerías*, line the elegant promenade. The small town beach often becomes crowded but there are bigger ones to the west, such as the Playa de Ostende.

ENVIRONS: Near the village of **Ramales de la Victoria**, 20 km (12 miles) south, are pre-historic caves containing etchings and engravings, reached by a very steep mountain road.

Small boats moored in the harbour at Castro Urdiales

THE BASQUE COUNTRY, NAVARRA AND LA RIOJA

VIZCAYA · GUIPÚZCOA · ÁLAVA · LA RIOJA · NAVARRA

GREEN HILLS MEET ATLANTIC BEACHES *in the Basque Country, land of an ancient people of mysterious origin. Navarra, also partly Basque, was a powerful medieval kingdom. The beautiful western Pyrenees form part of its charming countryside. The vineyards of La Rioja, to the south, produce many of Spain's finest wines.*

The Basques are a race apart – they will not let you forget that theirs is a culture different from any in Spain. Although the Basque regional government enjoys considerable autonomy, there is a strong separatist movement seeking to sever links with the government in Madrid.

The Basque Country (Euskadi is the Basque name) is an important industrial region. The Basques are great deep-sea fishermen and fish has a major role in their imaginative cuisine, regarded by many as the best in Spain.

Unrelated to any other tongue, the Basque language, *Euskera,* is widely used on signs and most towns have two names; the fashionable resort of San Sebastián, for example, is known to locals as Donostia. *Euskera* is also spoken in parts of Navarra, which is counted as part of the wider (unofficial) Basque Country. Many of its finest sights – the towns of Olite and Estella, and the monastery of Leyre – date from the Middle Ages when Navarra was a kingdom straddling the Pyrenees. Pamplona, its capital, is best known for its daredevil bull-running fiesta, which is held in July.

As well as its vineyards and bodegas, La Rioja is a region of market gardens. Among its many historic sights are the cathedral of Santo Domingo de la Calzada and the monasteries of San Millán de la Cogolla and Yuso.

Basque farmhouse near Gernika Lumo in the Basque Country

◁ A street in the village of Roncal, in the foothills of the Navarrese Pyrenees

---

Exploring the Basque Country, Navarra and La Rioja

THESE GREEN, HILLY REGIONS have diverse attractions. The Pyrenees in Navarra offer skiing in winter and climbing, caving and canoeing the rest of the year. The cliffs of the Basque Country are broken by rocky coves, rias, and wide bays with beaches of fine yellow sand, interspersed with fishing villages. Inland, minor roads wind through wooded hills, valleys and gorges past lonely castles and isolated homesteads. In La Rioja, to the south, they cross vineyards, passing villages and towns clustered round venerable churches and monasteries.

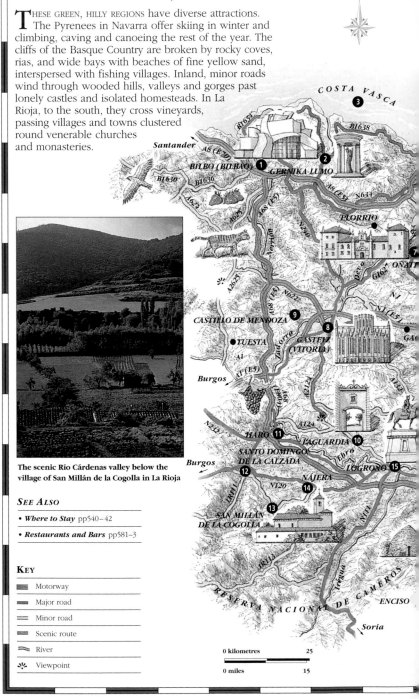

The scenic Río Cárdenas valley below the village of San Millán de la Cogolla in La Rioja

SEE ALSO

- *Where to Stay* pp540–42
- *Restaurants and Bars* pp581–3

KEY

▬	Motorway
▬	Major road
▬	Minor road
▬	Scenic route
≈	River
☼	Viewpoint

0 kilometres   25

0 miles   15

SIGHTS AT A GLANCE

Bilbo (Bilbao) **1**
Castillo de Javier **29**
Castillo de Mendoza **9**
Las Cinco Villas
de la Montaña **24**
Costa Vasca **3**
Donostia (San Sebastián) **4**
Elizondo **25**
Enciso **16**

Gasteiz (Vitoria) **8**
Gernika-Lumo **2**
Haro **11**
Hondarribia (Fuenterrabía) **5**
Iruña (Pamplona) **23**
Laguardia **10**
Lizarra (Estella) **22**
Logroño **15**
Monasterio de Leyre **28**
Monasterio de La Oliva **18**
Nájera **14**

Olite **20**
Oñati **7**
Orreaga (Roncesvalles) **26**
Puente la Reina **21**
Sangüesa **30**
San Millán de la Cogolla **13**
Santo Domingo de la Calzada **12**
Santuario de Loiola **6**
Tudela **17**
Ujué **19**
Valle de Roncal **27**

GETTING AROUND

The main road in the north, the A8 (E8), runs between Irún and Bilbao. The A68 (E8) runs southwards from Bilbao via Haro and follows the Ebro Valley, the area's east–west communications corridor, past Tudela. Motorway spurs extend to Vitoria and Pamplona. The rail network connects the cities and the larger towns, and most towns are served by coach. Bilbao has an international airport.

The fashionable Playa de Ondarreta, one of San Sebastián's three beaches

Buildings overlooking the Río Nervión in Bilbao

Bilbao ❶

Vizcaya. 🏛 *375,000.* ✈ 🚉 🚌 🚢
🛈 *Paseo del Arenal 1, 94 479 57
60.* 🎫 *Santiago (25 Jul), San Ignacio
(31 Jul), La Asunción (15 Aug).*
W *www.bilbao.net*

BILBAO (BILBO) is the centre
of Basque industry, Spain's
leading commercial port and
the largest Basque city. It is
surrounded by high, bare hills.
Its suburbs spread 16 km (10
miles) along the Río Nervión
(Nerbioi) to its estuary. The
river between Las Arenas and
the fishing port of Portugalete
is crossed via the **Puente Col-
gante**. This iron transporter
bridge, built in 1893, has a
suspended cabin for cars and
passengers. On the east bank
of the estuary is Santurtzi
(Santurce), from where ferries
sail to the UK *(see p628)*.

Bilbao has flourished as an
industrial city since the mid-
19th century, when iron ore
began to be extracted from
deposits northwest of the city.
Soon, steelworks and chemical
factories became a major part
of the local landscape.

The city is not beautiful, but
it is prosperous and its once
heavy pollution is now much
reduced. An urban development scheme has introduced
pieces of fascinating modernist
architecture to break up the
monotone industrial sprawl.

By the river, however, is the
city's medieval heart, the *casco
viejo*, built in the 14th century.
Here, amid alleys lively with
tapas bars, is the arcaded Plaza
Nueva and the **Catedral
Basílica de Santiago**. The
**Museo Arqueológico, Etno-
gráfico e Histórico Vasco**
displays Basque art, folk artifacts and photographs of
Basque life. In the cloister is
the Idol of Mikeldi, an animal-
like carving dating from the
3rd–2nd century BC.

In the newer town is the
large **Museo de Bellas Artes**
(Museum of Fine Art), one of
Spain's best art museums. It
displays art ranging from
12th-century Catalan masterpieces to works by modern
artists of international fame,
including Vasarely, Kokoschka,
Bacon, Delaunay and Léger.
There are also several rooms
of paintings by Basque artists.

The jewel in the area's
cultural crown is the **Museo
Guggenheim Bilbao** *(see
pp116–17)*, which opened in
1997. The museum is part of
a redevelopment of the city
which includes the expansion
of the capacity of its port and
the new metro system,
designed in a futuristic style
by Norman Foster. Another
striking new building is the
**Palacio de la Música y
Congresos Euskalduna**. Designed to resemble a ship, it
has an auditorium seating 2,200
people and is the home of the
Bilbao Symphony Orchestra.

West of the city, a funicular
railway ascends to the village
of La Reineta where there is a
panorama across the dock-
yards. On the estuary's east
bank is Algorta, a beach resort.

🏛 **Museo Arqueológico,
Etnográfico e Histórico
Vasco**
Plaza Miguel Unamuno 4. 📞 *94 415
54 23.* 🕐 *Tue–Sun.* 🔴 *public hols.*
🔲 🔲

🏛 **Museo de Bellas Artes**
Plaza del Museo 2. 📞 *94 439 60 60.*
🕐 *Tue–Sun.* 🔴 *public hols.* 🔲
🎭 **Palacio de la Música y
Congresos Euskalduna**
Ave Abandoibarra 4. 📞 *94 403 50
00.* 🕐 *for concerts.* 🔲

Gernika-Lumo ❷

Vizcaya. 🏛 *15,400.* 🚉 🚌
🛈 *Artekalea 8, 94 625 58 92.*
🔴 *Mon.* 🎫 *Aniversario del
Bombardeo de Guernica (26 Apr).*

THIS LITTLE TOWN is of great
symbolic significance to
the Basques. For centuries,
Basque leaders met in democratic assembly under an oak
on a hillside here. On 26 April
1937 Gernika-Lumo (Guernica)
was the target of the world's
first saturation bombing raid,
carried out by Nazi aircraft at
the request of General Franco.
Picasso's powerful painting
(see pp62–3) of this outrage can
be seen in Madrid *(see p289)*.

The town has since been
rebuilt and is rather dull. But
in a garden, inside a pavilion
and closely guarded, is the
300-year-old petrified trunk of
the oak tree, the *Gernikako
Arbola*, or Oak of Gernika,
symbol of the ancient roots of
the Basque people. A younger
oak, its successor, is planted
beside it. The Basque people
make visits to this ancient tree
as if on a pilgrimage.

Zuloaga's *Condesa Mathieu de Noailles* **(1913), Bilbao Museum of Fine Art**

Basque fishermen depicted in the stained-glass ceiling of the Casa de Juntas in Gernika-Lumo

The **Casa de Juntas**, nearby, is a former chapel where the parliament of the province of Vizcaya has convened since 1979, when the Basque provinces regained their autonomy. In one room a stained-glass ceiling depicts the Oak of Gernika with Basque citizens debating their rights.

The Europa Park, next door, has peace sculptures by Henry Moore and Eduardo Chillida.

ENVIRONS: Five km (3 miles) northeast of Gernika, near Kortézubi (Cortézubi), are the **Cuevas de Santimamiñe**. On the walls of a small chamber are drawings in charcoal of bison and other animals made by Cro-Magnon cave dwellers around 11,000 BC. They were discovered in 1917. A guide shows visitors these ancient drawings and then leads them down the Long Gallery, an underground passage full of oddly shaped stalagmites and stalactites, some of them shot through with brilliant colours. Santimamiñe is one of several huge cave complexes in this mountain area, but most are closed to the public.

🏛 **Casa de Juntas**
C/ Allende Salazar. ☎ *94 625 11 38.*
◯ *daily.* ● *15 Aug & 25 Dec.* ♿
🏛 **Cuevas de Santimamiñe**
Barrio Basondo, Kortézubi. ☎ *94 625 58 92.* ◯ *Mon–Fri.* ● *public hols.*

Costa Vasca ❸

Vizcaya & Guipúzcoa. 🚉 *Bilbao.*
🚌 *Bilbao.* 🛈 *Getxo, 94 491 08 00.*

THE BASQUE COUNTRY'S 176 km (110 miles) of coastline is heavily indented: rugged cliffs alternate with inlets and coves, the whole backed by wooded hills. Some of the fishing villages are over-developed, but the scenery inland is attractive.

There are good beaches north of Algorta (near Bilbao). **Plentzia** is a pleasant estuary town with a marina. Eastwards on the coast is **Bakio**, a large fishing village also known for its beaches. Beyond it the BI3101, a dramatic corniche road, winds high above the sea past the tiny island hermitage,

Anglers on the quayside at Lekeitio, a port on the Costa Vasca

San Juan de Gaztelugatxe, and Matxitxaco, a headland lighthouse. It passes Bermeo, a port with a fishery museum, the **Museo del Pescador**, and Mundaka, a small surfing resort. On the serene Ría de Guernica there are two sandy beaches, **Laida** and **Laga**.

Lekeitio, a fishing port to the east, has a pretty shoreline. Old Basque houses line the seafront below the 15th-century church of Santa María. One long beach, good for swimming, sweeps round the village of **Saturrarán** and the old port of **Ondarroa**. The Lekeitio–Ondarroa road is pleasantly planted with pines.

Zumaia is a beach resort with an old quarter. In the **Museo de Ignacio Zuloaga**, the former home of the well-known Basque painter who lived from 1870–1945, colourful studies of Basque rural and maritime life are on display. **Getaria**, along the coast, is a trawler port with lively cafés. and the 14th-century Iglesia de San Salvador. **Zarautz**, once a fashionable resort, has sizeable beaches and elegant mansions.

🏛 **Museo del Pescador**
Plaza Torrontero 1. ☎ *94 688 11 71.*
◯ *Tue–Sun.* ● *public hols.* ♿
🏛 **Museo de Ignacio Zuloaga**
Casa Santiago Zumaya, Carretera de San Sebastián. ☎ *943 86 23 41.*
◯ *Jan–Sep: Wed–Sun.* 🖼

Bilbao: Museo Guggenheim

THE MUSEO GUGGENHEIM is the jewel in Bilbao's cultural crown. The building itself is a star attraction: a mind-boggling array of silvery curves by the American architect Frank Gehry, which are alleged to resemble a ship or a flower. The Guggenheim's collection represents an intruigingly broad spectrum of modern and contemporary art, and includes works by Abstract Impressionists such as Willem de Kooning and Mark Rothko. Most of the art shown here is displayed as part of an ongoing series of temporary exhibitions and major retrospectives. Some of these are also staged at the Guggenheim museums in New York, Venice and Berlin.

Roofscape
The Guggenheim's prow-like points and metallic material make it comparable to a ship.

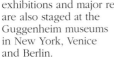

The tower, on the far side of the bridge, was designed to resemble a sail. It is not an exhibition space.

The Puente de la Salve was incorporated into the design of the building, which extends underneath it.

★ Titanium façade
Rarely used in buildings, titanium is more usually used for aircraft parts. In total 60 tons were used, but the layer is only 3 mm (0.1 inches) thick.

The Snake, by Richard Serra, was created in hot-rolled steel. It is over 30 m (100 ft) long.

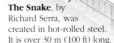

Fish Gallery
Dominated by Richard Serra's Snake, this gallery is the museum's largest. The fish motif, seen in the flowing shape, is one of architect Frank Gehry's favourites.

★ Atrium
The space in which visitors to the museum first find themselves is the extraordinary 60-m (165-ft) high atrium. It serves as an orientation point and its height makes it a dramatic setting for exhibiting large pieces.

VISITORS' CHECKLIST

Avenida Abandoibarra. **C** *944 35 90 80.* **M** *Moyua.* **☐** *1, 10, 11, 13, 18, 27, 38, 46, 48, 71.* **☐** *10am–8pm daily.* **●** *Mon (Sep–Jun), public hols.*
W www.guggenheim-bilbao.es

Puppy, by American artist Jeff Koons, has a coat of flowers irrigated by an internal system. Originally a temporary feature, the sculpture's popularity with Bilbao's residents earned it a permanent spot.

Second-floor balcony

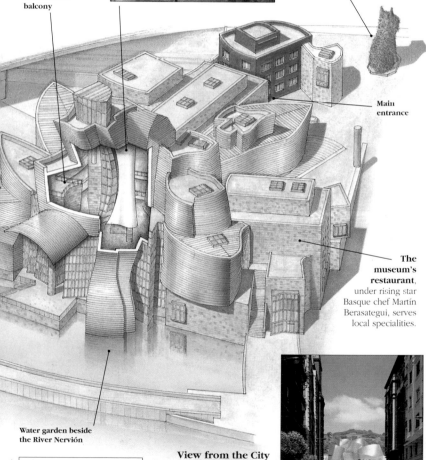

Main entrance

The museum's restaurant, under rising star Basque chef Martín Berasategui, serves local specialities.

Water garden beside the River Nervión

View from the City
Approaching along the Calle de Iparraguirre, the "Guggen", as the museum has been nicknamed by locals, stands out amid traditional buildings.

STAR SIGHTS

★ Titanium façade

★ Atrium

San Sebastián's Playa de Ondarreta, with its view across the bay

San Sebastián ❹

Guipúzcoa. 🏛 180,000. 🚉 🚌 🛈
Reina Regente 3, 943 48 11 66. 🚢
Sun. 🎭 San Sebastián (20 Jan);
Semana Grande (mid-Aug).
Ⓦ www.sansebastianturismo.com

GLORIOUSLY SITUATED on a neat, shell-shaped bay, San Sebastián (Donostia) is the most elegant and fashionable Spanish seaside resort. At either end of the bay is a tower-topped hill – Monte Urgull in the east and Monte Igueldo in the west. Between the two, in the mouth of the bay, lies a small island, the Isla de Santa Clara.

San Sebastián became a smart resort in the late 19th century, and has remained popular with the aristocracy. It still has many smart shops and one of Spain's grandest luxury hotels, the María Cristina *(see p542)*, but San Sebastián is now primarily a family resort.

The city is renowned for its great summer arts festivals. A jazz festival is held in July, a classical music festival in late August, and the San Sebastián International Film Festival in September. The Semana Grande in August focuses on traditional Basque folk culture.

Cuisine also plays a huge part in local life: many Basque men in San Sebastián belong to gastronomic clubs where they gather to cook, eat, drink and talk. Even these days, women are seldom invited to such gatherings.

The Old Town

San Sebastián's fascinating old town, called the Parte Vieja, is wedged between the bay and the Río Urumea. The alleys of the old town, packed with restaurants and tapas bars, are intensely animated at night. In the large local fish market, stalls piled high with delicacies testify to the key role of fish in the life of the town.

The heart of the old town is the **Plaza de la Constitución**, a handsome, arcaded square with blue and orange shutters. The numbers on the balconies date from when the square was used as a bullring – organizers sold a ticket for each numbered place. The church of **Santa María del Coro**, nearby, has a rich Baroque portal.

Monte Urgull rises behind the old town. On the summit are a statue of Christ and the ruined **Castillo de Santa Cruz de la Mota**, with old cannons.

Beaches

San Sebastián's two principal beaches follow the bay round to **Monte Igueldo**. The **Playa de Ondarreta** is the more fashionable of the two while the **Playa de la Concha** is the larger. Between them is the **Palacio Miramar**, built in 1889 by the Basque architect, José Goicoa, to designs by Selden Wornum, a British architect. The palace, built for Queen María Cristina as a summer residence, established San Sebastián as an aristocratic resort. The gardens are open to the public, and the palace often plays host to local events.

At the water's edge near the Playa de Ondarreta is a striking modern iron sculpture, *The Comb of the Winds* by Eduardo Chillida. A road and a funicular railway lead to the top of Monte Igueldo, where there is an amusement park.

To the east of the Playa de la Concha is the surfer's favourite beach, **Playa de la Zurriola**, which is overlooked by the hill, **Monte Ulía**.

Aquarium

Plaza Carlos Blasco de Imaz. ☎ 943
44 00 99. 🕐 Sep–Jun: 10am–8pm;
Jul–Aug: 10am–10pm daily.
⚫ 25 Dec & 1 Jan. 🈴
This remodeled aquarium boasts a 360º underwater tunnel, where visitors can view over 5,000 fish, including two small sharks. Tickets allow entry to the Naval Museum, containing exhibits of Basque naval history.

The Comb of the Winds by Eduardo Chillida

Josep Maria Sert's murals of Basque life in the Museo de San Telmo

Kursaal
Playa de la Zurriola. **(** 943 00 30 00
These giant cubes stand out as the most prominent feature on Zurriola beach, especially when lit up at night. Designed by Rafael Moneo, the cubes contain large auditoriums, for most of the year home to conferences and concerts.

🏛 Museo de San Telmo
Plaza Zuloaga. **(** 943 42 49 70.
○ Tue–Sun. ♿
This is a large museum in a 16th-century monastery below Monte Urgull. In the cloister is a collection of Basque funerary columns dating from the 15th–17th centuries.

The museum also contains displays of headdresses, furniture, tools and other artifacts, and paintings by local Basque artists: 19th-century works by Antonio Ortiz Echagüe, modern paintings

by Ignacio Zuloaga, portraits by Vicente López and masterpieces by El Greco. The chapel holds 16 murals by the Catalan artist Josep Maria Sert, depicting Basque legends, culture and the region's seafaring life.

🏛 Chillida-Leku
Caserío Zabalaga, Bº Jáuregui 66, Hernani. **(** 943 33 60 06. ○ Tue.
🖼 Ⓦ www.eduardo-chillida.com
Set in a 16th-century farmhouse surrounded by pleasant gardens, this new museum displays a permanent collection of 40 sculptures by the acclaimed Basque artist Eduardo Chillida

ENVIRONS: 5 km (3 miles) east of San Sebastián is **Pasaia Donibane**, a picturesque fishing village consisting of a jumble of houses with a cobbled main street which has some good fish restaurants.

The waterfront of the tiny fishing village of Pasaia Donibane

Old balconied houses in the upper town, Hondarribia

Hondarribia ❺

Guipúzcoa. 🏘 14,000. 🚇 Calle Javier Ugarte 6, 943 64 54 58.
📅 La Kutxa Entrega (25 Jul), Alarde (6–8 Sep).

Hondarribia (Fuenterrabía), the historic town at the mouth of the Río Bidasoa, was attacked by the French over many centuries. The upper town is protected by 15th-century walls and entered via their original gateway, the handsome **Puerta de Santa María**. They enclose alleys of old houses with carved eaves, balconies and coats of arms.

The streets cluster round the church of **Santa María de la Asunción**, with its massive buttresses, tall Baroque tower, and, inside, a gold reredos. At the town's highest point is the **castle**, which was founded in the 10th century and is now a parador *(see p541)*.

Hondarribia is a fishing port and there are seafront cafés in La Marina, the lively fishermen's quarter. It is also a seaside resort, with beaches stretching to the north.

ENVIRONS: A hill road climbs westwards to the shrine of the Virgin of Guadalupe. Further along this road are panoramic views of the coast and the mountains. From the **Ermita de San Marcial**, which stands on a hill 9 km (6 miles) to the south, there are views of the Bidasoa plain straddling the border – the French towns are neatly white, the Spanish ones are greyer.

SAN SEBASTIÁN FILM FESTIVAL

This festival, founded in 1953, is one of the five leading European annual film festivals. It is held in late September, drawing more than 100,000 spectators. The special Donostia Prize is awarded as a tribute to the career of a star or director: recent winners include Susan Sarandon, Jeanne Moreau and Jeremy Irons. Visiting celebrities have included Quentin Tarantino, Greta Scacchi and William Hurt. Prizes also go to individual new films. An early winner was Hitchcock's *Vertigo*. The festival's website is www. sansebastianfestival.ya.com

Lauren Bacall receiving an award

The Renaissance façade of the former Basque university in Oñati

Santuario de Loiola ❻

Loiola (Guipúzcoa). 943 81 65 08. daily.

SAINT IGNATIUS OF LOIOLA (San Ignacio de Loyola), founder of the Jesuits, was born in the 1490s in the Santa Casa (holy house), a stone manor near Azpeitia. In the 17th century it was enclosed by the Basílica de San Ignacio, and the rooms in which the aristocratic Loiola family lived were converted into chapels. The Chapel of the Conversion is the room in which Ignatius, as a young soldier, recovered from a war injury, and had a profound religious experience.

A diorama depicts episodes in the saint's life: dedicating his life to Christ at the Monastery of Montserrat (see pp208–209); writing his *Spiritual Exercises*

in a cave at Manresa; his imprisonment by the Inquisition; and his pilgrimage to the Holy Land. The basilica, built from 1681–1738, has a Churrigueresque dome and a circular nave, in which almost every surface is richly carved.

Oñati ❼

Guipúzcoa. 10,000. Plaza de los Fueros 4, 943 78 34 53. Sat. Corpus Christi (May/Jun), San Miguel (29 Sep).

THE HISTORIC TOWN of Oñati (Oñate) in the Udana Valley has a distinguished past. In the First Carlist War, 1833–9 (see p59), it was a seat of the court of Don Carlos, brother of King Fernando VII and pretender to the throne. Its former **university**, built in about 1540, was for centuries the only one in the Basque

Country. It has a Renaissance façade, decorated with statues of saints, and an elegant patio.

In the Plaza de los Fueros is the **Iglesia de San Miguel**, a Gothic church with a stone cloister in Plateresque (see p21) style. It contains the tomb of Bishop Zuázola of Ávila, the founder of the university. Opposite is the Baroque **town hall** (ayuntamiento).

ENVIRONS: A mountain road ascends to the **Santuario de Arantzazu**, overshadowed by the peak of Aitzgorri. In 1469 a shepherd reported seeing a vision of the Virgin here. Over the door of the church, built in the 1950s, are sculptures of the apostles by Jorge Oteiza.

🏛 Universidad de Sancti Spiritus
Avenida de la Universidad Vasca. 943 78 34 53. Mon–Fri for guided tours (phone in advance).

The imposing Santuario de Loiola, with its Churrigueresque cupola

---

THE FOUNDING OF THE JESUIT ORDER

The Society of Jesus was founded in Rome in 1539 by Saint Ignatius and a group of priests who were dedicated to helping the poor. Pope Paul III soon approved the order's establishment, with Ignatius as Superior General. The order, which grew wealthy, vowed military obedience to the Pope and became his most powerful weapon against the Reformation. Today, there are approximately 24,000 Jesuits working, mainly in education, in 110 countries.

Saint Ignatius of Loiola

Basque Culture

THE BASQUES may be Europe's oldest race. Anthropologists think they could be descended from Cro-Magnon people, who lived in the Pyrenees 40,000 years ago. The dolmens and carved stones of their ancestors are evidence of the Basques' pagan roots.

Long isolated in their mountain valleys, the Basques preserved their unique language, myths and art for millennia, almost untouched by other influences.

Many families still live in the isolated, chalet-style stone *caseríos*, or farmhouses, built by their forebears. Their music and high-bounding dances are unlike those of any other culture, and their cuisine is varied and imaginative.

The *fueros* or ancient Basque laws and rights were suppressed under General Franco, but since the arrival of democracy in 1975 the Basques have had their own parliament and police force, having won great autonomy over their own affairs.

Basque policeman

THE BASQUE REGION

Areas of Basque culture

The national identity *is symbolized by the region's flag:* La Ikurriña. *The white cross symbolizes Christianity. The green St Andrew's Cross commemorates a battle won on his feast day.*

Bertsolaris *are bards. They improvise witty, sometimes humorous songs, whose verses relate current events or legends. Bertsolaris sing, unaccompanied, to gatherings in public places, such as bars and squares, often in competition. This oral tradition has preserved Basque folklore, legends and history. No texts were written in* Euskera *(Basque) until the 16th century.*

Traditional sports *are highly respected in Basque culture. In pelota* (frontón), *teams hit a ball at a wall then catch it with a wicker scoop or their hands. Sports involving strength, such as log-splitting and weightlifting, are the most popular.*

The Basque economy *has always relied on fishing and associated industries, such as shipbuilding and agriculture. In recent history, heavy industries have made this region prosperous.*

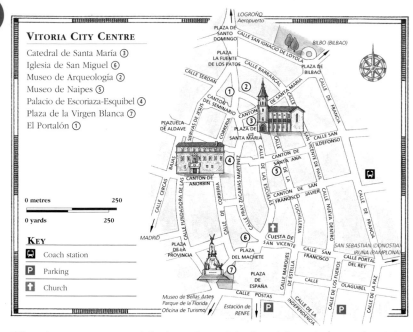

VITORIA CITY CENTRE

Catedral de Santa María ③
Iglesia de San Miguel ⑥
Museo de Arqueología ②
Museo de Naipes ⑤
Palacio de Escoriaza-Esquibel ④
Plaza de la Virgen Blanca ⑦
El Portalón ①

0 metres   250
0 yards   250

KEY

🚌   Coach station
🅿   Parking
✝   Church

Vitoria ❽

Álava. 🏠 *210,000.* ✈ 🚌 🚌
🛈 *Avenida de Gasteiz, 945 16 15
98.* 🍴 *Thu.* 🎭 *Romería de San
Prudencio (28 Apr), Fiestas de la Virgen
Blanca (4–9 Aug).*
🌐 *www.vitoria-gasteiz.org*

Vitoria (Gasteiz), the seat
of the Basque government,
was founded on a hill – the
province's highest point and
the site of an ancient Basque
town, Gasteiz. Vitoria's oldest
part, El Campillo, was rebuilt
in 1200 after a fire. The city
later grew rich on the iron
and wool trades.

The old town focuses on the
Plaza de la Virgen Blanca,
with its monument to a battle

fought nearby in 1813, when
the British Duke of Wellington
defeated the French. Around
the plaza are old houses with
miradores (glazed balconies).

On the hillside above the
plaza is the Gothic **Iglesia de
San Miguel**. An outside niche
contains a statue of the Virgen
Blanca (White Virgin), Vitoria's
patron saint. A big festival *(see
p128)* begins on her feast day,
4 August. On the wall of San
Miguel facing the **Plaza del
Machete** there is a recess that
once held a machete on which
the city's rulers swore to up-
hold the laws or be slain.

The old town has several
Renaissance palaces, including
the 16th-century **Palacio de
Escoriaza-Esquibel**, which

has a Plateresque *(see p21)*
patio. Around it is a charming
area of old alleys linked by
steep steps. Young people
throng the bars at night.

The city has two cathedrals.
The oldest, on the old town's
limit, is the Gothic **Catedral
de Santa María**, with a sculpted west porch. Close by, in
Calle Correría, a street of old
houses, is the enchanting **El
Portalón**, a merchant's house
and hostel from the 15th century. The building, which is full
of Basque country furniture
and art, is now a restaurant.

Among the city's later architectural gems are an arcaded
street, **Los Arquillos**, and the
adjoining **Plaza de España**,
also arcaded. They were built
in the late 18th century to link
the old town with the new
quarter then being built. South
of the old town is the Neo-
Gothic **Catedral de María
Inmaculada**, begun in 1907
and in use, though unfinished.

🏛 Museo de Arqueología

Calle Correría 116. 📞 *945 18
19 22.* 🕐 *Tue–Sun.*
The exhibits in this museum, in
a 16th-century half-timbered
house, include dolmens erected more than 4,000 years ago,
Roman sculptures found in
Álava, and medieval artifacts.

The quiet Plaza de España in the centre of Vitoria

The Gothic west door of Vitoria's Catedral de Santa María

🏛 Museo de Naipes

Palacio de Bendaña, C/ Cuchillería. 945 18 19 20. *Tue–Sun.*

The grandson of Heraclio Fournier, who founded a playing cards factory in Vitoria in 1868, displays his collection of more than 6,000 items in this museum. The oldest exhibits are late 14th-century Italian cards. Among the many sets of tarot cards are some designed by Salvador Dalí in the 1980s.

🏛 Museo de Armería

Paseo Fray Francisco 3. 945 18 19 25. *Tue–Sun.*

The weapons exhibited in this museum range in age from prehistoric axes to 20th-century pistols. There are also displays of medieval armour and an exhibit tracing the events of the 1813 Battle of Vitoria.

🏛 Museo Diocesano de Arte Sacro

Catedral de la Immaculada. 945 18 19 18. *10am–2pm, 4–6:30pm Tue–Fri, 10am–2pm Sat, 11am–2pm Sun & public hols.*

The design of this museum has been carefully blended into the style of the surrounding cathedral. Exhibits of religious art are displayed in sections which relate to their medium, such as stone, wood or silver.

Castillo de Mendoza **9**

Mendoza (Álava). 945 18 16 17. *Tue–Sun.*

In the centre of Mendoza village, 8 km (5 miles) west of Vitoria, stands this small, square, much restored fortress dating from the 13th century. There are marvellous views from the tops of the four towers. Once a ducal residence, the thick-walled castle now houses the **Museo Heráldica**. In it are displayed the coats of arms of noble Basque families and items relating to them.

ENVIRONS: On the A2622 Pobes–Tuesta road are the **Salinas de Añana**, a group of tiered saltpans that are fed by mineral springs. The nearby village of **Tuesta** boasts a Romanesque church with a decorated portal. Inside are capitals carved with historical scenes, and a medieval wood sculpture of St Sebastian.

Laguardia **10**

Álava. 1,500. Plaza San Juan, 941 60 08 45. *Tue.* *San Juan and San Pedro (24 Jun).*

This little wine town is the capital of La Rioja Alavesa, a part of southern Álava province where Rioja wines (*see pp74–5*) have been produced for centuries. It is a fertile, vine-clad plain, sheltered by high hills to the north. There are fine panoramic views from the road that climbs up to the Herrera pass. Laguardia is a medieval hill town, its encircling ramparts, towers and fortified gateways visible from afar. Along its steep, narrow cobbled streets there are many **bodegas** (wine cellars), offering wine tastings and tours throughout the year. It is usually necessary to make a booking in advance.

The Gothic **Iglesia de Santa María de los Reyes** has an austere façade with an unusual portal. A delicate statue of the Virgin and Child is displayed inside the church.

Virgin and child statue in Laguardia

Vineyards near Laguardia, capital of La Rioja Alavesa, a wine-producing region since the Middle Ages

Haro ⓫

La Rioja. 🏠 *9,000.* 🚉 🚌 ℹ️ *Plaza Monseñor Florentino Rodriguez, 941 30 33 66.* 🛒 *Tue & Sat.* 🎉 *Wine Battle (29 Jun), Virgen de la Vega (8 Sep).*

A GRACEFUL TOWN on the Río Ebro, Haro has a lively old quarter with wine taverns and mansions. It is crowned by the hilltop **Iglesia de Santo Tomás**, a Gothic church with a Plateresque *(see p21)* portal.

Haro is the centre for the vineyards and bodegas of the Rioja Alta wine region, which is higher and cooler than the Rioja Baja *(see pp74–5)*. The clay soil and the climate – Haro is sheltered by a sierra to the north – create the conditions in which the famous regional wines are produced. Many bodegas run tours of their cellars, including tastings. To join one, you usually need to book ahead at the bodega or the tourist office. There is sometimes a small charge.

The cafés in the main square offer local wines at low prices and a convivial atmosphere, especially in the evenings.

A wine-throwing orgy is the climax of the town's fiesta *(see p128)* held every June.

Rows of Rioja vines on the rolling hills near Haro

Tomb of St Dominic in the cathedral of Santo Domingo de la Calzada

Santo Domingo de la Calzada ⓬

La Rioja. 🏠 *5,800.* 🚌 ℹ️ *Calle Mayor 70, 941 34 12 30.* 🛒 *Sat.* 🎉 *Día del Patron (12 May), San Jerónimo Hermosilla (19 Sep).*

THIS TOWN on the Road to Santiago de Compostela *(see pp78–9)* is named after the 11th-century saint who built bridges and roads *(calzadas)* to help pilgrims. To tend sick travellers, St Dominic also built a hospital, which now serves as a parador *(see p542)*.

Miracles performed by the saint are recorded in carvings on his tomb in the town's part-Romanesque, part-Gothic **cathedral**, and in paintings on the wall of the choir. The most obvious and bizarre record is a sumptuously decorated cage set in a wall in which, for centuries, a live cock and hen have been kept. The cathedral has a carved walnut reredos at the high altar, the last work, in 1541, of the artist Damià Forment. The restored 14th-century **ramparts** of the town are also worth seeing.

THE COCK AND HEN OF ST DOMINIC

A live cock and hen are kept in the cathedral of Santo Domingo de la Calzada as a tribute to the saint's miraculous life-giving powers. Centuries ago, it is said, a German pilgrim refused the advances of a local girl, who denounced him as a thief. He was hanged as a consequence, but later his parents found him alive on the gallows. They rushed to a judge, who said, dismissively, "Nonsense, he's no more alive than this roast chicken on my plate". Whereupon, the chicken stood up on the plate and crowed.

The cock and hen in their decorated cage

San Millán de la Cogolla ⑬

La Rioja. ⚐ *300*. ℹ *Calle Mayor 50, 941 37 32 59*. 🎭 *Traslación de las Reliquias (26 Sep), San Millán (12 Nov)*.

THIS VILLAGE grew up around two monasteries. On a hillside above the village is the **Monasterio de San Millán de Suso**. It was built in the 10th century on the site of a community founded by St Emilian, a shepherd hermit, in 537. The church, hollowed out of pink sandstone, has Romanesque and Mozarabic features. It contains the carved alabaster tomb of St Emiliano and also the tomb of the 13th-century writer, Gonzalo de Berceo *(see p30)*, who was a monk here.

The **Monasterio de San Millán de Yuso** is below it, in the Cárdenas Valley. It was built between the 16th and 18th centuries on the site of an earlier monastery. The part-Renaissance church has Baroque golden doors and a rococo sacristy, where 17th-century paintings are hung.

In the treasury there is a collection of ivory plaques. They were once part of two 11th-century jewelled reliquaries, which were plundered by French troops in 1813.

Medieval manuscripts are also displayed in the treasury. Among them is a facsimile of one of the earliest known texts in Castilian Romance *(see p30)*. It is a commentary by a 10th-century Suso monk on a work by San Cesáreo de Arles, the *Glosas Emilianenses*.

The Monasterio de San Millán de Yuso in the Cárdenas valley

Cloister of the Monasterio de Santa María la Real, Nájera

Nájera ⑭

La Rioja. ⚐ *7,200*. 🚉 ℹ *Calle Constantino 1, 941 36 00 41*. 🚌 *Thu*. 🎭 *Fiestas de Nájera (24 Jun), Santa María la Real (16, 17 Sep)*.

THE OLD TOWN of Nájera, west of Logroño, was the capital of La Rioja and Navarra until 1076, when La Rioja was incorporated into Castile. The royal families of Navarra, León and Castile are buried in the **Monasterio de Santa María la Real**. It was founded in the 11th century beside a sandstone cliff where a statue of the Virgin was found in a cave. A 13th-century Madonna can be seen in the cave, beneath the carved choir stalls of the 15th-century church.

The 12th-century carved tomb of Blanca of Navarra, the wife of Sancho III, is the finest of many royal sarcophagi.

🏛 **Monasterio de Santa María la Real**
Nájera. 📞 *941 36 36 50*. ⏰ *Tue– Sun*. ⬤ *public hols*. 📷 ♿

Logroño ⑮

La Rioja. ⚐ *130,000*. 🚉 🚌 ℹ *Paseo del Espolón, Príncipe de Vergara 1, 941 29 12 60*. 🎭 *San Bernabé (11 Jun), Grape Harvest (21 Sep)*.

THE CAPITAL OF LA RIOJA is a tidy, modern city of wide boulevards and smart shops. It is the commercial centre of a fertile plain where quality vegetables are produced, in addition to Rioja wines.

In Logroño's pleasant old quarter of narrow streets abutting the Río Ebro is the Gothic **cathedral**, with twin towers. Above the south portal of the nearby **Iglesia de Santiago el Real** is a Baroque equestrian statue of St James in his role as Moorslayer *(see p51)*.

ENVIRONS: About 50 km (30 miles) south of Logroño, the N111 winds through the dramatic **Iregua Valley**, through tunnels and gorges and under twisted crags, before climbing into the Sierra de Cameros.

The ornate Baroque west door of Logroño cathedral

Enciso ⑯

La Rioja. ⚐ *220*. 🚌 *from Logroño*. ℹ *Plaza Mayor, 941 39 60 05*. 🎭 *San Roque (16 Aug)*.

NEAR THIS REMOTE hill village west of Calahorra is Spain's "Jurassic Park". Signposts point to the *huellas de dinosaurios* (dinosaur footprints). Embedded in rocks overhanging a stream are the prints of many giant, three-toed feet, up to 30 cm (1 ft) long. They were made around 150 million years ago, when dinosaurs moved between the marshes of the Ebro valley, at that time a sea, and these hills. Prints can also be seen at other locations in the area.

ENVIRONS: Arnedillo, 10 km (6 miles) to the north, is a spa with thermal baths once used by Fernando VI. In **Autol**, to the east, there are two unusual limestone peaks.

The intricately carved portal of Tudela cathedral

Tudela ⑰

Navarra. 🚶 25,600. 🚗 🚌
ℹ Plaza Vieja 1, 948 84 80 58.
🎪 Sat. 🎉 Santa Ana (26 Jul).

NAVARRA'S SECOND CITY is the great commercial centre of the vast agricultural lands of the Ebro valley in Navarra, the Ribera. Although much of Tudela consists of modern developments, its origins are ancient. Spanning the Ebro is a 13th-century bridge with 17 irregular arches. The old town has well-preserved Mudéjar and Jewish districts.

The delightful **Plaza de los Fueros** is old Tudela's main square. It is surrounded by houses with wrought-iron balconies. On their façades are paintings of bullfights, a reminder that the plaza was formerly used as a bullring.

The **cathedral**, begun in 1194, exemplifies the religious toleration under which Tudela was governed after the Reconquest. It is Early Gothic, with a carved portal depicting the Last Judgement. The Romanesque cloister encloses the ruins of a 9th-century mosque, and a Mudéjar chapel, which may have been a synagogue.

ENVIRONS: To the north is the **Bárdenas Reales**, an arid area of limestone cliffs and crags. About 20 km (12 miles) west of Tudela is the spa town of **Fitero**, with the 12th-century Monasterio de Santa María.

Monasterio de La Oliva ⑱

Carcastillo (Navarra). **📞** 948 72 50 06. 🚌 from Pamplona. 🕐 daily.

FRENCH CISTERCIAN MONKS built this small monastery on a remote plain in the 12th century. The church is simple, in typical Cistercian style, but adorned with rose windows.

One of the cloisters in the Monasterio de La Oliva

The serene cloister, dating from the 15th century, adjoins a 13th-century chapterhouse. The church also has a tower, erected in the 17th century.

Today, the monks survive by selling their honey, cheese and wine, and by accepting paying guests (see p532).

Ujué ⑲

Navarra. 🚶 280. **ℹ** Plaza Municipal, 948 73 81 85. 🎉 Virgen de Ujué (8 Sep).

ONE OF SPAIN'S least spoiled hill villages, Ujué commands a high spur at the end of a winding road. It has quaint façades, cobbled alleys and steep steps. The **Iglesia de Santa María** is in Gothic style with a Romanesque chancel and an exterior lookout gallery. Beside the church is a ruined fortress. From its terrace there are views of the Pyrenees.

On 25 April every year, pilgrims in black capes come here to visit the Virgin of Ujué, whose Romanesque image is displayed in the church.

Olite ⑳

Navarra. 🚶 3,000. 🚌
ℹ Calle Mayor 3, 948 74 17 03.
🎪 Wed. 🎉 Exaltación de la Santa Cruz (14–20 Sep).

THE HISTORIC TOWN of Olite was founded by the Romans and later chosen as a royal residence by the kings of Navarra. Part of the town's old walls can be seen. They

---

THE KINGDOM OF NAVARRA

Navarra emerged as an independent Christian kingdom in the 10th century, after Sancho I Garcés became king of Pamplona. Sancho III the Great expanded the kingdom, and at his death, in 1035, Navarra stretched all the way from Ribagorza in Aragón to Valladolid. Sancho VI the Wise, who reigned 1150–94, recognized the independent rights (fueros) of many towns. In 1234, Navarra passed by marriage to a line of French rulers. One, Carlos III the Noble, built Olite castle. His grandson, Carlos de Viana, wrote the Chronicle of the Kings of Navarra in 1455. In 1512 Navarra was annexed by Fernando II of Castile, as part of united Spain, but it kept its own laws and currency until the 1800s.

Prince Carlos de Viana, Carlos III's grandson

enclose a delightful jumble of steep, narrow streets and little squares, churches and the **Monasterio de las Clarisas**, begun in the 13th century. The houses along the Rúa Cerco de Fuera and the Rúa Mayor were built between the 16th and 18th centuries.

The castle, the **Palacio Real de Olite**, was built about 1406 by Carlos III, and has earned Olite its nickname "the Gothic town". It was heavily fortified, but was brilliantly decorated inside by Mudéjar artists with *azulejos* (ceramic tiles) and marquetry ceilings. The walkways were planted with vines and orange trees, and there was an aviary and a lions' den.

In the 19th century the castle was sacked by Carlists *(see pp58–9)* and the French. Since the 1920s, however, it has been restored to a semblance of its former glory. Part of it houses a parador *(see p541)*.

Today, the castle is a complex of courtyards, passages, steep stairs, large halls, royal chambers, battlements, towers and turrets. From the "windy tower" monarchs were able to watch tournaments.

Adjoining the castle is a 13th-century former royal chapel, the **Iglesia de Santa María la Real**, with a richly carved Gothic portal. Inside there is a 16th-century reredos.

Olite is in the Navarra wine region *(see pp74–5)* and the town has several bodegas.

♣ Palacio Real de Olite
Plaza de Carlos III. **[** 948 74 00 35. **○** daily. **[**

The battlements and towers of the Palacio Real de Olite

The five-arched, medieval pilgrims' bridge at Puente la Reina

Puente la Reina ㉑

Navarra. **[** 2,200. **[** Plaza de Mena 1, 948 34 08 45. **○** Sat. **[** Santiago (25 Jul).

FEW TOWNS along the Road to Santiago de Compostela *(see pp78–9)* evoke the past as vividly as Puente la Reina. The town takes its name from the graceful, humpbacked pedestrian bridge over the Río Arga. The bridge was built for pilgrims during the 11th century by royal command.

On Puente la Reina's narrow main street is the **Iglesia de Santiago**, which has a gilded statue by the west door showing the saint as a pilgrim. On the edge of town is the **Iglesia del Crucifijo**, another pilgrim church which was built in the 12th century by the Knights Templar. Contained within the church is a

Distinctive crucifix in Puente la Reina

Y-shaped wooden crucifix of a sorrowful Christ with arms upraised, which is said to have been a gift from a German pilgrim in the 14th century.

ENVIRONS: Isolated in the fields about 5 km (3 miles) to the east is the 12th-century **Iglesia de Santa María de Eunate**. This octagonal Romanesque church may once have been a cemetery church for pilgrims, as human bones have been unearthed here. Pilgrims would shelter beneath the church's external arcade. West of Puenta la Reina is the showpiece hill village of **Cirauqui**. It is also charming, if rather over-restored. Chic little balconied houses line tortuously twisting alleys linked by steps. The Iglesia de San Román, built in the 13th century on top of the hill, has a sculpted west door.

BASQUE COUNTRY, NAVARRA AND LA RIOJA'S FIESTAS

Los Sanfermines *(6–14 Jul)*, Pamplona (Navarra). In the famous *encierro* (bull running) six bulls are released at 8am each morning to run from their corral through the narrow, cobbled streets of the old town. On the last night of this week-long, non-stop party, crowds with candles sing Basque songs in the main square. The event gained worldwide fame after Ernest Hemingway described it in his novel *The Sun Also Rises.*

Bulls scattering the runners in Pamplona

Wine Battle *(29 Jun)*, Haro (La Rioja). People dressed in white clothes squirt each other with wine from leather drinking bottles in the capital of the Rioja Alta wine region.
Danza de los Zancos *(22 Jul and last Sat of Sep)*, Anguiano (La Rioja). Dancers on stilts, wearing ornate waistcoats and yellow skirts, hurtle down the stepped alley from the church to the main square.
La Virgen Blanca *(4 Aug)*, Vitoria (Álava). A dummy holding an umbrella (the *celedón*) is lowered from San Miguel church to a house below – from which a man in similar dress emerges. The mayor fires a rocket and the crowds in the square light cigars.

Pilgrims drinking from the wine tap near the monastery at Irache

Estella ②

Navarra. 🏛 *13,000.* 🚌 ℹ *Calle de San Nicolás 3, 948 55 63 01.* 🚌 *Thu.* 🎎 *San Andrés (early Aug).*

IN THE MIDDLE AGES Estella (Lizarra) was the centre of the royal court of Navarra and a major stopping point on the pilgrims' Road to Santiago de Compostela *(see pp78–9)*. The town was a stronghold of the Carlists *(see p59)* in the 19th century. A memorial rally is held here on the first Sunday of May every year.

The most important monuments in Estella are sited on the edge of town, across the bridge over the Río Ega. Steps climb steeply from the arcaded Plaza de San Martín to the remarkable 12th-century **Iglesia de San Pedro de la Rúa**, built on top of a cliff. It features a a Mudéjar-influenced, sculpted doorway. The carved capitals are all that now remain of the Romanesque cloister, which was destroyed when a castle overlooking the church was blown up in 1592. The **Palacio de los Reyes de Navarra**, on the other side of the Plaza de San Martín, is a rare example of civil Romanesque architecture. It also houses a gallery of Navarrese art.

In the town centre, on the arcaded Plaza de los Fueros, the **Iglesia de San Juan Bautista** has a Romanesque porch. The north portal of the **Iglesia de San Miguel** has Romanesque carvings of St Michael slaying a dragon.

ENVIRONS: The **Monasterio de Nuestra Señora de Irache**, 3 km (2 miles) southwest of Estella, was built by Cistercian monks, who sheltered pilgrims on their way to Santiago. The church is mainly Transitional Gothic in style, but it has Romanesque apses and a cloister in Plateresque style. It is capped by a remarkable dome.

A bodega next to the monastery provides pilgrims with wine from a tap in a wall.

A small road branches off the NA120 north of Estella and winds through a wooded gorge to reach the **Monasterio de Iranzu**, built in the 12th century. The graceful austerity of its church and cloisters are typically Cistercian features.

The Lizarraga Pass, further up the NA120, offers views of attractive beech woods.

Pamplona ②

Navarra. 🏛 *183,000.* ✈ 🚌 🚍 ℹ *C/ Eslava 1, 948 20 65 40.* 🎎 *Sanfermines (6–14 Jul).* 🌐 *www.pamplona.net*

THE OLD FORTRESS city of Pamplona (Iruña) is said to have been founded by the Roman general, Pompey. In the 9th century it became the capital of Navarra. This fairly busy city explodes into even more life in July during the fiesta of Los Sanfermines, with its daredevil bull running.

From the old **city walls** *(murallas)* you can get a good overview of Pamplona. The nearby **cathedral**, which is

Sumptuous interior of the Palacio de Navarra, Pamplona

Stone tracery in the elegant cloister of Pamplona cathedral

built in ochre-coloured stone, looks down on a loop in the Río Arga. It was built on the foundations of its 12th-century predecessor, and is mainly Gothic in style, with twin towers and an 18th-century façade. Inside there are lovely choir stalls and the alabaster tomb of Carlos III and Queen Leonor.

The southern entrance to the cloister is the beautifully carved, medieval Puerta de la Preciosa. The cathedral priests would gather here to sing an antiphon (hymn) to La Preciosa (Precious Virgin) before the night service.

The Museo Diocesano in the cathedral's 14th-century kitchen and refectory (closed for restoration) displays Gothic altarpieces, polychrome wood statues from all over Navarra, and a French 13th-century reliquary of the Holy Sepulchre.

West of the cathedral is the old town, the former Jewish quarter, cut through with many alleys. The Baroque **Palacio de Navarra** is near the Plaza del Castillo. Its opulent throne room of the kings of Navarra contains a portrait of King Fernando VII by Goya. Outside, a statue of 1903 shows a symbolic queen upholding the *fueros* (historic laws) of Navarra (*see p126*). North of the palace are the medieval **Iglesia de San Saturnino**, built on the site where St Saturninus is said to have baptized some 40,000 pagan townspeople, and the Baroque **town hall** *(ayuntamiento).*

Beneath the old town wall, in a 16th-century hospital with a Plateresque doorway, is the **Museo de Navarra**. This is a museum of regional archaeology, history and art. Exhibits include Roman mosaics and an 11th-century, Islam-inspired ivory casket. There are murals painted during the 14th–16th centuries, a portrait by Goya, and a collection of paintings by Basque artists.

To the southeast is the city's massive 16th-century **citadel**, erected in Felipe II's reign. It is designed with five bastions in a star shape. Beyond it are the spacious boulevards of the new town, and also the university's green campus.

🏛 **Museo de Navarra**
Calle Santo Domingo. 🄲 948 42 64 92. 🅾 Tue–Sun. 💷 &

🏛 **Palacio de Navarra**
Avenida Carlos III 2. 🄲 948 42 71 27. 🅾 by appointment. &

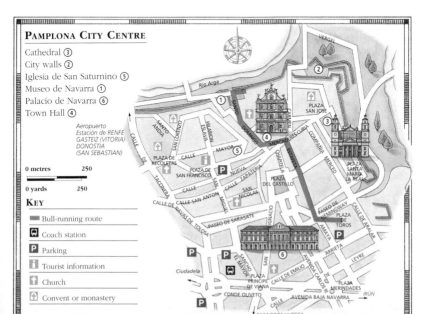

Sculpture in Pamplona depicting the encierro

PAMPLONA CITY CENTRE

Cathedral ③
City walls ②
Iglesia de San Saturnino ⑤
Museo de Navarra ①
Palacio de Navarra ⑥
Town Hall ④

0 metres   250
0 yards   250

KEY

▬ Bull-running route

🚌 Coach station

🅿 Parking

ℹ Tourist information

✝ Church

✝ Convent or monastery

Basque houses in the picturesque town of Etxalar, Valle de Bidasoa

Las Cinco Villas de la Montaña ❷

Navarra. 🚌 *Pamplona, San Sebastián.* 🏠 *Oieregi, 948 59 23 86.* 🅆 www.cfnavarra.es

FIVE ATTRACTIVE Basque towns lie in or near this valley, the most northerly being **Bera** (Vera). The houses in **Lesaka**

have wooden balconies under deep eaves. The road south passes hills dotted with white farmsteads to reach **Igantzi**, (Yanci), with its red-and-white houses. **Arantza** is the most remote town. Since the 12th century, pigeons have been caught in huge nets strung across a pass above **Etxalar** (Echalar). From the summit of La Rhune, on the French border above the valley, there is a great view of the Pyrenees.

Elizondo ❷

Navarra. 🏘 *3,000.* 🚌 🏠 *Baztandaren Ibiltzarra, 948 59 23 86.* 🛒 *Thu. Santiago (25 Jul), Feria (late Oct).*

THIS IS THE BIGGEST of a string of typical Basque villages in the very beautiful valley of Baztán. By the river are noble houses bearing coats of arms.
  Arizkun, further up the valley, has old fortified houses and a 17th-century convent. The **Cueva de Brujas**, near Zugarramurdi, was once a meeting place for witches.

Canopy over the Virgin and Child in the Colegiata Real

Roncesvalles ❷

Navarra. 🏘 *20.* 🏠 *Roncesvalles, 948 76 03 01.* 🎉 *Día de la Virgen de Roncesvalles (8 Sep).*

RONCESVALLES (ORREAGA), on the Spanish side of a pass through the Pyrenees, is a major halt on the Road to Santiago *(see pp78–9)*. Before it became associated with the pilgrim's way, Roncesvalles was the site of a major battle in 778, in which the Basques of Navarra slaughtered the rearguard of Charlemagne's army as it marched homeward. This event is described in the 12th-century French epic poem, *The Song of Roland*.
  The 13th-century **Colegiata Real**, which has served travellers down the centuries, has a silver-plated Virgin and Child below a high canopy. In the graceful chapterhouse, off the cloister, is the white tomb of Sancho VII the Strong (1154–1234), looked down upon by a stained-glass window of his great victory, the Battle of Las Navas de Tolosa *(see pp50–51)*. Exhibits in the church museum include "Charlemagne's chessboard", an enamelled reliquary which is so-called because of its chequered design.

Valle de Roncal ❷

Navarra. 🚌 *from Pamplona.* 🏠 *Roncal, 948 47 52 56.*

RUNNING perpendicular to the Pyrenees, this valley is still largely reliant on sheep, and the village of **Roncal** is known for its cheeses. Because of the relative isolation of the valley, the inhabitants have preserved their own identity and local costumes are worn

The forested countryside around Roncesvalles

during fiestas. The ski resort of **Isaba**, further up the valley, has a museum of local life and history. A spectacular road winds from Isaba to the tree-lined village of Ochagavia in the parallel **Valle de Salazar**. To the north, the pines and beeches of the **Bosque de Irati**, one of Europe's largest woodlands, spread over the Pyrenees into France, below the snowy summit of Monte Ori at 2,017 m (6,617 ft).

Colourful balconies of houses in the village of Roncal

Monasterio de Leyre ㉘

Yesa (Navarra). **(** *948 88 41 50.* 🚌 *Yesa.* ⬜ *daily.* 📷

THE MONASTERY of San Salvador de Leyre is situated high above a reservoir, alone amid grand scenery, backed by limestone cliffs. The abbey has been here since the 11th

century when it was a great spiritual centre. Sancho III and his successors made it the royal pantheon of Navarra.

The monastery began to decline in the 12th century. It was abandoned from the 19th century until 1954, when it was restored by Benedictines. They turned part of it into a modestly priced hotel *(see p542)*. To see the monastery you must join one of the tours run by the monks every morning and afternoon.

The big church, unadorned in the Cistercian manner, has three lofty apses. On its west portal are weatherworn carvings of strange beasts, as well as biblical figures. The 11th-century crypt has unusually short columns with chunky capitals. The monks' Gregorian chant *(see p358)* during services is wonderful to hear.

Castillo de Javier ㉙

Javier (Navarra). **(** *948 88 40 00.* 🚌 *from Pamplona.* ⬜ *daily.*

ST FRANCIS XAVIER, the patron saint of Navarra, a missionary and a co-founder of the Jesuit order *(see p120)*, was born in this romantic-looking 13th-century castle in 1506. It has since been completely restored and is now used by the Jesuits as a college. Visitors can see the saint's bedroom and a museum in the keep devoted to his life. In the oratory is a 13th-century polychrome Christ and a macabre 15th-century mural of grinning skeletons entitled *The Dance of Death*.

Crucifix in the oratory of the Castillo de Javier

Sangüesa ㉚

Navarra. 🏘 *4,500.* 🚌 **ℹ** *Calle Mayor 2, 948 87 14 11.* 🗓 *Fri.* 📅 *San Sebastián (11 Sep).*

SINCE MEDIEVAL TIMES this small town beside a bridge over the Río Aragón has been a stop on the Aragonese pilgrimage route to Santiago *(see pp78–9)*.

The richly sculpted south portal of the **Iglesia de Santa María la Real** is a 13th-century treasure of Romanesque art *(see p20)*. It is crammed with figures and details. Above the door, God is shown rejecting sinners and welcoming the chosen. This scene is surrounded by angels, musicians, warriors, artisans, geometric motifs and mythical animals.

The Romanesque **Iglesia de Santiago** and the 14th-century Gothic **Iglesia de San Francisco** are also worth seeing. On the main street is the **town hall** *(ayuntamiento),* formerly the palace of the Prince of Viana and a residence of the kings of Navarra. The interior is not open to visitors, but the Gothic and Baroque façades can be seen.

ENVIRONS: To the north of Sangüesa there are two deep, narrow gorges. The most impressive of them is the **Hoz de Arbayún**, whose limestone cliffs are inhabited by colonies of vultures. It is best seen from the NA178 north of Domeño. The **Hoz de Lumbier** can be seen from a point on the N240.

The roughly carved columns in the crypt of the Monasterio de Leyre

BARCELONA

Introducing Barcelona

BARCELONA, one of the Mediterranean's busiest ports, is more than the capital of Catalonia. In culture, commerce and sport it not only rivals Madrid, but also considers itself on a par with the greatest European cities. The success of the 1992 Olympic Games, staged in the Parc de Montjuïc, confirmed this to the world. Although there are plenty of historical monuments in the Old Town (Ciutat Vella), Barcelona is best known for the scores of buildings in the Eixample left by the artistic explosion of Modernisme *(see pp136–7)* in the decades around 1900. Always open to outside influences because of its location on the coast, not too far from the French border, Barcelona continues to sizzle with creativity: its bars and the public parks speak more of bold contemporary design than of tradition.

Casa Milà *(see p161) is the most avant-garde of all the works of Antoni Gaudí (see p160). Barcelona has more Art Nouveau buildings than any other city in the world.*

Palau Nacional *(see p168), on the hill of Montjuïc, dominates the monumental halls and fountain-filled avenue built for the 1929 International Exhibition. It now houses the Museu Nacional d'Art de Catalunya, an exceptional collection of medieval art, rich in Romanesque frescoes.*

MONTJUIC
(see pp164–9)

Montjuïc Castle *(see p169) is a massive fortification dating from the 17th century. Sited on the crest of the hill of Montjuïc, it offers panoramic views of the city and port, and forms a sharp contrast to the ultra-modern sports halls built nearby for the 1992 Olympic Games.*

Christopher Columbus *surveys the waterfront from the top of a 60-m (200-ft) column (see p152) in the heart of the Port Vell (Old Port). From the top, visitors can look out over the new promenades and quays that have revitalized the area.*

0 kilometres		1

0 miles		0.5

◁ **The Ramblas and the Old Town stretching out behind Barcelona's monument to Columbus**

The Sagrada Família
(see pp162–3), *Gaudí's unfinished masterpiece, begun in 1882, rises above the streets of the Eixample. Its polychrome ceramic mosaics and sculptural forms inspired by nature are typical of his work.*

EIXAMPLE
(see pp154–63)

Barcelona cathedral (see pp144–5) *is a magnificent 14th-century building in the heart of the Barri Gòtic (Gothic Quarter). It has 28 side chapels which encircle the nave and contain some splendid Baroque altarpieces. The keeping of white geese in the cloisters is a centuries-old tradition.*

OLD TOWN
(see pp138–53)

Parc de la Ciutadella (see p150), *between the Old Town and the Vila Olímpica, has something for everyone. The gardens full of statuary offer relaxation, the boating lake and the zoo are fun, while the three museums within its gates cover art, geology and zoology.*

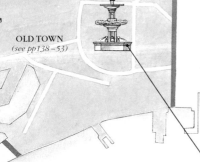

Las Ramblas (see pp146–7) *is the most famous street in Spain, alive at all hours of the day and night. A stroll down its length to the seafront, taking in its palatial buildings, shops, cafés and street vendors, makes a perfect introduction to Barcelona life.*

Gaudí and Modernisme

**Chimney,
Casa Vicens**

Towards the end of the 19th century a new style of art and architecture, Modernisme, a variant of Art Nouveau, was born in Barcelona. It became a means of expression for Catalan nationalism and counted Josep Puig i Cadafalch, Lluís Domènech i Montaner and, above all, Antoni Gaudí i Cornet *(see p160)* among its major exponents. Barcelona's Eixample district *(see pp154–63)* is full of the highly original buildings that they created for their wealthy clients.

All aspects of decoration in a Modernista building, even interior design, were planned by the architect. This door and its tiled surround are in Gaudí's 1906 Casa Batlló *(see p160)*.

A dramatic cupola covers the central salon, which rises through three floors. It is pierced by small round holes, inspired by Islamic architecture, giving the illusion of stars.

Upper galleries are richly decorated with carved wood and cofferwork.

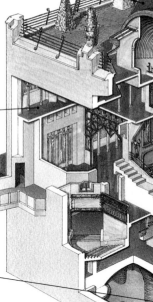

The spiral carriage ramp is an early sign of Gaudí's predilection for curved lines. He would later exploit this to the full in the wavy façade of his masterpiece, the Casa Milà (see p161).

THE EVOLUTION OF MODERNISME

Detail of Sagrada Família

1859 Civil engineer Ildefons Cerdà i Sunyer submits proposals for expansion of Barcelona

1878 Gaudí graduates as an architect

1883 Gaudí takes over design of Neo-Gothic Sagrada Família *(see pp162–3)*

1888 Barcelona Universal Exhibition gives impetus to Modernisme

1900 Josep Puig i Cadafalch builds Casa Amatller *(see p160)*

1903 Lluís Domènech i Montaner builds Hospital de la Santa Creu i de Sant Pau *(see p161)*

Hospital detail

1905 Domènech i Montaner builds Casa Lleó Morera *(see p160)*. Puig i Cadafalch builds Casa Terrades *(see p161)*

1910 Casa Milà completed

1926 Gaudí dies

1850	1865	1880	1895	1910	1925

Bizarrely decorated chimneys became one of the trademarks of Gaudí's later work. They reach a fantastic extreme on the gleaming, hump-backed roof of the Casa Batlló.

Elaborate wrought iron lamps light the grand hall.

Ceramic tiles decorate the chimneys.

GAUDÍ'S MATERIALS

Gaudí designed, or collaborated on designs, for almost every known media. He combined bare, undecorated materials – wood, rough-hewn stone, rubble and brickwork – with meticulous craftwork in wrought iron and stained glass. Mosaics of ceramic tiles were used to cover his fluid, uneven forms.

Stained-glass window in the Sagrada Família

Mosaic of ceramic tiles, Parc Güell *(see p174)*

Detail of iron gate, Casa Vicens *(see p160)*

Ceramic tiles on El Capricho *(see p107)*

Parabolic arches, used extensively by Gaudí, beginning in the Palau Güell, show his interest in Gothic architecture (see p20). These arches form a corridor in his 1890 Col·legio Teresiano, a convent school in the west of Barcelona.

Escutcheon alludes to the Catalan coat of arms.

PALAU GÜELL *(1889)*

Gaudí's first major building in the centre of the city *(see p147)* established his international reputation for outstandingly original architecture. Built for his life-long patron, the industrialist Eusebi Güell, the mansion stands on a small plot of land in a narrow street, making the façade difficult to view. Inside, Gaudí creates a sense of space by using carved screens, galleries and recesses. His unique furniture is also on display.

Organic forms inspired the wrought iron around the gates to the palace. Gaudí's later work teems with wildlife, such as this dragon, covered with brightly coloured tiles, which guards the steps in the Parc Güell.

Old Town

THE OLD TOWN, traversed by Barcelona's most famous avenue, the Ramblas, is one of the most extensive and harmonious medieval city centres in Europe. The Barri Gòtic (Gothic Quarter) contains the cathedral and ancient royal palace. Adjoining it is La Ribera, full of 14th-century mansions, one of which is occupied by the Museu Picasso. This area is bounded by the beautiful Parc de la Ciutadella, which contains the Museu d'Art Modern and the zoo. The revitalized seafront has several kilometres of reclaimed beaches, stretching from the modern Olympic Village to the Old Port, where there are historic shipyards, a fashionable marina and a promenade.

SIGHTS AT A GLANCE

Museums and Galleries
Museu d'Art Modern **20**
Museu Frederic Marès **2**
Museu de Geologia **18**
Museu d'Història de la Ciutat **4**
Museu Marítim and Drassanes **27**
Museu Picasso **13**
Museu de Zoologia **17**

Streets and Districts
Barceloneta **23**
Carrer Montcada **12**
Las Ramblas **9**
El Raval **8**

Harbour Sights
Golondrinas **26**
Port Vell **24**

Churches
Basílica de Santa Maria del Mar **11**
Cathedral (pp144–5) **7**

Historic Buildings
Casa de l'Ardiaca **1**
Casa de la Ciutat **5**
La Llotja **10**
Palau de la Generalitat **6**
Palau Reial Major **3**
Palau de la Música Catalana **14**

Modern Architecture
Vila Olímpica **22**

Monuments
Arc del Triomf **15**
Homenatge a Picasso **19**
Monument a Colom **25**

Parks and Gardens
Parc de la Ciutadella **16**
Parc Zoològic **21**

GETTING THERE
The area is well served by metro lines 1, 3 and 4; Jaume I station is in the heart of the Barri Gòtic. Many buses pass the Plaça de Catalunya, the centre of the modern city.

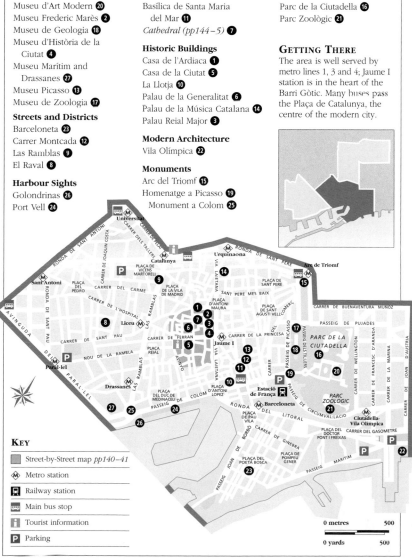

KEY

- Street-by-Street map *pp140–41*
- Ⓜ Metro station
- 🚆 Railway station
- 🚌 Main bus stop
- ℹ Tourist information
- 🅿 Parking

◁ **Stunning floral mosaic pillars in the Palau de la Música Catalana**

Street-by-Street: Barri Gòtic

Tᴴᴇ ʙᴀʀʀɪ ɢᴏᴛɪᴄ (Gothic Quarter) is the true heart of Barcelona. The oldest part of the city, it was the site chosen by the Romans in the reign of Augustus (27 BC–AD 14) on which to found a new *colonia* (town), and has been the location of the city's administrative buildings ever since. The Roman forum was on the Plaça de Sant Jaume, where now stand the medieval Palau de la Generalitat, Catalonia's parliament, and the Casa de la Ciutat, Barcelona's town hall. Close by are the Gothic cathedral and royal palace, where Columbus was received by Fernando and Isabel on his return from his voyage to the New World in 1492 *(see p53)*.

Wax candle, Cereria Subirà

Casa de l'Ardiaca
Built on the Roman city wall, the Gothic-Renaissance archdeacon's residence now houses Barcelona's historical archives ❶

To Plaça de Catalunya

S A N T   S E V E R

SANT DOMÈNEC DEL CALL

CARRER DEL CALL

SANT HONORAT

CARRER DEL BISBE

PIET

★ **Cathedral**
The façade and spire are 19th-century additions to the original Gothic building. Among the artistic treasures inside are medieval Catalan paintings ❼

Palau de la Generalitat
The seat of Catalonia's governor has superb Gothic features, which include the chapel and a stone staircase rising to an open-air, arcaded gallery ❻

PLAÇA DE SANT JAUME

CARRER DE FERRAN

To Las Ramblas

CARRER DE LA CIUTAT

Casa de la Ciutat
Barcelona's town hall was built in the 14th and 15th centuries. The façade is a Neo-Classical addition. In the entrance hall stands Three Gypsy Boys *by Joan Rebull (1899–1981), a 1976 copy of a sculpture he originally created in 1946* ❺

Kᴇʏ

– – – – Suggested route

Museu Frederic Marès
This medieval doorway is from an extensive display of Spanish sculpture – the mainstay of this museum's extraordinarily eclectic and high-quality collections **2**

LOCATOR MAP
See Street Finder map 5

EIXAMPLE

OLD TOWN

MONTJUIC

Roman city wall

TAPINERA

CARRER DELS COMTES DE BARCELONA

Saló del Tinell

★ Palau Reial Major
The 14th-century Capella Reial de Santa Àgata, with a 1466 altarpiece, is one of the best sur-viving sections of the palace **3**

Capella Reial de Santa Àgata

Plaça del Rei

Palau del Lloctinent

Cereria Subirà candle shop

VIA LAIETANA

CARRER DE JAUME I

Jaume I Metro

Museu d'Història de la Ciutat
Housed in a 14th-century mansion, which was moved from the Carrer dels Mercaders in 1931, the museum focuses on Barcelona's development in the 13th and 14th centuries, when commerce expanded dramatically **4**

CARRER DAGUERIA

SOTS-TINENT NAVARRA

The Centre Excursionista de Catalunya, housed in a medieval mansion, displays Roman columns from the Temple of Augustus, whose site is marked by a millstone in the street outside.

STAR SIGHTS
★ **Cathedral**
★ **Palau Rcial Major**

0 metres 100

0 yards 100

Decorated marble letterbox, Casa de l'Ardiaca

Casa de l'Ardiaca ❶

Carrer de Santa Llúcia 1. **Map** 5 B2.
☎ 93 318 11 95. Ⓜ Jaume I.
◷ 9am–9pm Mon–Fri, 9am–1pm
Sat. ● public hols.
🖳 www.bcn.es/arxiu/arxiuhistoric

S TANDING BESIDE what was
originally the Bishop's
Gate in the Roman wall is
the Archdeacon's House.
It was built in the 12th
century, but its present
appearance dates from
around 1500 when it was
remodelled and a colon-
nade added. In 1870 this
was extended to form
the Flamboyant Gothic
(see p20) patio around a
fountain. The Modernista
architect Domènech i Montaner
(1850–1923) added the fanciful
marble letterbox, carved with
three swallows and a tortoise,
beside the Renaissance portal.
Upstairs is the Arxiu Històric
de la Ciutat (City Archives).

Museu Frederic Marès ❷

Plaça de Sant Iu 5. **Map** 5 B2. ☎ 933
10 58 00. Ⓜ Jaume I. ◷ 10am–5pm
Tue & Thu, 10am–7pm Wed, Fri–Sat,
10am–3pm Sun. ● public hols.
🖼 (free first Sun of each month, &
Wed pm). ♿ 🄵 by appt.

T HE SCULPTOR Frederic Marès
i Deulovol (1893–1991) was
also a traveller and collector,
and this extraordinary museum
is a monument to his eclectic
taste. The building is part of
the Royal Palace complex and
was occupied by 13th-century
bishops, 14th-century counts
of Barcelona, 15th-century

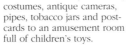

Virgin, Museu Frederic Marès

judges, and 18th-century nuns,
who lived here until they
were expelled in 1936. Marès,
who had a small apart-
ment in the building,
opened his museum in
1948. It is one of the
most fascinating in
the city and has an
outstanding collec-
tion of Roman-
esque and Gothic
religious art. In the
crypt there is an
assemblage of
stone sculpture and
two Romanesque
portals. Exhibits
on the three
floors above
range through
clocks, crucifixes,
costumes, antique cameras,
pipes, tobacco jars and post-
cards to an amusement room
full of children's toys.

Palau Reial Major ❸

Plaça del Rei. **Map** 5 B2. ☎ 93 315
11 11. Ⓜ Jaume I. ◷ Jun–Sep:
10am–8pm Tue–Sat, 10am–2pm Sun;
Oct–May: 4–8pm Tue–Sat, 10am–2pm
Sun. ● 1 Jan, 25 & 26 Dec. 🖼

T HE ROYAL PALACE was the
residence of the count-
kings of Barcelona from its
foundation in the 13th century.
The complex includes the 14th-
century Gothic Saló del Tinell,
a massive room with arches
spanning 17 m (56 ft). This is
where Isabel and Fernando
(see p66) received Columbus
after his triumphal return
from America. It is also where
the Inquisition (see p264) sat,
believing the walls would
move if lies were told.
On the right, built into the
Roman city wall, is the royal
chapel, the Capella de Santa

**Gothic nave of the Capella de
Santa Àgata, Palau Reial**

BARCELONA'S EARLY JEWISH COMMUNITY

Hebrew tablet

From the 11th to the 13th centuries Jews
dominated Barcelona's commerce and
culture, providing doctors and founding
the first seat of learning. But in 1243, 354
years after they were first documented in
the city, violent anti-Semitism led to the
Jews being consigned to a ghetto, El Call.
Ostensibly to provide protection, the
ghetto had only one entrance, which led
into the Plaça de Sant Jaume. Jews were
heavily taxed by the monarch, who
viewed them as "royal serfs"; but in return they also received
privileges, as they handled most of Catalonia's lucrative trade
with North Africa. However, official and popular persecution
finally led to the disappearance of the ghetto in 1401, 91
years before Judaism was fully outlawed in Spain (see p53).
Originally there were three synagogues, the main one being
in Carrer Sant Domènec del Call, but only the foundations
are left. A 14th-century Hebrew tablet is embedded in the wall
at No. 1 Carrer de Marlet, which reads: "Holy Foundation
of Rabbi Samuel Hassardi, for whom life never ends".

Àgata, with a painted wood ceiling and an altarpiece (1466) by Jaume Huguet. Its bell tower is part of a watchtower on the Roman wall. Stairs to the right of the altar lead to the 16th-century tower of Martí the Humane (who reigned from 1396–1410), the last ruler of the 500-year dynasty of the count-kings of Barcelona. From the top of the tower there are fine views over the royal complex.

Museu d'Història de la Ciutat **❹**

Plaça del Rei. **Map** 5 B2. **【** 93 315 11 11. **☁** Jaume I. **◐** 10am–2pm, 4–8pm Tue–Sat, 10am–2pm Sun & holy days. **●** 1 Jan, 25 & 26 Dec. **⌘**

THE CITY MUSEUM occupies the Casa Clariana-Padellàs, a Gothic building brought here stone by stone in 1931 from its original site in Carrer dels Mercaders. During the site's excavation, the remains of Roman water and drainage systems, baths, mosaic floors and a road were found. These can be seen in the basement, which extends beneath the Plaça de Rei. A stretch of the Roman city wall is accessible from the upper floors, devoted to Barcelona's post-Roman development.

Casa de la Ciutat **❺**

Plaça de Sant Jaume 1. **Map** 5 A2. **【** 934 02 70 00. **☁** Jaume I, Liceu. **◐** 10am–2pm Sun & public hols; 10am–8pm 12 Feb (St Eulàlia's Day) & 23 Apr (St Jordi's Day). **⌘ ♿**

THE MAGNIFICENT 14th-century city hall *(ajuntament)* faces the Palau de la Generalitat. Flanking the entrance of the Casa de la Ciutat are statues of Jaime (Jaume) I, who granted the city rights to elect councillors in 1249, and Joan Fiveller, who levied taxes on court members in the 1500s.

Inside is the huge council chamber, the 14th-century Saló de Cent, built for the city's 100 councillors. The Saló de les Cròniques, on the first floor, was commissioned for the 1929 International Exhibition and decorated by Josep-Marià Sert with murals of momentous events in Catalan history.

Palau de la Generalitat **❻**

Plaça de Sant Jaume 4. **Map** 5 A2. **【** 93 402 46 00. **☁** Jaume I. **◐** 23 Apr (St Jordi's Day), 2nd & 4th Sun of month; every Sat & Sun (write in advance for permission). **♿ ⌘**

SINCE 1403, the Generalitat has been the seat of the Catalonian Governor. Above

The Italianate façade of the Palau de la Generalitat

the entrance, in its Renaissance façade, is a statue of Sant Jordi (St George) – the patron saint of Catalonia – and the Dragon. The late Catalan-Gothic courtyard is by Marc Safont (1416).

Among the fine interiors are the Gothic chapel of Sant Jordi, also by Safont, and Pere Blai's Italianate Saló de Sant Jordi. At the back, one floor above street level, lies the *Pati dels Tarongers*, the Orange Tree Patio, by Pau Mateu, which has a bell tower built by Pere Ferrer in 1568.

The Catalan president has offices here as well as in the Casa dels Canonges. The two buildings are connected by a bridge across Carrer del Bisbe, built in 1928 and modelled on the famous Bridge of Sighs in Venice.

The magnificent council chamber, the Saló de Cent, in Casa de la Ciutat

Barcelona Cathedral ❼

The twin octagonal bell towers date from 1386–93. The bells were installed in this tower in 1545.

T HIS COMPACT GOTHIC CATHEDRAL, with a Romanesque chapel (Capella de Santa Llúcia) and beautiful cloister, was begun in 1298 under Jaime (Jaume) II, on the foundations of a site dating back to Visigothic times. It was not finished until the late 19th century, when the main façade was completed. A white marble choir screen, sculpted in the 16th century, depicts the martyrdom of St Eulàlia, the city's patron. Next to the font, a plaque records the baptism of six Caribbean Indians, whom Columbus brought back from the Americas in 1493.

Statue of St Eulalia

The main façade was not completed until 1889, and the central spire until 1913. It was based on the original 1408 plans of the French architect Charles Galters.

Nave Interior
The Catalan-style Gothic interior has a single wide nave with 28 side chapels. These are set between the columns supporting the vaulted ceiling, which rises to 26 m (85 ft).

★ **Choir Stalls**
The top tier of the beautifully carved 15th-century stalls contains the coats of arms (1518) of the 12 knights of the Order of Toisón del Oro.

Capella del Santíssim Sagrament
This small chapel houses the 16th-century Christ of Lepanto crucifix.

Capella de Sant Benet
This chapel, dedicated to the founder of the Benedictine Order and patron saint of Europe, houses a magnificent altarpiece showing The Transfiguration *by Bernat Martorell (1452).*

VISITORS' CHECKLIST

Plaça de la Seu. **Map** 5 A2.
📞 93 315 15 54. Ⓜ *Jaume I.*
🚌 17, 19, 45. 🕐 *8am–1:30pm, 4–7:30pm Mon–Fri, until 7pm Sat & Sun.* 🈺 ♿ **Sacristy Museum** 🕐 *11am–1pm daily.* 🈺 **Choir** 🕐 *9am–1pm, 4–7pm Mon–Fri, 9am–1pm Sat.* 🈺 ✝ *9am, 10am, 11am, noon, 7pm daily.*

★ Crypt
In the crypt, beneath the main altar, is the alabaster sarcophagus (1339) of St Eulàlia, martyred for her beliefs by the Romans during the 4th century AD.

★ Cloisters
The fountain, set in a corner of the Gothic cloisters and decorated with a statue of St George, provided fresh water.

Porta de Santa Eulàlia, entrance to Cloisters

The Sacristy Museum has a small treasury. Pieces include an 11th-century font, tapestries and liturgical artifacts.

Capella de Santa Llúcia

STAR FEATURES

★ **Choir Stalls**

★ **Crypt**

★ **Cloisters**

TIMELINE

400	700	1000	1300	1600	1900

559 Basilica dedicated to St Eulàlia and Holy Cross

877 St Eulàlia's remains brought here from Santa Maria del Mar

1339 St Eulàlia's relics transferred to alabaster sarcophagus

1046–58 Romanesque cathedral built under Ramon Berenguer I

1913 Central spire completed

1889 Main façade completed, based on plans dating from 1408 by architect Charles Galters

4th century Original Roman (paleo-Christian) basilica built

985 Building destroyed by the Moors

1257–68 Romanesque Capella de Santa Llúcia built

1298 Gothic cathedral begun under Jaime II

1493 Indians brought back from the Americas are baptized

Plaque of the Indians' baptism

The former dissecting room of the Antic Hospital de la Santa Creu

El Raval ❽

Map 2 E3. Ⓜ *Catalunya, Universitat.* **Museu d'Art Contemporani** Pl dels Angels 1. 📞 *93 412 08 10.* ⏰ *11am–7:30pm Mon–Fri, 10am– 8pm Sat, 10am–3pm Sun.* ⚫ *25 Dec, 1 Jan.* 📷 ♿ Ⓦ *www.macba.es*

THE DISTRICT of El Raval occupies the streets south of the Ramblas. Having grown up outside the city walls, it may lack the Barri Gòtic's architecture, but it is full of atmosphere and has some grand buildings.

The huge 14th-century Casa de la Caritat (Charity House) is now a cultural centre. Next to it stands the stunning, white Museu d'Art Contemporani, which opened in 1995. Close by, off the Carrer de l'Hospital, which has some of Barcelona's most intriguing shops, is the 15th-century Hospital de la Santa Creu, now housing the National Library of Catalonia.

The area formerly known as Barri Xinès (Chinese Quarter), towards the port, is the city's red light district. There is nothing Chinese about it save its name, given to it in the 1920s by a journalist after he had seen a film about San Francisco's Chinatown.

On Carrer Nou de la Rambla are Gaudí's Palau Güell *(see p137)*; the Hotel Espanya *(see p543)*, with its superb Modernista interior by Domènech i Montaner; and the city's most complete Romanesque church, Sant Pau del Camp, where Franciscans still sing Mass.

Las Ramblas ❾

THE HISTORIC AVENUE of Las Ramblas (Les Rambles in Catalan) is busy around the clock, especially in the evenings and at weekends. Newsstands, caged bird and flower stalls, tarot readers, musicians and mime artists throng the wide, tree-shaded central walkway. Among its famous buildings are the Liceu Opera House, the huge Boqueria food market and some grand mansions.

Exploring Las Ramblas
The name of this avenue, also known as La Rambla, comes from the Arabic *ramla*, meaning the dried-up bed of a seasonal river. Barcelona's 13th-century city wall followed the left bank of one such river that flowed from the Collserola hills to the sea.

Convents, monasteries and the university were built on the opposite bank in the 16th century. As time passed, the riverbed was filled in and those buildings demolished, but they are remembered in the names of the five Ramblas that make up the great avenue between the Plaça de Catalunya and Port Vell (Old Port). Today, it is lined with hotels, mansions, shops and cafés.

Palau Güell C/ Nou de la Rambla 3–5. **Map** 2 F3. 📞 *93 317 39 74.* Ⓜ *Liceu.* ⏰ *Tue–Sat.* ⚫ *public hols.* 📷 🎫 **Museu de Cera** Pg de la Banca 7. **Map** 2 F4. 📞 *93 317 26 49.* Ⓜ *Drassanes.* ⏰ *Jul–Sep: 10am–10pm daily; Oct– Jun: 10am–1:30pm, 4–7:30pm Mon–Fri, 11am–2pm, 4:30–8:30pm Sat, Sun & public hols.* 📷 ♿

The monument to Columbus at the bottom of the tree-lined Ramblas

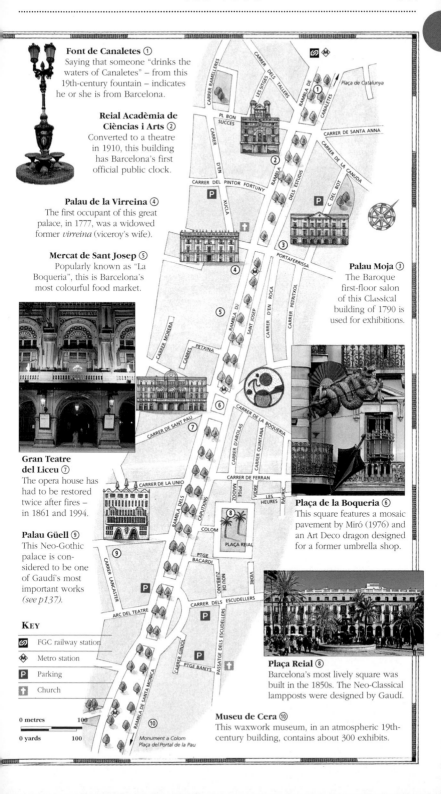

Font de Canaletes ①
Saying that someone "drinks the waters of Canaletes" – from this 19th-century fountain – indicates he or she is from Barcelona.

Reial Acadèmia de Ciències i Arts ②
Converted to a theatre in 1910, this building has Barcelona's first official public clock.

Palau de la Virreina ④
The first occupant of this great palace, in 1777, was a widowed former *virreina* (viceroy's wife).

Mercat de Sant Josep ⑤
Popularly known as "La Boqueria", this is Barcelona's most colourful food market.

Gran Teatre del Liceu ⑦
The opera house has had to be restored twice after fires – in 1861 and 1994.

Palau Güell ⑨
This Neo-Gothic palace is considered to be one of Gaudí's most important works *(see p137)*.

KEY

ⓕ	FGC railway station
◈	Metro station
P	Parking
✝	Church

0 metres	100
0 yards	100

Palau Moja ③
The Baroque first-floor salon of this Classical building of 1790 is used for exhibitions.

Plaça de la Boqueria ⑥
This square features a mosaic pavement by Miró (1976) and an Art Deco dragon designed for a former umbrella shop.

Plaça Reial ⑧
Barcelona's most lively square was built in the 1850s. The Neo-Classical lampposts were designed by Gaudí.

Museu de Cera ⑩
This waxwork museum, in an atmospheric 19th-century building, contains about 300 exhibits.

Statue of Poseidon in the courtyard of La Llotja

La Llotja ⑩

Carrer de Consolat de Mar 2. **Map** 5 B3. ⓦ *Jaume I.* 🖾 ⬤ *for restoration.*

LA LLOTJA (meaning commodity exchange) was built in the 1380s as the headquarters of the Consolat de Mar, the guild of Catalan sea-traders. It was remodelled in the Neo-Classical style in 1771 and housed the city's stock exchange until 1994. The original, three-aisled Gothic hall was retained, however, to act as the main trading room – it can be glimpsed through the large ground-floor windows.

The upper floors housed the Barcelona School of Fine Arts from 1849–1970, attended by the young Picasso and Joan Miró *(see p168)*. La Llotja is now home to a public library and local government offices.

Basílica de Santa Maria del Mar ⑪

Plaza Sta Maria 1. **Map** 5 B3. 🖾 93 310 23 90. ⓦ *Jaume I.* ⬤ *9am–1:30pm, 4:30–8pm daily (Sun from 10am).*

THE CITY'S favourite church with superb acoustics for concerts, is the only example of a church entirely in the Catalan Gothic style. It took just 55 years to build, with money donated by merchants and shipbuilders. The speed – unrivalled in the Middle Ages – gave it a unity of style both inside and out. The west front has a 15th-century rose window of the Coronation of the Virgin. More stained glass, from the 15th–18th centuries, lights the nave and aisles.

The choir and furnishings were burned in the Civil War *(see p63)*, adding to the sense of space and simplicity.

Carrer Montcada ⑫

Map 5 B3. ⓦ *Jaume I.* **Museu Tèxtil i de la Indumentària** 🖾 93 310 45 16. ⬤ *10am–6pm Tue–Sat, 10am–3pm Sun & public hols.* ⬤ *1 & 5 Jan, Good Fri, 1 May, 24 Jun, 25 & 26 Dec.* 🖾 🖾 🖾 *by appt.*

THE MOST AUTHENTIC medieval street in Barcelona is a narrow lane, overshadowed by gargoyles and protruding roofs. The Gothic palaces that line it, entered through great wooden doors and built around magnificent courtyards, date back to the expansion of Catalonia in the 13th century. A mural of the conquest of Mallorca, a rare secular Romanesque painting once in the 13th–15th-century Palau Berenguer d'Aguilar, is now in the Museu Nacional d'Art de Catalunya *(see p168)*.

Carrer Montcada's buildings were all modified over the years, particularly in the 17th

A wedding service in the Gothic interior of Santa Maria del Mar

Pablo Picasso, *Self-Portrait* in charcoal (1899–1900)

PABLO PICASSO IN BARCELONA

Picasso (1881–1973) was born in Málaga and was almost 14 when he came to Barcelona, where his father had found a job in the city's art academy. Picasso enrolled, and was a precocious talent among his contemporaries. He was a regular visitor to Els Quatre Gats, an artists' café still in existence in Carrer Montsió, where he held his first exhibition. He also exhibited in Sala Parks, a gallery still functioning in Carrer Petritxol. The family lived in Carrer Mercé and Picasso had a studio in Carrer Nou de la Rambla. It was among the prostitutes of Carrer d'Avinyò that he found inspiration for the work that many art historians see as the wellspring of modern art, *Les Demoiselles d'Avignon* (1906–7). Picasso left Barcelona for Paris in his early twenties and initially returned several times. After the Civil War his opposition to Franco kept him in France, but he designed a frieze for Barcelona's College of Architects in 1962 and was persuaded to allow the city to open a museum of his work, which it did the following year.

century when the Renaissance style prevailed. The only one to retain its original façade is the Casa Cervelló-Guidice at No. 25. The **Museu Tèxtil i de la Indumentària** in the Palau dels Marquesos de Lió at No. 12 (also called the Palau Mora) displays textiles and clothing from the 4th century onwards. The street also has the city's best-known champagne bar, *El Xampanyet (see p185).*

Museu Picasso ⓭

Carrer Montcada 15–23. **Map** 5 B1.
🔲 *93 319 63 10.* ⓜ *Jaume I.* 🔲
10am–7:30pm Tue–Sat & public hols,
10am–2:30pm Sun. 🔲 *1 Jan, Good*
Fri, 1 May, 24 Jun, 25–26 Dec. 🔲
🔲 🔲 www.museopicasso.bcn.es

O NE OF BARCELONA'S most popular attractions, the Picasso Museum, is housed in five adjoining palaces dating from medieval times on Carrer Montcada: Berenguer d'Aguilar, Baró de Castellet, Finestres, Mauri, and Meca.

The museum opened in 1963 using works donated by Jaime Sabartes, a friend of Picasso. Following Sabartes' death in 1968, Picasso himself donated paintings, including early examples. These were complemented by graphic works, left in his will, and 141 ceramic pieces given by his widow, Jacqueline.

The works are divided into two sections: paintings and drawings and ceramics. The strength of the 3,000-piece collection is Picasso's early works, demonstrating that even at the ages of 15 and 16

Glorious stained-glass dome, Palau de la Música Catalana

he was painting major works, such as *The First Communion* (1896). Few pictures are from his Blue and Rose periods. The most famous work is his series *Las Meninas*, based on Velázquez's masterpiece *(see p28)*, displayed in its entirety.

Palau de la Música Catalana ⓮

Carrer de Sant Francesc de Paula 2.
Map 5 B1. 🔲 *93 295 72 00.*
ⓜ *Urquinaona.* 🔲 *Sep–Jun: 10am–*
3:30pm; Jul: 10am–6pm daily. 🔲
Aug. 🔲 🔲 🔲 *every half hour.*
🔲 www.palaumusica.org

T HIS IS a real palace of music, a Modernista celebration of tile-work, sculpture and glorious stained glass. Designed by Lluís Domènech i Montaner, it was completed in 1908 on the site of a monastery dissolved in the 19th century. Although a few extensions have been added, the building still retains its

Painting in Picasso's series *Las Meninas* (1957), Museu Picasso

original appearance. The elaborate red brick façade is hard to appreciate fully in the confines of the narrow street. It is lined with mosaic-covered pillars topped by busts of Palestrina, Bach and Beethoven. The large stone sculpture of St George and other figures at the corner of the building is an allegory of Catalan folksong by Miquel Blay.

But it is the interior of the building which is truly inspiring. The auditorium on the first floor is lit by a huge inverted dome of stained glass depicting angelic choristers.

The sculptures of the composers Wagner and Clavé on the proscenium arch were designed by Domènech but finished by Pablo Gargallo. Josep Anselm Clavé's (1824–74) work in promoting Catalan song led to the creation of the Orfeó Català choral society in 1891, which became a focus of Catalan nationalism and the inspiration behind the Palau.

The pink brick façade of the late 19th-century Arc del Triomf

Arc del Triomf ⓯

Passeig Lluís Companys. **Map** 5 C1. Ⓜ *Arc de Triomf.*

THE MAIN GATEWAY to the 1888 Universal Exhibition, which filled the Parc de la Ciutadella, was designed by Josep Vilaseca i Casanovas. It is built of brick in the Mudéjar style *(see p51)*, with sculptured allegories of crafts, industry and business. The frieze by Josep Reynés on the main façade represents the city of Barcelona welcoming foreign visitors.

Parc de la Ciutadella ⓰

Avda del Marqués de l'Argentera. **Map** 6 D2. Ⓜ *Barceloneta, Ciutadella-Vila Olímpica.* ◯ *May–Aug: 10am–9pm daily; Mar–Apr & Sep–Oct: 10am–7pm or 8pm; Nov–Feb: 10am–6pm.* ♿

THIS POPULAR park has a large boating lake, orange groves and scores of naturalized parrots living in the palm trees. The 30-ha (75-acre) park was pre-

viously the site of a massive star-shaped citadel. Designed by Prosper Verboom, this was built for Felipe V between 1715 and 1720 following a 13-month siege of the city, brought about by Barcelona's opposition to the Bourbon succession *(see p58)*. The fortress was intended to house soldiers, but was never used for this purpose. It was converted into a prison, which became particularly notorious during the Napoleonic occupation *(see p59)*, and during the 19th-century liberal repressions, when it was hated as a symbol of centralized power.

In 1878, under the enlightened dictator General Prim, whose statue stands in the middle of the park, the citadel was pulled down and the park was given to the city, to become, in 1888, the venue of the Universal Exhibition.

Three buildings, however, survived: the arsenal, which was redesigned in 1932 for use by the Catalan parliament and is today shared by the Museu d'Art Modern; the Governor's Palace, which is now a school; and the chapel, still sometimes used by the military.

The gardens in the Plaça de Armes were laid out by the French landscape gardener Jean Forestier. They centre on a cascade based around a triumphal arch and partly inspired by the Trevi Fountain in Rome. It was designed by architect Josep Fontseré, with the help of Antoni Gaudí, who was then still a young student.

One of the galleries inside the spacious Museu de Zoologia

Museu de Zoologia ⓱

Passeig de Picasso, esquina Pujadas. **Map** 5 C2. 🕿 *93 319 69 12.* Ⓜ *Arc de Triomf, Jaume I.* ◯ *10am– 2pm Tue & Wed, Fri–Sun, public hols, 10am–6:30pm Thu.* 🔲 ♿ 🔲 *by appt.* 🔲 *www.museuzoologia.bcn.es*

AT THE ENTRANCE to the Parc de la Ciutadella is the fortress-like Castell dels Tres Dragons (Castle of the Three Dragons), named after a play by Frederic Soler. Decorated with a frieze of ceramic shields, it was built as a restaurant for the 1888 Universal Exhibition. The architect, Lluís Domènech i Montaner, modelled it on Valencia's Lonja *(see p241)*. He later used it as a workshop for Modernista design, and it became a focus of the movement. It has housed the city's Zoological Museum since 1937.

Ornamental cascade in the Parc de la Ciutadella designed by Josep Fontseré and Antoni Gaudí

Museu de Geologia ⑱

Parc de la Ciutadella. **Map** 5 C3.
[93 319 68 95. ⚋ Arc de Triomf, Jaume I. ☐ 10am–2pm Tue, Wed & Fri–Sun, 10am–6pm Thu. ● public hols. 🖼 ♿ ⛩ by appt.

Barcelona's oldest museum opened in 1882, the same year the Parc de la Ciutadella became a public space for the city. It has a large collection of fossils and minerals, including specimens from Catalonia and around the country.

Beside it is the Hivernacle, an iron-framed glasshouse, often used for concerts. Nearby is the Umbracle conservatory built by the park's architect, Josep Fontseré.

Glass cube of the *Homenatge a Picasso*, Parc de la Ciutadella

Homenatge a Picasso ⑲

Passeig de Picasso. **Map** 5 C3.
⚋ Barceloneta.

At the edge of the Parc de la Ciutadella, opposite the Avinguda del Marqués de l'Argentera, is Catalan sculptor Antoni Tàpies' intriguing 1983 work, *Homage to Picasso*.

Built to pay homage to Picasso's Cubist works, it is an intellectual sculpture that does not immediately suggest its title. A large, plain glass cube sits in a square pond, with water streaming down the sides. The cube contains an old sofa, chairs and a sideboard skewered by metal poles and draped with a blanket. The elements have not treated it kindly, and an air-conditioning system has had to be installed to prevent the glass from cracking.

***Dusk on the River Loing* by Alfred Sisley (1839–99)**

Museu d'Art Modern ⑳

Parc de la Ciutadella. **Map** 6 D3.
[93 319 50 23. ⚋ Arc de Triomf. ☐ 10am–7pm Tue–Sat, 10am–2:30pm Sun & public hols. 🖼 ♿
Ⓦ www.manac.es

The name of this museum is slightly misleading, as it really houses a collection of 19th- and 20th-century Catalan art, in which the main players – Miró, Picasso, Dalí and Tàpies – are under-represented as they have museums of their own. This should not, however, put potential visitors off, as much of the work is excellent and of great help in understanding Catalan life and culture.

In particular there are works by Catalonia's two main early 20th-century painters, Santiago Rusiñol (1861–1931) and Ramón Casas (1866–1932), considered to be the region's first Impressionist. Casas' line drawings record the faces of the great men of his day. Chief among them is a picture of Picasso, newly arrived in Paris. There is also a painting of Casas himself with Pere Romeu; the two men were founders of Barcelona's Els Quatre Gats café (*see p148*), where the painting was originally hung.

Picasso's contemporaries, the painters Joaquim Mir (1873–1940) and Isidre Nonell (1873–1911), are represented here, and there are some sculptures by Miquel Blay (1866–1936). There is also a landscape by Alfred Sisley (1839–99), *Dusk on the River Loing.*

The museum has a few excellent examples of Modernista furniture from homes around the Eixample, including an entire private altar.

Parc Zoològic ㉑

Parc de la Ciutadella. **Map** 6 D3.
[93 225 67 80. ⚋ Ciutadella-Vila Olímpica. ☐ Mar: 10am–6:30pm, Apr: 10am–7pm, May–Sep: 10am–7:30pm, Oct–Feb: 10am–5pm. 🖼
♿ Ⓦ www.zoobarcelona.com

Barcelona's zoo was laid out in the 1940s to a relatively enlightened design in which the animals are separated by moats instead of iron bars. The zoo is strong on primates and for years its mascot has been Floquet de Neu (Snowflake), a rare albino gorilla. Dolphin and whale shows are held in one of the aquariums. By the entrance is Roig i Soler's 1885 fountain sculpture, *The Lady with the Umbrella*, now a symbol of Barcelona.

Floquet de Neu, Barcelona zoo's rare albino gorilla

Smart boats and the twin skyscrapers at the Port Olímpic

Vila Olímpica 22

Map 6 F4. 🚇 Ciutadella-Vila Olímpica.

THE MOST DRAMATIC rebuilding for the 1992 Olympics was the demolition of the old industrial waterfront and the laying out of 4 km (2 miles) of promenade and pristine sandy beaches. Suddenly Barcelona seemed like a seaside resort. At the heart of the project was a 65-ha (160-acre) new estate of 2,000 apartments and parks called Nova Icària. The area is still popularly known as the Vila Olímpica because the buildings once housed the Olympic athletes.

On the sea front there are twin 44-floor blocks, Spain's tallest skyscrapers, one occupied by offices and the other by the Arts hotel *(see p544)*. They stand beside the Port Olímpic, which was also built for 1992. The main reason for visiting are the two levels of restaurants in a wonderful setting around the marina.

Barceloneta 23

Map 5 B5. 🚇 Barceloneta.

BARCELONA'S fishing "village", which lies on a triangular tongue of land jutting into the sea just below the city centre, is renowned for its fish restaurants and port-side cafés.

Barceloneta was built by the architect and military engineer Juan Martín de Cermeño in 1753 to rehouse people made homeless by the construction,

just inland, of a large fortress, La Ciutadella *(see p150)*. Since then it has housed largely workers and fishermen. Laid out on a grid system with narrow houses of two or three floors, in which each room has a window on the street, the area has a friendly air.

In the small Plaça de la Barceloneta, at the centre of the district, is the Baroque church of Sant Miquel del Port, also by Cermeño. A market is often held in the square here.

Today, Barceloneta's fishing fleet is still based in the nearby industrial docks by a small clock tower. On the opposite side of this harbour is the Torre de Sant Sebastià, terminus of the cable car that runs right across the port, via the World Trade Centre, to Montjuïc.

Port Vell 24

Map 5 A4. 🚇 Barceloneta, Drassanes.
Aquàrium 📞 93 221 74 74.
🕐 Oct–May: 9am–9pm Mon–Fri, 9:30am–9:30pm Sat, Sun, & public hols; Jun & Sep: 9:30am–9:30pm daily; Jul–Aug: 9:30am–11pm daily.
🎫 ♿ 🌐 www.aquariumbcn.com

THE CITY'S NEW leisure port is at the foot of Las Ramblas, just beyond the old customs house. This was built in 1902 at the Portal de la Pau, the former maritime entrance to the city, where steps lead into the water. To the south, the Moll de Barcelona, with a new World Trade Centre, serves as the passenger pier for visiting liners. In front of the customs house, Las Ramblas is linked to the yacht clubs on the Moll

d'Espanya by a swing bridge and pedestrian jetty. The Moll d'Espanya (*moll* meaning quay, wharf or pier) has a shopping and restaurant complex, the Maremàgnum, plus an IMAX cinema and the largest aquarium in Europe.

The Moll de la Fusta (Timber Wharf), with terrace cafés, has red structures inspired by Van Gogh's bridge at Arles. At the end of the wharf stands *El Cap de Barcelona (Barcelona Head)*, a 20-m (66-ft) sculpture by Pop artist Roy Lichtenstein.

Monument a Colom 25

Plaça del Portal de la Pau. **Map** 2 F4.
📞 93 302 52 24. 🚇 Drassanes.
🕐 Oct–Mar: 10am–1:30pm, 3:30–6:30pm Tue–Fri, 10am–6:30pm Sat, Sun & public hols; Apr–May: 10am–7:30pm daily; Jun–Sep: 9am–8:30pm daily. 🎫

THE COLUMBUS monument in the Portal de la Pau (the "Gate of Peace") was designed by Gaietà Buïgas for the 1888 Universal Exhibition.

The 60-m (200-ft) cast iron monument marks the spot where Columbus stepped ashore in 1493 after discovering America, bringing with him six Caribbean Indians. He was accorded a state welcome by the Catholic Monarchs in the Saló del Tinell *(see p142)*. The Indians' conversion to Christianity is commemorated in the cathedral *(see pp144–5)*.

A lift gives access to a viewing platform at the top of the monument, where a bronze statue, points out to sea.

Fishing boat moored at the quayside of Barceloneta

A *golondrina* departing from the Plaça del Portal de la Pau

Golondrinas ㉖

Plaça del Portal de la Pau. **Map** 2 F5.
[93 442 31 06. ⊕ *Drassanes.*
○ *times variable – phone ahead for information.* 📷

SIGHTSEEING TRIPS around Barcelona's harbour can be made on small double-decker boats called *golondrinas* (literally "swallows"). They moor beside the steps of the Plaça del Portal de la Pau in front of the Columbus Monument.

Tours last around half an hour. The boats go out beneath the steep, castle-topped hill of Montjuïc towards the industrial port. They usually stop off at the breakwater, which reaches out to sea from Barceloneta, to allow passengers to disembark for a stroll.

An alternative one-and-a-half-hour trip takes in Barcelona Harbour, the commercial port and beaches and stops off at the Port Olímpic.

Museu Marítim and Drassanes ㉗

Avinguda de les Drassanes. **Map** 2 F4.
[93 342 99 20. ⊕ *Drassanes.*
○ *10am–7pm daily.* ● *1 & 6 Jan, 25 & 26 Dec.* 📷 ♿ 📷 *12:30pm Sat–Sun*

THE GREAT GALLEYS that made Barcelona a major seafaring power were built in the sheds of the Drassanes (shipyards), which now house the maritime museum. These royal dry docks are the largest and most complete surviving medieval complex of their kind in the

world. They were founded in the mid-13th century, when dynastic marriages uniting the kingdoms of Sicily and Aragón meant that better maritime communications between the two became a priority. Three of the yards' four original corner towers survive.

Among the vessels to slip from the Drassanes' vaulted halls was the *Real*, flagship of Don Juan of Austria, Charles V's illegitimate son, who led the Christian fleet to victory against the Turks at Lepanto in 1571 *(see p55)*. The museum's showpiece is a full-scale replica decorated in red and gold.

The *Llibre del Consulat de Mar*, a book of nautical codes and practice, is a reminder that Catalonia was once the arbiter of Mediterranean maritime law. The expertise of its sailors is also evident in the collection of pre-Columbian charts and maps, including one of 1439 which was used by Amerigo Vespucci.

Stained-glass window in the Museu Marítim

EIXAMPLE

ARCELONA CLAIMS to have the greatest collection of Art Nouveau buildings of any city in Europe. The style, known in Catalonia as Modernisme, flourished after 1854, when it was decided to pull down the medieval walls to allow the city to develop into what had previously been a construction-free military zone.

The designs of the civil engineer Ildefons Cerdà i Sunyer (1815–76) were chosen for the new expansion *(eixample)* inland. These plans called for a rigid grid system of streets, but at each intersection the corners were chamfered to allow the buildings there to overlook the junctions or squares. The few exceptions

Jesus of the Column,
Sagrada Família

to this grid system include the Diagonal, a main avenue running from the wealthy area of Pedralbes down to the sea, and the Hospital de la Santa Creu i de Sant Pau by Modernista architect Domènech i Montaner (1850–1923). He hated the grid system and deliberately angled the hospital to look down the diagonal Avinguda de Gaudí towards Antoni Gaudí's church of the Sagrada Família, the city's most spectacular Modernista building *(see pp162–3)*. The wealth of Barcelona's commercial elite, and their passion for all things new, allowed them to give free rein to the age's most innovative architects in designing their residences as well as public buildings.

SIGHTS AT A GLANCE

Museums and Galleries
Fundació Antoni Tàpies ❷

Churches
Sagrada Família pp162–3 ❻

Modernista Buildings
Casa Milà, "La Pedrera" ❸
Casa Terrades, "Casa de les Punxes" ❹
Hospital de la Santa Creu i de Sant Pau ❺
Illa de la Discòrdia ❶

KEY

▨	Street-by-Street map *pp178–9*
Ⓜ	Metro station
▣	Railway station
▥	Main bus stop
ⓘ	Tourist information
Ⓟ	Parking

GETTING THERE

Metro line 3 has stations at either end of the Passeig de Gràcia (Catalunya and Diagonal), and one in the middle, at the Illa de la Discòrdia (Passeig de Gràcia). Metro line 5 takes you straight to the Sagrada Família and Hospital de Sant Pau (a long walk from other sights).

0 metres		500
0 yards		500

◁ **Nativity façade of the Sagrada Família – the only façade to be more or less completed in Gaudí's lifetime**

Street-by-Street: Quadrat d'Or

T HE HUNDRED OR SO city blocks centring on the Passeig de Gràcia are known as the Quadrat d'Or, "Golden Square", because they contain so many of Barcelona's best Modernista buildings *(see pp136–7)*. This was the area within the Eixample favoured by the wealthy bourgeoisie, who embraced the new artistic and architectural style with enthusiasm, not only for their residences, but also for commercial buildings. Most remarkable is the Illa de la Discòrdia, a single block containing houses by Modernisme's most illustrious exponents. Many interiors can be visited by the public, revealing a feast of stained glass, ceramics and ornamental ironwork.

Perfume bottle, Museu del Perfum

Diagonal Metro

Vinçon home decor store *(see p183)*

Passeig de Gràcia, the Eixample's main avenue, is a showcase of highly original buildings and smart shops. The graceful street lamps are by Pere Falqués (1850–1916).

RAMBLA DE CATALUNYA

PASSEIG DE GRÀCIA

Fundació Tàpies
Topped by Antoni Tàpies' wire sculpture Cloud and Chair, *this 1879 building by Domènech i Montaner houses a wide variety of Tàpies' paintings, graphics and sculptures* ❷

Casa Amatller

Museu del Perfum

Casa Ramon Mulleras

★ **Illa de la Discòrdia**
In this city block, four of Barcelona's most famous Modernista houses vie for attention. All were created between 1900 and 1910. This ornate tower graces the Casa Lleó Morera by Domènech i Montaner ❶

To Plaça de Catalunya

Casa Batlló

Casa Lleó Morera

Passeig de Gràcia Metro

Museu de la Música is housed in the Palau Baró de Quadras designed by Puig i Cadafalch in 1904. This carving adorns the doorway. The museum has displays of historical instruments collected from around the world.

LOCATOR MAP
See Street Finder map 3

EIXAMPLE

OLD TOWN

AVINGUDA DIAGONAL

CARRER DE PAU CLARIS

CARRER DE PROVENÇA

CARRER DE ROGER DE LLÚRIA

CARRER DE MALLORCA

CARRER DE VALÈNCIA

CARRER DEL BRUC

CARRER D'ARAGÓ

Casa Thomas

To Sagrada Família

Palau Ramon de Montaner

Casa Terrades
Built in red brick with carved stone ornamentation, this 1905 house by Puig i Cadafalch echoes the Gothic buildings of northern Europe ❹

★ Casa Milà "La Pedrera"
Gaudí put all his architectural daring into this, his most famous house. The result is a remarkable wave-like façade and a roofscape of chimneys and vents resembling abstract sculptures ❸

0 metres	100
0 yards	100

KEY

– – – Suggested route

STAR SIGHTS

★ **Illa de la Discòrdia**

★ **Casa Milà "La Pedrera"**

Sumptuous interior of the Casa Lleó Morera, Illa de la Discòrdia

Illa de la Discòrdia ❶

Passeig de Gràcia, between Carrer d'Aragó and Carrer del Consell de Cent. **Map** 3 A4. 🌀 *Passeig de Gràcia.* **Casa Amatller** 📞 *93 488 01 39.* ⬭ *10am–7pm Mon–Sat, 10am–2pm Sun & public hols.*

THE MOST famous group of Modernista *(see pp136–7)* buildings in Barcelona amply illustrates the range of styles involved in the movement. The city block in which they stand has been dubbed the Illa de la Discòrdia, "Block of Discord", owing to the startling visual argument between them.

The three most famous houses, on Passeig de Gràcia, were remodelled in Modernista style from existing houses early in the 20th century, but named after their original owners.

No. 35 is **Casa Lleó Morera** (1902–6), the first residential work of Lluís Domènech i Montaner. The ground floor was gutted to create a shop in 1943, but the Modernista interiors upstairs still exist.

Beyond the next two houses, one of which is a beauty shop containing a perfume museum, is **Casa Amatller**, designed by Puig i Cadafalch in 1898. Its façade is a harmonious blend of styles, featuring Moorish and Gothic windows encased in iron grilles. The stepped gable roof is dotted with tiles. Inside the wrought-iron main doors is a fine stone staircase beneath a stained-glass roof. The building is now used by the Institut Amatller d'Art Hispànic. Tickets for tours of the houses are available here.

Next door is Antoni Gaudí's **Casa Batlló** (1904–6). Its façade has heavily tiled walls and curving iron balconies pierced with holes to look like masks or skulls. The hump-backed, scaly-looking roof is thought to represent a dragon, with St George (the patron saint of Catalonia) as a chimney.

Fundació Antoni Tàpies ❷

Carrer d'Aragó 255. **Map** 3 A1. 📞 *93 487 03 15.* 🌀 *Passeig de Gràcia.* ⬭ *10am–8pm Tue–Sun & public hols.* ⬤ *1 & 6 Jan, 25 & 26 Dec.* 📷 ♿

ANTONI TAPIES, born in 1923, is Barcelona's best-known living artist. Inspired by Surrealism, his abstract work is executed in a variety of materials, including concrete and metal *(see p156)*. It is not easy to appreciate at first, but the exhibits should help those interested obtain a clearer perspective, even if there are not enough here to gain a full understanding of the artist's work. They are housed in the first domestic building in Barcelona to be built with iron (1880), designed by Domènech i Montaner for his brother's publishing firm.

ANTONI GAUDÍ (1852–1926)

Born in Reus (Tarragona) into a family of artisans, Gaudí was the leading exponent of Catalan Modernisme. Following a stint as a blacksmith's apprentice, he studied at Barcelona's School of Architecture. Inspired by a nationalistic search for a romantic medieval past, his work was supremely original. His first major achievement was the Casa Vicens (1888) at No. 24 Carrer de les Carolines. But his most celebrated building is the extravagant church of the Sagrada Família *(see pp162–3)*, to which he devoted his life from 1914. He gave all his money to the project and often went from house to house begging for more, until his death a few days after being run over by a tram.

Decorated chimney pot, Casa Vicens

◁ **Extraordinary sculptured and ceramic-encrusted chimneys of Gaudí's Casa Milà**

The rippled façade of Gaudí's apartment building, Casa Milà

Casa Milà ❸

Passeig de Gràcia 92. **Map** 3 B3.
☎ 93 484 59 80. Ⓜ Diagonal.
🕐 10am–7:30pm daily. ● public hols. W www.casacat.es/cccc

USUALLY CALLED "LA PEDRERA" ("the stone quarry"), the Casa Milà is Gaudí's greatest contribution to Barcelona's civic architecture, and his last work before he devoted himself entirely to the Sagrada Família (see pp162–3).

Built between 1906 and 1910, "La Pedrera" completely departed from the established construction principles of the time and, as a result, was ridiculed and strongly attacked by Barcelona's intellectuals.

Gaudí designed this corner apartment block, eight storeys high, around two circular courtyards. In the basement he incorporated the city's first underground car park. The intricate ironwork balconies, by Josep Maria Jujol, are like seaweed against the wave-like walls of white undressed stone. There are no straight walls anywhere in the building.

The Milà family had an apartment on the first floor. Regular guided tours from an office on the ground floor take in the extraordinary roof, where the multitude of sculpted air ducts and chimneys look so threatening they have been dubbed the *espantabruixes*, the witch-scarers.

Casa Terrades ❹

Avinguda Diagonal 416. **Map** 3 B3.
Ⓜ Diagonal. ● to public.

THIS FREE-STANDING, six-sided apartment block by Modernista architect Puig i Cadafalch gets its nickname, "Casa de les Punxes" (House of the Points), from the spires on its six corner turrets, which are shaped like witches' hats. It was built between 1903 and 1905 by converting three existing houses on the site and was Puig's largest work. It is an eclectic mixture of medieval and

Spire on the main tower, Casa Terrades

Renaissance styles. The towers and gables are influenced in particular by north European Gothic architecture. However, the deeply carved, floral stone ornament of the exterior, in combination with red brick as the principal building material, are typically Modernista.

Hospital de la Santa Creu i de Sant Pau ❺

Carrer de Sant Antoni Maria Claret 167.
Map 4 F1. ☎ 93 291 91 99. Ⓜ Hospital de Sant Pau. **Grounds** 🕐 daily; write in advance for permission.
♿ ✔ W www.hspau.com

LLUIS DOMÈNECH I MONTANER began designing a new city hospital in 1902. Totally innovative in concept, his scheme consisted of 26 attractive Mudéjar-style pavilions set in large gardens, as he strongly disliked huge wards and believed that patients would recover better amid fresh air and trees. All the connecting corridors and service areas were hidden underground.

Also believing art and colour to be therapeutic, he decorated the pavilions profusely. The turreted roofs were tiled with ceramics, and the reception pavilion embellished with sculptures by Pau Gargallo and mosaic murals. The vast project was completed after Domènech's death, in 1930, by his son Pere.

Statue of the Virgin, Hospital de la Santa Creu i de Sant Pau

Sagrada Família ❻

Bell Towers
Eight of the 12 spires, one for each apostle, have been built. Each is topped by Venetian mosaics.

EUROPE'S MOST unconventional church, the Temple Expiatori de la Sagrada Família, is an emblem of a city that likes to think of itself as individualistic. Crammed with symbolism inspired by nature and striving for originality, it is Gaudí's *(see pp136–7)* greatest work. In 1883, a year after work had begun on a Neo-Gothic church on the site, the task of completing it was given to Gaudí who changed everything, extemporizing as he went along. It became his life's work and he lived like a recluse on the site for 16 years. He is buried in the crypt. At his death only one tower on the Nativity façade had been completed, but work resumed after the Civil War and several more have since been finished to his original plans. Work continues today, financed by public subscription.

A carved whelk

THE FINISHED CHURCH

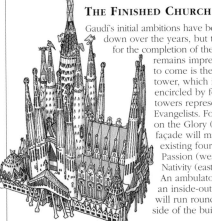

Gaudí's initial ambitions have been scaled down over the years, but the design for the completion of the building remains impressive. Still to come is the central tower, which is to be encircled by four large towers representing the Evangelists. Four towers on the Glory (south) façade will match the existing four on the Passion (west) and Nativity (east) façades. An ambulatory – like an inside-out cloister – will run round the outside of the building.

Tower with lift

The apse was the first part of the church Gaudí completed. Stairs lead down from here to the crypt below.

The altar canopy, designed by Gaudí, is still waiting for the altar.

★ Passion Façade
This bleak façade was completed in the late 1980s by artist Josep Maria Subirachs. A controversial work, its sculpted figures are angular and often sinister.

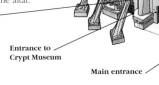

Entrance to Crypt Museum

Main entrance

Spiral Staircases
*Steep stone steps –
400 in each – allow
access to the towers
and upper galleries.
Majestic views
reward those who
climb or take the lift.*

**Tower
with lift**

★ **Nativity Façade**
*The most complete part of Gaudí's
church, finished in 1904, has
doorways which represent Faith,
Hope and Charity. Scenes of the
Nativity and Christ's childhood are
embellished with symbolism, such as
doves representing the congregation.*

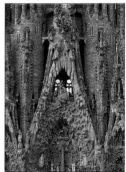

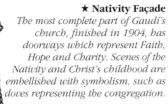

★ **Crypt**
*The crypt, where Gaudí is buried,
was built by the original architect,
Francesc de Paula Villar i Lozano,
in 1882. This is where services are
held. On the lower floor a museum
traces the careers of both architects
and the church's history.*

Nave
*In the nave, which is still under
construction, a forest of fluted
pillars will support four galleries
above the side aisles, while
skylights let in natural light.*

STAR FEATURES

★ **Passion Façade**

★ **Nativity Façade**

★ **Crypt**

MONTJUÏC

THE HILL OF MONTJUIC, rising to 213 m (699 ft) above the commercial port on the south side of the city, is Barcelona's biggest recreation area. Its museums, art galleries, gardens and nightclubs make it a popular place in the evenings as well as during the day.

There was probably a Celt-iberian settlement here before the Romans built a temple to Jupiter on their Mons Jovis, which may have given Montjuïc its name – though another theory suggests that a Jewish cemetery on the hill inspired the name Mount of the Jews.

The absence of a water supply meant that there were few buildings on Montjuïc until the castle was erected on the top in 1640.

The hill finally came into its own as the site of the 1929 International Fair. With great energy and flair, buildings were erected all over the north side, with the grand Avinguda de la Reina Maria Cristina, lined with huge exhibition halls, leading into it from the Plaça d'Espanya. In the middle of the avenue is the Font Màgica (Magic Fountain), which is regularly illuminated in colour. Above it is the Palau Nacional, home of the city's historic art collections. The Poble Espanyol is a crafts centre housed in copies of buildings from all over Spain. The last great surge of building on Montjuïc was for the 1992 Olympic Games, which left Barcelona with international-class sports facilities.

Statue, gardens of the Palau Nacional

SIGHTS AT A GLANCE

Historic Buildings
Castell de Montjuïc **7**

Modern Architecture
Estadi Olímpic de Montjuïc **8**
Pavelló Mies van der Rohe **4**

Museums and Galleries
Fundació Joan Miró **1**
Museu Arqueològic **2**
Museu Nacional d'Art de Catalunya **3**

Squares
Plaça d'Espanya **6**

Theme Parks
Poble Espanyol **5**

GETTING THERE

Apart from the exhibition halls near Espanya Metro station, reaching most of Montjuïc's attractions on foot involves a steep climb. However, buses 13 and 61 will take you up the hill from Plaça d'Espanya. For the castle, take the funicular from Metro Paral·lel, then the cable car. These run from 11am–7:30/8pm on winter weekends and daily in summer to 9:30/10pm.

KEY

■	Street-by-Street map *pp 166-7*
Ⓜ	Metro station
🚠	Cable car station
🚟	Funicular railway station
🚌	Main bus stop
P	Parking

0 metres   500

0 yards   500

◁ **Changing colours of the Font Màgica (Magic Fountain) on the grand avenue leading up to Montjuïc**

Street-by-Street: Montjuïc

MONTJUIC IS A SPECTACULAR vantage point from which to view the city. It has a wealth of art galleries and museums, as well as a funfair, and an open-air theatre adjoining a rose garden. The most interesting buildings lie around the Palau Nacional, where Europe's greatest Romanesque art collection is housed. Montjuïc is approached from the Plaça d'Espanya between brick pillars based on the campanile of St Mark's in Venice, which give a foretaste of the eclecticism of building styles. The Poble Espanyol illustrates the traditional architecture of Spain's regions, while the Fundació Joan Miró is boldly modern.

Pavelló Mies van der Rohe
This statue by Georg Kolbe (see p169) stands serenely in the steel, glass, stone and onyx pavilion built in the Bauhaus style as the German contribution to the 1929 International Exhibition ❹

AVINGUDA DEL MARQUES DE COMILLAS

AVINGUDA DELS MONTANYANS

PASSEIG DE LES CASC

★ **Poble Espanyol**
Containing replicas of buildings from many regions, this "village" provides a fascinating glimpse of vernacular styles ❺

AVINGUDA DE L'ESTADI

★ **Museu Nacional d'Art de Catalunya**
Displayed in the National Palace, the main building of the 1929 International Exhibition, is Europe's finest collection of early medieval frescoes. These were a great source of inspiration for Joan Miró (see p168) ❸

To Montjuïc castle and Olympic stadium

STAR SIGHTS

★ **Poble Espanyol**

★ **Museu Nacional d'Art de Catalunya**

★ **Fundació Joan Miró**

Fountains and cascades descend in terraces from the Palau Nacional. Below them is the Font Màgica (Magic Fountain). On summer evenings, from Thursday to Sunday, its jets are programmed to a multi-coloured music and light show. This marvel of water-and-electrical engineering was originally built by Carles Buigas (1898–1979) for the 1929 International Exhibition.

LOCATOR MAP
See Street Finder map 1

Museu Arqueològic
The museum displays important finds from prehistoric cultures in Catalonia and the Balearic Islands. The Dama de Ibiza, *a 4th-century sculpture, was found in Ibiza's Carthaginian necropolis* (see p487) ❷

Museu Etnològic displays artifacts from Oceania, Africa, Asia and Latin America.

o Plaça d'Espanya

RIUS I TAULET

CARRER DE LA GUARDIA URBANA

CARRER DE LLEIDA

PASSEIG DE LA SANTA MADRONA

PASSEIG DE LA SANTA MADRONA

PASSEIG DE LA SANTA MADRONA

SANTA MADRONA

AVINGUDA DE MIRAMAR

Mercat de les Flors theatre
(see p185)

Teatre Grec is an open-air theatre set among gardens.

★ **Fundació Joan Miró**
This tapestry by Joan Miró hangs in the centre he created for the study of modern art. In addition to Miró's works in various media, the modern building by Josep Lluís Sert is of architectural interest ❶

To funfair, Montjuïc castle and cable car

KEY

– – – Suggested route

0 metres 100

0 yards 100

Flame in Space and Naked Woman (1932) by Joan Miró

Fundació Joan Miró ❶

Parc de Montjuïc. **Map** 1 B3. 🛈 *93 329 19 08.* ⓜ *Espanya, then bus 50.* 🔵 *Jul–Sep: 10am–8pm Tue, Wed, Fri, Sat, Thu 9:30pm; Oct–Jun: 10am–7pm Tue, Wed, Fri & Sat; all year: 10am–9:30pm Thu, 10am–2:30pm Sun & public hols.* 🔴 *1 Jan, 25, 26 Dec.* 🖼 🖼 Ⓦ *www.bcn.fjmiro.es*

JOAN MIRÓ (1893–1983) studied at the fine art school at La Llotja *(see p148).* From 1919, he spent much of his time in Paris. Though opposed to Franco, he returned to Spain in 1940 and from then on lived mainly in Mallorca, where he died.

An admirer of primitive Catalan art and Gaudí's Modernisme *(see p136)*, Miró always remained a Catalan painter but developed a Surrealistic style, with vivid colours and fantastical forms suggesting dream-like situations.

In 1975, after the return of democracy to Spain *(see p64)*, his friend, the architect Josep Lluís Sert, designed the stark, white building to house a permanent collection of paintings, sculptures and tapestries lit by natural light. Miró himself donated the works and some of the best pieces on display include his *Barcelona Series* (1939–44), a set of 50 black-and-white lithographs. Periodic exhibitions of other artists' work are also held.

Museu Arqueològic ❷

Passeig Santa Madrona 39–41. **Map** 1 B3. 🛈 *93 423 21 49.* ⓜ *Espanya, Poble Sec.* 🔵 *9:30am–7pm Tue–Sat, 10am–2:30pm Sun & public hols.* 🔴 *1 Jan, 25, 26 Dec.* 🖼 *(free 11 Feb, 23 Apr, 18 May, 11 & 24 Sep).* 🖼

HOUSED IN the Renaissance-inspired 1929 Palace of Graphic Arts, the museum shows artifacts from prehistory to the Visigothic period (AD 415–711). Highlights are finds from the Greco-Roman town of Empúries *(see p206)* and Iberian silver treasure. There is also a splendid collection of Visigothic jewellery.

Museu Nacional d'Art de Catalunya ❸

Parc de Montjuïc, Palau Nacional. **Map** 1 A2. 🛈 *93 622 03 60.* ⓜ *Espanya.* 🔵 *10am–7pm Tue–Sat, 10am–2:30pm Sun & public hols.* 🖼 🖼 🖼 🖼 *noon by appt (93 622 03 75).*

THE AUSTERE Palau Nacional was built for the 1929 International Exhibition, but in 1934 it was used to house an art collection that has since become the most important in the city.

The museum includes what is probably the greatest display of Romanesque items in the world, centred around a series of magnificent 12th-century frescoes. These have been peeled from Catalan Pyrenean churches and re-pasted on to replicas of the original vaulted ceilings and apses they adorned, to save them from plunder and the ravages of time. The most remarkable are the wall paintings from Santa Maria de Taüll *(see p201)* and from Sant Climent de Taüll *(see p20)*.

There is also an impressive Gothic collection, covering the whole of Spain but particularly good on Catalonia. Notable artists of the time are exhibited, including the 15th-century Spanish artists Lluís Dalmau and Jaume Huguet.

Distinguished works by El Greco, Velázquez and Zurbarán are on display in the Baroque and Renaissance collection. A photographic collection was also started in 1996.

12th-century *Christ in Majesty*, **Museu Nacional d'Art de Catalunya**

Morning by Georg Kolbe (1877–1945), Pavelló Mies van der Rohe

Pavelló Mies van der Rohe **❹**

Avinguda del Marqués de Comillas.
Map 1 B2. 93 423 40 16.
 Espanya. 50. 10am–8pm
daily. 1 Jan, 25 Dec.

I F THE SIMPLE lines of the
glass and polished stone
German Pavilion look modern
today, they must have
shocked visitors to the International Exhibition in 1929.
Designed by Ludwig Mies van
der Rohe (1886–1969), director
of the Avant-Garde Bauhaus
school, it includes his famous
Barcelona Chair. The building
was demolished after the exhibition, but a replica was built
on the centenary of his birth.

Poble Espanyol **❺**

Avinguda del Marqués de Comillas.
Map 1 A2. 93 508 63 00.
 Espanya. 9am–8pm Mon,
9am–2am Tue–Thu, 9am–4am Fri &
Sat, 9am–midnight Sun.
 www.poble-espanyol.com

T HE IDEA BEHIND the Poble
Espanyol (Spanish Village)
was to display Spanish architectural styles and crafts. It was
laid out for the 1929 International Exhibition, but has
proved enduringly popular.
 Building styles from all over
Spain are illustrated by 116
houses. These are arranged on
streets radiating from a main
square and were created by
many well-known architects

and artists of the time. The
village was refurbished at the
end of the 1980s and is now a
favourite place to visit for both
tourists and native *Barcelonins*.
 Resident artisans produce a
wide range of crafts including
hand-blown glass, ceramics,
sculpture, Toledo damascene
(*see p372*) and Catalan canvas
sandals. The Torres de Avila
(*see p185*), which form the
huge main entrance, have been
converted into one of the city's
most popular nightspots, with
an interior by designers Alfredo
Arribas and Javier Mariscal.
There are also shops, cafés,
bars and a children's theatre.

**View from Palau Nacional down-
hill towards the Plaça d'Espanya**

Plaça d'Espanya **❻**

Avinguda de la Gran Via de les Corts
Catalanes. **Map** 1 B1. Espanya.

T HE FOUNTAIN in the middle
of this road junction, the
site of public gallows until they
were transferred to Ciutadella
in 1715, is by Josep Maria Jujol,
one of Gaudí's followers. The
sculptures are by Miquel Blay.
The 1899 bullring to one side
is by Font i Carreras, but
Catalans have never taken to
bullfighting and the arena is
now used as a music venue.
 On the Montjuïc side of the
roundabout is the Avinguda
de la Reina Maria Cristina.
This is flanked by two 47-m
(154-ft) high brick campaniles
by Ramon Raventós, modelled
on the bell towers of St Mark's
in Venice and built as the
entrance way to the 1929
International Exhibition. The
avenue, lined with exhibition
buildings, leads up to Carles
Buigas's illuminated *Font
Màgica* (Magic Fountain) in
front of the Palau Nacional.

Castell de Montjuïc **❼**

Parc de Montjuïc. **Map** 1 B5. 93
329 86 13. Paral·lel, then funicular
& cable car (only Sat & public hols in
winter). **Museum** Nov–15 Mar:
9:30am–5:30pm Tue–Sun; 16 Mar–
Oct: 9:30am–8pm. 1 Jan, Good
Fri, 1 May, 25–26 Dec.

T HE WHOLE OF THE summit of
Montjuïc is occupied by
an 18th-century castle with
views over the port. The first
castle was built in 1640, but
was destroyed by Felipe V in
1705. The present fortress was
built for the Bourbon family.
During the War of Independence it was captured by
French troops. After the Civil
War it became a prison, where
the Catalan leader Lluís Companys was executed in 1940.
 The castle is now a military
museum with a display of
ancient weaponry.

Estadi Olímpic de Montjuïc **❽**

Passeig Olímpic 17–19. **Map** 1 A3.
 93 426 20 89. Espanya, Poble
Sec. 50, 51. Oct–May: 10am–
6pm daily; Jun–Sep: 10am– 8pm
daily. 1 Jan.

T HE NEO-CLASSICAL FAÇADE has
been preserved from the
original stadium, built by Pere
Domènech i Roura for the
1936 "Alternative" Olympics,
cancelled at the outbreak of
the Civil War. The arena was
refitted to a capacity of 70,000
for the 1992 Olympics.
 Nearby are the steel-and-
glass **Palau Sant Jordi** indoor
stadium, by Japanese architect
Arata Isozaki, and swimming
pools by Ricardo Bofill.

**Entrance to the refurbished 1992
Olympic Stadium**

FURTHER AFIELD

THE RADICAL redevelopment of Barcelona's outskirts in the late 1980s and early 1990s gave it a wealth of new buildings, parks and squares. The city's main station, Sants, was rebuilt and the neighbouring Parc de l'Espanya Industrial and Parc de Joan Miró were created, containing lakes, modern sculpture and futuristic architecture. The Parc de Clot, beyond the new national theatre *(see p184)*, is also of striking modern design. In the west of the city, where

the streets start to climb steeply, are the historic royal palace and monastery of Pedralbes, and Gaudí's famous Parc Güell, dating from 1910. Beyond is the Serra de Collserola, the city's closest rural area. Two funiculars provide an exciting way of reaching its heights, which offer superb views of the city. Tibidabo, the highest point, with a funfair, the Neo-Gothic church of the Sagrat Cor and a modern steel-and-glass communications tower, is a favourite place among *Barcelonins* for a day out.

Parc Güell gateway signs

SIGHTS AT A GLANCE

Museums and Galleries
Museu de la Ciència **8**
Museu del Futbol Club Barcelona **3**

Historic Buildings
Monestir de Pedralbes **5**
Palau Reial de Pedralbes **4**

Modern Buildings
Torre de Collserola **6**

Parks and Gardens
Parc de l'Espanya Industrial **2**
Parc Güell **9**
Parc de Joan Miró **1**

Theme Parks
Tibidabo **7**

0 metres   500
0 yards   500

KEY

▨	Street-by-Street map
▢	Built-up area
🚉	Railway station
🚟	Funicular railway station
▬	Motorway
▬	Major road
═	Minor road

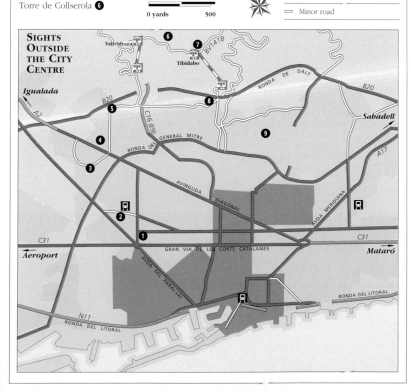

SIGHTS OUTSIDE THE CITY CENTRE

Dona i Ocell (1983) by Joan Miró
in the Parc de Joan Miró

Parc de Joan Miró ❶

Carrer d'Aragó 1. 🚇 *Tarragona.*

BARCELONA'S 19th-century
slaughterhouse *(escorxa-
dor)* was transformed in the
1980s into this unusual park,
hence its alternative name, Parc
de l'Escorxador.

It is constructed on two levels,
the lower of which is devoted
to football pitches interspersed
with landscaped sections of
palms, pines, eucalyptus trees
and flowers. The upper level is
completely paved and is dominated by a magnificent 1983
sculpture by the Catalan artist
Joan Miró *(see p168)* entitled
Dona i Ocell (Woman and
Bird). Standing 22 m (72 ft)
high in the middle of a pool,
its surface is coated with colourful pieces of glazed tile.

Parc de l'Espanya Industrial ❷

Plaça de Joan Peiró. 🚇 *Sants-Estació.*

THIS MODERN PARK, designed
by the Basque architect
Luis Peña Ganchegui, owes its
name to the textile mill that
used to stand on the 5-hectare
(12-acre) site.

Laid out in 1986 as part of
Barcelona's policy to provide
more open spaces within the
city, the park has canals and a
rowing lake – with a Classical
statue of Neptune at its centre.
Tiers of steps rise around the
lake like an amphitheatre and
on one side a row of ten futuristic watchtowers dominates the
entire area. Their only function
is to serve as public viewing
platforms and lamp standards.

Six contemporary sculptors
are represented in the park,
among them Andrés Nagel,
whose huge metal dragon incorporates a children's slide.

Museu del Futbol Club Barcelona ❸

Avda de Aristides Maillol. 📞 *93 496
36 00.* 🚇 *Maria Cristina, Collblanc.*
🕐 *10am–6:30pm Mon–Sat, 10am–
2pm Sun & public hols.* ⬤ *1 & 6 Jan,
24 Sep, 25 & 26 Dec.* 📷 ♿
🌐 *www.fcbarcelona.com*

CAMP NOU, Europe's largest
football stadium, is home
to the city's famous football
club, Barcelona FC (Barça, as it
is known locally). Founded in
1899, it is one of the world's
richest soccer clubs, and has
more than 100,000 members.

The stadium is a magnificent,
sweeping structure, built in 1957

Line of watchtowers in the Parc
de l'Espanya Industrial

to a design by Francesc Mitjans.
An extension was added in
1982 and it can now comfort-
ably seat 100,000 fans.

The club's museum, which
displays club memorabilia and
trophies on two floors, and has
a souvenir shop, is one of the
most popular in Barcelona.
There are also paintings and
sculptures of famous club
footballers commissioned for
the Blau-grana Biennial, an
exhibition held in celebration
of the club in 1985 and 1987.
Blau-grana (blue-burgundy)
are the colours of Barça's strip.
The club's flags were used as
an expression of local nationalist feelings during the Franco
dictatorship, when the Catalan
flag was banned.

As well as hosting its own
high-profile matches (mainly
at weekends), Camp Nou also
accommodates affiliated local
soccer clubs and promotes a
number of other sports in its
sports centre, ice rink and
mini-stadium.

View across Camp Nou stadium, prestigious home of the Futbol Club Barcelona

Palau Reial de Pedralbes ❹

Avinguda Diagonal 686. ⓜ *Palau Reial.* ⬤ *to the public.* **Museu de Ceràmica & Museu de Arts Decoratives** 🛈 *93 280 50 24.* ◖ *10am–6pm Tue–Sat, 10am–3pm Sun & public hols.* ⬤ *1 Jan, 1 May, 24 Jun, 25 & 26 Dec.* ♿ ⛔ 📷 *by appt*

T
HE PALACE OF PEDRALBES was once the main house on the estate of Count Eusebi Güell. In 1919 he offered it to the Spanish royal family. The first visit was from Alfonso XIII in 1926, before which the interior was refurbished and a new throne, supported by golden lions, was created for him.

Two fascinating museums and the gardens are open to the public. The Museu de Arts Decoratives, opened in 1937, displays period furniture from other great houses in the city and fine household items from the Middle Ages to the present. A genealogical tree traces the 500-year dynasty of the count-kings of Barcelona.

The palace also houses the Museu de Ceràmica, which has displays of historic Catalan and Moorish pottery and modern ceramics, including works by Miró and Picasso *(see p148).*

The palace gardens are well laid out with small ponds and paths. Just behind the gardens, in Avinguda de Pedralbes, is the entrance to the original Güell estate. It is guarded by a black wrought-iron gate, its top forged into a great, open-jawed dragon, and two gate houses, all by Gaudí *(see pp136–7).*

Madonna of Humility, **Monestir de Santa Maria de Pedralbes**

Monestir de Santa Maria de Pedralbes ❺

Carrer de Montevideo 14. **Monastery** ⬤ *to the public.* **Thyssen-Bornemisza Collection** *Baixada del Monestir 9.* 🛈 *93 203 92 82.* ⓜ *Reina Elisenda.* ◖ *10am–2pm Tue–Sun.* ⬤ *public hols.* ♿ ⛔ *not 1st floor.*

A
PPROACHED through an arch in its walls, the monastery of Pedralbes still has the air of a living enclosed community. This is heightened by its furnished cells, kitchens, infirmary and refectory. But the nuns of the Order of St Clare

moved to an adjoining building in 1983. The monastery was founded in 1326 by Elisenda de Montcada de Piños, fourth wife of Jaime II of Catalonia and Aragón. Her tomb lies between the church and the cloister. On the church side her effigy is dressed in royal robes; on the other as a nun.

The most important room in the monastery is the Capella (chapel) de Sant Miquel, with murals of the *Passion* and the *Life of the Virgin*, both painted by Ferrer Bassa in 1346, when Elisenda's niece, Francesca Saportella, was abbess.

In 1989, some 60 paintings forming part of the Thyssen-Bornemisza Collection (most of which is in Madrid – *see pp278–9*) were donated to the monastery. They now hang in the former dormitory and one of Queen Elisenda's rooms and are mainly religious in theme. The collection is strong in Italian and Spanish works, including examples by Fra Angelico, Tiepolo, Canaletto, Velázquez and Zurbarán.

Torre de Collserola ❻

Carretera de Vallvidrera al Tibidabo. 🛈 *93 406 93 54.* ⓜ *Peu de Funicular, then Funicular de Vallvidrera & bus 211.* ◖ *11am–2:30 & 3:30– 6pm (7 or 8pm summer) Wed–Sun.* ⬤ *1 & 6 Jan, 25 Dec.* ♿ ⛔

I
N A CITY that enjoys thrills, the ultimate ride is offered by the communications tower near Tibidabo mountain *(see p174).* A glass-sided lift takes less than two minutes to reach the top of this 288-m (944-ft) tall structure standing on the summit of a 445-m (1,460-ft) hill – not a pleasant experience for those who fear heights.

The tower was designed by English architect Norman Foster for the 1992 Olympic Games. Needle-like in form, it is a tubular steel mast on a concrete pillar. There are 13 levels. The top one has an observatory with a powerful telescope, and a public viewing platform with a 360° view encompassing Barcelona, the sea and the mountain chain on which Tibidabo sits.

BARCELONA V REAL MADRID

FC Barcelona

Més que un club is the motto of Barcelona FC: "More than a club". More than anything else it has been a symbol of the struggle of Catalan nationalism against the central government in Madrid. To fail to win the league is one thing. To come in behind Real Madrid is a complete disaster. Each season the big question is which of the two teams will win the title. Under the Franco regime in a memorable episode in 1941, Barça won 3–0 at home. At the return match in Madrid, the crowd was so hostile that the police and referee "advised" Barça to prevent trouble. Demoralized by the intimidation, they lost 11–1. Loyalty is paramount: one Barça player who left to join Real Madrid received death threats.

Real Madrid

Merry-go-round, Tibidabo

Tibidabo **7**

Plaça del Tibidabo 3–4. **C** 93 211 79 42. ✪ Avda Tibidabo, then Tramvia Blau & Funicular. **Amusement Park** ☐ variable – phone ahead for times. ● Oct–Apr: Mon–Fri. ♿ **Temple del Cor** **C** 93 417 56 86. ☐ 10am–2pm, 3–7pm daily. ♿

T HE HEIGHTS OF TIBIDABO are reached by the Tramvia Blau (Blue Tram), Barcelona's one last surviving tram, and a funicular railway. The name, inspired by Tibidabo's views of the city, comes from the Latin *tibi dabo* (I shall give you) – a reference to the Temptation of Christ when Satan took him up a mountain and offered him the world spread at his feet.

The hugely popular Parc d'Atraccions (*see p185*) first opened in 1908. The rides were completely renovated in the 1980s. While the old ones retain their charm, the newer ones provide the latest in vertiginous experiences. Their hilltop location at 517 m (1,696 ft) adds to the thrill. Also in the park is the Museu d'Automates, displaying automated toys, juke boxes and gaming machines.

Tibidabo is crowned by the Temple Expiatori del Sagrat Cor (Church of the Sacred Heart), built with religious zeal but little taste by Enric Sagnier between 1902 and 1911. A lift takes you up to the feet of an enormous figure of Christ.

Just a short bus ride away is another viewpoint worth visiting – the Torre de Collserola (*see p173*).

Museu de la Ciència **8**

Carrer Teodor Roviralta 55. **C** 93 212 60 50. ✪ Avinguda del Tibidabo, then Tramvia Blau. ☐ 10am–8pm Tue–Sun. ● public hols. ♿ (free first Sun of every month). ♿

T HE CITY'S science museum provides some excellent hands-on experiences. Here you can test your physical abilities and learn about world ecology. Floors are devoted to sound and light. There is a weather station, a planetarium staging 35-minute shows, and outside is a full-sized submarine, which you can enter through holes cut in the hull.

Parc Güell **9**

Carrer d'Olot. **C** 93 424 38 09. Ⓜ Lesseps. ☐ summer 10am–9pm daily, winter 10am–6pm daily. ♿ **Casa-Museu Gaudí** **C** 93 219 38 11. ☐ Apr–Sep: 10am–8pm daily; Oct–Mar: 10am–6pm daily. ● 1 Jan. ♿

D ESIGNATED a World Heritage Site by UNESCO, the Parc Güell is Antoni Gaudí's

(*see pp136–7*) most colourful creation. He was commissioned in the 1890s by Count Eusebi Güell to design a garden city on 20 hectares (50 acres) of the family estate. Little of the grand design for decorative public buildings and 60 houses among landscaped gardens became reality. What we see today was completed between 1910 and 1914, and the park opened in 1922.

Most atmospheric is the Room of a Hundred Columns, a cavernous covered hall of 84 crooked pillars, which is brightened by glass and ceramic mosaics. Above it, reached by a flight of steps flanked by ceramic animals, is the Gran Plaça Circular, an open space with a snaking balcony of coloured mosaics, said to have the longest bench in the world. It was executed by Josep Jujol, one of Gaudí's collaborators.

Two pavilions at the entry are by Gaudí, but the Casa-Museu Gaudí, a gingerbread-style house where Gaudí lived from 1906–26, was built by Francesc Berenguer. It contains drawings and furniture by Gaudí.

Mosaic-encrusted chimney by Gaudí at the entrance of the Parc Güell

BARCELONA STREET FINDER

T HE MAP REFERENCES given with the sights, shops and entertainment venues described in the Barcelona section of the guide refer to the street maps on the following pages. Map references are also given for Barcelona hotels (see *pp543–5)*, and for bars and restaurants *(see pp584–6)*. The schematic map below shows the area of Barcelona covered by the *Street Finder*. The symbols used for sights and other features and services are listed in the key at the foot of the page.

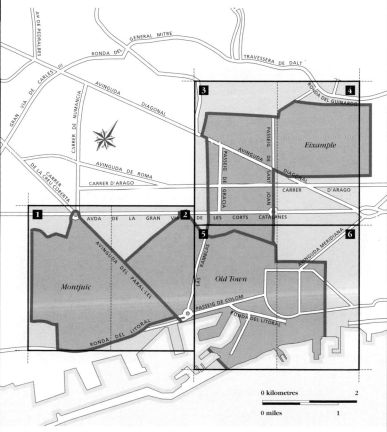

KEY TO STREET FINDER

■ Major sight	⬛ Golondrina boarding point	✚ Church
■ Place of interest	🚡 Cable car	⊠ Post office
■ Other building	🚞 Funicular railway station	= Railway line
⮂ Main railway station	🚕 Taxi rank	→ One-way street
🚇 Local (FF CC) railway station	P Parking	▬ Pedestrianized street
Ⓜ Metro station	ℹ Tourist information	
🚌 Main bus stop	✚ Hospital with casualty unit	**SCALE OF MAP PAGES**
🚍 Coach station	🚓 Police station	0 metres 250
		0 yards 250

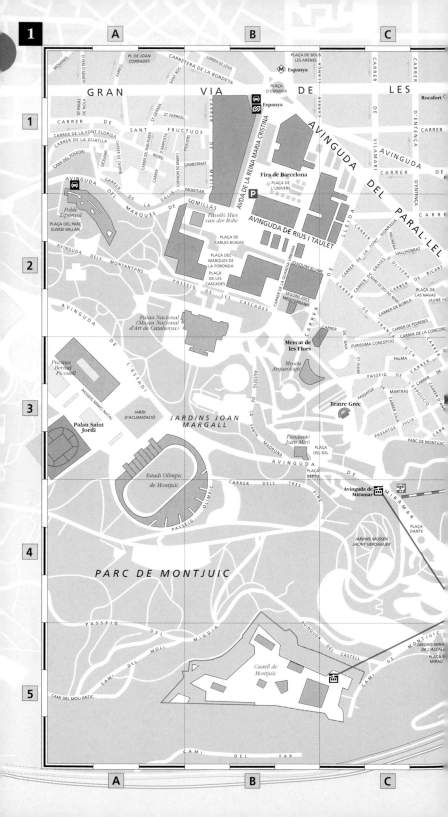

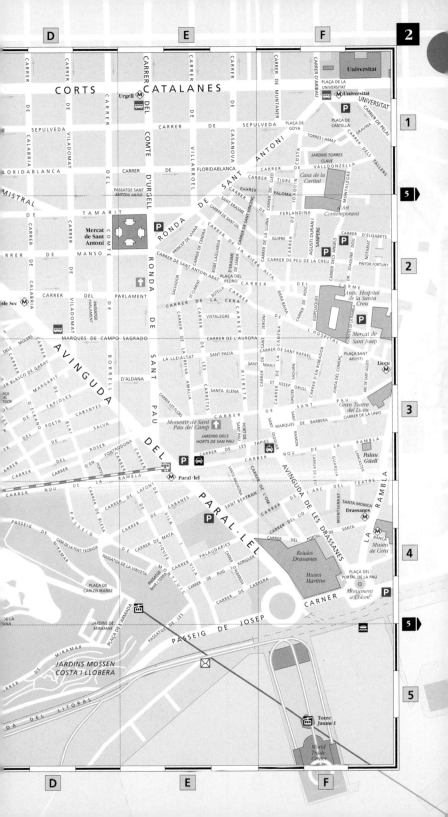

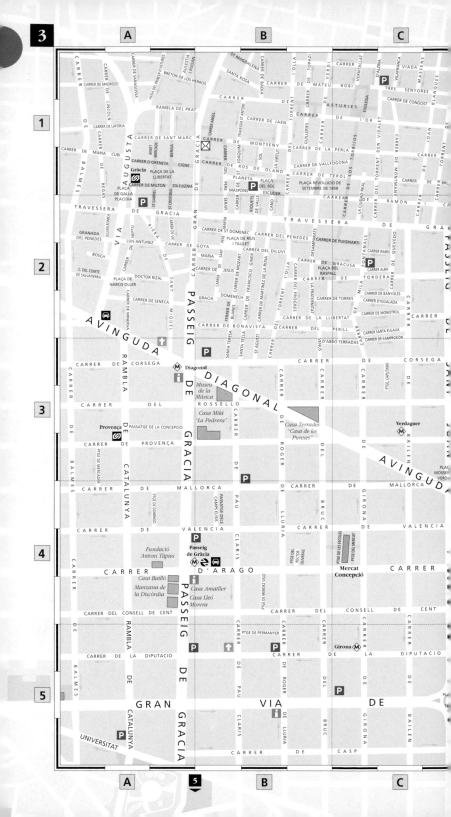

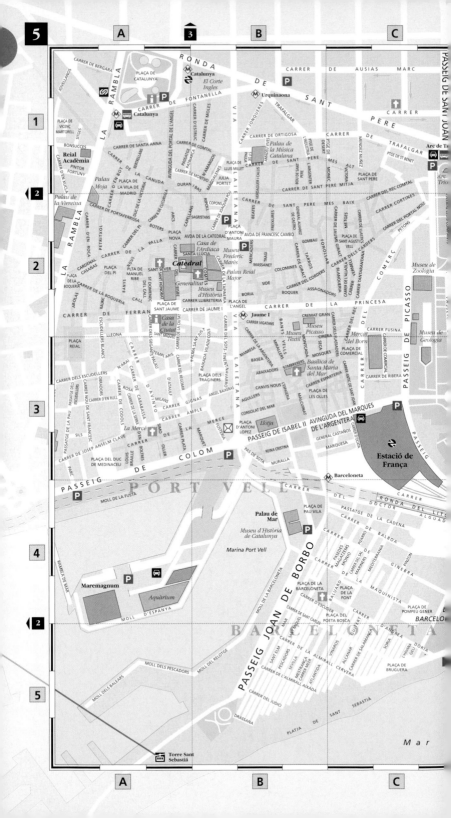

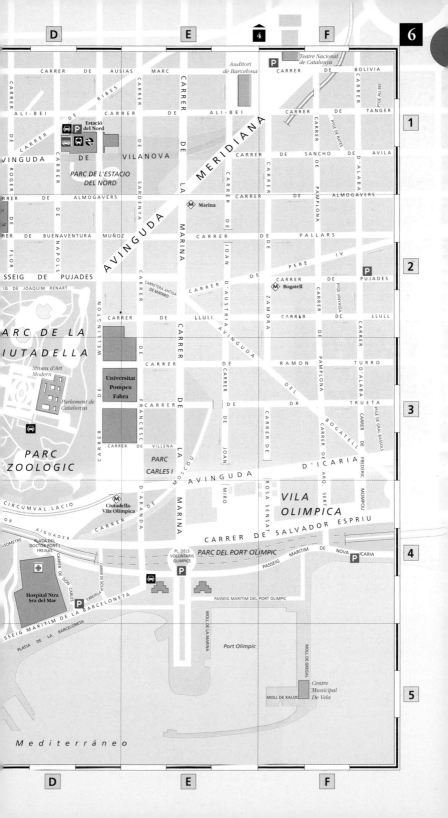

SHOPPING IN BARCELONA

A CITY WITH impeccable style, Barcelona is where you'll find the best in Catalan, Spanish and international design. For those in search of fashion, a good place to begin a tour of Barcelona is on the streets around the Passeig de Gràcia, which make up the most important shopping area, and where crowds browse among the well-known fashion and design stores. In this area there are also many interesting

Wall tile outside La Manual Alpargatera

old shops such as food stores, herbalists and pharmacies – some displaying beautiful Modernista frontages. For those who enjoy the hustle and bustle of small crowded streets, the Barri Gòtic, in the heart of the city, has something for everyone. Particularly interesting are the antique dealers and the shops specializing in traditional crafts such as carnival masks, ceramics and handmade espadrilles.

Some of the beautifully displayed confectionery at Escribà

FOOD AND DRINK

B ARCELONA's cake shops are sights in themselves and, with its displays of chocolate sculptures, no *pastisseria* is more enticing or spectacular than **Escribà**. Other food shops also have a great deal of character, none more so than **Colmado Quilez** in the Eixample. This wonderful old store stocks a huge range of hams, cheeses and preserves, in addition to a comprehensive selection of Spanish and foreign wines and spirits.

DEPARTMENT STORES AND GALERÍAS

T HE BRANCH of **El Corte Inglés**, Spain's largest department store chain, on Plaça Catalunya, is a Barcelona landmark and a handy place to find everything under one roof, including plug adaptors and services like key-cutting. Other branches are located around the city. Barcelona's hypermarkets also sell a wide

range of goods. As they are on the outskirts of the city – south along the Gran Vía towards the airport, and on the Avinguda Meridiana to the north – a car is the best way to reach them.

The fashion malls or *galerías*, built mostly during the affluent 1980s, are hugely popular. The branch of **Bulevard Rosa**, on the Passeig de Gràcia has a good choice of shops selling clothes and accessories. On the Avinguda Diagonal is **La Illa**, a large, lively shopping mall containing such popular chain stores as Mango as well as specialist retailers.

FASHION

I NTERNATIONAL fashion labels are found alongside clothes by young designers on and around the Passeig de Gràcia. **Adolfo Domínguez** stocks classically styled clothes for men and women; **Armand Basi** sells quality leisure and sportswear; and discount designer fashion is available at

Contribuciones. Many shops offer traditional, fine-quality tailoring skills and **Calzados E Solé**, which is situated in the Old Town, specializes in classic handmade shoes and boots.

SPECIALITY SHOPS

A WALK AROUND Barcelona can reveal a wonderful choice of shops selling traditional craft items and handmade goods that in most places have now been largely replaced by the production line. **La Caixa de Fang** has a good variety of Catalan and Spanish ceramics, among them traditional Catalan cooking pots and colourful tiles. **L'Estanc** has everything for the smoker, including the best Havana cigars. **La Manual Alpargatera** is an old shoe shop that specializes in Catalan-style espadrilles. These are handmade on the premises and come in all colours. The city's oldest shop, **Cereria Subirà** *(see pp140–41)*, sells candles in every imaginable form.

Menswear department in Adolfo Domínguez

DESIGN, ART AND ANTIQUES

IF YOU ARE interested in modern design, or just looking for gifts, you should pay a visit to **Vinçon**, the city's most famous design emporium. Situated on the Passeig de Gràcia, it has everything for the home, including beautiful fabrics and furniture. A must is **BD-Ediciones de Diseño**, which has the feel of an art gallery. Housed in a building designed by Domènech i Montaner, the shop has furniture based on designs by Gaudí and Charles Rennie Mackintosh, and sells wonderful contemporary furniture and accessories.

Most of the commercial art galleries and print shops are found on Carrer Consell de

Mouthwatering fruit stalls in La Boqueria market

The stylishly sparse display of furniture at Vinçon

Cent, in the Eixample, while the Barri Gòtic – especially the Carrer de la Palla and Carrer del Pi – is the best place to browse around small but fascinating antique shops. As well as fine furniture and old dolls, **L'Arca de l'Avia** sells antique silks and lace, all of which are set out in pretty displays.

BOOKS AND NEWSPAPERS

MOST CITY-CENTRE news kiosks stock English-language newspapers, but the most comprehensive stock of foreign newspapers and magazines is in **Crisol**, which also sells books, videos, CDs and photographic equipment.

MARKETS

NO ONE SHOULD miss the chance to look around **La Boqueria** on the Ramblas, one of the most spectacular food markets in Europe. There is an antiques market in the Plaça del Pi on the 1st and 3rd Friday and Saturday of each month. On Sunday mornings coin, stamp and book collectors set up stall in the Plaça Reial, and a craft market is held near the Sagrada Família. The city's traditional flea market, **Encants Vells**, takes place on Mondays, Wednesdays, Fridays and Saturdays. It offers a variety of jewellery and clothes.

ENTERTAINMENT IN BARCELONA

FEW CITIES CAN MATCH the vitality of Barcelona and nowhere is this more evident than in its live arts scene. The stunning Palau de la Música Catalana has keen and critical audiences. It regularly hosts some of the world's greatest classical musicians, including Montserrat Caballé and José Carreras, who are both *Barcelonins*. Equally dynamic are the many exciting theatre and dance companies performing all year round at numerous indoor and outdoor venues.

Busker in the Barri Gòtic

Modern music fans are well catered for by any number of rock venues and live jazz and salsa clubs, not to mention the buskers on the Ramblas or in the squares of the Barri Gòtic. A tradition of old Barcelona that continues to thrive is its brash, glittering music halls.

The magnificent interior of the Palau de la Música Catalana

ENTERTAINMENT GUIDES

THE MOST COMPLETE guide to what's going on each week in Barcelona is the *Guía del Ocio*, out every Thursday. It includes a cinema listings section. The Friday *El País* also has a very useful entertainments supplement.

SEASONS AND TICKETS

THEATRE and concert seasons for the main venues run from September to June, with limited programmes at other times. In general, the city's varied menu of entertainments reflects its rich multicultural artistic heritage. In summer the city hosts the Festival del Grec, a showcase of international music, theatre and dance, in open-air venues such as the Teatre Grec in Montjuïc and the Plaça del Rei in the Barri Gòtic. There is also a wide variety of concerts to choose from during the Festa de la Mercé *(see p153)* in

September. The simplest way to get theatre and concert tickets is to buy them at the box office of the relevant venue, although tickets for many theatres can also be bought from branches of the Caixa de Catalunya or La Caixa savings banks. Tickets for the Festival should be obtained from tourist offices.

CLASSICAL MUSIC

BARCELONA'S **Palau de la Música Catalana** *(see p149)* is one of the world's most beautiful concert halls. Also inspiring is the **Auditori de Barcelona**, opened in 1999 to give the city two modern halls for large-scale and chamber concers. It is now home to the Orquestra Simfònica de Barcelona, which performs there throughout the season.

Barcelona's status as the opera capital of Spain took something of a knock when the **Gran Teatre del Liceu** burned down in 1994, after welders working on the stage set fire to the curtain. Five

years later, however, following extensive reconstruction work, the opera house reopened in October 1999 with a performance of Puccini's *Turandot*. Today, the theatre's internationally respected opera season runs from September to July every year.

THEATRE AND DANCE

WORTH SEEING are Catalan contemporary theatre groups such as Els Comedians or La Cubana whose original style combines a thrilling mélange of theatre, music, mime and elements from traditional Mediterranean fiestas.

The **Mercat de les Flors** *(see p167)*, a converted former flower market in Montjuïc, is an exciting theatre presenting high-quality productions of classic and modern plays in Catalan. The new **Teatre Nacional de Catalunya**, near the Plaza de Toros Monumental, is another fine showcase for Catalan drama.

The Liceu is the main venue for international and domestic

Outrageous stage show at one of Barcelona's many clubs

The façade of the modern Teatre Nacional de Catalunya

classical ballet performances. There are many contemporary dance companies and regular performances are staged at the Mercat de les Flors in Montjuïc.

CAFÉS, BARS AND CLUBS

AMONG BARCELONA'S most famous modern sights are the high-tech design bars built in the 1980s. These include the **Mirablau**, looking out over the city, and the **Torres de Ávila**, in the Poble Espanyol *(see p169)*, which is the height of post-modernism. **Otto Zutz** has DJs. Less chic, but still fun, are the **Apolo**, and **La Paloma**, a dance hall complete with a 1904 interior where various music is played, including the paso doble.

The best-known champagne bar in the old city is **El Xampanyet**, while cocktails can be found at **Boadas**. **El Bosc de les Fades** is a fascinating café which is decorated in the style of a fairy's woodland grotto.

ROCK, JAZZ AND WORLD MUSIC

BIG NAMES like David Byrne and Paul McCartney have performed at **Zeleste**, while **La Boîte** has live folk and blues. In summer, festivals and open-air concerts are held around the city. Jazz venues include the **Harlem Jazz Club** and **Jamboree**, with live music, and salsa fans will enjoy **Antilla Barcelona**.

AMUSEMENT PARKS

IN SUMMER and at other times, Barcelona's giant amusement park on the summit of **Tibidabo** *(see p174)* is busy until late in the evening. A visit to Tibidabo is more enjoyable by tram, funicular or cable car.

SPORTS

THE UNDOUBTED KINGS of sport in this city are **FC Barcelona**. They boast the largest football stadium in Europe, the Nou Camp *(see p173)*, and have a fanatical following. Barcelona also has a high-ranking basketball team.

Packed house at the gigantic Nou Camp stadium

DIRECTORY

CLASSICAL MUSIC

Auditori de Barcelona
Carrer de Lepant 150.
Map 4 E1.
[93 247 93 00.
[w] www.autidori.com

Gran Teatre del Liceu de Barcelona
Las Ramblas 51–59.
Map 2 F3.
[93 485 99 13.
[w] www.liceubarcelona.com

Palau de la Música Catalana
Carrer de Sant Francesc de Paula 2.
Map 5 B1.
[93 295 72 00.
[w] www.palaumusica.org

THEATRE AND DANCE

Mercat de les Flors
Carrer de Lleida 59.
Map 1 B3.
[93 426 18 75.

Teatre Nacional de Catalunya
Pl de les Arts 1. **Map** 4 F5.
[93 306 57 00.

CAFÉS, BARS AND CLUBS

Apolo
Carrer Nou de la Rambla 113. **Map** 2 E3.
[93 441 40 01.

El Bosc de les Fades
Pasaje de Banca 7.
Map 2 F4.
[93 317 26 49.

Boadas
C/ dels Tallers 1. **Map** 5 A1.
[93 318 88 26.

Mirablau
Plaça Doctor Andreu.
[93 418 58 79.

Otto Zutz
Carrer de Lincoln 15.
Map 3 A1.
[93 238 07 22.

La Paloma
C/ Tigre 27. **Map** 2 F1.
[93 301 68 97.

Torres de Ávila
Poble Espanyol, Avinguda M de Comillas. **Map** 1 A1.
[93 424 93 09.

El Xampanyet
Carrer Montcada 22.
Map 5 B2.
[93 319 70 03.

ROCK, JAZZ AND WORLD MUSIC

Antilla Barcelona
Carrer de Aragó 141–3.
[93 451 21 51.

Jamboree
Plaça Reial 17.
Map 5 A3.
[93 319 17 89.

Harlem Jazz Club
Carrer de la Comtessa de Sobradiel 8.
[93 310 07 55.

Zeleste
Carrer de Almogàvers 122.
Map 6 F2.
[93 309 12 04.

AMUSEMENT PARKS

Tibidabo
[93 211 79 42.

SPORTS

FC Barcelona
Nou Camp, Avinguda Aristides Maillol.
[93 496 36 00.

EASTERN SPAIN

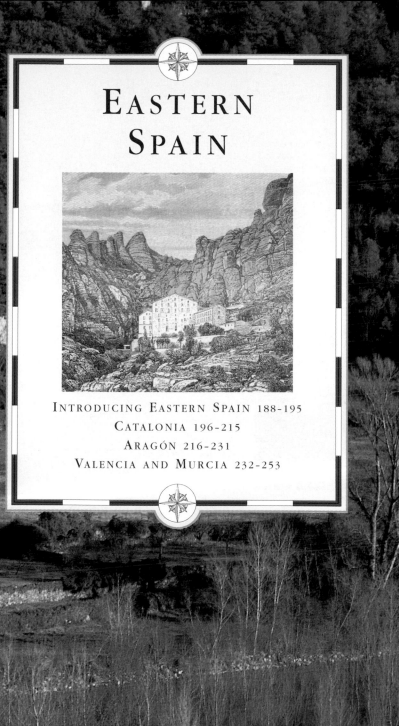

Introducing Eastern Spain

EASTERN SPAIN covers an extraordinary range of climates and landscapes, from the snowbound peaks of the Pyrenees in Aragón to the beaches of the Costa Blanca and Costa Cálida, popular for their winter warmth and sunshine. The region has a wealth of historical sights including ancient monasteries near Barcelona, magnificent Roman ruins in Tarragona, Mudéjar churches and towers in Aragón and the great cathedrals of Valencia and Murcia. Away from the busy coasts, the countryside is often attractive but little visited.

Ordesa National Park *(see pp222–3) in the Pyrenees has some of the most dramatic mountain scenery in Spain. It makes excellent walking country.*

Zaragoza *(see pp226–7) has many striking churches, especially the cathedral, the Basílica de Nuestra Señora del Pilar, and the Mudéjar-style Iglesia de la Magdalena.*

Zaragoza

ARAGÓN
(see pp216–31)

Teruel

Valencia *(see pp240–43) is Spain's third largest city. It has an old centre of narrow streets overlooked by venerable houses and monuments, such as El Miguelete, the cathedral's conspicuous bell tower. The city hosts a spectacular festival, Las Fallas, in March.*

**VALENC
AND MURC**
(see pp232–

Valenci

Murcia cathedral *(see p252), built in the 14th century, has a Baroque façade and belfry, and two ornate side chapels – one in late-Gothic style and the other Renaissance. In Murcia, you can also visit an elegant 19th-century gentlemen's club, the Casino.*

Alican

| 0 kilometres | 50 |
| 0 miles | 50 |

Murcia

◁ **The 12th-century monastery at Gerri de la Sal in Catalonia**

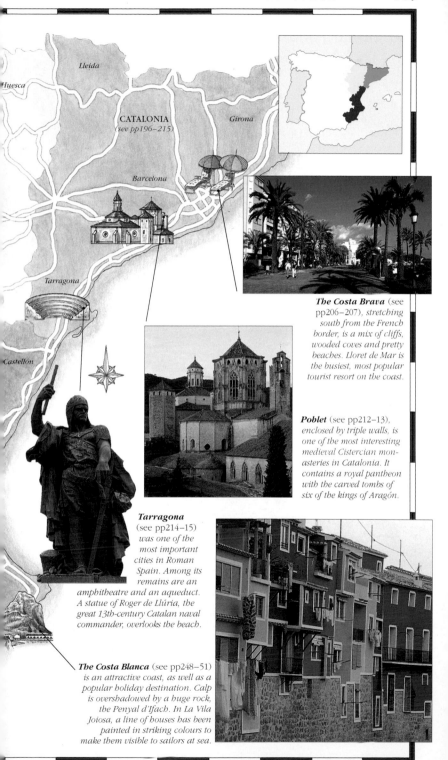

Lleida

Huesca

CATALONIA
(see pp196–215)

Girona

Barcelona

Tarragona

Castellón

The Costa Brava (see pp206–207), *stretching south from the French border, is a mix of cliffs, wooded coves and pretty beaches. Lloret de Mar is the busiest, most popular tourist resort on the coast.*

Poblet (see pp212–13), *enclosed by triple walls, is one of the most interesting medieval Cistercian monasteries in Catalonia. It contains a royal pantheon with the carved tombs of six of the kings of Aragón.*

Tarragona *(see pp214–15) was one of the most important cities in Roman Spain. Among its remains are an amphitheatre and an aqueduct. A statue of Roger de Llúria, the great 13th-century Catalan naval commander, overlooks the beach.*

The Costa Blanca (see pp248–51) *is an attractive coast, as well as a popular holiday destination. Calp is overshadowed by a huge rock, the Penyal d'Ifach. In La Vila Joiosa, a line of houses has been painted in striking colours to make them visible to sailors at sea.*

Regional Food: Eastern Spain

THE MEDITERRANEAN CUISINE of the east coast has been enriched by centuries of foreign influence, from the Romans and the Moors especially. Olives, rice, oranges, almonds and saffron are combined with produce from the sea and the mountains. The varied cooking of Catalonia embraces sweet and savoury combinations, fish stews, snails and several classic sauces, like spicy *romesco* made from red peppers, tomatoes and chillies. High-quality fruit and vegetables, such as ñora peppers, grow on the fertile coastal plains of Valencia and Murcia. Paella is the best known of the many rice dishes of these two regions. The cold, dry, mountain air of Aragón is ideal for curing hams.

Ñora peppers

Amanida *is a Catalan salad that combines vegetables with cured meat or cheese, or some kind of fish or shellfish.*

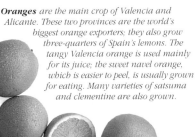

Oranges *are the main crop of Valencia and Alicante. These two provinces are the world's biggest orange exporters; they also grow three-quarters of Spain's lemons. The tangy Valencia orange is used mainly for its juice; the sweet navel orange, which is easier to peel, is usually grown for eating. Many varieties of satsuma and clementine are also grown.*

Parrillada de mariscos *is an assortment of shellfish grilled on a barbecue and served with allioli (garlic mayonnaise).*

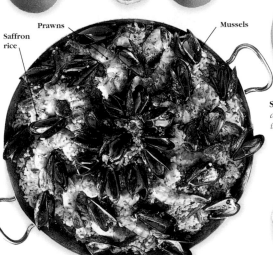

Prawns

Saffron rice

Mussels

Suquet, *one of the famous fish and shellfish stews of Catalonia, is made with saffron, wine, tomatoes and potatoes.*

Paella, *a Valencian rice dish known the world over, is cooked in a large, shallow, two-handled pan, traditionally over an open fire. Short-grain Spanish rice, flavoured and perfumed with saffron, is simmered with a variety of colourful ingredients: seafood, chicken or rabbit; tomatoes, herbs and fresh and dried beans.*

Fideus a la cassola *is a dish of fideus (a kind of noodle) with red peppers, pork chops or fillet, and sausages.*

Butifarra amb mongetes *is a traditional Catalan dish of grilled black sausage with dried white beans.*

Cochifrito, *a simple peasant dish from Aragón, is prepared from lamb fried with lemon, garlic and paprika.*

Pollo al ajillo *is chicken grilled with garlic. It is served with a white wine or sherry sauce made with the juices of the chicken.*

Pastel de carne, *a Murcian pie of Middle Eastern origin, consists of minced meat and chopped boiled eggs in a puff pastry case.*

Llagosta i pollastre *is a typical Catalan combination of lobster with chicken in a tomato and hazelnut sauce.*

Crema catalana *is a rich egg custard with a golden brown layer of grilled sugar on top. It is served very cold.*

Orange
Cherry
Apple
Pear
Pumpkin

Candied fruits (frutas escarchadas) *are a popular way of preserving the abundant produce of the region. In Aragón they are often chocolate coated.*

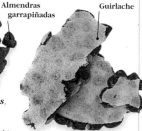

Almendras garrapiñadas
Guirlache

Almond sweets, *like almendras garrapiñadas (almonds coated in a crunchy sugar) and* guirlache *(containing toasted almonds), were introduced to Spain by the Moors. Turrón comes in two main varieties: one white and hard and studded with whole nuts; the other made from a soft paste of ground almonds.*

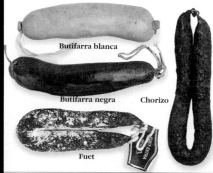

Butifarra blanca
Butifarra negra
Chorizo
Fuet

SAUSAGES

Catalan sausages, especially those from the mountain town of Vic, are renowned. The white *butifarra* sausage contains pork, tripe and pine nuts, while the black variety uses blood, pork belly and spices. Both can be grilled or served with beans. The region produces many types of cured sausage, such as the firm, finely textured *llangonisseta*, and the long, dry *fuet*. The coarser, scarlet-coloured chorizo, particularly beloved of Aragón and Murcia, contains paprika, and can be sliced finely and eaten with bread, perhaps as a tapa, or served in stew or soup.

Wines of Eastern Spain

SPAIN'S EASTERN SEABOARD offers a wide spread of wines of different styles. Catalonia deserves pride of place, and here the most important region is Penedès, home of *cava* (traditional-method sparkling wine) and some high quality still wine. In Aragón, Cariñena reds can be good, and Somontano, in the Pyrenees, has fine, international-style varietals. Valencia and Murcia provide large quantities of easy-drinking reds, whites and *rosados* (rosés). Most notable among these are the rosés of Utiel-Requena, the Valencian Moscatels and the strong, full-bodied reds made in Jumilla.

Cabernet Sauvignon vines

Monastery of Poblet and Las Murallas vineyards in Catalonia

Somontano has had remarkable success because of the COVISA company's cultivation of international grape varieties such as Chardonnay and Pinot Noir.

0 kilometres   100

0 miles   50

KEY FACTS ABOUT WINES OF EASTERN SPAIN

Location and Climate

The climate of Eastern Spain varies mainly with altitude – low-lying parts are hot and dry; it also gets hotter the further south you go. The wine regions of Catalonia have a Mediterranean climate along the coast, which becomes drier futher inland. The middle Penedès is a favoured location with a range of climates which suits many grape varieties. Somontano has a cooler, altitude-tempered climate. Valencia and Murcia can be, in contrast, unrelentingly hot.

Grape Varieties

The most common native red grape varieties planted in much of Eastern Spain are Garnacha, Tempranillo – which is called Ull de Llebre in Catalonia – Monastrell and Cariñena. Bobal makes both reds and, to a greater extent, rosés in Utiel-Requena. For whites, Catalonia has Parellada, Macabeo and

Xarel·lo (the trio most commonly used for *cava*), while in Valencia, Merseguera and Moscatel predominate. In the regions furthest to the southeast, Airén and Pedro Ximénez are sometimes found. French grape varieties, such as Chardonnay, Merlot, Cabernet Sauvignon and Sauvignon Blanc, flourish in the regions of Penedès, Costers del Segre and Somontano.

Good Producers

Somontano: COVISA (Viñas del Vero), Viñedos del Altoaragón. ***Alella:*** Marqués de Alella, Parxet. ***Penedès:*** Codorníu, Conde de Caralt, Freixenet, Juvé y Camps, Masía Bach, Mont-Marçal, René Barbier, Miguel Torres. ***Costers del Segre:*** Castell del Remei, Raimat. ***Priorato:*** Cellers Scala Dei, Masía Barril. ***Valencia:*** Vicente Gandía. ***Utiel-Requena:*** C. Augusto Egli. ***Alicante:*** Gutiérrez de la Vega. ***Jumilla:*** Asensio Carcelén (Sol y Luna), Bodegas Vitivino.

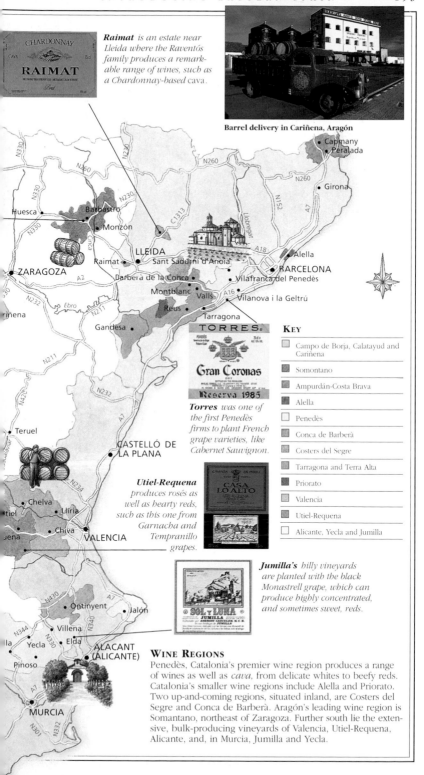

Raimat is an estate near Lleida where the Raventós family produces a remarkable range of wines, such as a Chardonnay-based cava.

Barrel delivery in Cariñena, Aragón

Torres was one of the first Penedès firms to plant French grape varieties, like Cabernet Sauvignon.

Utiel-Requena produces rosés as well as hearty reds, such as this one from Garnacha and Tempranillo grapes.

Jumilla's hilly vineyards are planted with the black Monastrell grape, which can produce highly concentrated, and sometimes sweet, reds.

KEY

- Campo de Borja, Calatayud and Cariñena
- Somontano
- Ampurdán-Costa Brava
- Alella
- Penedès
- Conca de Barberà
- Costers del Segre
- Tarragona and Terra Alta
- Priorato
- Valencia
- Utiel-Requena
- Alicante, Yecla and Jumilla

WINE REGIONS

Penedès, Catalonia's premier wine region produces a range of wines as well as *cava*, from delicate whites to beefy reds. Catalonia's smaller wine regions include Alella and Priorato. Two up-and-coming regions, situated inland, are Costers del Segre and Conca de Barberà. Aragón's leading wine region is Somantano, northeast of Zaragoza. Further south lie the extensive, bulk-producing vineyards of Valencia, Utiel-Requena, Alicante, and, in Murcia, Jumilla and Yecla.

Flowers of the Matorral

Yellow bee orchid

THE MATORRAL, a scrubland rich in wild flowers, is the distinctive landscape of Spain's eastern Mediterranean coast. It is the result of centuries of woodland clearance, during which the native holm oak was felled for timber and to provide land for grazing and cultivation. Many colourful plants have adapted to the extremes of climate here. Most flower in spring, when hillsides are daubed with pink and white cistuses and yellow broom, and the air is perfumed by aromatic herbs such as rosemary, lavender and thyme. Buzzing insects feed on the abundance of nectar and pollen.

Spanish broom is a small bush with yellow flowers on slender branches. The black seed pods split when dry, scattering the seeds on the ground.

The century plant's flower stalk can reach 10 m (32 ft).

Jerusalem sage, *an attractive shrub which is often grown in gardens, has tall stems surrounded by bunches of showy yellow flowers. Its leaves are greyish-white and woolly.*

Aleppo pine   Rosemary

Rose garlic *has round clusters of violet or pink flowers at the end of a single stalk. It survives the summer as the bulb familiar to all cooks.*

FOREIGN INVADERS

Several plants from the New World have managed to colonize the bare ground of the *matorral*. The prickly pear, thought to have been brought back by Christopher Columbus, produces a delicious fruit which can be picked only with thickly gloved hands. The rapidly growing century plant, a native of Mexico which has tough spiny leaves, sends up a tall flower shoot only when it is 10–15 years old, after which it dies.

Prickly pear in bloom

Flowering shoots of the century plant

Common thyme *is a low-growing aromatic herb which is widely cultivated for us in the kitchen.*

The mirror orchid, a small plant which grows on grassy sites, is easily distinguished from other orchids by the brilliant metallic blue patch inside the lip, fringed by brown hairs.

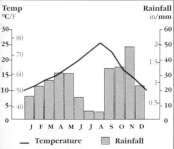

CLIMATE CHART
Most plants found in the *matorral* come into bloom in the warm, moist spring. The plants protect themselves from losing water during the dry summer heat with thick leaves or waxy secretions, or by storing moisture in bulbs or tubers.

Temp °C/F — Rainfall in/mm
— Temperature ☐ Rainfall

J F M A M J J A S O N D

WILDLIFE OF THE MATORRAL

The animals which live in the *matorral* are most often seen early in the morning, before the temperature is high. Countless insects fly from flower to flower, providing a source of food for birds. Smaller mammals, such as mice and voles, are active only at night when it is cooler and there are few predators around.

Holm oaks are very common in Eastern Spain. The leaves are tough and rubbery to prevent water loss.

The strawberry tree is an evergreen shrub with glossy serrated leaves. Its edible strawberry-like fruit turns red when ripe.

Ladder snakes feed on small mammals, birds and insects. The young are identified by a black pattern like the rungs of a ladder, but adults are marked with two simple stripes.

Tree heather

Scorpions hide under rocks or wood by day. When disturbed, the tail is curled quickly over the body in a threatening gesture. The sting, lethal to small animals, can cause some irritation to humans.

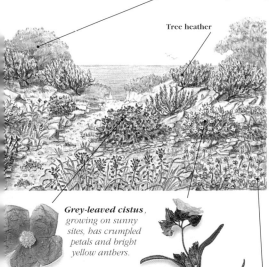

The Dartford warbler, a skulking bird which has dark plumage and a cocked tail, sings melodiously during its mating display. Males are more vividly coloured than females.

Grey-leaved cistus, growing on sunny sites, has crumpled petals and bright yellow anthers.

Narrow-leaved cistus exudes a sticky aromatic gum used in perfumes.

The swallow-tail butterfly is one of the most conspicuous of the great many insects living in the matorral. *Bees, ants and grasshoppers are also extremely common.*

Star clover is a low-growing annual whose fruit develops into a star-shaped seed head. Its flowers are often pale pink.

CATALONIA

··

LLEIDA · ANDORRA · GIRONA
BARCELONA PROVINCE · TARRAGONA

C ATALONIA *is a proud nation-within-a-nation which was once, under the count-kings of Barcelona-Aragón, one of the Mediterranean's great sea powers. It has its own semi-autonomous regional government and its own language, Catalan, which has all but replaced Spanish in place names and on road signs throughout the region.*

The Romans first set foot on the Iberian Peninsula at Empúries on Catalonia's Costa Brava ("wild coast"). They left behind them great monuments, especially in and around Tarragona, the capital of their vast province of Tarraconensis. Later, Barcelona emerged as the region's capital, economically and culturally important enough to rival Madrid.

In the 1960s the Costa Brava became one of Europe's first mass package-holiday destinations. Although resorts such as Lloret de Mar continue to draw the crowds, former fishing villages such as Cadaqués remain relatively unspoiled on this naturally attractive coast.

Inland, there is a rich artistic heritage to be explored. Catalonia has several spectacular monasteries, especially Montserrat, its spiritual heart, and Poblet. There are also many medieval towns, such as Montblanc, Besalú and Girona – which contain a wealth of monuments and museums.

In the countryside there is a lot to seek out, from the wetland wildlife of the Río Ebro delta to the vineyards of Penedès (where most of Spain's sparkling wine is made). In the high Pyrenees rare butterflies brighten remote mountain valleys, and little hidden villages encircle exquisite Romanesque churches.

Aigüestortes y E. Sant Maurici National Park in the central Pyrenees, in the province of Lleida

◁ **A fisherman inspects his nets in Cadaqués on the Costa Brava**

Exploring Catalonia

CATALONIA INCLUDES a long stretch of the Spanish Pyrenees, whose green, flower-filled valleys hide picturesque villages with Romanesque churches. The Parc Nacional d'Aigüestortes and Vall d'Aran are paradises for naturalists, while Baqueira-Beret offers skiers reliable snow. Sun-lovers can choose between the rugged Costa Brava or the long sandy stretches of the Costa Daurada. Tarragona is rich in Roman monuments. Inland are the monasteries of Poblet and Santes Creus and the well-known vineyards of Penedès.

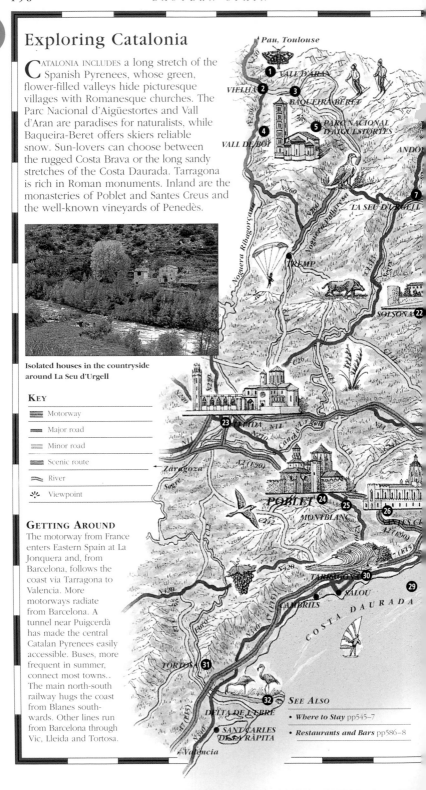

Isolated houses in the countryside around La Seu d'Urgell

KEY

- ▬ Motorway
- ▬ Major road
- ▬ Minor road
- ▬ Scenic route
- ∼ River
- ☼ Viewpoint

GETTING AROUND

The motorway from France enters Eastern Spain at La Jonquera and, from Barcelona, follows the coast via Tarragona to Valencia. More motorways radiate from Barcelona. A tunnel near Puigcerdà has made the central Catalan Pyrenees easily accessible. Buses, more frequent in summer, connect most towns.. The main north-south railway hugs the coast from Blanes southwards. Other lines run from Barcelona through Vic, Lleida and Tortosa.

SEE ALSO

- **Where to Stay** pp545–7
- **Restaurants and Bars** pp586–8

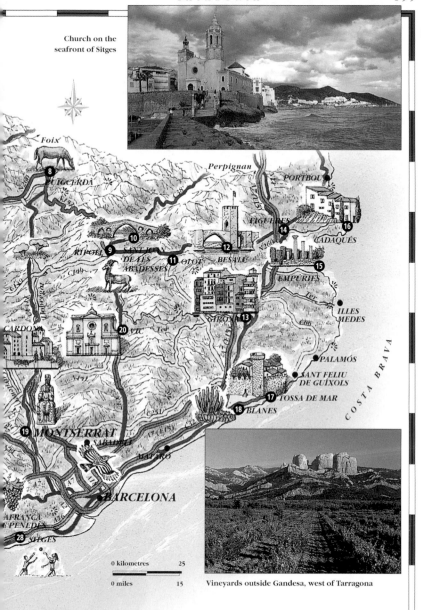

Church on the seafront of Sitges

Vineyards outside Gandesa, west of Tarragona

SIGHTS AT A GLANCE

The Vall d'Aran, surrounded by the snow-capped mountains of the Pyrenees

BUTTERFLIES OF THE VALL D'ARAN

A huge variety of butterflies and moths is found high in the mountains and valleys of the Pyrenees. In particular, the isolated Vall d'Aran is the home of several unique and rare subspecies. The best time of year to see the butterflies is between May and July.

Grizzled Skipper
(Pyrgus malvae)

Checkered Skipper
(Carterocephalus palaemon)

Clouded Apollo
(Parnassius mnemosyne)

Vall d'Aran ❶

Lleida N230. 🚌 Vielha. 🛈 Vielha 973 64 01 10.

THIS VALLEY OF VALLEYS – *aran* means valley – is a beautiful 600-sq km (230-sq mile) haven of forests and flower-filled meadows, surrounded by towering mountain peaks.

The Vall d'Aran was formed by the Riu Garona, which rises in the area and flows out to France as the Garonne. With no proper link to the outside world until 1924, when a road was built over the Bonaigua Pass, the valley was cut off from the rest of Spain for most of the winter. Snow still blocks the narrow pass from November to April, but today access is easy through the Túnel de Vielha from El Pont de Suert.

The fact that the Vall d'Aran faces north means that it has a climate similar to that found on the Atlantic coast. Many rare wild flowers and butterflies flourish in the perfect conditions created by the damp breezes and shady slopes. It is also a noted habitat for many species of narcissus.

Tiny villages have grown up beside the Riu Garona, often around Romanesque churches, notably at **Bossòst**, **Salardú**, **Escunhau** and **Arties**. The valley is also ideal for outdoor sports such as skiing and is popular with walkers.

Vielha ❷

Lleida. 🏘 2,700. 🚌 🛈 Carrer Sarriulera 10, 973 64 01 10. 🚍 Thu. 🎉 Fiesta de Vielha (8 Sep), Feria de Vielha (8 Oct).

NOW A MODERN ski resort, the capital of the Vall d'Aran preserves relics of its medieval past. The Romanesque church of **Sant Miquel** has an octagonal bell tower, a tall, pointed roof and a superb wooden 12th-century crucifix, the *Mig Aran Christ*. It once formed part of a larger carving, since lost, which represented the Descent from the Cross. The **Museu de la Vall d'Aran** is a museum devoted to Aranese history and folklore.

🏛 **Museu de la Vall d'Aran**
Carrer Major 26. 📞 973 64 18 15. 🕐 daily. ● public hols. 🈲 ♿

Mig Aran Christ (12th-century), Sant Miquel church, Vielha

Baqueira-Beret ❸

Lleida. 🚠 *100.* 🚌 🛈 *Baqueira-Beret, 973 63 90 00.* 🎪 *Romería de Nuestra Señora de Montgarri (2 Jul).*

THIS EXTENSIVE ski resort, one of the best in Spain, is popular with both the public and the Spanish royal family. There is reliable winter snow cover and a choice of over 40 pistes at altitudes from 1,520 m to 2,470 m (4,987 ft to 8,104 ft).

Baqueira and Beret were separate mountain villages before skiing became popular, but they have now merged to form a single resort. The Romans took full advantage of the thermal springs located here, which are nowadays appreciated by tired skiers.

Vall de Boí ❹

Lleida N230. 🚌 *La Pobla de Segur.* 🚌 *El Pont de Suert.* 🛈 *Barruera, 973 69 40 00.*

THIS SMALL VALLEY on the edge of the Parc Nacional d'Aigüestortes is dotted with tiny villages, many of which are built around magnificent Catalan Romanesque churches.

Dating from the 11th and 12th centuries, these churches are distinguished by their tall belfries, such as the **Església de Santa Eulàlia** at Erill-la-Vall, which has six floors.

The two churches at Taüll, **Sant Climent** *(see p20)* and **Santa Maria**, have superb frescoes. Between 1919 and 1923 the originals were taken for safekeeping to the Museu Nacional d'Art de Catalunya in Barcelona *(see p168)* and replicas now stand in their place. You can climb the towers of Sant Climent for superb views of the surrounding countryside.

Other churches in the area worth visiting include those at **Coll**, for its fine ironwork, **Barruera**, and **Durro**, which has another massive bell tower.

At the head of the valley is the hamlet of **Caldes de Boí**, popular for its thermal springs and ski facilities. It is also a good base for exploring the Parc Nacional d'Aigüestortes, the entrance to which is only 5 km (3 miles) from here.

The tall belfry of Sant Climent church at Taüll in the Vall de Boí

Parc Nacional d'Aigüestortes ❺

Lleida. 🚌 *La Pobla de Segur.* 🚌 *El Pont de Suert, La Pobla de Segur.* 🛈 *Barruera, 973 69 40 00.*

THE PRISTINE mountain scenery of Catalonia's only national park *(see pp26 -7)* is among the most spectacular to be seen in the Pyrenees.

Established in 1955, the park covers an area of 102 sq km (40 sq miles). Its full title is Parc Nacional d'Aigüestortes i Estany de Sant Maurici, named after the lake *(estany)* of Sant Maurici in the east and the Aigüestortes (literally, twisted waters) area in the west. The main village is the mountain settlement of Espot, on the park's eastern edge. Dotted around the park are waterfalls and the sparkling, clear waters of around 150 lakes and tarns which, in an earlier era, were scoured by glaciers to depths of up to 50 m (164 ft).

The finest scenery is around Sant Maurici lake, which lies beneath the twin shards of the Serra dels Encantats, (Mountains of the Enchanted). From here, there is a variety of walks, particularly along the string of lakes that lead north to the towering peaks of Agulles d'Amitges. To the south is the dramatic vista of Estany Negre, the highest and deepest tarn in the park.

Early summer in the lower valleys is marked by a mass of pink and red rhododendrons, while later in the year wild lilies bloom in the forests of fir, beech and silver birch.

The park is also home to a variety of wildlife. Chamois (also known as izards) live on the mountain screes and in the meadows, while beavers and otters can be spotted by the lakes. Golden eagles nest on mountain ledges, and grouse and capercaillie are found in the woods.

During the summer the park is popular with walkers, while in winter, the snow-covered mountains are ideal for cross-country skiing.

A crystal-clear stream, Parc Nacional d'Aigüestortes

Catalonia's national emblem

Catalan has now fully recovered from the ban it suffered under Franco's dictatorship and has supplanted Castilian (Spanish) as the language in everyday use all over Catalonia. Spoken by more than eight million people, it is a Romance language akin to the Provençal of France. Previously it was suppressed by Felipe V in 1717 and only officially resurfaced in the 19th century, when the Jocs Florals (medieval poetry contests) were revived during the rebirth of Catalan literature. A leading figure of the movement was the poet Jacint Verdaguer (1845–1902).

Andorra ❻

Principality of Andorra. 🏠 65,000. 🚌 Andorra la Vella. ❗ Calle Dr Vilanova, Andorra la Vella, 00 376 82 02 14. 🌐 www.andorra.ad

A NDORRA OCCUPIES 464 sq km (179 sq miles) of the Pyrenees between France and Spain. In 1993, it became fully independent and held its first ever democratic elections. Since 1278, it had been an autonomous feudal state under the jurisdiction of the Spanish bishop of La Seu d'Urgell and the French Count of Foix (a title adopted by the President of France). These are still the ceremonial joint heads of state.

Andorra's official language is Catalan, though French and Castilian are also spoken. The currency changed from the peseta to the Euro in 2002.

For many years Andorra has been a tax-free paradise for shoppers, reflected in the crowded shops of the capital **Andorra la Vella**. Les Escaldes (near the capital), as well as Sant Julià de Lòria and El Pas de la Casa (near the Spanish and French borders), have also become shopping centres.

Most visitors never see Andorra's rural charms, which match those of other parts of the Pyrenees. The region is excellent for walkers. One of the main routes leads to the **Cercle de Pessons**, a bowl of lakes in the east, and past Romanesque chapels such as **Sant Martí** at La Cortinada. In the north is the picturesque Sorteny valley where traditional farmhouses have been converted into snug restaurants.

La Seu d'Urgell ❼

Lleida. 🏠 13,000. 🚌 ❗ Avda Valles de Andorra 33, 973 35 15 11. 🚌 Tue & Sat. 🎪 Fiesta Mayor (Aug).

T HIS ANCIENT Pyrenean town was made a bishopric by the Visigoths in the 6th century. Feuds between the bishops of Urgell and the Counts of Foix over land ownership led to the emergence of Andorra in the 13th century.

The 12th-century **cathedral** has a much venerated Romanesque statue of Santa Maria d'Urgell. The **Museu Diocesà** contains medieval works of art and manuscripts, including a 10th-century copy of St Beatus of Liébana's *Commentary on the Apocalypse* (see p106).

🏛 Museu Diocesà
Plaça del Deganat. 📞 973 35 32 42. 🕐 daily. ● public hols. 🎟 ♿

Carving, La Seu d'Urgell cathedral

Puigcerdà ❽

Girona. 🏠 7,000. 🚌 🚌 ❗ Carrer Querol 1, 972 88 05 42. 🚌 Sun. 🎪 Fiesta del Lago (third Sun of Aug). 🌐 www.puigcerda.com

P UIG IS CATALAN for hill. Although Puigcerdà sits on a relatively small hill compared with the encircling mountains, which rise to 2,900 m (9,500

ft), it nevertheless has a fine view right down the beautiful Cerdanya valley, watered by the trout-filled Riu Segre.

Puigcerdà, very close to the French border, was founded in 1177 by Alfonso II as the capital of Cerdanya, which shares a past and its culture with the French Cerdagne. The Spanish enclave of **Llívia**, an attractive little town with a medieval pharmacy, lies 6 km 4 miles) inside France.

Cerdanya is the largest valley in the Pyrenees. At its edge is the nature reserve of **Cadí-Moixeró**, which has a population of alpine choughs.

Portal of Monestir de Santa Maria

Ripoll ❾

Girona. 🏠 11,000. 🚌 🚌 ❗ Plaça Abat Oliva, 972 70 23 51. 🚌 Sat. 🎪 Fiesta Mayor (11–12 May). 🌐 www.elripolles.com

O NCE A TINY mountain base from which raids against the Moors were made, Ripoll is now best known for the **Monestir de Santa Maria**, built in AD 888. The town has been called "the cradle of Catalonia" as the monastery was both the power base and cultural centre of Guifré el Pélos (Wilfred the Hairy), founder of the 500-year dynasty of the House of Barcelona. He is buried in the monastery.

In the later 12th century, the huge west portal gained a series of intricate carvings, which are perhaps the finest Romanesque carvings in Spain. They depict historical and biblical scenes. The two-storey cloister is the only other part of the original monastery to have survived wars and anti-clerical purges. The rest is a 19th-century reconstruction.

The medieval town of Besalú on the banks of the Riu Fluvià

Sant Joan de les Abadesses ⑩

Girona. 🚶 3,800. 🚌 🚺 Plaza de Abadia 9, 972 72 05 99. 🚍 Sun. 🎪 Fiesta Mayor (second week of Sep). 🖥 www.santjoandelesabadesses.com

A FINE, 12th-century Gothic bridge arches over the Riu Ter to this unassuming market town, whose main attraction is its **monastery**.

Founded in AD 885, it was a gift from Guifré, first count of Barcelona, to his daughter, the first abbess. The church is unadorned except for a superb wooden calvary, *The Descent from the Cross*. Made in 1150, it looks modern; part of it, a thief, was burnt in the Civil War and replaced with such skill that it is hard to tell which is new. The monastery's museum has Baroque and Renaissance altarpieces.

12th-century calvary, Sant Joan de les Abadesses monastery

Environs: To the north is **Camprodon**, a small town full of grand houses, and shops selling local produce. The region is especially noted for its *llonganisses* (sausages).

Olot ⑪

Girona. 🚶 28,000. 🚌 🚺 Bisbe Lorenzana 15, 972 26 01 41. 🚍 Mon. 🎪 Corpus Christi (Jun), Fiesta del Tura (8 Sep). 🖥 www.olot.org

T HIS SMALL MARKET TOWN is at the centre of a landscape pockmarked with the conical hills of extinct volcanoes. But it was an earthquake in 1474 which last disturbed the town, destroying its medieval past.

During the 18th century the town's textile industry spawned the "Olot School" of art: finished cotton fabrics were printed with drawings, and in 1783 the Public School of Drawing was founded.

Much of the school's work, which includes sculpted saints and paintings such as Joaquim Vayreda's *Les Falgueres*, is in the **Museu Comarcal de la Garrotxa**, housed in an 18th-century hospice. There are also pieces by Modernista sculptor Miquel Blay, whose damsels support the balcony at No. 38 Passeig Miquel Blay.

🏛 Museu Comarcal de la Garrotxa

Calle Hospici 8. 📞 972 27 91 30. 🕐 Wed–Mon. 🔴 1 Jan, 25 Dec. 🎫 🚻

Besalú ⑫

Girona. 🚶 2,000. 🚌 🚺 Plaça de la Llibertat 1, 972 59 12 40. 🚍 Tue. 🎪 Sant Vicenç (22 Jan), Fiesta Mayor (last weekend of Sep).

A MAGNIFICENT medieval town, with a striking approach across a fortified bridge over the Riu Fluvià, Besalú has two fine churches. These are the Romanesque **Sant Vicenç** and **Sant Pere**, the sole remnant of Besalú's Benedictine monastery. It was founded in AD 948, but pulled down in 1835 leaving a big, empty square.

In 1964 a **mikvah**, a ritual Jewish bath, was discovered by chance. It was built in 1264 and is one of only three of that period to survive in Europe. The tourist office has the keys to all the town's attractions.

To the south, the sky-blue lake of **Banyoles**, where the 1992 Olympic rowing contests were held, is ideal for picnics.

Sausage shop in the mountain town of Camprodon

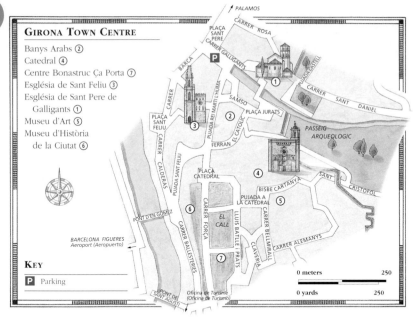

GIRONA TOWN CENTRE

Banys Arabs ②
Catedral ④
Centre Bonastruc Ça Porta ⑦
Església de Sant Feliu ③
Església de Sant Pere de
　Galligants ①
Museu d'Art ⑤
Museu d'Història
　de la Ciutat ⑥

KEY

P Parking

0 meters　　　　　250
0 yards　　　　　250

Girona ⑬

Girona. 🏛 75,000. ✈ 🚉 🚌 🛈
*Rambla de la Llibertat 1, 972 22 65
75.* 🏛 *Tue, Sat.* 🎭 *El Pedal (last fortnight of Sep), San Narciso (late Oct).*
🖥 *www.ajuntament.gi*

THIS HANDSOME TOWN puts
on its best face beside the
Riu Onyar, where tall, pastel-
coloured buildings rise above
the water. Behind them, in
the old town, the Rambla de
la Llibertat is lined with busy
shops and street cafés.
　The houses were built in the
19th century to replace sections of the city wall damaged
during a seven-month siege
by French troops in 1809. Most
of the rest of the ramparts, first
raised by the Romans, are still
intact and have been turned
into the **Passeig Arqueològic**
(Archaeological Walk), which
runs right around the city.
　The starting point of the
walk is on the north side of
the town, near the **Església
de Sant Pere de Galligants**
(St Peter of the Cock Crows).
The church now houses the
city's archaeological collection.
　From here a narrow street into the old part of town passes
through the north gate, where
huge Roman foundation stones
are still visible. They mark the
route of the Via Augusta, the
road which originally ran
from Tarragona to Rome. The
most popular place of devotion for the people of Girona
is the **Església de Sant Feliu**.
The church, begun in the
14th century, was built over
the tombs of St Felix and St
Narcissus, both patrons of the
city. Next to the high altar are
eight Roman sarcophagi
embedded in the apse wall.
　Despite their name, the
nearby **Banys Arabs** (Arab
Baths), lit by a fine octagonal
lantern, were built in the late
12th century, about 300 years
after the Moors had left.

🏛 Centre Bonastruc Ça Porta
Carrer de la Força 8. 📞 *972 21
67 61.* ◯ *daily.* ● *public hols* ♿
🖥 ♿ 🖥 *www.ajuntament.gi*
Amid the maze of alleyways
and steps in the old town is
the former, partially restored,
Jewish quarter of El Call. The
Centre Bonastruc Ça Porta
gives a history of Girona's
Jews, who were expelled in
the late 15th century.

⛪ Cathedral
The style of Girona Cathedral's
solid west face is pure Catalan
Baroque, but the rest of the
building is Gothic. The single
nave, built in 1416 by Guillem
Bofill, is the widest Gothic
span in Christendom. Behind
the altar is a marble throne
known as "Charlemagne's
Chair" after the Frankish king

Painted houses crowded along the bank of the Riu Onyar in Girona

whose troops took Girona in 785. In the chancel is a 14th-century jewel-encrusted silver and enamel altarpiece, the best example in Catalonia. Among the fine Romanesque paintings and statues in the cathedral's museum are a 10th-century illuminated copy of St Beatus of Liébana's *Commentary on the Apocalypse*, and a 14th-century statue of the Catalan king, Pere the Ceremonious.

The collection's most famous item is a tapestry, called *The Creation*, decorated with lively figures. The rich colours of this large 11th- to 12th-century work are well preserved.

Tapestry of *The Creation*

🏛 Museu d'Art

Pujada de la Catedral. **C** 972 20 95 36. 🕐 *Tue–Sun.* ● *1, 6 Jan, 25–26 Dec.* 🈲 ♿
Ⓦ www.ddgi.es/museu

This former episcopal palace is one of Catalonia's best art galleries, with works ranging from the Romanesque period to the 20th century. Items from churches destroyed through war or neglect give an idea of church interiors long ago. Highlights are 10th-century carvings, a silver-clad altar from the church at Sant Pere de Rodes and a 12th-century beam from Cruilles.

🏛 Museu d'Història de la Ciutat

Carrer de la Força 27. **C** 972 22 22 29. 🕐 *10am–2pm daily, 5–7pm Tue–Sat.* ● *1, 6 Jan, 25–26 Dec.*

The city's history museum is housed in an 18th-century former convent. Parts of the cemetery are preserved, including the recesses where the bodies of members of the Capuchin Order were placed while decomposing. The collection includes old *sardana* (*see p215*) instruments.

Figueres ⑭

Girona. 🏘 *35,000.* 🚆 🚌 ℹ *Plaça del Sol, 972 50 31 55.* 🚌 *Thu.* 🎉 *Santa Cruz (3 May), San Pedro (29 Jun).* Ⓦ www.figueres.org

FIGUERES is in the north of the Empordà (Ampurdán) region, the fertile plain that sweeps inland from the Gulf of Roses. Every Thursday, the market here fills with fruit and vegetables from the area.

The **Museu de Joguets** (Toy Museum) is housed on the top floor of the old Hotel de Paris, on the Rambla, Figueres' main street. Inside are exhibits from all over Catalonia. At the lower end of the Rambla is a statue of Narcís Monturiol i Estarriol (1819–85), claimed to be the inventor of the submarine.

A much better known son of the town is Salvador Dalí, who founded the **Teatro-Museo Dalí** in 1974. The most visited museum in Spain after the Prado, the galleries occupy Figueras's old main theatre. Its roof has an eye-catching glass dome. Not all the work shown is by Dalí, and none of his best-known works are here.

***Rainy Taxi*, a monument in the garden of the Teatro-Museu Dalí**

But the displays, including *Rainy Taxi* – a black Cadillac being sprayed by a fountain – are a monument to the man who, fittingly, is buried here.

🏛 Museu de Joguets

Calle Sant Pere 1. **C** 972 50 45 85. 🕐 *daily.* 🈲 ♿
🏛 Teatre-Museu Dalí

Plaça Gala-Salvador Dalí. **C** 972 67 75 05. 🕐 *Oct–Jun: Tue–Sun; Jul–Sep: daily.* ● *1 Jan, 25 Dec.* 🈲 📷 *by appt.*
Ⓦ www.salvador-dali.org

THE ART OF DALÍ

Salvador Dalí e Domènech was born in Figueres in 1904 and mounted his first exhibition at the age of 15. After studying at the Escuela de Bellas Artes in Madrid, and dabbling with Cubism, Futurism and Metaphysical painting, the young artist embraced Surrealism in 1929, becoming the movement's best-known painter. Never far from controversy, the self-publicist Dalí became famous for his hallucinatory images – such as *Woman-Animal Symbiosis* – which he described as "hand-painted dream photographs". Dalí's career also included writing and film-making, and established him as one of the 20th century's greatest artists. He died in his home town in 1989.

Ceiling fresco in the Wind Palace Room, Teatro-Museu Dalí

Empúries **⑮**

Girona. 🚌 L'Escala. 📞 972 77 02 08. ⏰ Oct–May: 10am–6pm daily; Jun–Sep & Easter: 10am–8pm daily. ⛔ 1 Jan, 25 Dec. 🎫 for ruins.

THE EXTENSIVE ruins of the Greco-Roman town of Empúries (Ampurias) occupy an imposing site beside the sea. Three separate settlements were built between the 7th and 3rd centuries BC: the old town (known to archaeologists as Palaiapolis); the new town (Neapolis), and the Roman town, which was founded by Julius Caesar in 49 BC.

The **old town** (Palaiapolis) was founded by the Greeks in 600 BC as a trading port. Built on what was then a small offshore island, it is now the site of the tiny walled hamlet of Sant Martí de Empúries.

Around 550 BC this was replaced by a larger colony which the Greeks named Emporion ("trading place"). In 218 BC, the Romans landed at Empúries and built a city next to the new town. From here they began their subjugation of the peninsula *(see p46)*.

Excavations in the **new town** have uncovered several temples. On the main street are the remains of the agora (meeting place), and floor mosaics. A museum nearby exhibits some finds from the site; the best are now in the Museu Arqueològic of Barcelona *(see p168)*. The extensive **Roman town** was located on the hill behind the museum. So far excavations have revealed the ruins of two villas and a forum.

An excavated Roman pillar in the ruins of Empúries

Looking south along the Costa Brava from Tossa de Mar

Cadaqués **⑯**

Girona. 🏘 2,000. 🚌 ℹ️ Carrer Cotxe 2, 972 25 83 15. 🚐 Mon. 🎭 Santa Esperanza (18 Dec), Fiesta Mayor de Verano (Sep).

THIS PRETTY, whitewashed resort, overlooked by the large, Baroque **Església de Santa Maria**, is the most easterly in the country. In the 1960s it was dubbed "Spain's St Tropez", largely because of the young crowd which sought out Salvador Dalí in the nearby unspoiled creek of Portlligat.

The **Centre d'Art Perrot-Moore** contains fine examples of Dalí's work, some excellent Picassos, and a room dedicated to contemporary artists.

🏛 **Centre d'Art Perrot-Moore**
Carrer Vigilant 1. 📞 972 25 82 31. ⏰ Tue–Sun. ⛔ Nov–Apr. 🎫 ♿

Tossa de Mar **⑰**

Girona. 🏘 4,000. 🚌 ℹ️ Avinguda Pelegri 25, 972 34 01 08. 🚐 Thu. 🎭 Fiesta de Verano (29 Jun–2 Jul), Fiesta de Invierno (22 Jan). 🌐 www.tossademar.com

AT THE END of a corniche, the Roman town of Turissa is one of the prettiest along the Costa Brava. Above the new town is the **Vila Vella** (old town), a protected national monument. The medieval walls, with three towers, enclose fishermen's cottages, a 14th-century church and bars.

Within the old town is the **Museu Municipal**. This collection of local archaeological finds and modern art includes *The Flying Violinist*, by the Russian artist Marc Chagall.

🏛 **Museu Municipal**
Plaça Roig y Soler 1. 📞 972 34 07 09. ⏰ Tue–Sun (call to check). 🎫

Blanes **⑱**

Girona. 🏘 30,000. 🚌 🚉 ℹ️ Plaça de Catalunya 21, 972 33 03 48. 🚐 Mon. 🎭 El Bilar (6 Apr), Sta Ana (late Jul). 🌐 www.blanes.net

THE WORKING PORT of Blanes has one of the longest beaches on the Costa Brava, but the highlight of the town is the **Jardí Botànic Mar i Murtra**. These fine gardens, designed by the German Karl Faust in 1928, are spectacularly sited above cliffs. There are 7,000 species of Mediterranean and tropical plants.

✈ **Jardí Botànic Mar i Murtra**
Passeig Karl Faust 10. 📞 972 33 08 26. ⏰ daily. ⛔ 1 & 6 Jan, 24 & 25 Dec. 🎫 ♿

A few of the many species of cacti, Jardí Botànic Mar i Murtra

The Costa Brava

THE COSTA BRAVA ("wild coast") runs for some 200 km (125 miles) from Blanes northwards to the region of Empordà (Ampurdán), which borders France. It is a mix of pine-backed sandy coves, golden beaches and crowded, modern resorts. The busiest resorts – Lloret de Mar, Tossa de Mar and La Platja d'Aro – are to the south. Sant Feliu de Guíxols and Palamós are still working towns behind the summer rush. Just inland there are medieval villages to explore, such as Peralada, Peratallada and Pals. Wine, olives and fishing were the mainstays of the area before the tourists came in the 1960s.

Cadaqués retains an air of seclusion as it is accessible only by a steep road. It has an arty atmosphere and its small, stony beaches remain unspoiled and less crowded than others.

L'Estartit is a good base for the Illes Medes, a former pirates' lair, which now form a marine reserve with clear waters perfect for skin diving.

Palamós is a working port with modern hotels to the south, and secluded beaches and coves lapped by clear water to the north.

La Platja d'Aro's long and sandy beach is lined with modern hotel blocks. It is one of the most popular resorts on the coast.

Tossa de Mar has a golden beach and a small cove beneath the fortified old town.

Cadaqués

Roses

L'Escala

L'Estartit
Illes Medes

Begur

Llafranc
Calella de Palafrugell
Palamós

La Platja d'Aro
S'Agaró
Sant Feliu de Guixols

Tossa de Mar

Lloret de Mar

Blanes

0 kilometres 10

0 miles 5

Roses lies at the head of a sweeping bay. Its sandy beach, the longest on the Costa Brava, has become a mecca for lovers of water sports.

L'Escala is a small resort, popular mainly with local tourists. It has fine beaches and a small port where fishing nets dry in the sun.

Begur is a hilltop town just inland. It has good views of the coast, and small coves are tucked at its feet.

Llafranc, a whitewashed resort, with a promenade leading to neighbouring Calella, is one of the coast's most pleasant resorts.

Lloret de Mar has more hotels than anywhere else on the coast. But there are unspoiled beaches nearby, such as Santa Cristina,

Monestir de Montserrat ⑲

T HE "SERRATED MOUNTAIN" (*mont serrat*), its highest peak rising to 1,236 m (4,055 ft), is a magnificent setting for Catalonia's holiest place, the Monastery of Montserrat, which is surrounded by chapels and hermits' caves. The monastery was first mentioned in the 9th century, enlarged in the 11th century, and in 1409 became independent of Rome. In 1811, when the French attacked Catalonia in the War of Independence (*see p59*), the monastery was destroyed and the monks killed. Rebuilt and repopulated in 1844, it was a beacon of Catalan culture during the Franco years. Today Benedictine monks live here.

A Benedictine monk

Visitors can hear the Escolania singing the *Salve Regina y Virolai* (the Montserrat hymn) at 1pm and 7:10pm every day (except Sunday), and not in July and during the Christmas period, in the basilica.

Plaça de Santa Maria
The focal points of the square are two wings of the Gothic cloister built in 1477. The modern monastery façade is by Françesc Folguera.

Plaça de la Creu   **Gothic cloister**

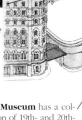

The Museum has a collection of 19th- and 20th-century paintings and many Catalan works.

The Way of the Cross
This path passes 14 statues representing the stations of the Cross. It begins near the Plaça de l'Abat Oliba.

STAR FEATURES

★ **Basilica Façade**

★ **Black Virgin**

View of Montserrat
The complex includes shops, cafés and a hotel. Funicular railways take visitors from the Plaça de la Creu to the Cova Santa and the hermitage of Sant Joan.

★ Basilica Façade
Agapit and Venanci Vallmitjana sculpted Christ and the apostles on the basilica's Neo-Renaissance façade. It was built in 1900 to replace the Plateresque façade of the original church, consecrated in 1592.

VISITORS' CHECKLIST

Montserrat (Barcelona province).
📞 93 877 77 77. 🚋 Aeri de Montserrat, then cable car. 🚌 from Barcelona. **Basilica** ◯ Oct–Jun: 7:30am–7:30pm daily; Jul–Sep: 7:30am–8:15pm daily.
✝ all day, from 9am Mon–Fri, from 7:30am Sat, from 8am Sun & religious hols. 📷 ♿
Museum ◯ 10am–6pm Mon–Fri, 9:30am–6:30pm Sat & Sun & public hols. 📷 ♿ 🎫 🍴

★ Black Virgin
La Moreneta looks down from behind the altar. Protected behind glass, her wooden orb protrudes for pilgrims to touch.

Basilica Interior
The sanctuary in the domed basilica is adorned by a richly enamelled altar and paintings by Catalan artists.

The Escolania is the famous choir of 50 boy choristers, who sing twice a day in the basilica.

Terminus for cable car from Aeri de Montserrat railway station

THE VIRGIN OF MONTSERRAT

The small wooden statue of La Moreneta (the dark one) is the soul of Montserrat. It is said to have been made by St Luke and brought here by St Peter in AD 50. Centuries later, the statue is believed to have been hidden from the Moors in the nearby Santa Cova (Holy Cave). Carbon dating suggests, however, that the statue was carved around the 12th century. In 1881 Montserrat's Black Virgin became patroness of Catalonia.

The blackened Virgin of Montserrat

Inner Courtyard
On one side of the courtyard is the baptistry (1902), with sculptures by Carles Collet. Pilgrims may approach the Virgin through a door to the right.

Vic ⓴

Barcelona. 🏠 *31,000.* 🚊 🚌 ℹ️ *Calle Ciutat 4, 93 886 20 91.* 🚌 *Tue & Sat.* 📷 *Mercat del Ram (Sat before Easter), Sant Miquel (5–15 Jul), Música Viva (Sep), Mercat Medieval (6–8 Dec).*

M ARKET DAYS – Tuesdays and Saturdays – are the best time to go to this small country town. This is when the excellent local sausages (*embotits*), for which the area is renowned, are piled high in the large Gothic Plaça Major, along with other produce from the surrounding plains.

In the 3rd century BC Vic was the capital of an ancient Iberian tribe, the Ausetans. The town was then colonized by the Romans – the remains of a Roman temple survive today. Since the 6th century the town has been a bishop's see. In the 11th century, Abbot Oliva commissioned the El Cloquer tower, around which the cathedral was built in the 18th century. The interior of the cathedral is covered with vast murals by Josep Maria Sert (1876–1945). They are painted in reds and golds, and represent scenes from the Bible.

Adjacent to the cathedral is the **Museu Episcopal de Vic**, which has one of the best collections of Romanesque artifacts in Catalonia. Its large display of mainly religious art and relics includes bright, simple murals and wooden sculptures from rural churches. Also on display are 11th- and 12th-century frescoes.

Cardona dominating the surrounding area from its hilltop site

🏛 Museu Episcopal
Plaça Bisbe Oliba. 📞 *93 889 44 17.* ⭕ *daily (except Mon Apr–Sep).* ♿ 📷

Cardona ㉑

Barcelona. 🏠 *6,000.* 🚊 ℹ️ *Avinguda Rastrillo, 93 869 27 98.* 🚌 *Sun.* 📷 *Fiesta Mayor (2nd Sun of Sep).* 🌐 *www.salcardona.com*

T HE 13TH-CENTURY castle of the Dukes of Cardona, constables to the crown of Aragón, is set on the top of a hill. The castle was rebuilt in the 18th century and is now a parador (*see p534*). Beside the castle is an early 11th-century church, the **Església de Sant Vicenç**, where the Dukes of Cardona are buried.

The castle gives views of the town below and of the Montanya de Sal (Salt Mountain), a huge salt deposit beside the Riu Cardener which has been mined since Roman times.

Solsona ㉒

Lleida. 🏠 *7,000.* 🚊 ℹ️ *Carrelera de Bassella 1, 973 48 23 10.* 🚌 *Tue & Fri.* 📷 *Carnival (Feb); Corpus Christi (May/Jun), Fiesta Mayor (8–11 Sep).* 🌐 *www.elsolsones.com*

N INE TOWERS and three gateways remain of Solsona's fortifications. Inside the walls is an ancient town of noble mansions. The cathedral has a black stone Virgin. The **Museu Diocesà i Comarcal** contains Romanesque paintings and archaeological finds.

🏛 Museu Diocesà i Comarcal
Plaça Palau 1. 📞 *973 48 21 01.* ⭕ *Tue–Sun.* ⚫ *1 Jan & 25 Dec.* ♿

Lleida ㉓

Lleida. 🏠 *120,000.* 🚊 🚌 ℹ️ *Avinguda de Madrid 36, 973 27 09 97.* 🚌 *Thu & Sat.* 📷 *Sant Anastasi (11 May), Sant Miquel (29 Sep).* 🌐 *www.lleidatur.es*

D OMINATING Lleida (Lérida), the capital of Catalonia's only landlocked province, is **La Suda**, a large, ruined fort taken from the Moors in 1149. The old cathedral, **La Seu Vella**, founded in 1203, is situated within the walls of the fort, high above the town. It was transformed into barracks by Felipe V in 1707 but today, sadly, is desolate. It remains imposing, however, with Gothic windows in the cloister.

A lift descends from the Seu Vella to the Plaça de Sant Joan in the town below. This square is at the mid-point of a busy

Twelfth-century altar frontal, Museu Episcopal de Vic

street sweeping round the foot of the hill. The new cathedral is here, as are manorial buildings such as the rebuilt 13th-century town hall, the **Paeria**.

Poblet ㉔

See pp212–13.

Montblanc ㉕

Tarragona. 🏃 *6,000.* 🚆 🚌
ℹ️ *Antigua Iglesia de Sant Françesc, 977 86 17 33.* 🚌 *Tue, Fri.* 🎉 *Fiesta Mayor (8–11 Sep).*

THE MEDIEVAL grandeur of Montblanc lives on within its walls, which are considered to be Catalonia's finest piece of military architecture. At the **Sant Jordi** gate, St George allegedly slew the dragon. The **Museu Comarcal de la Conca de Barberà** has interesting displays on local crafts.

🏛 **Museu Comarcal de la Conca de Barberà**
Carrer Josa 6. 📞 *977 86 03 49.*
⏰ *Tue–Sun & public hols.* 🈳

Santes Creus ㉖

Tarragona. 🏃 *150.* 🚆 ℹ️ *Plaça de Sant Bernard 1, 977 63 83 01.* 🚌 *Sat & Sun.* 🎉 *Sta Llúcia (13 Dec).*

HOME TO THE the prettiest of the "Cistercian triangle" monasteries is the tiny village of Santes Creus. The other

two, Vallbona de les Monges and Poblet *(see pp212–13),* are nearby. The **Monestir de Santes Creus** was founded in 1150 by Ramon Berenguer IV *(see p50)* during his reconquest of Catalonia. The Gothic cloisters are decorated with figurative sculptures, a style first permitted by Jaime II, who ruled from 1291 to 1327. His finely carved tomb, along with that of other nobles, is in the 12th-century church. The austerity of the interior is relieved by a beautiful rose window.

🔓 **Monestir de Santes Creus**
📞 *977 63 83 29.* ⏰ *Tue–Sun.* 🈳

Vilafranca del Penedès ㉗

Barcelona. 🏃 *30,000.* 🚆 🚌
ℹ️ *Carrer Cort 14, 93 892 03 58.*
🚌 *Sat.* 🎉 *Fiesta Mayor (29–31 Aug).*
🌐 *www.ajvilafranca.es*

THIS BUSY MARKET town is set in the heart of Catalonia's main wine-producing region *(see pp192–3).* The **Museu del Vi** (Wine Museum), in a 14th-century palace, documents the history of the area's wine trade. Local bodegas can be visited for wine tasting.

Eight km (5 miles) to the north is **Sant Sadurní**, the capital of Spain's sparkling wine, *cava (see pp576–7).*

🏛 **Museu del Vi**
Plaça Jaume I. 📞 *93 890 05 82.*
⏰ *Tue–Sun & public hols.* 🈳

Anxaneta **climbing to the top of a tower of** *castellers*

CATALONIA'S FIESTAS

Human Towers *(various dates and locations).* The province of Tarragona is famous for its *castellers* festivals, where teams of men stand on each others' shoulders in an effort to build the highest human tower. Each tower, which can be up to seven people high, is topped by a small boy called the *anxaneta. Castellers* can be seen in action in many towns, especially Vilafranca del Penedès and Valls.
Dance of Death *(Maundy Thu),* Verges (Girona). Men dressed as skeletons perform a macabre dance.
St George's Day *(23 Apr).* Lovers give each other a rose and a book on the day of Catalonia's patron saint. The book is in memory of Cervantes, who died on this day in 1616.
La Patum *(Corpus Christi, May/Jun),* Berga (Barcelona province). Giants, devils and bizarre monsters parade through the town.
Midsummer's Eve *(23 Jun).* Celebrated all over Catalonia with bonfires and fireworks.

Monestir de Santes Creus, surrounded by poplar and hazel trees

Monestir de Poblet ㉔

THE MONASTERY OF SANTA MARIA DE POBLET is a haven of tranquillity and a resting place of kings. It was the first and most important of three sister monasteries, known as the "Cistercian triangle" *(see p211)*, that helped to consolidate power in Catalonia after it had been recaptured from the Moors by Ramon Berenguer IV. In 1835, during the Carlist upheavals, it was plundered and seriously damaged by fire. Restoration of the impressive ruins, now largely complete, began in 1930 and monks returned in 1940.

The dormitory is reached by stairs from the church. The vast 87-m (285-ft) gallery dates from the 18th century. Half of it is still in use by the monks.

The 13th-century refectory is a vaulted hall with an octagonal fountain and a pulpit.

View of Poblet
The abbey, its buildings enclosed by fortified walls that have hardly changed since the Middle Ages, is in an isolated valley near the Riu Francolí's source.

Museum

Wine cellar

Library
The Gothic scriptorium was converted into a library in the 17th century, when the Duke of Cardona donated his book collection.

Former kitchen

Royal doorway

Royal palace

TIMELINE

1157 Founding of sister monastery at Vallbona de les Monges		*Royal tombs*			
	14th century Main cloister finished			**1812** Poblet desecrated by French troops	
1168 Santes Creus founded – third abbey in Cistercian triangle		**1479** Juan II, last king of Aragón, buried here			**1940** Monks return

1100	1300	1500	1700	1900

1196 Alfonso II is the first king to be buried here	**1336–87** Reign of Pere the Ceremonious, who designates Poblet a royal pantheon			**1953** Tombs reconstructed. Royal remains returned
1151 Poblet monastery founded by Ramon Berenguer IV		**1788–1808** Reign of Carlos IV, who has main reredos installed	**1835** Disentailment *(p59)* of monasteries. Poblet ravaged	

Chapterhouse
This perfectly square room, with slender columns, has tiers of benches for the monks. It is paved with the tombstones of 11 abbots who died between 1393 and 1693.

Parlour cloister

San Esteve cloister

New sacristy

VISITORS' CHECKLIST

Off N240, 10 km (6 miles) from Montblanc. 977 86 22 91.
L'Espluga de Francolí, then taxi. 10am–12:30pm, 3–5:30pm (6pm Jun–Sep) daily. public hols. 8am Mon-Sat; 8am, 10am, 1pm & 6pm Sun & public hols.

★ **High Altar Reredos**
Behind the stone altar, supported by Romanesque columns, an impressive alabaster reredos fills the apse. It was carved by Damià Forment in 1527.

The Abbey Church, large and unadorned, with three naves, is a typical Cistercian building.

★ **Royal Tombs**
The tombs in the pantheon of kings were begun in 1359. In 1950 they were reconstructed by the sculptor Frederic Marès.

Baroque church façade

★ **Cloisters**
The evocative, vaulted cloisters were built in the 12th and 13th centuries and were the centre of monastic life. The capitals are beautifully decorated with carved scrollwork.

STAR FEATURES

★ High Altar Reredos

★ Royal Tombs

★ Cloisters

Palm trees lining the waterfront at Sitges

Sitges ㉘

Barcelona. 🚶 20,000. 🚊 🚌 ℹ️
Carrer Sinia Morera 1, 93 894 50 04.
🚢 Jul–Sep: every Thu; Oct–Jun:
every other Thu. 🎆 Fiesta Mayor
(23–24 Aug). W www.sitges.org

Lively bars line the seafront
at Sitges which is popular
with both locals and foreigners.
Modernista artist Santiago
Rusiñol (1861–1931) spent a lot
of time here. He bequeathed
his collection of ceramics,
sculptures and paintings to
the **Museu Cau Ferrat**.

🏛 Museu Cau Ferrat

Carrer Fonollar. ☎ 93 894 03 64.
🕐 Tue–Sun. 🕐 public hols. 🎆

Costa Daurada ㉙

Tarragona. 🚌 🚌 🚢 Calafell, San Vicente,
Salou. ℹ️ Tarragona, 977 23 34 15.

The entire coast of Tarragona
province is known as the
Costa Daurada, the Golden
Coast, because of its long,
sandy beaches. **Vilanova i la
Geltrú** and **El Vendrell** are
two of the many ports along it
that are still active. The **Casa
Nadiva de Pau Casals** in El
Vendrell is dedicated to the
life of the famous cellist.
   Port Aventura, south of
Tarragona, is one of Europe's
largest theme parks. Its exoti-
cally inspired attractions are
named Mediterrània, México,

China, Polynesia and Wild
West. **Salou** and **Cambrils** to
the south are the liveliest resorts – the others are mostly
low-key, family holiday places.

🏛 Casa Nadiva de Pau Casals

Avda Palfuriana 59–61. ☎ 977 68 42
76. 🕐 daily. 🎆 ♿
🎢 Port Aventura

Autovia Salou–Vila-seca. ☎ 977 77
90 00. 🕐 16 Mar–6 Jan. 🎆 ♿

Tarragona ㉚

Tarragona. 🚶 110,000. ✈️ 🚌 🚌
ℹ️ Carrer Fortuny 4, 977 23 34 15.
🚢 Tue & Thu. 🎆 Santa Tecla (23 Sep).

Tarragona is now a major
industrial port with a large
petrochemical industry, but it
also preserves many remnants
of its Roman past. It was then

the capital of Tarraconensis.
The Romans chose it as their
base for the conquest of the
peninsula, which began in the
3rd century BC (see pp46–7).
   The avenue of Rambla Nova
ends abruptly above the sea on
the clifftop Balcó de Europa,
from which the extensive ruins
of the **Anfiteatro Romano** can
be seen. Within them is the
ruined 12th-century church of
Santa Maria del Miracle.
   Nearby is the Praetorium,
a Roman tower that was converted into a palace in medieval times. It is sometimes
known as the Castell de Pilato
(named after Pontius Pilate),
and it now houses the **Museu
de la Romanitat**. This displays Roman and medieval
finds, and gives access to the
cavernous passageways of the
excavated Roman circus, built

The remains of the Roman amphitheatre, Tarragona

in the 1st century AD. Adjoining the Praetorium is the **Museu Nacional Arqueològic,** containing the most important collection of Roman artifacts in Catalonia. It has a large collection of bronze implements, stone busts and beautiful mosaics, including the *Head of Medusa.*

Among the most impressive remains in the city are the gigantic pre-Roman stones on which the Roman wall is built. An archaeological walk runs along a 1-km (1,100-yd) long stretch of the wall and its towers.

Behind it is the 12th-century **cathedral,** built on the site of a Roman temple to Jupiter and a subsequent Arab mosque. The structure evolved over many centuries, as seen from the harmonious blend of styles of the exterior. Inside is an alabaster altarpiece of St Tecla carved by Pere Johan in 1434. The large 13th-century cloister, which is filled with orange trees, features early Gothic vaulting, but the doorway is Romanesque in its geometric decoration.

In the west of town is a 3rd- to 6th-century Christian cemetery (ask about opening times in the archaeological museum). Some of the carved sarcophagi, in the site museum were originally used as pagan tombs.

Ruins of the Palaeo- Christian Necropolis

ENVIRONS: The well-preserved **Aqüeducte de les Ferreres** lies just outside the city, next to the A7 motorway. (There is a lay-by for viewing.) This 2nd-century aqueduct was built to bring water to the city from the Riu Gaià, 30 km (19 miles) to the north. The **Arc de Barà,** a 1st-century triumphal arch on the Via Augusta, is 20 km (12 miles) northeast on the N340.

🏛 **Museu Nacional Arqueològic de Tarragona**
Plaça del Rei 5. 📞 977 23 62 09.
⭘ *Tue–Sun.* 🎟 *(free Tue).* 🦽
🏛 **Museu de la Romanitat**
Plaça del Rei. 📞 977 24 19 52.
⭘ *Tue–Sun.* 🎟

Tortosa ㉛

Tarragona. 🏘 *30,000.* 🚉 *Avda Generalitat, 977 51 08 22.* ☯ *Mon.* 🎭 *Nuestra Señora de la Cinta (late Aug & early Sep).* W *www.tortosa.altanet.org*

A RUINED CASTLE and medieval walls are clues to Tortosa's historical importance. Sited at the lowest crossing point on the Riu Ebre (Río Ebro), it has been strategically significant since Iberian times. The Moors held the city from the 8th century until 1148. The old Moorish castle, known as La Zuda, is all that remains of their defences. It has been renovated as a parador *(see p547).* The Moors also built a mosque in 914. Its foundations were used for the cathedral, on which work began in 1347. Although not completed for 200 years, the style is Gothic.

Tortosa was badly damaged in 1938–39 during one of the fiercest battles of the Civil War *(see pp62–3),* when the Ebre formed the front line between the opposing forces.

Delta de L'Ebre ㉜

Tarragona. 🚉 *Aldea.* 🚌 *Deltebre, Aldea.* 🛈 *Deltebre 977 48 96 79.* W *www.ebre.com/delta*

T HE DELTA of the Riu Ebre is a prosperous rice-growing region and wildlife haven. Some 70 sq km (27 sq miles) have been turned into a nature reserve, the **Parc Natural del Delta de L'Ebre.** In Deltebre there is an information centre and an interesting **Eco-Museu,** with an aquarium containing species found in the delta.

The main towns in the area are **Amposta** and **Sant Carles de la Ràpita,** both of which serve as good bases for exploring the reserve.

The best sites for seeing wildlife are along the shore, from the Punta del Fangar in the north to the Punta de la Banya in the south. Everywhere is accessible by car except Illa de Buda. Flamingoes breed on this island and other water birds, such as avocets, can be seen from tourist boats that leave from Riumar and Deltebre.

🏛 **Eco-Museu**
Carrer Martí Buera 22. 📞 *977 48 96 79.* ⭘ *daily (by appt).* ⬤ *1 & 6 Jan, 25 & 26 Dec.* 🎟 🦽

THE SARDANA

Catalonia's national dance is more complicated than it appears. The success of the Sardana depends on all of the dancers accurately counting the complicated short- and long-step skips and jumps, which accounts for their serious faces. Music is provided by a *cobla,* an 11-person band consisting of a leader playing a three-holed flute *(flabiol)* and a little drum *(tabal),* five woodwind players and five brass players. When the music starts, dancers join hands and form circles. The Sardana is performed during most local fiestas *(see p211)* and at special day-long gatherings called *aplecs.*

A group of Sardana dancers captured in stone

ARAGÓN

···

HUESCA · TERUEL · ZARAGOZA

*S*TRETCHING ALMOST HALF *the length of Spain, and bisected by the Ebro, one of the country's longest rivers, Aragón takes in a wide variety of scenery, from the snow-capped summits of Ordesa National Park in the Pyrenees to the dry plains of the Spanish interior. This largely unsung and undervisited region contains magnificent Mudéjar architecture and many unspoiled medieval towns.*

From the 12th–15th centuries Aragón was a powerful kingdom, or, more accurately, a federation of states, including Catalonia. In its heyday, in the 13th century, its dominions stretched across the Mediterranean as far as Sicily. By his marriage to Isabel of Castile and León in 1469, Fernando II of Aragón paved the way for the unification of Spain.

After the Reconquest, Muslim architects and craftsmen were treated more tolerantly here than elsewhere, and they continued their work in the distinctive Mudéjar style, building with elaborate brickwork and patterned ceramic decoration. Their work can be seen in churches all over Aragón and there are outstanding examples in the cities of Teruel and the capital, Zaragoza, Spain's fifth largest city, which stands on the banks of the Ebro.

The highest peaks of the Pyrenees lie in Huesca province. Some of the region's finest sights are in the Pyrenean foothills, which are crossed by the Aragonese variation of the pilgrims' route to Santiago de Compostela. Probably the most spectacular of them is the monastery of San Juan de la Peña – half-concealed beneath a rock overhang – which was founded in the 9th century.

The climate of the region varies as much as the landscape: winters can be long and harsh and summers hot.

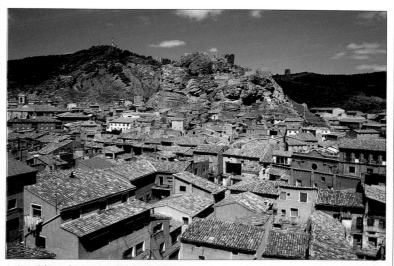

A view of the rooftops and medieval walls of Daroca

◁ **Torla village church, on the edge of Ordesa National Park**

Exploring Aragón

Stone carving, San Juan de la Peña

THE LANDSCAPES OF ARAGÓN range from the high Pyrenees, north of Huesca, through the desiccated terrain around Zaragoza to the forested hills of Teruel province. The cities of Teruel and Zaragoza have some of the most striking Mudéjar monuments in Spain. There are many small, picturesque preserved towns in the region. Ordesa National Park contains stunning mountain scenery, but it can only be visited fully after the snow melts in spring, and even then much of it has to be explored on foot. Pretty Los Valles offers less dramatic but equally enjoyable landscapes and is a popular tourist destination. Other attractive places include the impressively sited Castillo de Loarre and Monasterio de San Juan de la Peña, and the waterfalls of Monasterio de Piedra.

The Puerto de Somport, near Panticosa

SIGHTS AT A GLANCE

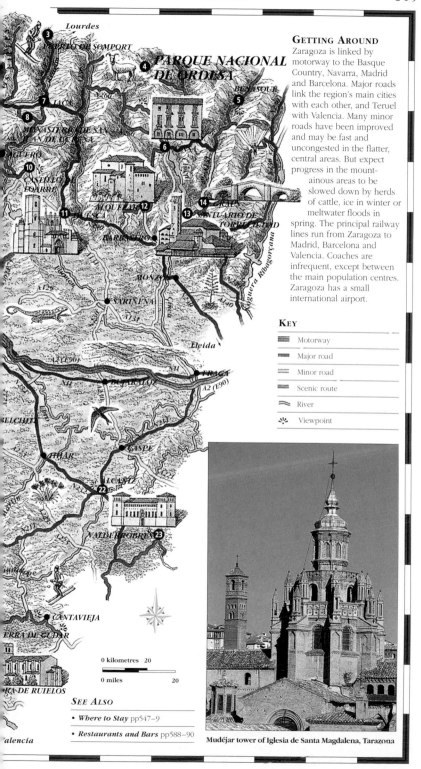

Lourdes

PUERTO DE SOMPORT

3

PARQUE NACIONAL DE ORDESA

4

BENASQUE

5

7 JACA

8

MONASTERIO DE SAN JUAN DE LA PEÑA

6

VALERO

10

CASTILLO DE LOARRE

11 HUESCA

12 ALQUÉZAR

13

14

SANTUARIO DE TORRECIUDAD

BARBASTRO

MONZÓN

SARIÑENA

Lleida

BUJARALOZ

FRAGA

A2 (E90)

BELCHITE

AZAILA

CASPE

ALCAÑIZ

22

VALDERROBRES **23**

CANTAVIEJA

SIERRA DE GÚDAR

RA DE RUIELOS

GETTING AROUND

Zaragoza is linked by motorway to the Basque Country, Navarra, Madrid and Barcelona. Major roads link the region's main cities with each other, and Teruel with Valencia. Many minor roads have been improved and may be fast and uncongested in the flatter, central areas. But expect progress in the mountainous areas to be slowed down by herds of cattle, ice in winter or meltwater floods in spring. The principal railway lines run from Zaragoza to Madrid, Barcelona and Valencia. Coaches are infrequent, except between the main population centres. Zaragoza has a small international airport.

KEY

▬▬▬	Motorway
▬▬▬	Major road
▬▬▬	Minor road
▬▬▬	Scenic route
≈≈	River
✵	Viewpoint

0 kilometres   20

0 miles   20

SEE ALSO

Valencia

Mudéjar tower of Iglesia de Santa Magdalena, Tarazona

The town hall, Sos del Rey Católico

Sos del Rey Católico ❶

Zaragoza. 🏘 *900*. 🚗 🛈 *Emilio Alfaro 5, 948 88 85 35 (summer); Plaza de la Villa 1, 948 88 80 65 (winter)*. 🚌 *Fri.* 🎉 *Fiestas mayores (third Thu of Aug)*.

FERNANDO OF ARAGÓN – the so-called "Catholic King" who married Isabel of Castile, thereby uniting Spain *(see pp52–3)* – was born in this small town in 1452, hence its distinguished royal name.

The **Palacio de Sada**, the king's reputed birthplace, with a beautiful inner courtyard, is among the town's grandest stone mansions. It stands in a small square amid a maze of narrow cobbled streets. At the top of the town are the remnants of a castle and the **Iglesia de San Esteban**. The church's font and carved capitals are noteworthy, as are the 13th-century frescoes in two of the crypt's apses. From here there are fine views over the surrounding hills.

The Gothic-arched **Lonja** (commodities exchange) and the 16th-century **town hall** *(ayuntamiento)* are located on the adjacent main square.

ENVIRONS: The "Cinco Villas" are five towns recognized by Felipe V for their loyalty during the War of the Spanish Succession *(see p58)*. **Sos del Rey Católico** is the most appealing of these. The others are Ejea de los Caballeros, Tauste, Sádaba and **Uncastillo**. This last town, 20 km (12 miles) to the southeast, has a fortress and a Romanesque church, the Iglesia de Santa María.

Los Valles ❷

Huesca. 🚉 *Jaca.* 🚌 *from Jaca to Hecho.* 🛈 *Carretera de Oza, (ayuntamiento) 974 37 50 02.*

THE DELIGHTFUL VALLEYS of Ansó and Hecho, formed by the Veral and Aragón Subordán rivers respectively, were isolated until recently due to poor road links. Their villages have retained traditional customs and a local dialect called *cheso*, passed down the generations. Now the area's crafts and costumes have made it popular with tourists. The Pyrenean foothills and pine forests above the valleys are particularly good for walking, fishing and cross-country skiing.

Ansó lies in the prettiest valley, which becomes a shadowy gorge where the Río Veral and the road next to it squeeze between vertical crags and through rock tunnels. Many of its buildings have stone façades and steep, tiled roofs. In the Gothic church (16th century) there is a museum dedicated to local costume. **Hecho** is host to an open-air festival of modern sculpture. Previous years' exhibits lie scattered around the village. The bucolic village of **Siresa**, which contains the 11th-century church of San Pedro, lies to the north of Hecho.

Puerto de Somport ❸

Huesca. 🚌 *Somport, Astun or Jaca.* 🛈 *Pl Ayuntamiento 1, Canfranc, 974 37 31 41.*

JUST INSIDE THE BORDER with France, the Somport Pass was for centuries a strategic crossing point for the Romans and Moors, and for medieval pilgrims en route to Santiago de Compostela *(see pp78–9)*. Today the austere scenery is specked with holiday apartments built for skiing. **Astún** is modern and well organized, while **El Formigal**, to the east, is a stylish, purpose-built resort. Non-skiers can enjoy the scenery around the Panticosa gorge. **Sallent de Gállego** is popular for rock-climbing and fishing.

Steep, tiled roofs of Hecho, with a typical pepperpot chimney

Rough and craggy landscape around Benasque

Parque Nacional de Ordesa **4**

See pp222–3.

Benasque **5**

Huesca. 🏠 *1,250.* **i** *Calle de San Sebastián 5, 974 55 12 89.* 🚌 *Tue.* 📅 *San Marcial (San Pedro 29 Jun).*

TUCKED AWAY IN THE northeast corner of Aragón, at the head of the Esera valley, the village of Benasque presides over a ruggedly beautiful stretch of Pyrenean scenery. Although the village has expanded greatly to meet the holiday trade, a sympathetic use of wood and stone has resulted in buildings which complement the existing older houses. A stroll through the old centre filled with aristocratic mansions is a delight.

The most striking buildings in Benasque are the 13th-century **Iglesia de Santa María Mayor**, and the **Palacio de los Condes de Ribagorza**. The latter has a Renaissance façade.

Above the village rises the Maladeta massif. There are magnificent views from its ski slopes and hiking trails. Several local mountain peaks, including **Posets** and **Aneto**, exceed 3,000 m (9,800 ft).

ENVIRONS: For walkers, skiers and climbers, the area around Benasque has a great deal to offer, for all levels of ability.

The neighbouring resort of **Cerler** was developed with care from a rustic village into a popular base for skiing and other winter sports.

At Castejón de Sos, 15 km (9 miles) south of Benasque, the road passes through the **Congosto de Ventamillo**, a scenic rocky gorge.

Ainsa **6**

Huesca. 🏠 *1,600.* 🚌 **i** *Cruce de Carreteras, Avda Pirinaica 1, 974 50 07 67.* 🚌 *Tue.* 📅 *San Sebastián (20 Jan).*

THE CAPITAL of the kingdom of Sobrarbe in medieval times, Ainsa has retained its charm. The Plaza Mayor, a broad cobbled square, is surrounded by neat terraced arcades of brown stone. On one side stands the shapely belfry of the **Iglesia de Santa María** – consecrated in 1181 – and beyond, old streets lead up to the restored castle.

Jaca **7**

Huesca. 🏠 *12,000.* 🚌 🚍 **i** *Avda Regimento de Galicia 2, 974 36 00 98.* 🚌 *Fri.* 📅 *La Victoria (first Fri of May), Santa Orosia (late Jun).* 🌐 *www.aytojaca.es*

JACA DATES BACK as far as the 2nd century AD. In the 8th century the town bravely repulsed the Moors – an act which is commemorated in the festival of La Victoria – and in 1035 became the first capital of the kingdom of Aragón. Jaca's 11th-century **cathedral**, one of Spain's oldest, is much altered inside. Traces of its original splendour can be seen on the restored south porch and doorway, where carvings depict biblical scenes. The dim nave and chapels are decorated with ornate vaulting and sculpture. A museum of sacred art, in the cloisters, contains a collection of Romanesque and Gothic frescoes and sculptures from local churches. The streets that surround the cathedral form an attractive quarter.

Sculpture in Jaca cathedral

Jaca's only other significant tourist sight is its 16th-century **citadel**, a fort decorated with corner turrets, on the edge of town. Today the town serves as a principal base for the Aragonese Pyrenees.

The arcaded main square of Ainsa with the Iglesia de Santa María

Parque Nacional de Ordesa **4**

Signpost in Ordesa National Park

WITHIN ITS BORDERS the Parque Nacional de Ordesa y Monte Perdido combines all the most dramatic elements of Spain's Pyrenean scenery. At the heart of the park are four glacial canyons – the Ordesa, Añisclo, Pineta and Escuain valleys – which carve the great upland limestone massifs into spectacular cliffs and chasms. Most of the park is accessible only on foot: even then, snow during autumn and winter makes it inaccessible to all, except those with specialist climbing equipment. In high summer, however, the crowds testify to the park's well-earned reputation as a paradise for walkers and nature lovers alike.

Valle de Ordesa
The Río Arazas cuts through forested limestone escarpments, providing some of Ordesa's most popular walks.

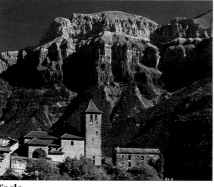

Torla
This village, at the gateway to the park, huddles beneath the forbidding slopes of Mondarruego. With its core of cobbled streets and slate-roofed houses around the church, Torla is a popular base for visitors to Ordesa.

El Taillón
Brecha de Rolando
3,144 m (10,315 ft)
Gruta de Casteret
Mondarruego
2,848 m (9,344 ft)
VALLE DE ORDESA
Cascada Torrombotera
SIERRA DE LAS CUTA
Torla
BIESCAS
Broto
Fa
Oto
Sarvisé
Jalle
AINSA

PYRENEAN WILDLIFE

Spanish Ibex

Ordesa is a spectacle of flora and fauna, with many of its species unique to the region. Trout streams rush along the valley floor, where slopes provide a mantle of various woodland harbouring all kinds of creatures, including otters, marmots and capercaillies (large grouse). On the slopes, flowers burst out before the snow melts, with gentians and orchids sheltering in crevices and edelweiss braving the most hostile crags. Higher up, the Pyrenean chamois is still fairly common; but the unique Ordesa ibex, or mountain goat, is now becoming scarce and is a protected species. The rocky pinnacles above are the domain of birds of prey.

Spring gentian (*Gentiana verna*)

0 kilometres   2

0 miles   2

KEY

Major road

Minor road

-- Footpath

Spanish/French border

National park boundary

🅷 Tourist information

Viewpoint

View from Parador de Bielsa

The parador (see p548), at the foot of Monte Perdido, looks out at stunning sheer rock faces streaked by waterfalls.

(see p548)

VISITORS' CHECKLIST

🛈 Visitors' centre, 9 km (5.5 miles) north of Torla on road to Valle de Ordesa, 974 24 33 61.
🚍 Change at Sabiñánigo for Torla. 🚉 Sabiñánigo.

(Map showing:)

Parador de Bielsa 🅿

Monte Perdido
3,355 m (11,008 ft)

VALLE DE PINETA

Cinca

BIELSA

Refugio de Góriz

SIERRA DE LAS TUCAS

Cascada Cola de Caballo

...das de Soaso

Vellos

CAÑON DE AÑISCLO

GARGANTA DE ESCUAIN

Revilla

Escuaín

BIELSA

Tella

...uisán • Nerín

Bestué •

Puértolas •

Vellos

Cola de Caballo

The 70-m (230-ft) "Horse's Tail" waterfall makes a scenic stopping point near the northern end of the long hike around the Circo Soaso. It provides a taste of the spectacular scenery found along the route.

Hikers in Ordesa National Park

TIPS FOR WALKERS

Several well-marked trails follow the valleys and can be easily tackled by anyone reasonably fit, though walking boots are a must. The mountain routes may require climbing gear so check first with the visitors' centre and get a detailed map. Pyrenean weather changes rapidly – beware of ice and snow early and late in the season – but in case of need there are several *refugios*, which provide basic overnight shelter.

Cañon or Garganta de Añisclo

A wide path leads along this beautiful, steep-sided gorge, following the wooded course of the turbulent Río Vellos through dramatic limestone scenery.

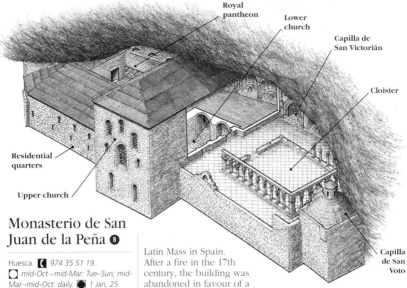

Royal pantheon

Lower church

Capilla de San Victorián

Cloister

Residential quarters

Upper church

Capilla de San Voto

Monasterio de San Juan de la Peña ❽

Huesca. 📞 974 35 51 19.
🕐 mid-Oct – mid-Mar: Tue–Sun; mid-Mar–mid-Oct: daily. ⬤ 1 Jan, 25 Dec. 🛇 ✇ ✓ ▣
🌐 www.monasteriosanjuan.com

SET UNDER a bulging rock, this monastery was an early guardian of the Holy Grail *(see p240)*. In the 11th century it underwent reformation in Cluniac style, and was the first monastery to introduce the Latin Mass in Spain. After a fire in the 17th century, the building was abandoned in favour of a newer one further up the hillside. This was later sacked by Napoleon's troops, although the Baroque façade survives.

The church of the old monastery is on two floors. The lower one is a primitive rock-hewn crypt built in the early 10th century. The upper floor contains an 11th-century church with a simple triple apse hollowed out of the side of the cliff. The well-preserved Romanesque pantheon contains the stacked tombs of the early Aragonese kings. The exterior cloister is San Juan de la Peña's *pièce de résistance*, the capitals of its columns carved with biblical scenes.

Agüero ❾

Huesca. 👥 181. ℹ San Jaime 1, 974 38 04 89. 🎏 San Roque (15–19 Aug). 🌐 www.agueroturincon.com

THE PICTURESQUE setting of this attractive village, clustered against a dramatic crag of eroded pudding stone, amply rewards a brief detour from the main road. The most important reason for visiting Agüero, however, is to see the 12th-century **Iglesia de Santiago**. This Romanesque church is reached by a long stony track leading uphill just before the village.

The capitals of the columns in this unusual triple-naved building are carved with fantastical beasts as well as scenes from the life of Jesus and the Virgin Mary. The beautiful carvings on the doorway display biblical events, including scenes from the Epiphany and Salome dancing ecstatically. The lively, large-eyed figures are attributed to the mason responsible for the superb carvings in the monastery at San Juan de la Peña.

Castillo de Loarre ❿

Loarre (Huesca). 📞 974 38 27 22.
🚌 Ayerbe. 🚉 from Huesca.
🕐 mid-Mar–Jun & Sep–mid-Oct: Tue–Sun; Jun–Aug: daily; mid-Oct–mid-Mar: Wed–Sun.

THE RAMPARTS of this sturdy fortress stand majestically above the road approaching from Ayerbe. It is so closely moulded around the contours of a rock that at night or in poor visibility it could be mistaken for a natural outcrop. On a clear day, the hilltop setting is stupendous, with views of the surrounding orchards and reservoirs of the

Village of Agüero, situated under a rocky crag

Ebro plain. Inside the curtain walls lies a complex founded in the 11th century on the site of a Roman castle. It was later remodelled under Sancho I (Sancho Ramírez) of Aragón, who established a religious community here, placing the complex under the rule of the Order of St Augustine.

Within the castle walls is a Romanesque church decorated with alabaster windows, a chequered frieze and carved capitals. Its crypt contains the remains of St Demetrius.

Sentry paths, iron ladders and flights of steps ramble precariously around the castle's towers, dungeons and keep.

The formidable Castillo de Loarre looming above the surrounding area

Huesca ⓫

Huesca. 🏠 48,000. 🚇 🚉 🛈 Plaza de la Catedral 1, 974 29 21 70. 🚌 Mon, Tue & Thu. 🎇 San Vicente (22 Jan); San Lorenzo (9–15 Aug).

Altarpiece by Damià Forment, in Huesca cathedral

Founded in the 1st century BC, the independent state of Osca (present-day Huesca) had a senate and an advanced education system. From the 8th century, the area grew into a Moorish stronghold. In 1096 it was captured by Peter of Aragón and was the region's capital until 1118, when the title passed to Zaragoza.

Huesca is now the provincial capital. The pleasant old town has a Gothic **cathedral**. The eroded west front is surmounted by an unusual wooden gallery in Mudéjar style. Above the nave is slender-ribbed star vaulting studded with golden bosses. The cathedral's best feature is an alabaster altarpiece by the master sculptor,

Damià Forment. On the altarpiece, a series of energetic Crucifixion scenes in relief are highlighted by illumination.

Opposite the cathedral is the Renaissance **town hall** (ayuntamiento). Inside hangs La Campana de Huesca, a gory 19th-century painting depicting the town's most memorable event: the beheading of a group of troublesome nobles in the 12th century by order of King Ramiro II.

The massacre occurred in the Sala de la Campana of the 17th-century university. This now houses the superb **Museo Arqueológico Provincial**, containing archaeological finds and a collection of art.

🏛 Museo Arqueológico Provincial

Plaza de la Universidad 1. 📞 974 22 05 86. ◯ 10am–2pm, 5–8pm Tue–Sat, 10am–2pm Sun & public hols. ● 1 & 6 Jan, 24, 25, & 31 Dec.

Alquézar ⓬

Huesca. 🏠 310. 🛈 Calle Arrabal, 974 31 89 40. 🎇 San Sebastián (20 Jan); San Ipolito (12 Aug).

This moorish village attracts much attention because of its spectacular setting. Its main monument, the stately 16th-century **collegiate church**, dominates a hill jutting above the strange rock formations of the canyon of the Río Vero. Inside, the church's cloisters have capitals carved with biblical scenes. Next to it is the chapel built after Sancho I recaptured Alquézar from the Moors. Nearby are the ruined walls of the original alcazar, which gives the village its name.

Santuario de Torreciudad ⓭

Huesca. 📞 974 30 40 25. 🚌 to El Grado from Barbastro. ◯ daily. 🕭

This shrine was built to honour the devotion of the founder of the Catholic lay order of Opus Dei – Josemaría Escrivá de Balaguer – to the Virgin. It occupies a promontory, with picturesque views over the waters of the **Embalse de El Grado** at Torreciudad. The huge church is made of angular red brick in a stark, modern design.

Inside, the elaborate modern altarpiece of alabaster, sheltering a glittering Romanesque Virgin, is in contrast to the bleak, functional nave.

Environs: The small town of **Barbastro**, which lies 20 km (12 miles) to the south, has an arcaded *plaza mayor* and a 16th-century cathedral with an altar by Damià Forment.

The ruins of Alquézar castle, rising above the village

Houses with frescoed façades on the Plaza de España, Graus

Graus ⓮

Huesca. 🏠 3,300. 🚉 🛈 Calle
Fermin Muri 25, 974 54 61 63. 🅰
Mon. 🎭 Santo Cristo and San
Vicente Ferrer (12–15 Sep).

CONCEALED IN THE HEART of
Graus's old town lies the
unusual **Plaza de España**, surrounded by brick arcades and
brightly frescoed half-timbered
houses. One of these was the
home of the infamous Tomás
de Torquemada, the Inquisitor
General (see p52). The old
quarter, with its narrow streets,
is best explored on foot. At
fiesta time, this small town is
a good place to see typical
Aragonese dancing.

ENVIRONS: About 20 km (12
miles) northeast, the hill village
of **Roda de Isábena** has the
smallest cathedral in Spain.
Dating from 1067, this striking
building has a 12th-century
cloister off which is a chapel
with 13th-century frescoes.
North of the village is the
picturesque Isábena valley.

Tarazona ⓯

Zaragoza. 🏠 11,000. 🚉 🛈 Plaza
San Francisco 1, 976 64 00 74. 🅰
every other Thu. 🎭 San Atilano (27
Aug–1 Sep). 🇼 www.tarazona.org

MUDEJAR TOWERS stand high
above the earth-coloured,
mottled pantiles of this ancient
bishopric. On the outskirts of
the old town is the **cathedral**,
all turreted finials and pierced
brickwork with Moorish cloister tracery and Gothic tombs.
In the upper town on the

other side of the river, more
churches, in typical Mudéjar
style, can be found amid the
maze of narrow hilly streets.
More unusual perhaps are the
former bullring, now a circular
plaza enclosed by houses, and
the splendid Renaissance **town
hall** (ayuntamiento). The
town hall, built of golden
stone, has a façade carved with
mythical giants and a frieze
showing Carlos V's homage
to Tarazona.

Monasterio de Veruela ⓰

Vera de Moncayo (Zaragoza). 📞 976
64 90 25. 🚉 Vera de Moncayo.
🕐 Tue–Sun. 🎟 ♿

THIS ISOLATED CISTERCIAN retreat, set in the green
Huecha valley near the Sierra
de Moncayo, is one of the
greatest monasteries in Aragón.
Founded in the 12th century
by French monks, the huge
abbey church has a mixture
of Romanesque and Gothic

features. Worn green and blue
Aragonese tiles line the floor
of its handsomely vaulted triple
nave. The well-preserved
cloisters sprout exuberantly
decorated beasts, heads of
human beings and foliage in
the Plateresque style (see p21).
The plain, dignified chambers
make a suitable venue for art
exhibitions in the summer.

ENVIRONS: In the hills to the
west the small **Parque Natural
de Moncayo** rises to a height
of 2,315 m (7,600 ft). Streams
race through the woodland
of this nature reserve, which
throngs with bird life. A tortuous potholed road leads to
a chapel at the highest point.

Zaragoza ⓱

Zaragoza. 🏠 600,000. ✈ 🚉 🚌
🛈 Plaza del Pilar, 976 20 12 00.
🅰 Wed, Sun. 🎭 San Valero (29 Jan),
Cincomarzada (5 Mar), San Jorge
(23 Apr), Virgen del Pilar (12 Oct).
🇼 www.turismozaragoza.com

A CELTIBERIAN settlement
called Salduba existed on
the site of the present city; but
it is from the Roman settlement
of Cesaraugusta that Zaragoza
takes its name. Its location on
the fertile banks of the Río
Ebro ensured its ascendancy,
now Spain's fifth largest city
and the capital of Aragón.
Badly damaged during the
War of Independence (see
p58), the city was largely rebuilt but the old centre retains
a number of interesting buildings. Most of the city's main
sights are grouped around the
vast Plaza del Pilar. The most

Entrance and tower of the Monasterio de Veruela

impresssive of them is the **Basílica de Nuestra Señora del Pilar**, with its huge church sporting 11 brightly tiled cupolas. Inside, the Santa Capilla (Lady Chapel) by Ventura Rodríguez contains a small statue of the Virgin on a pillar amid a blaze of silver and flowers. Her long skirt-like *manta* is changed every day, and devout pilgrims pass behind the chapel to kiss an exposed section of the pillar.

Nearby, on the square, stand the **town hall** *(ayuntamiento)*, the Gothic-Plateresque **Lonja** (commodities exchange) and the **Palacio Episcopal**.

Occupying the east end of the square is Zaragoza's cathedral, **La Seo**, displaying a great mix of styles. Part of the exterior is faced with typical Mudéjar brick and ceramic decoration, and inside are a fine Gothic reredos and splendid Flemish tapestries.

Close by is the flamboyant Mudéjar bell tower of the **Iglesia de la Magdalena**, and remains of the Roman forum. Parts of the **Roman walls** can also be seen at the opposite side of the Plaza del Pilar, near the **Mercado de Lanuza**, a market with sinuous ironwork in Art Nouveau style.

Some of the cupolas of the Basílica de Nuestra Señora del Pilar

The **Museo Camón Aznar** exhibits the eclectic collection of a wealthy local art historian, whose special interest was Goya. The top floor contains a collection of his etchings. Many minor works by artists of other periods can be seen, as well as good contemporary art. The **Museo de Zaragoza** contains many paintings, as well as archaeological artifacts.

The **Museo Pablo Gargallo** is a showroom for the Aragonese sculptor after whom it is named, who was active at the beginning of the 20th century.

One of the most important monuments in Zaragoza lies on the busy road to Bilbao. The **Alfajería** is an enormous Moorish palace built in the 11th century. A courtyard of lacy arches surrounds a sunken garden and a small mosque.

🏛 **Museo Camón Aznar**
Calle Espoz y Mina 23. ☎ 976 39 73 28. ◯ Tue–Sun. 🎦 🅰 ⚹ by appt.
🏛 **Museo de Zaragoza**
Plaza de los Sitios 6. ☎ 976 22 21 81. ◯ Tue–Sun. ⚹
🏛 **Museo Pablo Gargallo**
Plaza de San Felipe 3. ☎ 976 39 20 58. ◯ Tue–Sun. ⚹

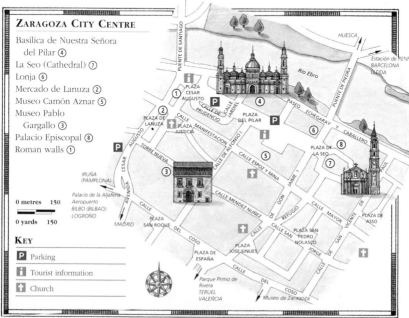

Zaragoza City Centre

0 metres   150
0 yards   150

Key

🅿 Parking
ℹ Tourist information
✝ Church

Gateway through the medieval walls of Daroca

Calatayud ⓲

Zaragoza. 👥 20,000. 🚊 🚌
ℹ️ Plaza del Fuerte, 976 88 63 22.
🗓️ Tue. 🎭 San Roque (14–17 Aug).

THE HUGE MOORISH FORTRESS
and minaret-like church
towers of Calatayud are visible
far across the surrounding clay
hills and fertile red plains. Only
ruins are left of the 8th-century
Arab castle of the ruler, Ayub,
which gave the town its name
(*Kalat Ayub* means castle of
Ayub). The church of **Santa
María la Mayor** has a Mudéjar
tower and an elaborate façade
in the Plateresque style.

The ruins of the Roman settlement of Bilbilis, birthplace
of the poet Martial, are east of
Calatayud, near Huérmeda.

Monasterio de Piedra ⓳

3 km (2 miles) south of Nuévalos.
📞 976 84 90 11. 🚊 Calatayud. 🚌
from Zaragoza. ⭕ daily. 🎨 🎫 ♿

FOUNDED BY Alfonso II of
Aragón in 1195, this
Cistercian monastery suffered
damage in the 19th century
and was subsequently rebuilt.

Some of the original buildings
survive, however, including the
chapterhouse, refectory and
hostel – all of which date back
to the 13th century.

In the damp, blackened cellars, the monks once distilled
strong potions of herbal liqueur in a large alembic. The
kitchen was allegedly the first
place in Europe where drinking
chocolate, from Mexico, was
prepared *(see p55)*.

The park in which the monastery stands is a picturesque
nature reserve full of grottoes
and waterfalls. A hotel is now
located in the old monastery
buildings *(see p549)*.

Daroca ⓴

Zaragoza. 👥 2,900. ℹ️ Plaza de
España 4, 976 80 01 29. 🚌 Thu.
🎭 Santo Tomás (7 Mar).

AN IMPRESSIVE ARRAY of battlemented medieval walls
stretches approximately 4 km
(2 miles) around this old Moorish stronghold. Although parts
of the walls have decayed, the
114 towers and fortified gateways are still a remarkable
sight, particularly from the
main road to Zaragoza.

The **Colegial de Santa
María**, a church in the central
square, houses the Holy Cloths
from the Reconquest *(see
pp50–51)*. After a surprise
attack by the Moors in 1239,
priests celebrating Mass in the
countryside hastily bundled
the consecrated bread into the
linen sheets used to cover the
altar. When the cloths were
unwrapped they were miraculously stained with blood.

ENVIRONS: The agricultural
town of **Monreal del Campo**,
42 km (26 miles) south of
Daroca, has a saffron museum.
The backbreaking labour of
harvesting the autumn crocus,
formerly an important crop, is
no longer profitable.

Fuendetodos ㉑

Zaragoza. 👥 180. ℹ️ Calle Zuloaga
24, 976 14 38 01. 🎭 San Roque (last
Sat of May), San Bartolomé (24 Aug).

THIS SMALL VILLAGE was the
birthplace of one of Spain's
best-known artists of the late
18th and early 19th centuries,

Interior of Goya's cottage in Fuendetodos

Castle-parador above Alcañiz

Francisco de Goya. The **Casa-Museo de Goya** is a neat cottage said to be the painter's home. It has been restored and furnished in appropriate period style. On display are some of the artist's personal effects as well as engravings.

ENVIRONS: Lying 20 km (12 miles) east of Fuendetodos is **Belchite**, the site of one of the most horrific battles of the Spanish Civil War *(see pp62–3)*, for control of the strategic Ebro valley. Remains of the old, shell-torn town have been left tottering as a monument to the horrors of war.

In **Cariñena**, 25 km (16 miles) west of Fuendetodos, bodegas offer the opportunity to sample and buy the excellent, full-bodied red wine for which the region is justly renowned *(see pp192–3)*.

🏛 **Casa-Museo de Goya**
Calle Zuluaga 3. 📞 976 14 38 30.
⬚ 11am–2pm, 4–7pm Tue–Sun. 🖼

Alcañiz ㉒

Teruel. 🏘 14,000. 🚌 ℹ️ Calle Mayor 1, 978 83 12 13. 🚍 Tue. 🎉 Fiestas Patronales (8–13 Sep).

FROM A DISTANCE, two buildings rise above the town of Alcañiz. One is the **castle**, which was the headquarters of the Order of Calatrava in the 12th century. This historic building has been converted into a parador *(see p548)*. The keep, the Torre del Homenaje, has a collection of 14th-century frescoes depicting the conquest of Valencia by Jaime I.

The other building is the **Colegiata de Santa María**. This church, on the sloping Plaza de España, has a Gothic tower and a Baroque façade.

On the same square are the elegantly galleried **Lonja** (commodities exchange), with its lacy Gothic arches, and the **town hall** *(ayuntamiento)*, with one Mudéjar and one Renaissance façade.

FRANCISCO DE GOYA

Self-portrait by Goya

Born in Fuendetodos in 1746, Francisco de Goya specialized in designing cartoons for the tapestry industry *(see p296)* in his early life, and in decorating churches such as Zaragoza's Basílica del Pilar with vivacious frescoes. In 1799 he became painter to Carlos IV, and depicted the king and his wife María Luisa with unflattering accuracy *(see p29)*. The invasion of Madrid by Napoleon's troops in 1808 *(see pp58–9)* and its attendant horrors had a profound and lasting effect on Goya's temperament, and his later works are imbued with cynical despair and isolation. He died in Bordeaux in 1828.

ARAGÓN'S FIESTAS

Las Tamboradas
(Maundy Thursday and Good Friday), Teruel province. During Easter Week, brotherhoods of men wearing long black robes beat drums in mourning for Christ. Las Tamboradas begins with "the breaking of the hour" at midnight on Thursday in Híjar. The Tamborada in Calanda begins the following day at midday. The solemn drum rolls continue for several hours. Aching arms and bleeding hands are considered to be signs of religious devotion.

Young drummer in Las Tamboradas, Alcorija

Carnival *(Feb/Mar)*, Bielsa (Huesca). The protagonists of this fiesta, known as *Trangas*, have rams' horns on their heads, blackened faces and teeth made of potatoes. They are said to represent fertility.
Romería de Santa Orosia *(25 Jun)*, Yebra de Basa (Huesca). Pilgrims in folk costume carry St Orosia's skull to her shrine.
Día del Pilar *(12 Oct)*, Zaragoza. Aragón's distinctive folk dance, the *jota*, is performed everywhere during the city's festivities in honour of its patroness, the Virgin of the Pillar *(see p227)*. On the Día del Pilar there is a procession with cardboard giants, and a spectacular display of flowers dedicated to the Virgin.

Alcalá de la Selva castle, overlooking the town

Valderrobres ❷❸

Teruel. ⩍ 2,000. ⊟ ⅱ Avda
Cortes de Aragón 25, 978 85 06 44.
🚌 Sat. 🎪 San Roque (mid-Aug).

JUST INSIDE Aragón's border
with Catalonia, the delightful
town of Valderrobres overlooks
the shallow, trout-filled Río
Matarrana. Dominating the
town is the restored **castle**,
which was formerly a palace
for Aragonese royalty. Below
it stands the imposing Gothic
**Iglesia de Santa María la
Mayor**, with a huge rose
window in Catalan Gothic
style. The unusual arcaded
plaza has a pleasing town hall
(ayuntamiento) completed in
the end of the 16th century.

ENVIRONS: To the south lies
tiny **Mirambel**, a carefully
restored medieval village.

♣ **Castillo de Valderrobres**
⬚ Jul–Sep: Tue–Sun, Oct–Jun: Sat,
Sun & public hols. 🎟

Sierra de Gúdar ❷❹

Teruel. 🚌 Mora de Rubielos. 🚌 Alcalá
de la Selva. ⅱ Plaza de la Iglesia 4,
Alcalá, 978 80 10 00.

THIS RANGE OF HILLS, northeast of Teruel, is a region
of pine woods and jagged
limestone outcrops erupting
from scrub-covered slopes. At
2,019 m (6,624 ft), **Peñarroya**
is the highest point. Nearby
Valdelinares, Aragón's third-
highest village, is a ski station.
From the access roads there
are panoramic views of the
hills. Especially noteworthy are
the views from the towns of
Linares de Mora and **Alcalá**

de la Selva, which has a castle
set against a backdrop of rock
faces. Its Baroque church, with
shell motifs and twisted columns, shelters the shrine of
the Virgen de la Vega.

Mora de Rubielos ❷❺

Teruel. ⩍ 1,400. ⅱ Diputación 1,
978 80 61 32 (summer); 978 80 00
00 (winter). 🚌 Mon & Fri. 🎪 San
Miguel (28 Sep–1 Oct).

DOMINATED BY one of the
best-preserved castles in
Aragón, Mora de
Rubielos has a
medieval old town.
Its **collegiate
church** has chapels
decorated with
azulejos from
Manises. There is a
fountain nearby
which depicts
dolphins
playing.

ENVIRONS: Rubielos de Mora,
lying 10 km (6 miles) to the
southeast, is worth exploring
simply for its well-preserved
stone and timber buildings.
Among the balconied houses
is an Augustinian convent with
a Gothic reredos.

Teruel ❷❻

Teruel. 🚗 31,000. ⊟ ⊟ ⅱ Calle
Tomás Nougués 1, 978 60 22 79.
🚌 Thu. 🎪 Día del Sermón de las
Tortillas (Tue of Easter week), La
Vaquilla del Ángel (mid-Jul), Feria del
Jamón (mid-Sep). ⓦ www.teruel.org

THIS INDUSTRIAL TOWN has
been the scene of much
desperate fighting throughout
the centuries. It began with
the Romans, the first to capture
and civilize Celtiberian Turba.
During the Reconquest the
town became a strategic frontier prize. In 1171 Alfonso II
recaptured Teruel for Christian
Spain, but many Muslims continued to live peacefully in
the city, which they embellished with beautiful Mudéjar
towers. The last mosque was
closed only at the height of
the Inquisition (see p264), in
1502. More recently, during
the terrible, freezing winter of
1937, the bitterest battle of
the Civil War (see pp62–3)
was fought here. There were
many thousands of casualties.
The old quarter is home to
the wedge-shaped Plaza del
Torico, with a monument of a

Tiled towers and rooftops of Teruel cathedral

Balconied café above Albarracín's main square

small bull, the city's emblem. Within walking distance lie the five remaining Mudéjar towers. Most striking are those of **San Salvador** and **San Martín**, both dating back to the 12th century. The latter has multi-patterned brickwork studded with blue and green ceramics.

Inside the **Iglesia de San Pedro** are the tombs of the famous Lovers of Teruel. The **cathedral** has more colourful Mudéjar work, including a lantern dome of glazed tiles, and a tower completed in the 17th century. The dazzling coffered ceiling is painted with lively scenes of medieval life.

The **Museo Provincial**, one of Aragón's best museums, is housed in an elegant mansion. It has a large collection of ceramics, testifying to an industry for which Teruel has long been known. North of the centre is the **Acueducto de los Arcos**, a 16th-century aqueduct.

🏛 **Museo Provincial**
Pl Fray Anselmo Polanco 3. ⬛ 978 60 01 50. ⬤ Tue–Sun.

Albarracín ㉗

Teruel. 🏘 1,200. 🚌 ⓘ Calle Diputación 4, 978 71 02 51. ⬤ Wed. 🎉 Los Mayos (30 Apr–1 May), Fiestas Patronales (13–17 Sep). Ⓦ www.albarracin.org

I T IS EASY TO SEE WHY this picturesque town earned an international award for historical preservation. A dramatic cliff above the Río Guadalaviar is the perfect setting for this attractive cluster of mellow

pink buildings. Standing on a ridge behind the town are the defensive walls and towers which date from Muslim times.

There is a good view of the town from below the **Palacio Episcopal** (Bishop's Palace). Inside the neighbouring 16th-century **cathedral**, which is topped by a belfry, there is a Renaissance carved wooden altarpiece depicting scenes from the life of St Peter. The treasury museum contains 16th-century Brussels tapestries and enamelled chalices.

Some of Albarracín's sturdy beamed and galleried houses have an unusual two-tier structure. The ground floor is limestone, and the overhanging upper storey is covered in rough coral-pink plasterwork.

Many have been restored to their medieval form. Just outside the town are the caves of Navazo and Callejón, with their prehistoric rock paintings. Reproductions can be seen in Teruel's Museo Provincial.

ENVIRONS: In the surrounding **Montes Universales**, which rise to 1,170 m (3,840 ft), is the source of the Tagus, one of Spain's longest rivers. From fertile cereal plains to crumbling rocks, this area is a colourful mixture of poplars, junipers and thick pine woods, with poppies in spring. At **Cella**, northeast of Albarracín, the Río Jiloca has its source.

Rincón de Ademuz ㉘

Valencia. 🏘 1,200. 🚌 Ademuz. ⓘ Plaza del Ayuntamiento 1, 978 78 20 00. ⬤ Wed. 🎉 Fiestas de la Virgen del Rosario (early Oct).

T HIS REMOTE ENCLAVE south of Teruel officially belongs to the Comunidad Valenciana (see p233); but is effectively an island of territory, stranded between the borders of Aragón and Castilla-La Mancha. The area has not prospered in recent years. But it still has its own austere charm and some peaceful tracts of country scattered with red rocks.

THE LOVERS OF TERUEL

According to legend, in 13th-century Teruel two young people, Diego de Marcilla and Isabel de Segura, fell in love and wished to marry. She came from a wealthy family, but he was poor, and her parents forbade the match. Diego was given five years in which to make his fortune and establish a name for himself. At the end of this time he returned to Teruel, laden with wealth, only to find his bride-to-be already married to a local nobleman. Diego died of a broken heart and Isabel, full of despair at his death, died the following day.

Isabel de Segura   **Diego de Marcilla**

VALENCIA AND MURCIA

CASTELLÓN · VALENCIA · ALICANTE · MURCIA

TODAY, THE CENTRAL REGION *of Spain's eastern Mediterranean coast is an important holiday destination – the beaches of the Costa Blanca, the Costa del Azahar and the Costa Cálida draw millions of tourists annually. Centuries ago, Muslim settlers made these regions bloom, and the fertile fields and citrus groves of the coastal plains are still Spain's citrus orchard and market garden.*

These productive lands have been occupied for more than 50,000 years. The Greeks, Phoenicians, Carthaginians and Romans all settled here before the Moors arrived, trading the products of land and sea.

The provinces of Castellón, Valencia and Alicante (which make up the Comunidad Valenciana) were reconquered from the Moors by a Catalan army. The language these troops left behind them developed into a dialect, *valenciano*, which is widely spoken and increasingly seen on signposts. Murcia, to the south, is one of Spain's smallest autonomous regions.

The population is concentrated on the coast where the historic towns and cities of Valencia, Alicante and Cartagena have been joined by modern package holiday resorts, such as Benidorm and La Manga del Mar Menor. Inland, where tourism has barely reached, the landscape rises into the chains of mountains that stand between the coast and the plateau of Central Spain. The scenery inland ranges from picturesque valleys and hills in the Maestrat, in the north of Castellón, to the semi-desert terrain around Lorca in southern Murcia.

The warm climate encourages outdoor life and exuberant fiestas. Most famous of these are Las Fallas of Valencia; the mock battles between Moors and Christians staged in Alcoi; and the lavish, costumed Easter processions in Murcia and Lorca.

Hill terraces of olive and almond trees ascending the hillsides near Alcoi

◁ The Penyal d'Ifach, rising directly out of the sea to tower above the Costa Blanca near Calp

Exploring Valencia and Murcia

THE COASTS OF VALENCIA AND MURCIA are popular for seaside holidays and ideal for water sports almost all year round. Principal resorts include Benidorm, Benicassim and La Manga del Mar Menor. Some coastal towns such as Peñíscola, Gandia, Denia, Alicante and Cartagena have charming old quarters, castles and other monuments well worth visiting. Close to the sea are several scenic nature reserves: the freshwater lagoon of L'Albufera, and, on the Costa Blanca, the saltpans of Santa Pola and the striking limestone crag of the Penyal d'Ifach.

Inland, the region offers excursions to such undiscovered beauty spots as El Maestrat and the mountains around Alcoi, as well as the undervisited historic towns of Xàtiva and Lorca. The two regional capitals, Valencia and Murcia, are both lively university cities with fine cathedrals and numerous museums.

Fishing nets strung out in the lagoon of L'Albufera

GETTING AROUND

The region's principal roads are the A7 (E15) motorway (toll-paying from Alicante northwards except for the Valencia bypass) and the N332 along the coast. Other motorways connect Valencia with Madrid, A3 (E901), and Alicante with Madrid, N330. There are main rail lines from Alicante, Valencia and Murcia to Madrid, but the rest of the rail network is rather fragmented and buses are often quicker than trains. A scenic narrow-gauge railway line along the Costa Blanca connects Denia to Alicante via Benidorm. The region's international airports are at Alicante and Valencia.

0 kilometres   25

0 miles   20

SEE ALSO

• *Where to Stay* pp549–51

• *Restaurants and Bars* pp590–92

Orange groves outside Denia

SIGHTS AT A GLANCE

KEY

≡ Motorway
━ Major road
━ Minor road
━ Scenic route
≈ River
☼ Viewpoint

One of the many coves on Xàbia's rugged coast

(Map labels)
Zaragoza
MORELLA
Barcelona
C. Eval
EL MAESTRAT
VINAROS
PEÑISCOLA
VILLAFAMES
BENICÀSSIM
CASTELLÓ
DE LA PLANA
ONDA
SANT JOSEP
SAGUNT
MONASTERIO
DE EL PUIG
VALENCIA
L'ALBUFERA
CULLERA
XÀTIVA
GANDIA
DENIA
XÀBIA
GUADALEST
PENYAL
D'IFACH
BENIDORM
ILLA DE
TABARCA
EVIEJA
COSTA DEL AZAHAR
COSTA BLANCA

The unbroken medieval wall surrounding the historic hilltop town of Morella in El Maestrat

El Maestrat ❶

Castellón & Teruel. 🚌 Morella.
🏠 Morella, 964 17 30 32.

CRUSADING WARLORDS of the
Knights Templar and the
Knights of Montesa – known
as *maestres* (masters) – gave
their name to this lonely upland region. To rule over this
frontier land, which straddles
the border between Valencia
and Aragón, they built fortified
settlements in dramatic defensive positions, often on rocky
crags. The best preserved of
them is **Morella**, the principal
town. **Forcall**, not far from
Morella, has two 16th-century
mansions on its porticoed

**The Torre de la Sacristía, in the
restored village of Mirambel**

square. To the south, the village of **Ares del Maestre** is
spectacularly sited beneath a
1,318-m (4,300-ft) high rock.
Cantavieja is the most important town in the Aragonese
part of El Maestrat (where it
is known as El Maestrazgo). It
has a handsome, arcaded
square. The walled village of
Mirambel, nearby, has been
meticulously restored to its
medieval condition.
There are several spooky
but fascinating shrines to the
Virgin in El Maestrat, notably
the cave at **La Balma**, which
is reached via a rocky ledge.
The scenery in most parts is
striking: fertile valleys alternate
with breathtaking cliffs and
bare, flat-topped mountains
overflown by eagles and vultures. Tourism is developing
very slowly here: there are few
places to stay and the roads
can be windy and slow.

Morella ❷

Castellón. 🏘 2,800. 🚌 🏠 Plaza de
San Miguel, 964 17 30 32. 🔄 Sun.
🎊 Fiestas patronales (Aug).

BUILT ON a high, isolated
outcrop and crowned by
a ruined castle, Morella cuts a
dramatic profile. Its unbroken
medieval walls retain six gateways, which lead into a fan-
shaped maze of streets and

steep, tapering alleys, many
of which are shaded by the
eaves of ancient houses. The
main street is lined with shady
porticoes. In the upper part of
town is the **Basílica de Santa
María la Mayor**. Its unique
raised choirloft is reached by
a finely carved spiral staircase.

EN ESTA CASA OBRÓ SAN VICENTE FERRER EL PRODIGIOSO
ILAGRO DE LA RESURRECCIÓN DE UN NIÑO QUE SU MADRE
NAJENADA HABÍA DESCUARTIZADO Y GUISADO EN
OBSEQUIO AL SANTO (1414)

MORELLA'S MIRACLE

A plaque on the wall of
Morella's Calle de la Virgen
marks the house in which
St Vincent Ferrer is said to
have performed a bizarre
miracle in the early 15th
century. A housewife, dis-
traught at having no meat
to offer the saint, cut up
her son and put him in
the cooking pot. When St
Vincent discovered this,
he reconstituted the boy –
except for one of his little
fingers, which his mother
had eaten to see if the dish
was sufficiently salted.

Peñíscola ❸

Castellón. 🏠 5,000. 🚉 ℹ️ Paseo Marítimo, 964 48 02 08. 🚌 Mon. 🎉 Fiestas Patronales (2nd week Sep).

T HE FORTIFIED OLD TOWN of Peñíscola clusters around the base of a castle built on a rocky promontory, surrounded on three sides by the sea. This labyrinth of narrow winding streets and white houses is enclosed by massive ramparts. These are entered by either the Fosch Gate – reached by a ramp from the Plaza del Caudillo – or through the San Pedro Gate, from the harbour.

The **Castell del Papa Luna** was built on the foundations of an Arab fortress in the late 13th century by the Knights Templar. Their cross is carved above the door. It later became the residence of the papal pretender Pedro de Luna, cardinal of Aragón. He was elected Pope Benedict XIII during the Great Schism that split the Catholic Church at the end of the 14th century. Although he was deposed by the Council of Constance in 1414, he continued to proclaim his right to the papacy until his death as a nonagenarian in 1423.

The uppermost battlements of the castle are false: they were built for a scene from the 1961 film El Cid. Modern Peñíscola is now a thriving holiday resort.

⚑ Castell del Papa Luna
Calle Castillo. 📞 964 48 00 21. 🕐 daily. 🌙 1 Jan, 9 Sep, 9 Oct, 25 Dec. 📷

Sunset view of the beach and old town of Peñíscola

Costa del Azahar ❹

Castellón. 🚉 Castelló de la Plana. 🚉 Castelló de la Plana. ℹ️ Castelló de la Plana, 964 35 86 88.

T HE "ORANGE BLOSSOM COAST" of Castellón province is named after the dense citrus groves of the coastal plain. The two principal resorts are Benicàssim, where handsome old villas have been supplemented by modern hotels and other tourist amenities, and Peñíscola. Alcossebre and Oropesa also have popular beaches. Vinaròs – the most northerly point – and Benicarló are key fishing ports supplying prawns and date-mussels to local restaurants.

Sculpture in the Casa del Batle

Villafamés ❺

Castellón. 🏠 1,500. 🚉 ℹ️ Plaza del Ayuntamiento 1, 964 32 90 01. 🚌 Fri. 🎉 Patronales (mid-Aug).

T HIS MEDIEVAL TOWN climbs from a flat plain along a rocky ridge to the restored round keep of its castle. The older, upper part of the town is a warren of sloping streets filled with sturdy houses.

A 15th-century mansion houses the **Casa del Batle**, a museum of contemporary art. The works on display, some of which are for sale, date from 1959 to the present.

🏛 Casa del Batle
Calle Diputación 20. 📞 964 32 91 52. 🕐 Tue–Sun. 📷

Castelló de la Plana's planetarium, close to the beach

Castelló de la Plana ❻

Castellón. 🏠 160,000. 🚉 🚉 ℹ️ Plaza María Agustina 5, 964 35 86 88. 🚌 Mon. 🎉 Fiesta de la Magdalena (3rd Sat of Lent).

O RIGINALLY FOUNDED on high ground inland, the capital of Castellón province was relocated nearer to the coast in the 13th century.

The city centre, the Plaza Mayor, is bordered by the market, the town hall, the cathedral and **El Fadri**, a 58-m (190-ft) high octagonal bell tower erected in the 1590s.

The **Museo Provincial de Bellas Artes** contains a collection of artifacts dating from the middle Palaeolithic era, paintings from the 15th to the 20th centuries and modern ceramics from the region. On temporary display is José de Ribera's Saint Jerome.

The **Convento de las Madres Capuchinas** has an important collection of paintings which are attributed to Francisco de Zurbarán.

In **El Planetario** there are demonstrations of the night sky, the solar system and the nearest stars. It also has a permanent exhibit on holography.

🏛 Museo Provincial de Bellas Artes
Avda Hermanos Bou 28. 📞 964 72 75 00. 🕐 Tue–Sun. 📷 (free Sun).
⛪ Convento de las Madres Capuchinas
Calle Núñez de Arce 11. 📞 964 22 06 41. 🕐 4–8pm daily.
🎪 El Planetario
Paseo Marítimo 1, El Grao. 📞 964 28 29 68. 🕐 11am 2pm Sat & Sun, 4:30–8pm Tue–Sat. 🌙 Sep. 📷 (planetarium). ♿

Onda ❼

Castellón. 🚶 *22,000.* 🚌 ℹ️ *Calle Cervantes 6, 964 77 08 73.* 📅 *Thu.* 🎉 *Feria del Santísimo Salvador (6 Aug).*

ONDA, HOME to a thriving ceramics industry, is overlooked by a ruined **castle**, which was known to its Moorish founders as the "Castle of the Three Hundred Towers". The old quarter of the town has some character, especially the charming square of **Plaza del Almudín**, with its medieval porticoes.

But the main reason to visit Onda is to take a look at the **Museo El Carmen**, a natural history museum belonging to a Carmelite monastery.

The collection was begun in 1952 by the monks for their own private scientific study. It was only opened to the public a decade later. The clever use of subdued lighting lends dramatic effect to the 10,000 plant and animal specimens which are exhibited over three floors. Objects include large stuffed animals placed in naturalistic settings, butterflies and other insects, shells, fossils, minerals and grisly, preserved anatomical specimens.

🏛 **Museo El Carmen**
Carretera de Tales. 📞 *964 60 07 30.* 🕐 *Tue–Sun.* ⬛ *20 Dec–6 Jan.* 📷

Two butterfly exhibits in the Museo El Carmen

Boat ride through the winding Coves de Sant Josep

Coves de Sant Josep ❽

Vall d'Uixó (Castellón). 📞 *964 69 05 76.* 🚌 *Vall d'Uixó.* 🕐 *daily.* 📷

THE CAVES OF St Joseph were first explored in 1902. The subterranean river that formed them, and which still flows through them, has been charted for almost 3 km (2 miles). However, its source has not yet been discovered and only part of this distance can be explored on a visit.

Boats take visitors along the serpentine course of the river. You may have to duck to avoid projections of rock on the way. Here and there the narrow caves open out into large chambers such as the *Sala de los Murciélagos* (Hall of the Bats – the bats left when the floodlights were installed). The water reaches its deepest point of 12 m (39 ft) in the *Lago Azul* (Blue Lake). You can explore a further 255 m (837 ft) along the *Galería Seca* (Dry Gallery) on foot. The caves are often closed to visitors after heavy rain.

Alto Turia ❾

Valencia. 🚌 *Chelva.* ℹ️ *CV35 Valencia–Ademúz km 73, 96 163 50 84.*

THE ATTRACTIVE WOODED HILLS of the upper reaches of the Río Turia in Valencia (Alto Turia) are popular with hikers and day-trippers. **Chelva**, the main town, has an unusual clock on its church which shows not only the hour but the day and month as well. The town is overlooked by the **Pico del Remedio** (1,054 m/ 3,458 ft), from the summit of which there is a fine panoramic view of the region. In a valley near Chelva, at the end of an unsurfaced but drivable track, are the remains of a Roman aqueduct, **Peña Cortada**.

The most attractive and interesting village in Alto Turia is **Alpuente**, situated above a dry gorge. Between 1031 and 1089, when it was captured by El Cid (*see p352*), Alpuente was the capital of a small *taifa*, a Moorish kingdom. In the 14th century it was still important enough for the kingdom of Valencia's parliament to meet here. The town hall is confined to a small tower over a 14th-century gateway, which was later extended in the 16th century by the addition of a rectangular council chamber.

Requena, to the south is Valencia's main wine town. Further south, Valencia's other principal river, the Xúquer (Júcar), carves tremendous gorges near Cortes de Pallas on its way past the **Muela de Cortes**. This massive, wild plateau and nature reserve is crossed by one small road and a lonely dirt track.

LA TOMATINA

The highpoint of the annual fiesta in Buñol (Valencia) is a sticky food fight on the last Wednesday of August, which attracts thousands of visitors dressed in their worst clothes. Lorry loads of ripe tomatoes are provided by the town council at 11am for participants to hurl at each other. No one in range of the combatants is spared: foreigners and photographers are prized targets.

The battle originated in 1944. Some say it began with a fight between friends. Others say irreverent locals pelted civic dignitaries with tomatoes during a procession. Increasing national and international press coverage means that more people attend, and more tomatoes are thrown, every year.

Sagunt's ruined fortifications, added to by successive rulers of the town

Sagunt ⑩

Valencia. 🏘 61,000. 🚉 🚌 ℹ Pl
Cronista Chabret, 96 266 22 13. 🅰
Wed. 🎭 Fiestas (mid-Jul–mid-Aug).

SITED NEAR THE JUNCTION of
two Roman roads, Sagunt
(Sagunto) played a crucial
role in Spain's ancient history.

In 219 BC Hannibal, the
Carthaginian commander in
southern Spain, stormed and
sacked Rome's ally Saguntum.
All the inhabitants of the town
were said to have died in the
assault, the last throwing themselves on to bonfires rather
than fall into the hands of
Hannibal's troops. The incident sparked off the Second
Punic War, a disaster for the
Carthaginians, which ended

with Rome's occupation of the
peninsula (see pp46–7).

The town still contains several reminders of the Roman
occupation, including the 1st-
century AD **Roman theatre**.
Built out of limestone in a
natural depression on the hillside above the town, it has
been controversially restored
by the regional government
using modern materials. The
theatre is now used as a venue
for music, plays and Sagunt's
annual theatre festival.

The ruins of the **castle**,
sprawling along the crest of
the hill above the modern-
day town, mark the original
site of Saguntum. Superim-
posed on each other are the
excavated remains of various
civilizations, including the

Iberians, the Carthaginians,
the Romans and the Moors.
The ruins of the castle are divided into seven divisions, the
highest being La Ciudadella,
and the most important Armas.

⚑ **Castillo de Sagunt**
🞔 Tue–Sun. 🎟

Monasterio de
El Puig ⑪

El Puig (Valencia). ☎ 96 147 02 00.
🚉 🚌 El Puig. 🞔 10am–1pm, 4–7pm
(4–6pm in winter) Tue–Sun. 🎟 🅲

THIS MERCEDARIAN monastery
was founded by King
Jaime I of Aragón, who
conquered Valencia from the
Moors in the 13th century.

The monastery is now
home to a collection of 240
paintings from between the
16th and 18th centuries and
the Museo de la Imprenta y
de la Obra Gráfica (Museum
of Printing and Graphic Art).
The museum commemorates
the printing of the first book
in Spain – thought to have
been in Valencia in 1474 –
and illustrates the development of the printing press.
Exhibits include printers'
blocks and a copy of the
smallest book in the world.

Messy participants throwing tomatoes at each other in the annual fiesta of La Tomatina

Valencia ⑫

Spain's third largest city is sited in the middle of the *huerta*: a fertile plain of orange groves and market gardens, which is one of Europe's most intensively farmed regions. With its warm coastal climate, Valencia is known for its exuberant outdoor living and nightlife. In March the city stages one of Spain's most spectacular fiestas, Las Fallas *(see p245)*, in which giant papier-mâché sculptures are burned in the streets. Modern Valencia is a centre for trade and manufacturing, notably ceramics. A ferry service connects the city with the Balearic Islands.

Flowers in honour of Valencia's patroness, Virgen de los Desamparados

Exploring Valencia

Valencia stands on the course of the Río Turia. The city centre and the crumbling old quarter of El Carmen are on the right bank. Most of the monuments are within walking distance of the Plaza del Ayuntamiento, the triangular main square which is presided over by the town hall.

The city was founded by the Romans in 138 BC and later conquered by the Moors. It was captured by El Cid *(see p352)* in 1096, retaken by the Moors, and finally recaptured by Jaime I, the Conqueror, in 1238, to become absorbed into the kingdom of Aragón.

The three finest buildings in Valencia were built during its economic and cultural heyday in the 14th and 15th centuries: the Torres de Serranos, a gateway that survived the demolition of the medieval walls in the 19th century, La Lonja and the cathedral.

♛ Palau de la Generalitat
Plaza des Manises. 【 96 386 61 00.
◯ *by prior appointment only.*
This palace, which is now used by the Valencian regional government, was built in Gothic style between 1482 and 1579 but added to in the 17th and 20th centuries. It surrounds an enclosed stone patio from which two staircases ascend to splendidly decorated rooms.

The larger of the two Salas Doradas (Golden Chambers), on the mezzanine level, has a multicoloured coffered ceiling and tiled floor. The walls of the parliament chamber are decorated with frescoes.

♙ Basílica de la Virgen de los Desamparados
Pl de la Virgen. 【 96 391 86 11.
◯ *7am–2pm, 4pm–9pm daily.*
The ornately dressed statue of Valencia's patroness, the Virgin of the Helpless, stands above an altar in this 17th-century church, lavishly adorned with flowers and candles. She is honoured during Las Fallas by La Ofrenda ("the Offering"), a display of flowers in the square outside the church.

♙ Cathedral
Pl de la Reina 【 96 391 81 27
Museo ◯ *Mon–Sat.* Miguelete
◯ *daily.* 🎫 🗗
Built originally in 1262, the cathedral has been added to over the ages, and its three doorways are all in different styles. The oldest is the Romanesque Puerta del Palau but the main entrance is the 18th-century Baroque portal, the Puerta de los Hierros.

A unique court meets on Thursdays at noon in front of the other doorway, the Gothic Puerta de los Apóstoles. For an estimated 1,000 years, the Water Tribunal has settled disputes between farmers over irrigation in the *huerta*.

Inside the cathedral, a chapel holds an agate cup, claimed to be the Holy Grail. According

The Miguelete, the cathedral's bell tower on Plaza de la Reina

to legend it arrived in Valencia from Jerusalem by way of San Juan de la Peña monastery in Aragón *(see p224)*.

The cathedral's 68-m (223-ft) high octagonal bell tower, the Miguelete, built between 1380 and 1420, is Valencia's main landmark. The cathedral also houses a museum.

♒ La Lonja
Plaza del Mercado. **(** 96 352 54 78. **◯** *Tue–Sun.*
An exquisite Late Gothic hall, built between 1482 and 1498 as a commodities exchange, La Lonja is now used for hosting cultural events. The outside walls are decorated with gargoyles and a variety of other grotesque figures. The high ceiling of the transactions hall is formed by star-patterned vaulting which is supported on graceful spiral columns.

▣ Mercado Central
Plaza del Mercado. **(** 96 382 91 01. **◯** *Mon–Sat am.*
This huge iron, glass and tile Art Nouveau building, with its parrot and swordfish weather-

Ornate toilet sign outside Valencia's Mercado Central

vanes, opened in 1928 and is one of the largest and most attractive markets in Europe. Every morning its thousand or so stalls are filled with a bewildering variety of food.

▥ Museo Nacional de Cerámica Gonzalez Martí
Poeta Querol 2. **(** 96 351 63 92. **◯** *Tue–Sun.* **●** *1 & 22 Jan, 1 May, 24, 25 & 31 Dec.* **✎** *(free Sat pm & Sun).* **&**
Spain's Ceramics Museum is housed in the mansion of the Marqués de Dos Aguas, an 18th-century fantasy of

coloured plasterwork. The doorway is surrounded by a carving by Ignacio Vergara. The 5,000 exhibits include prehistoric, Greek and Roman ceramics, pieces by Picasso and a tiled Valencian kitchen.

♙ Colegio del Patriarca
This seminary was built in the mid-16th century. The walls and ceiling of the church are covered with frescoes by Bartolomé Matarana. During Friday morning Mass, the painting above the altar, *The Last Supper* by Francisco Ribalta, is lowered to reveal a painting of the crucifixion by an anonymous 15th-century German artist.

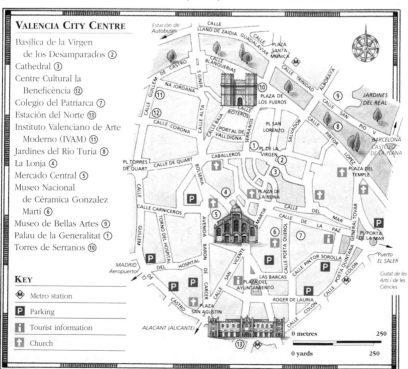

KEY

◉	Metro station
P	Parking
▯	Tourist information
✝	Church

0 metres   250

0 yards   250

The Palau de la Música, Valencia's prestigious concert hall

Beyond the Centre

The centre of the city is bordered by the Gran Vía Marqués del Turia and the Gran Vía Ramón y Cajal. Beyond these lie the 19th-century suburbs laid out on a grid plan.

The best way to get around beyond the centre is by the metro, one line of which is a tramway to the beaches of El Cabañal and La Malvarrosa.

Ecce Homo by Juan de Juanes in the Museo de Bellas Artes

♣ Jardines del Río Turia

Where once there was a river there is now a 5-km (3-mile) long strip of gardens, sports fields and playgrounds crossed by a dozen bridges. In a prominent position above the riverbed stands the Palau de la Música, an international-class

concert hall built in the 1980s. The centrepiece of the nearby children's playground is the giant figure of Gulliver pinned to the ground and covered with steps and slides.

The best of Valencia's other public gardens stand near the banks of the river. The largest of them, the Jardines Reales – known locally as Los Viveros – contain a small zoo. The intimate Italian-style Monforte Gardens are dotted with marble statues and filled with hibiscus and magnolia. The Jardín Botánico, created in 1802, is planted with 7,000 species of shrubs and trees.

🏛 Museo De Bellas Artes

Museo San Pio V, Calle San Pio V 9. [96 360 57 93.] Tue–Sun. ● 1 Jan, Good Fri, 25 & 31 Dec. & 🗹
An important collection of 2,000 paintings and statues dating from antiquity to the last century is housed in this former seminary, which was built between 1683 and 1744.

Valencian art dating from the 14th and 15th centuries is represented by a series of golden altarpieces by Alcanyis, Pere Nicolau and Maestro de Bonastre. Velázquez's self-portrait and works by Bosch, El Greco, Murillo, Ribalta, Van Dyck and the local Renaissance painter Juan de Juanes hang on the first floor.

On the top floor there are six paintings by Goya and pictures by important Valencian artists from the 19th and 20th centuries: Ignacio Pinazo, Joaquín Sorolla and Antonio Muñoz Degrain. A large collection of the latter's hallucinatory coloured paintings are gathered together in one room, among them the disturbing *Amor de Madre*.

♠ Torres de Serranos

Plaza de los Fueros. [96 391 90 70.] Tue–Sun.
Erected in 1238 as a triumphal arch in the city's walls, this gateway combines defensive and decorative features. Its two towers are crowned with battlements and lightened by delicate Gothic tracery.

The towering gateway of the Torres de Serranos

🏛 Instituto Valenciano de Arte Moderno (IVAM)

Calle Guillem de Castro 118. **96 386 30 00.** ⬤ *10am–8pm Tue–Sun.* 🎟 *(free Sun).* 🚻 🅦 *www.ivam.es*

The Valencian Institute of Modern Art is in two buildings. Works by Julio González, the father of 20th-century Spanish sculpture, are included in the modern main building. A 13th-century Carmelite convent has temporary exhibitions of contemporary works.

🏛 Centre Cultural la Beneficència

Calle Corona 36. **96 388 35 65.** ⬤ *10am–9pm (Oct–Mar 8pm) Tue–Sun.* 🚻

Displays of prehistoric and ethnographic objects here include part of a collection of 5,000 Stone Age engravings of deer and horses made on limestone plaques that were found in the Cueva de Parpalló, in the hills near Gandia *(see p244).*

Art Nouveau-style column in the Estación del Norte

🚆 Estación del Norte

Calle Játiva 24. **902 24 02 02.** ⬤ *daily.*

Valencia's mainline railway station was built from 1906–17 in a style inspired by Austrian Art Nouveau. Inside, ceramic murals and stained glass in the foyer and cafeteria depict the life and crops of the *huerta* and L'Albufera *(see p244).*

🏛 Ciutat de les Arts i de les Ciències

Avenida Autovia del Saler. **90 210 00 31.** ⬤ *daily.* 🎟 🚻

Valencia's most impressive modern project, the City of Arts and Sciences, is still

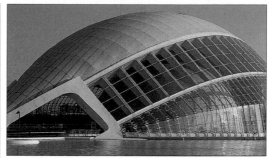

The hemispherical IMAX cinema at the Ciutat de les Arts i de les Ciències

under construction. Situated out of the centre towards the port, this futuristic collection of buildings constructed around a lake was largely designed by local architect Santiago Calatrava.

The IMAX cinema and planetarium was the first space to open. The other spaces are a hall for the performing arts, a science museum and an oceanographic park, containing a variety of marine creatures and an underwater restaurant.

🏛 Museo del Gremio Artistas Falleros

Avda San José Artesano 17. **96 347 96 23.** ⬤ *Mon–Sat.* 🎟 🚻

Up to 170 artists and craftsmen labour all year round in the *barrio* of Ciudad Fallera to build the elaborate papier-mâché sculptures that are burned during Las Fallas *(see p245).* They sometimes show visitors around their workshops – except during their busiest period in the months leading up to March. Each year the best *ninots* (papier-mâché cartoon-like figures) are saved from the flames and put on display in this craft guild

museum, along with posters, photographs and other memorabilia dating from 1902.

El Cabañal and La Malvarrosa Beaches

To the east of the city, the beaches of El Cabañal and La Malvarrosa are bordered by a broad and lively esplanade about 2 km (1 mile) long. Although these two former fishermen's districts were carelessly developed in the 1960s and 1970s, they retain some quaint, traditional houses tiled on the outside to keep them cool in summer. The light of La Malvarrosa inspired the Impressionist painter Joaquín Sorolla *(see p295).* The Paseo de Neptuno, near the port, is lined with restaurants, many of which specialize in paella.

ENVIRONS: The intensively farmed plain of the *huerta* is a maze of fields planted with artichokes and *chufas,* the raw ingredient of *horchata.*

Manises, near the airport, is renowned for its ceramics, which are sold in shops and factories. There is also a ceramics museum.

VALENCIA'S SUMMER SPECIALITY

In summer, the bars and cafés of Valencia offer a thirst-quenching drink unique to the area. *Horchata,* a sweet, milky drink produced mainly in the nearby town of Alboraia, is made from *chufas* (earth almonds). It is served semi-frozen and usually eaten with *fartons –* soft, sweet bread sticks – or *rosquilletas –* crunchy biscuit sticks. The oldest *horchatería* in the city centre is Santa Catalina, off the Plaza de la Virgen.

Painted tiles showing woman serving *horchata*

Fishing boats on the shore of the freshwater lake, L'Albufera

L'Albufera ⓭

Valencia. 🚉 🛈 *Carretera del Palmar, Raco de l'Olla, 96 162 73 45.*

A FRESHWATER LAKE situated on the coast just south of Valencia, L'Albufera is one of the prime wetland habitats for birds in Eastern Spain.

It is cut off from the sea by a wooded sandbar, the Dehesa, and fringed by a network of paddy fields which produce a third of Spain's rice.

L'Albufera is fed by the Río Turia and connected to the sea by three channels, which are fitted with sluice gates to control the water level. The lake reaches a maximum depth of 2.5 m (8 ft), and is gradually shrinking because of natural silting and the reclamation of land. In the Middle Ages the lake encompassed an area over ten times its present size.

Over 250 species of birds – including large numbers of egrets and herons – have been recorded in the lake's reed beds and marshy islands, the *matas*. L'Albufera was declared a nature reserve in 1986 to protect its birdlife. Many birds can be seen with binoculars from the shores of the lake.

A visitors' centre at Raco de l'Olla provides information on the ecology of lake, the paddy fields and the Dehesa.

Xàtiva ⓮

Valencia. 🚶 27,000. 🚉 🚉 🛈 *Calle Alameda de Jaime I 50, 96 227 33 46.* 🚐 *Tue & Fri.* 🎉 *Las Fallas (16–19 Mar); Fira de agosto (15–20 Aug).*

A LONG THE NARROW RIDGE of Mount Vernissa, above Xàtiva, run the ruins of a once-grand **castle** of 30 towers. It was largely destroyed by Felipe V in the War of the Spanish Succession *(see p58)*. Felipe also set fire to the town, which continues to wreak its revenge in an extraordinary way – by hanging Felipe's full-length portrait upside down in the **Museo Municipal**.

Until the attack, Xàtiva was the second town of the kingdom of Valencia. It is thought

Felipe V's full-length portrait hanging upside down in Xàtiva

to have been founded by the Phoenicians. Under the Moors it became prosperous, and in the 12th century it was the first European city to make paper.

Among the sights in the narrow streets and squares of the old town are a former hospital with a Plateresque façade, and a medieval fountain in the Plaça de la Trinidad.

The oldest church in Xàtiva is the **Ermita de San Feliú** (Chapel of St Felix) on the road up to the fortress. It dates from around 1269 and is hung with a number of 14th- to 16th-century icons.

⛰ **Castillo de Xàtiva**
Subida del Castillo. 📞 *96 227 42 74.* 🕐 *Tue–Sun.* 💳
🏛 **Museo Municipal**
Carrer de la Corretgeria 46. 📞 *96 227 65 97.* 🕐 *Tue–Sun.* 💳 🚻

Gandia ⓯

Valencia. 🚶 62,000. 🚉 🛈 *Calle Marqués de Campo, 96 287 77 88.* 🚐 *Thu, Sat.* 🎉 *Las Fallas (16–19 Mar).* 🖥 *www.gandia.org*

I N 1485, Rodrigo Borja (who became Pope Alexander VI) was granted the title of Duchy of Gandia. He founded the Borgia clan and, together with his children, was later implicated in murder and debauchery.

Rodrigo's great-grandson later redeemed the family name by joining the Jesuit order. He was canonized as St Francis Borja by Pope Clement X in 1671.

The house in which he was born and lived, the **Palacio Ducal** (Duke's Palace), is now owned by the Jesuits. Its simple Gothic courtyard belies the richly decorated chambers within, especially the Baroque Golden Gallery. The small patio has a tiled floor depicting the four elements of earth, air, fire and water.

🏛 Palacio Ducal
Duc Alfons el Vell 1. 📞 96 287 14
65. ◯ Tue–Sun. 🌕 ▯

The ornate and gilded interior of the Palacio Ducal, Gandia

Denia ⑯

Alicante. 🏙 30,000. 🚌 🚍 ⛴ ℹ
Plaza Oculista Buigues 9, 96 642 23
67. ⛴ Mon. 🎭 Fiestas Patronales
(early Jul). 🌐 www.denia.net

THIS TOWN was founded as a Greek colony. It takes its name from the Roman goddess Diana – a temple in her honour was excavated here. In the 11th century it became the capital of a short-lived Muslim kingdom, whose dominion extended from Andalusia to the Balearic Islands.

It is now a fishing port and holiday resort. The town centre spreads around the base of a low hill. A large **castle**, once an Arab fortress, on its summit overlooks the harbour. The entrance gate, the Portal de la Vila, survives, but it was altered in the 17th century.

The Palacio del Gobernador (Governor's House), within the castle, contains an archaeological museum which shows the development of Denia from 200 BC to the 18th century.

North of the harbour is the sandy beach of Las Marinas. To the south is the rocky and less developed Las Rotas beach, which is good for snorkelling.

♠ Castillo de Denia
Calle San Francisco. 📞 96 642 06
56. ◯ daily. ● 1 Jan, 25 Dec. 🌕

Xàbia ⑰

Alicante. 🏙 24,000. 🚌 ℹ Plaza de
la Iglesia 6, 96 579 43 56. ⛴ Thu.
🎭 Aduanas de Mar (first week of Sep).

PIRATES AND SMUGGLERS once took advantage of the hiding places afforded by the cliffs, caves, inlets and two rocky islands that make up Xàbia's attractive coastline.

The town centre is perched on a hill a short way inland, on the site of an Iberian walled settlement. Many of the buildings lining its streets are made from the local Tosca sandstone. The 16th-century **Iglesia de San Bartolomé** was fortified to serve its congregation as a refuge in times of invasion. It has openings over the door through which missiles could be dropped on to attackers.

The seafront is overlooked by ruined 17th- and 18th-century windmills. Because of council policy, Xàbia's beaches have been kept mercifully free of the high-rise apartment blocks that dominate many other Spanish resorts.

Entrance to the Gothic Iglesia de San Bartolomé in Xàbia

The ceremonial burning of Las Fallas on St Joseph's Day

VALENCIA AND MURCIA'S FIESTAS

Las Fallas (19 Mar). Huge papier-mâché monuments (fallas) are erected in the crossroads and squares of Valencia around 15 March and ceremonially set alight on the night of the 19th, St Joseph's Day. Costing thousands of euros each, the fallas depict satirical scenes and can take up to a year to build. During the fiesta, the city echoes to the sound of fire crackers.
Good Friday, Lorca (Murcia). The "blue" and "white" brotherhoods compete to outdo each other in pomp and finery during a grand procession of biblical characters.
Moors and Christians (22–4 Apr), Alcoi (Alicante). Two costumed armies march into the city, where they perform ceremonies and fight mock battles in commemoration of the Reconquest.
Bous en la Mar (early Jul), Denia (Alicante). People dodge bulls on the quay until one or the other falls into the sea (see p35).
Misteri d'Elx (14–15 Aug), Elx (Alicante). This choral play, in the Iglesia de Santa María, has spectacular special effects.
La Tomatina (last Wed of Aug), Buñol (Valencia). Thousands of participants pelt each other with ripe tomatoes (see pp238–9).

The Costa Blanca

Less hectic than the Costa del Sol *(see pp448–9)* and with warmer winters than the Costa Brava *(see p207)*, the Costa Blanca occupies a prime stretch of Spain's Mediterranean coastline. Alicante, with its airport and mainline railway station, is the arrival and departure point for most tourists. Between Alicante and Altea there are long stretches of sandy beach which have been heavily built up with apartment blocks and hotels. North of Altea there are more fine beaches, but they are broken by cliffs and coves. South from Alicante, as far as the resort of Torrevieja, the scenery is drier and more barren, relieved only by the wooded sand dunes of Guardamar del Segura.

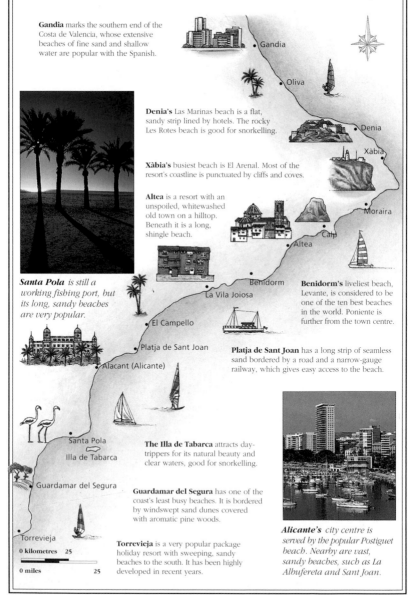

Gandia marks the southern end of the Costa de Valencia, whose extensive beaches of fine sand and shallow water are popular with the Spanish.

Denia's Las Marinas beach is a flat, sandy strip lined by hotels. The rocky Les Rotes beach is good for snorkelling.

Xàbia's busiest beach is El Arenal. Most of the resort's coastline is punctuated by cliffs and coves.

Altea is a resort with an unspoiled, whitewashed old town on a hilltop. Beneath it is a long, shingle beach.

Santa Pola is still a working fishing port, but its long, sandy beaches are very popular.

Benidorm's liveliest beach, Levante, is considered to be one of the ten best beaches in the world. Poniente is further from the town centre.

Platja de Sant Joan has a long strip of seamless sand bordered by a road and a narrow-gauge railway, which gives easy access to the beach.

The Illa de Tabarca attracts day-trippers for its natural beauty and clear waters, good for snorkelling.

Guardamar del Segura has one of the coast's least busy beaches. It is bordered by windswept sand dunes covered with aromatic pine woods.

Torrevieja is a very popular package holiday resort with sweeping, sandy beaches to the south. It has been highly developed in recent years.

0 kilometres   25

0 miles   25

Alicante's city centre is served by the popular Postiguet beach. Nearby are vast, sandy beaches, such as La Albufereta and Sant Joan.

Gandia · Oliva · Denia · Xàbia · Moraira · Calp · Altea · Benidorm · La Vila Joiosa · El Campello · Platja de Sant Joan · Alacant (Alicante) · Santa Pola · Illa de Tabarca · Guardamar del Segura · Torrevieja

◁ **Entrance of the Moorish army, part of a festival to commemorate the Reconquest, Ontinyent, Valencia**

Penyal d'Ifach ⑱

Alicante. 🚆 *Calp.* 🚌 *Calp.* 🛈
*Avda de los Ejércitos Españoles 44,
Calp, 96 583 69 20.*

Ｗ HEN VIEWED from afar, the rocky outcrop of the Penyal d'Ifach seems to rise vertically out of the sea. One of the Costa Blanca's most dramatic sights, this 332-m (1,089-ft) tall block of limestone looks virtually unclimbable. However, a short tunnel, built in 1918, allows walkers access to the much gentler slopes on its seaward side.

Allow about two hours for the round trip, which starts at the visitors' centre above Calp harbour. It takes you up gentle slopes covered with juniper and fan palm, with the waves crashing below. As you climb, and at the exposed summit, there are spectacular views of a large stretch of the Costa Blanca. On a clear day you can see the hills of Ibiza *(see p486)*.

The Penyal d'Ifach is also home to 300 types of wild plant, including several rare species. Migrating birds use it as a landmark, and the salt flats below it are an important habitat for them. The rock was privately owned until 1987, when the regional government acquired it and turned it into a nature reserve.

Situated below the rock is the Iberian town of Calp, renowned for its beaches.

Guadalest ⑲

Alicante. 🚶 *200.* 🛈 *Avenida de Alicante, 96 588 52 98.* 🎉 *Fiestas de los Jóvenes (1st week of Jun), Virgen de la Asunción (14–17 Aug).*

Ｄ ESPITE DRAWING coach loads of day-trippers from Benidorm, the pretty mountain village of Castell de Guadalest remains relatively unspoiled. This is largely because its older part is accessible only on foot by a single entrance: a sloping tunnel cut into the rock on which the castle ruins and the church's distinctive belfry are precariously perched.

Guadalest was founded by the Moors, who carved the surrounding hillsides into ter-

The magnificent limestone rock Penyal d'Ifach

races and planted them with crops. These are still irrigated by the original ditches constructed by the Moors. The village was badly damaged by earthquakes in 1644 and 1748.

From the **castle** there are fine views of the surrounding mountains. The only access to the castle is through the **Museo de Micro-Miniaturas**, where you can see a microscopic version of Goya's *Fusilamiento 3 de Mayo* painted on a grain of rice, his *The Naked Maja (see p283)*, painted on the wing of a fly, and a sculpture of a camel passing through the eye of a needle.

🏛 Museo de Micro-Miniaturas
Calle de la Iglesia 5. 📞 *96 588 50 62.* 🕐 *daily (until 9pm Apr–Sep).* 🌐

The belfry of Guadalest, perched on top of a rock

Alcoi ⑳

Alicante. 🚶 *62,000.* 🚆 🚌 🛈 *San Lorenzo 2, 965 53 71 55.* 🎉 *Moors and Christians (21–4 Apr).* 🌐 *www.alcoi.com*

Ｓ ITED AT THE confluence of three rivers and surrounded by high mountains, Alcoi is an industrial city. But it is best known for its mock battles between Moors and Christians *(see p245)* and its *peladillas* – almonds coated in sugar.

On the slopes above it is **Font Roja** (the red spring), a nature reserve and shrine, marked by a towering statue of the Virgin Mary.

ENVIRONS: To the north of Alcoi is the **Sierra de Mariola**, a mountain range famed for its herbs. The best point of access is the village of **Agres**. A scenic route runs from here to the summit of Mont Cabrer at 1,390 m (4,560 ft). It passes two ruined *neveras* – pits once used to store ice for preserving fish and meat.

The bullring of **Bocairent**, 10 km (6 miles) west of Agres, was carved out of rock in 1813. A nearby cliff is pockmarked with **Les Covetes dels Moros** ("the Moors' Caves"). Despite their name, the origin of these man-made caves is a mystery.

Benidorm ㉑

Alicante. 🏠 55,000. 🚌 🚉 🚏 **ℹ** *Calle Martínez Alejos 16, 96 585 13 11.*
🚢 *Wed, Sun.* 🎭 *Virgen del Carmen (16 Jul), Las Fallas (16–19 Mar).*
W *www.benidorm.org*

WITH FORESTS of skyscrapers overshadowing its two long beaches, this famous holiday resort is more reminiscent of Manhattan than the obscure fishing village it still was in the early 1950s.

Benidorm boasts more accommodation than any other resort on the Mediterranean, but its clientele has changed since the 1980s when its name was synonymous with "lager louts". A huge public park and open-air auditorium used for cultural events, the **Parque de l'Aigüera**, is emblematic of the facelift Benidorm has gone through in recent years. The town now attracts more elderly holidaymakers from the north of Spain than youths from England. Even so, the top attractions are still said to be sex, sun, night-clubs and "English" pubs.

A park on a promontory between the Levante and Poniente beaches, the **Balcón del Mediterráneo**, ends in a giant waterspout – a single-jet fountain. From here there is a panoramic view of the town. A short way out to sea is the Illa de Benidorm, a wedge-

Main staircase with floral lamp in the Casa Modernista, Novelda

shaped island served by ferries from the harbour. The island is being converted into a nature reserve for sea birds.

ENVIRONS: La Vila Joiosa (Villajoyosa), to the south, is much older than Benidorm. Its principal sight is a line of brightly painted houses that overhang the riverbed. They were painted in such vivid colours, it is said, so that their fishermen owners would be able to identify their homes when they were out at sea.

The older part of **Altea**, to the north of Benidorm, stands on a hill above modern beach-front developments. It is a delightful jumble of white houses, narrow streets and alleys, and long flights of steps arranged round a prominent, blue-domed church.

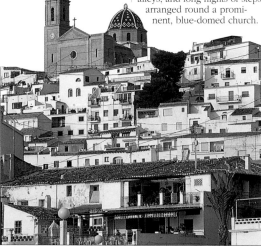

The old town of Altea, dominated by its domed church

Novelda ㉒

Alicante. 🏠 24,000. 🚌 🚉 **ℹ** *Calle Mayor 6, 96 560 92 28.* 🚢 *Wed, Sat.* 🎭 *Santa María Magdalena (20–25 Jul).* **W** *www.novelda.net*

THE INDUSTRIAL TOWN of Novelda is dominated by its many marble factories. But it is the exquisitely preserved Art Nouveau house, the **Casa Modernista**, that is of special interest. It was built in 1903 and rescued from demolition in 1975 by a local bank. The building's three floors are furnished in period style. There are few straight lines or functional shapes and almost every inch of wall-space has some floral or playful motif.

ENVIRONS: Villena town hall has a collection of Bronze Age gold objects, the **Tesoro de Villena** (*see pp44–5*).

🏛 **Casa Modernista**
Calle Mayor 24. 📞 965 60 02 37.
🕐 *Mon–Sat.* 🎟 *by appt.*
🏛 **Tesoro de Villena**
Ayuntamiento. 📞 965 80 11 50.
🕐 *Tue–Sun.*

Alicante ㉓

Alicante. 🏠 290,000. ✈ 🚉
🚌 🚢 **ℹ** *Rambla Méndez Núñez 23, 96 514 93 21.* 🚢 *Thu, Sat.* 🎭 *Hogueras (third week of Jun).* **W** *www.alicanteturismo.com*

A PORT AND SEASIDE resort built around a natural harbour, Alicante (Alacant) is the principal city of the Costa Blanca. Both the Greeks and Romans established settlements here. In the 8th century the Moors refounded the city under the shadow of Mount Benacantil. The summit of this hill is now occupied by the **Castillo de Santa Bárbara**, which dates mainly from the 16th century. From its top battlements there is a view over the whole city.

The focus of the city is the **Explanada de España**, a palm-lined promenade along the waterfront. The 18th-century **town hall** (*ayuntamiento*), is worth seeing for the Salón Azul (Blue Room). A metal disc on the marble staircase is used as a reference

Yachts moored in Alicante harbour, beside the Explanada de España

point in measuring the sea level all around Spain. A fine collection of 20th-century art can be seen at the small **Casa de la Asegurada**. Local artist Eusebio Sempere (1924–85) assembled works by Dalí, Miró, Picasso *(see pp28–9)*, and others. The exhibit changes every four months to allow all the collection to be viewed.

⚓ **Castillo de Santa Bárbara**
Playa del Postiguet. **[** 96 526 31 31.
🔲 *daily.* 🎫 *(for elevator only).* 👤
🏛 **Ayuntamiento**
Plaza del Ayuntamiento. **[** 96 514 91 00. 🔲 *9am–2pm Mon–Fri.*
🏛 **Casa de la Asegurada**
Plaza de Santa María 3. **[** 96 514 09 59. 🔲 *Tue–Sun.* 🎫

Illa de Tabarca 🄬

Alicante. 🚢 *from Santa Pola/Alicante.*
ℹ *Santa Pola, 966 69 22 76.*

T HE BEST POINT of departure for the Illa de Tabarca is Santa Pola. This small, flat island is divided into two parts: a stony, treeless area of level ground known as *el campo* (the countryside), and a walled settlement, which is entered through three gateways. The settlement was laid out on a grid plan in the 18th century, on the orders of Carlos III, to deter pirates.

Tabarca is a popular place to swim and snorkel and it can get crowded in the summer.

Fish and salt have long been important to the economy of Santa Pola. A Roman fish salting works has been excavated here, and outside the town are some modern saltpans.

Elx 🄫

Alicante. 🚶 *200,000.* 🚃 🚌
ℹ *Portell de Granyana, 96 545 38 31.*
🔲 *Mon, Sat.* 🎉 *Virgen de la Asunción (second week of Aug).*

T HE FOREST of over 300,000 palm trees that surrounds Elx (Elche) on three sides is said to have been planted by the Phoenicians around 300 BC. Part of it has been enclosed as a private garden called the **Huerto del Cura**. Some of the palms – one with a trunk which has divided into eight branches – are dedicated to various notable people, such as the Empress Elizabeth of Austria, who visited here in 1894.

The first settlement in the area, around 5000 BC, was at La Alcudia, where a 5th-century BC Iberian stone bust of a priestess, *La Dama de Elche (see p44)*, was discovered in 1897. The original is in Madrid, but there are several replicas scattered around Elx.

The blue-domed Baroque church, the **Basílica de Santa María**, was built in the 17th century to house the **Misteri d'Elx** *(see p37)*. Next to it is **La Calahorra**, a Gothic tower, which is a surviving part of the city's defences.

A clock on the roof next to the town hall has two 16th-century mechanical figures, which strike the hours on bells.

🌴 **Huerto del Cura**
Porta de la Morera 49. **[** 96 545 19 36. 🔲 *daily.* 🎫 👤 🎫
W www.huertodelcura.com
🏛 **La Calahorra**
Calle Uberna. **●** *closed to public.*

Orihuela 🄭

Alicante. 🚶 *62,000.* 🚃 🚌 **ℹ** *Calle Francisco Die 25, 96 530 27 47.*
🔲 *Tue.* 🎉 *La Reconquista (17 Jul).*

I N THE 15TH CENTURY Orihuela was prosperous enough for Fernando and Isabel to stop and collect men and money on their way to do battle against the Moors at Granada. The Gothic **cathedral**, with its Romanesque cloister, contains Velázquez's *The Temptation of St Thomas Aquinas*. Among the 18th-century processional floats displayed in the **Museo San Juan de Dios** is one bearing a statue of a she-devil, *La Diablesa*.

🏛 **Museo San Juan de Dios**
Calle del Hospital. **[** 96 674 31 54.
🔲 *Tue–Sun.* 👤 🎫

***La Diablesa*, Orihuela**

Torrevieja 🄮

Alicante. 🚶 *72,000.* **ℹ** *Plaza Ruiz Capdepont, 96 571 59 36.* 🔲 *Fri.*
🎉 *Habaneras (late Jul–early Aug).*

D URING THE 1980s, Torrevieja grew at a prodigious rate as thousands of Europeans purchased homes here. Before tourism, the town's source of income was sea salt. The salt works are the most productive in Europe and the second most important in the world.

Torrevieja stages a festival of *habaneras*, melodic songs originating in Cuba, brought back to Spain by salt exporters.

Capilla del Junterón, Murcia

Murcia ㉘

Murcia. 🏛 350,000. 🚃 ✈
ℹ Plaza Julián Romea 4, 902 10 10
70. 🚌 Thu. 🎭 Semana Santa
(Easter Week).
ⓦ www.murcia-turismo.com

A REGIONAL CAPITAL and university city on the River
Segura, Murcia was founded in
825 by the Moors, following
successful irrigation of the
surrounding fertile plain.

The centre of the modern
city is the 18th-century square,
La Glorieta. The pedestrianized Calle de la Trapería, linking the cathedral and the former marketplace (now the
Plaza Santo Domingo), is the
city's main street.

On it stands a gentlemen's
club founded in 1847, the
Casino (ask the doorman for
permission to look round). It is
entered through an Arab-style
patio, fashioned on the royal
chambers of the Alhambra. The
huge ballroom has a polished
parquet floor and is illuminated by five crystal chandeliers.
A painting covering the ceiling of the ladies' cloakroom
depicts the goddess Selene.

Work on the **cathedral**
began in 1394 over the foundations of Murcia's central
mosque, and it was finally
consecrated in 1467. The large
tower was added much later
and constructed in stages from
the 16th to the 18th centuries.
The architect Jaime Bort built
the main, Baroque façade
between 1739 and 1754.

The cathedral's finest features
are two exquisitely ornate side
chapels. The first, the Capilla
de los Vélez, is in Late Gothic

style and was built between
1490 and 1507. The second,
the Renaissance Capilla del
Junterón, dates from the early
16th century.

The **cathedral museum**
displays grand Gothic altarpieces, a frieze from a Roman
sarcophagus and the third
largest monstrance in Spain.

Francisco Salzillo (1707–83),
one of Spain's greatest sculptors, was born in Murcia, and
a museum in the **Iglesia de
Jesús** (Church of Jesus)
exhibits nine of his *pasos* –
sculptures on platforms. These
are carried through the streets

Arab-style patio, Murcia Casino

of the city on Good Friday
morning. The figures are so
lifelike that a fellow sculptor
is said to have told the men
carrying a *paso*: "Put it down,
it will walk by itself".

ENVIRONS: The folk museum,
the **Museo Etnológico de la
Huerta de Murcia**, stands
beside a large water wheel –
a 1955 copy in iron of the

original 15th-century wooden
wheel. The three galleries display agricultural and domestic
items, some of them 300 years
old. A traditional, thatched
Murcian farmhouse *(barraca)*
forms part of the museum.

🎰 **Casino**
Calle Trapería 18. 📞 968 21 22 55.
🕐 9am–10pm daily. 🈳
🏛 **Museo Etnológico de la
Huerta de Murcia**
Avda del Príncipe. 📞 968 89 38 66.
🕐 Tue–Sun. ♿

Mar Menor ㉙

Murcia. ✈ San Javier. 🚏 to
Cartagena, then bus. 🚌 La Manga.
ℹ La Manga, 968 14 61 36.
ⓦ www.marmenor.net

T HE ELONGATED, high-rise
holiday resort of La Manga,
built on a long, thin, sandy
strip, separates the Mediterranean and the Mar Menor,
literally "the Smaller Sea".

Really a large lagoon, the
sheltered Mar Menor can be
5°C (9°F) warmer than the
Mediterranean in summer. Its
high mineral concentrations
first drew rest-cure tourists in
the early 20th century. They
stayed at the older resorts of
Santiago de la Ribera and Los
Alcázares, which still have
pretty wooden jetties.

From either La Manga or
Santiago de la Ribera you can
make a ferry trip to the Isla
Perdiguera, one of the five
islands in the Mar Menor.

The old saltpans at Lo Pagán,
near San Pedro del Pinatar, are
now a nature reserve.

The resort of Los Alcázares on the edge of the Mar Menor

View of the domes and spires of Cartagena's town hall from the seafront

Cartagena ⓸

Murcia. 🚶 *179,000.* ✈ *San Javier.*
🚌 🚍 ⛴ 🅸 *Plaza Bastareges, 968
50 64 83.* 🅰 *Wed.* 🎭 *Semana Santa
(Easter Week), Carthaginians and
Romans (last two weeks Sep).*

THE FIRST SETTLEMENT founded in the natural harbour
of Cartagena was constructed
in 223 BC by the Carthaginians,
who called it *Quart Hadas*
(New City). After conquering
the city in 209 BC, the Romans
renamed it *Carthago Nova*
(New Carthage). Although the
city declined in importance in
the Middle Ages, its prestige
increased in the 18th century
when it became a naval base.
     You can get an overview of
the city from the park which
surrounds the ruins of the
Castillo de la Concepción,
Cartagena's castle. On the
quayside below is a prototype
submarine designed by Isaac
Peral in 1888. The city hall,
opposite, marks the end of
the Calle Mayor, a street overlooked by balconies and lined
with handsome buildings. Excavations in the city include a
Roman street and the **Muralla
Bizantina** (Byzantine Wall),
built between 589 and 590.
     The **National Underwater
Archaeology Museum** has
an interesting collection of
ancient Roman and Greek jars.

🅽 **Muralla Bizantina**
Calle Nueva. 🄲 *968 50 79 66.*
🅾 *Tue–Sun.*
🏛 **Museo Nacional de
Arqueología Submarino**
Carretera Faro de Navidad. 🄲 *968 50
84 15.* 🅾 *10am–3pm Tue–Sun.*
🅰 *(except Sun).* 🎦

Costa Cálida ⓶

Murcia. 🚍 *Murcia.* 🚍 *Murcia.*
🅸 *Águilas, 968 49 32 85.*
🆆 *www.aguilas.org*

THE MOST POPULAR RESORTS of
Murcia's "Warm Coast" are
around the Mar Menor. Between Cabo de Palos and Cabo
Tinoso the few small beaches
are dwarfed by cliffs. The
resorts of the southern part of
the coast are relatively quiet.
There are several fine beaches
at Puerto de Mazarrón; and at
nearby Bolnuevo the wind has
eroded soft rocks into strange
shapes. The growing resort of
Águilas marks the southern
limit of the coast, at the border
with Andalusia.

Lorca ⓷

Murcia. 🚶 *77,000.* 🚌 🚍
🅸 *Calle Lope Gisber, 968 46 61 57.*
🅰 *Thu.* 🎭 *Semana Santa (Easter
Week), Feria (3rd week of Sep), Día
de San Clemente (23 Nov).*

THE FERTILE FARMLAND
around Lorca, Murcia's
third most important town,
is an oasis in one of the
most arid areas of Europe.
Lorca was an important
staging post on the Via
Heraclea, as witnessed
by the Roman milepost
standing in a corner
of the Plaza San
Vicente. During the
wars between Moors
and Christians in the 13th
to 15th centuries, Lorca
became a frontier town
between Al Andalus and
the Castilian territory of

Murcia. Its castle dates from
this era, although only two of
its original 35 towers remain.
After Granada fell the town
lost its importance and, except
for one surviving gateway, its
walls were demolished.
     The centre of the town, the
Plaza de España, is lined with
handsome stone buildings.
One side is occupied by the
Colegiata de San Patricio
(Church of St Patrick), built
between 1533 and 1704, the
only church in Spain dedicated
to the Irish saint. At the head
of the square is the town hall.
A former prison, it was built in
two blocks between 1677 and
1739, and later connected by
an arch that spans the street.

Caravaca de
la Cruz ⓹

Murcia. 🚶 *22,000.* 🅸 *Calle de las
Monjas 17, 968 70 24 24.* 🅰 *Mon,
3rd Sun of month (crafts).* 🎭 *Vera Cruz
(1–5 May).* 🆆 *www.caravacas.org*

ATOWN OF ancient churches,
Caravaca de la Cruz's
fame lies in its castle which
houses the **Santuario de la
Vera Cruz** (Sanctuary of the
True Cross). This is where a
double-armed cross is said to
have appeared miraculously
in 1231 – 12 years before the
town was seized by Christians.
The highlight of the Vera Cruz
fiesta is the Race of the Wine
Horses, which commemorates
the lifting of a Moorish siege
of the castle. The cross was
dipped in wine which the
thirsty defenders then
drank and recovered
their fighting strength.

     ENVIRONS: Just to the
north is the village of
Moratalla, a jumble of
steep streets and brightly painted houses lying
beneath a 15th-
century castle. The
village is among the
foothills marking Murcia's
western border.
     Cehegín, east of
Caravaca, is a partially
preserved medieval town.

**Roman milepost topped by a
statue of St Vincent, Lorca**

MADRID

Introducing Madrid

Spain's capital, a city of over three million people, is situated close to the geographical centre of the country, at the hub of both road and rail networks. Because of its distance from the sea and its altitude – 660 m (2,150 ft) – the city endures cold winters and hot summers, making spring and autumn the best times to visit. Madrid's attractions include three internationally famous art galleries, a royal palace, grand public squares and many museums filled with the treasures of Spain's history. The city is surrounded by its own small province, the Comunidad de Madrid, which takes in the Sierra de Guadarrama and one of Spain's most famous monuments, the palace of El Escorial.

The Palacio Real (see pp266–7), *the royal palace built by Spain's first Bourbon kings, dominates the western part of Old Madrid. Its lavishly decorated chambers include the throne room.*

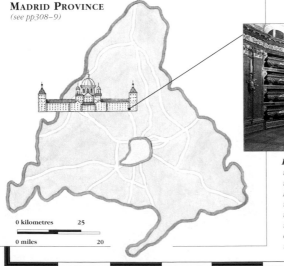

The Plaza Mayor (see p263), *Old Madrid's great 17th-century square, has been a focal point of the city since the days when it was used as a public arena for bullfights, trials by the Inquisition and executions (see p264). An equestrian statue of Felipe III stands in the middle of the square.*

OLD MADRID
(see pp258–71)

MADRID PROVINCE
(see pp308–9)

El Escorial (see pp312–13), *the massive, architecturally austere monastery-palace built by Felipe II, has some sumptuous apartments decorated with great works of art. Marble sarcophagi in the octagonal Royal Pantheon contain the mortal remains of most Spanish monarchs.*

| 0 kilometres | 25 |
| 0 miles | 20 |

◁ **Sculpted fountain of the Goddess Cybele in the Plaza de Cibeles, with the main post office behind**

The Museo Thyssen-Bornemisza (see pp278–9), *one of the most important privately assembled art collections in the world, was sold to Spain in 1993. The 18th-century palace houses major works by Titian, Rubens, Goya, Van Gogh and Picasso.*

The Plaza de Cibeles (see p276), *one of the city's most impressive squares, is ringed by distinctive buildings, including the 19th-century Banco de España and Madrid's main post office, with sculptures on its white façade.*

BOURBON MADRID
(see pp272–89)

The Parque del Retiro (see p287) *has leafy paths and avenues, and a boating lake overlooked by a majestic colonnade. It is an ideal place in which to relax between visits to the great art galleries and museums of Bourbon Madrid.*

The Museo del Prado (see pp282–5) *is one of the world's greatest art galleries. It has important collections of paintings by Velázquez and Goya, whose statue stands outside the main entrance.*

| 0 metres | 500 |
| 0 yards | 500 |

The Centro de Arte Reina Sofía (see pp288–9), *an outstanding museum of 20th-century art, is entered by highly original exterior glass lifts. Inside, the star exhibit is Guernica, Picasso's famous painting of the horrors of the Civil War.*

OLD MADRID

WHEN FELIPE II chose Madrid as his capital in 1561, it was a small Castilian town of little real significance. In the following years, it was to grow into the nerve centre of a mighty empire.

According to tradition, it was the Moorish chieftain Muhammad ben Abd al Rahman who established a fortress above the Río Manzanares. Magerit, as it was called in Arabic, fell to Alfonso VI of Castile between 1083 and 1086. Narrow streets with houses and medieval churches began to grow up on the higher ground behind the old Arab alcazar, which was replaced by a Gothic palace in the 15th century.

Drawer designed for storing herbs, Palacio Real

When this burned down in 1734, it was replaced in turn by the present Bourbon palace, the Palacio Real.

The population had scarcely reached 20,000 when Madrid was chosen as capital, but by the end of the century it had more than trebled. The 16th-century city is known as the "Madrid de los Austrias", after the reigning Habsburg dynasty. During this period royal monasteries were endowed and churches and private palaces were built. In the 17th century, the Plaza Mayor was added and the Puerta del Sol, the "Gate of the Sun", became the spiritual and geographical heart not only of Madrid but of all Spain.

SIGHTS AT A GLANCE

Historic Buildings
Palacio Real pp266–7 **9**

Museums and Galleries
Real Academia de
  Bellas Artes **14**

Churches and Convents
Catedral de la
  Almudena **7**
Colegiata de San Isidro **2**
Iglesia de San Nicolás **5**

Monasterio de las
  Descalzas Reales **13**
Monasterio de la
  Encarnación **10**

Streets, Squares and Parks
Campo del Moro **8**
Gran Vía **12**
Plaza de España **11**
Plaza Mayor **4**
Plaza de Oriente **6**

Plaza de la Villa **3**
Puerta del Sol **1**

GETTING THERE
The metro is the fastest and easiest way to get to Old Madrid. Take line 1 to Gran Vía or Sol; alternatively, lines 2, 3, 5, and 10 are good for getting to the main sights. Buses 51, 52, 150 and 153 to the Puerta del Sol are useful.

KEY

	Street-by-Street map pp260–61
M	Metro station
	Main bus stop
i	Tourist information
P	Parking

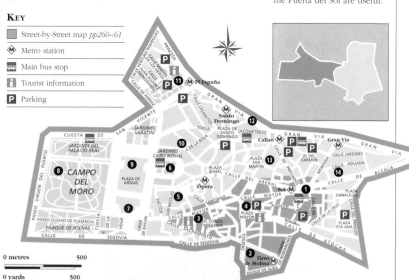

| 0 metres | 500 |
| 0 yards | 500 |

◁ **Monument to Cervantes by Lorenzo Coullaut-Valera in the Plaza de España**

Street-by-Street: Old Madrid

S TRETCHING FROM THE CHARMING Plaza de
la Villa to the busy Puerta del Sol, the
compact heart of Old Madrid is steeped
in history and full of interesting sights.
Trials by the Inquisition *(see p264)* and
executions were once held in the Plaza
Mayor. This porticoed square is Old
Madrid's finest piece of architecture, a
legacy of the Habsburgs *(see pp54–7)*.
Other buildings of note are the Colegiata
de San Isidro and the Palacio de Santa
Cruz. For a more relaxing way of enjoying Old Madrid, sit in one of the area's
numerous cafés or browse among the
stalls of the Mercado de San Miguel.

★ **Plaza Mayor**
*This beautiful 17th
century square
competes with the
Puerta del Sol as
the focus of Old
Madrid. The
arcades at the base
of the three-storey
buildings are filled
with cafés and
craft shops* ❹

The Mercado de San Miguel is
housed in a 19th-century building
with wrought-iron columns. The
market sells a variety of food and
household goods.

To Palacio
Real

CALLE MAYOR

PLAZA MORENAS

PLAZA DE LA VILLA

CALLE DE SACRAMENTO

CORDÓN

PUÑONROSTRO

Town hall
(ayuntamiento)

Casa de Cisneros

Arco de Cuchilleros

★ **Plaza de la Villa**
*The 15th-century Torre de
los Lujanes is the oldest of
several historic buildings
standing on this square* ❸

0 metres	100
0 yards	100

**The Basílica Pontificia
de San Miguel** is an
imposing 18th-century
church with a beautiful
façade and a graceful
interior. It is one of very
few churches in Spain
inspired by the Italian
Baroque style.

STAR SIGHTS

★ **Plaza Mayor**

★ **Plaza de la Villa**

★ **Puerta del Sol**

★ Puerta del Sol
With its shops and cafés, the Puerta del Sol is one of the city's liveliest areas. This sign for Tío Pepe, a brand of sherry, has become synonymous with the square ❶

LOCATOR MAP
See Street Finder map 2

Iglesia de San Ginés

Sol Metro

Casa de Correos

Equestrian statue of Carlos III

To Bourbon Madrid

BORDADORES

CALLE DEL ARENAL

PUERTA DEL SOL

CALLE DE ALCALÁ

CALLE MAYOR

CALLE DE POSTAS

CALLE PAZ

CALLE DE CARRETAS

BARCELONA

ESPOZ Y MINA

PLAZA MAYOR

PLAZA PROVINCIA

PLAZA DE JACINTO BENAVENTE

SALVADOR

DUQUE DE RIVAS

CALLE DE LA COLEGIATA

The Palacio de Santa Cruz was built as the court prison in the 17th century. This Baroque *(see p21)* palace is now occupied by the Foreign Ministry.

Colegiata de San Isidro
This was Madrid's provisional cathedral until La Almudena was completed (see p265). It is named after the city's patron, St Isidore, a local 12th-century farmer ❷

Tirso de Molina Metro

KEY

‒ ‒ ‒ Suggested route

Kilometre Zero, the centre of Spain's road network, Puerta del Sol

Puerta del Sol ❶

Map 2 F3. ⓦ *Sol.*

Noisy with traffic, chatter and policemen's whistles, the Puerta del Sol ("Gateway of the Sun") makes a fitting centre for Madrid. This is one of the city's most popular meeting places, and huge crowds converge on this famous square on their way to the shops and sights in the old part of the city.

The square marks the site of the original eastern entrance to the city, once occupied by a gatehouse and castle. These disappeared long ago and in their place came a succession of churches. In the late 19th century the area was turned into a square and became the centre of café society.

Today the "square" is shaped like a half moon. A recent addition is the imposing statue of Carlos III in its centre. The square's southern side is edged by an austere red-brick building, originally the city's post office, built in the

The bronze bear and strawberry tree of Madrid, Puerta del Sol

1760s under Carlos III. In 1847 it became the headquarters of the Ministry of the Interior. In 1866 the clocktower, which gives the building much of its identity, was added. During the Franco regime *(see pp 62–3)*, the police cells beneath the building were the site of many human rights abuses. In 1963, Julián Grimau, a member of the underground Communist party, allegedly fell from an upstairs window and miraculously survived, only to be executed shortly afterwards.

The building is now home to the regional government and is the focus of many festive events. At midnight on New Year's Eve dense crowds fill the square and people swallow a grape on each stroke of the clock, a tradition supposed to bring good luck for the rest of the year. Outside it, a symbol on the ground marks Kilometre Zero, considered the centre of Spain's huge road network.

The buildings opposite are arranged in a semicircle and contain modern shops and cafés. On the corner of Calle del Carmen is a bronze statue of the symbol of Madrid – a bear reaching for the fruit of a *madroño* (strawberry tree).

The Puerta del Sol has witnessed many important historical events. On 2 May 1808 the uprising against the occupying French forces began here, but the crowd, pitted against the well-armed French troops, was crushed *(see p59)*. In 1912 the liberal prime minister José Canalejas was assassinated in the square and, in 1931, the Second Republic *(see p 61)* was proclaimed from the balcony of the Ministry of the Interior.

Colegiata de San Isidro ❷

Calle de Toledo 37. **Map** 2 E4.
▮ 91 369 20 37. ⓦ *La Latina.* ◻
8am–12.45pm, 6–8:30pm daily.

Built in the Baroque style *(see p21)* for the Jesuits in the mid-17th century, this twin-towered church served as Madrid's cathedral until La Almudena *(see p265)* was completed in 1993.

After Carlos III expelled the Jesuits from Spain in 1767 *(see p58)*, Ventura Rodríguez was commissioned to redesign the interior of the church. It was then rededicated to Madrid's patron saint, St Isidore, and two years later the saint's remains were moved here from the Iglesia de San Andrés. San Isidro was returned to the Jesuits during the reign of Fernando VII (1814–33).

Altar in the Catedral de San Isidro

Plaza de la Villa ❸

Map 2 D4. ⓦ *Ópera, Sol.*

The much restored and frequently remodelled Plaza de la Villa is one of the most atmospheric spots in Madrid. Some of the city's most historic secular buildings are situated around this square.

The oldest building is the early 15th-century Torre de los Lujanes, with its Gothic portal and Mudéjar-style horseshoe arches. François I of France was allegedly imprisoned in it following his defeat at the Battle of Pavia in 1525. The Casa de Cisneros was built in 1537 for the nephew

Portal of the Torre de los Lujanes

of Cardinal Cisneros, founder of the historic University of Alcalá *(see pp314–15)*. The main façade, on the Calle de Sacramento, is an excellent example of the Plateresque style *(see p21)*.

Linked to this building, by an enclosed bridge, is the town hall *(ayuntamiento)*. Designed in the 1640s by Juan Gómez de la Mora, architect of the Plaza Mayor, it exhibits the same combination of steep roofs with dormer windows, steeple-like towers at the corners and an austere façade of brick and stone. Before construction was finished – more than 30 years later – the building had acquired handsome Baroque doorways. A balcony was later added by Juan de Villanueva, the architect of the Prado *(see pp282–5)*, so that the royal family could watch Corpus Christi processions passing by.

Plaza Mayor ❹

Map 2 E4. Sol.

THE PLAZA MAYOR forms a splendid rectangular square, all balconies and pinnacles, dormer windows and steep slate roofs. The square, with its theatrical atmosphere, is very Castilian in character. Much was expected to happen here and a great deal did – bullfights, executions, pageants and trials by the Inquisition *(see p264)* – all watched by crowds, often in the presence of the reigning king and queen.

The first great public scene was the beatification of Madrid's patron, St Isidore, in 1621. In the same year, the execution of Rodrigo Calderón, secretary to Felipe III, was held here. Although hated by the Madrid populace, Calderón bore himself with such dignity on the day of his death that the phrase "proud as Rodrigo on the scaffold" survives to this day. Perhaps the greatest occasion of all, however, was the arrival here – from Italy – of Carlos III in 1760.

The square was started in 1617 and built in just two years, replacing slum houses. Its architect, Juan Gómez de la Mora, was successor to Juan de Herrera, designer of Felipe II's austere monastery-palace, El Escorial *(see pp312–13)*. Mora echoed the style of his master, softening it slightly. The fanciest part of the arcaded construction is the Casa de la Panadería (bakery). Its façade, recently and crudely reinvented, is decorated with allegorical paintings.

The equestrian statue in the centre is of Felipe III, who ordered the square's construction. Started by the Italian Giovanni de Bologna and finished by his pupil Pietro Tacca in 1616, the statue was moved here in 1848 from the Casa de Campo *(see p292)*. Nowadays the square is lined with outdoor cafés, and is the venue for a collectors' market on Sundays *(see p305)*. The southern exit of the square leads into the Calle de Toledo towards the streets where the Rastro, Madrid's famous flea-market *(see p292)*, is held. A flight of steps in the southwest corner takes you under the Arco de Cuchilleros to the Calle de Cuchilleros, where there are a number of *mesones*, traditional restaurants.

Allegorical paintings on the Casa de la Panadería, Plaza Mayor

The Spanish Inquisition

THE SPANISH INQUISITION was set up by Fernando and Isabel in 1480 to create a single, monolithic Catholic ideology in Spain. Protestant heretics and alleged "false converts" to Catholicism from the Jewish and Muslim faiths were tried, to ensure the religious unity of the country. Beginning with a papal bull, the Inquisition was run like a court, presided over by the Inquisitor-General. However, the defendants were denied counsel, not told the charges facing them and tortured to obtain confessions. Punishment ranged from imprisonment to beheading, hanging or burning at the stake. A formidable system of control, it gave Spain's Protestant enemies a major propaganda weapon by contributing to the *Leyenda Negra* (Black Legend) which lasted, along with the Inquisition, into the 18th century.

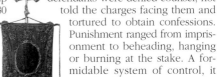

Inquisition banner

A Protestant heretic appears before the royal family, his last chance to repent and convert.

A convicted defendant, forced to wear a red *sanbenito* robe, is led away to prison.

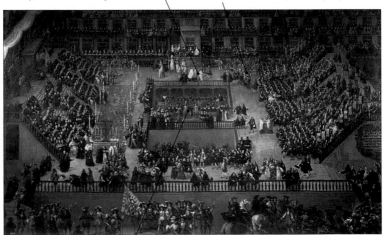

Those who have refused to confess are sentenced in public by day, and then executed before nightfall.

AUTO-DA-FÉ IN THE PLAZA MAYOR

This painting by Francisco Rizi (1683) depicts a trial, or *auto-da-fé* – literally, show of faith – held in Madrid's main square on 30 June 1680. Unlike papal inquisitions elsewhere in Europe, it was presided over by the reigning monarch, Carlos II, accompanied by his queen.

Torture *was widely used by the Inquisitors and their assistants to extract confessions from their victims. This early 19th-century German engraving shows a man being roasted on a wheel.*

The Procession of the Flagellants *(c.1812) by Goya shows the abiding influence of the Inquisition on the popular imagination. The penitents in the picture are wearing the tall conical hats of heretics tried by the Inquisition. These hats can still be seen in Easter Week processions (see p34) throughout Spain.*

Iglesia de San Nicolás ❺

Plaza de San Nicolás 1. **Map** 1 C3.
☎ 91 559 40 64. Ⓜ *Ópera.*
◷ *8:30am–1:30pm, 5:30–8:30pm Mon, 6:30–8:30pm Tue–Sat, 10am–2pm, 6:30–8:30pm Sun.*

THE FIRST MENTION of the church of San Nicolás is in a document of 1202. Its brick tower, with horseshoe arches, is the oldest surviving ecclesiastical structure in Madrid. It is thought to be 12th-century Mudéjar in style, and may have originally been the minaret of a Moorish mosque.

Plaza de Oriente ❻

Map 1 C3. Ⓜ *Ópera.*

DURING HIS DAYS as king of Spain, Joseph Bonaparte *(see p59)* carved out this stirrup-shaped space from the jumble of buildings to the east of the Palacio Real *(see pp266–7)*, providing the view of the palace enjoyed today.

The square was once an important meeting place for state occasions; kings, queens and dictators all made public appearances on the palace balcony facing the plaza. The many statues of early kings which stand here were originally intended for the palace roofline, but proved too heavy. The equestrian statue of Felipe IV in the centre of the square is by Italian sculptor Pietro

Equestrian statue of Felipe IV, by Pietro Tacca, Plaza de Oriente

View of the Catedral de la Almudena and the Royal Palace

Tacca, and is based on drawings by Velázquez. Facing the palace, across the square, is the imposing Teatro Real, or Teatro de la Ópera, inaugurated in 1850 by Isabel II.

Catedral de la Almudena ❼

Calle de Bailén 8–10. **Map** 1 B3.
☎ 91 542 22 00. Ⓜ *Ópera.*
◷ *10am–2pm, 5pm–9pm daily.* ♿

DEDICATED TO the city's patron, the cathedral of La Almudena was begun in 1879 and completed over a century later. Construction was slow – ceasing completely during the Civil War – and involved several architects. The cathedral's Neo-Gothic grey and white façade is similar to that of the Palacio Real, which stands opposite. The crypt houses a 16th-century image of the Virgen de la Almudena.

Further along the Calle Mayor is the site of archaeological excavations which have uncarthed the remains of Madrid's Moorish and medieval city walls.

Campo del Moro ❽

Map 1 A3. Ⓜ *Príncipe Pío.*
◷ *Apr–Sep: 10am–8pm Mon–Sat.*

THE CAMPO DEL MORO (the "Field of the Moor") is a pleasing park, rising steeply from the Río Manzanares to offer one of the finest views of the Palacio Real *(see pp266–7)*.

The park has a varied history. In 1109 a Moorish army, led by Ali ben Yusuf bivouacked here, hence the name. The park went on to become a jousting ground for Christian knights. In the late 19th century it was used as a lavish playground for royal children. Around the same time it was landscaped in what is described as English style, with winding paths, grass and woodland, fountains and statues. It was reopened to the public in 1931 under the Second Republic *(see p61)*, closed again under Franco, and not reopened until 1983. The Museo de Carruajes is situated in the lower part of the park, but is closed indefinitely. It houses official royal carriages and sedan chairs.

Palacio Real ⑨

ADRID'S VAST AND LAVISH ROYAL PALACE was
built to impress. The site, on a high bluff
over the Río Manzanares, had been
occupied for centuries by a royal fortress, but
after a fire in 1734, Felipe V commissioned a
truly palatial replacement. Construction lasted 26 years, spanning the
reign of two Bourbon monarchs,
and much of the exuberant decor
reflects the tastes of Carlos III and
Carlos IV *(see p67)*. The palace

Statue of   was used by the royal family until
Carlos III   the abdication of Alfonso XIII in
1931. The present king, Juan Carlos I, lives in the
more modest Zarzuela Palace outside Madrid, but the
Royal Palace is still used for state occasions.

**★ Dining
Room**
*This gallery was
decorated in 1879.
With its chandeliers,
ceiling paintings and
tapestries, it evokes
the grandeur of
regal Bourbon
entertaining.*

★ Porcelain Room
*The walls and ceiling
of this room, built on
the orders of Carlos III,
are entirely covered in
royal porcelain from the
Buen Retiro factory. Most
of the porcelain is green
and white, and depicts
cherubs and wreaths.*

**First
floor**

**The Hall of
Columns**, once used
for royal banquets, is
decorated with 16th-
century bronzes and
Roman imperial busts.

★ Gasparini Room
*Named after its Neapolitan
designer, the Gasparini
Room is decorated with
lavish rococo chinoiserie.
The adjacent antechamber,
with painted ceiling and
ornate chandelier, houses
Goya's portrait of Carlos IV.*

STAR FEATURES

★ Dining Room

★ Porcelain Room

★ Gasparini Room

★ Throne Room

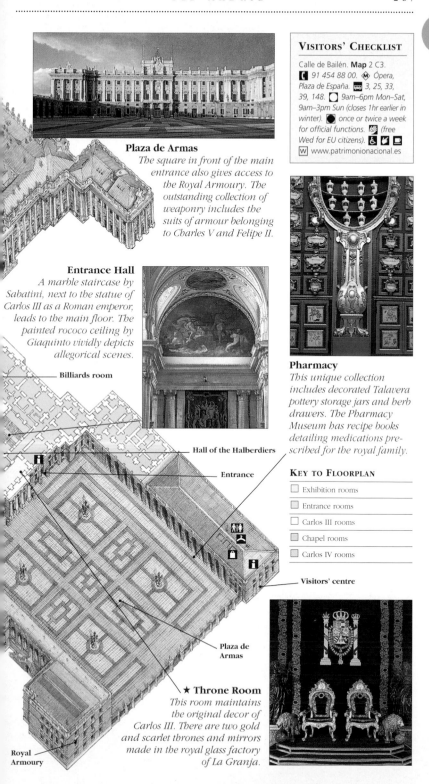

Plaza de Armas
The square in front of the main entrance also gives access to the Royal Armoury. The outstanding collection of weaponry includes the suits of armour belonging to Charles V and Felipe II.

Entrance Hall
A marble staircase by Sabatini, next to the statue of Carlos III as a Roman emperor, leads to the main floor. The painted rococo ceiling by Giaquinto vividly depicts allegorical scenes.

Billiards room

Hall of the Halberdiers

Entrance

Plaza de Armas

★ Throne Room
This room maintains the original decor of Carlos III. There are two gold and scarlet thrones and mirrors made in the royal glass factory of La Granja.

Royal Armoury

VISITORS' CHECKLIST

Calle de Bailén. **Map** 2 C3.
91 454 88 00. Ópera, Plaza de España. 3, 25, 33, 39, 148. 9am–6pm Mon–Sat, 9am–3pm Sun (closes 1hr earlier in winter). once or twice a week for official functions. (free Wed for EU citizens).
W www.patrimonionacional.es

Pharmacy
This unique collection includes decorated Talavera pottery storage jars and herb drawers. The Pharmacy Museum has recipe books detailing medications prescribed for the royal family.

KEY TO FLOORPLAN

☐ Exhibition rooms
☐ Entrance rooms
☐ Carlos III rooms
☐ Chapel rooms
☐ Carlos IV rooms

Visitors' centre

Entrance to the Convento de la Encarnación

Monasterio de la Encarnación ⓾

Plaza de la Encarnación 1. **Map** 1 C2.
☎ 91 454 88 00. Ⓜ *Ópera, Santo Domingo.* ◌ *10:30am–12:45pm, 4–5:45pm Tue–Thu & Sat, 10:30am–12:45pm Fri, 11am–1:45pm Sun.*
🎫 *(free Wed for EU residents).* ♿

STANDING in a delightful tree-shaded square, this tranquil Augustinian convent was founded in 1611 for Margaret of Austria, wife of Felipe III. The architect, Juan Gómez de la Mora, also built the Plaza Mayor *(see p263)* and the façade clearly reveals his work.

The interior of the convent, which is still inhabited by nuns, has the atmosphere of old Castile, with its blue and white Talavera tiles, wooden doors, exposed beams and portraits of royal benefactors.

Inside is a collection of 17th-century art, with paintings by José de Ribera and Vincente Carducho lining the walls. Polychromatic wooden statues include *Cristo Yacente* (*Lying Christ*), by Fernández.

The convent's main attraction is the reliquary chamber with a ceiling painted by Carducho. It is used to store the skulls and bones of saints. There is also a phial containing the dried blood of St Pantaleon. According to a popular myth, the blood liquefies each year on 27 July, the anniversary of the saint's death. Should the blood fail to liquefy, it is said that disaster will befall

Madrid. The church, rebuilt by Ventura Rodríguez after a fire in 1767, has paintings by Francisco Bayeu and frescoes by brothers González Velázquez.

Plaza de España ⓫

Map 1 C1. Ⓜ *Plaza de España.*

ONE OF MADRID'S busiest traffic intersections and most popular meeting places is the Plaza de España, which slopes down towards the Palacio Real *(see pp266–7)* and the Sabatini Gardens. In the 18th and 19th centuries the square was occupied by military barracks, built here because of the square's close proximity to the palace. However, further expansion of Madrid resulted in its being left as a public space.

The square acquired its present appearance during the Franco period *(see pp62–3)*, with the construction, on the northern side, of the massive Edificio de España in 1948. Across the square is the Torre de Madrid (1957), known as

La Jirafa (the Giraffe), which, for a while, was the tallest concrete structure in the world. The most attractive part of the square is its centre, occupied by a massive stone obelisk built in 1928. In front of it is a statue of the author Cervantes *(see p315)*. Below him, Don Quixote *(see pp376–7)* rides his horse Rocinante while the plump Sancho Panza trots alongside on his donkey. On the left-hand side is Dulcinea, Don Quixote's sweetheart.

Gran Vía ⓬

Map 2 D1. Ⓜ *Plaza de España, Santo Domingo, Callao, Gran Vía.*

A MAIN TRAFFIC ARTERY of the modern city, the Gran Vía was inaugurated in 1910. Its construction spanned several decades and required the demolition of large numbers of run-down buildings and small lanes between the Calle de Alcalá and the Plaza de España. This somewhat haphazard road-building scheme soon became the subject of a

Stone obelisk with statue of Miguel de Cervantes, Plaza de España

◁ **Night-time traffic on the Gran Vía, seen from the Plaza de España**

One of the many 1930s buildings lining the Gran Vía

zarzuela – a comic opera – that most *Madrileño* of art forms *(see p306)*. Nowadays, the Gran Vía is at the centre of city life and, following a much-needed restoration programme, has become an architectural showpiece.

The most interesting buildings are clustered at the Alcalá end, starting with the Corinthian columns, high-level statuary and tiled dome of the Edificio Metrópolis *(see p274)*.

A temple with Art Nouveau mosaics on its upper levels crowns No. 1 Gran Vía. One striking feature of buildings at this end of the street is colonnaded galleries on the upper floors, imitating medieval Aragonese and Catalan architecture. Another is the fine wrought-iron balconies and carved stone details, such as the gargoyle-like caryatids at No. 12. This part of the Gran Vía has a number of old-world Spanish shops.

On the Red de San Luis, an intersection of four major roads, is the Telefónica building. As the first skyscraper to be erected in the capital – in 1929 – it caused a sensation. Beyond here, the Gran Vía becomes much more American in character, with cinemas, tourist shops and many cafés.

Opposite Callao metro station, on the corner of the Calle Jacometrezo, is another of Madrid's well-known buildings, the Art Deco Capitol cinema and bingo hall, which was built in the 1930s.

Monasterio de las Descalzas Reales ⑬

Plaza de las Descalzas 3. **Map** 2 E3.
☎ 91 454 88 00. ⚇ Sol, Callao.
◷ 10:30am–12:45pm, 4–5:45pm
Tue–Thu & Sat, 10:30am–12:45pm
Fri, 11am–1:45pm Sun & public hols.
⊠ (free Wed for EU residents).
ⓦ www.patrimonionacional.es

MADRID'S MOST notable religious building has a fine exterior in red brick and granite. This is one of the few surviving examples of 16th-century architecture in the city.

Around 1560 Felipe II's sister, Doña Juana, decided to convert the original medieval palace which stood here into a convent for nuns and women of the royal household. Her high rank, and that of her fellow nuns, accounts for the massive store of art and wealth of the Descalzas Reales (Royal Barefoot Sisters).

The stairway has a fresco of Felipe IV's family looking down, as if from a balcony, and a fine ceiling by Claudio Coello and his pupils. It leads up to a small first-floor cloister, which is ringed with chapels containing works of art and precious objects relating to the lives of the former nuns. The main chapel contains the tomb of Doña Juana. The Sala de Tapices contains a series of

Decorated chapel, Monasterio de las Descalzas Reales

tapestries, one woven in 1627 for Felipe II's daughter, Isabel Clara Eugenia. Another, *The Triumph of the Eucharist,* is based on cartoons by Rubens. Major paintings on show include works by Brueghel the Elder, Titian, Zurbarán, Murillo and Ribera.

***Fray Pedro Machado* by Zurbarán**

Real Academia de Bellas Artes ⑭

Calle de Alcalá 13. **Map** 3 A5. ☎ 91 524 08 64. ⚇ Sevilla, Sol. ◷ 9am–7pm Tue–Fri, 10am–2pm Sat–Mon. ● public hols. ⊠ (free Wed & Sun). ♿
ⓦ www.rabasf.insde.es

FAMOUS FORMER STUDENTS of this arts academy, housed in an 18th-century building by Churriguera *(see p21)*, include Dalí and Picasso. Its art gallery's collection includes works such as drawings by Raphael and Titian. Among the old masters are paintings by Rubens and Van Dyck. Spanish artists from the 16th to the 19th centuries are well represented, with several magnificent works by Ribera, Murillo, El Greco and Velázquez. One of the highlights is Zurbarán's *Fray Pedro Machado*, typical of the artist's paintings of monks.

An entire room is devoted to Goya, a former director of the academy. On show here are his painting of a relaxed Manuel Godoy *(see p58)*, the *Burial of the Sardine (see p35)*, the grim *Madhouse*, and a self-portrait painted in 1815.

BOURBON MADRID

To the east of Old Madrid, there once lay an idyllic district of market gardens known as the Prado, the "Meadow". In the 16th century a monastery was built on this rising ground. The Habsburgs extended it to form a palace (see p287), of which only fragments now remain; the palace gardens are now the popular Parque del Retiro. The Bourbon monarchs, especially Carlos III, chose this area to expand and embellish the city in the 18th century. Around the Paseo del Prado they built grand squares with fountains, a triumphal gateway, and what was to become the Museo del Prado, one of the world's greatest art galleries. A more recent addition to the area is the Centro de Arte Reina Sofía, a collection of modern Spanish art.

SIGHTS AT A GLANCE

Historic Buildings

Ateneo de Madrid **13**
Café Gijón **15**
Casa de Lope de Vega **10**
Congreso de los Diputados **14**
Estación de Atocha **21**
Hotel Ritz **1**
Real Academia de la Historia **11**
Teatro Español **12**

Museums and Galleries

Centro de Arte Reina Sofía pp288–9 **22**
Museo Arqueológico Nacional **18**
Museo del Ejército **7**
Museo Nacional de Artes Decorativas **6**
Museo del Prado pp282–5 **9**
Museo Thyssen-Bornemisza pp278–9 **3**

Churches

Iglesia de San Jerónimo el Real **8**

Monuments

Puerta de Alcalá **5**

Streets, Squares and Parks

Calle de Serrano **17**
Parque del Retiro **19**
Plaza Cánovas del Castillo **2**
Plaza de Cibeles **4**
Plaza de Colón **16**
Real Jardín Botánico **20**

GETTING THERE

The metro is the fastest and easiest way to get to and around Bourbon Madrid. Lines 1, 2 and 4 serve all of the main sights. Useful buses include routes 2, 8, 14, 15, 27, 74, and 146 to the Plaza de Cibeles.

KEY

- Street-by-Street map pp272–3
- Metro station
- Railway station
- Main bus stop
- Tourist information
- Parking

0 metres 200
0 yards 200

The expansive Parque del Retiro, which once formed the gardens of a Habsburg palace

Street-by-Street: Paseo del Prado

Façade of Banco de España

IN THE LATE 18TH CENTURY, before the museums and lavish hotels of Bourbon Madrid took shape, the Paseo del Prado was laid out and soon became a fashionable spot for strolling. Today the Paseo's main attraction lies in its museums and art galleries. Most notable are the Museo del Prado (just south of the Plaza Cánovas del Castillo) and the Museo Thyssen-Bornemisza, both displaying world famous collections. Among the grand monuments built under Carlos III are the Puerta de Alcalá, the Fuente de Neptuno and the Fuente de Cibeles, which stand in the middle of busy roundabouts.

The Paseo del Prado, based on the Piazza Navona in Rome, was built by Carlos III as a centre for the arts and sciences in Madrid.

Banco de Espana Metro

The Edificio Metrópolis
(see p271), on the corner of Gran Vía and Calle de Alcalá, was built in 1905. Its façade is distinctively Parisian.

Banco de España

★ Museo Thyssen-Bornemisza
This excellent art collection occupies the Neo-Classical Villahermosa Palace, completed in 1806 ❸

Congreso de los Diputados
Spain's parliament witnessed the transition from dictatorship to democracy (see pp64–5) ⓮

Plaza de Canovas del Castillo
In the middle of this large square stands a sculpted fountain of the god Neptune in his chariot ❷

PLAZA DE LAS CORTES

PLAZA CANOVAS DEL CASTILLO

To Museo del Prado

Hotel Palace

STAR SIGHTS

★ **Museo Thyssen-Bornemisza**

★ **Puerta de Alcalá**

★ **Plaza de Cibeles**

---

0 metres   100

0 yards   100

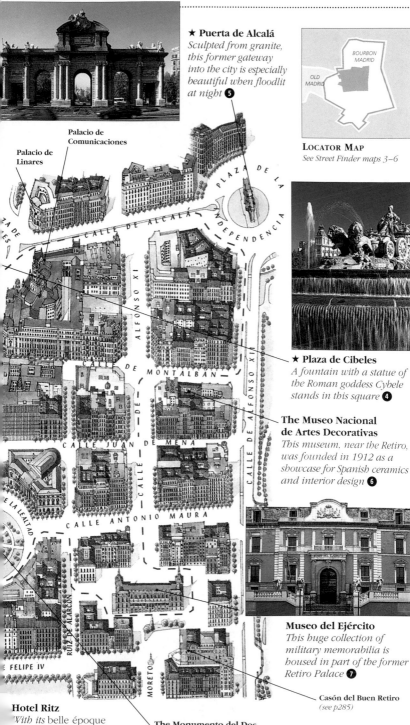

★ Puerta de Alcalá
*Sculpted from granite,
this former gateway
into the city is especially
beautiful when floodlit
at night* ❺

LOCATOR MAP
See Street Finder maps 3–6

Palacio de
Comunicaciones

Palacio de
Linares

★ Plaza de Cibeles
*A fountain with a statue of
the Roman goddess Cybele
stands in this square* ❹

**The Museo Nacional
de Artes Decorativas**
*This museum, near the Retiro,
was founded in 1912 as a
showcase for Spanish ceramics
and interior design* ❻

Museo del Ejército
*This huge collection of
military memorabilia is
housed in part of the former
Retiro Palace* ❼

Casón del Buen Retiro
(see p285)

Hotel Ritz
*With its belle époque
interior, the Ritz is one of
the most elegant hotels in
Spain* ❶

**The Monumento del Dos
de Mayo** commemorates the
War of Independence
against the French *(see p59).*

KEY

– – – Suggested route

Hotel Ritz ❶

Plaza de la Lealtad 5. **Map** 5 C1.
🅲 91 521 28 57. Ⓜ *Banco de España.* 🚫 ♿ 🆆 www.ritz.es

A FEW MINUTES' walk from the Prado, this hotel is said to be Spain's most extravagant. It was part of the new breed of hotels constructed as luxury accommodation for the wedding guests of Alfonso XIII in 1906.

The opulence of the Ritz *(see p553)* is reflected in its prices. Each of the 158 rooms is beautifully decorated in a different style, with carpets made by hand at the Real Fábrica de Tapices *(see p296)*.

At the start of the Civil War *(see pp62–3)* the hotel was converted into a hospital, and it was here that the Anarchist leader Buenaventura Durruti died of his wounds in 1936.

The Fuente de Neptuno

Plaza Cánovas del Castillo ❷

Map 5 C1. Ⓜ *Banco de España.*

T HIS BUSY ROUNDABOUT is named after Antonio Cánovas del Castillo, one of the leading statesmen of 19th-century Spain *(see p60)*, who was assassinated in 1897.

Dominating the plaza is the Fuente de Neptuno – a fountain with a statue depicting Neptune in his chariot, being pulled by two horses. The statue was designed in 1780 by Ventura Rodríguez as part of Carlos III's scheme to beautify eastern Madrid.

Visitors admiring the works of art in the Museo Thyssen-Bornemisza

Museo Thyssen-Bornemisza ❸

See pp278–9.

Plaza de Cibeles ❹

Map 3 C5. Ⓜ *Banco de España.* **Casa de América** 🅲 91 595 48 00. ⬤ *to the public.*

A S WELL AS BEING one of Madrid's best-known landmarks, the Plaza de Cibeles is also one of the most beautiful.

The Fuente de Cibeles stands in the middle of the busy traffic island at the junction of the Paseo del Prado and the Calle de Alcalá. This fine sculpted fountain is named after Cybele, the Graeco-Roman goddess of nature, and shows her sitting in her chariot, drawn by a pair of lions. Designed in the late 18th century by José Hermosilla and Ventura Rodríguez, it is considered a symbol of Madrid.

Around the square rise four important buildings, the most impressive of which is the main post office, the Palacio de Comunicaciones, mockingly known as "Our Lady of Communications". Its appearance – white, with high pinnacles – is often likened to a wedding cake. It was built between 1905 and 1917 on the site of former gardens.

On the northeast side of the square is the stone façade of the Palacio de Linares, built by the Marquis of Linares at the time of the second Bourbon restoration of 1875 *(see p60)*. At one time threatened with demolition, the palace was reprieved and converted into the Casa de América, and now displays a collection of paintings by Latin American artists. It is also used as a venue for theatrical performances and lectures.

In the northwest corner of the Plaza de Cibeles, surrounded by attractive gardens, is the heavily guarded Army Headquarters, which is housed in the buildings of the former Palacio de Buenavista. The palace was commissioned by the Duchess of Alba in 1777 as a family residence, though its construction was twice delayed by fires.

Occupying a whole block on the opposite corner is the Banco de España, constructed between 1884 and 1891. Its design was inspired by the Venetian Renaissance style, with delicate ironwork adorning the roof and windows. Much-needed renovation work has returned the bank to its late 19th-century magnificence.

The Fuente de Cibeles, with the Palacio de Linares in the background

View through the central arch of the Puerta de Alcalá

Puerta de Alcalá **5**

Map 4 D5. Retiro.

THIS CEREMONIAL GATEWAY is the grandest of the monuments erected by Carlos III in his attempt to improve the looks of eastern Madrid. It was designed by Francesco Sabatini to replace a smaller Baroque gateway which had been built by Felipe III for the entry into Madrid of his wife, Margaret of Austria.

Construction of the gate began in 1769 and lasted nine years. It was built from granite in Neo-Classical style, with a lofty pediment and sculpted angels. It has five arches – three central and two outer rectangular ones.

Until the mid-19th century the gateway marked the city's easternmost boundary. It now stands in the busy Plaza de la Independencia, and is best seen when floodlit at night.

Museo Nacional de Artes Decorativas **6**

Calle de Montalbán 12. **Map** 4 D5.
91 532 64 99. Retiro, Banco de España. 9:30am–3pm Tue–Fri, 10am–2pm Sat, Sun & public hols. (free Sun). W ww.mcu.es

HOUSED IN A 19th-century palace overlooking the Parque del Retiro, the National Museum of Decorative Arts contains an interesting collection of furniture and *objets d'art*. The exhibits are mainly from Spain and date back as far as Phoenician times.

One of the finest exhibits on the museum's five floors is a kitchen, moved here from an 18th-century Valencian mansion. Its 1,500 tiles depict a domestic scene from the era. There are also some excellent ceramic pieces from Talavera de la Reina *(see p368)*, and ornaments from the Far East.

Museo del Ejército **7**

Calle Méndez Núñez 1. **Map** 6 D1.
91 522 89 77. Retiro.
10am–2pm Tue–Sun. public hols. (free Sat). by appt.

SPAIN'S ARMY MUSEUM occupies one of the remaining parts of the 17th-century Palacio del Buen Retiro. Displays are dedicated to the military history of different periods and house an array of weapons, from Moorish times to the present day.

One of the highlights of the museum is the sword of El Cid – *La Tizona* – on display in the Sala de Armas. The tunic and sword of Boabdil, the last Moorish ruler of Granada *(see pp52–3)*, are exhibited in the Sala Árabe.

In the Sala Colonial is a fragment of the cross which was planted in the ground by Columbus upon reaching the New World. In the same room is a piece of the tree under which Hernán Cortés sheltered during a rebellion by the Aztecs in Mexico *(see p54)*.

More recent events are illustrated by busts and flags from Spain's War of Independence *(see p59)*, in the Sala del Dos de Mayo. There are also several rooms devoted to the Spanish Civil War *(see pp62–3)*, as well as an entire room of tin soldiers. The building is to become part of the Prado *(see pp282–85)* in 2004 or 5, when the army museum will be moved to Toledo's Alcazar *(see p372)*.

The sword of El Cid, *La Tizona*, in the Museo del Ejército

Museo Thyssen-Bornemisza ❸

This MAGNIFICENT MUSEUM is based on the collection assembled by Baron Heinrich Thyssen-Bornemisza and his son, Hans Heinrich, the present baron. In 1992 it was installed in Madrid's 18th-century Villahermosa Palace, and was sold to the nation the following year. From its beginnings in the 1920s, the collection was intended to illustrate the history of Western art, from Italian and Flemish primitives, through to 20th-century Expressionism and Pop Art. The museum's outstanding collection, consisting of some 800 paintings, includes masterpieces by Titian, Goya, Van Gogh and Picasso, and by 2003 it will include the Baroness's collection of mainly impressionist art. It is regarded by many critics as the most important private art collection in the world.

★ **Our Lady of the Dry Tree** (c.1450)
This tiny painted panel is by Bruges master Petrus Christus. The letter A hanging from the tree stands for "Ave Maria".

★ **Harlequin with a Mirror**
The figure of the harlequin was a frequent subject of Picasso's. The careful composition in this 1923 canvas, which is thought by some to represent the artist himself, is typical of Picasso's "Classical" period.

STAR PAINTINGS

* ★ **Our Lady of the Dry Tree** by Christus

* ★ **Harlequin with a Mirror** by Picasso

* ★ **The Toilet of Venus** by Rubens

GALLERY GUIDE

The galleries are arranged around a covered central courtyard, which rises the full height of the building. The top floor starts with early Italian art and goes through to the 17th-century. The first floor continues the story with 17th-century Dutch works and ends with German Expressionism. The ground floor is dedicated to 20th-century paintings.

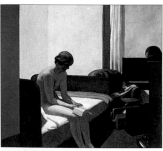

Hotel Room (1931)
Edward Hopper's painting is a study of urban isolation. The solitude is made less static by the suitcases and the train timetable on the woman's knee.

Portrait of Baron Thyssen-Bornemisza
This informal portrait of the present baron, against the background of a Watteau painting, was painted by Lucian Freud between 1981 and 1982.

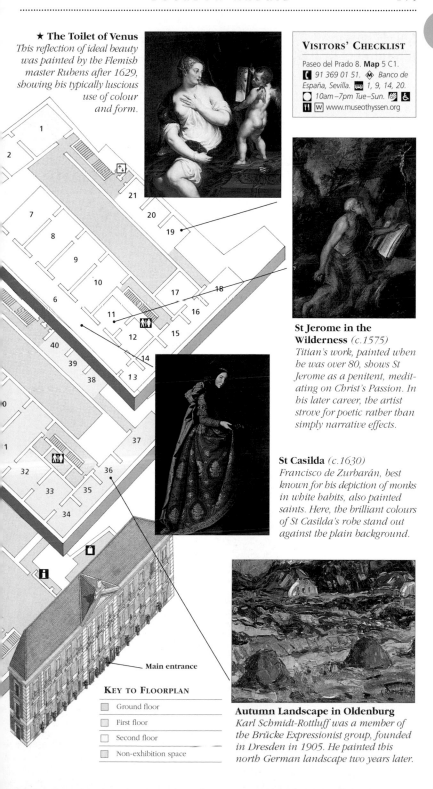

★ The Toilet of Venus
This reflection of ideal beauty was painted by the Flemish master Rubens after 1629, showing his typically luscious use of colour and form.

VISITORS' CHECKLIST

Paseo del Prado 8. **Map** 5 C1.
91 369 01 51. *Banco de España, Sevilla.* 1, 9, 14, 20.
10am–7pm Tue–Sun.
www.museothyssen.org

St Jerome in the Wilderness *(c.1575)*
Titian's work, painted when he was over 80, shows St Jerome as a penitent, meditating on Christ's Passion. In his later career, the artist strove for poetic rather than simply narrative effects.

St Casilda *(c.1630)*
Francisco de Zurbarán, best known for his depiction of monks in white habits, also painted saints. Here, the brilliant colours of St Casilda's robe stand out against the plain background.

Main entrance

KEY TO FLOORPLAN

- Ground floor
- First floor
- Second floor
- Non-exhibition space

Autumn Landscape in Oldenburg
Karl Schmidt-Rottluff was a member of the Brücke Expressionist group, founded in Dresden in 1905. He painted this north German landscape two years later.

Iglesia de San Jerónimo el Real ❽

Calle del Moreto 4. **Map** 6 D1. ☎ *91 420 35 78.* Ⓜ *Banco de España.* ⏱ *Oct–Jun: 8:30am–1:30pm, 5–8:30pm daily, (6–8:30pm Jul–Sep).* ♿

BUILT IN THE 16TH century for Queen Isabel, but since remodelled, San Jerónimo is Madrid's royal church. From the 17th century it became virtually a part of the Retiro palace which once stood here *(see p287).* The church was

Castizos during San Isidro

MADRID'S FIESTAS

San Isidro *(15 May).* Madrid's great party around 15 May is in honour of St Isidore, the humble 12th-century farmworker who became the city's patron. With a *corrida* every day, this is Spain's biggest bullfighting event. Throughout the city there are also art exhibitions, open-air concerts and fire-works. Many people dress in *castizo (see p292)* folk costume for the occasion.
The Passion *(Easter Saturday),* Chinchón. A passion play is performed in the town's atmospheric arcaded Plaza Mayor.
Dos de Mayo *(2 May).* This four-day holiday marks the city's uprising against Napoleon's troops in 1808 *(see p59).*
New Year's Eve. The nation focuses on the Puerta del Sol *(see p262)* at midnight as crowds gather to swallow a grape on each chime of the clock.

originally attached to the Hieronymite monastery. Parts of it are due to form an annexe of the Prado Museum.

The church was the setting for the marriage of Alfonso XIII and Victoria Eugenia of Battenberg in 1906, and is a popular venue for weddings. King Juan Carlos I's coronation was held here in 1975.

Museo del Prado ❾

See pp282–5.

Casa de Lope de Vega ❿

Calle de Cervantes 11. **Map** 5 B1. ☎ *91 429 92 16.* Ⓜ *Antón Martin.* ⏱ *9:30am–2pm Tue–Fri, 10am–2pm Sat.* ● *public hols.* 🎫 *(free Wed).* 📷 🎥

FELIX LOPE DE VEGA, a leading Golden Age writer *(see p30),* moved into this sombre house in 1610. Here he wrote over two-thirds of his plays,

Félix Lope de Vega

thought to total almost 2,000. Meticulously restored in 1935 using some of Lope de Vega's own furniture, the house gives a great feeling of Castilian life in the early 17th century. A dark chapel with no external windows occupies the centre, separated from the writer's bedroom by only a barred window. The small garden at the rear is planted with the flowers and fruit trees mentioned by the writer in his works. He died here in 1635.

Statue of Goya in front of the Prado

Sunlit balcony of the magnificent Teatro Español

Real Academia de la Historia ⓫

Calle León 21. **Map** 5 A2. 91 429 06 11. Antón Martín.

THE ROYAL ACADEMY of History is an austere brick building built by Juan de Villanueva in 1788. Its location, in the so-called Barrio de los Literatos (Writers' Quarter), is apt.

In 1898, the great intellectual and bibliophile, Marcelino Menéndez Pelayo, became director of the academy, living here until his death in 1912. The library contains more than 200,000 books and several important manuscripts.

Recently, a museum housing the pictures and antiques of the Academy was constructed; it is due to open in 2003.

Teatro Español ⓬

Calle del Príncipe 25. **Map** 5 A1. 91 429 62 97. Sol, Sevilla. for performances from 7pm Tue–Sun.

DOMINATING the Plaza Santa Ana is the Teatro Español, one of Madrid's oldest and most beautiful theatres. From 1583 many of Spain's finest plays, by leading dramatists of the time such as Lope de Rueda, were first performed in the Corral del Príncipe which originally stood on this site. In 1802 this was replaced by the Teatro Español. The Neo-Classical façade, with pilasters and medallions, is by Juan de Villanueva. Engraved on it are the names of great Spanish dramatists, including that of celebrated writer Federico García Lorca (see p31).

Ateneo de Madrid ⓭

Calle del Prado 21. **Map** 5 B1. 91 429 17 50. Antón Martín, Sevilla. 9am–2pm Mon–Fri.

FORMALLY FOUNDED IN 1835, this learned association has strongly liberal political leanings. It is similar to a gentlemen's club in atmosphere, with a grand stairway and panelled hall hung with the portraits of famous fellows. Closed down during past periods of repression and dictatorship, is still a mainstay of liberal thought in Spain. Many leading Socialists are members of the Ateneo, along with writers and other Spanish intellectuals.

Carving on the façade of the Ateneo de Madrid

Congreso de los Diputados ⓮

Plaza de las Cortes. **Map** 5 B1. 91 390 60 00. Sevilla. 10:30am–12:30pm Sat, by appt Mon–Fri. Aug.

THIS IMPOSING YET attractive building is home to the Spanish parliament, the Cortes. Built in the mid-19th century on the site of a former convent, it is characterized by Classical columns, heavy pediments and guardian bronze lions. It was here, in 1981, that Colonel Tejero of the Civil Guard held the deputies at gunpoint on national television, as he tried to spark off a military coup (see p64). His failure was seen as an indication that democracy was now firmly established in Spain.

Bronze lion guarding the Cortes

Café Gijón ⓯

Paseo de Recoletos 21. **Map** 3 C4. 91 521 54 25. Banco de España. 8am–1:30am Sun–Fri, 8am–2am Sat & public hols.

MADRID'S CAFÉ LIFE (see pp306–7) was one of the most attractive features of the city from the turn of the 20th century, right up to outbreak of the Civil War. Of the many intellectuals' cafés which once thrived, only the Gijón survives. Today the café continues to attract a lively crowd of literati. With its cream-painted wrought-iron columns and black and white table tops, it is perhaps better known for its atmosphere than for its appearance.

Museo del Prado ➒

THE PRADO MUSEUM contains the world's greatest assembly of Spanish painting – especially works by Velázquez and Goya – ranging from the 12th to 19th centuries. It also houses impressive foreign collections, particularly of Italian and Flemish works. The Neo-Classical building was designed in 1785 by Juan de Villanueva on the orders of Carlos III and it opened as a museum in 1819. The Prado is being renovated in several phases over the next few years. The Casón del Buen Retiro annexe has 19th- and 20th-century paintings and sculptures. It is undergoing restoration and will re-open in mid-2003.

★ Velázquez Collection
The Triumph of Bacchus (1629), Velázquez's first portrayal of a mythological subject, shows the god of wine (Bacchus) with a group of drunkards.

The Three Graces *(c.1635)*
This was one of the last paintings by the Flemish master Rubens, and was part of the artist's personal collection. The three women dancing in a ring – the Graces – are the daughters of Zeus, and represent Love, Joy and Revelry.

The Martyrdom of St Philip
(c.1639) José de Ribera moved from his native Valencia to Naples as a young man. There he was influenced by Caravaggio's dramatic use of light and shadow, known as chiaroscuro, as seen in this work.

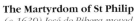

STAR EXHIBITS

★ **Velázquez Collection**

★ **Goya Collection**

The Garden of Delights *(c.1505)*
Hieronymus Bosch (El Bosco in Spanish), one of Felipe II's favourite artists, is especially well represented in the Prado. This enigmatic painting de-picts paradise and hell.

Main entrance

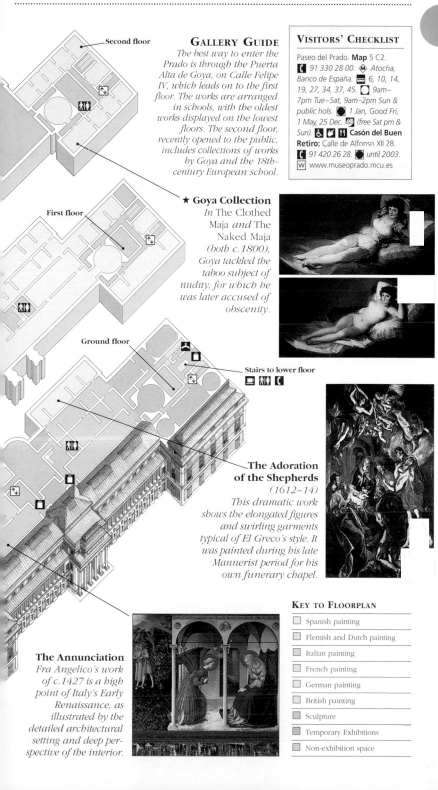

Second floor

GALLERY GUIDE
The best way to enter the Prado is through the Puerta Alta de Goya, on Calle Felipe IV, which leads on to the first floor. The works are arranged in schools, with the oldest works displayed on the lowest floors. The second floor, recently opened to the public, includes collections of works by Goya and the 18th-century European school.

VISITORS' CHECKLIST

Paseo del Prado. **Map** 5 C2.
91 330 28 00. ⊕ Atocha,
Banco de España. 🚌 6, 10, 14,
19, 27, 34, 37, 45. ◯ 9am–
7pm Tue–Sat, 9am–2pm Sun &
public hols. ● 1 Jan, Good Fri,
1 May, 25 Dec. 📷 (free Sat pm &
Sun). ♿ 📷 🍴 **Casón del Buen
Retiro:** Calle de Alfonso XII 28.
91 420 26 28. ● until 2003.
W www.museoprado.mcu.es

★ **Goya Collection**
In The Clothed Maja *and* The Naked Maja *(both c.1800), Goya tackled the taboo subject of nudity, for which he was later accused of obscenity.*

First floor

Ground floor

Stairs to lower floor

The Adoration of the Shepherds
*(1612–14)
This dramatic work shows the elongated figures and swirling garments typical of El Greco's style. It was painted during his late Mannerist period for his own funerary chapel.*

The Annunciation
Fra Angelico's work of c.1427 is a high point of Italy's Early Renaissance, as illustrated by the detailed architectural setting and deep perspective of the interior.

KEY TO FLOORPLAN

☐ Spanish painting
☐ Flemish and Dutch painting
☐ Italian painting
☐ French painting
☐ German painting
☐ British painting
☐ Sculpture
☐ Temporary Exhibitions
☐ Non-exhibition space

Exploring the Prado's Collection

THE IMPORTANCE OF THE PRADO is founded on its royal collections. The wealth of foreign art, including many of Europe's finest works, reflects the historical power of the Spanish crown (see pp54–9). The Low Countries and parts of Italy were under Spanish domination for centuries. The 18th century was an era of French influence, following the Bourbon accession to the Spanish throne. The Prado is worthy of repeated visits, but if you go only once, see the Spanish works of the 17th century.

St Dominic of Silos Enthroned as Abbot (1474–7) by Bermejo

SPANISH PAINTING

RIGHT UP TO THE 19th century, Spanish painting focused on religious and royal themes. Although the limited subject matter was in some ways a restriction, it also offered a sharp focus that seems to have suited Spanish painters.

Spain's early medieval art is represented somewhat sketchily in the Prado but there are some examples such as the anonymous mural paintings from the Holy Cross hermitage in Maderuelo, which show a Romanesque heaviness of line and forceful characterization.

Spanish Gothic art can be seen in the Prado in the works of Bartolomé Bermejo and Fernando Gallego. The sense of realism in their paintings was borrowed from Flemish masters of the time.

Renaissance features began to emerge in the works of painters such as Pedro de Berruguete, whose Auto-da-fé is both chilling and lively. St Catherine, by Fernando Yáñez de la Almedina, shows the influence of Leonardo da Vinci, for whom Yáñez probably worked while training in Italy.

What is often considered as a truly Spanish style – with its highly wrought emotion and deepening sombreness – first started to emerge in the 16th century in the paintings of the Mannerists. This is evident in Pedro Machuca's fierce Descent from the Cross and in the Madonnas of Luis de Morales, "the Divine". The elongation of the human figure in Morales' work is carried to a greater extreme by Domenikos Theotocopoulos, better known as El Greco (see p28). Although many of his masterpieces remain in his adopted town

Saturn Devouring One of his Sons (1820–23) by Francisco de Goya

of Toledo (see p373), the Prado has an impressive collection, including The Nobleman with his Hand on his Chest.

The Golden Age (see pp56–7) was a particularly productive time for Spanish art. José de Ribera, who lived in (Spanish) Naples, followed Caravaggio in combining realism of character with the techniques of chiaroscuro and tenebrism. Another master who used this method was Francisco Ribalta, whose Christ Embracing St Bernard is here. Zurbarán, known for his still lifes and portraits of saints and monks, is also a notable presence in the Prado.

This period, however, is best represented by the work of Diego Velázquez. As Spain's leading court painter from his late twenties until his death, he produced scenes of heightened realism, royal portraits, and religious and mythological paintings. Examples of all of these are displayed in the Prado. Perhaps his greatest work is Las Meninas (see pp28–9).

Another great Spanish painter, Goya, revived Spanish art in the 18th century. He first specialized in cartoons for tapestries, then became a court painter. His work went on to embrace the horrors of war, as seen here in The 3rd of May (see pp58–9), and culminated in a sombre series known as The Black Paintings.

Still Life with Four Vessels (c.1658–64) by Francisco de Zurbarán

CASÓN DEL BUEN RETIRO

On the hill behind the Prado is its annexe, the Casón del Buen Retiro, once part of the Palacio del Buen Retiro *(see p287)*. Its exhibits have included late 19th-century and early 20th-century works, as well as Neo-Classical and Romantic art, and paintings on historical themes. However, the Casón del Buen Retiro is currently closed for refurbishment and is not due to reopen until the middle of 2003.

Children at the Beach (1910) by Joaquín Sorolla

FLEMISH AND DUTCH PAINTING

Spain's long connection with the Low Countries *(see pp56–7)* led naturally to an intense admiration for the so-called Flemish primitives. Many exceptional works now hang in the Prado. *St Barbara*, by Robert Campin, has a quirky intimacy, and Rogier van der Weyden's *The Deposition* is an unquestioned masterpiece. Most notable of all, however, are Hieronymus Bosch's weird and eloquent inventions, which were collected by Felipe II. The Prado has some of his major paintings, including the *Temptation of St Anthony* and *The Haywain*. Works from the 16th century include the magnificent *Triumph of Death* by Brueghel the Elder. There are nearly 100 canvases by the 17th-century Flemish painter Peter Paul Rubens, of which the greatest is *The Adoration of the Magi*. The two most notable Dutch paintings on display are by Rembrandt: *Artemisia*, and a fine self-portrait.

David Victorious over Goliath (c.1600) by Caravaggio

ITALIAN PAINTING

The Prado is the envy of many museums, not least for its vast collection of Italian paintings. Botticelli's dramatic wooden panels telling *The Story of Nastagio degli Onesti*, a vision of a knight forever condemned to hunt down and kill his own beloved, are a sinister high point. Raphael contributes the superb *Christ Falls on the Way to Calvary* and the sentimental *The Holy Family of the Lamb*.

Christ Washing the Disciples' Feet, by Tintoretto, is a profound masterpiece. Venetian masters Veronese and Titian are also very well represented. Titian served as court painter to Charles V, and few works express the drama of Habsburg rule so deeply as his sombre painting *The Emperor Charles V at Mühlberg*. Also on display are works by Giordano, Caravaggio and Tiepolo, master of Italian rococo.

FRENCH PAINTING

Marriages between French and Spanish royalty in the 17th century, culminating in the Bourbon accession to the throne in the 18th century, brought French art to Spain. The Prado has eight works attributed to Poussin, among them his serene *Parnassus* and *Landscape with St Jerome*. The magnificent *Landscape with the Embarkation of St Paula Romana at Ostia* is the best work here by Claude Lorrain. Among the 18th-century artists featured are Antoine Watteau and Jean Ranc. *Felipe V* is the work of the royal portraitist Louis-Michel van Loo.

GERMAN PAINTING

Although German art is not especially well represented in the Prado, there are several paintings by Albrecht Dürer, such as his lively *Self-Portrait*, painted at the age of 26. Lucas Cranach also figures. Works by the late 18th-century painter Anton Raffael Mengs include portraits of Carlos III.

The Deposition (c.1430) by Rogier van der Weyden

Floor mosaic in the Museo Arqueológico Nacional

Plaza de Colón ⓖ

Map 4 D3. Ⓜ *Serrano, Colón.*

THIS LARGE SQUARE, one of Madrid's focal points, is dedicated to Christopher Columbus (Colón in Spanish).

It is overlooked by huge tower blocks, built in the 1970s to replace the 19th-century mansions which stood here.

On the south side is a palace housing the National Library and Archaeological Museum. The Post-Modernist skyscraper of the Heron Corporation towers over the square from the far side of the Paseo de la Castellana.

The real feature of the square, however, is the pair of monuments dedicated to the discoverer of the Americas. The prettiest, and oldest, is a Neo-Gothic spire made in 1885, with Columbus at its top, pointing west. Carved reliefs on the plinth give highlights of his discoveries. Across the square is the second, more modern monument – a cluster of four large concrete shapes inscribed with quotations about Columbus's journey to America *(see p53)*.

Constantly busy with traffic, the plaza may seem an unlikely venue for cultural events. Beneath it, however, is an extensive complex, the Centro Cultural de la Villa de Madrid, which includes the city's municipal art centre,

exhibition halls, lecture rooms, a theatre and a café. The terminal for the bus which runs to and from the airport *(see p626)* is also located underground.

Calle de Serrano ⓗ

Map 4 D4. Ⓜ *Serrano.*

NAMED AFTER a 19th-century politician, Madrid's smartest shopping street runs north from the Plaza de la Independencia to the Plaza del Ecuador, in the district of Salamanca. The street is lined with shops *(p304)* – many specializing in luxury items – housed in old-fashioned mansion-blocks. Several of the country's top designers, including Adolfo Domínguez and Roberto Verino, have boutiques towards the north, near the ABC Serrano *(see p305)* and the Museo Lázaro Galdiano *(see p295)*. Branches of the Italian shops Versace, Gucci, Escada and Armani, as well as the French Chanel, can be found on the Calle de José Ortega y Gasset. Lower down the Calle de Serrano, towards Serrano metro station, is a branch of El Corte Inglés. On the Calle de Claudio Coello, which runs parallel with Serrano, there are several lavish antique shops, in keeping with the area's up-market atmosphere.

Statue of Columbus, Plaza de Colón

Museo Arqueológico Nacional ⓘ

Calle de Serrano 13. **Map** 4 D3.
📞 91 577 79 12. Ⓜ *Serrano.*
⭘ 9:30am – 8:30pm Tue – Sat,
9:30am – 2:30pm Sun. ⬤ public
hols. 🎫 (free Sat pm & Sun). ♿
Ⓦ www.man.es

WITH HUNDREDS of exhibits, ranging from prehistoric times to the 19th century, this museum is one of Madrid's best. Founded by Isabel II in 1867, it consists mainly of material uncovered during excavations all over Spain, as well as pieces from Egypt, Ancient Greece and the Etruscan civilization.

The earliest finds – from the prehistoric era – are arranged in chronological order in the basement. Highlights include an exhibition on the ancient civilization of El Argar in Andalusia *(see p44)*, and a display of jewellery uncovered at the Roman settlement of Numantia, near Soria *(see p359)*.

The museum's ground floor is largely devoted to the period between Roman and Mudéjar Spain. Iberian culture is also represented, with two notable sculptures – *La Dama de Elche (see p44)* and *La Dama de Baza*. The Roman period is illustrated with some impressive mosaics, including *Monks and Seasons*, from Hellín (Albacete), and *Bacchus and his Train*, from Zaragoza.

Outstanding pieces from the Visigothic period include a collection of 7th-century gold votive crowns from Toledo province, known as the Treasure of Guarrazar.

On show from the Islamic era is pottery uncovered from Medina Azahara in Andalusia *(see p453)*, and metal objects. Romanesque exhibits include an ivory crucifix carved in 1063 for Fernando I of Castilla-León and his Queen, Doña Sancha, and the *Madonna and Child* from Sahagún, considered a masterpiece of Spanish art.

Steps outside the museum's entrance lead underground to an exact replica of the Altamira caves in Cantabria *(see p108)* – complete with their paintings of the Paleolithic era.

Parque del Retiro ⓓ

Map 6 E1. █ 91 409 23 36. Ⓜ *Retiro, Ibiza, Atocha.* ⬤ *at night.* ♿

THE RETIRO PARK, in Madrid's smart Jerónimos district, takes its name from Felipe IV's royal palace complex, which once stood here. Today, all that remains of the palace is the **Casón del Buen Retiro** (*see p285*) and the **Museo del Ejército** (*see p277*).

Used privately by the royal family from 1632, the park became the scene of elaborate pageants, bullfights and mock naval battles. In the 18th century it was partially opened to the public, provided visitors were formally dressed, and in 1869 it was fully opened. Today, the Retiro remains one of the most popular places for relaxing in Madrid.

A short stroll from the park's northern entrance down the tree-lined avenue leads to the pleasure lake, where rowing boats can be hired. On one side of the lake is a half-moon colonnade in front of which an equestrian statue of Alfonso XII rides high on a column. Opposite, portrait painters and fortune-tellers ply their trade.

To the south of the lake are two attractive palaces. The Neo-Classical **Palacio de Velázquez** and the **Palacio de Cristal** (Crystal Palace) were built by Velázquez Bosco in 1887 as venues for exhibitions held in that year.

Statue of Bourbon king Carlos III in the Real Jardín Botánico

Real Jardín Botánico ⓔ

Plaza de Murillo 2. **Map** 6 D2. █ 91 420 30 17. Ⓜ *Atocha.* ◯ *10am–dusk daily.* 📷 ♿

SOUTH OF the Prado (*see pp282–5*), and a suitable place for resting after visiting the gallery, are the Royal Botanical Gardens. Inspired by Carlos III, they were designed in 1781 by botanist Gómez Ortega and Juan de Villanueva, the architect of the Prado.

Interest in the plants of South America and the Philippines took hold during the Spanish Enlightenment (*see p58*), and the neatly laid out beds offer a huge variety of flora, ranging from trees and shrubs to medicinal plants and herbs.

Estación de Atocha ⓕ

Plaza del Emperador Carlos V. **Map** 6 D4. █ 902 240 202. Ⓜ *Atocha RENFE.* ◯ *5:30am–midnight daily.* ♿

MADRID'S FIRST railway service, from Atocha to Aranjuez, was inaugurated in 1851. Forty years later Atocha station was replaced by a new building, which, in the 1980s, was given a modern extension. The older part of the station, built of glass and wrought iron, now houses a pleasant indoor palm garden. Adjoining it is the modern terminus for the high-speed AVE trains to Córdoba and Seville (*see p630*).

The Ministerio de Agricultura, across the road, is a splendid late 19th-century building adorned with tiled corner domes and rooftop statuary.

Entrance of Madrid's Estación de Atocha, busy with travellers

Monument of Alfonso XII (1901), facing the Retiro's boating lake

Museo Nacional Centro de Arte Reina Sofía ㉒

THE HIGHLIGHT of this museum of 20th-century art is without doubt Picasso's *Guernica*. There are, however, other major works not to be missed, by influential artists including Miró and Picasso. The collection is housed in the former premises of Madrid's General Hospital, which was built in the late 18th century. Exterior glass lifts were added in 1990 when the building was converted into the National Museum. The museum is being extended with the addition of three new glass buildings that will leave more exhibition space by 2004.

Portrait II *(1938* *Joan Miró's huge, enigmatic work shows elements of Surrealism, despi being painted mo than ten years after the end of his true Surrealist period.*

★ Woman in Blue *(1901) Picasso disowned this work after it won only an honourable mention in a national competition. Decades later it was located and acquired by the Spanish state.*

Guernica

Landscape at Cadaqués

Salvador Dalí was born in Figueres in Catalonia. He became a frequent visitor to the town of Cadaqués, on the Costa Brava (see p207), where he painted this landscape in the summer of 1923.

Second floor

Accident
Alfonso Ponce de León's disturbing work, painted in 1936, prefigured his death in a car crash later that same year.

STAR EXHIBITS

★ **Woman in Blue**
 by Picasso

★ **La Tertulia del Café
 de Pombo** by Solana

★ **Guernica** by Picasso

★ **La Tertulia del Café de Pombo** *(1920)*
José Gutiérrez Solana depicts a gathering of intellectuals (tertulia) in a famous café in Madrid, which no longer exists.

Glass lift

Entrance

Toki-Egin
(Homenaje a San Juan de la Cruz) *(1952)*
In his abstract sculptures, Eduardo Chillida used a variety of materials, such as wood, iron and steel, to convey strength.

VISITORS' CHECKLIST

Calle Santa Isabel 52. **Map** 5 C3.
91 467 50 62. Atocha.
6, 14, 18, 19, 27, 45, 55, 68.
10am–9pm Mon & Wed–Sat,
10am–2:30pm Sun. 1 Jan,
24, 25, 31 Dec & some public
hols. (free Sat pm & Sun).
www.
museoreinasofia.mcu.es

GALLERY GUIDE

The permanent collection is on the second and fourth floors, arranged around an open courtyard. It traces art through the 20th century, from its beginnings to the present day. The second floor is dedicated to the historic vanguards, with individual rooms allocated to significant artists such as Dalí, Miró and Picasso. The fourth floor continues with post-World War II to contemporary works, via movements such as Abstract Art, Pop Art and Minimal Art.

KEY TO FLOORPLAN

☐ Exhibition space

▨ Non-exhibition space

Visitors admiring *Guernica*

★ PICASSO'S *GUERNICA*

The most famous single work of the 20th century, this Civil War protest painting *(see pp62–3)* was commissioned by the Spanish Republican government in 1937 for a Paris exhibition. The artist found his inspiration in the mass air attack of the same year on the Basque town of Gernika-Lumo *(see p114)*, by German pilots flying for the Nationalist air force. The painting hung in a New York gallery until 1981, reflecting the artist's wish that it should not return to Spain until democracy was re-established. It was moved here from the Prado in 1992.

FURTHER AFIELD

SEVERAL OF MADRID's best sights, including some interesting but little-known museums, lie outside the city centre. The axis of modern Madrid is the Paseo de la Castellana, a long, wide avenue lined by skyscraper offices and busy with traffic. A journey along it gives a glimpse of Madrid as Spain's commercial and administrative capital. La Castellana skirts the Barrio de Salamanca, an upmarket district of stylish boutiques, named after the 19th-century aristocrat who built it, the Marquis de Salamanca.

Statue in Plaza de Cascorro

The districts around Old Madrid, especially Malasaña and La Latina, offer a more typically authentic *Madrileño* atmosphere. On Sundays, some of the old streets are crowded with bargain-hunters at the sprawling second-hand market, El Rastro. If you need to escape from the bustle of the city for a while, west of Old Madrid, across the Río Manzanares, is Madrid's vast, green recreation ground, the Casa de Campo, with its pleasant pine woods, boating lake, amusement park and zoo.

SIGHTS AT A GLANCE

Historic Buildings
Palacio de Liria 9
Real Fábrica de Tapices 16
Templo de Debod 6

Churches and Convents
Ermita de San Antonio de la Florida 5

Museums and Galleries
Museo de América 7
Museo Cerralbo 8
Museo Lázaro Galdiano 13

Museo Municipal 11
Museo Sorolla 12

Streets, Squares and Parks
Casa de Campo 4
La Latina 2
Malasaña 10
Paseo de la Castellana 14
Plaza de la Paja 3
Plaza de Toros de Las Ventas 15
El Rastro 1

0 kilometres   2

0 miles   1

KEY

Main sightseeing area

Parks and open spaces

Railway station

Motorway

Major road

Minor road

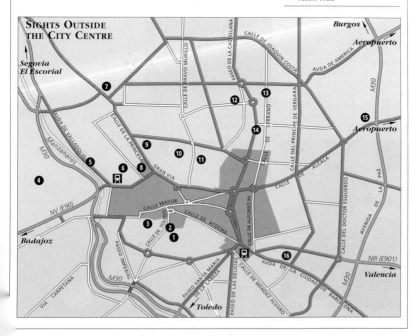

SIGHTS OUTSIDE THE CITY CENTRE

Mudéjar arches and tilework on the exterior of the Plaza de Toros de Las Ventas

El Rastro ❶

Calle Ribera de Curtidores. **Map** 2 E5.
🚇 *La Latina, Embajadores.* ⊙ *10am–2pm Sun & public hols.*

MADRID'S CELEBRATED flea market *(see p305)*, established in the Middle Ages, has its hub in the Plaza de Cascorro and sprawls downhill towards the Río Manzanares. The main street is the Calle Ribera de Curtidores, or "Tanners' Riverbank", once the centre of the slaughterhouse and tanning industry.

Although some people claim that the Rastro has changed a great deal since its heyday during the 19th century, there are still plenty of *Madrileños*, as well as tourists, who shop here. They come in search of a bargain from the stalls which sell a huge range of wares – anything from new furniture to second-hand clothes. The wide range of goods and the lively crowds in the Rastro make it an ideal way to spend a Sunday morning.

The Calle de Embajadores is the market's other main street. It runs down past the dusty Baroque façade of the Iglesia de San Cayetano, designed by José Churriguera and Pedro de Ribera. Its interior has been restored since fire destroyed it during the Civil War.

Further along the street is the former Real Fábrica de Tabacos (the Royal Tobacco Factory), begun as a state enterprise in 1809. Its female labour force long had a reputation for taking a hard-line stance in industrial disputes.

Shoppers browsing around the Rastro flea market

La Latina ❷

Map 2 D5. 🚇 *La Latina, Lavapiés.*

THE DISTRICT OF La Latina, together with the adjacent Lavapiés, is considered to be the heart of *castizo* Madrid. This term is used to describe the culture of the traditional working classes of Madrid – that of the true *Madrileño*.

La Latina runs along the city's southern hillside from the Plaza Puerta de Moros, southwards through the streets where the Rastro is held. To the east it merges with Lavapiés. La Latina's steep streets are lined with tall, narrow houses, renovated to form an attractive neighbourhood. There are old-fashioned bars around the Plaza del Humilladero, although this square and the streets to the north of La Latina, around the Puerta del Sol, have sadly become notorious for petty crime.

Bottles of wine for sale in an old-style bar in Lavapiés

Plaza de la Paja ❸

Map 1 C4. 🚇 *La Latina.*

ONCE THE FOCUS of medieval Madrid, the area around the Plaza de la Paja – literally Straw Square – is still atmospheric. Despite its location, in a less than affluent district, many interesting buildings are located on the square.

Climbing upwards from the Calle de Segovia, a glimpse left along the Calle Príncipe Anglona yields a view of the Mudéjar-style brick tower of the Iglesia de San Pedro, dating

Interior of San Francisco el Grande

from the 14th century. Up past the fountain, the Plaza de la Paja ends with the harsh stone walls of the Capilla del Obispo, or Bishop's Chapel, belonging originally to the adjoining Palacio Vargas. The superb Plateresque altarpiece is by Francisco Giralte. Up to the left, the Baroque, cherub-covered dome of the Iglesia de San Andrés stands out.

Nearby is a small cluster of interlinked squares, ending in the Plaza Puerta de Moros, a reminder of the Muslim community which once occupied the area. From here, a right turn leads to the domed bulk of San Francisco el Grande, an impressive landmark. Inside the church is a painting by Goya and his brother-in-law Francisco Bayeu. The choir-stalls were moved here from the monastery of El Paular *(see pp310–11)*.

Casa de Campo ❹

Avenida de Portugal. 🄲 *91 463 63 34.* 🚇 *Batán, Lago, Príncipe Pío.*

THIS FORMER ROYAL hunting ground, with pines and scrubland stretching over 1,740 ha (4,300 acres), lies in western Madrid. Its wide range of amenities make it a popular recreation area for *Madrileños*.

Attractions include a boating lake, a zoo, and an amusement park – the Parque de Atracciones *(see p307)* – with over 50 rides. Sports enthusiasts can make use of the swimming pool and jogging track. In the summer the park is also used as a venue for rock concerts.

Egyptian temple of Debod, with two of its original gateways

Ermita de San Antonio de la Florida ❺

Glorieta San Antonio de la Florida 5.
📞 91 542 07 22. 🚇 Príncipe Pío.
🕐 10am–2pm, 4–8pm Tue–Fri,
10am–2pm Sat & Sun. ● public
hols. 📷 (free Wed & Sun). 🚫 ♿

GOYA ENTHUSIASTS should not miss a visit to the Neo-Classical Ermita de San Antonio de la Florida, built during the reign of Carlos IV. The present church stands on the site of two previous ones, and is dedicated to St Anthony. It is named after the pastureland of la Florida, on which the original church was built.

Goya took just four months, in 1798, to paint the cupola with an immense fresco. It depicts the resurrection of a murdered man who rises in order to prove the innocence of the falsely accused father of St Anthony. The characters in it are everyday people of the late 18th century: lurking, low-life types and lively *majas (see p283)* – shrewd but elegant women. The fresco is considered by many art critics to be among Goya's finest works.

The tomb of the artist is housed in the chapel. His remains were brought here from Bordeaux, where he died in exile in 1828 *(see p229)*.

Templo de Debod ❻

Paseo de Pintor Rosales. **Map** 1 B1.
📞 91 366 74 15. 🚇 Ventura
Rodríguez, Plaza de España. 🕐
9:45am–1:45pm Tue–Sun;
Apr–Sep: 6–8pm Tue–Fri;
Oct–Mar: 4–6pm Tue–Fri. ●
public hols. 📷 (free Wed & Sun).

THE EGYPTIAN temple of Debod, built in the 2nd century BC, was rescued from the area flooded by the Aswan Dam and given to Spain as a tribute to Spanish engineers involved in the project. The temple is carved with shallow reliefs, and stands in a line with two of its original three gateways. They are situated on high ground above the Río Manzanares, in the gardens of the Parque del Oeste. From the park there are sweeping views over the Casa de Campo to the Guadarrama mountains.

The park is the site of the former Montaña barracks, which were stormed by the populace at the start of the Civil War in 1936.

Further to the west, below the brow of the hill, there is an attractive rose garden.

Museo de América ❼

Avenida de los Reyes Católicos 6. 📞
91 549 26 41. 🚇 Moncloa. 🕐
10am–3pm Tue–Sat, 10am–2:30pm
Sun. ● some public hols. 📷 (free
Sun). ♿ 🌐 www.mcu.es

THIS HANDSOME MUSEUM houses artifacts related to Spain's colonization of parts of the Americas. Many of the exhibits, which range from prehistoric times to the present, were brought back to Europe by early explorers of the New World *(see pp54–5)*.

The collection is arranged on the first and second floors, and individual rooms are given a cultural theme such as society, communication and religion. There is documentation of the Atlantic voyages by the first explorers, and examples of the objects which they found. The highlight of the museum is perhaps the rare Mayan *Códice Trocortesiano* (AD 1250–1500) from Mexico, a type of parchment illustrated with hieroglyphics of scenes from everyday life. Also worth seeing are the solid gold funereal ornaments from Colombia, the Treasure of the Quimbayas (AD 500–1000), and the collection of contemporary folk art from some of Spain's former American colonies.

Piece of the Treasure of the Quimbayas

Museo Cerralbo ⑧

Calle Ventura Rodríguez 17. **Map** 1 C1. 91 547 36 46. Plaza de España, Ventura Rodríguez. 15 Jun– 15 Sep: 10am– 2pm Tue–Sat; 10:30am–1:30pm Sun. (free Wed & Sun). w www.mcu.es

THIS 19TH-CENTURY mansion near the Plaza de España is a monument to Enrique de Aguilera y Gamboa, the 17th Marquis of Cerralbo. A compulsive collector of art and artifacts, he bequeathed his lifetime's collection to the nation in 1922, stipulating that the exhibits be arranged exactly as he left them. They range from Iberian pottery to 18th-century marble busts.

One of the star exhibits is El Greco's *The Ecstasy of Saint Francis of Assisi*. There are also lesser-known paintings by Ribera, Zurbarán, Alonso Cano and Goya, which hang in the Picture Gallery.

The focal point of the main floor is the ballroom, lavishly decorated with mirrors. A large collection of weaponry is on display on this floor.

Main staircase of the exuberant Museo Cerralbo

Palacio de Liria ⑨

Calle de la Princesa 20. 91 547 53 02. Ventura Rodríguez. write a year in advance for permission.

THE LAVISH but much restored Palacio de Liria was completed by Ventura Rodríguez in 1780. Once the residence of the Alba family, and still owned by the Duchess, it can be visited by appointment only.

The palace houses the Albas' outstanding collection of art, and Flemish tapestries. There are paintings by Titian, Rubens and Rembrandt. Spanish art is particularly well represented, with major works by Goya, such as his 1795 portrait of the Duchess of Alba, as well as El Greco, Zurbarán and Velázquez.

Behind the palace is the **Cuartel del Conde-Duque**, the former barracks of the Count-Duke Olivares, Felipe IV's minister. They were built in 1720 by Pedro de Ribera, who adorned them with a Baroque façade. The barracks now house a cultural centre.

Rooftops in the Malasaña district

Malasaña ⑩

Map 2 F1. Tribunal, Bilbao.

A FEELING OF the authentic old Madrid pervades this district of narrow, sloping streets and tall houses. For some years it was the centre of the *movida*, the frenzied nightlife which began after the death of Franco.

A walk along the Calle San Andrés leads to the Plaza del Dos de Mayo. In the centre is a monument to artillery officers Daoiz and Velarde, who defended the barracks which stood here at the time of the uprising against the French in 1808 *(see p59)*.

On Calle de la Puebla is the Iglesia de San Antonio de los Alemanes. The church was founded by Felipe III in the 17th century as a hospital for Portuguese immigrants, and was later given over for use by German émigrés. Inside, the walls are decorated with 18th-century frescoes by Giordano.

Museo Municipal ⑪

Calle de Fuencarral 78. **Map** 3 A3. 91 588 86 72. Tribunal. 9:30am– 8pm Tue–Fri, 10am–2pm Sat & Sun (15 Jun–15 Sep: 9:30am–2pm Tue–Sun). public hols. (free Wed & Sun).

THE MUNICIPAL MUSEUM is worth visiting just for its Baroque doorway *(see p21)* by Pedro de Ribera, arguably the finest in Madrid. Housed in the former hospice of St

Ferdinand, the museum was inaugurated in 1929. The basement is devoted to the city's archaeology, while upstairs is a series of bird's-eye views and maps showing how Madrid has been transformed over the years. Among them is Pedro Texeiro's map of 1656, thought to be the oldest of the city. There is also a model of Madrid, made in 1830 by León Gil de Palacio.

Modern exhibits include a reconstruction of the collage-filled study of Ramón Gómez de la Serna, a key figure of the famous literary gatherings in the Café de Pombo *(see p289)*. In the garden is a Baroque fountain, also by Ribera.

Sorolla's former studio in the Museo Sorolla

Baroque façade of the Museo Municipal, by Pedro de Ribera

Museo Sorolla ⑫

Paseo del General Martínez Campos 37.
Ⅽ 91 310 15 84. Ⓜ *Rubén Darío, Iglesia, Gregorio Marañón.* ◻ *10am–3pm Tue–Sat, 10am–2pm Sun.* ▨ *(free Sun).*

THE FORMER studio-mansion of Valencian Impressionist painter Joaquín Sorolla, now a museum housing his paintings, has been left virtually as it was when he died in 1923.

Although Sorolla is perhaps best known for his brilliantly lit Mediterranean beach scenes, the changing styles of his paintings are well represented in the museum, with examples of his gentle portraiture and a series of works representing people from different parts of Spain. Also on display are various objects amassed during the artist's lifetime, including Span-ish tiles and ceramics. The house, constructed in 1910, has an Andalusian-style garden designed by Sorolla himself.

Museo Lázaro Galdiano ⑬

Calle de Serrano 122. **Ⅽ** 91 56 ✦ 60 84. Ⓜ *Núñez de Balboa, Rubén Darío, Gregorio Marañón.* ◗ *for restoration until early 2004.* Ⓦ www.flg.es

THIS IS ONE OF the best art museums in the city. It is housed in the former mansion-home of the writer José Lázaro Galdiano, and consists of his private collection of fine and applied art, bequeathed to the nation in 1947.

Charles V's fob watch

A colossal central hall, rising through two floors, dominates the mansion. The collection contains items of exceptional quality, ranging from less familiar Goya portraits to a mass of fob watches, including a cross-shaped pocket-watch worn by Charles V when hunting. Among the most beautiful objects are a series of Limoges enamels, miniature sculptures, and *The Saviour*, a portrait attributed to Leonardo da Vinci. The Museo features paintings by English artists Constable, Turner, Gainsborough and Reynolds, as well as 17th-century paintings by the likes of Spanish painters Velázquez, Zurbarán, Ribera, Murillo and El Greco.

Poster for Almodóvar's *Women on the Verge of a Nervous Breakdown*

LA MOVIDA

With Franco's death in 1975 came a new period of personal and artistic liberty. For the young, this was translated into the freedom to stay out late, drinking and sometimes sampling drugs. The phenomenon was known as *la movida*, "the action", and it was at its most intense in Madrid. Although analysts at the time saw it as having serious intellectual content, *la movida* has had few lasting cultural results, except for the emergence of satirical film director Pedro Almodóvar.

Torre de Picasso towering over the Paseo de la Castellana

Paseo de la Castellana ⓮

Ⓜ *Santiago Bernabéu, Cuzco, Plaza de Castilla.*

THE BUSY TRAFFIC artery which cuts through eastern Madrid comprises several parts. Its southernmost portion – the Paseo del Prado *(see pp274–5)* – starts just north of the Estación de Atocha *(see p287)*. The oldest section of the road, it dates from the reign of Carlos III, who built it as part of his embellishment of eastern Madrid *(see p287)*. At the Plaza de Cibeles, the avenue becomes the handsome Paseo de Recoletos, which boasts fashionable cafés, including the Café Gijón *(see p281)*.

The Plaza de Colón marks the start of the Paseo de la Castellana, whose pavement cafés have become a focal point for young Madrid's social life. This northernmost section has several notable examples of modern architecture, including the huge grey Nuevos Ministerios building, completed under Franco. Further on, before reaching the Plaza de Lima, is the Torre de Picasso *(see p21)*, one of Spain's tallest buildings. East of the square is the Estadio Bernabéu, home of Real Madrid Football Club *(see p173)*. The building that dominates the Paseo, however, is the Puerta de Europa, locally known as "Torres Kio": twin glass blocks on either side of the road, built at an angle as if leaning toward each other.

Plaza de Toros de Las Ventas ⓯

Calle de Alcalá 237. [91 356 22 00.
Ⓜ *Ventas.* ⬚ *for bullfights and concerts only.* **Museo Taurino** [91 725 18 57. ⬚ *Mar–Oct: 9:30am–2:30pm Tue–Fri, 10am–1pm Sun; Nov– Feb: 9:30am–2:30pm Mon–Fri.* ♿

WHATEVER your opinion of bullfighting, Las Ventas is undoubtedly one of the most beautiful bullrings in Spain. Built in 1929 in Neo-Mudéjar style, it replaced the city's original bullring which stood near the Puerta de Alcalá. With its horseshoe arches around the outer galleries and the elaborate tilework decoration, it makes an attractive venue for the *corridas* held during the bullfighting season, from May to October. The statues outside the bullring are monuments to two renowned Spanish bullfighters: Antonio Bienvenida and José Cubero.

Adjoining the bullring is the Museo Taurino. The museum contains a varied collection of memorabilia, including portraits and sculptures of famous matadors, as well as the heads of several bulls killed during fights at Las Ventas. Visitors can view close up the tools of the bullfighter's trade: capes and *banderillas* – sharp darts used to wound the bull *(see pp32–3)*. For some people, the gory highlight of the exhibition is the blood-drenched *traje de luces* worn by the legendary Manolete during his fateful bullfight at Linares

in Andalusia in 1947. Also on display is a costume which belonged to Juanita Cruz, a female bullfighter of the 1930s who was forced, in the face of prejudice, to leave Spain. In September and October, the bullring is used as a venue for a season of rock concerts.

Real Fábrica de Tapices ⓰

Calle Fuenterrabia 2. [91 434 05 51. Ⓜ *Menéndez Pelayo.* ⬚ *10am–2pm Mon–Fri.* ● *Easter & Aug.* 🌐 Ⓦ www.realfatapices.com

FOUNDED BY Felipe V in 1721, the Royal Tapestry Factory is the sole survivor of several factories which were opened by the Bourbons *(see pp58–9)* during the 18th century. In 1889 the factory was relocated to this building just south of the Parque del Retiro.

Visitors can see the making of the carpets and tapestries by hand, a process which has changed little. Goya and his brother-in-law Francisco Bayeu created drawings, or cartoons, which were the inspiration for tapestries made for the royal family. Some of the cartoons are on display here; others can be seen in the Museo del Prado *(see pp282–5)*. Some of the tapestries can be seen at El Pardo *(see p314)* and at El Escorial *(see pp312–13)*. Nowadays one of the factory's main tasks is making and repairing the beautiful carpets decorating the Hotel Ritz *(see p276)*.

Plaza de Toros de Las Ventas, Madrid's beautiful bullring

MADRID STREET FINDER

THE MAP REFERENCES given with the sights, shops and entertainment venues described in the Madrid section of the guide refer to the street maps on the following pages. Map references are also given for Madrid hotels *(see pp552–4)*, and for bars and restaurants *(pp592–4)*. The schematic map below shows the area of Madrid covered by the *Street Finder*. The symbols used for the sights and other features are listed in the key at the foot of the page.

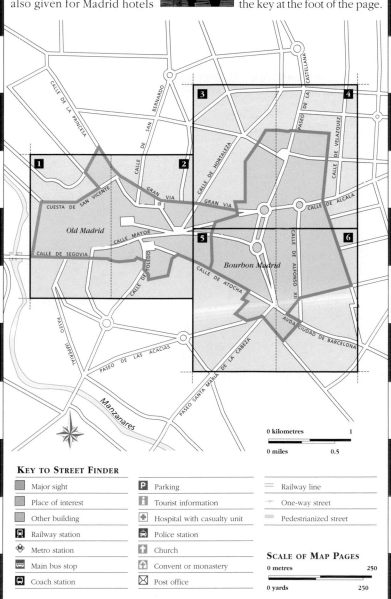

KEY TO STREET FINDER

Major sight	
Place of interest	
Other building	
Railway station	
Metro station	
Main bus stop	
Coach station	

P	Parking
i	Tourist information
	Hospital with casualty unit
	Police station
	Church
	Convent or monastery
⊠	Post office

Railway line
One-way street
Pedestrianized street

SCALE OF MAP PAGES

0 metres   250

0 yards   250

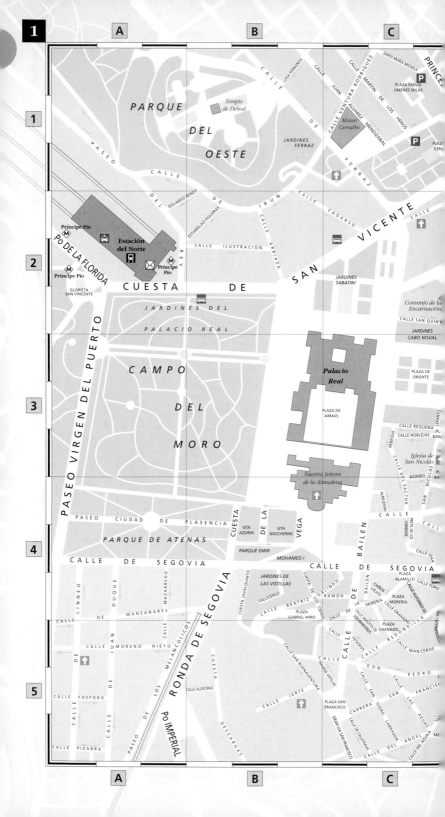

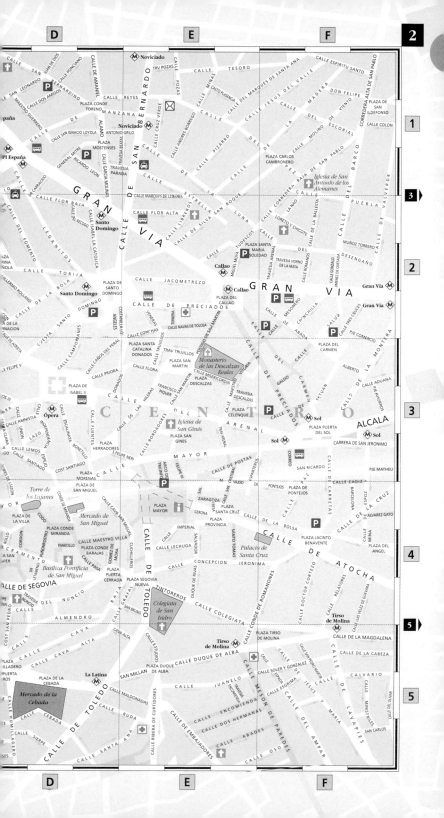

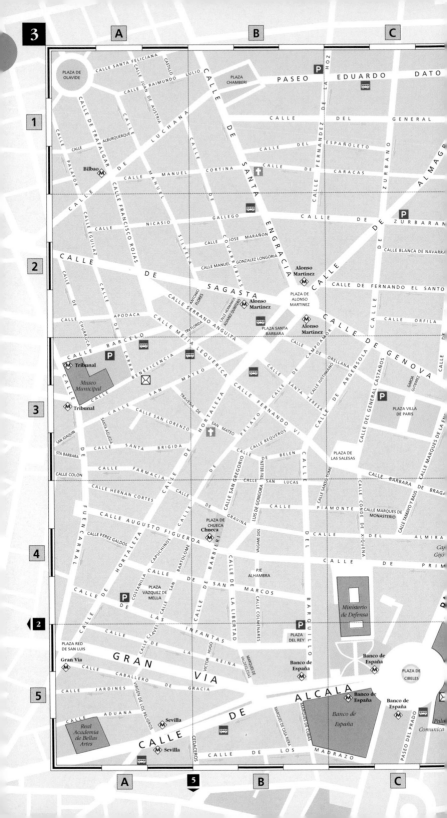

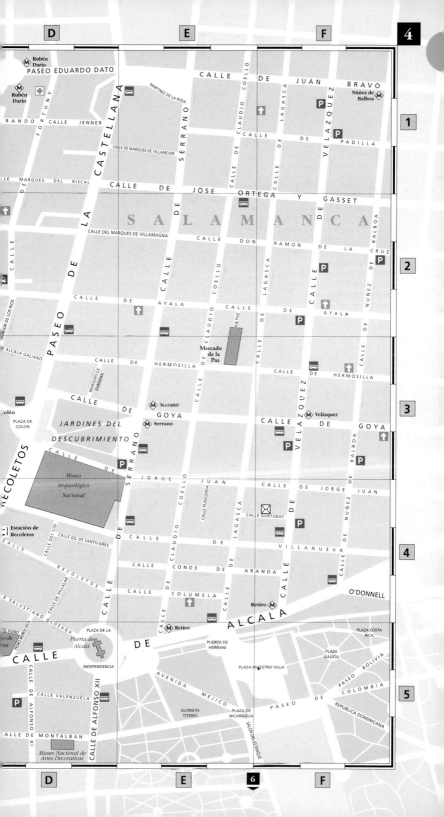

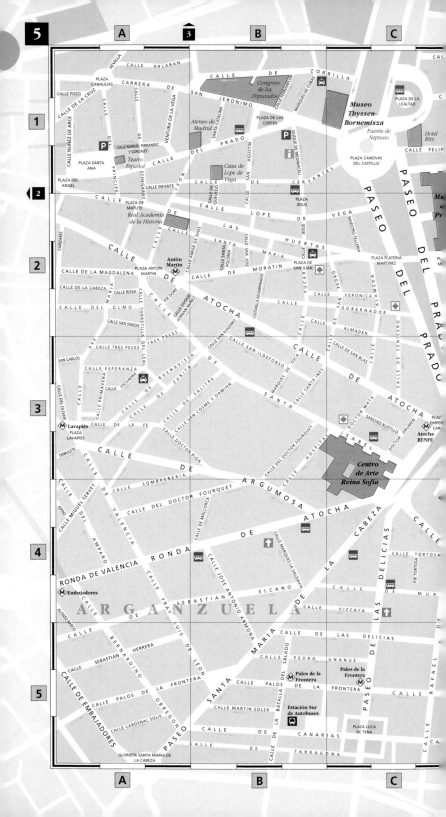

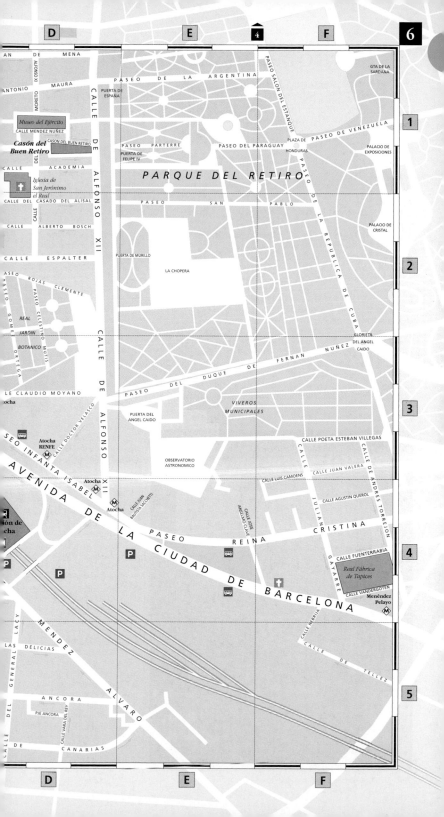

AN DE MENA

ALFONSO XII

ANTONIO MORETO MAURA

CALLE MENDEZ NUÑEZ

Museo del Ejército

Casón del Buen Retiro CASON DEL BUEN RETIRO

CALLE DEL

CALLE ACADEMIA

Iglesia de San Jerónimo el Real

CALLE DEL CASADO DEL ALISAL

CALLE ALBERTO BOSCH

CALLE

CALLE ESPALTER

ASEO ROJAS CLEMENTE

PASEO CELESTINO MUTIS

GOMEZ ORTEGA

REAL

JARDIN

BOTANICO

LE CLAUDIO MOYANO

tocha

SEO INFANTA ISABEL

Atocha RENFE

CALLE DOCTOR VELASCO

CALLE DE ALFONSO XII

PUERTA DE ESPAÑA

PASEO DE LA ARGENTINA

PASEO SALON DEL ESTANQUE

GTA DE LA SARDANA

PASEO PARTERRE

PUERTA DE FELIPE IV

PASEO DEL PARAGUAY

PLAZA DE PASEO DE VENEZUELA

HONDURAS

PALACIO DE EXPOSICIONES

PARQUE DEL RETIRO

PASEO SAN PABLO

PASEO DE LA REPUBLICA DE CUBA

PALACIO DE CRISTAL

PUERTA DE MURILLO

LA CHOPERA

GLORIETA DEL ANGEL CAIDO

PASEO DEL DUQUE DE FERNAN NUÑEZ

PUERTA DEL ANGEL CAIDO

VIVEROS MUNICIPALES

CALLE POETA ESTEBAN VILLEGAS

OBSERVATORIO ASTRONOMICO

CALLE JUAN VALERA

CALLE LUIS CAMOENS

CALLE AGUSTIN QUEROL

CALLE DE ANDRES TORREJON

CALLE JULIAN

ón de cha

AVENIDA DE LA CIUDAD DE BARCELONA

MENDEZ ALVARO

GENERAL LACY

LAS DELICIAS

CALLE DEL

ANCORA

PJE ANCORA

CALLE VARA DEL REY

DE CANARIAS

Atocha

CALLE JUAN BAUTISTA SACCHETTI

PASEO REINA

CALLE JOSE ANGELINO CLAVE

CRISTINA

CALLE FUENTERRABIA

GAYARRE

Real Fábrica de Tapices

CALLE VANDERGOTEN

Menéndez Pelayo

CALLE NEBRIJA

CALLE DE TELLEZ

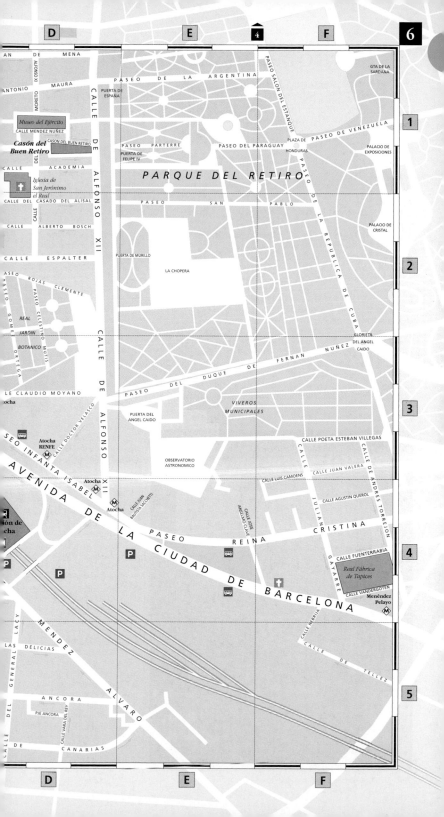

SHOPPING IN MADRID

MADRID IS A CITY that offers the best of everything, from its handmade Spanish guitars to the latest designer clothes. That the city's shopping areas are quite well defined is an additional bonus. The elegant, upmarket fashion stores are mostly concentrated in the Salamanca district and the latest in street fashion is available in

Selection of Madrid's cakes

the Chueca district, while most of the general clothes shops are situated in the city centre. There are food markets throughout the city, though the best speciality food and wine stores are to be found within Old Madrid. Not to be missed is the centuries-old Rastro *(see p292)* every Sunday, one of the greatest flea markets in the world.

FOOD AND DRINK

EVERY DISTRICT in Madrid has a food market with fresh meat, fish, fruit and vegetables. For gourmet specialities, take a walk around Old Madrid, where branches of the **Museo del Jamón** have enormous selections of the many different types of Spanish hams, cured sausages and cheeses. They also have bars and restaurants inside. A comprehensive stock of Spanish wines is sold in the beautiful **Mariano Madrueño**, which was established in 1895. North of Old Madrid is the

Horno San Onofre with its mouthwatering displays of cakes, breads and savouries, especially at Christmas.

DEPARTMENT STORES AND SHOPPING MALLS

THE DEPARTMENT STORE CHAIN, **El Corte Inglés**, has branches all over the city, selling clothes, foods and virtually everything else. They also offer services like photo-developing and shoe repairing.
  Shopping malls have grown rapidly in Madrid in recent years and among the best are

the **Las Rozas Village**, the **Jardín de Serrano** and **ABC Serrano**. For everything under one roof, go to the huge **La Vaguada** mall on the north side of the city. There are also several hypermarkets, mostly around the M30 ring road.

FASHION

A VARIED MIX of clothes stores are located around the Calle de Preciados in the centre of town, but the best-known Spanish and international fashion names are on the Calle de Serrano *(see p286)* and Calle Ortega y Gasset in the Salamanca district. **Ekseption** has a wide range of top designer labels, while the young, eccentric **Agatha Ruíz de la Prada** displays

On the catwalk in Madrid

her unique creations in a shop on a street off the west side of the Paseo de la Castellana.
  The best place for clothes by young designers is the Chueca district, in and around the Calle del Almirante, with shops such as **Ararat**.

CRAFTS, DESIGN AND GIFTS

MADRID'S specialist craft shops are concentrated around the Plaza Mayor. They sell traditional craftwork like lace, embroidery and, at **Almoraima**, fans. **Arco de Cuchilleros** sells ceramics, leather and jewellery.
  Two other districts, Huertas and Lavapiés, have many unusual old shops such as

The enticing frontage of the Museo del Jamón

Inside one of the many antique shops in the streets around the Rastro

Cerámica El Alfar for modern and traditional ceramics and Guitarrería F Manzanero for handmade guitars.

Among the best modern design shops is La Oca at the Puerta de Toledo, which has striking contemporary kitchen and household goods.

ART AND ANTIQUES

THE COMMERCIAL galleries and antiques shops of Madrid are conveniently grouped together. In the Salamanca district, especially along Calle de Claudio Coello, are some of the most exclusive antique shops. Cheaper and more unusual antiques can be found in the Huertas and La Latina districts, particularly around the streets where the Rastro is held. Here, there are several arcades of small shops which open on weekdays, as well as during the Sunday market.

BOOKS AND NEWSPAPERS

THE GIANT French-owned FNAC book and video store has a good selection of books and magazines in English and other languages, and also a very efficient theatre and concert ticket desk. Booksellers is a good English-language bookshop.

The second-hand bookstalls on the Calle Claudio Moyano, near the Parque del Retiro, are a permanent fixture. Here, rare volumes as well as cheap paperbacks can be acquired.

MARKETS

EACH SUNDAY thousands pack the long, narrow hill of Calle Ribera de Curtidores, centre of El Rastro market (see p292) which spreads over into the surrounding streets. At the top of the hill, in the Plaza de Cascorro, the stalls sell mostly clothes and jewellery, but elsewhere you can find just about anything.

The coin and stamp market, which is held every Sunday morning in the Plaza Mayor, is a little less hectic and also fascinating. There are also stalls selling second-hand books and magazines, badges and other collectables.

Sunday morning in the busy Rastro flea market

DIRECTORY

FOOD AND DRINK

Horno San Onofre
Calle San Onofre 3.
Map 2 F2.
[91 532 90 60.

Mariano Madrueño
Calle Postigo de San Martín 3. **Map** 2 E2.
[91 521 19 55.

Museo del Jamón
Carrera de San Jerónimo 6.
Map 5 A1.
[91 521 03 46.

DEPARTMENT STORES AND SHOPPING MALLS

ABC Serrano
C/ Serrano 61. **Map** 4 E1.
[91 577 50 31.

Centro Comercial La Vaguada
Avenida Monforte de Lemos 36.
[91 730 10 00.

El Corte Inglés
C/ Preciados 3. **Map** 2 F3.
[91 309 05 35.

Las Rozas Village
A6 (autovía). Exit (salida) 19, Las Rozas.
[91 640 49 08.

Jardín de Serrano
Calle de Goya 6–8.
Map 4 E3.
[91 577 00 12.

FASHION

Agatha Ruíz de la Prada
Calle Marqués de Riscal 8.
Map 4 D1.
[91 310 44 83.

Ararat
Calle del Almirante 10.
Map 3 C4.
[91 531 81 56.

Ekseption
Calle de Velázquez 28.
Map 4 F3.
[91 577 43 53.

CRAFTS, DESIGN AND GIFTS

Almoraima
Plaza Mayor 12.
Map 2 E4.
[91 365 42 89.

Arco de Cuchilleros
Plaza Mayor 9.
Map 2 E4.
[91 365 26 80.

Cerámica El Alfar
Calle de Claudio Coello 112. **Map** 4 E2.
[91 411 35 87.

Guitarrería F Manzanero
Calle Santa Ana 12.
Map 2 D5.
[91 366 00 47.

La Oca
Ronda de Toledo 1.
[91 365 13 01.

BOOKS AND NEWSPAPERS

Booksellers
Calle José Abascal 48.
[91 442 79 59.

FNAC
C/ Preciados 28.
Map 2 E3.
[91 595 61 00.

MARKETS

El Rastro
Calle Ribera de Curtidores.
Map 2 E5.

ENTERTAINMENT IN MADRID

MADRID'S NIGHTLIFE is not for the faint-hearted. On a typical Saturday night the first stirrings of activity start in the cafés in the early evening, with the accent gradually shifting to tapas bars, restaurants and clubs; like the city's clamouring traffic, the revelling goes on through the night. Those with a slightly less frenetic evening

Flamenco guitarist in Parque del Retiro

in mind will find the best in all the Spanish arts – particularly flamenco and Madrid's own comic opera style, *zarzuela*. There is a good choice of classical music, and thriving jazz and rock circuits. Theatre lovers can choose between Spanish Golden Age classics, or modern mainstream and experimental drama.

Madrid's Teatro Real

ENTERTAINMENT GUIDES

THE BEST GUIDE to what's on currently in Madrid is the *Guía del Ocio*, which includes complete cinema listings and is on sale every Friday. Three daily newspapers have weekly entertainment supplements on Friday: *ABC*, *El Mundo*, and *El País*.

SEASONS AND TICKETS

THE MAIN CONCERT and theatre seasons run from September to June. May's San Isidro fiesta *(see p280)* and the Festival de Otoño – from September to November – attract many top Spanish and international names in music, theatre and other arts – enquire at tourist offices for details.

The FNAC bookstore *(see p305)* sells concert and theatre tickets with little or no commission. State-funded theatres, like the **Auditorio Nacional** and **Teatro de la Zarzuela**, sell their own and each other's tickets. Tickets for other events can be bought in advance by phone at **Caja de Madrid**.

CLASSICAL MUSIC, DANCE AND ZARZUELA

THE TWO CONCERT HALLS of the **Auditorio Nacional** host a range of programmes each year by the Orquesta Nacional de España and international orchestras. Opera in Madrid is due to move into the **Teatro Real**, currently being restored.

The main dance company is the contemporary Compañía Nacional de Danza. **Teatro Albéniz** hosts dance performance as well as Madrid's own musical form, *zarzuela*, comic opera similar to operetta. There are productions at the **Teatro de la Zarzuela** and other theatres in summer.

THEATRE

MADRID'S MOST prestigious theatres are the **Teatro de la Comedia**, home to the Compañía Nacional de Teatro Clásico and its productions of Spanish Golden Age classics, and the **Teatro María Guerrero**, which presents modern drama in Spanish and

also hosts foreign productions. (The theatre is closed until mid-2003.) In addition, there is a thriving network of fringe venues, among the best of which is the often provocative **Teatro Alfil**. An enormous range of Spanish and international theatre talent takes part in the annual Festival de Otoño.

FLAMENCO

ANDALUSIA MAY BE the home of flamenco *(see pp406–7)*, but Madrid's (often expensive) clubs are where the best exponents are based. A club like **Casa Patas**, catches the raw power of genuine flamenco guitar and *cante* singing at its finest with no amplification. The **Café de Chinitas** is a good place to see spontaneous flamenco dancing.

CAFÉS, BARS AND CLUBS

MADRID'S BARS have a style of their own. The city has conserved many of its old grand cafés, which are wonderful places to sit and

Dancing the night away at the Joy Eslava dance club

Exterior of the historic Café Gijón

people-watch or chat. Of the literary cafés, the most famous is **Café Gijón** *(see p281)*.

A plush, popular club that attracts a lively young crowd is **Joy Eslava**, which doesn't hot up till well after midnight.

Wherever the night has been spent, an excellent way to finish is with a breakfast of *chocolate con churros (see p576)* at the **Chocolatería San Ginés**, just as the people of Madrid have been doing since it opened in 1894.

ROCK, JAZZ AND WORLD MUSIC

MAJOR INTERNATIONAL acts play regularly in Madrid's stadiums and sports halls, but **La Riviera** is a small, lively venue that has hosted acts such as Bob Dylan and The Cranberries. In summer there are open-air rock concerts in

the Casa de Campo's **Parque de Atracciones**. The **Café Central**, one of Europe's best jazz clubs, is near the Plaza Santa Ana, site of several good jazz and Latin music clubs, where you can see a live act, then dance the night away to the sinuous rhythms of salsa.

AMUSEMENTS

THE **Parque de Atracciones** funfair, in the Casa de Campo *(see p292)*, is popular with young and old. Modern water parks are also popular, and Aquamadrid, outside the city centre, is a good choice.

BULLFIGHTING AND FOOTBALL

BULLFIGHTING remains hugely popular in Madrid, and **Las Ventas** bullring *(see p296)*, the most important in Spain, holds *corridas* every Sunday from March to October. During the fiesta of San Isidro, in May, there are fights every day.

Real Madrid *(see p173)* are the local aristocrats of football and their Bernabéu stadium is one of the great theatres of the game. The ground of their rivals **Atlético de Madrid** is smaller and cheaper, and often has a better atmosphere.

Las Ventas bullring on the day of a bullfight

MADRID PROVINCE

MADRID PROVINCE (the Comunidad de Madrid) sits high on Spain's central plateau. There is plenty of superb scenery and good walking country in the sierras to the north, which are a refuge for city dwellers who go there to ski in winter or cool down during the torrid summers. In the western foothills of these mountains stands El Escorial, the royal palace-cum-monastery built by Felipe II, from which he ruled his empire. Close by is the Valle de los Caídos, the war monument erected by Franco. The smaller royal palace of El Pardo is on the outskirts of Madrid, and south of the city is the 18th-century summer palace of Aranjuez, set in lush parkland. Historic towns include Alcalá de Henares, which has a Renaissance university building, and Chinchón, where taverns cluster around a picturesque arcaded market square.

SIGHTS AT A GLANCE

Towns and Cities
Alcalá de Henares **9**
Buitrago del Lozoya **2**
Chinchón **10**
Manzanares el Real **7**

Historic Buildings
El Escorial pp312–13 **6**
Monasterio de Santa María de El Paular **3**
Palacio de El Pardo **8**

Palacio Real de Aranjuez **11**
Santa Cruz del Valle de los Caídos **5**

Mountain Ranges
Sierra Centro de Guadarrama **4**
Sierra Norte **1**

KEY

Madrid city

Madrid province

✈ Barajas Airport

Motorway

Major road

Minor road

Province boundary

0 kilometres 25

0 miles 20

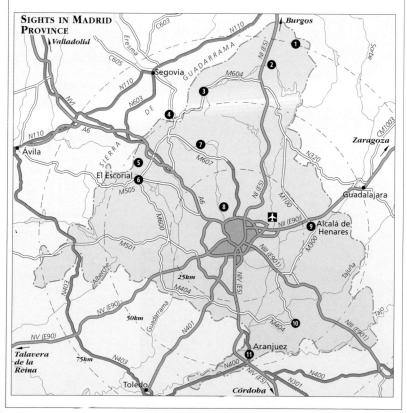

SIGHTS IN MADRID PROVINCE

◁ **Celebration of Mass in the church of the Monasterio de Santa María de El Paular**

The village of Montejo de la Sierra in the Sierra Norte

Sierra Norte ❶

Madrid. 🚌 *Montejo.* 🛈 *Calle Real 64, Montejo, 91 869 70 58.*

T HE BLACK SLATE HAMLETS of the Sierra Norte, which were once known as the Sierra Pobre (Poor Sierra), are located in the most attractively rural part of Madrid province.

At **Montejo de la Sierra**, the largest village in the area, an information centre organizes riding, the rental of traditional houses (*see p531*), and visits to the nearby nature reserve of the **Hayedo de Montejo de la Sierra**. This is one of the most southern beech woods (*see p76*) in Europe, and a relic of a previous era, when climatic conditions here were more suitable for the beech. From Montejo, you can drive on to picturesque hamlets such as **La Hiruela** or **Puebla de la Sierra**, both of which are set in lovely walking country.

The drier southern hills slope down to the **Embalse de Puentes Viejas**, a reservoir where summer chalets cluster around artificial beaches. On the eastern edge

of the sierra is the village of **Patones**, which is thought to have escaped invasion by the Moors and Napoleon's troops because of its isolated location.

Buitrago del Lozoya ❷

Madrid. 🚶 *1,700.* 🚌 🛈 *Calle Tahona 11, 91 868 00 56.* 🛒 *Sat.* 🎉 *La Asunción and San Roque (15 Aug), Cristo de los Esclavos (15 Sep).*

P ICTURESQUELY SITED above a meander in the Río Lozoya is the walled town of Buitrago del Lozoya. Founded by the Romans, it was fortified by the Arabs, and became an important market town in medieval times. The 14th-century Gothic-Mudéjar castle is in ruins, although the gatehouse, arches and stretches of the original Arab wall have survived. Today, the castle is used as a venue for bullfights and hosts a festival of ancient theatre and music in the summer.

The old quarter, within the walls, retains its charming

atmosphere. The church of **Santa María del Castillo**, dating from the 15th century, has a Mudéjar tower and ceilings which were moved here from the old hospital. The **town hall** *(ayuntamiento)*, in the newer part of Buitrago, preserves a 16th-century processional cross. In the basement is the **Museo Picasso**. The prints, drawings and ceramics were collected by the artist's friend, Eugenio Arias.

🏛 **Museo Picasso**
Plaza de Picasso 1. 📞 *91 868 00 56.* ⬤ *Mon.*

Altarpiece in the Monasterio de Santa María de El Paular

Monasterio de Santa María de El Paular ❸

Southwest of Rascafría on M604. 📞 *91 869 14 25.* 🚌 *Rascafría.* ⬤ *noon–5pm Mon–Sat, 1–6pm Sun.* 🎟

F OUNDED IN 1390 as Castile's first Carthusian monastery, Santa María de El Paular stands on the site of a medieval royal hunting lodge. Although it is mainly Gothic in style, Plateresque and Renaissance features were added later. The monastery was abandoned in 1836 when government minister Mendizábal ordered the sale of church goods (*see p59*). It fell into disrepair until the state restored it in the 1950s. Today the complex comprises a working Benedictine monastery, a church and a private hotel (*see p554*).

The church's delicate alabaster altarpiece, attributed to

Buitrago del Lozoya, standing next to the river

Flemish craftsmen, dates from the 15th century. Its panels depict scenes from the life of Jesus. The lavish Baroque *camarín* (chamber), behind the altar, was designed by Francisco de Hurtado in 1718.

Every Sunday, the monks sing an hour-long Gregorian chant in the church. If they are not busy, they will show you the cloister's Mudéjar brick vaulting and double sun-clock.

The monastery is a good starting point for exploring the country towns of **Rascafría** and **Lozoya** in the surrounding Lozoya valley. To the south-west is the nature reserve of **Lagunas de Peñalara**.

Sierra Centro de Guadarrama **❹**

Madrid. 🚉 *Puerto de Navacerrada, Cercedilla.* 🚌 *Navacerrada, Cercedilla.* ℹ️ *Navacerrada, 91 856 00 06.*

THE CENTRAL SECTION of the Sierra de Guadarrama was little visited until the 1920s, when the area was first linked by train to Madrid. Today, the granite slopes are planted with pines and specked by holiday chalets. Villages such as **Navacerrada** and **Cercedilla** have grown into popular resorts for skiing, mountain-biking, rock-climbing and horse riding. Walkers wanting to enjoy the pure mountain air can follow marked routes from Navacerrada.

The **Valle de Fuenfría**, a nature reserve of wild forests, is best reached via Cercedilla. It has a well-preserved stretch of the original Roman road, as well as several picnic spots and marked walking routes.

The gigantic cross at Valle de los Caídos

Santa Cruz del Valle de los Caídos **❺**

North of El Escorial on M600. 📞 *91 890 56 11.* 🚌 *from El Escorial.* 🕐 *Tue–Sun.* ⬤ *some public hols.* 🎫 *(free Wed for EU residents).* 🌐 *www.patrimonionacional.es*

GENERAL FRANCO had the Holy Cross of the Valley of the Fallen built as a memorial to those who died in the Civil War *(see pp62–3)*. The vast cross is located some 13 km (8 miles) north of El Escorial *(see pp312–13)*, and dominates the surrounding countryside. Some Spanish people find it too chilling a symbol of the dictatorship to be enjoyable, while for others its sheer size is rewarding.

The cross is 150 m (490 ft) high and rises above a basilica carved 250 m (820 ft) deep into the rock by prisoners. A number of them are said to have died in the 20-year-plus project.

Next to the basilica's high altar is the plain white tomb-stone of Franco, and, opposite, that of José Antonio Primo de Rivera, founder of the Falange Española party. A further 40,000 coffins of soldiers from both sides in the Civil War lie here out of sight, including those of two unidentified victims.

From the arms of the cross, there are magnificent views over the pine forests.

Navacerrada pass in the Sierra de Guadarrama

El Escorial ❻

Fresco by Luca Giordano

FELIPE II'S IMPOSING GREY PALACE of San Lorenzo de El Escorial stands out against the foothills of the Sierra de Guadarrama to the northwest of Madrid. It was built between 1563 and 1584 in honour of St Lawrence, and its unornamented severity set a new architectural style which became one of the most influential in Spain. The interior was conceived as a mausoleum and contemplative retreat rather than a splendid residence. Its artistic wealth, which includes some of the most important works of art of the royal Habsburg collections, is concentrated in the museums, chapterhouses, church, royal pantheon and library. In contrast, the royal apartments are remarkably humble.

★ Royal Pantheon
The funerary urns of Spanish monarchs line the marble mausoleum.

Main entrance

Bourbon Palace

Architectural Museum

Sala de Batallas

Basilica
The highlight of this huge decorated church, is the lavish altarpiece. The chapel houses a superb marble sculpture of the cruci-fiction by Cellini.

The Alfonso XII College
was founded by monks in 1875 as a boarding school.

Patio de los Reyes

Entrance to Basilica only

★ Library
This impressive array of 40,000 books incorporates Felipe II's personal collection. On display are precious manuscripts, including a poem by Alfonso X the Learned. The 16th-century ceiling frescoes are by Tibaldi.

STAR FEATURES

★ Royal Pantheon

★ Library

★ Museum of Art

The royal apartments, on the second floor of the palace, consist of Felipe II's modestly decorated living quarters. His bedroom opens directly on to the high altar of the basilica.

★ **Museum of Art**
Flemish, Italian and Spanish paintings hang in the museum, located on the first floor. One of the highlights is The Calvary, *by 15th-century Flemish artist Rogier van der Weyden.*

VISITORS' CHECKLIST

Avda de Juan de Borbon Y Battemberg. ☎ 91 890 59 04. 🚇 from Atocha, Chamartín. 🚌 661, 664 from Moncloa. ☐ Apr–Sep: 10am–6pm (Oct–Mar: 5pm). ⬤ public hols. 🎫 (free Wed for EU residents). ✝ 9:30am daily; 7pm, 8pm Sat & Sun. 🎦 🛒 🅆 www.patrimonionacional.es

The Patio de los Evangelistas is a temple by Herrera. The Jardin de los Frailes makes a nice walk.

Chapterhouses
On display here is Charles V's portable altar. The ceiling frescoes depict monarchs and angels.

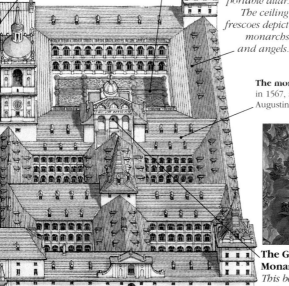

The monastery was founded in 1567, and has been run by Augustinian monks since 1885.

The Glory of the Spanish Monarchy by Luca Giordano
This beautiful fresco, above the main staircase, depicts Charles V and Felipe II, and scenes of the building of the monastery.

The Building of El Escorial
When chief architect Juan Bautista de Toledo died in 1567 he was replaced by Juan de Herrera, royal inspector of monuments. The plain architectural style of El Escorial is called desornamentado, *literally,* "unadorned".

Climber resting on a rock face of La Pedriza, near Manzanares el Real

Manzanares el Real 🐧

Madrid. 🏛 4,500. 🚌 ℹ Plaza del Pueblo 1, 91 853 00 09. 🚐 Tue & Fri. 🎭 Fiesta de Verano (early Aug), Cristo de la Nave (14 Sep).

F ROM A DISTANCE, the skyline of Manzanares el Real is dominated by its restored 15th-century castle. Although the castle is equipped with some traditionally military features, such as double machicolations and turrets, it was used mainly as a residential palace by the Dukes of Infantado. Below the castle is a 16th-century church,

a Renaissance portico and fine capitals. Behind the town, bordering the foothills of the Sierra de Guadarrama, is **La Pedriza**, a mass of granite screes and ravines, very popular with climbers. It now forms part of an attractive nature reserve.

ENVIRONS: Colmenar Viejo, 12 km (7.5 miles) to the southeast of Manzanares, has a superb Gothic-Mudéjar church.

Palacio de El Pardo 🐧

El Pardo, northwest of Madrid on N605. 📞 91 376 15 00. 🚌 from Moncloa. ⬜ daily. ⬤ during royal visits. 🎟 (free Wed for EU residents). 🌐 www.patrimonionacional.es

T HIS ROYAL HUNTING lodge and palace, set in parkland just outside Madrid's city limits, boasts General Franco among its former residents. A guided tour takes visitors round the moated palace's Habsburg wing and the identical 18th-century extension, designed by Francesco Sabatini.

The ornamental Bourbon interior is heavy with frescoes, gilt mouldings and tapestries, many of which were woven to designs by Goya *(see p296)*. Today the palace lodges visiting heads of state and

entertains royal guests. Surrounding the palace and the elegant 18th-century village of El Pardo is an enormous forest of holm oak. The area is popular for picnicking, and some game animals still run free.

Façade of Colegio de San Ildefonso in Alcalá de Henares

Alcalá de Henares 🐧

Madrid. 🏛 170,000. 🚌 🚐 ℹ Callejón Santa María, 91 889 26 94. 🚐 Mon, Wed. 🎭 Feria de Alcalá (late Aug).

A T THE HEART of a modern industrial town is one of Spain's most renowned university quarters. Founded in 1499 by Cardinal Cisneros, Alcalá's

Lavish 18th-century tapestry inside the Palacio de El Pardo

university became one of the foremost places of learning in 16th-century Europe. The most historic college, **San Ildefonso**, survives. Former students include Golden Age playwright Lope de Vega *(see p280)*. In 1517 the university produced Europe's first polyglot bible, with text in Latin, Greek, Hebrew and Chaldean.

Alcalá's other sights are the cathedral and the **Casa-Museo de Cervantes**, birthplace of the Golden Age author. The newly restored 19th-century palace, **Palacio de Laredo** has splendid decorations that can be seen only on a guided tour.

🏛 **Casa-Museo de Cervantes**
Calle Mayor. ☎ *91 889 96 54.*
🕐 *Tue–Sun.* ● *public hols.*

Chinchón's unique porticoed Plaza Mayor

Chinchón ⑩

Madrid. 👥 *4,500.* 🚉 🚌 ℹ️ *Plaza Mayor 3, 91 894 00 84.* 🚌 *Sat.* 📅 *Semana Santa (Easter Week), San Roque (12–18 Aug).*

CHINCHÓN IS arguably Madrid province's most picturesque town. The 16th-century, typically Castilian, porticoed **Plaza Mayor** has a splendidly theatrical air. It comes alive for the Easter passion play, acted out by the townspeople *(see p280)*, and during the August bullfights. The 16th-century church, perched above the square, has an altar painting by Goya, whose brother was a priest here. Just off the square is the 18th-century Augustinian monastery, which has been converted into a **parador**

with a peaceful patio garden *(see p554)*. A ruined 15th-century castle is on a hill to the west of town. Although it is closed to the public, there are views of Chinchón and the countryside from outside it.

Chinchón is a popular weekend destination for *Madrileños*, who come here to sample the excellent chorizo and locally produced *anís (see p577)* in the town's many taverns.

Palacio Real de Aranjuez ⑪

Plaza de Parejas, Aranjuez. ☎ *91 891 13 44.* 🚉 🚌 🕐 *10am–6:15pm Tue–Sun (Oct–Mar: until 5:15pm).* 🎟 *(free Wed for EU residents).* ♿ 🚺

THE ROYAL SUMMER PALACE and gardens of Aranjuez grew up around a medieval hunting lodge standing beside a natural weir, the meeting point of the Tagus and Jarama rivers.

Today's palace of brick and white stone was built in the 18th century by the Habsburgs and redecorated by the Bourbons. A guided tour takes you through numerous Baroque rooms, among them the

Chinese Porcelain Room, the Hall of Mirrors and the Smoking Room, modelled on the Alhambra in Granada. It is worth visiting Aranjuez for the simple pleasure of walking in the 300 hectares (740 acres) of shady royal gardens which inspired Joaquín Rodrigo's *Concierto de Aranjuez*. The Parterre Garden and the Island Garden, between the rivers, survive from the original 16th-century palace.

Between the palace and the River Tagus is the 18th-century Prince's Garden, decorated with sculptures, fountains and lofty trees from the Americas. In the garden is the Casa de Marinos (Sailors' House), a museum housing the launches once used by the royal family for trips along the river. At the far end of the garden is the Casa del Labrador (Labourer's Cottage), a decorative royal pavilion built by Carlos IV.

The town's restaurants are deservedly popular because of the exceptional quality of the asparagus and strawberries. In summer, a 19th-century steam train, built to carry strawberries, runs between here and the capital.

MIGUEL DE CERVANTES

Miguel de Cervantes Saavedra, Spain's greatest literary figure *(see p30)*, was born in Alcalá de Henares in 1547. After fighting in the naval Battle of Lepanto (1571), he was held captive by the Turks for more than five years. In 1605, when he was almost 60 years old, the first of two parts of his comic masterpiece *Don Quixote (see p377)* was published to popular acclaim. He continued writing novels and plays until his death in Madrid on 23 April 1616, the same day that Shakespeare died.

Gardens surrounding the Royal Palace at Aranjuez

CENTRAL
SPAIN

Introducing Central Spain

MUCH OF SPAIN'S VAST CENTRAL PLATEAU, the *meseta*, is covered with wheat fields or dry, dusty plains, but there are many attractive places to explore. Central Spain's mountains, gorges, forests and lakes are filled with wildlife. A deep sense of history permeates the towns and cities of the tableland, reflected in some stunning architecture: the Roman ruins of Mérida, the medieval mansions of Cáceres, the Gothic cathedrals of Burgos, León and Toledo, the Renaissance grandeur of Salamanca, and castles almost everywhere.

León Cathedral (see p336–7), an outstanding Gothic building, was completed during the 14th century. As well as many glorious windows of medieval glass, it has superb carved choir stalls depicting biblical scenes and everyday life.

León

CASTILLA Y LEÓN
(see pp328–59)

Zamora

Vallado

Salamanca (see pp340–43) is the site of some of the finest Renaissance and Plateresque architecture in Spain. Among the city's most notable buildings are the university, its façade a mass of carved detail; the old and new cathedrals (built side by side); and the handsome Plaza Mayor, built in warm golden sandstone.

Salamanca

Ávila

Cáceres

Tole

EXTREMADURA
(see pp382–95)

The Museo Nacional de Arte Romano in Mérida (see p392) houses Roman treasures. The city has a well-preserved Roman theatre.

Badajoz

0 kilometres	50
0 miles	50

◁ **Roofs and walls in the old part of Toledo**

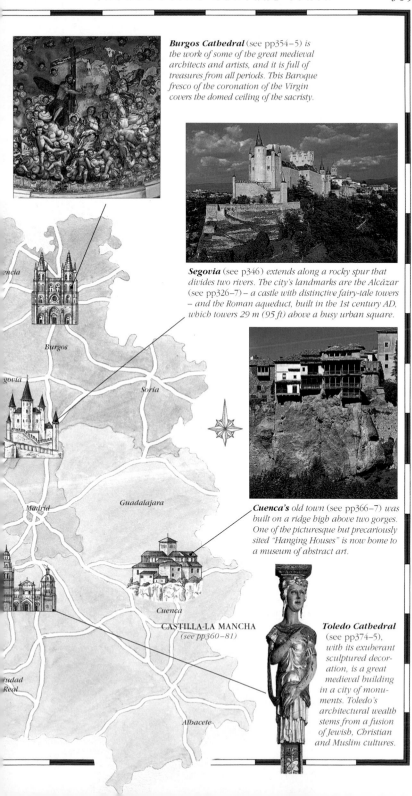

Burgos Cathedral (see pp354–5) is the work of some of the great medieval architects and artists, and it is full of treasures from all periods. This Baroque fresco of the coronation of the Virgin covers the domed ceiling of the sacristy.

Segovia (see p346) extends along a rocky spur that divides two rivers. The city's landmarks are the Alcázar (see pp326–7) – a castle with distinctive fairy-tale towers – and the Roman aqueduct, built in the 1st century AD, which towers 29 m (95 ft) above a busy urban square.

Cuenca's old town (see pp366–7) was built on a ridge high above two gorges. One of the picturesque but precariously sited "Hanging Houses" is now home to a museum of abstract art.

CASTILLA-LA MANCHA
(see pp360–81)

Toledo Cathedral (see pp374–5), with its exuberant sculptured decoration, is a great medieval building in a city of monuments. Toledo's architectural wealth stems from a fusion of Jewish, Christian and Muslim cultures.

Burgos

Soria

Guadalajara

Madrid

Cuenca

Albacete

Regional Food: Central Spain

T HE RESTAURANTS OF MADRID are a rich source of specialities from every Spanish region, along with superb fresh fish that is often on the table within a few hours of being caught. Game, such as wild boar, pheasant and partridge, is plentiful throughout Central Spain, but especially in Extremadura, where wild frog and tench are also eaten. Castilla y León and Castilla-La Mancha maintain a tradition of homely, robust cooking with a variety of warming one-pot pulse stews. The north also produces excellent bread, which is eaten with everything. Sausages and simple rabbit or pork dishes, spiced with cumin and garlic, are **Garlic** typical of Castilla-La Mancha; while Castilla y León is known for its suckling pig and milk-fed lamb, roasted whole in enormous bread ovens. Little cakes, such as Toledo's famous marzipans, are popular and many convents continue to make and sell their own.

Patatas a la importancia *are egg-coated potatoes fried and then simmered in wine seasoned with onions and saffron.*

Saffron *(azafrán) comes from the purple autumn crocus, which has three deep red stigmas. Introduced by the Moors centuries ago, it is the world's most expensive spice because it must be picked by hand. The plains of La Mancha (see p376) yield Spain's highest quality saffron, which is sold in strands and date stamped. Saffron is soaked, crushed or toasted to add its taste and golden colour to a variety of dishes.*

Pollo al padre Pero, *a dish of Extremadura, is half a young chicken simmered in a spicy pepper and tomato sauce.*

Chickpeas

Beef

Chicken

Cabbage

Salt pork belly

Sausage

Cocido madrileño *is a widely available meat dish and every region has its own variation. It is essentially a slow-simmered stew of beef, chicken, ham and pork belly with chickpeas. Cabbage, chorizo and morcilla (black sausage) are also included. The broth is drunk first, as soup, and the rest often served as two further courses.*

Sopa de ajo *is a warming garlic soup which is thickened with bread. Poached egg and paprika are often added to it.*

Migas, *originally a shepherd's dish, is fried breadcrumbs. It is often served with fried peppers or, in Extremadura, with bacon.*

Perdiz con chocolate *is braised partridge with carrots and onions, served with a rich, dark, chocolate-tasting gravy.*

Pisto, *La Mancha's best dish, is Spain's version of ratatouille. It combines peppers, tomatoes, onions and courgettes.*

El frite, *from Extremadura, is a dish of fried lamb with garlic, onion and lemon, flavoured with the local paprika.*

Sausages *are made in most of the villages of Extremadura and Castilla, and are of varying types. Those made in Guijuelo (including chorizo) and Montanchez are particularly good, as are the hams, cured loins and shoulders produced in Extremadura.*

Menestra de ternera *is a stew in which veal is simmered gently with young vegetables, such as carrots and peas.*

Cabrito al ajillo *is kid fried with onions and herbs. This savoury dish can also include pounded goat's liver.*

Manchego, *made from sheep's milk on the plains of La Mancha, is widely regarded as Spain's greatest cheese. When fully mature it becomes very hard, similar to Parmesan. The texture and the taste vary depending on whether it is* fresco *(young),* curado *(over 13 weeks old) or* añejo *(at least 7 months old).*

Yemas *means yolks, which these sugary cakes resemble in their shape, colour and content. The best come from Ávila (see p344).*

PULSES

An enormous variety of pulses, in all colours, shapes and sizes is grown on the plains of Castilla y León. The best pulses are expensive, and their names are legally protected. The best-known white beans are the *alubias blancas* of Barco de Ávila; the best chickpeas are grown in Fuentesauco; and the finest lentils come from La Armuña.

Chickpeas   **Lentils**   **Pinto beans**

Wines of Central Spain

THE WINES OF CENTRAL SPAIN originate in either the
small, high-quality regions of northwest Castilla
y León or in the vast wine-producing plains of La
Mancha and Valdepeñas. Ribera del Duero has become
Spain's most fashionable red wine region, with its
aromatic, rich yet fine reds made from Tinto Fino
grapes (the local name for Tempranillo) and, more
recently, lighter, fruity wines. Rueda makes a good
white wine, made from the Verdejo grape. La Mancha
and Valdepeñas both produce lots of simple white
wine, and reds which can be mellow and fruity.

Harvesting Viura grapes at Rueda

*Toro makes the
most powerful
and fiery of all
red wines from
the ubiquitous
Tempranillo grape.*

Artesian well for irrigating vines in La Mancha

KEY FACTS ABOUT WINES OF CENTRAL SPAIN

**Location and
Climate**
Ribera del
Duero, Rueda
and Toro are all high-lying
areas with extreme climates
– very hot summer days combined with cool nights, and
cold winters. The marked
difference of temperature
between day and night helps
to preserve the acidity in the
grapes. Both La Mancha and
Valdepeñas are extremely
hot and dry areas. In recent
years, droughts have caused
a severe shortage of grapes.

Grape Varieties
The Tempranillo
grape – also
known as Tinto
Fino, Tinto del Toro and
Cencibel – produces nearly
all the best red wines of
Central Spain. Cabernet
Sauvignon is permitted in
some regions; it is used in
some Ribera del Duero wines

and occasionally surfaces as
a single varietal, as at the estate of the Marquis of Griñón
in Méntrida. Verdejo, Viura
and Sauvignon Blanc are
used for white Rueda. The
white Airén grape predomi-
nates in the vineyards of
Valdepeñas and La Mancha.

Good Producers
Toro: Fariña (Gran
Colegiata). ***Rueda:***
Álvarez y Diez, Los
Curros, Marqués
de Riscal, Sanz. ***Ribera del
Duero:*** Alejandro Fernández
(Pesquera), Boada, Hermanos
Pérez Pascuas (Viña Pedrosa),
Ismael Arroyo (Valsotillo),
Vega Sicilia, Victor Balbás.
Méntrida: Marqués de
Griñón. ***La Mancha:*** Fermín
Ayuso Roig (Estola), Vinícola
de Castilla (Castillo de
Alhambra). ***Valdepeñas:***
Casa de la Viña, Félix Solís,
Luis Megía (Marqués de
Gastañaga), Los Llanos.

Villafranca
del Bierzo
Cacabelos
Ponferrada
LE
ZAMOR
Duero
SALAMANCA
N122
N620
N110
N630

**Traditional earthenware *tinaja*,
still used for fermenting wine**

0 kilometres　　　　100

0 miles　　　50

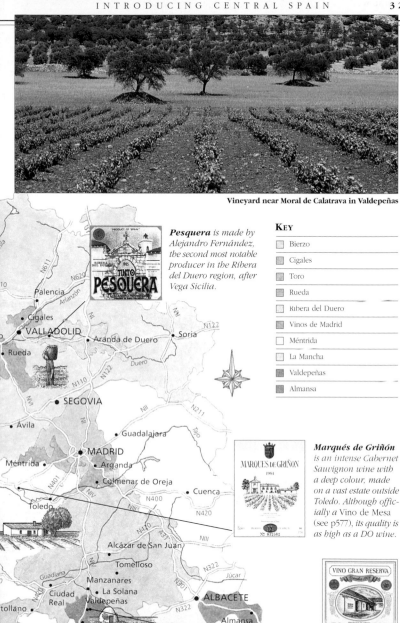

Vineyard near Moral de Calatrava in Valdepeñas

Pesquera is made by Alejandro Fernández, the second most notable producer in the Ribera del Duero region, after Vega Sicilia.

KEY

	Bierzo
	Cigales
	Toro
	Rueda
	Ribera del Duero
	Vinos de Madrid
	Méntrida
	La Mancha
	Valdepeñas
	Almansa

Marqués de Griñón is an intense Cabernet Sauvignon wine with a deep colour, made on a vast estate outside Toledo. Although officially a Vino de Mesa (see p577), its quality is as high as a DO wine.

Señorío de los Llanos is produced in Valdepeñas. Its fine reds – made from Cencibel (Tempranillo) and aged in oak – are of excellent value.

WINE REGIONS

The wine regions of Ribera del Duero, Toro and Rueda, are situated on remote, high plateaus, straddling the Río Duero. To the northwest lies the isolated region of Bierzo, whose wines have more in common with neighbouring Valdeorras in Galicia. Some wine is produced around Madrid, and southwest of the capital is the largely undistinguished region of Méntrida. Most of Central Spain's wine is produced in La Mancha – the world's largest single wine region – and in the smaller enclave of Valdepeñas, which produces a great deal of "vino de mesa".

Birds of Central Spain

Bee-eater

THE VAST AND VARIED wild habitats of Central Spain are home to the richest avifauna in the peninsula. White storks' nests are a common sight on the church towers and chimneypots of towns. Grebes, herons and shovelers can be seen in the marshlands; the distinctive hoopoe is often spotted in woods; and grasslands are the nesting grounds of bustards and cranes. The mountains and high plains are the domain of birds of prey such as the imperial eagle, peregrine falcon and vultures. Deforestation, changing agricultural practices and hunting have all taken their toll in recent decades. Today, almost 160 bird species are the subject of conservation initiatives.

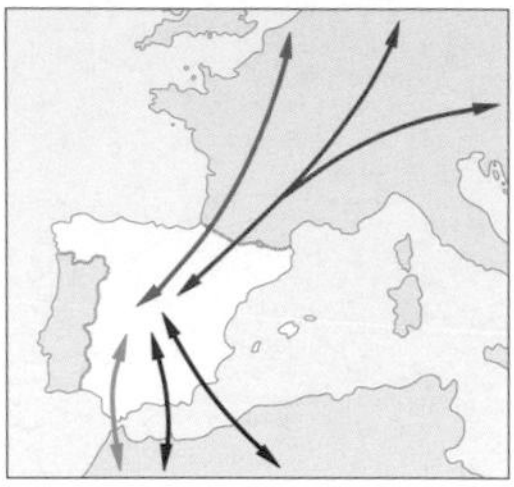

Migration Routes

- Cranes
- Storks
- Raptors
- Wildfowl

Marshland and Wet Meadow

Wetlands, such as Lagunas de Ruidera *(see p379)*, on the edge of the plains of La Mancha, are vital feeding grounds for a wide range of waterfowl, some of which may remain in Spain throughout the year. Other migratory species use such sites as stopover points to feed, rest and build up enough energy to enable them to complete their journeys.

__Little egrets__ are recognized by their snow white plumage and graceful slow flight. They feed largely on frogs, snails and small fish.

__Shovelers__ feed on the water surface with a characteristic shovelling motion. The male has brightly coloured plumage but the female is a dull brown.

Woodland and Scrub

Habitats in areas of woodland, such as the Parque Nacional de Cabañeros *(see p369)*, and scrub support many species, such as rollers and woodpeckers, throughout the year. Food is plentiful and there are many places to roost and nest. Early in the morning is the best time for spotting some of the rarer species, such as the bluethroat.

__Rollers__ are commonly found in woodland, often nesting in tree stumps or holes left by woodpeckers. Their food includes grasshoppers, crickets and beetles.

__Hoopoes__ can be easily identified by their striking plumage and by the crest which can be raised if the bird is alarmed. They feed on ground insects.

STORKS

Both the white and the (much rarer) black stork breed in Spain. They can be recognized in flight by their slow, steady wingbeats and may occasionally be seen soaring on thermals, usually during migrations. During the breeding season they put on elaborate courtship displays, which involve "dancing", wing-beating and bill-clapping. Their large nests, made of branches and twigs and lined with grasses, are constructed on roofs, towers, spires and chimneypots, where they are easy to watch. They feed on insects, fish and amphibians. Stork populations are threatened by wetland reclamation and the use of pesticides.

The endangered black stork

Nesting on a monastery roof

GRASSLAND AND FIELD

Many of Spain's natural grasslands have been ploughed over to plant cereals and other crops. Remaining vestiges are rich in wild grasses and flowers and are vital habitats for species such as bustards and larks.

Cranes perform elegant courtship dances and are also stately birds in flight, their long necks extended to the limit. They are omnivores, feeding on amphibians, crustaceans, plants and insects.

Great bustards nest in shallow depressions formed in open grassland and cultivated fields. Spain is home to half of the world's population.

MOUNTAIN AND HIGH PLAIN

Some of Spain's most spectacular birds of prey live in mountain ranges, such as the Sierra de Gredos *(see p344)*, and the high plains of Central Spain. The broad wingspans of eagles and vultures allow them to soar on currents of warm air as they scan the ground below for prey and carrion.

Imperial eagles, with their vast wingspan of 2.25 m (7 ft), are extremely rare – only around 100 pairs are left in the whole of Spain.

Griffon vultures, a gregarious species, nest in trees and on rocky crags, often using the same place from year to year. Their broad wingspans can exceed 2 m (6 ft).

The Castles of Castile

13th-century fresco of the siege of a castle

THE GREATEST CONCENTRATION of Spain's 2,000 castles is in Castile (now part of Castilla y León), which derived its name from the word *castillo*, or castle. In the 10th and 11th centuries this region was the battleground between Moors and Christians. Villages and towns were fortified as protection against one side or the other. Most of the surviving castles in Castile, however, were built as noble residences after the area had been reconquered and there was no longer a military purpose for them. Fernando and Isabel *(see pp52–3)* banned the building of new castles at the end of the 15th century; many existing ones were converted to domestic use.

Coca Castle *(see p347)*, a classic Mudéjar design in brick

La Mota Castle (see p348), *at Medina del Campo, near Valladolid, was originally a Moorish castle but was rebuilt after 1440 and later became the property of Fernando and Isabel. The square-shaped Torre del Homenaje has twin bartizan turrets at its corners and machiolations beneath its battlements. Great curtain walls surround the castle.*

Patio de armas (courtyard)

Bartizan turrets

The Torre de Juan II contained the dungeons.

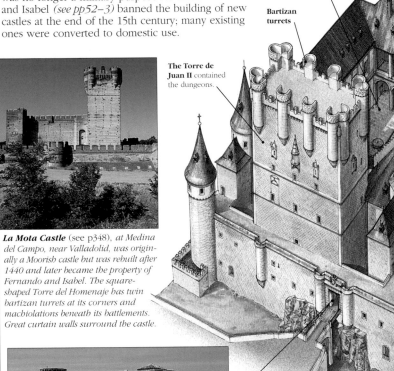

The barbican, with the coat of arms of the Catholic Monarchs carved over the gate, contains the portcullis and guards' watchrooms.

Belmonte Castle (see p376) *was built in the 15th century as the stronghold of the quarrelsome Marquis of Villena, Juan Pacheco. Late-Gothic in style, it has a sophisticated, hexagonal ground plan, with a triangular bailey.*

SEGOVIA ALCÁZAR

The plan of the royal castle of Segovia *(see p346)* is determined by the contours of the rocky outcrop on which it stands. Begun in the 12th century, the Alcázar was mostly built between 1410 and 1455. It had to be largely rebuilt following a fire in 1862. The fortress's formidable walls conceal several sumptuous apartments.

Torre del Homenaje has pointed turrets, atypical of Spanish castles.

Curtain wall

The King's Room, the most important room in the castle, is Gothic in style.

The Pine Cone Room gets its name from the golden pine cones on the ceiling.

The Galley Room

The Throne Room has ornate plasterwork and a Mudéjar ceiling.

Peñafiel Castle (see p349) has been compared to a battleship because of its long, narrow shape. The site above the Duero valley has been defended since the 10th century, but the present castle is 15th-century.

TERMS USED IN THIS GUIDE

Alcazar: Castle or palace used as a royal residence.

Bartizan: A small turret which projects from the battlements of a tower above attackers.

Cross and orb loophole: Narrow slit, shaped to allow archers to shoot at various angles.

Curtain wall: Outer, windowless wall, often low enough for archers to fire over it from the keep and other towers.

Machicolation: A projection overhanging the wall beneath a battlement to allow boiling oil, missiles or human waste to be dropped on to the enemy.

Torre del Homenaje: The fortified tower or keep at the heart of a castle, often built to a square plan, in which the nobleman's family lived.

THE CASTLES OF CASTILLA Y LEÓN

Some of Central Spain's finest surviving castles can be visited today. A few, such as Ciudad Rodrigo *(see p339)*, have been turned into luxurious paradors *(see pp534–5)*.

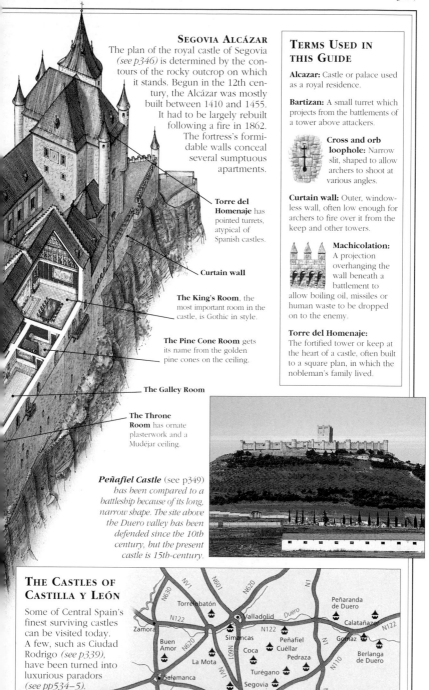

Castilla y León

LEÓN · ZAMORA · SALAMANCA · ÁVILA · SEGOVIA
VALLADOLID · PALENCIA · BURGOS · SORIA

Awesome expanses of ochre plains *stretch to hills crowned with the castles that cover this vast region. Through Spain's history, these central provinces have had a major influence on its language, religion and culture. Their many historic cities preserve some of the country's most magnificent architectural sights.*

The territories of the two rival medieval kingdoms of Castile and León, occupying the northern half of the great plateau in the centre of Spain, now form the country's largest region, or *comunidad autónoma*.

Castile and León were first brought together under one crown in 1037 by Fernando I; but the union was not consolidated until the early 13th century. The kingdom of Castile and León was one of the driving forces of the Reconquest. El Cid, the legendary hero, was born near Burgos.

Wealth pouring in from the wool trade and the New World, reaching a peak in the 16th century, financed the many great artistic and architectural treasures that can be seen today in the cities of Castilla y León. Burgos has an exuberantly decorated Gothic cathedral. León cathedral is famous for its wonderful stained glass. At the heart of the monumental city of Salamanca is the oldest university in the peninsula. Segovia's aqueduct is the largest Roman structure in Spain and its Alcázar is the country's most photographed castle. Ávila is surrounded by an unbroken wall, built by Christian forces against the Moors. In Valladolid, the regional capital, a superb collection of multicoloured sculpture is displayed in a magnificent 15th-century building.

Beyond the cities, in Castilla y León's varied countryside, there are many attractive small towns which preserve outstanding examples of the region's vernacular architecture.

Cereal fields and vineyards covering the fertile Tierra de Campos in Palencia province

◁ The battle-scarred castle of Calatañazor (Soria), site of a Christian victory against the Moors in 1002

Exploring Castilla y León

COVERING THE NORTHERN PART of Central Spain's vast
tableland, Castilla y León has a huge variety of
sights. Many – the university of Salamanca, the Alcázar
and aqueduct of Segovia, the medieval walls of Ávila,
the monastery at Santo Domingo de Silos, and the
great cathedrals of Burgos and León – are well known.
Other historic towns and villages worthy of a detour
include Ciudad Rodrigo, Covarrubias, Pedraza
de la Sierra and Zamora. This region also
has beautiful mountainous
countryside in the Sierra de
Francia, Sierra de Bejar
and Sierra de Gredos.

SIGHTS AT A GLANCE

SEE ALSO

0 kilometres   50
0 miles   30

GETTING AROUND

Madrid makes a convenient springboard for touring in Castilla y León. The major cities of the region are connected by rail but the coach is often a quicker alternative. If you intend exploring rural areas or visiting small towns it is advisable to hire a car. The region's motorways and main roads tend to be dominated by trucks. Minor roads, which are generally in good condition, are a more enjoyable way of seeing the countryside.

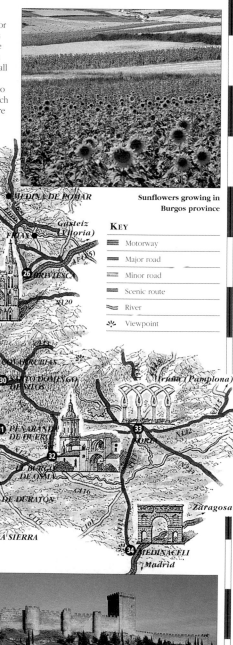

Sunflowers growing in Burgos province

KEY

▬▬	Motorway
▬▬	Major road
▭▭	Minor road
▬▬	Scenic route
≈	River
☀	Viewpoint

Peñaranda de Duero castle

El Bierzo ❶

León. 🚊 *Ponferrada.* 🚌 *Ponferrada.*
ℹ️ *Ponferrada, 987 42 42 36.*
🌐 *www.bierzonet.es*

THIS NORTHWESTERN region of León province was at one time the bed of an ancient lake. Sheltered by hills from the worst extremes of Central Spain's climate, its sun-soaked, alluvial soils make for fertile orchards and vineyards. Over the centuries, the area has also yielded rich mineral pickings including coal, iron and gold. Many hiking routes and picnic spots are within reach of the main towns of Ponferrada and Villafranca del Bierzo.

In the eastern section, you can trace the course of the old Road to Santiago *(see pp78–9)* through the **Montes de León**, past the pilgrim church and medieval bridge of Molinaseca. Turning off the road at the remote village of Acebo you pass through a deep valley where there are signs pointing to the **Herrería de Compludo**, a fascinating water-powered 7th-century ironworks. The equipment is still in working order and is demonstrated regularly.

The **Lago de Carucedo**, to the southwest of Ponferrada, is an ancient artificial lake. It acted as a reservoir in Roman times, a by-product of a vast gold-mining operation. Using slave labour, millions of tonnes of alluvium were washed from

A *palloza* in the Sierra de Ancares

the hills of Las Médulas by a complex system of canals and sluice gates. The ore was then panned, and the gold dust collected on sheep's wool. It has been estimated that more than 500 tonnes of precious metal were extracted from the hills between the 1st and 4th centuries AD. These ancient workings lie within a memorable landscape of wind-eroded crags, and hills pierced by tunnels and colonized by gnarled chestnut trees. You can best appreciate the area from a viewpoint at Orellán, which is reached via a rough, steep track. **Las Médulas**, a village south of Carucedo, is another place to go for a fine view.

To the north of the NVI highway lies the Sierra de Ancares, a wild region of rounded, slate mountains marking the borders of Galicia and Asturias. Part of it now forms the **Reserva Nacional de los Ancares Leoneses**, an attractive nature reserve. The heathland dotted with oak and birch copses is home to deer, wolves, brown bears and capercaillies.

Several isolated villages high in the hills contain *pallozas* – primitive, pre-Roman stone dwellings thatched with rye. One of the most striking collections of these huts can be found in the isolated village of **Campo del Agua**, in the west.

🏛 **Herrería de Compludo**
Compludo. 📞 *987 69 54 21.*
🕐 *Tue–Sun.*

Villafranca del Bierzo ❷

León. 👥 *3,900.* 🚌 ℹ️ *C/ Diez Ovelar 10, 987 54 00 28.* 🛒 *Tue.* 🎉 *Winter Fiesta (28 Jan), Fiesta del Cristo (14 Sep).*

EMBLAZONED MANSIONS line the ancient streets of this delightful town on the Road to Santiago. The solid, early 16th-century, drum-towered castle is still inhabited. Near the Plaza Mayor a number of imposing churches and convents compete for attention. Particularly worth seeing are the fine sculptures adorning the north portal of the simple, Romanesque **Iglesia de Santiago**. At the church's Puerta del Perdón (Door of Mercy), pilgrims who

Craggy, tree-clad hills around the ancient gold workings near the village of Las Médulas

were too weak to make the final gruelling hike across the hills of Galicia could obtain dispensation. Visitors to the town can also sample the local speciality, cherries marinated in *aguardiente*, a spirit.

ENVIRONS: One of the finest views over El Bierzo is from **Corullón**, to the south. This pretty village with grey stone houses is set in a sunny location above the broad, fertile basin of the Río Sil where the vines of the Bierzo wine region flourish (*see pp74–5*). Two churches, the late 11th-century San Miguel and the restored, Romanesque San Esteban, are worth a visit. Down in the valley, the Benedictine monastery at **Carracedo del Monasterio** stands in ruined splendour. Founded in 990, it was at one time the most powerful religious community in El Bierzo.

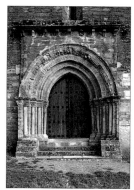

Puerta del Perdón of Villafranca's Iglesia de Santiago

Ponferrada ❸

León. 🏘 *63,000.* 🚉 🚌 🛈 *C/ Gil y Carrasco 4, 987 42 42 36.* 🛒 *Wed & Sat.* 🎉 *Virgen de la Encina (7 Sep).*

A MEDIEVAL BRIDGE reinforced with iron (*pons ferrata*), erected for the benefit of pilgrims on their way to Santiago de Compostela, gave this town its name. Today, prosperous from both iron and coal deposits, Ponferrada has expanded into a sizeable town.

Most of its attractions are confined to the small old quarter. Ponferrada's majestic **castle** was constructed between the

The imposing Templar castle of Ponferrada

12th and 14th centuries by the Knights Templar to protect pilgrims. During the Middle Ages it was one of the largest fortresses in northwest Spain.

Standing on the main square is the Baroque **town hall** (*ayuntamiento*). One entrance to the square is straddled by a tall clock tower which sits above one of the gateways of the medieval wall. Nearby is the Renaissance **Basílica de la Virgen de la Encina**. The older **Iglesia de Santo Tomás de las Ollas** is hidden away in the town's village-like northern suburbs. Mozarabic, Romanesque and Baroque elements combine in the architecture of this simple church. The 10th-century apse has beautiful horseshoe arches. Ask at the nearest house for the key.

ENVIRONS: A pleasant drive through the idyllic **Valle de Silencio** (Valley of Silence), south of Ponferrada, follows a poplar-fringed stream past several bucolic villages. The last and most beautiful of these is **Peñalba de Santiago**, sheltering beneath an attractive ring of mountains. The 10th-century Mozarabic church of Santiago de Peñalba has horseshoe arches above its double portal.

Puebla de Sanabria ❹

Zamora. 🏘 *1,700.* 🚌 🛈 *Plaza Mayor 1, 980 62 07 34.* 🛒 *Fri.* 🎉 *Las Victorias (9 Sep).*

THIS ATTRACTIVE OLD village lies beyond the undulating broom and oak scrub of the Sierra de la Culebra. A steep cobbled street leads past stone and slate houses with huge, overhanging eaves and walls bearing coats of arms, to a hilltop church and castle.

The village has become the centre of a popular inland holiday resort based around the largest glacial lake in Spain, the **Lago de Sanabria**, now a nature reserve. Among the many activities available are fishing, walking and water sports.

Local touring routes beckon visitors to Ribadelago on the lakeshore, though the road to the quaint hill village of **San Martín de Castañeda** gives better views. There's a small visitors' centre for the nature reserve in San Martín's restored monastery. The village is so traditional that you may still see cattle yoked to wooden carts, and women dressed in black from head to toe.

The 12th-century church and 15th-century castle of Puebla de Sanabria

The nave of Astorga cathedral

Astorga ❺

León. 👥 12,400. 🚗 🚌 ℹ️ *Glorieta Eduardo de Castro 5.* 📞 *987 61 82 22.* 🚌 *Tue.* 🎉 *Santa Marta (late Aug).*

THE ROMAN TOWN of Asturica Augusta was a strategic halt on the Vía de la Plata (Silver Road), a Roman road linking Andalusia and northwest Spain. Later it came to form a stage on the pilgrimage route to Santiago *(see pp78–9)*.

Soaring above the ramparts in the upper town are Astorga's two principal monuments, the cathedral and the Palacio Episcopal. The **cathedral** was built between the 15th and the 18th centuries and displays a variety of architectural styles ranging from its Gothic apse to the effusive Baroque of its two towers, which are carved with various biblical scenes. The gilt altarpiece by Gaspar Becerra is a masterpiece of the Spanish Renaissance. Among the many fine exhibits found in the cathedral's museum are the 10th-century carved casket of Alfonso III the Great, the jewelled Reliquary of the True Cross and a lavish silver monstrance which is studded with enormous emeralds.

Opposite the cathedral is a fairy-tale building of multiple turrets and quasi-Gothic windows. The unconventional **Palacio Episcopal** (Bishop's Palace) was designed at the end of the 19th century by Antoni Gaudí, the highly original Modernista architect *(see p160)*, for the incumbent bishop, a fellow Catalan, after a fire in 1887 had destroyed the previous building. Its bizarre appearance as well as its phenomenal cost so horrified the diocese that no subsequent bishops ever lived in it. Today it houses an assembly of medieval religious art devoted to the history of Astorga and the pilgrimage to Santiago. Roman relics, including coins unearthed in the Plaza del Parque, are evidence of Astorga's importance as a Roman settlement. The palace's interior is decorated with Gaudí's ceramic tiles and stained glass.

Reliquary of the True Cross

🏛️ Palacio Episcopal
Pl Eduardo de Castro. 📞 *987 61 68 82.* 🕐 *Tue–Sun.* ⬤ *1 & 6 Jan, 25 Dec.* 🎉

Cuevas de Valporquero ❻

Valporquero. 📞 *987 57 64 08.* 🚌 *from León.* 🕐 *Apr–May: Fri–Sun; Jun–Sep: daily; Oct: Fri–Sun.* 🎉

THIS COMPLEX OF limestone caves – technically a single cave with three separate entrances – is directly beneath the village of Valporquero de Torío in the northern part of León province. The caves were formed in the Miocene period between 5 and 25 million years ago. Severe weather conditions in the surrounding mountains make the water-sculpted caverns inaccessible between December and Easter. Less than half of the huge system, which stretches 3,100 m (10,200 ft) under the ground, is open to the public. Guided tours take parties through an impressive series of galleries in which lighting picks out the beautiful limestone concretions. Iron and sulphur oxides have tinted the rocks many subtle shades of red, grey and black. The massive Gran Rotonda, covering an area of 5,600 sq m (18,350 sq ft) and reaching a height of 20 m (65 ft), is the most stunning cave in the complex.

As the interior is cold, and the surface often slippery to walk on, it is advisable to wear warm clothes and sturdy shoes.

Illuminated stalactites hanging from the roof of one of the chambers in the Cuevas de Valporquero

León **7**

León. 139,800. 🏠 🚊 🚌 ℹ️ *Plaza de la Regla 4, 987 23 70 82.* 🛒 *Wed & Sat.* 🎉 *San Juan and San Pedro (24–9 Jun).* 🌐 www.jcyl.es

FOUNDED AS a camp for the Romans' Seventh Legion, León became the capital of a kingdom in the Middle Ages. As such it played a central role in the early years of the Reconquest *(see pp48–9)*.

The city's most important building – apart from its great **cathedral** *(see pp336–7)* – is the **Colegiata de San Isidoro**, built into the Roman walls which encircle the city. A separate entrance leads through to the Romanesque **Panteón Real** (Royal Pantheon), the last resting place of more than 20 monarchs. It is superbly decorated with carved capitals and 12th-century frescoes illustrating a variety of biblical and mythical subjects, as well as scenes of medieval life.

The alleyways in the picturesque old quarter around the Plaza Mayor are interspersed with bars and cafés, decrepit mansions and churches. Two well-preserved palaces stand near to the Plaza de Santo Domingo: the **Casa de los Guzmanes**, with its elegantly arcaded Renaissance patio, and Antoni Gaudí's unusually restrained **Casa de Botines** (which is now a bank).

The **Hostal de San Marcos**, down beside the river, is a prime example of Spanish

Frescoes in Basílica de San Isidoro showing medieval seasonal tasks

Renaissance architecture *(see p21)*. It was founded during the 12th century as a monastery to lodge travellers en route to Santiago. The present building was begun in 1513 as the headquarters of the Knights of Santiago. The incredibly elaborate project continued into the 18th century, when a Baroque pediment added a final flourish to the beautiful Plateresque façade studded with scallop shells. The main hall has a fine 16th-century coffered ceiling. A parador *(see p534)* now occupies the main part of the Hostal de San Marcos. In the vaulted galleries off the church and cloister is the **Museo de León**, whose many treasures include a haunting little ivory crucifix, the *Cristo de Carrizo*.

ENVIRONS: Around 30 km (20 miles) east of León is the **Iglesia de San Miguel de Escalada**. Dating from the 10th century, it is one of the finest surviving churches built by the Mozarabs – Christians influenced by the Moors. Notice the Visigothic panels and the exterior gallery of stately horseshoe arches resting on carved capitals. At **Sahagún**, 70 km (40 miles) southeast of León, are the Mudéjar churches of San Tirso and San Lorenzo, with triple apses and belfries. A colossal ruined castle overlooks the Río Esla beside **Valencia de Don Juan,** 40 km (25 miles) south of León.

🏛 Museo de León
Plaza de San Marcos. 📞 *987 24 50 61.* 🕐 *Tue–Sun am.* 🎫 *(free Sat & Sun).*

THE MARAGATOS

Astorga is the principal town of the Maragatos, an ethnic group of unknown origin, thought to be descended from 8th-century Berber invaders. By marrying only among themselves, they managed to preserve their customs through the centuries and keep themselves apart from the rest of society. Although the demise of their traditional trade of mule-driving has changed their way of life, the Maragatos still keep to their communities. Their costumes can be seen during fiestas.

Maragatos dressed in traditional costume

León Cathedral

Carved detail from the choir

Tʜᴇ ᴍᴀsᴛᴇʀ ʙᴜɪʟᴅᴇʀs of this Spanish Gothic cathedral *par excellence* *(see p20)* were inspired by French techniques of vaulting and buttressing. The present structure of golden sandstone, built on the site of King Ordoño II's 10th-century palace, was begun in the mid-13th century and completed less than 100 years later.

It combines a slender but very high nave with the huge panels of stained glass which are the cathedral's most magnificent feature. Although it has survived for 700 years, today there is concern about air pollution attacking the soft stone.

West Rose Window
This window, measuring 8 m (26 ft) in diameter, dates from the 13th century, making it one of the cathedral's oldest.

The 13th- to 14th-century cloister galleries are decorated with Gothic frescoes by Nicolás Francés.

The silver reliquary is an ornate chest dating from the 16th century.

Cathedral Museum
Pedro de Campaña's panel, The Adoration of the Magi, *is one of the many magnificent treasures displayed in the museum.*

Entrance

★ **West Front**
The three portals are decorated with 13th-century carvings. Those above the Portada del Juicio *depict a scene from the Last Judgment, where the Blessed pass into paradise.*

Inside the Cathedral

The plan of the building is a Latin cross. The tall nave is slender but long, measuring 90 m (295 ft) by 40 m (130 ft) at its widest. To appreciate the dazzling colours of the stained glass it is best to visit on a sunny day.

The altarpiece includes five original panels created by Gothic master Nicolás Francés.

The Virgen Blanca is a Gothic sculpture of a smiling Virgin. The original is kept in this chapel. A copy stands by the west door.

The choir has two tiers of 15th-century stalls. Behind it is the carved and gilded retrochoir, in the shape of a triumphal arch.

★ Stained Glass

The windows, covering an area of 1,800 sq metres (19,350 sq ft), are the outstanding feature of the cathedral.

STAR FEATURES

★ West Front

★ Stained Glass

LEÓN'S STAINED GLASS

León cathedral's great glory is its magnificent glasswork. The 125 large windows and 57 smaller, round ones date from every century from the 13th to the 20th. They cover an enormous range of subjects, from fantastical beasts to plants. Many depict saints and characters from biblical stories.

Window with plant motif

Some of the windows reveal fascinating details about medieval life: *La Cacería*, in the north wall, depicts a typical hunting scene, while the rose window in the Capilla del Nacimiento shows pilgrims worshipping at the tomb of St James in Santiago de Compostela in Galicia *(see pp88–9).*

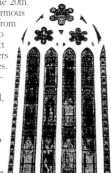

A large window in the south wall

Zamora ❽

Zamora. 👥 65,000. 🚆 🚌 ℹ️ *Calle de Santa Clara 20, 980 53 18 45.* 🗓 *Tue.* 🎉 *Semana Santa (Easter Week), San Pedro (29 Jun).* 🌐 www.jcyl.es

L ITTLE REMAINS of Zamora's past as an important strategic frontier town. In Roman times, it was on the Vía de la Plata *(see p334),* and during the Reconquest was fought over fiercely. The city has now expanded far beyond its original boundaries, but the old quarter contains a wealth of Romanesque churches.

The ruins of the **city walls**, built by Alfonso III in 893, are pierced by the Postigo de la Traición (Traitor's Gate), where Sancho II was stabbed to death in 1072. The **parador** *(see p558)* is in an old palace with a Renaissance courtyard adorned with coats of arms.

Two other palaces, the **Casa de los Momos** and the **Casa del Cordón**, have ornately carved façades and windows.

Zamora's most important monument is its unique **cathedral**, a 12th-century structure built in Romanesque style but with a number of later Gothic additions. The building's most eye-catching feature is its striking, scaly, hemispherical dome. Inside, there are superb iron grilles and Mudéjar pulpits surround Rodrigo Alemán's 15th-century choir stalls. The

Peaceful gardens of the Colegiata de Santa María in Toro

allegorical carvings of nuns and monks on the misericords and armrests were once considered risqué. The museum, off the sober cloisters, displays an important collection of 15th-century Flemish tapestries known as the *Black Tapestries*. These illustrate classical and military scenes.

Nearby, several churches exhibit features characteristic of Zamora's architectural style, notably multi-lobed arches and heavily carved portals. The best are the 12th-century **Iglesia de San Ildefonso** and the **Iglesia de la Magdalena**.

Another reason for visiting Zamora is for its lively Easter Week celebrations, when elaborate *pasos* (sculpted floats) are paraded through the streets. During the rest of the year the *pasos* can be admired in the **Museo de Semana Santa**.

ENVIRONS: The 7th-century Visigothic church of **San Pedro de la Nave**, 12 km (7.5 miles) northwest of Zamora, has charming carvings adorning its

Sierra de Francia and Sierra de Bejar ❿

T HESE ATTRACTIVE schist hills buttress the western edges of the Sierra de Gredos *(see p344).* Narrow roads wind their way through picturesque chestnut, olive and almond groves, and quaint rural villages of wood and stone. The highest point of the range is La Peña de Francia, which, at 1,732 m (5,700 ft), is easily recognizable from miles around. The views from the peak, and from the roads leading up to it, offer a breathtaking panorama of the surrounding empty plains and rolling hills.

La Peña de Francia ①
Crowning the peak is a windswept Dominican monastery sheltering a blackened, Byzantine-style statue of the Virgin and Child.

La Alberca ②
This pretty and much-visited village sells local honey, hams and handicrafts. On 15 August each year it celebrates the Assumption with a traditional mystery play performed in costume.

The unmistakable peak of La Peña de Francia

| 0 kilometres | 5 |
| 0 miles | 5 |

KEY

▬▬ Tour route

═══ Other roads

⚜ Viewpoint

Las Batuecas ③
The road from La Alberca careers down into a green valley, pa the monastery where Luis Buñuel made his film *Tierra sin Pan (Land without Bread*

Fish-scale tiling on dome of Zamora cathedral

capitals and friezes. **Toro**, 33 km (21 miles) east of Zamora, is at the heart of a wine region *(see pp322–3)*. The highlights of its **Colegiata de Santa María** are the west portal, and, inside, a fine Hispano-Flemish painting, *La Virgen de la Mosca* (The Virgin and the Fly). In 1476, the forces of Isabel I *(see pp52–3)* secured a crucial victory over the Portuguese at Toro, confirming her succession to the throne of Castile.

Ciudad Rodrigo ⑨

Salamanca. 🏃 *16,000.* 🚌 🚉 🛈
Plaza de Amayuelas 5, 923 46 05 61.
🚌 *Tue.* 🎉 *San Sebastián (20 Jan),
Carnaval del Toro (before Faster)*
🌐 *www.ciudadrodrigo.net*

DESPITE ITS LONELY setting – stranded on the country's western marches miles from anywhere – this lovely old town is well worth a detour. Its frontier location inevitably gave rise to fortification, and its robust 14th-century castle is now an atmospheric **parador** *(see p556)* with good views over the Río Agueda. The prosperous 15th and 16th centuries were Ciudad Rodrigo's heyday. In 1812, during the War of Independence *(see p58–9)*, the city, then occupied by the French, was besieged for 11 days before falling to the Duke of Wellington's forces.

The golden stone buildings within the ramparts are delightful. The main monument is the **cathedral**, whose belfry still bears the marks of shellfire from the siege. The exterior has a shapely curved balustrade and accomplished portal carvings. Inside, it is worth seeing the cloisters and the choir stalls, carved with lively scenes by Rodrigo Alemán. The main attraction of the adjacent **Capilla de Cerralbo** (Cerralbo Chapel) is an altarpiece attributed to Ribera's school. Off the chapel's south side is the quiet, arcaded Plaza del Buen Alcalde.

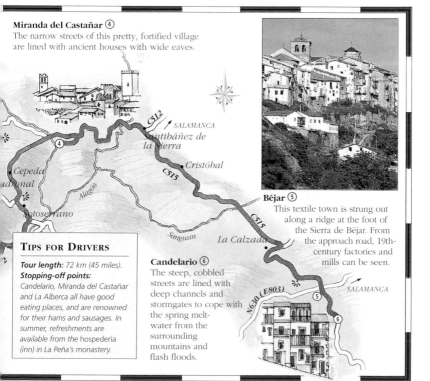

Miranda del Castañar ④
The narrow streets of this pretty, fortified village are lined with ancient houses with wide eaves.

SALAMANCA
Santibáñez de la Sierra
Cristóbal
Cepeda
Alagón
Sotoserrano
Sangusín
La Calzada
SALAMANCA

Béjar ⑤
This textile town is strung out along a ridge at the foot of the Sierra de Béjar. From the approach road, 19th-century factories and mills can be seen.

Candelario ⑥
The steep, cobbled streets are lined with deep channels and stormgates to cope with the spring meltwater from the surrounding mountains and flash floods.

TIPS FOR DRIVERS

Tour length: *72 km (45 miles).*
Stopping-off points:
Candelario, Miranda del Castañar and La Alberca all have good eating places, and are renowned for their hams and sausages. In summer, refreshments are available from the hospedería (inn) in La Peña's monastery.

Street-by-Street: Salamanca ⓫

Shell detail, façade of the Casa de las Conchas

THE GREAT UNIVERSITY CITY of Salamanca is Spain's finest showcase of Renaissance and Plateresque architecture. Founded as an Iberian settlement in pre-Roman times, the city fell to Hannibal in 217 BC. Preeminent among its artists and master craftsmen of later years were the Churriguera brothers *(see p21)*. Their work can be seen in many of Salamanca's golden stone buildings, notably in the Plaza Mayor. Other major sights are the two cathedrals and the 13th-century university, one of Europe's oldest and most distinguished.

The Casa de las Conchas is easily identifiable from the stone scallop shells that stud its walls. It is now a library.

The Palacio de Monterrey is a Renaissance mansion.

★ **Universidad**
In the centre of the university's elaborate façade is this medallion, carved in relief, which depicts the Catholic Monarchs.

★ **Catedral Vieja and Catedral Nueva**
Despite being in different architectural styles, the adjoining old and new cathedrals blend well together. This richly coloured altarpiece painted in 1445 is in the old cathedral.

Puente Romano
The Roman bridge across the Río Tormes, built in the 1st century AD, retains 15 of its original 26 arches. It provides an excellent view of the city.

STAR SIGHTS

★ **Universidad**

★ **Catedral Vieja and Catedral Nueva**

★ **Plaza Mayor**

| 0 metres | 100 |
| 0 yards | 100 |

Museo Art Nouveau y Art Deco

KEY

- - - Suggested route

CALLE DE LA COMPAÑÍA
CALLE DE SERRANOS
CALLE DE LOS LIBREROS
CALLE VERACRUZ
PASEO DE

★ Plaza Mayor
This 18th-century square is one of Spain's largest and grandest. On the east side is the Royal Pavilion, decorated with a bust of Felipe V, who built the square.

VISITORS' CHECKLIST

Salamanca. 🏘 160,000. ✈ 15 km (9 miles) east. 🚉 Paseo de la Estación, 902 24 02 02. 🚌 Avda de Filiberto Villalobos 71, 923 23 67 17. ℹ Plaza Mayor 14, 923 21 83 42. 🛍 Sun. 🎉 San Juan de Sahagún (12 Jun), Virgen de la Vega (8 Sep). 🌐 www.jcyl.es

Iglesia de San Martín

The Palacio de Fonseca was built in 1538 by Archbishop Alonso de Fonseca.

Torre del Clavero
This 15th-century tower still has its original turrets. They are adorned with the coats of arms of its founders, and Mudéjar trelliswork.

Iglesia-Convento de San Esteban
The Plateresque façade of the church is carved with delicate relief. Above the door is a frieze decorated with medallions and coats of arms.

Convento de las Dueñas
Sculptures on the capitals of the beautiful two storey cloister show demons, skulls and tormented faces, which contrast with serene carvings of the Virgin.

Exploring Salamanca

The majority of Salamanca's monuments are located inside the city centre, which is compact enough to explore on foot. The university, the Plaza Mayor, and the old and new cathedrals are all unmissable.

🔒 Catedral Vieja and Catedral Nueva

Unusually, the 16th-century new cathedral did not replace the old, but was constructed beside it. It is in a mix of architectural styles, being mainly Gothic, with Renaissance and Baroque additions. The west front has elaborate Late Gothic stonework, and a central panel carved with religious scenes.

The 12th- to 13th-century Romanesque old cathedral is entered through the new one. The highlight is a wonderful altarpiece of 53 panels, painted in lustrous colours by Nicolás Florentino. It frames a statue of Salamanca's patron saint, the 12th-century Virgen de la Vega, which was crafted in Limoges enamel. In the vault above it is a fresco depicting scenes from the Last Judgment, which is also by Florentino.

The 15th-century Capilla de Anaya (Anaya Chapel) contains the superb 15th-century alabaster tomb of Diego de Anaya, an archbishop of Salamanca.

Façade of Salamanca University, on the Patio de las Escuelas

🏛 Universidad

Patio de las Escuelas 1. ☎ 923 29 44 00. ⭕ daily. ⚫ 25 Dec. 📷

Salamanca's historic university was founded by Alfonso IX of León in 1218. The extravagant 16th-century façade of the Patio de las Escuelas (Schools Square) is a perfect example of the Plateresque style (see p21). Opposite is a statue of Fray Luis de León, who taught theology at the university. Inside, his former lecture room is preserved in its original style. Off the Patio de las Escuelas is the Escuelas Menores building, which houses a huge zodiac fresco, *The Salamanca Sky.*

🏛 Plaza Mayor

This magnificent square was built by Felipe V to thank the city for its support during the War of the Spanish Succession (see p58). Designed by the Churriguera brothers (see p21) in 1729 and completed in 1755, it was once used for bullfights, but nowadays is a delightful place to stroll or shop. Within the harmonious blend of arcaded buildings and cafés are the Baroque town hall and, opposite, the Royal Pavilion, from where the royal family used to watch events in the square. The Plaza Mayor is built of warm golden sandstone, and is especially resplendent at dusk.

Royal Pavilion in Salamanca's beautiful Plaza Mayor

🔒 Iglesia-Convento de San Esteban

The 16th-century church of this Dominican monastery is particularly interesting for its superb ornamented façade. The relief on the central panel, completed by Juan Antonio Ceroni in 1610, depicts the stoning of St Stephen, to whom the monastery is dedicated. Above this is a frieze, delicately carved with figures of children and horses.

The interior of the large single-nave church is equally stunning. The ornate altarpiece, of twisted gilt columns decorated with vines, is the work of José Churriguera and dates from 1693. Below it is one of Claudio Coello's last paintings, another representation of the martyrdom of St Stephen.

The double-galleried Claustro de los Reyes, completed in Plateresque style in 1591, has capitals which are carved with the heads of the prophets.

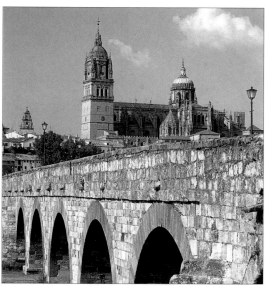

Salamanca's double cathedral, towering over the city

Sculpted shells on the walls of the Casa de las Conchas

♜ Casa de las Conchas
Calle de la Compañía 2. ☎ 923 26 93 17. ◯ daily. **Library** ◯ Mon–Sat.
The name of this mansion – House of the Shells – derives from the golden stone scallop shells that cover most of its walls. The shells are a symbol of the Order of Santiago, one of whose knights, Rodrigo Maldonado, built the mansion at the beginning of the 16th century. He also adorned the building with his family's coat of arms. It is now a library.

⛪ Convento de las Dueñas
Plaza del Concilio de Trento.
☎ 923 21 54 42. ◯ daily. 🖼
The main feature of this Dominican convent, which stands opposite San Esteban, is its Renaissance double cloister, whose tranquil gardens seem strangely at odds with the grotesques carved on the capitals. The cloister also preserves a tiled Moorish arch.

🏛 Museo Art Nouveau y Art Deco
Calle Gibraltar 14. ☎ 923 12 14 25.
◯ Tue–Sun. 🖼 (free Thu am).
This important art collection, housed in a 19th-century building, includes paintings, jewellery and furniture from all over Europe. Individual rooms are devoted to porcelain and Limoges enamel, and stained-glass work by Lalique.

♜ Colegio de los Irlandeses
Calle de Fonseca 4. ☎ 923 29 45 70.
◯ daily. 🖼 (free Mon am).
The Archbishop of Toledo, Alonso de Fonseca, built this Renaissance palace in 1512 and the coat of arms of the Fonseca family appears over the main entrance. Its name arises from the fact that it became a seminary for Irish priests at the end of the 16th century. The interior Italianate courtyard has a first-floor gallery and a chapel. Today the building is used as council and university offices.

⛪ Convento de las Úrsulas
Calle de las Úrsulas 2. ☎ 923 21 98 77. ◯ Mon–Sat. 🖼
In the church of this convent is the superbly carved tomb of its founder, Alonso de Fonseca, the powerful 16th-century Archbishop of Santiago. The museum includes fine paintings by Luis de Morales.

♜ Casa de las Muertes
Calle Bordadores. ● to public.
The House of the Dead takes its name from the small skulls that embellish its façade. Grotesques and other figures feature, and there is a cornice

Skull carving on the façade of the Casa de las Muertes

decorated with cherubs. The façade is a wonderfully accomplished example of the early Plateresque style.

The adjacent house is where author and philosopher Miguel de Unamuno died in 1936. The Casa-Museo de Unamuno, next door to the university, contains information about his life.

♜ Torre del Clavero
Plaza de Colón.
The tower is the last vestige of a palace that once stood here. It was built around 1480 and is named after a former resident, the key warden (*clavero*) of the Order of Alcántara.

Tower opposite Casa de las Muertes

ENVIRONS: To the northwest of the city, the course of the Río Tormes leads through the fortified old town of **Ledesma**, across lonely countryside to the Arribas del Duero, a series of massive reservoirs near to the Portuguese border.

Dominating the town of **Alba de Tormes**, 20 km (12 miles) east of Salamanca, is the Torre de la Armería, the only remaining part of the castle of the Dukes of Alba. The Iglesia de San Juan was built in the 12th century in Romanesque style. The Iglesia-Convento de las Madres Carmelitas was founded by St Teresa of Ávila in 1571, and is where her remains are now kept.

The castle of **Buen Amor**, 26 km (16 miles) to the north, was founded in 1227. Later, it was converted into a palace and used by the Catholic Monarchs while fighting Juana la Beltraneja (*see p52*).

Sierra de Gredos

Ávila. 🚌 *Hoyos del Espino.*
ℹ️ *Hoyos del Espino, 920 34 90 07
(920 34 90 35 Jul & Aug).*

THIS GREAT mountain range,
west of Madrid, has abun-
dant wildlife, especially ibex
and birds of prey. Some parts
have been developed to cater
for weekenders who come skiing, fishing, hunting or hiking.
Tourism here isn't a recent
phenomenon – Spain's first
parador opened in Gredos in
1928 *(see p556)*. Despite this,
there are many traditional villages off the beaten track.

The slopes on the south side
of the range, extending into
Extremadura, are fertile and
sheltered, with pinewoods, and
apple and olive trees. The
northern slopes, in contrast,
have a covering of scrub and
a scattering of granite boulders.

A single main road, the
N502, crosses the centre of the
range via the Puerto del Pico, a
pass at 1,352 m (4,435 ft), leading to Arenas de San Pedro, the
largest town of the Sierra
de Gredos. On this road is the
castle of **Mombeltrán**, built
at the end of the 14th century.

Near Ramacastañas, south of
the town of Arenas de San
Pedro, are the limestone caverns of the **Cuevas del Águila**.

The sierra's highest summit,
the Pico Almanzor (2,592 m,
8,500 ft) dominates the west.
Around it lies the **Reserva
Nacional de Gredos**, protecting the mountain's wildlife.

The Toros de Guisando near El Tiemblo in the Sierra de Gredos

Near El Tiemblo, in the east,
stand the **Toros de Guisando**,
four stone statues resembling
bulls, believed to be of Celt-
iberian origin *(see pp44–5).*

Ávila ®

Ávila. 🏘️ *50,000.* 🚉 🚌 ℹ️ *Plaza de
la Catedral 4, 920 21 13 87.* 😊 *Fri.*
🎭 *San Segundo (2 May); Santa
Teresa (15 Oct).* 🌐 *www.jcyl.es*

AT 1,131 M (3,710 FT)
above sea level,
Ávila de los Caballeros
("of the Knights") is the
highest provincial capital
in Spain. In winter access
roads can be blocked
with snow, and at night
the temperature plummets.
The centre of the city is
encircled by the finest-
preserved **medieval
walls** in Europe. One
of the best views of the   *Tuna* **in Ávila**
walls is from Los Cuatro
Postes (Four Posts) on the road
to Salamanca. This is the place
where the young St Teresa,

who had run away from home,
was caught by her uncle. Built
in the 11th century, the walls
are over 2 km (1 mile) long.
They are punctuated by 88
sturdy turrets, on which storks
can be seen nesting in season.
The ground falls away very
steeply from the walls on three
sides, making the city practically impregnable. The east
side, however, is relatively
flat, and there-
fore had to be for-
tified more heavily.
The oldest sections
of the wall are here.
They are guarded by
the most impressive of
the city's nine gate-
ways, the **Puerta de
San Vicente**. The apse
of the **cathedral** also
forms part of the walls.
The cathedral's warlike
(and unfinished) ex-
terior, decorated with
beasts and scaly wild
men, is an unusual design.
The interior is a mixture of
Romanesque and Gothic styles

The superbly preserved 11th-century walls, punctuated with 88 cylindrical towers, which encircle Ávila

using an unusual mottled red and white stone. Finer points to note are the carvings on the retrochoir and, in the apse, the tomb of a 15th-century bishop known as El Tostado, "the Tanned One", because of his dark complexion.

Many churches and convents in Ávila are linked to St Teresa, who was born in the city. The **Convento de Santa Teresa** was built on the site of her home within the walls and she also lived for more than 20 years in the **Monasterio de la Encarnación** outside the walls. There is even a local sweetmeat, *yemas de Santa Teresa*, named after the saint.

The **Iglesia de San Vicente**, also located just outside the eastern walls, is Ávila's most important Romanesque church, distinguished by its ornamented belfry. It was begun in the 12th century but has some Gothic features which were added later. The west door-

Cloisters of the Real Monasterio de Santo Tomás in Ávila

way is often compared to the Pórtico da Gloria of Santiago cathedral *(see p88)*. Inside, the carved tomb of St Vincent and his sisters depicts their hideous martyrdom in graphic detail. Another Romanesque-Gothic church worth seeing is the **Iglesia de San Pedro.**

Some way from the centre is the **Real Monasterio de Santo Tomás**, with three cloisters. The middle one, carved with the yoke and arrow emblem of the Catholic Monarchs, is the most beautiful. The last cloister leads to a museum displaying chalices and processional crosses. The church contains the tomb of Prince Juan, the only son of Fernando and Isabel. In the sacristy lies another historic figure: Tomás de Torquemada, head of the Inquisition *(see p52)*.

In Ávila, you may see groups of *tunas* – students dressed in traditional costume walking the town's streets while singing songs and playing guitars.

Beautiful gardens and palace of San Ildefonso

La Granja de San Ildefonso ⑩

Segovia. 【 921 47 00 19. 🚍 *from Madrid or Segovia.* ◐ *mid-Oct–mid-Mar: 10am–1:30pm, 3–5pm Tue–Sat, 10am–2pm Sun; mid-Mar–mid-Oct: 10am–6pm Tue–Sun.* 🔲 *(free Wed for EU residents).* ✔

This sumptuous royal pleasure palace is set against the backdrop of the Sierra de Guadarrama mountains. It stands on the site of a hunting lodge built by Enrique IV during the 15th century.

In 1720, Felipe V embarked on a project to create a fine palace. A succession of different artists and architects contributed to the rich furnishings inside and the splendid gardens without.

Some rooms were damaged in a fire in 1918 but they have been sumptuously restored.

A guided tour meanders through countless impressive salons decorated with ornate *objets d'art* and Classical frescoes against settings of marble, gilt and velvet. Huge glittering chandeliers, produced in the local crystal factory, hang from the ceiling. In the private apartments there are superb court tapestries. The church is fittingly adorned in lavish high Baroque style, and the Royal Mausoleum contains the tomb of Felipe V and his queen.

In the gardens, stately chestnut trees, clipped hedges and statues frame a complex series of pools. On 30 May, 25 July and 25 August each year the spectacular fountains are set in motion.

St Teresa of Jesus

Teresa de Cepeda y Ahumada (1515–82) was one of the Catholic Church's greatest mystics and reformers. When aged just seven, she ran away from home in the hope of achieving martyrdom at the hands of the Moors, only to be recaptured by her uncle on the outskirts of the city. She became a nun at 19 but rebelled against her order. From 1562, when she founded her first convent, she travelled around Spain with her disciple, St John of the Cross, founding more convents for the followers of her order, the Barefoot Carmelites. Her remains are in Alba de Tormes near Salamanca *(see p343)*.

Statue of St Teresa in the cathedral museum

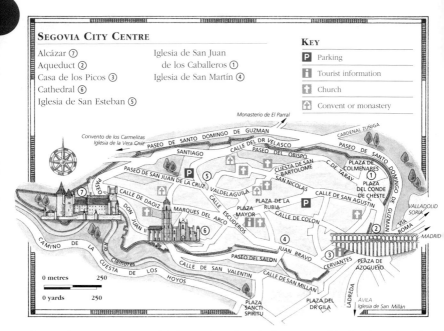

SEGOVIA CITY CENTRE

Alcázar ⑦
Aqueduct ②
Casa de los Picos ③
Cathedral ⑥
Iglesia de San Esteban ⑤

Iglesia de San Juan
de los Caballeros ①
Iglesia de San Martín ④

KEY

🅿 Parking

ℹ Tourist information

🛉 Church

⛪ Convent or monastery

Segovia ⑮

Segovia. 🏛 54,000. 🚉 🚌 ℹ *Plaza Mayor 10, 921 46 03 34.* 🛒 *Tue, Thu & Sat.* 🎉 *San Juan (24 Jun); San Pedro (29 Jun).* 🆆 *www.infosegovia.com*

SEGOVIA IS THE MOST spectacularly sited city in Spain. The old town is set high on a rocky spur and surrounded by the Río Eresma and Río Clamores. It is often compared to a ship – the Alcázar on its sharp crag forming the prow, the pinnacles of the cathedral rising like masts, and the aqueduct trailing behind like a rudder. The view of it from the valley below at sunset is magical.

The **aqueduct**, in use until the late 19th century, was built at the end of the 1st century AD by the Romans, who turned the ancient town into an important military base.

The **cathedral**, dating from 1525 and consecrated in 1678, is the last great Gothic church in Spain. It was built to replace the old cathedral, which was destroyed in 1520 during the revolt of the Castilian towns (*see p54*). The cloister, however, survived and was rebuilt on the new site. The pinnacles, flying buttresses, tower and dome form an impressive silhouette, while the interior is

light and elegantly vaulted. Graceful ironwork grilles enclose the side chapels. The chapterhouse museum, with a coffered ceiling, houses 17th-century Brussels tapestries.

At the city's western end is the **Alcázar** *(see pp326–7)*. Rising sheer above crags with a multitude of gabled roofs, turrets and crenellations, it appears like the archetypal fairy-tale castle. The present building is mostly a fanciful reconstruction following a fire in 1862. It contains a museum of weaponry and a series of elaborately decorated rooms.

Notable churches in Segovia include the Romanesque **San Juan de los Caballeros**, which has an outstanding sculptured portico, **San Esteban** with a striking five-storey tower, and **San Martín** with its beautiful arcades and capitals. Just inside the city walls is the **Casa de los Picos**, a mansion whose unique façade is adorned with diamond-shaped stones.

ENVIRONS: The vast palace of **Riofrío**, 11 km (7 miles) to the southwest, is set in a deer park. It was built as a hunting lodge by Felipe V's widow, Isabel

The imposing Gothic cathedral of Segovia

SEGOVIA'S AQUEDUCT

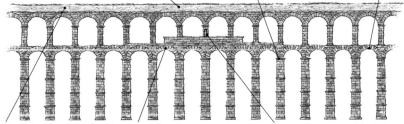

Water channel

Slots used to support blocks of ashlar

Arches reach a maximum height of 29 m (95 ft).

Water from the Río Frío flowed into the city, filtered through a series of tanks along the way.

Two tiers of arches – a total of 728 m (2,400 ft) in length – were needed to cope with the ground's gradient.

In this niche a statue of the Virgin Mary replaces an earlier inscription relating to the founding of the aqueduct.

Segovia's distinctive Alcázar, towering over the city

Farnese, in 1752, and has richly decorated rooms. It also houses a hunting museum.

♠ Alcázar de Segovia
Plaza de la Reina Victoria Eugenia.
[921 46 07 59. **◯** daily. **●** 1 & 6 Jan, 25 Dec. **▓** (free Tue). **[** **[**
☷ Palacio de Riofrío
[921 47 00 19. **◯** Tue–Sun. **▓** (free Wed EU residents).

Pedraza de la Sierra ⓰

Segovia. **▓** 470. **[** C/ Real 3, 921 50 86 66. **◄** Nuestra Señora la Virgen del Carrascal (8 Sep).

THE ARISTOCRATIC little town of Pedraza de la Sierra is perched high over rolling countryside. Within its medieval walls, old streets lead past mansions, emblazoned with coats of arms, to the porticoed **Plaza Mayor** (see p23). The huge, austere **castle**, standing on a rocky outcrop, was the home of local artist Ignacio

Zuloaga (1870–1945). The castle museum shows some of his works. On July evenings, torchlit classical music concerts are held throughout the town.

ENVIRONS: The main sight at **Turégano**, 30 km (19 miles) north, is a large hilltop castle which incorporates the 15th-century Iglesia de San Miguel.

Sepúlveda ⓱

Segovia. **▓** 1,350. **[** Plaza del Trigo 1, 921 54 02 37. **◄** Wed. **◄** Patronales (last week of Aug).

SPECTACULARLY SITED on a slope above the Río Duratón, this picturesque town offers views of the Sierra de Guadarrama. Parts of its medieval walls and castle survive. Of its several Romanesque churches, the **Iglesia del Salvador**, behind the main square, is purely 11th century and is notable for possessing one of the oldest side doors in Spain (1093).

ENVIRONS: Winding through a canyon haunted by griffon vultures is the Río Duratón, 7 km (4 miles) west of Sepúlveda. This area of striking beauty has been designated a natural park, the **Parque Natural de las Hoces del Duratón**.

Ayllón, 45 km (28 miles) northeast of Sepúlveda, has an arcaded main square and the Plateresque (see p21) Palacio de Juan de Contreras of 1497.

The Iberian and Roman ruins at **Tiermes**, 28 km (17 miles) further southeast, have been partially excavated, and finds can be seen in Soria's Museo Numantino (see p359).

Castillo de Coca ⓲

Coca (Segovia). **[** 617 57 35 54. **◄** from Segovia. **◯** Wed–Mon. **▓** **[**

BUILT IN THE late 15th century for the influential Fonseca family, Coca castle (see p326) is one of Castilla y León's most memorable fortresses. It was used more as a residential palace than a defensive castle, although its multiplicity of turrets and battlements are a fine example of Mudéjar military architecture. Built of thin, rose-tinted bricks, it is a complex moated structure comprising three concentric walls around a massive keep. It is now a forestry school, with a display of Romanesque woodcarvings.

ENVIRONS: The 14th-century castle of **Arévalo** in Avila, 26 km (16 miles) southwest, is where Isabel I spent her childhood. The porticoed Plaza de la Villa is surrounded by some attractive half-timbered houses.

Massive keep of the 15th-century Castillo de Coca

Medina del Campo ⑲

Valladolid. 👥 20,000. 🚗 🚌
ℹ️ Plaza Mayor 27, 983 81 13 57.
🕐 Sun. 🎭 San Antolín (2–8 Sep).

MEDINA BECAME wealthy in medieval times on the proceeds of huge sheep fairs and is still an important agricultural centre today. The vast brick Gothic-Mudejár **Castillo de la Mota** (see p326), on its outskirts, was built in 1440 by the powerful Fonseca family. However, the town transferred the castle's ownership to the Crown in 1475. Isabel I and her daughter Juana "la Loca" ("the Mad") both stayed here. Later, it served as a prison – Cesare Borja, one of its more celebrated inmates, was incarcerated here from 1506–08. In a corner of the Plaza Mayor stands the modest house (built over an arch) where Isabel died in 1504; her statue presides over the square.

ENVIRONS: Towering over the plains, some 25 km (16 miles) to the south of Medina del Campo, are the walls of **Madrigal de las Altas Torres**. In 1451 Isabel was born here in a palace that later became the Monasterio de las Agustinas in 1527.

Statue of Isabel, Medina del Campo

⛰ **Castillo de la Mota**
📞 983 80 10 24. 🕐 daily.
🔴 public hols.

Castillo de la Mota at Medina del Campo

son Pedro the Cruel into a residence for his mistress, María de Padilla. Pining for her native Andalusia, she had the convent decorated with fine Moorish arches, baths and tiles. Most impressive are the patio and the main chapel. There is a display of royal musical instruments, including the portable organ of Juana "la Loca". After the death of her husband, Juana spent 46 years in semi-confinement here until her own death in 1555. In the old quarter, the **Iglesia de San Antolín** now houses an art museum.

🏛 **Convento de Santa Clara**
📞 983 77 00 71. 🕐 Tue–Sun. 🎫
🏛 **Iglesia de San Antolín**
Calle Postigo. 📞 983 77 09 80.
🕐 Tue–Sun. 🎫 🎫

Tordesillas ⑳

Valladolid. 👥 8,000. 🚗 🚌 ℹ️ Casa del Tratado, 983 77 10 67. 🕐 Tue. 🎭 Semana de la Peña (16–22 Sep).

THIS PLEASANT TOWN is where the historic treaty between Spain and Portugal was signed in 1494, dividing the lands of the New World (see p53). A fateful oversight by the Spanish map makers left the immense prize of Brazil to Portugal.

The town's main sight is the **Convento de Santa Clara**. It was constructed by Alfonso XI in 1350 and converted by his

Moorish patio in the Convento de Santa Clara, Tordesillas

Valladolid ㉑

Valladolid. 👥 320,000. 🚗 🚌
ℹ️ Calle Santiago 19, 983 35 18 01.
🕐 Sun. 🎭 San Pedro Regalado (13 May); San Mateo (21–9 Sep).
🌐 www.dip-valladolid.es

THE ARABIC CITY of Belad-Walid (meaning "Land of the Governor") is located at the confluence of the Río Esgueva and Río Pisuerga. Although it has become sprawling and industrialized, Valladolid has some of Spain's best Renaissance art and architecture.

Fernando and Isabel (see pp52–3) were married in the Palacio Vivero in 1469 and, following the completion of the Reconquest in 1492, they made Valladolid their capital. Less spectacularly, Columbus died here, alone and forgotten, in 1506. In 1527 Felipe II was born in the Palacio de los Pimentel. José Zorrilla, who popularized the legendary Don Juan in his 1844 play (see p31), was also born in the city.

The city's **university** dates from the 15th century. The Baroque façade (see p21) was begun in 1715 by Narciso Tomé, who later created the remarkable Transparente of Toledo cathedral (see p375).

The **Iglesia de San Pablo** has a spectacular façade, embellished with angels and coats of arms in Plateresque style. Among the other noteworthy churches are **Santa María la Antigua**, with its Romanesque belfry, and the **Iglesia de Las Angustias,** where Juan de Juni's fine sculpture of the Virgen de los Cuchillos (Virgin of the Knives) is on display.

🏛 Casa de Cervantes
Calle Rastro 7. **[** 983 30 88 10. **○** Tue–Sun. **●** public hols. **◰** (free Sun am) **◲**
The author of *Don Quixote* (*see p30*) lived in this simple house with white-washed walls for the last years of his life. The rooms have been restored and contain some of Cervantes' original furnishings.

⛪ Cathedral
Calle Arribas 1. **[** 983 30 43 62. **◰**
Work started on the unfinished cathedral in 1580 by Felipe II's favourite architect, Juan de Herrera, but gradually lost momentum over the centuries. Churrigueresque (*see p21*) flourishes on the façade are in contrast to the sombre, square-pillared interior, whose only redeeming flamboyance is a Juan de Juni altarpiece. The Museo Diocesano inside, however, contains some fine pieces of religious art and sculpture.

🏛 Museo Nacional de Escultura
Cadenas de S Gregorio 1–2. **[** 983 25 03 75. **○** Tue–Sun. **●** public hols. **◰** (free Sat pm & Sun am for EU residents). **◲**
Ⓦ www.pymes.tsai.es/museoescultura
This art collection, usually in the Colegio de San Gregorio, has moved to the nearby Palacio de Villena until 2006. The display consists mainly of wooden religious sculptures

Façade of Colegio de San Gregorio, Valladolid

Berruguete's *Natividad*, in Museo Nacional de Escultura, Valladolid

from the 13th–18th centuries. They include Juan de Juni's emotive depiction of the burial of Christ and *Recumbent Christ* by Gregorio Fernández. An Alonso Berruguete altarpiece, and walnut choir stalls by Diego de Siloé and other artists, are among the other fine works to be found here.

The building itself is worthy of attention, particularly the Plateresque staircase, the chapel by Juan Güas, and the patio of twisted columns and delicate basket arches. The façade is an fine example of Isabelline (*see p20*) sculpture, portraying a mêlée of naked children scrambling about in thorn trees, hairy wild men, and strange birds and beasts. It is attributed mainly to Gil de Siloé, Simon of Cologne and Juan Güas.

🏛 Museo Oriental
Paseo de los Filipinos 7. **[** 983 30 69 00. **○** daily. **◰**
Beyond the Parque de Campo Grande is this small but interesting museum. The Museo Oriental is housed in the Real Colegio de los Agustinos Filipinos, a grandiose Neo-Classical Augustinian college, and contains an important collection of curios and art brought from China and the Philippines by missionaries.

ENVIRONS: The moated grey castle that dominates the village of **Simancas**, 11 km (7 miles) southwest of Valladolid, was converted by Charles V into Spain's national archive.

The Visigothic church in the village of **Wamba**, 15 km (9 miles) to the west, contains the tomb of King Reccesvinth.

An unusual long, narrow 15th-century castle on a ridge overlooks the wine town of **Peñafiel**, 60 km (40 miles) east of Valladolid (*see p327*).

Medina de Rioseco ❷

Valladolid. **⌂** 5,000. **🚌 ⓘ** Plaza Mayor, 983 70 08 25. **○** Wed. **�** San Juan (24–9 Jun).

DURING THE MIDDLE AGES this town, like Medina del Campo, grew wealthy from the profitable wool trade. These riches enabled it to commission leading artists, mainly of the Valladolid school, to decorate its churches. The dazzling star vaulting and superb woodwork of the **Iglesia de Santa María de Mediavilla**, near the centre of town, are evidence of this. Inside, the Benavente Chapel is a *tour de force*, with a colourful stucco ceiling by Jerónimo del Corral (1554), and an altarpiece by Juan de Juni. The enormous monstrance (1585) in the treasury is by Antonio de Arfe.

The interior of the **Iglesia de Santiago** is equally stunning, with a triple altarpiece by the Churriguera brothers of Salamanca (*see p21*).

The ancient buildings on Medina de Rioseco's main street, the Calle de la Rúa, are supported on wooden pillars, forming shady porticoes.

Altarpiece by Juan de Juni, Iglesia de Santa María de Mediavilla

CASTILLA Y LEÓN'S FIESTAS

El Colacho *(Sun after Corpus Christi, May/Jun),* Castrillo de Murcia (Burgos). Babies born during the previous 12 months are dressed in their best Sunday clothes and laid on mattresses in the streets. Crowds of people, including the anxious parents, watch as *El Colacho* – a man dressed in a bright red and yellow costume – jumps over the babies in order to free them from illnesses, especially hernias. He is said to represent the devil fleeing from the sight of the Eucharist. This ritual is thought to have originated in 1621.

El Colacho **jumping over babies in Castrillo de Murcia**

St Agatha's Day *(Sun closest to 5 Feb),* Zamarramala (Segovia). Every year two women are elected as mayoresses to run the village on the day of St Agatha, patron saint of married women. They ceremonially burn a stuffed figure representing a man. **Good Friday**, Valladolid. The procession of 28 multi-coloured sculptures which depict various scenes of the Passion is one of the most spectacular in Spain. **Fire-walking** *(23 Jun),* San Pedro Manrique (Soria). Men, some carrying people on their backs, walk barefoot over burning embers. It is said that only local people can do this without being burned.

The beautiful carved retrochoir of Palencia cathedral

Palencia ㉓

Palencia. 🏘 *80,000.* 🚉 🚌 ℹ️ *Calle Mayor 105, 979 74 00 68.* 🗓 *Tue, Wed & Thu.* 🎉 *Virgen de la Calle (2 Feb).* 🌐 www.jcyl.es

IN MEDIEVAL TIMES, Palencia was a royal residence and the site of Spain's first university, founded in 1208. The city gradually diminished in importance following its involvement in the failed revolt of the Castilian towns of 1520 *(see p54).*

Although Palencia has since expanded considerably on profits from coal and wheat, its centre, by the old stone bridge over the Río Carrión, remains almost village-like.

The city's main sight is the **cathedral**, known as *La Bella Desconocida* (the Unknown Beauty). It is especially worth a visit for its superb works of art, many the result of Bishop Fonseca's generous patronage. The retrochoir, exquisitely sculpted by Gil de Siloé and Simon of Cologne, and the two altarpieces, are also noteworthy. The altarpiece above the high altar was carved by Philippe de Bigarny early in the 16th century. The inset panels are by Juan de Flandes, Isabel I's court painter. Behind the high altar is the Chapel of the Holy Sacrament, with an altarpiece dating from 1529 by Valmaseda. In this chapel, high on a ledge to the left, is the colourful tomb of Doña Urraca of Navarra. Below the retrochoir, a Plateresque *(see p21)* staircase leads down to the fine Visigothic crypt.

ENVIRONS: Baños de Cerrato, 12 km (7 miles) to the south, contains the tiny Visigothic Iglesia de San Juan Bautista. Founded in 661, it is alleged to be the oldest intact church in Spain. Typical Visigothic carved capitals and horseshoe arches decorate the interior.

Frómista ㉔

Palencia. 🏘 *1,000.* ℹ️ *Paseo Central, 979 81 01 80 (summer); 979 81 07 63 (winter).* 🗓 *Fri.* 🎉 *Patrón de Frómista (week after Easter).* 🌐 www.fromista.com

THIS TOWN on the Road to Santiago de Compostela *(see pp78–9)* is the site of one of Spain's purest Romanesque churches. The **Iglesia de San Martín** is the highlight of the town, partly due to a restoration in 1904, leaving the church, dating from 1066, entirely Romanesque in style. The presence of Pagan and Roman motifs suggest it may have pre-Christian origins.

ENVIRONS: Carrión de los Condes, 20 km (12 miles) to the northwest, is also on the Road to Santiago. The frieze on the door of the Iglesia de Santiago depicts not religious figures but local artisans. There are carvings of bulls on the façade of the 12th-century Iglesia de Santa María del Camino. The Convento de San Zoilo has a Gothic cloister and offers simple accommodation.

Located at **Gañinas**, 20 km (12 miles) to the northwest (just south of Saldaña), is the well-preserved Roman villa,

Interior of the Iglesia de San Juan Bautista at Baños de Cerrato

Posada of the Monasterio de Santa María la Real, Aguilar de Campoo

La Olmeda. It has a number of impressive mosaics, including a hunting scene with lions and tigers. Finds from the villa are displayed in the archaeological museum located in the Iglesia de San Pedro in Saldaña.

⋔ Villa Romana La Olmeda
Pedrosa de la Vega. ☐ *Tue–Sun.* ● *23 Dec–31 Jan.* ☑ *ticket also covers archaeological museum.* ☑

Aguilar de Campoo **㉕**

Palencia. ㊙ *7,700.* ▤ **ℹ** *Plaza España 32, 979 12 36 41.* ☐ *Tue.* 📷 *San Pedro (29 Jun); Romería de la Virgen del Llano (9 Sep).* Ⓦ *www.turwl.com/aguilar*

SITUATED BETWEEN the parched plains of Central Spain and the lush green foothills of the Cantabrian Mountains is the old fortified town of Aguilar de Campoo. At one end of its ancient porticoed main square is the impressive bell tower of the **Colegiata de San Miguel**. In this church is a mausoleum containing the tomb of the Marquises of Aguilar.

Among the other places of interest are the **Ermita de Santa Cecilia**, and the restored Romanesque-Gothic **Monasterio de Santa María la Real**, which has a small, friendly *posada* (inn), ideal for a night's stay *(see p555)*.

ENVIRONS: Six km (4 miles) south, at **Olleros de Pisuerga**, is a church built in a cave. From the parador at **Cervera de Pisuerga**, 25 km (15 miles) northwest of Aguilar, there are stunning views, and tours of the **Reserva Nacional de Fuentes Carrionas**. This is a rugged region overlooked by Fuentes Carrionas, a 2,487-m (8,159-ft) peak.

Briviesca **㉖**

Burgos. ㊙ *6,200.* ▤ ▤ **ℹ** *Calle Santa María Encimera 1, 947 59 39 39.* ☐ *Sat.* 📷 *Feria de San José (19 Mar), Santa Casilda (9 May).*

THIS LITTLE WALLED TOWN, in the northeast of Burgos province, has an arcaded main square and several dignified mansions. The best known of its churches is the **Convento de Santa Clara**, with its 16th-century walnut reredos carved with religious scenes. In 1388 Juan I of Aragón created the title Príncipe de Asturias for his son, Enrique, in the town. The Santuario de Santa Casilda, situated outside Briviesca, has a collection of votive objects.

ENVIRONS: Oña, 25 km (15 miles) north, is an attractive town. A Benedictine monastery was founded here in 1011.

Overlooking a fertile valley, 20 km (12 miles) further northeast, is the little hilltop town of **Frías**. Its castle overlooks cobbled streets and pretty old houses. Crossing the Río Ebro is a fortified medieval bridge, still with its central gate tower.

At **Medina de Pomar**, 30 km (20 miles) north of Oña, there is a 15th-century castle, once the seat of the Velasco family. Inside are the ruins of a palace with fine Mudéjar stucco decoration and Arabic inscriptions.

The medieval bridge over the Río Ebro at Frías, with its central gate tower

Flemish triptych inside the collegiate church in Covarrubias

Covarrubias ㉗

Burgos. 🏠 650. 🚌 🚖 Calle Monseñor Vargas, 947 40 64 61 (Mar–Nov). 🚍 Tue. 🎭 San Cosme and San Damián (26–27 Sep).

Named after the reddish caves on its outskirts, Covarrubias stands on the banks of the Río Arlanza. Medieval walls surround the charming old centre with its arcaded half-timbered houses (see p22). The distinguished **collegiate church** shows the historical importance of Covarrubias: here is the tomb of Fernán González, first independent Count of Castile, and one of the great figures in Castilian history. By uniting several fiefs against the Moors in the 10th century, he started the rise in Castilian power that ensured the resulting kingdom of Castile would play a leading role in the unification of Spain. The church museum in the sacristy contains treasures, notably a Flemish triptych of the Adoration of the Magi, attributed to Gil de Siloé, and a 17th-century organ.

Environs: A short distance east along the Río Arlanza lies the ruins of the 11th-century Romanesque monastery of **San Pedro de Arlanza**. At **Quintanilla de las Viñas**, 24 km (15 miles) north of Covarrubias, is a ruined 7th-century Visigothic church. The reliefs on the columns of the triumphal arch are remarkable, depicting sun and moon symbols that may be pagan.

Burgos ㉘

Burgos. 🏠 162,000. ✈ 🚌 🚖 🅸 Plaza de Alonso Martínez 7, 947 20 31 25. 🚍 Wed, Sat, Sun. 🎭 San Lesmes (30 Jan); Pedro and San Pablo (30 Jun). 🌐 www.patroturisbur.es

Founded in 884, Burgos has played a significant political and military role in Spanish history. It was the capital of the united kingdoms of Castile and León from 1073 until losing that honour to Valladolid after the fall of Granada in 1492 (see pp52–3). During the 15th and 16th centuries Burgos grew rich from the wool trade and used its riches to finance most of the great art and architecture which can be seen in the city today. Less auspiciously, Franco chose Burgos as his headquarters during the Civil War (see pp62–3).

The city's strategic location on the main Madrid–France highway and on the route to Santiago (see pp78–9) ensure many visitors; but even without this Burgos would justify a long detour. Despite its size and extremes of climate, it is one of most agreeable provincial capitals in Castilla y León.

Approach via the bridge of Santa María, which leads into the old quarter through the **Arco de Santa María**, a gateway carved with statues of various local worthies. The main bridge into the city, however, is the Puente de San Pablo, where a statue commemorates the city's hero, El Cid. Not far

from the bridge stands the **Casa del Cordón**, a 15th-century palace (now a bank) which has a Franciscan cord motif carved over the portal. A plaque declares that this is the spot where the Catholic Monarchs welcomed Columbus on his return, in 1497, from the second of his famous voyages to the Americas.

The lacy, steel-grey spires of the **cathedral** (see pp354–5) are a prominent landmark from almost anywhere in the city. On the rising ground behind it stands the **Iglesia de San Nicolás**, whose main feature is a superb altarpiece by Simon of Cologne (1505). The crowded carvings vividly depict a number of scenes from the life of St Nicholas. Other churches worth visiting are the **Iglesia de San Lorenzo**, with its superb Baroque ceiling, and the **Iglesia de San Esteban**, which has a museum of altarpieces. The **Iglesia de Santa Águeda**, is the place where El Cid made King Alfonso VI swear that he

The Arco de Santa María in Burgos, adorned with statues and turrets

EL CID (1043–99)

Rodrigo Díaz de Vivar was born into a noble family in Vivar del Cid, north of Burgos, in 1043. He served Fernando I, but was banished from Castile after becoming embroiled in the fratricidal squabbles of the king's sons, Sancho II and Alfonso VI. He switched allegiance to fight for the Moors, then changed side again, capturing Valencia for the Christians in 1094, ruling the city until his death. For his heroism he was named El Cid, from the Arabic Sidi (Lord). He was a charismatic man of great courage, but it was an anonymous poem, El Cantar del Mío Cid, in 1180, that immortalized him as a romantic hero of the Reconquest (see pp50–51). The tombs of El Cid and his wife, Jimena, are in Burgos cathedral.

Statue of El Cid in Vivar del Cid

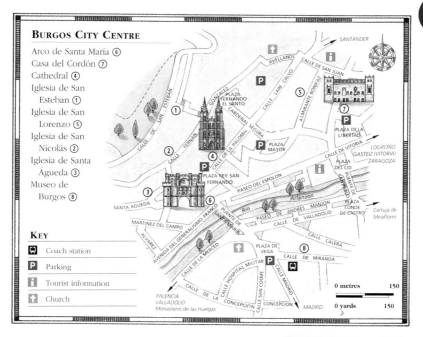

BURGOS CITY CENTRE

Arco de Santa María ⑥
Casa del Cordón ⑦
Cathedral ④
Iglesia de San
  Esteban ①
Iglesia de San
  Lorenzo ⑤
Iglesia de San
  Nicolás ②
Iglesia de Santa
  Águeda ③
Museo de
  Burgos ⑧

KEY

🚌 Coach station

🅿 Parking

ℹ Tourist information

✠ Church

0 metres   150
0 yards   150

---

played no part in the murder of his elder brother, King Sancho II *(see p338)*.

Across the river, the palace of the Casa de Miranda houses the archaeological section of the **Museo de Burgos,** with finds from the Roman city of Clunia. Nearby, the **Casa de Angulo** contains the Fine Arts section, whose prize exhibits are Juan de Padilla's tomb by Gil de Siloé, and a Moorish casket in enamelled ivory.

Two religious houses, on the outskirts of Burgos, are worth visiting. Just west of the city is the **Real Monasterio de**

Sculpted tomb of Juan de Padilla by Gil de Siloé, in Museo de Burgos

Huelgas, a Cistercian convent founded in 1187 by Alfonso VIII. It was lavishly endowed and soon achieved great prestige. One of the most interesting parts is the **Museo de Ricas Telas,** a textile museum containing ancient fabrics from the convent's many royal tombs. Other highlights include a Romanesque cloister dating from the late 12th century, and the Gothic cloister of San Fernando, decorated with Moorish designs. In the Capilla de Santiago is a curious wooden figure of St James holding a sword, with which, according to tradition, royal princes were dubbed Knights of Santiago.

To the east of Burgos is the **Cartuja de Miraflores,** a Carthusian monastery founded during the 15th century. The church includes two of Spain's most notable tombs, attributed to Gil de Siloé. One holds the bodies of Juan II and Isabel of Portugal (the parents of Isabel the Catholic); the other contains that of her brother, Prince Alfonso. Equally spectacular is the multicoloured altarpiece by Gil de Siloé, allegedly gilded with the first consignment of gold brought back to Spain from the New World.

Polychrome altarpiece by Gil de Siloé, in Cartuja de Miraflores

🏛 **Museo de Burgos**
Calle Calera 25. 【 947 26 58 75.
◯ Tue–Sun. 🏷 (free Sat & Sun). ♿

✠ **Real Monasterio de Huelgas**
Calle de las Huelgas. 【 947 20 16 30. ◯ Tue–Sun. 🏷 ♿ ✔

✠ **Cartuja de Miraflores**
Ctra de San Pedro Cardeña. ◯ daily.

ENVIRONS: Ten km (6 miles) southeast of Burgos is the **Monasterio de San Pedro de Cardeña.** El Cid led his family to safety here while he rode into exile after King Alfonso VI had banished him from the territory of Castile.

Burgos Cathedral

SPAIN'S THIRD-LARGEST CATHEDRAL was founded in 1221 by Bishop Mauricio under Fernando III. The groundplan – a Latin cross – measures 84 m (92 yds) by 59 m (65 yds). Its construction was carried out in several stages over three centuries and involved many of the greatest artists and architects in Europe. The style is almost entirely Gothic, and shows influences from Germany, France, and the Low Countries. First to be built were the nave and cloisters, while the intricate, crocketed spires and the richly decorated side chapels are mostly later work. The architects cleverly adapted the cathedral to its sloping site, incorporating stairways inside and out.

Christ at the Column, by Diego de Siloé

West Front
The lacy, steel-grey spires soar above a sculpted balustrade depicting Castile's early kings.

★ **Golden Staircase**
This elegant Renaissance staircase by Diego de Siloé (1523) links the nave with a tall door (kept locked) at street level.

Lantern

Tomb of El Cid

STAR FEATURES

★ **Golden Staircase**

★ **Constable's Chapel**

★ **The Crossing**

Capilla de Santa Tecla

Puerta de Santa María (main entrance)

Capilla de Santa Ana
The altarpiece (1490) in this chapel is by the sculptor Gil de Siloé. The central panel shows the Virgin with St Joachim.

Capilla de la Presentación (1519–24) is a funerary chapel with a star-shaped, traceried vault.

Retrochoir

Several of the reliefs around the chancel were carved by Philippe de Bigarny. This expressive scene, which was completed in 1499, depicts the road to Calvary.

Capilla de San Juan Bautista and museum

★ Constables' Chapel
The tomb of the High Constable of Castile and his wife lies beneath the openwork vault of this chapel of 1496.

Sacristy *(1765)*
The sacristy was rebuilt in Baroque style, with an exuberant plasterwork vault and rococo altars

Capilla de la Visitación

Puerta de la Coronería
The tympanum of this portal of 1240 shows Christ flanked by the Evangelists. Statues of the apostles sit below.

★ The Crossing
The magnificent star-ribbed central dome, begun in 1539, rises on four huge pillars. It is decorated with effigies of prophets and saints. Beneath it is the tomb of El Cid and his wife.

Capilla del Santisímo Cristo

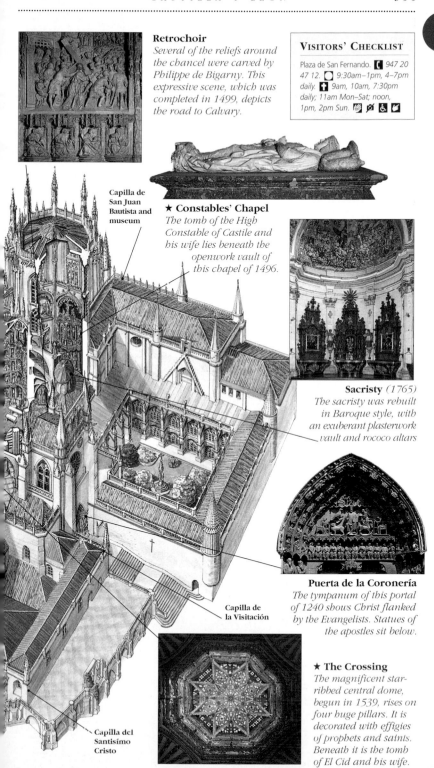

Lerma 29

Burgos. 🏛 2,500. 🚌 🚆 🏥 Calle
Audiencia 6, 947 17 70 02. 🚌 Wed.
🎪 Nuestra Señora de la Ascensión
(7–8 Sep). 🌐 www.cliente.csa.es

THE GRANDIOSE APPEARANCE of
this town is largely due to
the ambition of the notorious
first Duke of Lerma (see p56),
Felipe III's corrupt favourite
and minister from 1598–1618.
He misused vast quantities of
Spain's new-found wealth on
new buildings in his home
town – all strictly Classical in
style, in accordance with prevailing fashion. At the top of
the town, the haughty **Palacio
Ducal**, built in 1605 as his
residence, is currently
undergoing reconstruction to
transform it into a parador.

There are good views over
the Río Arlanza from the archways near to the **Convento
de Santa Clara** and also from
the **Colegiata de San Pedro**
church, which has a bronze
statue of the Duke's uncle.

**The narrow, sloping streets of the
old town of Lerma**

**Cloisters of the Monasterio de
Santo Domingo de Silos**

Monasterio de Santo Domingo de Silos 30

Santo Domingo de Silos (Burgos).
📞 947 39 00 68. 🚌 from Burgos.
🕐 Tue–Sat. 🎪 🏥 9am Mon–Fri,
noon Sat & Sun.

ST DOMINIC gave his name to
the monastery that he re-
built in 1042 over the ruins of
a Visigothic abbey destroyed
by the Moors. It is a place of
spiritual and artistic pilgrimage,
and its tranquil setting has inspired countless poets.

Others come to admire the
beautiful Romanesque cloisters,
whose capitals are sculpted in
a great variety of designs, both
symbolistic and realistic. The
carvings on the corner piers
depict various scenes from the
Bible and the ceilings are coffered in Moorish style. The
body of St Dominic rests in a
sarcophagus, supported by
three Romanesque lions, in
the north gallery. The old pharmacy, just off the cloister, has
a display of jars from Talavera
de la Reina (see p368).

The Benedictine community
holds regular services in Gregorian chant in the Neo-Classical
church by Ventura Rodríguez.
The monastery offers accommodation for male guests.

ENVIRONS: Just to the southwest lies the **Garganta de la
Yecla** (Yecla Gorge), where a
path leads down to a narrow
fissure cut by the river. To the
northeast are the peaks and
wildlife reserve of the **Sierra
de la Demanda**, extending
over the border into La Rioja.

**The 15th-century castle of
Peñaranda de Duero**

Peñaranda de Duero 31

Burgos. 🏛 660. 🚌 🏥 Calle Real 1,
947 55 20 68 (Jun–Sep: 947 55 20
34). 🚌 Fri. 🎪 Santiago (25 Jul);
Virgen de la Asunción (15 Aug).

THE CASTLE OF Peñaranda was
built during the Reconquest
(see pp50–51) by the Castilians,
who had driven the Moors
back south of the Río Duero.
From its hilltop site, there are
views down to one of the most
charming villages in old Castile,
where pantiled houses cluster
around a huge church. The
main square is lined with porticoed, timber-framed buildings
and the superb Renaissance
Palacio de Avellaneda.
Framing its main doorway are
various heraldic devices, and
inside is a patio which has

GREGORIAN PLAINCHANT

At regular intervals throughout the
day, the monks of Santo Domingo
de Silos sing services in plainchant,
an unaccompanied singing of Latin
texts in unison. The origins of
chant date back to the beginnings
of Christianity, but it was Pope
Gregory I (590–604) who codified
this manner of worship. It is an
ancient and austere form of music
which has found a new appeal
with modern audiences. In 1994 a
recording of the monks became a
surprise hit all over the world.

**Manuscript for an 11th-
century Gregorian chant**

◁ **View from the castle over the church and town of Peñaranda, on the Río Duero**

Curtain walls and drum towers of Berlanga de Duero castle

double galleries and fine decorated ceilings. On Calle de la Botica, off the square, is a 17th-century **pharmacy** with antique blue and white apothecary jars.

ENVIRONS: In the old quarter of **Aranda de Duero**, 20 km (12 miles) to the west, the **Iglesia de Santa María**, has an Isabelline façade (see p20).

🏛 **Palacio de Avellaneda**
Plaza Condes de Miranda 1.
🕻 947 55 20 13. ◯ Tue–Sun.

El Burgo de Osma ②

Soria. 🏘 5,000. 🚻 Plaza Mayor 9, 975 36 01 16. 🚍 Sat. 🎪 Virgen del Espino and San Roque (14–19 Aug).

THE MOST INTERESTING sight in this attractive village is the **cathedral**. Although it is mostly Gothic (dating from 1232), with Renaissance additions, the tall tower is Baroque (1739). Its treasures include a Juan de Juni altarpiece, a white marble pulpit and the tomb of the founder, San Pedro de Osma. The museum contains a valuable collection of illuminated manuscripts and codices.

Porticoed buildings line the streets and the Plaza Mayor, and storks nest on the Baroque Hospital de San Agustín.

ENVIRONS: Overlooking the Río Duero at **Gormaz**, 15 km (9 miles) south, is a massive castle with 28 towers. There are also mighty medieval fortresses at **Berlanga de Duero**, 12 km (7 miles) further to the

southeast, and at **Calatañazor**, 25 km (16 miles) northeast of El Burgo de Osma, near to the place where the Moorish leader al Mansur was killed in battle in 1002 (see p49).

Soria ③

Soria. 🏘 34,000. 🚻 Plaza Ramón y Cajal, 975 21 20 52. 🚍 Thu. 🎪 San Juan (late Jun). ⓦ www.jcyl.es

CASTILLA Y LEON'S smallest provincial capital stands on the banks of the Río Duero. Soria's stylish, modern parador (see p557) is named after the poet Antonio Machado (1875–1939, see p31), who wrote in praise of the town and the surrounding plains. Many of the older buildings are gone, but notable among those remaining are the imposing russet **Palacio de los Condes de Gómara**, and the handsome **Concatedral de San Pedro**, both built in the 16th century.

The **Museo Numantino**, opposite the municipal gardens, displays a variety of finds from the nearby Roman ruins

of Numantia and Tiermes (see p347). Across the Duero is the ruined monastery of **San Juan de Duero**, with a 13th-century cloister of interlacing arches.

ENVIRONS: North of Soria are the ruins of **Numantia**. The Celtiberian inhabitants endured a year-long Roman siege in 133 BC before defiantly burning the town and themselves (see p46). To the northwest is the Sierra de Urbión, a range of pine-clad hills with a lake, the **Laguna Negra de Urbión**.

🏛 **Museo Numantino**
Paseo de Espolón. 🕻 975 22 14 28.
◯ Tue–Sun. 🎫 (free Sat, am Sun). ♿

Medinaceli ④

Soria. 🏘 725. 🚉 🚻 Campo de San Nicolás, 689 73 41 76.
🎪 Julián de San Agustín (28 Aug); Cuerpos Santos (13 Nov).

ONLY a triumphal arch remains of Roman Ocilis, perched on a high ridge over the Río Jalón. Built in the 2nd or 3rd century AD, it is the only one in Spain with three arches. It has been adopted as the symbol for ancient monuments on Spanish road signs.

ENVIRONS: Lying just to the east are the red cliffs of the Jalón gorges. On the Madrid–Burgos road is the Cistercian monastery of **Santa María de Huerta**, founded in 1179. Its glories include a 13th-century Gothic cloister and the superb, crypt-like Monks' Refectory.

🏠 **Monasterio de Santa María de Huerta**
🕻 975 32 70 02. ◯ daily. 🎫 ♿

Decorative arches in the cloister of the monastery of San Juan de Duero

CASTILLA-LA MANCHA

GUADALAJARA · CUENCA · TOLEDO · ALBACETE · CIUDAD REAL

L A MANCHA'S EMPTY BEAUTY, *its windmills and medieval castles, silhouetted above the sienna plains, was immortalized by Cervantes in Don Quixote's epic adventures. Its brilliantly sunlit, wide horizons are one of the classic images of Spain. This scarcely visited region has great, scenic mountain ranges, dramatic gorges and the two monument-filled cities of Toledo and Cuenca.*

You will always find a castle nearby in this region – as the name Castilla suggests. Most were built in the 9th–12th centuries, when the region was a battleground between Christians and Moors. Others mark the 14th- and 15th-century frontiers between the kingdoms of Aragón and Castile. Sigüenza, Belmonte, Alarcón Molina de Aragón and Calatrava La Nueva are among the most impressive.

Toledo, which was the capital of Visigothic Spain, is an outstanding museum city. Its rich architectural and artistic heritage derives from a coalescence of Muslim, Christian and Jewish cultures with medieval and Renaissance ideas and influences.

Cuenca is another attractive city. Its old town is perched above converging gorges; on two sides it spills down steep hillsides. Villanueva de los Infantes, Chinchilla, Alcaraz and Almagro are towns of character built between the 16th and 18th centuries. Ocaña and Tembleque each has a splendid *plaza mayor* (main square).

La Mancha's plains are brightened by natural features of great beauty in its two national parks – the Tablas de Daimiel, and Cabañeros, within the Montes de Toledo. Rimming the plains are beautiful upland areas: the olive groves of the Alcarria; Cuenca's limestone mountains; and the peaks of the Sierra de Alcaraz. The wine region of La Mancha is the world's largest expanse of vineyards. Around Consuegra and Albacete fields turn mauve in autumn as the valuable saffron crocus blooms.

Windmills above Campo de Criptana on the plains of La Mancha

◁ Old houses in Cuenca, a city dramatically located over two gorges

Exploring Castilla-La Mancha

THE HISTORIC CITY OF TOLEDO is Castilla-La Mancha's major tourist destination. Less crowded towns with historical charm include Almagro, Oropesa, Alcaraz and Guadalajara. At Sigüenza, Calatrava, Belmonte and Alarcón there are medieval castles, reminders of the region's eventful past. Some towns on the plains of La Mancha, such as El Toboso and Campo de Criptana, are associated with the adventures of Don Quixote (see p377). The wooded uplands of the Serranía de Cuenca, the Alcarria and the Sierra de Alcaraz provide picturesque scenic routes. A haven for bird lovers is the wetland nature reserve of the Tablas de Daimiel.

The village of Alcalá del Júcar

SIGHTS AT A GLANCE

SEE ALSO

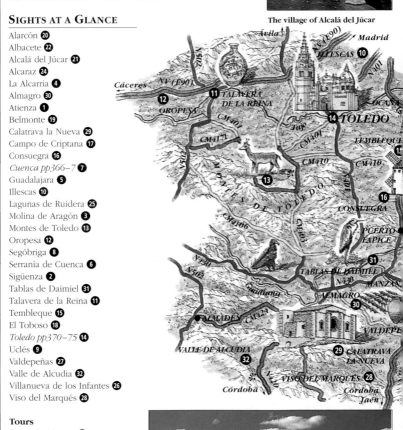

Cattle grazing on the isolated plains of La Mancha

GETTING AROUND

Castilla-La Mancha is best explored by car as it is well-endowed with a network of motorways radiating outwards from Madrid: the N401 to Toledo, the NII (E90) to Sigüenza, the NIII (E901) to Albacete, the NIV (E5) to Valdepeñas and the NV (E90) to Talavera de la Reina and Oropesa. The region is also served by the high-speed AVE train which runs between Madrid and Seville, stopping at Ciudad Real. Otherwise, public transport is infrequent and slow.

KEY

Motorway
Major road
Minor road
Scenic route
River
Viewpoint

The tranquil Montes de Toledo

Atienza

Guadalajara. *500.* **i** *Plaza de España 11, 949 39 90 01.* *Fri.* *La Caballada (early Jun).*

RISING HIGH above the valley it once protected, Atienza contains vestiges of its medieval past. Crowning the hill are a ruined 12th-century castle. The arcaded Plaza Mayor and the Plaza del Trigo are joined by an original gateway. The **Museo de San Gil**, a religious art museum, is in the church of the same name. The **Iglesia de Santa María del Rey**, at the foot of the hill, displays a Baroque altarpiece.

ENVIRONS: Campisábalos, to the west, has an outstanding 12th-century Romanesque church. The **Hayedo de Tejera Negra**, further west, is a nature reserve of beech woods.

Museo de San Gil
Calle General Franco. **(** *949 39 90 14.* *Sep–Jun: Sat & Sun; Jul–Aug: daily.*

Sigüenza

Guadalajara. *5,000.* **i** *Ermita del Humilladero, 949 34 70 07.* *Sat.* *San Juan (24 Jun); San Roque (15 Aug).*

DOMINATING the hillside town of Sigüenza is its impressive castle-parador *(see p559).* The **cathedral**, is Romanesque, with later additions, such as the Gothic-Plateresque cloisters. In one of the chapels is the Tomb of El Doncel, built for Martín

Semi-recumbent figure of El Doncel on his tomb in Sigüenza cathedral

Vázquez de Arce, Isabel of Castile's page *(see p52).* He was killed in battle against the Moors in 1486. The sacristy has a beautiful ceiling carved with flowers and cherubs.

Molina de Aragón

Guadalajara. *3,500.* **i** *C/ Carmen 1, 949 83 20 98 (summer); Plaza de España 1, 949 83 00 01 (winter).* *Thu.* *Día del Carmen (16 Jul), Ferias (30 Aug –5 Sep).*

MOLINA'S ATTRACTIVE medieval quarter is at the foot of a hill next to the Río Gallo. The town was disputed during the Reconquest and captured from the Moors by Alfonso I of Aragón in 1129. Many monuments were destroyed during the War of Independence *(see p59),* but the 11th-century hilltop castle preserves six original towers. It is possible to visit the Romanesque **Iglesia de Santa Clara**.

ENVIRONS: West of Molina is the chapel of the **Virgen de la Hoz**, set in a beautiful rust-red ravine. Further southwest is a nature reserve, the **Parque Natural del Alto Tajo**.

Arab ramparts above Molina de Aragón's old town

La Alcarria

Guadalajara. *Guadalajara.* **i** *Pastrana, 949 37 06 72 (closed Sat in Winter).*

THIS VAST STRETCH of undulating olive groves and fields east of Guadalajara is still evocative of Camilo José Cela's *(see p31)* classic book *Journey to the Alcarria.* Driving through the rolling hills, it seems that little has changed since this account of the hardship of Spanish rural life was written in the 1940s.

Towards the centre of the Alcarria are three immense, adjoining reservoirs called the **Mar de Castilla** (Sea of

Olive groves in La Alcarria in the province of Guadalajara

Castile). The first reservoir was built in 1946, and holiday homes have subsequently sprung up close to the shores and on the outskirts of villages.

Historic **Pastrana**, which is situated 40 km (25 miles) southeast of Guadalajara, is one of the most attractive towns in the Alcarria. It grew up around a mansion, the **Palacio Mendoza**, and by the 17th century had become larger and more affluent than Guadalajara. The **Iglesia de la Asunción** contains four 15th-century Flemish tapestries and a painting by El Greco.

Brihuega, 30 km (19 miles) northeast of Guadalajara, has a pleasant old centre.

Guadalajara ❺

Guadalajara. 👥 70,000. 🚊 🚌 ℹ️
Plaza de los Caidos 6, 949 21 16 26.
🏛 Tue, Sat. 🎉 Virgen de la Antigua
(Sep). 🌐 www.jccm.es

G UADALAJARA'S HISTORY is largely lost within the modern city, although traces of its Renaissance splendour survive. The **Palacio de los Duques del Infantado**, built between the 14th and 17th centuries by the powerful Mendoza dynasty, is an out-standing example of Gothic-Mudéjar architecture *(see p20)*. The main façade and patio are adorned with carving. The restored palace now houses the Museo Provincial. Among the churches in the town is the **Iglesia de Santiago**, with a Gothic-

Detail of the façade of the Palacio de los Duques del Infantado

Sculpted rock figures in Ciudad Encantada

Plateresque chapel by Alonso de Covarrubias. The 15th-century **Iglesia de San Francisco** is home to the mausoleum of the Mendoza family. The cathedral is built on the site of a mosque.

ENVIRONS: At **Lupiana**, 11 km (7 miles) east of Guadalajara, is the two-storey Monasterio de San Bartolomé, which was founded in the 14th century.

🏛 Palacio de los Duques del Infantado
Avenida del Infantado del Ejército.
📞 949 21 33 01. ⏰ Tue–Sun. 📷

Serranía de Cuenca ❻

Cuenca. 🚌 Cuenca. ℹ️ Cuenca,
969 23 21 19. 🌐 www.cuenca.org

T O THE NORTH AND EAST of Cuenca stretches the vast *serranía*, a mountainous area of forests and pastures dissect-ed by deep gorges. Its two most popular beauty spots are the **Ciudad Encantada**

(Enchanted City), where the limestone has been eroded into spectacular shapes, and the moss-clad waterfalls and rock pools of the **Nacimiento del Río Cuervo** (Source of the River Cuervo).

The main river flowing through the area, the Júcar, carves a gorge near Villalba de la Sierra. The viewpoint of the **Ventana del Diablo** gives the best view of the gorge.

Between Beteta and Priego (known for its pottery and canework), to the north, is an-other spectacular river canyon, the **Hoz de Beteta**, where the Río Guadiela has cut its way through the surrounding cliffs. There are good views from the convent of **San Miguel de las Victorias**. A small road leads to the 18th-century royal spa of **Solán de Cabras**

In the emptier eastern and southern tracts is **Cañete**, a pretty fortified old town with a parish church displaying 16th-century paintings. To the southeast of Cañete are the eerie ridgetop ruins of the abandoned town of **Moya**.

Street-by-Street: Cuenca ❼

CUENCA'S PICTURESQUE OLD TOWN sits astride a steeply sided spur which drops precipitously on either side to the deep gorges of the Júcar and Huécar rivers. Around the Moorish town's narrow, winding streets grew the Gothic and Renaissance city, its monuments built with with the profits of the wool and textile trade. The main sight is the cathedral, one of the most original works of Spanish Gothic, with Anglo-Norman influences. One of the picturesque Hanging Houses, which jut out over the Huécar ravine, has been converted into the excellent Museum of Abstract Art.

The Plaza de la Merced buildings contrast with the modern Museo de las Ciencias (Science Museum).

Museo de las Ciencias

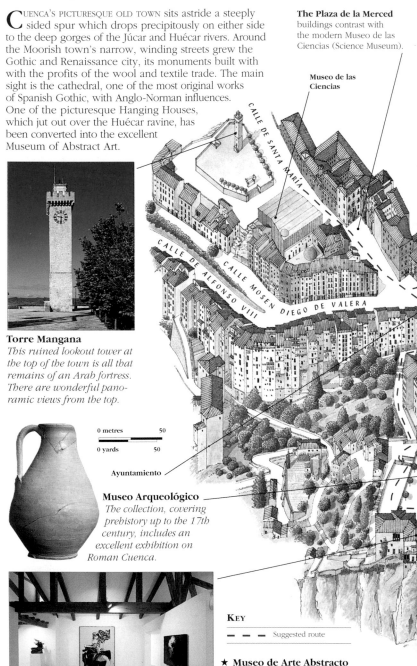

Torre Mangana
This ruined lookout tower at the top of the town is all that remains of an Arab fortress. There are wonderful panoramic views from the top.

| 0 metres | 50 |
| 0 yards | 50 |

Ayuntamiento

Museo Arqueológico
The collection, covering prehistory up to the 17th century, includes an excellent exhibition on Roman Cuenca.

KEY

– – – Suggested route

★ **Museo de Arte Abstracto**
Spain's abstract art museum is inside one of the Hanging Houses. It contains works by the movement's leading artists, including Antoni Tàpies and Eduardo Chillida.

Plaza Mayor
This café-lined, arcaded square is in the heart of the old town. The 18th-century Baroque town hall (ayuntamiento), *built over arches, stands at the south end.*

The Iglesia de San Miguel, perched over the Júcar gorge, was built in the Gothic style. It has a beautiful Mudéjar ceiling.

SEVERO CATALINA

PLAZA MAYOR

CALLE DE SAN PEDRO

CALLE DE JULIÁN ROMERO

DE OBISPO VALERO

To Parador de Cuenca

Museo Diocesano
The cathedral's treasures, which are housed in the Palacio Episcopal, include paintings by El Greco.

★ **Cathedral**
Highlights of the 12th- to 16th-century building are the decorated altar, chapterhouse and the side chapels.

★ **Hanging Houses**
The 14th-century beamed Casas Colgadas were once used as a summer residence for the royal family.

STAR SIGHTS

★ **Museo de Arte Abstracto**

★ **Hanging Houses**

★ **Cathedral**

Remains of a Roman building in Segóbriga

Segóbriga **8**

Saelices (Cuenca). **[** 969 13 20 64. **○** Tue–Sun. **Museum ●** public hols, 24, 25 & 31 Dec. **▨**

THE SMALL RUINED Roman city of Segóbriga, near the town of Saelices, is located in open, unspoiled countryside close to the Madrid–Valencia motorway. The Romans who lived here exploited the surrounding area, growing cereals, felling timber and mining minerals.

Many parts of the city can be explored. The 3rd-century theatre – which has a capacity of 2,000 people – is sometimes used for dramatic performances today. Segóbriga also had a necropolis, an amphitheatre, a temple to Diana and public baths. The quarries which supplied the stone to build the city can also be seen.

Nearby, there is a small museum containing some of the site's finds, although the best statues are in Cuenca's Museo Arqueológico (see p366).

Monasterio de Uclés **9**

Uclés (Cuenca). **[** 969 13 50 58. **○** 9am–dusk daily. **▨**

THE SMALL VILLAGE OF Uclés, to the south of the Alcarria, is dominated by its impressive castle-monastery, nicknamed "El Escorial de La Mancha" for the similarity of its church's profile to that of El Escorial (see pp312–13). Originally an impregnable medieval fortress, Uclés became the monastery seat of the Order of Santiago from 1174, because of its cen-

tral geographical location. The austere building you see today, used as a seminary school, is mainly Renaissance, but overlaid with ornamental Baroque detail. Among its attractive features are a magnificent carved wooden ceiling and staircase.

Illescas **10**

Toledo. **▨** 12,200. **▨ ▯** Plaza Mayor 1, 925 51 10 51. **△** Thu. **▨** Fiesta de Milagro (11 Mar); Fiesta Patronal (31 Aug).

JUST OFF THE Madrid–Toledo motorway, Illescas was the summer location for Felipe II's court. While there is little to see of its old town, the 16th-century **Hospital de la Caridad**, next to the Iglesia de la Asunción (which is easily identified by its Mudéjar tower), is important for its art collection. The hospital has five outstanding late El Grecos

Ceramics in Talavera workshop

(see p373) hanging in its 16th-century interior. The subjects of three of these are the Nativity, the Annunciation and the Coronation of the Virgin.

🛈 Hospital de la Caridad
Calle Cardenal Cisneros 2. **[** 925 54 00 35. **○** daily. **▨ ♿**

Talavera de la Reina **11**

Toledo. **▨** 80,000. **▯ ▨ ▯** Ronda del Cañillo, 925 82 63 22. **△** Wed & 1st Sat of month. **▨** Virgen del Prado (24 May); San Mateo (27 Sep).

A RUINED 15TH-CENTURY bridge across the Tagus marks the entrance to the old part of this busy market town, famous for its ceramics. From the bridge you can walk past the surviving section of the Roman and medieval wall to the **collegiate church**. This is the largest of the town's four Gothic-Mudéjar churches and is notable for its fine rose window.

Talavera's ceramic workshops are on the western edge of town. They still produce the blue and yellow *azulejos* (tiles) which have been a trademark of the town since the 16th century; but nowadays they also make domestic and decorative objects.

A good selection of the town's *azulejos* can be seen in the large **Ermita del Virgen del Prado** by the river. Many of the interior walls have superb 16th- to 20th-century tile friezes of religious scenes.

Part of a frieze of tiles in Talavera's Ermita del Virgen del Prado

Traditional embroidery work in Lagartera, near Oropesa

Oropesa ⑫

Toledo. 🏛 *2,800*. 🚉 🛈 *Plaza del Navarro 9, 925 43 00 02*. 🚌 *Mon.* 🎭 *Virgen de Peñitas (8–9 Sep), Beato Alonso de Orozco (19 Sep)*.

Oropesa's medieval and Renaissance splendour as one of Toledo's satellite communities has left a charming old quarter at the centre of today's small farming town. A circular Ruta Monumental starts from the massive, mainly 15th-century **castle** on the top of the hill. A Renaissance extension – thought to be the work of Juan de Herrera, coarchitect of El Escorial (*see pp312–13*) – was added to the castle in the 16th century by the wealthy and influential Álvarez family. A large part of the castle has been converted into a parador (*see p559*).

The Ruta Monumental continues around the town, taking in a number of churches, convents, a small ceramics museum and the town hall which presides over the main square.

ENVIRONS: The area around Oropesa is excellent for buying handicrafts. **Lagartera**, just to the west of the town, is famous for the embroidery and lacework by the women in the village and **El Puente del Arzobispo**, 12 km (7 miles) south of Oropesa, is a good source of painted ceramics and *esparto* (grass-weaving) work. **Ciudad de Vascos**, further southeast, is a ruined 10th-century Arab city in splendid countryside around Azután,

Montes de Toledo ⑬

Toledo. 🚉 *San Martín de Montalbán.* 🛈 *Toledo, 925 22 08 43.*

To the southwest of Toledo a range of low mountains sweeps towards Extremadura. In medieval times the Montes de Toledo were owned by bishops and the kings. They cover an area of approximately 1,000 sq km (386 sq miles).

The attractive new nature reserve of the **Parque Nacional de Cabañeros** (*see pp26–7*) encloses a sizeable area of woodland and pastures used for grazing sheep. The easiest access to the park is from **Pueblo Nuevo del Bullaque**. From here it is possible to make four-hour guided trips in Land Rovers, during which you may spot wild boar, deer and imperial eagles. In the pasturelands stand *chozos*, conical refuges for shepherds and their families.

In the eastern foothills of the Montes de Toledo is **Orgaz**, with a parish church which contains works by El Greco. Nearby villages, such as **Los Yébenes** and **Ventas con Peña Aguilera**, are known for their leather goods and restaurants serving game.

On the plains stands the small church of **Santa María de Melque**, believed to date back to the 8th century. Close by is the Templar castle of **Montalbán**, a vast but ruined 12th-century fortress. Nearer to Toledo, at **Guadamur**, there is another handsome castle.

A *chozo* (shepherd's cabin) in the Parque Nacional de Cabañeros

CASTILLA-LA MANCHA'S FIESTAS

La Endiablada (*2–3 Feb*) Almonacid del Marquesado (Cuenca). At the start of the two-day-long "Fiesta of the Bewitched", men and boys, gaudily dressed as "devils", with cowbells strapped to their backs, gather in the house of their leader, the *Diablo Mayor*. They accompany the images of the Virgen de la Candelaria (Virgin of Candlemas) and St Blaise in procession. As the devils dance alongside the floats bearing the saints' images, they ring their bells loudly and incessantly.

One of the so-called "devils" in La Endiablada fiesta

Romería del Cristo del Sahúco (*Pentecost, May/ Jun*), Peñas de San Pedro (Albacete). A cross-shaped coffin bearing a figure of Christ is carried 15 km (9 miles) here from its shrine by men dressed in white.
La Caballada (*early Jun*), Atienza (Guadalajara). Horsemen follow the route across country taken by the 12th-century muleteers of Atienza, who are said to have saved the boy King Alfonso VIII of Castile from his uncle, Fernando II.
Corpus Christi (*May/ Jun*), Toledo. One of Spain's most dramatic Corpus Christi (*see p34*) processions. The cathedral monstrance (*see p374*) is paraded in the streets.

Street-by-Street: Toledo ⑭

Damascene work, typical of Toledo

PICTURESQUELY SITED on a hill above the River Tagus is the historic centre of Toledo. Behind the old walls lies much evidence of the city's rich history. The Romans built a fortress on the site of the present-day Alcázar. The Visigoths made Toledo their capital in the 6th century AD, and left behind several churches. In the Middle Ages, Toledo was a melting pot of Christian, Muslim and Jewish cultures, and it was during this period that the city's most outstanding monument – its cathedral – was built. In the 16th century the painter El Greco came to live in Toledo, and today the city is home to many of his works.

The Iglesia de San Román, of Visigothic origin, now contains a museum relating the city's past under the Visigoths.

Puerta de Valmardón

| 0 metres | 100 |
| 0 yards | 100 |

CARDENAL LORENZANA

CALLE DE SAN ROMÁN

CALLE DE ALFONSO X

★ Iglesia de Santo Tomé
This church, with a beautiful Mudéjar tower, houses El Greco's masterpiece, The Burial of the Count of Orgaz *(see p28).*

CALLE DE ALFONSO XII

CALLE DE LA TRINIDAD

To Sinagoga de Santa María la Blanca and Monasterio de San Juan de los Reyes

To Sinagoga del Tránsito and Casa-Museo de El Greco

Archbishop's Palace

Taller del Moro
Once used as a workshop by craftsmen building the cathedral, this Mudéjar palace now houses a museum of Mudéjar ceramics and tiles.

STAR SIGHTS

- **★ Iglesia de Santo Tomé**

- **★ Museo de Santa Cruz**

- **★ Cathedral**

he Puerta del
l has a double
oorish arch and
two towers.

Ermita del Cristo de la Luz

This small mosque, the city's only remaining Muslim building, dates from around AD 1000.

To tourist information,
Estación de Autobuses,
and Estación de RENFE

VISITORS' CHECKLIST

Toledo. 🏛 *67,000.* ✈ 🚉
Paseo de la Rosa, 902 24 02 02.
🚌 *Avenida de Castilla-
La Mancha, 925 21 58 50.*
ℹ *Puerta de Bisagra, 925 22 08
43.* 🗓 *Tue.* 🎉 *Corpus Christi
(May/Jun); Virgen del Sagrario
(15 Aug).* **Iglesia de San
Román** ◯ *Tue–Sun.* 🎫 **Taller
del Moro** ◯ *Tue–Sun.* 🎫

The Plaza de Zocodover
is named after the market
which was held here in
Moorish times. It is still the
city's main square, with
many cafés and shops.

PLAZA DE
ZOCODOVER

CALLE DEL COMERCIO

CUESTA DE CARLOS V

LFILERITOS

SIXTO RAMÓN PARRO

NAL CISNEROS

★ Museo de Santa Cruz

*The city's main fine arts
collection includes several
tapestries from Flanders.
Among them is this
15th-century zodiac
tapestry, with well-
preserved rich colours.*

KEY

 — — — Suggested route

★ Cathedral

*Built on the site of a Visigothic
cathedral and a mosque, this
impressive structure is one of
the largest cathedrals in
Christendom (see pp374–5).
The Flamboyant Gothic high
altar reredos (1504) is the
work of several artists.*

Alcázar

*In the central patio of the
fortress is a replica of the
statue Carlos V y el Furor:
the original is housed in
the Prado Museum.*

Toledo cathedral rising above the rooftops of the medieval part of the city

Exploring Toledo

Toledo is easily reached from Madrid by rail, bus or car, and is then best explored on foot. To visit all the main sights you need at least two days, but it is possible to walk around the medieval and Jewish quarters in a long morning. To avoid the heavy crowds, go midweek and stay for a night, when the city is at its most atmospheric.

🏰 Alcázar

Cuesta de Carlos V. 🔔 *925 22 30 38.* ⏰ *Tue–Sun.* 🎟 *(free Wed).* 📷

Charles V's fortified palace stands on the site of former Roman, Visigothic and Muslim fortresses. Its severe square profile suffered damage by fire three times before being almost completely destroyed in 1936 when the Nationalists survived a 70-day siege by the Republicans. Restoration followed the original plans and the building now houses an army museum. The siege headquarters have been preserved as a monument to Nationalist heroism. Between 2004–2005 the army museum, the Museo del Ejército *(see p277)* will move here from central Madrid, making this the main army museum in Spain.

The Borbón-Lorenzana Library contains more than 100,000 books from the 16th to 19th centuries and more than 1,000 manuscripts.

🏛 Museo de Santa Cruz

Calle Miguel de Cervantes 3. 🔔 *925 22 10 36.* ⏰ *daily (am Sun).* 🎟

This museum is housed in a 16th-century hospital founded by Cardinal Mendoza. The building has some outstanding Renaissance architectural features, including the main doorway, staircase and cloister. The four main wings, laid out in the shape of a Greek cross, are dedicated to the fine arts. The collection is especially strong in medieval and Renaissance tapestries, paintings and sculptures. There are also works by El Greco, including one of his last paintings, *The Assumption* (1613), still in its original altarpiece. Decorative

The Assumption by El Greco (1613) in the Museo de Santa Cruz

arts on display include two typically Toledan crafts: armour and damascened swords, made by inlaying blackened steel with gold wire. Damascene work, such as plates and jewellery (as well as swords), is still produced in the city.

⛪ Iglesia de Santo Tomé

Plaza del Conde 4. 🔔 *925 25 60 98.* ⏰ *daily.* 🎟 *(free Wed pm for EU residents).*

Visitors come to Santo Tomé mainly to admire El Greco's masterpiece, *The Burial of the Count of Orgaz (see p28).* The Count paid for much of the 14th-century building that stands today. The painting, commissioned in his memory by a parish priest, depicts the miraculous appearance of St Augustine and St Stephen at his burial, to raise his body to heaven. It has never been moved from the setting for which it was painted, nor restored. Nevertheless, it is remarkable for its contrast of glowing and sombre colours. In the foreground, allegedly, are the artist himself and his son (both looking out) as well as Cervantes. The church itself is thought to date back to the 12th century, and its tower is one of the best examples of Mudéjar architecture in the city.

Nearby is the **Pastelería Santo Tomé**, a good place to buy locally made marzipan.

♙ Sinagoga de Santa María la Blanca

Calle de los Reyes Católicos 4. ☎ 925 22 72 57. ⏰ *daily.* ☷ *(free Wed pm).*

The oldest and largest of the city's eight original synagogues, this monument dates back to the 12th century. In 1405 it was taken over as a church by the military-religious Order of Calatrava. Restoration has returned it to its original beauty – carved stone capitals and wall panels stand out against white horseshoe arches and plasterwork. In the main chapel is a Plateresque altarpiece. In 1391 a massacre of Jews took place on this site, a turning point after years of religious tolerance in the city.

Mudéjar arches in the Sinagoga de Santa María la Blanca

♙ Sinagoga del Tránsito

Calle Samuel Leví. ☎ 925 22 36 65. ◐ *until mid-2003.* ☷

The most elaborate Mudéjar interior in the city is hidden behind the deceptively humble façade of this former synagogue, built in the 14th century by Samuel Ha-Leví, the Jewish treasurer to Pedro the Cruel. The interlaced frieze of the lofty prayer hall harmoniously fuses Islamic, Gothic and Hebrew geometric motifs below a wonderful coffered ceiling.

Adjoining the synagogue is an interesting museum dedicated to Sephardi (Spanish Jewish) culture. The manuscripts, tombstones, wedding costumes and sacred objects of worship date from both before and after the Jews' expulsion from Spain at the end of the 15th century *(see p53).*

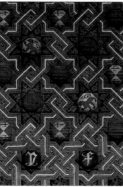

Ornate ceiling in the Monasterio de San Juan de los Reyes

♙ Monasterio de San Juan de los Reyes

Calle de los Reyes Católicos 17. ☎ 925 22 38 02. ⏰ *daily.* ☷ *(free Wed pm, for Spanish only).*

A wonderful mixture of architectural styles, this monastery was commissioned by the Catholic Monarchs in honour of their victory over the Portuguese at the battle of Toro in 1476 *(see p339).* Originally, it was intended to be their burial place, but they were actually laid to rest in Granada *(see p462).* Largely the work of Juan Güas, the church's main Isabelline structure was completed in 1492. Although it was badly damaged by Napoleon's troops in 1808 *(see p59),* it has been restored to its original splendour with features such as a Gothic cloister (1510) which has a multicoloured Mudéjar ceiling. Near to the church is a stretch of the Jewish quarter's original wall.

▥ Casa-Museo de El Greco

Calle Samuel Leví. ☎ 925 22 40 46. ⏰ *Tue–Sun.* ☷ *(free Sat pm, Sun).*

It is not clear whether El Greco actually lived in or simply near to this house in the heart of the Jewish quarter, now a museum housing a collection of his works. Canvases on display include *View of Toledo,* a detailed depiction of the city at the time, and the superb series *Christ and the Apostles.* Underneath the museum, on the ground floor, is a domestic chapel with a fine Mudéjar ceiling and a collection of art by painters of the Toledan School, such as Luis Tristán, a student of El Greco.

♙ Iglesia de Santiago del Arrabal

Calle Arrabal

This is one of Toledo's most beautiful Mudéjar monuments. It can be easily identified by its tower, which dates from the 12th-century Reconquest *(see pp50–51).* The church, which was built slightly later, has a beautiful woodwork ceiling. The ornate Mudéjar pulpit and Plateresque altarpiece stand out against the otherwise plain Mudéjar interior.

♙ Puerta Antigua de Bisagra

When Alfonso VI conquered Toledo in 1085, he entered it through this gateway, alongside El Cid. It is the only gateway in the city to have kept its original 10th-century military architecture. The huge towers are topped by a 12th-century Arab gatehouse.

EL GRECO

Born in Crete in 1541, El Greco ("the Greek") came to Toledo in 1577 to paint the altarpiece in the convent of Santo Domingo el Antiguo. Enchanted by the city, he stayed here, painting religious portraits and altarpieces for other churches. Although El Greco was trained in Italy and influenced by masters such as Tintoretto, his works are closely identified with the city where he settled. He died in Toledo in 1614.

Domenikos Theotocopoulos, better known as El Greco

Toledo Cathedral

THE SPLENDOUR OF TOLEDO'S massive cathedral reflects its history as the spiritual heart of the Spanish church and the seat of the Primate of all Spain. Still today, the Mozarabic Mass, which dates back to Visigothic times, is said here. The present cathedral was built on the site of a 7th-century church. Work began in 1226 and spanned three centuries, until the completion of the last vaults in 1493. This long period of construction explains the cathedral's mixture of styles: pure French Gothic – complete with flying buttresses – on the exterior; with Spanish decorative styles, such as Mudéjar and Plateresque work, used in the interior.

★ **Sacristy**
El Greco's The Denuding of Christ, *above the marble altar, was painted especially for the cathedral. Also here are works by Titian, Van Dyck and Goya.*

The Cloister, on two storeys, was built in the 14th century on the site of the old Jewish market.

View of Toledo Cathedral
Dominating the city skyline is the Gothic tower at the west end of the nave. The best view of the cathedral, and the city, is from the parador (see p560).

The belfry in the tower contains a heavy bell known as *La Gorda* ("the Fat One").

The Puerta del Mollete, on the west façade, is the main entrance to the cathedral. From this door, *mollete*, or soft bread, was distributed to the poor.

Monstrance
In the Treasury is the 16th-century Gothic silver and gold monstrance. It is carried through the streets of Toledo during the Corpus Christi celebrations (see p369).

STAR FEATURES

★ **Sacristy**

★ **Transparente**

★ **High Altar Reredos**

★ **Choir**

★ Transparente
This Baroque altarpiece of marble, jasper and bronze, by Narciso Tomé, is illuminated by an ornate sky-light. It stands out from the mainly Gothic interior.

Capilla de Santiago

The Capilla de San Ildefonso contains the superb Plateresque tomb of Cardinal Alonso Carrillo de Albornoz.

Chapterhouse
Above 16th-century frescoes by Juan de Borgoña is this multicoloured Mudéjar ceiling, unique in the city.

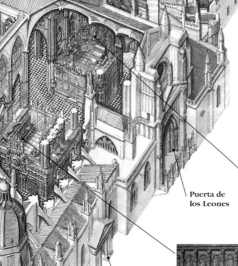

Puerta de los Leones

★ High Altar Reredos
The polychrome reredos, one of the most beautiful in Spain, depicts scenes from Christ's life.

Puerta Llana

The Puerta del Perdón, or Door of Mercy, has a tympanum decorated with religious characters.

The Capilla Mozárabe has a beautiful Renaissance ironwork grille, carved by Juan Francés in 1524.

★ Choir
The carvings on the wooden lower stalls depict scenes of the fall of Granada. The alabaster upper ones show figures from the Old Testament.

Windmills on the ridge above Consuegra, overlooking the plains of La Mancha

Tembleque ⓯

Toledo. 🏠 *2,200.* 🚹 *Plaza Mayor 1, 925 14 52 61.* 🚌 *Wed.* 🎎 *Jesús de Nazareno (late Aug).*

T HE WELL-PRESERVED timbered Plaza Mayor *(see p23)* at Tembleque dates from the 17th century. It is decorated with the red cross of the Knights Hospitallers, the military order which once ruled the town.

ENVIRONS: Ocaña, 30 km (20 miles) north of Tembleque, centres on the enormous yet elegant, late 18th-century brick *plaza mayor*. It is of the largest squares in Spain, after those in Madrid and Salamanca.

Consuegra ⓰

Toledo. 🏠 *10,000.* 🚉 🚹 *Cerro Calderico, 925 47 57 31.* 🚌 *Sat.* 🎎 *La Rosa de Azafrán (late Oct).*

C ONSUEGRA'S ELEVEN windmills *(see p23)* and ruined castle stand on a ridge above the town, overlooking the plains of La Mancha. One windmill has working machinery which is set in motion every year during the town's festival to celebrate the autumn harvest of a colourful local crop: saffron *(see p320)*. During the fiesta, pickers compete to see who can strip petals from the saffron crocus the fastest.

ENVIRONS: About 4 km (2 miles) along the road to **Urda** is a ruined Roman dam. An old restaurant *(see p598)* at **Puerto Lápice**, off the NIV 20 km (13 miles) south of Consuegra, claims to be the inn in which Don Quixote was "knighted" by the indulgent landlord.

Campo de Criptana ⓱

Ciudad Real. 🏠 *14,700.* 🚉 🚹 *Calle Barbero 1, 926 56 22 31.* 🚌 *Tue.* 🎎 *Virgen de Criptana (17 Apr).*

T HE REMAINING TEN windmills of what was originally La Mancha's largest collection – 32 – stand on a hillcrest above wheat plains. Three date back to the 16th century and have their original machinery intact. One windmill is the tourist information office. Another four contain museums of local life.

ENVIRONS: More windmills stand above nearby **Alcázar de San Juan** and **Mota del Cuervo**, a good place to buy *queso Manchego*, La Mancha sheep's cheese *(see p321)*.

El Toboso ⓲

Toledo. 🏠 *2,100.* 🚹 *C/ Daoíz y Velarde 3, 925 56 82 26.* 🚌 *Wed.* 🎎 *San Agustín (27–30 Aug).*

O F ALL THE villages of La Mancha claiming links to Don Quixote, El Toboso has the clearest ties. It was chosen by Cervantes as the birthplace of Dulcinea, Don Quixote's sweetheart. The **Casa de Dulcinea**, the home of Doña Ana Martínez Zarco, on whom Dulcinea was allegedly based, has been refurbished in its original 16th-century style.

The village was considered to be of such cultural importance that the French army is said to have refused to attack it during the War of Independence *(see pp58–9)*.

🏛 **Casa de Dulcinea** 🚹 *925 19 72 88.* 🕐 *Tue–Sun.* 🎟 *(free pm Sat & am Sun).*

Belmonte ⓳

Cuenca. 🏠 *2,600.* 🚉 🚹 *Plaza del Caudillo 1, 967 17 00 08.* 🚌 *Mon.* 🎎 *San Bartolomé (late Aug); Virgen de Gracia (second week of Sep).*

B ELMONTE'S MAGNIFICENT 15th-century **castle** *(see p326)* is one of the best preserved in the region. It was built by Juan Pacheco, Marquis of Villena, after Enrique IV gave him the town in 1456. Inside it has decorative carved coffered ceilings, and Mudéjar plasterwork. The **collegiate church** is especially

Belmonte's splendid 15th-century castle

remarkable for its richly decorated chapels and Gothic choir stalls, which were brought here from Cuenca cathedral *(see p367)*. There is also outstanding ironwork, a Renaissance reredos and the font at which the Golden Age poet Fray Luis de León (1527–91), was baptized.

ENVIRONS: Two villages near Belmonte also flourished under the Marquis of Villena. The church at **Villaescusa de Haro**, 6 km (4 miles) to the northeast, has an outstanding 16th-century reredos. **San Clemente**, some 40 km (25 miles) further southeast, clusters around two near-perfect Renaissance squares. There is a Gothic alabaster cross in the Iglesia de Santiago Apóstol.

🏰 **Castillo de Belmonte**
📞 627 40 66 80 🕐 *Tue–Sun.* 📷

The castle of Alarcón, which has been converted into a parador

Alarcón ⑳

Cuenca. 🏘 *210.* ℹ *Plaza Infante Don Juan Manuel 1, 969 33 03 54.*
🎉 *Cristo de la Fé (14 Sep).*

PERFECTLY PRESERVED, the fortified village of Alarcón guards a narrow loop of the Río Júcar from on top of a rock. As you drive through its defences, you may have the impression of entering a film-set for a medieval epic.

The village dates back to the 8th century. It became a key military base for the Reconquest *(see pp50–51)* and was recaptured from the Moors by Alfonso VIII in 1184 following a nine-month siege. It was later acquired by the Marquis

The chalk cliffs of Alcalá del Júcar, honeycombed with tunnels

of Villena. Alarcón has dramatic walls and three defensive precincts. The small, triangular **castle**, high above the river, has been turned into a parador *(see p558)*, preserving much of its medieval atmosphere.

Two churches in the village are worth visiting. The **Iglesia de Santa María** is a lovely Renaissance church, with a fine portico and an altarpiece attributed to the Berruguete school. The nearby **Iglesia de Santísima Trinidad** is in Plateresque style *(see p21)*.

Alcalá del Júcar ㉑

Albacete. 🏘 *1,500.* ℹ *Avenida de los Robles 1, 967 47 30 90.* 🚌 *Sun (Apr–Oct).* 🎉 *San Lorenzo (7–15 Aug).*

WHERE THE RÍO JÚCAR runs through the chalk hills to the northeast of Albacete, it cuts a deep, winding gorge,

the Hoz de Júcar, along which you can drive for a stretch of 40 km (25 miles). Alcalá del Júcar is dramatically sited on the side of a spur of rock jutting out into the gorge. The town is a warren of steep alleys and flights of steps. At the top of the town, below the castle, houses have been extended by digging caves into the soft rock. Some of these have been transformed into tunnels cut from one side of the spur to the other.

ENVIRONS: To the west, the gorge runs past fertile orchards to the Baroque **Ermita de San Lorenzo**. Further on is the picturesque village of **Jorquera**, which was an independent state for a brief period during the Middle Ages, refusing to be ruled by the crown. It retains its Arab walls. A collection of shields is on display in the Casa del Corregidor.

DON QUIXOTE'S LA MANCHA

Cervantes *(see p315)* doesn't specify where his hero was born but several places are mentioned in the novel. Don Quixote is knighted in an inn in Puerto Lápice, believing it to be a castle. His sweetheart, Dulcinea, lives in El Toboso. The windmills he tilts at, imagining them to be giants, are thought to be those at Campo de Criptana. Another adventure takes place in the Cueva de Montesinos *(see p379)*.

Illustration from a 19th-century edition of *Don Quixote*

Albacete ㉒

Albacete. 🏛 147,500. 🚃 🚌 🛈
Calle del Tinte 2, 967 58 05 22. 🚌
Tue. 🎉 Virgen de los Llanos (8 Sep).

DESPITE BEING LABELLED one of Spain's least interesting cities, this provincial capital is not without its attractions. The main one is the excellent **Museo Provincial**, which has exhibits ranging from Iberian sculptures and unique Roman amber and ivory dolls to 20th-century paintings. The city's **cathedral**, begun in 1515, has a Renaissance altarpiece.

Albacete is also known for its daggers and jackknives, crafted here since Muslim times, and the agricultural fair, held each September.

🏛 Museo Provincial
Parque Abelardo Sánchez. 📞 967 22 83 07. 🕐 Tue–Sun. 🎟 free Sat pm & Sun am. ♿

The castle of Chinchilla de Monte Aragón, overlooking the town

ENVIRONS: Chinchilla de Monte Aragón, 12 km (7 miles) to the southeast, has a well-preserved old quarter around a main square. Above the town is the picturesque shell of its 15th-century castle.

Almansa, 70 km (43 miles) further east, is dominated by another imposing castle, which is of Moorish origin.

Alcaraz ㉔

Albacete. 🏛 1,700. 🛈 Plaza Mayor 1, 967 38 00 02. 🚌 Wed. 🎉 Rosario de Cortes (1 May), Feria (4–9 Sep).

AN IMPORTANT ARAB and Christian stronghold, Alcaraz's military power waned after the Reconquest but its economy flourished around its (now defunct) carpet-making industry.

Standing in the attractive Renaissance Plaza Mayor are the "twin towers" of **Tardón** and **Trinidad**, and an 18th-century commodity exchange,

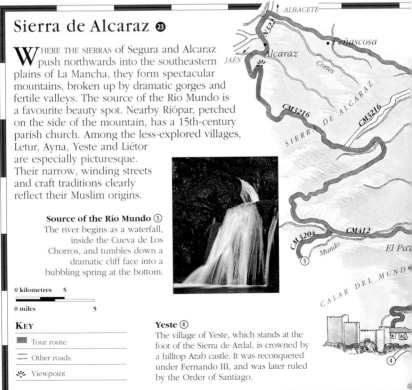

Sierra de Alcaraz ㉓

WHERE THE SIERRAS of Segura and Alcaraz push northwards into the southeastern plains of La Mancha, they form spectacular mountains, broken up by dramatic gorges and fertile valleys. The source of the Río Mundo is a favourite beauty spot. Nearby Riópar, perched on the side of the mountain, has a 15th-century parish church. Among the less-explored villages, Letur, Ayna, Yeste and Liétor are especially picturesque. Their narrow, winding streets and craft traditions clearly reflect their Muslim origins.

Source of the Río Mundo ⑤
The river begins as a waterfall, inside the Cueva de Los Chorros, and tumbles down a dramatic cliff face into a bubbling spring at the bottom.

0 kilometres   5

0 miles   5

KEY

▬▬ Tour route

╌╌ Other roads

🌠 Viewpoint

Yeste ④
The village of Yeste, which stands at the foot of the Sierra de Ardal, is crowned by a hilltop Arab castle. It was reconquered under Fernando III, and was later ruled by the Order of Santiago.

the **Lonja del Corregidor**, with Plateresque decoration. The square is surrounded by lively, narrow streets with traditional houses. On the out-skirts of the town are the castle ruins and the one surviving arch of a Gothic aqueduct. Alcaraz also makes a good base for touring the sierras of Alcaraz and Segura.

The twin towers of Tardón and Trinidad on Alcaraz's main square

Lagunas de Ruidera ㉕

Cuidad Real. 🚍 Ossa de Montiel.
🛈 Ruidera, 926 52 81 16.
🆆 www.lagunaruidera.com

ONCE NICKNAMED "The Mir-rors of La Mancha", the 16 interconnected lakes which make up the Parque Natural de las Lagunas de Ruidera stretch for 20 km (12 miles) through a valley. They allegedly take their name from a story in *Don Quixote (see p377)* in which a certain Mistress Ruidera, her daughters and her nieces are said to have been turned into lakes by a magician.

Although La Mancha's falling water table has led to a decline in the amount of water in the lakes, they are still worth visit-ing for their wealth of wildlife, which includes great and little bustards, herons and many types of duck. The wildlife has recently come under threat due to the increasing number of

One of the lakes in the Parque Natural de las Lagunas de Ruidera

tourists, and the development of holiday chalets on the lakes' shores. Near one of the lakes, the Laguna de San Pedro, is the **Cueva de Montesinos**, a deep, explor-able cave which was also used as the setting for an episode in *Don Quixote*.

To the northwest, the lakes link up with the Embalse de Peñarroya reservoir, which is overlooked by a castle.

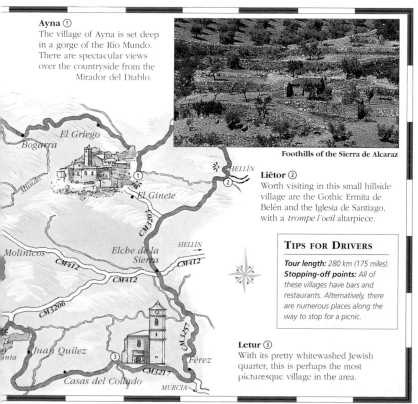

Ayna ①
The village of Ayna is set deep in a gorge of the Río Mundo. There are spectacular views over the countryside from the Mirador del Diablo.

Foothills of the Sierra de Alcaraz

Liétor ②
Worth visiting in this small hillside village are the Gothic Ermita de Belén and the Iglesia de Santiago, with a *trompe l'oeil* altarpiece.

TIPS FOR DRIVERS

Tour length: 280 km (175 miles).
Stopping-off points: All of these villages have bars and restaurants. Alternatively, there are numerous places along the way to stop for a picnic.

Letur ③
With its pretty whitewashed Jewish quarter, this is perhaps the most picturesque village in the area.

Villanueva de los Infantes ㉖

Ciudad Real. 🏘 5,800. 🚌
ℹ️ Plaza Mayor 3, 926 36 13 21. 🚐
Fri. 🎭 Ferias (late Aug), Virgen de
Antigua (8 Sep), Santo Tomás (18 Sep).

VILLANUEVA'S OLD TOWN, which
centres on the graceful
Neo-Classical Plaza Mayor, is
one of the most attractive in
La Mancha. Many buildings
on the square have wooden
balconies and arcades. Also on
the square is the **Iglesia de
San Andrés**, which has a
Renaissance façade. Inside
are a Baroque altarpiece and
organ, as well as the now
empty tomb of the Golden Age
author Francisco de Quevedo.
He lived and died in the
Convento de los Domínicos.

ENVIRONS: The village of **San
Carlos del Valle**, 16 km
(10 miles) to the northwest,
has a perfectly preserved 18th-
century square and galleried
houses built of rust-red stone.

Valdepeñas ㉗

Ciudad Real. 🏘 27,000. 🚆 🚌 ℹ️
Pl de España, 926 31 25 52. 🚐 Thu.
🎭 Grape Harvest (first week of Sep).

VALDEPEÑAS is the capital of
La Mancha's vast wine
region, the world's largest
expanse of vineyards, producing vast quantities of red
wine (see pp192–3). This
largely modern town comes
alive for its September wine
festival. In the network of

older streets around the café-
lined Plaza de España are the
Iglesia de la Asunción and
the municipal museum.
Valdepeñas has over 30
bodegas which can be visited.
One of them, **Bodega Museo**,
has some of the few remaining
traditional cellars, with huge
earthenware jars, *tinajas*.

🍷 Bodega Museo
Salida a Ciudad Real. 📞 926 31 28 49.
◯ daily.

**Courtyard of the Palacio del Viso
in Viso del Marqués**

Viso del Marqués ㉘

Ciudad Real. 🏘 3,100. 🚌 ℹ️ Plaza
de la Oretania 8, 926 33 60 01.
🚐 Tue. 🎭 San Andrés (second Sun
of May), Feria (24 – 8 Jul).

THE SMALL VILLAGE of Viso
del Marqués in La Mancha
is the unlikely setting of the
Palacio del Viso, a grand
Renaissance building. This

mansion was commissioned
in 1564 by the Marquis of
Santa Cruz, the admiral of the
fleet which defeated the Turks
at Lepanto in 1571 (see p55).
One of the main features of
the house is a Classical patio.
Inside, the principal rooms
have been decorated with
Italian frescoes.

ENVIRONS: About 25 km
(16 miles) to the northeast of
Viso del Marqués is Spain's
oldest bullring at **Las Virtudes**.
Square and galleried, it was
built in 1641 next to a 14th-
century church, which has a
Churrigueresque altarpiece.

🏛 Palacio del Viso
Plaza del Pradillo 12. 📞 926 33
60 08. ◯ Tue –Sun. 🌑 Aug.

Calatrava la Nueva ㉙

Cuidad Real. Aldea de Rey.
📞 926 22 13 37.
◯ Tue –Sun.

MAGNIFICENT in its isolated
hilltop setting, the ruined
castle-monastery of Calatrava la
Nueva is reached by a stretch
of original medieval road.
It was founded in 1217
by the Knights of Calatrava,
Spain's first military-religious
order (see p50), to be their
headquarters. The complex is
of huge proportions, with a
double patio and a church
with a triple nave. The church
has been restored and is illuminated by a beautiful rose
window above the entrance.

Expanse of vineyards near Valdepeñas

Calatrava la Nueva castle-monastery, dominating the plains of La Mancha

After the Reconquest, the building continued to be used as a monastery until it was abandoned in 1802 following earthquake damage.

Opposite the castle are the ruins of a Muslim frontier fortress, **Salvatierra**, which was captured from the Moors by the Order of Calatrava in the 12th century.

Almagro ③⓪

Ciudad Real. 🏯 8,300. 🚗 🚌
🛈 Palacio del Conde de Valparaiso, 926 86 07 17. 🗓 Wed. 🎉 Virgen de las Nieves (5 Aug), San Bartolomé (25 Aug). 🖵 www.ciudad-almagro.com

ALMAGRO was disputed during the Reconquest, until the Order of Calatrava captured it and built the castle of Calatrava la Nueva to the southwest of the town. The rich architectural heritage of the atmospheric old town is partly the legacy of the Fugger brothers, the Habsburgs' bankers who settled in nearby Almadén during the 16th century.

The town's main attraction is its colonnaded stone plaza, with characteristic enclosed, green balconies. On one side is a 17th-century courtyard-theatre – the **Corral de Comedias** – where a drama festival is held every July in honour of St Bartholomew.

Other monuments worth seeing include the Fuggers' Renaissance warehouse and former university, and also the parador (see p558).

ENVIRONS: To the northwest is **Ciudad Real**, founded by Alfonso X the Learned in 1255. Among its sights are the cathedral, the Iglesia de San Pedro, and the Mudéjar gateway, the Puerta de Toledo.

Raised walkway in the Parque Nacional de Las Tablas de Daimiel

Tablas de Daimiel ③①

Ciudad Real. 🚌 Daimiel. 🛈 Daimiel, Plaza de España 1, 926 26 06 39.

THE MARSHY WETLANDS of the Tablas de Daimiel, northeast of Ciudad Real, are the feeding and nesting grounds of a huge range of aquatic and migratory birds. Despite being national parkland since 1973, they have become an ecological cause célèbre due to the growing threat from the area's lowering water table. This has affected the area's wildlife in recent years.

One corner of the park is open to the public, with walking routes to islets and observation towers. Breeding birds here include great crested grebes and mallards. Otters and red foxes are among the mammals which have traditionally inhabited the park.

Valle de Alcudia ③②

Ciudad Real. 🚌 Fuencaliente.
🛈 Ciudad Real, Calle Alarcos 21, 926 20 00 37.

ALCUDIA'S LUSH lowlands, which border the Sierra Morena foothills to the south, are among central Spain's most unspoiled countryside. The area is used largely as pasture land. In late autumn it is filled with sheep, whose milk makes the farmhouse cheese for which the valley is known.

The mountain village of **Fuencaliente** has thermal baths that open in the summer. Further north, **Almadén** is the site of a large mercury mine. **Chillón**, to the northwest, has a late Gothic church.

Small isolated farmhouse in the fertile Valle de Alcudia

EXTREMADURA

CÁCERES · BADAJOZ

O F ALL THE SPANISH REGIONS, *far-flung Extremadura – "the land beyond the River Douro" – is the most remote from the modern world. Green sierras run southwards through rolling hills strewn with boulders. Forests and reservoirs shelter rare wildlife. The towns, with their atmospheric old quarters, have a romantic, slow-paced charm. In winter, storks nest on their spires and chimneys.*

The finest monuments in Extremadura are the ruins of ancient settlements scattered across the region. Many are exceptionally well preserved. Some of Spain's finest Roman architecture is to be seen in Mérida, capital of the Roman province of Lusitania, which has an aqueduct and a magnificent theatre. Other Classical remains dot the countryside – notably a Tartessan temple at Cancho Roano and a Roman bridge at Alcántara. Smaller finds are displayed in Badajoz museum.

Modern development has bypassed the old town of Cáceres, whose ancient walls, winding streets and nobles' mansions are still marvellously intact. Trujillo, Zafra and Jerez de los Caballeros have medieval and Renaissance quarters; and there are small, splendidly decorated cathedrals in Plasencia, Coria and Badajoz. The castles and stout walls of Alburquerque and Olivenza mark frontiers embattled through history. Many cathedrals and monasteries were built in the troubled times during and after the Reconquest by the large military-religious orders which then governed the region for the crown.

Extremadura was the birthplace of many conquistadors and emigrants to the New World; the riches they found there financed a surge of building. Guadalupe monastery, in the eastern hills, is the most splendid monument to the region's New World ties.

View over the rooftops of the historic town of Cáceres

◁ An old stone cross in the woods near Yuste, a Hieronymite monastery founded in 1404

Exploring Extremadura

EXTREMADURA IS IDEAL for nature lovers and those who want to get off the beaten track to discover the old Spain. It offers beautiful driving and walking country in its northern sierras and valleys, and exceptional wildlife in Monfragüe Natural Park. Some of the best Roman ruins in Spain can be found throughout Extremadura, especially in the regional capital, Mérida. The walled old town of Cáceres, with its well-preserved Jewish quarter, and the monasteries of Guadalupe and Yuste, are other historic sights not to be missed. To the south, the Templar towns in the Sierra Morena, such as Jerez de los Caballeros, have fine old buildings, while the small, historic towns of Coria, Zafra and Llerena all make charming bases for excursions.

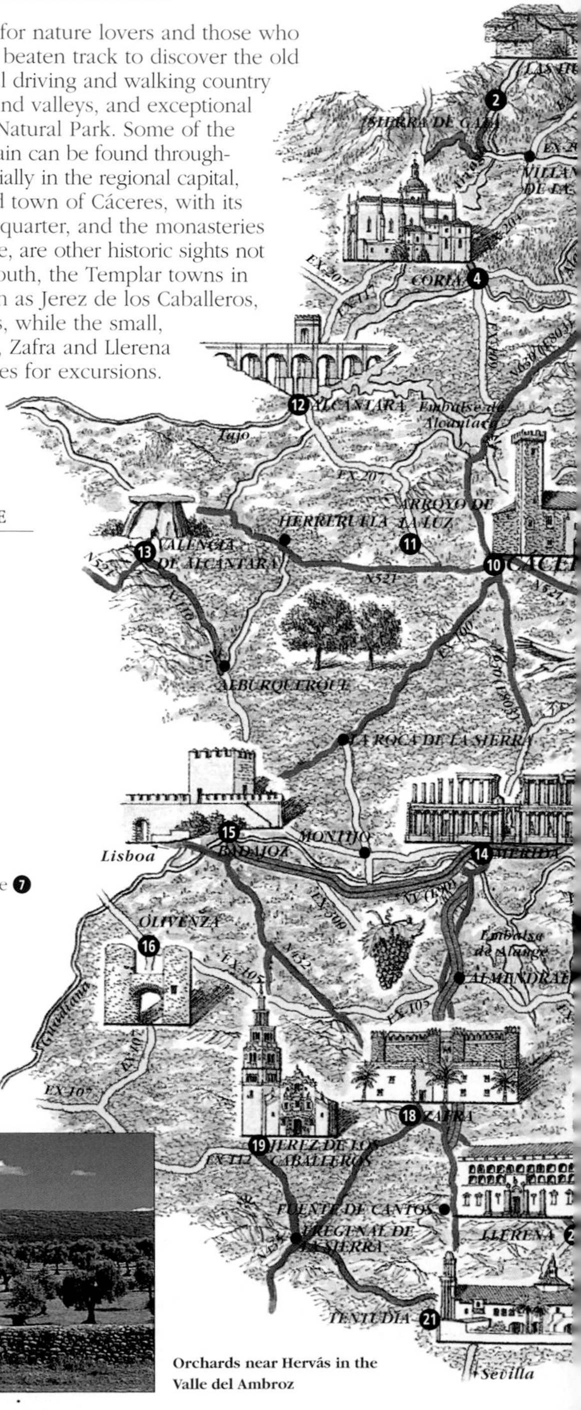

SIGHTS AT A GLANCE

Alcántara ⑫
Arroyo de la Luz ⑪
Badajoz ⑮
Cáceres pp.390–91 ⑩
Cancho Roano ⑰
Coria ④
Guadalupe ⑧
Hervás ③
Las Hurdes ①
Jerez de los Caballeros ⑲
Llerena ⑳
Mérida ⑭
Monasterio de Yuste ⑥
Olivenza ⑯
Parque Natural de Monfragüe ⑦
Plasencia ⑤
Sierra de Gata ②
Tentudía ㉑
Trujillo ⑨
Valencia de Alcántara ⑬
Zafra ⑱

**Orchards near Hervás in the
Valle del Ambroz**

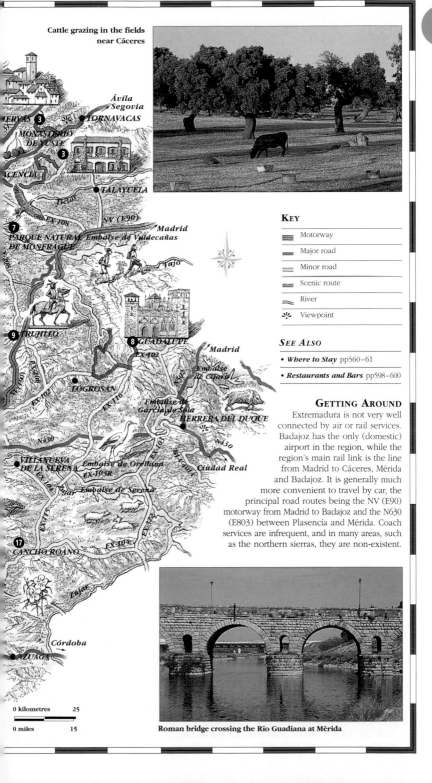

Cattle grazing in the fields
near Cáceres

TORNAVACAS

MONASTERIO
DE YUSTE

CENCIA

TALAYUELA

EX-108 NV (E90)

Madrid

PARQUE NATURAL
DE MONFRAGÜE

Embalse de Valdecañas

Tajo

TRUJILLO

GUADALUPE
EX-102

Madrid

Embalse
de Cíjara

LOGROSÁN

Embalse de
García de Sola

HERRERA DEL DUQUE

N430

VILLANUEVA
DE LA SERENA

EX-103R

Embalse de Orellana

Embalse de Serena

Ciudad Real

N430

CANCHO ROANO

EX-104

Zújar

Córdoba

AZUAGA

KEY

▬▬	Motorway
▬▬	Major road
▬▬	Minor road
▬▬	Scenic route
≈	River
☼	Viewpoint

SEE ALSO

• *Where to Stay* pp560–61

• *Restaurants and Bars* pp598–600

GETTING AROUND

Extremadura is not very well
connected by air or rail services.
Badajoz has the only (domestic)
airport in the region, while the
region's main rail link is the line
from Madrid to Cáceres, Mérida
and Badajoz. It is generally much
more convenient to travel by car, the
principal road routes being the NV (E90)
motorway from Madrid to Badajoz and the N630
(E803) between Plasencia and Mérida. Coach
services are infrequent, and in many areas, such
as the northern sierras, they are non-existent.

Roman bridge crossing the Río Guadiana at Mérida

0 kilometres	25
0 miles	15

Beehives, a common sight in Las Hurdes

Las Hurdes ❶

Cáceres. 🚌 *Pinofranqueado, Caminomorisco, Nuñomoral.*
🛈 *Pinofranqueado, 927 67 41 81.*

LAS HURDES' slate mountains, goats and beehives were memorably caught in the 1932 Luis Buñuel film, *Tierra sin Pan (Land without Bread)*. The area's legendary poverty disappeared with the arrival of roads in the 1950s, but the black slopes, riverbeds and hill terraces remain.

From Pinofranqueado or Vegas de Coria, roads climb past picturesque "black" villages like Batuequilla, Fragosa, and El Gasco, which sits under an extinct volcano. The more developed **Lower Hurdes** area, crossed by the Río Hurdano and the main access route (C512), is dotted with camp sites and restaurants serving traditional cuisine.

Sierra de Gata ❷

Cáceres. 🚌 *Cáceres.* 🛈 *Moraleja, 927 14 70 88.*

THERE ARE 40 hamlets in the Sierra de Gata, scattered between olive groves, orchards and fields. The area has retained its old-fashioned rural charm by conserving hunters' paths for woodland walking, and its local crafts, most notably lace-making. In the lowland towns of **Valverde de Fresno** and **Acebo**, the local dialect, *chapurriau*, is still spoken. On the higher slopes, **Eljas**, **Gata** and **Villamiel** have ruins of medieval fortresses. The old granite houses have carved family crests on the front and distinctive outside staircases.

Coat of arms on a house front in Acebo

Hervás ❸

Cáceres. 🏘 *4,000.* 🛈 *C/ Braulio Navas 6, 927 47 36 18.* 🗓 *Sat.*
🎉 *Nuestra Señora de la Asunción (14–17 Aug).* 🌐 *www.hervas.com*

SITTING AT THE TOP of the wide Valle del Ambroz, Hervás is known for its medieval Jewish quarter, with its whitewashed houses. The tiny streets, dotted with taverns and craft workshops, slope down towards the Río Ambroz. Just off the main plaza is the **Museo Pérez Comendador-Leroux**, named after the town's noted 20th-century sculptor, whose work is exhibited here.

The next town up towards the Béjar pass is **Baños de Montemayor**, whose name comes from its sulphurous baths, which date back to Roman times. These were revived in the early 1900s and are open to the public. At **Caparra**, southwest of Hervás, a triumphal arch stands on the Roman road, the Vía de la Plata (*see p334*).

🏛 **Museo Pérez Comendador-Leroux**
Calle Asensio Nelia 5. 📞 *927 48 16 55.* ⏱ *pm Tue–Sun.* ⬤ *public hols.*

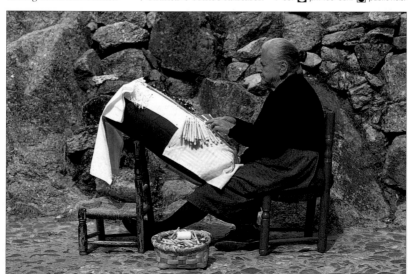

Traditional lace-making in one of the villages of the Sierra de Gata

Ancient wall and olive groves in the Valle del Ambroz

Coria ❹

Cáceres. 🏘 13,000. 🚉 🚌 *Avenida de Extremadura 39, 927 50 13 51.* 🛒 *Thu.* 🎉 *Día de la Virgen (week after Easter).* 🌐 www.coria.org

Coria's walled old town, perched above the Río Alagón, boasts a Gothic-Renaissance **cathedral** with rich Plateresque carving, and the 16th-century **Convento de la Madre de Dios**, which has a fine Renaissance cloister.

Forming part of the town walls, which are a Muslim and medieval patchwork, are an impressive castle tower, and four gates, two of which date back to Roman times. The gates are closed during the fiesta of San Juan in June for night-time bull-running. Situated below the old town is the **Puente Seco**, a Roman bridge over the river.

Plasencia ❺

Cáceres. 🏘 36,500. 🚉 🚌 🚌 🛈 *Plaza de la Catedral, 927 42 38 43.* 🛒 *Tue.* 🎉 *Ferias (8–11 Jun).*

Plasencia's golden-grey walls, rising above a curve in the banks of the Río Jerte, tell of the town's past as a military bastion. Nowadays Plasencia is best known for its Tuesday market, dating back to the 12th century, which is held in the main square.

A short walk away are the town's two cathedrals, which are built back-to-back. The 16th-century **Catedral Nueva** has a Baroque organ and carved wooden choir stalls. The Romanesque **Catedral Vieja**, next to it, has a museum with works by Ribera, and a late 14th-century Bible.

The nearby **Museo Etnográfico y Textil**, housed in a 14th-century hospital, has displays of crafts and costumes.

The rest of the Jerte valley has pockets of outstanding beauty, such as the **Garganta de los Infiernos**, a nature reserve with dramatic, rushing waterfalls.

🏛 **Museo Etnográfico y Textil**
Plaza del Marqués de la Puebla. 📞 927 42 18 43. ⏱ Wed–Sun.

Monasterio de Yuste ❻

Cuacos de Yuste (Cáceres). 📞 927 17 21 30. ⏱ daily 🎫

The Hieronymite monastery of Yuste, where Charles V *(see p55)* retired from public life in 1556 and died two years later, is remarkable for its simplicity and its lovely setting in the wooded valley of La Vera.

The church's Gothic and Plateresque cloisters and the austere palace are open to visitors. Just below it is **Cuacos de Yuste**, the most unspoiled of La Vera's old villages, where peppers, for making paprika, hang outside the houses.

Paprika peppers hanging up around a door in Cuacos de Yuste

A *Carantoña*, during the fiesta of St Sebastian, Acehuche

EXTREMADURA'S FIESTAS

Carantoñas *(20 Jan)*, Acehuche (Cáceres). During the fiesta of St Sebastian, the *Carantoñas* take to the streets of the town dressed up in animal skins, with their faces covered by grotesque masks designed to make them look terrifying. They represent the wild beasts which are said to have left the saint unharmed.

Pero Palo *(Carnival Feb/Mar)*, Villanueva de la Vera (Cáceres). In this ancient ritual a wooden figure dressed in a suit and representing the devil is paraded around the streets and then destroyed – except for the head, which is reused the year after.

Los Empalaos *(Maundy Thursday)*, Valverde de la Vera (Cáceres). Men do penance by walking in procession through the town with their arms outstretched and bound to small tree trunks.

Encamisá *(7 Dec)*, Torrejoncillo (Cáceres). Riders on horseback parade around town, where bonfires are set alight for the occasion.

Los Escobazos *(7 Dec)*, Jarandilla de la Vera (Cáceres). At night, the town is illuminated by bonfires in the streets, and torches are made from burning brooms.

Parque Natural de Monfragüe ❼

Cáceres. 🚍 *Villareal de San Carlos.* ℹ *Villareal de San Carlos, 927 19 91 34.*

T O THE SOUTH of Plasencia, rolling hills drop from scrubby peaks through wild olive, cork and holm oak woods to the dammed Tagus and Tiétar river valleys. In 1979, some 500 sq km (200 sq miles) of these hills were granted natural park status in order to safeguard the area's outstandingly varied wildlife species, which includes a large proportion of Spain's protected bird species *(see pp324–5)*.

The many species of bird which breed here include the black-winged kite, black vulture and, most notably, the black stork, as well as more

Birdwatchers in the Parque Natural de Monfragüe

common aquatic species on and near the water. Mammals living here include the lynx, red deer and wild boar. At **Villareal de San Carlos**, a hamlet founded in the 18th century, there is parking and an information centre which gives out maps of walks. An ideal time to visit the park is September, when many migrating birds stop off here.

Guadalupe ❽

Cáceres. 🏠 *2,500.* 🚍 ℹ *Plaza de Santa María de Guadalupe 1, 927 15 41 28.* **Monasterio** ◯ *daily.* 🎭 *Wed.* 🎉 *Cruz de Mayo (first Sun of May).*

T HIS VILLAGE grew around the magnificent Hieronymite **Monasterio de Guadalupe**, founded in 1340. In the main square there are shops that sell handmade ceramics and beaten copper cauldrons, both traditional monastic crafts, now made as souvenirs.

The turreted towers of the monastery, which is set in a deep wooded valley, help give it a fairy-tale air. According to legend, a shepherd found a wooden image of the Virgin Mary here in the early 14th century. The monastery grew to splendour under royal patronage, acquiring schools of

grammar and medicine, three hospitals, an important pharmacy and one of the largest libraries in Spain.

The 16th-century *hospedería* where royalty once stayed was destroyed by fire; the 20th-century reconstruction is now a hotel run by the monks *(see p560)*. The old hospital has been converted into a parador. In the car park is a plaque commemorating Spain's first human dissection, which took place here in 1402.

By the time the New World was discovered, the monastery was very important and in 1496 was the site of the baptism of some of the first native Caribbeans brought to Europe by Columbus *(see pp52–3)*.

The monastery was sacked by Napoleon in 1808 but was refounded by Franciscans a century later. Today it is still a

major centre of Catholicism, visited every year by thousands of pilgrims from around the Spanish-speaking world.

Guided tours (in Spanish only) begin in the museums of illuminated manuscripts, embroidered vestments and fine art. They continue to the choir and the magnificent Baroque sacristy, nicknamed "the Spanish Sistine Chapel", because of Zurbarán's portraits of monks hanging on the highly decorated walls. For many, the chance to touch or kiss the tiny Virgin's dress in the *camarín* (chamber) behind the altar is the highlight of the tour. Finally, you can linger in the 16th-century Gothic cloister which has two tiers of horseshoe arches around an ornate central pavilion. The church, with a magnificent 16th-century iron grille partly forged from the chains of freed slaves, may be visited separately.

ENVIRONS: The surrounding **Villuercas** and **Los Ibores** sierras, where herbs were once picked for the monastery pharmacy, have good woodland walks. The road south also gives access to the pasture lands of **La Serena**, a vital breeding ground for birds of the steppe *(see pp324–5)*, and the huge reservoir of **Cíjara**, surrounded by a game reserve.

Monasterio de Guadalupe, overlooking the town

Trujillo ❾

Cáceres. 👥 9,000. 🚉 ℹ️ *Plaza Mayor, 927 65 90 39.* 🚌 *Thu.* 🎭 *Feria del Queso (Apr/May), San Miguel (Sep).* ⓦ www.ayto-trujillo.com

W HEN THE PLAZA MAYOR of the medieval hilltop town of Trujillo is floodlit at night, it is one of the most beautiful squares in Spain. By day, there is much to visit, including the **Iglesia de Santa María la Mayor**, on one of the town's winding streets, which contains various sarcophagi.

At the top of the hill there is an Islamic fortress, which defended the town against the Christian advance during the Reconquest *(see pp50–51)*; but in 1232 it was retaken by the forces of Fernando III. Trujillo was the birthplace of

Statue of Francisco Pizarro in Trujillo's main square

several conquistadors, most notably Francisco Pizarro, who conquered Peru *(see p54)*, of whom there is a statue in the main square. His brother, Hernando Pizarro, founded

the **Palacio del Marqués de la Conquista**, one of several palaces and convents built with New World wealth. It has an elaborate corner window with carved stone heads of the Pizarro brothers and their Inca wives. The beautiful 16th-century **Palacio de Orellana-Pizarro** was built by Francisco de Orellana, the explorer of Ecuador and the Amazon. It has a fine Plateresque patio.

Once a year, in late April or early May, gourmets descend on the town for its renowned week-long cheese fair.

🏛 **Palacio del Marqués de la Conquista**
Plaza Mayor. ⬤ *to the public.*
🏛 **Palacio de Orellana-Pizarro**
Plaza de Don Juan Tena. 📞 *927 32 11 62.* ⬜ *daily.*

The Virgin of Guadalupe, her face blackened by smoke from smouldering lamps, is worshipped by pilgrims from around the world. She is kept in the camarín, *and dressed up for feast days. On her lap sits the infant Jesus.*

Gothic cloister

Embroidery museum

Painting and sculpture museum

Church

The chapterhouse has 87 illuminated manuscripts by the monks of Guadalupe.

The sacristy contains Zurbarán's Father Gonzalo de Illescas at Work.

Street-by-Street: Cáceres ⓾

Aᴀ FTER ALFONSO IX OF LEON conquered Cáceres in 1227, its growing prosperity as a free trade town attracted merchants, and later aristocracy, to settle here. They rivalled each other with stately homes and palaces fortified by watchtowers, most of which Isabel and Fernando, the reigning monarchs *(see pp52–3)*, ordered to be demolished in 1476 to halt the continual jostling for power. Today's serene Renaissance town dates from the late 15th and 16th centuries, after which economic decline set in. Untouched by the wars of the 19th and 20th centuries, Cáceres became Spain's first listed heritage city in 1949.

★ Casa de los Golfines de Abajo
The ornamental façade of this 16th-century mansion displays the shield of one of the town's leading families, the Golfines.

Casa y Torre de Carvajal
This typical Renaissance mansion has a 13th-century round Arab tower and a peaceful garden with a patio.

PLAZA DE
SANTA MARÍA

★ Iglesia de Santa María
Facing the Palacio Episcopal, this Gothic-Renaissance church has a beautiful cedarwood reredos and a 15th-century crucifix – the Cristo Negro *(Black Christ).*

| 0 metres | 50 |
| 0 yards | 50 |

KEY

– – – Suggested route

Arco de la Estrella
This low-arched gateway was built by Manuel Churriguera in 1726. It leads through the city walls from the Plaza Mayor into the old town and is flanked by a 15th-century watchtower.

Barrio de San Antonio
This quaint old Jewish quarter, with narrow streets of whitewashed houses restored to their original condition, takes its name from the nearby hermitage of St Anthony.

★ Museo Provincial
Housed in the Casa de las Veletas, this museum has contemporary art and archaeology from the region.

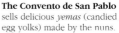

The Convento de San Pablo sells delicious *yemas* (candied egg yolks) made by the nuns.

Casa y Torre de la Cigüeña
The slender, battlemented tower of the House of the Stork was allowed to remain after 1476 because of the owner's loyalty to Isabel. It is now owned by the army.

The Iglesia de San Mateo, built between the 14th and 17th centuries, is one of Cáceres' earliest churches.

Casa del Sol (Casa de los Solís)
The façade of this elegant Renaissance building, once home of the Solís family, is emblazoned with a sun (sol) motif.

STAR SIGHTS

★ Casa de los Golfines de Abajo

★ Iglesia de Santa María

★ Museo Provincial

Arroyo de la Luz

Cáceres. 🏠 6,650. 🚌 🚉 ℹ️ *Plaza de la Constitución 16, 927 27 00 02.* 🚌 *Thu.* 🎉 *Día de la Patrona (Easter Mon).*

T HE SMALL TOWN of Arroyo de la Luz is home to one of the artistic masterpieces of Extremadura. Its **Iglesia de la Asunción**, completed in 1565, contains a spectacular altarpiece which incorporates 20 paintings by the mystical religious painter Luis de Morales.

ENVIRONS: The area has a large population of white storks *(see p325)*. Nearby **Malpartida** is home to the largest colony, whose nests adorn the church roof. There are some good picnic spots in the surrounding countryside.

Alterpiece in the Iglesia de la Asunción, Arroyo de la Luz

Alcántara

Cáceres. 🏠 1,900. 🚌 ℹ️ *Avenida de Merida 21, 927 39 08 63.* 🚌 *Tue.* 🎉 *Feria (15–17 Apr); San Pedro (19 Oct).*

A LCÁNTARA has two important sights. One is the drystone **Roman bridge**, 71 m (233 ft) above the Tagus river, which has an honorary arch and a temple. The other is the restored **Convento de San Benito**. This was built as the headquarters of the Knights of the Order of Alcántara, during the 16th century, and was sacked by Napoleon. Its surviving treasures are in the **Iglesia de Santa María de Almocóvar**.

Walls of the 16th-century Convento de San Benito, Alcántara

Valencia de Alcántara

Cáceres. 🏠 6,300. 🚌 🚉 ℹ️ *Calle de Hernan Cortes, 927 58 25 43.* 🚌 *Mon.* 🎉 *Día de los Mayos (1 May).*

T HE GOTHIC QUARTER of this hilltop frontier town is given an elegant air by its fountains and shady orange trees. The **Castillo de Piedra Buena**, which was built by the Knights of the Order of Alcántara, now houses a youth hostel. On the outskirts of the town are more than 40 dolmens, or megalithic burial sites.

ENVIRONS: Alburquerque, to the southeast, is sited on a rocky outcrop with a magnificent panoramic view from the ramparts and keep of its castle. Below is the walled old town and the 15th-century Iglesia de Santa María del Mercado.

Mérida

Badajoz. 🏠 50,400. 🚌 🚉 ℹ️ *Avenida José Álvarez Saez de Buruaga, 924 31 53 53.* 🚌 *Tue.* 🎉 *Fiestas Patronales (10 Dec).*

F OUNDED BY AUGUSTUS in 25 BC, Augusta Emerita grew into the cultural and economic capital of Rome's westernmost province, Lusitania, but lost its eminence under the Moors. Though a small city, Mérida, the capital of Extremadura, has many fine Roman monuments.

The best approach is from the west of town, via the modern suspension bridge over the Río Guadiana, bringing you to the original entrance of the Roman city and Arab fortress.

The city's centrepiece is the **Roman theatre** *(see pp46–7)*. One of the best-preserved Roman theatres anywhere, it is still used in summer for the city's drama festival and is part of a larger site with an **amphitheatre** *(anfiteatro)* and gardens. Nearby are the remains of a Roman house, the **Casa del Anfiteatro**, where there are underground galleries and large areas of well-preserved mosaics.

Opposite stands Rafael Moneo's stunning red-brick **Museo Nacional de Arte Romano**. The semicircular arches of its main hall are built to the same height as the city's Los Milagros aqueduct. Off this hall, which features sculptures from the Roman theatre, there are three galleries exhibiting ceramics, mosaics, coins and statuary. There is also an excavated Roman street. Near

Megalithic tomb on the outskirts of Valencia de Alcántara

Mérida's well-preserved Roman theatre, still used as a venue for classical drama

the museum are several other monuments, namely two villas with fine mosaics, and a racecourse (closed for excavation).

A chapel in front of the 3rd-century **Iglesia de Santa Eulalia** is dedicated to the child saint who was martyred on this site in Roman times. Towards the centre of the town are the **Templo de Diana** (1st century AD), with tall, fluted columns,

Sculpture of
Emperor Augustus

and the **Arco de Trajano**. The **Museo de Arte Visigodo** (Museum of Visigothic Art) is in the Convento de Santa Clara, which is situated off its main square. From the huge **Puente de Guadiana** there is a good view of the massive walls of the **Alcazaba**, one of Spain's oldest Moorish buildings (AD 835), whose precinct includes towers, a cistern and more Roman ruins. To the

east of the town stands the **Casa del Mithraeo**, with its Pompeiian-style frescoes and superb mosaics.

The magnificent, ruined Los Milagros aqueduct, with its granite and brick arches, are off the N630 towards Cáceres.

🏛 **Museo de Arte Visigodo**
Calle Santa Julia. 📞 *924 30 01 06.*
◯ *Tue –Sun.* ⬤ *1 May, 25 Dec.*
🏛 **Museo Nacional de Arte Romano**
Calle José Ramón Mélida. 📞 *924 31 16 90.* ◯ *Tue–Sun.* 🈺 *(free Sat pm & Sun).* ♿ 🆆 www.mnar.es

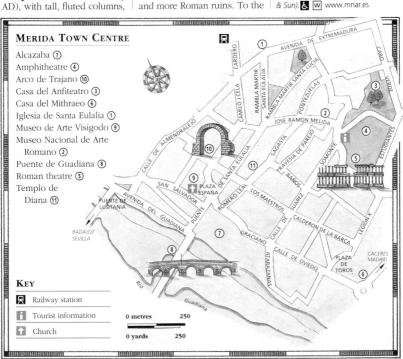

MERIDA TOWN CENTRE

Alcazaba ⑦
Amphitheatre ④
Arco de Trajano ⑩
Casa del Anfiteatro ③
Casa del Mithraeo ⑥
Iglesia de Santa Eulalia ①
Museo de Arte Visigodo ⑨
Museo Nacional de Arte Romano ②
Puente de Guadiana ⑧
Roman theatre ⑤
Templo de Diana ⑪

KEY

🚉 Railway station

ℹ️ Tourist information

✝ Church

0 metres   250

0 yards   250

Badajoz 🅖

Badajoz. 🏛 136,600. ✈ 🚌 🚍
ℹ Pasaje de San Juan, 924 22 49
81. 🏪 Tue & Sun. 🎪 Feria (24 Jun).

BADAJOZ is a plain, modern
city, though it retains traces
of its former importance. It was
a major city under the Moors
but centuries of conflict robbed
Badajoz of its former glories.

The Alcazaba now houses
the **Museo Arqueológico**,
which has over 15,000 pieces
from around the province, as
far back as Paleolithic times.
Nearby is the cathedral, dating
from the 13th–18th centuries,
with a stunning tiled cloister.
A new museum of contem-
porary art has also opened on
Calle Museo and is open every
day except Saturday.

🏛 **Museo Arqueológico**
Pl José Álvarez Saez de Buruaga. 📞
924 22 23 14. ⬜ Tue–Sun. 🖼 ♿

Olivenza 🅖

Badajoz. 🏛 10,700. 🚍 ℹ Plaza de
España, 924 49 01 51. 🏪 Sat.
🎪 Muñecas de San Juan (23 Jun).

A PORTUGUESE ENCLAVE until
1801, Olivenza has a
colourful character. Within
the walled town are the
medieval castle, housing the
**Museo Etnográfico Gonzalez
Santana**, a museum of rural
life, and three churches.
Santa María del Castillo has
a naive family tree of the
Virgin Mary. **Santa María
Magdalena**, is a fine example
of the 16th-century Portuguese

**Interior of Santa María Magdalena
church, Olivenza**

Manueline style. The 16th-
century **Santa Casa de
Misericordia** has blue and
white tiled friezes. In one, God
is shown banishing Adam and
Eve from the Garden of Eden.
Off the main square is the
Pasteleria Fuentes, which
sells custard cake.

🏛 **Museo Etnogràfico
Gonzalez Santana**
Plaza de Santa María.
📞 924 49 02 22.
⬜ Tue–Sun. ♿

Cancho Roano 🅖

Zalamea de la Serena. 📞 924 78
01 53. ⬜ Tue–Sun.

THIS SANCTUARY-PALACE, which
is thought to have been
built under the civilization of
Tartessus (see p45), was discovered in 1978. Excavations
on this small but unique site
have revealed a moated temple
that was rebuilt three times –

many of the walls and slate
floors are still intact. Each
temple was constructed on a
grander scale than the previous one and then burned in
the face of invasion during
the 6th century BC.

Most of the artifacts unearthed, including jewellery, ceramics and furniture, are on
display in the archaeological
museum at Badajoz.

ENVIRONS: A Roman funereal
monument stands next to the
church in nearby **Zalamea de
la Serena**. The town comes
alive during the September
fiestas, when the townsfolk
act out the classic 17th-century
play, *The Mayor of Zalamea*,
by Calderón de la Barca (see
p30), which was supposedly
based on a local character.
Shops in the town also sell
torta de la Serena, a cheese
made of sheep's milk.

**Remains of the Tartessan
sanctuary at Cancho Ruano**

Zafra 🅖

Badajoz. 🏛 15,000. 🚌 🚍
ℹ Plaza de España 8, 924 55 10 36.
🏪 Fri. 🎪 San Miguel (30 Sep–6 Oct).
🌐 www.zafraturismo.com

AT THE HEART of this graceful
town, nicknamed "little
Seville" because of its similarity
to the capital of Andalusia,
are two arcaded squares. The
Plaza Grande, the larger of the
two, is the site of the **Iglesia
de la Candelaria**, which has a
Zurbarán altarpiece. Converging on it is the older, 15th-
century **Plaza Chica**, which
used to be the marketplace.

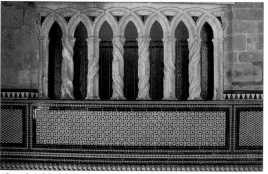
The colourful tiled cloister in the cathedral of Badajoz

Altarpiece by Zurbarán in the Iglesia de la Candelaria at Zafra

On Calle Sevilla is the 15th-century Convento de Santa Clara and the **Alcázar de los Duques de Feria**, now a parador *(see p561)* with a patio attributed to Juan de Herrera.

Environs: Some 25 km (16 miles) to the south, in **Fuente de Cantos**, is the house in which the painter Francisco de Zurbarán was born in 1598.

Jerez de los Caballeros ⓓ

Badajoz. 🏠 *9,600.* 🚌 🚆 ℹ *Plaza de San Agustin 1, 924 73 03 72.* 🗓 *Wed.* 🎪 *Feria del Jamón (early May).* 🌐 *www.dip-badajoz.es*

THE HILLSIDE PROFILE of Jerez, which is broken by three Baroque church towers, is one of the most picturesque in Extremadura. This small town is also historically important – Vasco Núñez de Balboa, who discovered the Pacific, was born here. In the **castle**, now laid out as gardens, knights of the Order of Knights Templar were beheaded in the Torre Sangrienta (Bloody Tower) in 1312. The old quarters of the town grew up around three churches: **San Bartolomé**, its façade studded with glazed ceramics; **San Miguel**, whose brick tower dominates the Plaza de España; and **Santa María de la Encarnación**.

Environs: Fregenal de la Sierra, 25 km (16 miles) to the south, is an attractive old town with a bullring.

Llerena ⓔ

Badajoz. 🏠 *5,700.* 🚌 🚆 ℹ *Calle Aurora 2, 924 87 05 51.* 🗓 *Thu.* 🎪 *Nuestra Señora de la Granada (1–15 Aug.* 🌐 *www.llerena.org*

EXTREMADURA'S southeastern gateway to Andalusia, the town of Llerena, is a mixture of Mudéjar and Baroque buildings. In the pretty main square, which is lined with palm trees, stands the arcaded, whitewash-and-brick church of **Nuestra Señora de la Granada**, its sumptuous interior reflecting its former importance as a seat of the Inquisition *(see p264).* At one end of the square is a fountain designed by Zurbarán, who lived in the town for 13 years. Also worth seeing is the 16th-century **Convento de Santa Clara**, on a street leading out of the main square.

Environs: At **Azuaga**, 30 km (20 miles) east of Llerena, is the Iglesia de la Consolación, which contains Renaissance and Mudéjar tiles.

Tentudía ㉑

Badajoz. 🚆 *Calera de León.* ℹ *Calera de León, 924 584 101* **Monasterio** ⚪ *Tue–Sun.* 🎫

WHERE THE SIERRA MORENA runs into Andalusia, fortified towns and churches founded by the medieval military orders stand among the wooded hills of Tentudía. Here, on a hilltop, stands the tiny **Monasterio de Tentudía**. Founded in the 13th century by the Order of Santiago, the monastery contains a superb Mudéjar cloister, and reredos with Seville *azulejos* (tiles).

At **Calera de León**, just 6 km (4 miles) north of Tentudía, there is a Renaissance convent, which was also founded by the Order of Santiago. The convent has a Gothic church and a cloister on two floors.

Bullring at Fregenal de la Sierra

SOUTHERN
SPAIN

Southern Spain at a Glance

O NE LARGE REGION – Andalusia – extends across
the south of Spain. Its landscape varies from
the deserts of Almería in the east, to the wetlands
of Doñana National Park in the west; and from
the snow-capped peaks of the Sierra Nevada to
the beaches of the Costa del Sol. Three inland
cities between them share the greatest of Spain's
Moorish monuments: Granada, Córdoba and
Seville, the capital, which stands on the banks of
the Río Guadalquivir. Andalusia has many other
historic towns as well as attractive, whitewashed
villages, important nature reserves and the sherry
producing vineyards around Jerez de la Frontera.

Córdoba's Mezquita *(see pp456–70)*
has a remarkable forest of arches in its
interior and an exquisitely decorated
mihrab (prayer niche) facing Mecca.

SEVILLE

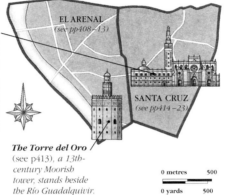

EL ARENAL
(see pp408–13)

SANTA CRUZ
(see pp414–23)

Córdoba

ANDALUSI
(see pp434–7)

La Giralda *(see pp418–*
19), the Moorish bell tower
of Seville cathedral, was
built as a minaret in 1198,
but extended to include a
belfry in the 16th century.

The Torre del Oro
(see p413), a 13th-
century Moorish
tower, stands beside
the Río Guadalquivir.

| 0 metres | 500 |
| 0 yards | 500 |

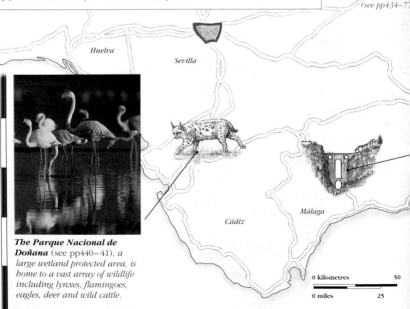

Huelva

Sevilla

Cádiz

Málaga

The Parque Nacional de
Doñana *(see pp440–41), a*
large wetland protected area, is
home to a vast array of wildlife
including lynxes, flamingoes,
eagles, deer and wild cattle.

| 0 kilometres | 50 |
| 0 miles | 25 |

◁ **Whitewashed houses with red-tiled roofs in Montefrío, near Granada**

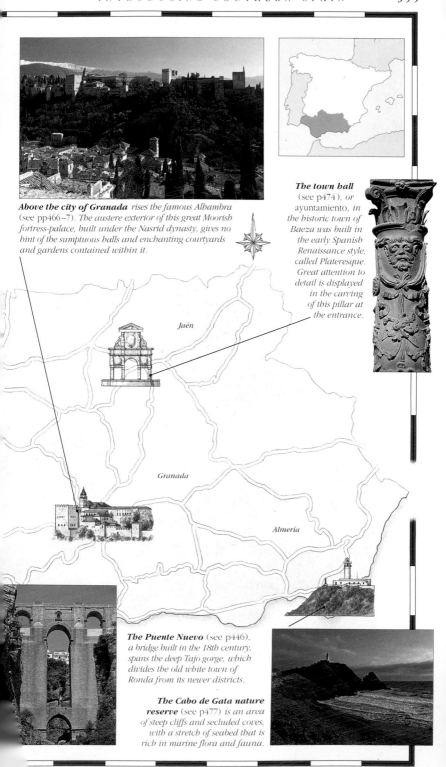

Above the city of Granada rises the famous Alhambra (see pp466–7). The austere exterior of this great Moorish fortress-palace, built under the Nasrid dynasty, gives no hint of the sumptuous halls and enchanting courtyards and gardens contained within it.

The town hall (see p474), or ayuntamiento, in the historic town of Baeza was built in the early Spanish Renaissance style, called Plateresque. Great attention to detail is displayed in the carving of this pillar at the entrance.

Jaén

Granada

Almería

The Puente Nuevo (see p446), a bridge built in the 18th century, spans the deep Tajo gorge, which divides the old white town of Ronda from its newer districts.

The Cabo de Gata nature reserve (see p477) is an area of steep cliffs and secluded coves, with a stretch of seabed that is rich in marine flora and fauna.

Regional Food: Southern Spain

THE ARAB PRESENCE made a lasting impact on the cuisine of Southern Spain. Rice, lemons, oranges, olives and vines were introduced, as well as many new vegetables and spices. Typical today are barbecued meats, sauces flavoured with cumin or saffron and sweets made from crushed almonds. Tomatoes and peppers are much used. Local sherry vinegars are used for dressing salads. The region is famous for its grilled fish, especially sardines, and deep-fried *calamares* (squid). Quality ham and pork are used widely in sausages; and in the mountains, stews of tripe or chickpeas are common fare. Tapas *(see pp574–5)* were invented in Andalusia and a wide variety of them is still served throughout the region.

Old sherry vinegar

Cachorreñas *is a fish soup from Cádiz. It is made with bread, and often clams, and flavoured with bitter orange peel.*

Olives and olive oil have been an important product of Andalusia since Roman times. Today, a third of Europe's olive oil is made here. Fruity green extra virgin oil comes from the olive mills of Baena and the Sierra de Segura. The many types of table olives include fat gordales, *small green* manzanillas *and stuffed olives.*

Aceitunas aliñadas *are marinated, cracked olives.*

Olive oil and olives

Fritura de pescado *is a typical dish from Málaga and Cádiz, where squid and fish are served with wedges of fresh lemon.*

Red pepper

Cold gazpacho soup

Croutons

Cucumber

Fideos a la malagueña *is a variation on paella made with the local spaghetti (instead of rice), shellfish and peppers.*

Gazpacho *is a chilled raw soup that is made by pounding bread and garlic with tomatoes, cucumber and peppers. Olive oil makes it creamy and vinegar gives it a refreshing tang. It is usually garnished with diced vegetables and croutons.*

Pescado a la sal *is fish baked whole in a crust of salt. It is often eaten accompanied by garlic mayonnaise or parsley sauce.*

Habas a la rondeña, *broad beans with cured ham, are so well known they are often called "Spanish-style" beans.*

Rabo de toro *is bull's tail braised with vegetables and red wine – one of the best dishes to employ bull's meat.*

Ternera con alcachofas, *a traditional Cordoban dish, combines veal and artichoke hearts in a Montilla wine sauce.*

Huevos a la flamenca *is a simple gypsy meal of eggs baked in small dishes with vegetables. Chorizo is often included.*

Tocino de cielo *is the most luscious of the custard and caramel desserts; the name means "heavenly bacon".*

Biscuits *include* roscones or rings, round cinnamon- and almond-flavoured *mantecados and soft fried* empanadillas.

FRUITS

Everything grows in the south, the market garden of Europe. Crops include strawberries, apples and pears as well as oranges and lemons. Tropical fruit is grown too, and Spain is also known for its melons. Figs grow wild, while the city of Granada owes its name to the locally grown pomegranate.

Figs

Oranges

Melon

Pomegranates

Persimmons

Strawberries

HAMS AND SAUSAGES

Some of the best *jamón serrano* (cured ham) comes from the mountains of Andalusia, in particular from Jabugo *(see p438)* and Trevélez *(see p460)*. Cooking sausages include paprika-flavoured chorizos and black *morcillas*, made using blood and spices. Cured sausages like chorizo and *salchichones* are often sliced and served as tapas.

Jamón serrano

Chorizo

Morcilla

Salchichón

Wines of Southern Spain

A NDALUSIA IS A LAND of fortified wines, and the best of these is *Jerez* (sherry). Andalusians drink the light, dry fino and manzanilla styles of sherry as wines (they only have 15.5 per cent alcohol) – always chilled, and often as an accompaniment to tapas *(see pp576–7)*. The longer-aged, richer, yet still dry styles of amontillado and oloroso sherry go well with the cured *jamón serrano (see p574)*. Other wines include fino, which may or may not be fortified, and Madeira-like Málaga.

González Byass logo

Working the soil in Jerez

Tío Pepe *is one of the finos of Jerez, which are noted for their bouquet of flor (yeast), pale colour and appetizing finish.*

WINE REGIONS

The Jerez wine region covers the chalky downs between the towns of Jerez, Sanlúcar and El Puerto de Santa María. South of the Montilla-Moriles region are Málaga's vineyards, which have been reduced by urban development.

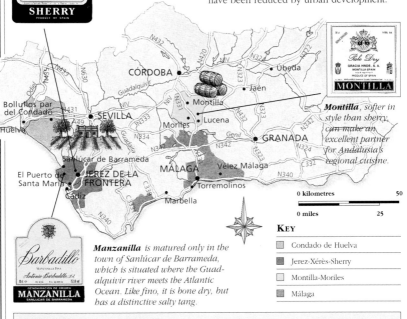

Montilla, softer in style than sherry, can make an excellent partner for Andalusia's regional cuisine.

Manzanilla *is matured only in the town of Sanlúcar de Barrameda, which is situated where the Guadalquivir river meets the Atlantic Ocean. Like fino, it is bone dry, but has a distinctive salty tang.*

KEY

☐	Condado de Huelva
☐	Jerez-Xérès-Sherry
☐	Montilla-Moriles
☐	Málaga

0 kilometres   50
0 miles   25

KEY FACTS ABOUT WINES OF SOUTHERN SPAIN

Location and Climate
The Jerez region has one of the sunniest climates in Europe – summer heat tempered by ocean breezes. The best type of soil is white, chalky *albariza*. In Montilla it is more clayey.

Grape Varieties
The best dry sherry is produced from the Palomino grape. Pedro Ximénez is used for the sweeter styles and is the main grape in Montilla and Málaga. Moscatel is also grown in Málaga.

Good Producers
Condado de Huelva: Manuel Sauci Salas (Riodiel), A.Villarán (Pedro Ximénez Villarán). **Jerez:** Barbadillo (Solear), Blázquez (Carta Blanca), Caballero (Puerto), Garvey (San Patricio), González Byass (Alfonso, Tío Pepe), Hidalgo (La Gitana, Napoleón), Lustau, Osborne (Quinta), Pedro Domecq (La Ina), Sandeman. **Montilla-Moriles:** Alvear (C.B., Festival), Gracia Hermanos, Pérez Barquero, Tomás García. **Málaga:** Scholtz Hermanos, López Hermanos.

HOW SHERRY IS MADE

Sherry is mixed from two principal grape varieties: Palomino, which makes a drier, more delicate sherry; and Pedro Ximénez, which is made into a fuller, sweeter type of sherry.

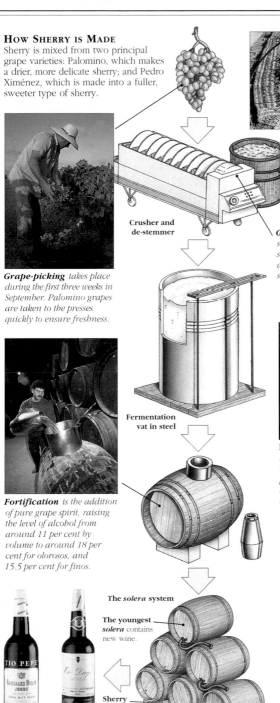

Crusher and de-stemmer

Grape-picking *takes place during the first three weeks in September. Palomino grapes are taken to the presses quickly to ensure freshness.*

Fermentation vat in steel

Fortification *is the addition of pure grape spirit, raising the level of alcohol from around 11 per cent by volume to around 18 per cent for olorosos, and 15.5 per cent for finos.*

The *solera* system

The youngest *solera* contains new wine.

Sherry for bottling is taken from the oldest *solera* on the bottom row.

The finished product

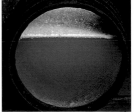

Grape-drying *is only required for Pedro Ximénez grapes. They are laid on esparto mats to shrivel in the sun, concentrating the sugar.*

Grape-pressing *and de-stalking, in cylindrical stainless steel vats, is usually done at night to avoid the searing Andalusian heat.*

Flor, *a yeast, may form on the exposed surface of young wine in the fermentation vat, preventing oxidization and adding a delicate taste. If flor develops, the wine is a fino.*

The solera system *assures that the qualities of a sherry remain constant. The wine from the youngest solera is mixed with the older in the barrels below and as a result takes on its character.*

Moorish Architecture

THE FIRST SIGNIFICANT PERIOD of Moorish architecture
arrived with the Cordoban Caliphate. The Mezquita
was extended lavishly during this period and possesses
all the enduring features of the Moorish style: arches,
stucco work and ornamental use of calligraphy. Later,
the Almohads imported a purer Islamic style, as can
be seen in La Giralda *(see p418–9)*. The Nasrids built
the superbly crafted Alhambra *(see p466–7)* while the
Mudéjares *(see p51)* used their skill to create beautiful
Moorish-style buildings such as the Palacio Pedro I
in Seville's Reales Alcázares *(see pp422–3)*.

Reflections *in water, combined
with an overall play of light, were
central to Moorish architecture.*

Moorish domes
*were frequently
unadorned on the
outside. Inside, an
intricate lattice of
stone ribs supported
the dome's weight.
Like this one in the
Mezquita* (see pp456–
7), *they were inlaid
with multi-coloured
mosaics featuring
stylized flowers.*

Defensive walls

Moorish gardens were
often arranged around
gently rippling pools
and channels.

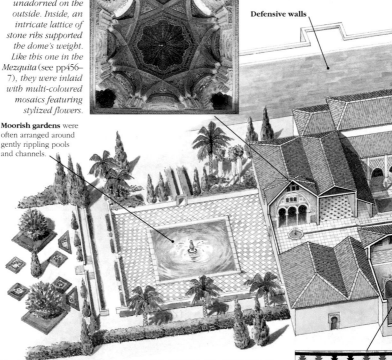

DEVELOPMENT OF MOORISH ARCHITECTURE

Pre-Caliphal era 710–929	Caliphal era 929–1031	Almoravid and Almohad era 1091–1248	Nasrid era 1238–1492
	1031–91 *Taifa* period *(see p50)*		c.1350 Alhambra palace

700	800	900	1000	1100	1200	1300	1400
	785 Mezquita in Córdoba begun		**1184** La Giralda in Seville begun		**c.1350** Palacio Pedro I		
		936 Medina Azahara near Córdoba begun		**Mudéjar era, after c.1215**			

Azulejos (see p420), *glaze
tiles, often adorned walls i
geometric patterns, as here
the Reales Alcázares (p422*

MOORISH ARCHES

The Moorish arch was developed from the horseshoe arch that the Visigoths used in the construction of churches. The Moors modified it and used it as the basis of great architectural endeavours, such as the Mezquita. Subsequent arches show more sophisticated ornamentation and the slow demise of the basic horseshoe shape.

Caliphal arch, Medina Azahara *(see p453)*

Almohad arch, Reales Alcázares *(see p422)*

Mudéjar arch, Reales Alcázares *(see p422)*

Nasrid arch, the Alhambra *(see p466)*

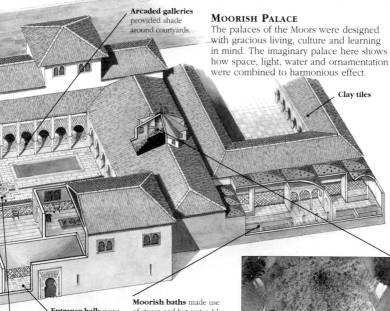

Arcaded galleries provided shade around courtyards.

MOORISH PALACE

The palaces of the Moors were designed with gracious living, culture and learning in mind. The imaginary palace here shows how space, light, water and ornamentation were combined to harmonious effect.

Clay tiles

Entrance halls were complex to confuse unwanted visitors.

Moorish baths made use of steam and hot water. Like Roman baths, they often had underfloor heating.

Water *cooled the Moors' elegant courtyards and served a contemplative purpose, as here in the Patio de los Leones in the Alhambra* (see p467).

Elaborate stucco work *typifies the Nasrid style of architecture. The Sala de los Abencerrajes in the Alhambra* (see p467) *was built using only the simplest materials, but it is nevertheless widely regarded as one of the most outstanding monuments of the period of the Moorish occupation.*

Flamenco, the Soul of Andalusia

Seville feria poster 1953

MORE THAN JUST A DANCE, flamenco is a forceful artistic expression of the sorrows and joys of life. Although it has interpreters all over Spain and even the world, it is a uniquely Andalusian art form, traditionally performed by gypsies. There are many styles of *cante* (song) from different parts of Andalusia, but no strict choreography – dancers improvise from basic movements, following the rhythm of the guitar and their feelings. Flamenco was neglected in the 1960s and 1970s, but recent years have seen a revival of serious interest in traditional styles and the development of exciting new forms.

***Sevillanas**, a folk dance that strongly influenced flamenco, is danced by Andalusians in their bars and homes.*

At a *tablao* (flamenco club) there will be at least four people on stage, including the hand clapper.

The origins of flamenco *are hard to trace. Gypsies may have been the main creators of the art, mixing their own Indian-influenced culture with existing Moorish and Andalusian folklore, and with Jewish and Christian music. There were gypsies in Andalusia by the early Middle Ages, but only in the 18th century did flamenco begin to develop into its present form.*

THE SPANISH GUITAR

Classical guitar

The guitar has a major role in flamenco, traditionally accompanying the singer. The flamenco guitar developed from the modern classical guitar, which evolved in Spain in the 19th century. Flamenco guitars have a lighter, shallower construction and a thickened plate below the soundhole, used to tap rhythms. Today, flamenco guitarists often perform solo. One of the greatest, Paco de Lucía, began by accompanying singers and dancers, before making his debut as a soloist in 1968. His inventive style, which combines traditional playing with Latin, jazz and rock elements, has influenced many musicians outside the realm of flamenco, such as the group Ketama, who play flamenco-blues.

Expert guitarist Paco de Lucía

Singing *is an integral part of flamenco and the singer often performs solo. Camarón de la Isla (1952 – 92), a gypsy born near Cádiz, was among the most famous contemporary* cantaores *(flamenco singers). He began as a singer of expressive* cante jondo *(literally, "deep songs"), from which he developed his own, rock-influenced style. He has inspired many singers.*

WHERE TO ENJOY FLAMENCO

Most of the leading performers are based in Madrid (see p306). In Granada, Sacromonte's caves (p465) are an exciting venue. In Seville, the Barrio de Santa Cruz (pp414–23) has good tablaos.

The proud yet graceful posture of the *bailaora* is suggestive of a restrained passion.

A harsh, vibrating voice is typical of the singer.

La Chanca *is a* bailaora *(female dancer) who is renowned for her fiery and forceful movements. Cristina Hoyos, another dancer famous for her highly polished personal style, leads her own flamenco dance company, which received world-wide acclaim in the 1980s.*

Traditional polka-dot dress

The bailaor *(male dancer) plays a less important role than the* bailaora. *However, many have achieved fame, including Antonio Canales. He has introduced a new beat through his original foot movements.*

THE FLAMENCO TABLAO
These days it is rare to come across spontaneous dancing at a *tablao,* but if dancers and singers are inspired, an impressive show usually results. Artists performing with *duende* ("magic spirit") will hear appreciative *olés* from the audience.

FLAMENCO RHYTHM
The unmistakable rhythm of flamenco is created by the guitar. Just as important, however, is the beat created by hand-clapping and by the dancer's feet in high-heeled shoes. The *bailaoras* may also beat a rhythm with castanets; Lucero Tena (born in 1939) became famous for her solos on castanets. Graceful hand movements are used to express the dancer's feelings of the moment – whether pain, sorrow, or happiness. Like the movements of the rest of the body, they are not choreographed, and the styles used vary from person to person.

Castanets made of wood

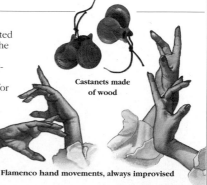

Flamenco hand movements, always improvised

EL ARENAL

OUNDED BY the Río Guadalquivir and guarded by the 13th-century Torre del Oro, El Arenal used to be a district of munitions stores and shipyards. Today this quarter is dominated by the dazzling white bullring, the Plaza de Toros de la Maestranza, where the Sevillians have been staging *corridas* for more than two centuries. The many bars and bodegas in the neighbouring streets are especially busy during the summer bullfighting season.

Once central to the city's life, the influence of the Guadalquivir declined as it silted up during the 17th century. By then El Arenal had become a notorious underworld haunt clinging to the city walls. The river was converted into a canal in the early 20th century but restored to its former navigable glory in time for Expo '92. The east bank was transformed into a tree-lined promenade with excellent views of Triana and La Isla de la Cartuja across the water *(see p428)*.

The Hospital de la Caridad testifies to the city's continuing love affair with the Baroque. Its church is filled with famous paintings by Murillo, and the story of the Seville School is told in the immaculately restored Museo de Bellas Artes further north. The city's stunning collection of art includes great works by Zurbarán, Murillo and Valdés Leal.

Torre del Oro shown on 20th-century tiles

SIGHTS AT A GLANCE

Historic Buildings
Hospital de la Caridad 4
Plaza de Toros de la Maestranza 3
Torre del Oro 5

Museums
Museo de Bellas Artes 1

Churches
Iglesia de la Magdalena 2

GETTING THERE
This area is well served by the orange Tussam buses. Take the C4, which runs along the Paseo de Colón. Alternatively, use one of the numerous routes to Plaza Nueva.

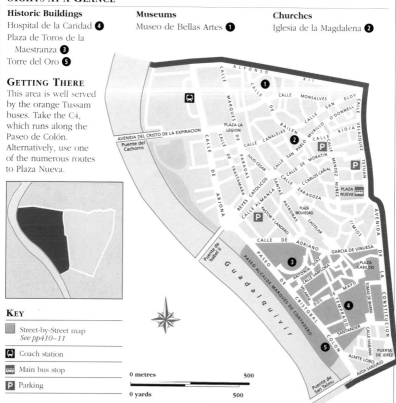

KEY

▨	Street-by-Street map *See pp410–11*
🚌	Coach station
🚌	Main bus stop
P	Parking

0 metres 500
0 yards 500

◁ **Pasting up an advertisement for a bullfight on the walls of the Plaza de Toros de la Maestranza**

Street-by-Street: El Arenal

ONCE HOME TO THE PORT of Seville, El Arenal also housed the ammunition works and the artillery headquarters. Now its atmosphere is set by the city's bullring, the majestic Plaza de Toros de la Maestranza. During the bullfighting season *(see p412)* the area's bars and restaurants are packed, but for the rest of the year El Arenal's backstreets remain quiet. The riverfront is dominated by one of Seville's best-known monuments, the Moorish Torre del Oro, while the long, tree-lined promenade beside the Paseo de Cristóbal Colón is perfect for a slow, romantic walk along the Guadalquivir.

Statue of Carmen

★ **Plaza de Toros de la Maestranza**
Seville's 18th-century bullring, one of Spain's oldest, has a Baroque façade in white and ochre ❸

Carmen
(see p427), sculpted in bronze, stands opposite the bullring.

CALLE DE ADRIANO

CALLE ANTONIA DÍAZ

PASEO DE CRISTÓBAL COLÓN

The Teatro de la Maestranza, a show-piece theatre and opera house, was opened in 1991. Home of the Orquesta Sinfónica de Sevilla, the theatre also features international opera and dance companies.

Paseo Alcalde Marqués de Contadero

STAR SIGHTS

★ **Plaza de Toros de la Maestranza**

★ **Hospital de la Caridad**

★ **Torre del Oro**

The Guadalquivir used to cause catastrophic inundations. Following floods in 1947 a barrage was constructed. Today, tourists enjoy peaceful boat trips, starting from the Torre del Oro.

El Buzo ("The Diver") is one of many traditional tapas bars and *freidurías* on or just off Calle Arfe. Nearby is Mesón Sevilla Jabugo I, a bar where jamón ibérico *(see p438)* is served.

LOCATOR MAP
See Street Finder map 3

El Postigo is an arts and crafts market.

GARCÍA VINUESA

To the Cathedral

El Torno, in the secluded Plaza de Cabildo, sells sweets made in a convent.

ARFE

AVENDA DE LA CONSTITUCIÓN

DE MAYO

TOMÁS DE IBARRA

TEMPRADO

★ Hospital de la Caridad
The walls of this Baroque hospital church are hung with fine paintings by Bartolomé Esteban Murillo and Juan de Valdés Leal ❹

To Reales Alcázares

Maestranza de Artillería

CALLE SANTANDER

Bodegón Torre del Oro
(see p600)

| 0 metres | 75 |
| 0 yards | 75 |

KEY

– – – Suggested route

★ Torre del Oro
Built in the 13th century to protect the port, this crenellated Moorish tower now houses a small maritime museum ❺

Madonna and Child in the Baroque Iglesia de la Magdalena

Museo de Bellas Artes ❶

Plaza del Museo 9. **Map** 1 B5. 95 422 07 90. 43, C3. 3–8pm Tue, 9am–8pm Wed–Sat, 9am–2pm Sun Groups of 20: by appt. (free for EU citizens)

T HE CONVENTO de la Merced Calzada has been restored to create one of the best art museums in Spain. Completed in 1612 by Juan de Oviedo, the building is designed around three patios which today are adorned with trees, flowers and some fine *azulejos (see p420).* The Patio Mayor is the largest of these, remodelled by the architect Leonardo de Figueroa in 1724. The convent church is notable for its Baroque domed ceiling, painted by Domingo Martínez.

The museum's collection of Spanish art and sculpture, from the medieval to the modern, focuses on the work of Seville School artists. Among the star attractions is *La Servilleta*, a Virgin and Child (1665–8), which is said to be painted on a napkin *(servilleta)*. One of Murillo's most popular works, it may be seen in the restored convent church. The boisterous *La Inmaculada* (1672) by Juan de Valdés Leal is on display in a gallery devoted to the artist's forceful religious

San Jerónimo Penitente in the Museo de Bellas Artes

paintings. The museum also contains several fine works by Zurbarán including *San Hugo en el Refectorio* (1655), which was painted for the monastery at La Cartuja *(see p428).*

Iglesia de la Magdalena ❷

Calle San Pablo 10. **Map** 3 B1. 95 422 96 03. 43. 7:30–11am, 6:30–9pm Mon–Sat, 7:30am–1:30pm, 6:30–9pm Sun.

T HIS IMMENSE BAROQUE church by Leonardo de Figueroa, completed in 1709, is gradually being restored to its former glory. In its southwest corner stands the Capilla de la Quinta Angustia, a Mudéjar chapel with three cupolas. This chapel survived from an earlier church where the great Seville School painter Bartolomé Murillo was baptized in 1618. The font that was used for his baptism is now in the baptistry of the present building. The church's west front is topped by a belfry which is painted in vivid colours.

Among the religious works in the church are a painting by Francisco de Zurbarán, *St Dominic in Soria*, housed in the Capilla Sacramental (to the right of the south door), and frescoes by Lucas Valdés over the sanctuary. On the wall of the north transept there is a cautionary fresco of a medieval *auto-da-fé (see p264).*

Plaza de Toros de la Maestranza ❸

Paseo de Cristóbal Colón 12. **Map** 3 B2. 95 422 45 77. C4, 12. 9:30am–2pm, 3–7pm daily.

S EVILLE'S FAMOUS bullring, built between 1761–1881, is arguably the most magnificent in Spain and well worth a visit.

The arcaded arena holds up to 14,000 spectators. Guided tours of this immense building start from the main entrance on Paseo de Cristóbal Colón. On the west side is the Puerta del Príncipe (Prince's Gate), through which the triumphant matadors are carried aloft by admirers from the crowd.

Just beyond the *enfermería* (emergency hospital) is a museum of portraits, posters and costumes, including a purple cape painted by Pablo Picasso. The tour continues on to the chapel where matadors pray for success, and then to the stables where the horses of the *picadores* (lance-carrying horsemen) are kept.

The bullfighting season starts on Easter Sunday and continues intermittently until October. Most *corridas* take place on Sunday evenings. Tickets can be bought from the *taquilla* (booking office) at the bullring.

Next door to the Plaza de Toros, and echoing its circular bulk, is the Teatro de la Maestranza. Seville's austere opera house and theatre, designed by Luis Marín de Terán and Aurelio de Pozo, opened in 1991. Fragments of ironwork from the 19th-century ammunition works that first occupied the site adorn the river façade.

Arcaded arena of the Plaza de Toros de la Maestranza, begun in 1761

Finis Gloriae Mundi by Juan de Valdés Leal in the Hospital de la Caridad

Hospital de la Caridad ❹

Calle Temprado 3. **Map** 3 B2. 📞 95 422 32 32. 🚌 C4. 🕐 9am–1:30pm, 3:30–7:30pm Mon–Sat, 9am–1pm Sun & public hols. 🏛 🚫

THIS CHARITY HOSPITAL was founded in 1674 and it is still used today as a sanctuary for elderly and infirm people. In the gardens stands a statue of its benefactor, Miguel de Mañara, whose dissolute life before he joined a brotherhood is said to have inspired the story of Don Juan. The façade of the hospital church, with its whitewashed walls, reddish stonework and framed *azulejos*, provides a glorious example of Sevillian Baroque.

Inside are two square patios decorated with plants, 18th-century Dutch tiles, and fine fountains with Italian statues depicting Charity and Mercy. At their northern end a passage to the right leads to another patio, containing a 13th-century arch which survives from the city's shipyards. Here, too, a bust of Mañara stands amid pretty rose bushes.

Inside the church there are a number of original canvases by some of the leading painters of the 17th century, despite the fact that some of its greatest artworks were looted by Marshal Soult during the Napoleonic occupation of 1808–14 *(see p58)*.

Directly above the entrance is the ghoulish *Finis Gloriae Mundi* (The End of the World's Glory) by Juan de Valdés Leal, and opposite hangs his morbid *In Ictu Oculi* (In the Blink of an Eye). Many of the other works that can be seen are by Murillo, including *St John of God Carrying a Sick Man* and portraits of the Child Jesus and *St John the Baptist as a Boy*.

Torre del Oro ❺

Paseo de Cristóbal Colón.
Map 3 B2. 📞 95 422 24 19.
🚌 C2, C3, C4, 21. 🕐 10am–2pm Tue–Fri, 11am–2pm Sat & Sun. ⚫ Aug & Mon. 🏛 (free Tue). 🚫

IN MOORISH SEVILLE the Tower of Gold formed part of the walled defences, linking up with the Reales Alcázares *(see pp422–3)*. It was built as a defensive lookout in 1220, with a companion tower on the opposite bank. A metal chain stretched between them to prevent hostile ships from sailing upriver. The turret was added in 1760. The gold in its name may be the gilded *azulejos* that once clad its walls, or treasures from the Americas unloaded here. The tower has had many uses: a gunpowder store, a chapel, a prison and port offices. Now, as the Museo Marítimo, it exhibits maritime maps and antiques.

The Torre del Oro, built by the Almohads

SEVILLE'S FIESTAS

April Fair *(two weeks after Easter)*. Life in the city moves over the river to the fairground for a week. Here, members of clubs, trade unions and neighbourhood groups meet in numerous *casetas* (entertainment booths) to drink and dance all night to the infectious, non-stop rhythm of *sevillanas*. (Access to booths may be limited to private parties.) Every day, from around 1pm, elegant, traditionally dressed riders on horseback and mantilla-crowned women in open carriages show off their finery in parades. During the afternoons, bullfights are often staged in the Maestranza bullring.

Float in Holy Week procession

Holy Week *(Mar/Apr)*. Over 100 gilded *pasos* (floats bearing religious images) are borne through the streets between Palm Sunday and Easter Day. Singers in the crowds often spontaneously burst into *saetas*, fragments of song in praise of Christ or the Virgin. Emotions are high in the early hours of Good Friday as the images of the Virgen de la Macarena and the Virgen de la Esperanza of Triana emerge from their churches.
Corpus Christi *(May/Jun)*. The *Seises*, boys dressed in Baroque costume, dance before the main altar of the cathedral *(see p419)*.

SANTA CRUZ

SEVILLE'S OLD JEWISH QUARTER, the Barrio de Santa Cruz, is a warren of white alleyways and patios that has long been the most picturesque corner of the city. Many of the best-known sights are located here: the cavernous Gothic cathedral with its landmark tower, La Giralda; the splendid Real Alcázar, with the royal palaces and lush gardens of Pedro I and Carlos V; and the Archivo de Indias, whose documents tell of Spain's exploration and conquest of the Americas.

Spreading northeast from these great monuments is an enchanting maze of whitewashed streets. The Golden Age artist Bartolomé Esteban

Ornate streetlamp, Plaza del Triunfo

Murillo lived here in the 17th century, while his contemporary, Juan de Valdés Leal, decorated the Hospital de los Venerables with superb Baroque frescoes.

Further north is one of Seville's favourite shopping streets, the Calle de las Sierpes. The market squares around it, such as the charming Plaza del Salvador, provided backdrops for some of the stories of Cervantes. Nearby, the ornate façades and interiors of the Ayuntamiento (town hall) and the Casa de Pilatos, a gem of Andalusian architecture, testify to the great wealth that flowed into the city from the New World during the 16th century, much of it spent on art.

SIGHTS AT A GLANCE

Historic Buildings

Archivo de Indias **6**
Ayuntamiento **2**
Casa de Pilatos **4**
Hospital de los Venerables **5**
Real Alcázar pp422–3 **7**

Churches

Cathedral and La Giralda pp418–19 **1**

Streets and Plazas

Calle de las Sierpes **3**

GETTING THERE

This area is well served by orange Tussam buses. Take any of routes 21, 22, 23, 25, 26, 30, 31, 33, 34, 40, 41 or 42 to reach the Avenida de la Constitución, convenient for most of the sights. *Circular* C3 or C4 will take you instead to the Puerta de Jerez.

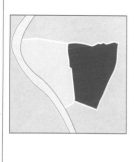

KEY

Street-by-Street map (pp416–17)

Tourist information

0 metres 400
0 yards 400

◁ **La Giralda seen from the gardens of the Real Alcázar**

Street-by-Street: Santa Cruz

Window grille, Santa Cruz

THE MAZE of narrow streets to the east of Seville cathedral and the Real Alcázar represents Seville at its most romantic and compact. As well as the expected souvenir shops, tapas bars and strolling guitarists, there are plenty of picturesque alleys, hidden plazas and flower-decked patios to reward the casual wanderer. Once a Jewish ghetto, its restored buildings, with characteristic window grilles, are now a harmonious mix of up-market residences and tourist accommodation. Good bars and restaurants make the area well worth an evening visit.

Plaza Virgen de los Reyes is often lined by horse-drawn carriages. In the centre of the square is an early 20th-century fountain by José Lafita.

Palacio Arzobispal, the 18th-century Archbishop's Palace, is still used by Seville's clergy.

★ **Cathedral and La Giralda**
This huge Gothic cathedral and its Moorish bell tower are Seville's most popular sights ❶

AVENIDA DE LA CONSTITUCION

Convento de la Encarnación

SANTO TOMAS

ROMERO M

MA

MIGUEL MAÑARA

Museo de Arte Contemporáneo

Plaza del Triunfo has a Baroque column celebrating the city's survival of the great earthquake of 1755. In the centre is a modern statue of the Virgin Mary (Immaculate Conception).

Archivo de Indias
Built in the 16th century as a merchants' exchange, the Archive of the Indies now houses documents relating to the Spanish colonization of the Americas ❻

Calle Mateos Gago is shaded by orange trees and filled with souvenir shops, cafés and tapas bars. Bar Giralda at No. 2, whose vaults are the remains of a Moorish bath house, is popular for its wide variety of tapas.

LOCATOR MAP
See Street Finder maps 3–4

LA MACARENA

EL ARENAL SANTA CRUZ

Guadalquivir

Plaza Santa Cruz is adorned by an ornate iron cross from 1692.

MESON DEL MORO

RODRIGO CARO

XIMENEZ ENCISO

SANTA TERESA

PLAZA STA CRUZ

JAMERDANA

REINOSO

LOPE DE RUEDA

GLORIA

JUSTINO DE NEVE

PL DOÑA ELVIRA

SUSONA

PIMIENTA

CALLEJON DEL AGUA

VIDA

★ Hospital de los Venerables
The 17th-century home for elderly priests has a splendidly restored Baroque church ⑤

Callejón del Agua is a whitewashed alleyway offering glimpses into enchanting plant-filled patios. It is called "Water Street" because it was once a water conduit to the Real Alcázar.

0 metres 50

0 yards 50

★ Real Alcázar
Seville's Royal Palaces are a rewarding combination of exquisite Mudéjar (see pp422–3) craftsmanship, regal grandeur and landscaped gardens ⑦

KEY

— — — Suggested route

STAR SIGHTS

★ **Cathedral and La Giralda**

★ **Hospital de los Venerables**

★ **Real Alcázar**

Seville Cathedral and La Giralda ❶

16th-century stained glass

Sᴇᴠɪʟʟᴇ's ᴄᴀᴛʜᴇᴅʀᴀʟ occupies the site of a great mosque built by the Almohads (see p50) in the late 12th century. La Giralda, its bell tower, and the Patio de los Naranjos are a legacy of this Moorish structure. Work on the Christian cathedral, the largest in Europe, began in 1401 and took just over a century to complete. As well as enjoying its Gothic immensity and the works of art in its chapels and sacristy, visitors can climb La Giralda for stunning views over the city.

★ La Giralda
The bell tower is crowned by a bronze weathervane (giraldillo) *portraying Faith, from which it takes its name. A replica has replaced the original vane.*

Entrance

★ Patio de los Naranjos
In Moorish times worshippers would wash their hands and feet in the fountain under the orange trees before praying.

Tʜᴇ Rɪsᴇ ᴏғ Lᴀ Gɪʀᴀʟᴅᴀ

The tower was built as a minaret in 1198. In the 14th century the bronze spheres at its top were replaced by Christian symbols. A new belfry was planned in 1557, but built to a more ornate design by Hernán Ruiz in 1568.

1198

1400

1557 (plan)

1568

Puerta del Perdón

Roman pillars
brought from Itálica (see p452) surround the cathedral steps.

Retablo Mayor
Santa María de la Sede, the cathedral's patron saint, sits at the high altar below a waterfall of gold. The 44 gilded relief panels of the reredos were carved by Spanish and Flemish sculptors between 1482 and 1564.

**The Sacristía
Mayor** houses
many works of
art, including
paintings by
Murillo.

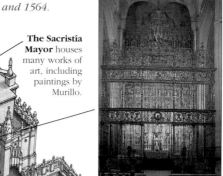

★ **Capilla Mayor**
*Monumental iron grilles
forged in 1518–32
enclose the main
chapel, which is
dominated by the
overwhelming
Retablo Mayor.*

**The Tomb of
Columbus** dates from
the 1890s. His coffin
is carried by bearers
representing the king-
doms of Castile, León,
Aragón and Navarra *(see p50).*

**Puerta
del Bautismo**

Iglesia del Sagrario,
a large 17th-century
chapel, is now used
as a parish church.

STAR FEATURES

★ **La Giralda**

★ **Patio de los
Naranjos**

★ **Capilla Mayor**

Puerta de la Asunción
*Though Gothic in style, this portal
was not completed until 1833. A
stone relief of the Assumption of the
Virgin decorates the tympanum.*

Genoese fountain in the Mudéjar Patio Principal of the Casa de Pilatos

Ayuntamiento ❷

Plaza Nueva 1. **Map** 3 C1. ☎ 95 459 01 01. 🚌 21, 23, 25, 30, 33, 34, 35. ◐ 5:30–6:30pm Tue–Thu, 11:30am–12:30pm Sat. Ø
🆆 www.ayunt-sevilla.es

SEVILLE'S CITY HALL stands between the Plaza de San Francisco, where *autos-da-fé* (public trials of heretics) were held, and the Plaza Nueva.

Building was completed between 1527 and 1534. The side bordering the Plaza de San Francisco is a fine example of ornate Plateresque style *(see p21)* favoured by the architect Diego de Riaño. The west front is Neo-Classical, built in 1891. Sculpted ceilings survive in the vestibule and the lower Casa Consistorial (Council Meeting Room), containing Velázquez's *Imposition of the Chasuble on St Ildefonso*. The upper Casa Consistorial has a dazzling coffered ceiling and paintings by Zurbarán and Valdés Leal.

Calle de las Sierpes ❸

Map 3 C1. 🚌 21, 30. **Casa de la Condesa Lebrija** ☎ 95 421 81 83. ◐ 10:30am–1pm, 4:30–7pm Mon–Fri, 10am–1pm Sat.

SEVILLE'S MAIN shopping promenade, the "Street of the Snakes", runs north from Plaza de San Francisco. Long-established stores selling hats, fans and traditional *mantillas* (lace headdresses) stand alongside clothes and souvenir shops. The parallel streets of Cuna and Tetuán also offer some enjoyable window-shopping. Halfway up the road walking north, Calle Jovellanos to the left leads to the 17th-century Capillita de San José. Further on, at the junction with Calle Pedro Caravaca, is the anachronistic, upholstered world of the Real Círculo de Labradores, a private men's club founded in 1856.

Opposite – with its entrance in Calle Cuna – is a 15th-century private mansion, the Casa de la Condesa Lebrija. Among the Lebrija family's treasures on display is a Roman mosaic from the ruins of nearby Itálica *(see p452)* and a collection of *azulejos*

Right at the end of the street, take the opportunity to buy a cake in La Campana, Seville's best-known *pastelería*.

Casa de Pilatos ❹

Plaza de Pilatos 1. **Map** 4 D1. ☎ 95 422 52 98. 🚌 C3, C4. ◐ **Ground floor** 9am–6pm in winter, 9am–7pm in summer. **First floor** 10am–2pm, 3–7pm. 📷 🎫 Ø ♿ ground floor.

ENRAPTURED BY by the architectural and decorative wonders of High Renaissance Italy and the Holy Land, the first Marquis of Tarifa built the Casa de Pilatos. So called because it was thought to resemble Pontius Pilate's home in Jerusalem, today it is the residence of the Dukes of Medinaceli and is one of the finest palaces in Seville.

Visitors enter through a marble portal, commissioned by the Marquis in 1529 from Genoese craftsmen. Across the arcaded Apeadero (carriage yard) is the Patio Principal. This courtyard is essentially Mudéjar *(see p51)* in style and decorated with *azulejos* and intricate plasterwork. In its corners are three Roman statues, depicting Minerva, a dancing muse and Ceres, and a Greek statue of Athena, dating from the 5th century BC. In its centre is a fountain which was imported from Genoa. To the right, through the Salón del Pretorio with its coffered ceiling and marquetry, is the Corredor de

---

AZULEJOS

Colourful *azulejos*, glazed ceramic tiles, are a striking feature of Seville. The craft was introduced to Spain by the Moors, who created fantastic mosaics in sophisticated geometric patterns for palace walls – the word *azulejo* derives from the Arabic for "little stone". New techniques were introduced in the 16th century and later mass production extended their use to decorative signs, shop façades and advertising hoardings.

Azulejo billboard for Studebaker Motor Cars (1924), Calle Tetuán

Fresco by Juan de Valdés Leal in the Hospital de los Venerables

Zaquizamí. The antiquities on display in adjacent rooms include a bas-relief of *Leda and the Swan* and two Roman reliefs commemorating the Battle of Actium of 31 BC.

Coming back to the Patio Principal, you turn right into the Salón de Descanso de los Jueces. Beyond is a rib-vaulted Gothic chapel, with Mudéjar plasterwork walls and ceiling. On the altar is a copy of a 4th-century sculpture in the Vatican, *The Good Shepherd*. Left through the Gabinete de Pilatos, with its small central fountain, is the Jardín Grande.

Returning once more to the main patio, behind the statue of Ceres, a tiled staircase leads to the upper floor. It is roofed with a wonderful *media naranja* (half orange) cupola built in 1537. There are Mudéjar ceilings in some rooms, which are filled with family portraits, antiques and furniture.

Hospital de los Venerables ❺

Plaza de los Venerables 8. **Map** 3 C2.
📞 95 456 26 96. 🚌 C3, C4. 🕐
10am–2pm, 4–8pm daily. 🔴 25 Dec,
1 Jan, Good Friday. 🎫 ♿ 📷

SET IN THE HEART of the Barrio de Santa Cruz, this home for elderly priests was begun in 1675 and completed around 20 years later by Leonardo de Figueroa. It has recently been restored as a cultural centre by FOCUS (Fundación Fondo de Cultura de Sevilla).

Stairs from the central, rose-coloured, sunken patio lead to the upper floors, which, along with the infirmary and cellar, are used as exhibition galleries.

A separate guided tour visits the Hospital church, a show-case of Baroque splendours, with frescoes by both Juan de Valdés Leal and his son Lucas Valdés. Other highlights of the church include sculptures of St Peter and St Ferdinand by Pedro Roldán, flanking the east door; and *The Apotheosis of St Ferdinand* by Lucas Valdés, top centre in the reredos of the main altar. Its frieze (inscribed in Greek) advises to "Fear God and Honour the Priest".

In the sacristy, the ceiling has an effective *trompe l'oeil* depicting *The Triumph of the Cross* by Juan de Valdés Leal.

Archivo de Indias ❻

Avda de la Constitución. **Map** 3 C2.
📞 95 421 12 34. 🚌 C3, C4, 21, 26,
31, 33, 34, 40. 🔴 closed for
refurbishment until 2003. 📷

THE ARCHIVE of the Indies illustrates Seville's pre-eminent role in the coloniza-tion and exploitation of the New World. Built between 1584–98 to designs by Juan de Herrera, co-architect of El Escorial *(see pp312–13)*, it was originally a *lonja* (exchange), where merchants traded. In 1785, Carlos III had all Spanish documents relating to the "Indies" collected under one roof. Among the archive's 86 million handwritten pages and 8,000 maps and drawings are letters from Columbus, Cortés, and Cervantes and the extensive correspondence of Felipe II. Some documents are now stored on CD-ROM.

Upstairs, the library rooms contain regularly changing displays of drawings, maps and facsimile documents.

Façade of the Archivo de Indias by Juan de Herrera

Real Alcázar ❼

Mudéjar stucco

IN 1364 PEDRO I ordered the construction of a royal residence within the palaces which had been built by the city's Almohad *(see p50)* rulers. Within two years, craftsmen from Granada and Toledo had created a jewel box of Mudéjar patios and halls, the Palacio Pedro I, now at the heart of Seville's Real Alcázar. Later monarchs added their own distinguishing marks: Isabel I *(see p52)* dispatched navigators to explore the New World from her Casa de la Contratación, while Carlos I (the Holy Roman Emperor Charles V – *see p54*) had grandiose, richly decorated apartments built.

Jardín de Troya

Gardens of the Alcázar
Laid out with terraces, fountains and pavilions, these gardens provide a delightful refuge from the heat and bustle of Seville.

★ Charles V Rooms
Vast tapestries and lively 16th-century azulejos *decorate the vaulted halls of the apartments and chapel of Charles V.*

Patio del Crucero lies above the old baths.

PLAN OF THE REAL ALCÁZAR

The complex has been the home of Spanish kings for almost seven centuries. The palace's upper floor is used by the royal family today.

KEY

☐ Area illustrated above

☐ Gardens

★ Patio de las Doncellas
The Patio of the Maidens boasts plasterwork by the top craftsmen of Granada.

★ Salón de Embajadores
Built in 1427, the dazzling dome of the Ambassadors' Hall is of carved and gilded, interlaced wood.

VISITORS' CHECKLIST

Patio de Banderas. **Map** 3 C2. 📞
95 450 23 23. 🚌 *C3, C4, 23, 25, 26.* ⏰ *9:30am–7pm Tue–Sat, 9:30am–5pm Sun & public hols (Oct–Mar: until 5pm Tue–Sat).* 🎫

Horseshoe Arches
Azulejos and complex plasterwork decorate the Ambassadors' Hall, which has three symmetrically arranged, ornate archways, each with three horseshoe arches.

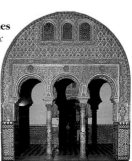

Casa de la Contratación

The Patio de la Montería was where the court met before hunting expeditions.

Patio de las Muñecas
The Patio of the Dolls and its surrounding bedrooms formed the domestic heart of the palace. It derives its name from two tiny faces on one of its arches.

The façade of the Palacio Pedro I is a prime example of Mudéjar style.

Puerta del León (entrance)

Patio del Yeso
The Patio of Plaster, a garden with flower beds and a water channel, retains features of the earlier, 12th-century Almohad Alcázar.

STAR FEATURES

★ **Charles V Rooms**

★ **Patio de las Doncellas**

★ **Salón de Embajadores**

FURTHER AFIELD

THE NORTH OF Seville, La Macarena, is a character-ful mix of decaying Baroque and Mudéjar churches, and old-style tapas bars. The place to visit here is the Basílica de la Macarena, a shrine to Seville's much-venerated Virgen de la Esperanza Macarena. Among the many convents and churches in the area, the Convento de Santa Paula offers a rare opportunity to peep behind the walls of an enclosed community.

The area south of the city is dominated by the exten-sive, leafy Parque María Luisa. A large part of the park originally formed the grounds of the Baroque Palacio de San Telmo. Many of the historic build-ings in the park were erected for the Ibero-American Exposition of 1929. The grand five-star Hotel Alfonso XIII

and the crescent-shaped Plaza de España are the most striking legacies of this upsurge of Andalusian pride. Nearby is the Royal Tobacco Factory, forever associated with the fictional gypsy heroine Carmen, who toiled in its sultry halls. Today, it is part of the Universidad, Seville's university.

There is more to see across the river from the city centre. With its cobbled streets and shops selling ceramics, the Triana quarter retains the feel of old Seville. In the 15th century a Carthusian monastery, the Monasterio de Santa María de las Cuevas, was built north of Triana. Columbus resided there and, largely due to this connection, the area around it, the Isla de la Cartuja, was chosen as the site for Expo '92. Today the site is being developed as cultural and educational theme parks.

**Roman column,
Alameda de Hércules**

SIGHTS AT A GLANCE

Historic Buildings
Palacio de San Telmo ❹
Universidad ❺

Churches and Convents
Basílica de la Macarena ❶
Convento de Santa Paula ❷
Iglesia de San Pedro ❸

Historic Areas
Isla de la Cartuja ❽
Parque María Luisa ❻
Triana ❼

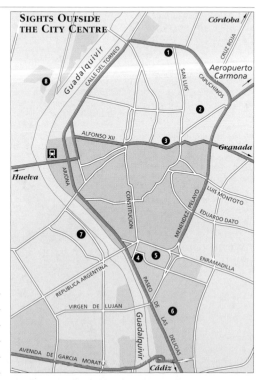

**SIGHTS OUTSIDE
THE CITY CENTRE**

Córdoba

Aeropuerto
Carmona

Granada

Huelva

Cádiz

0 kilometres   1
0 miles   0.5

KEY

▢ City centre

▢ Parks and open spaces

🚉 Railway station

▬ Major road

═ Minor road

◁ **Pabellón de Andalucía, built on the Isla de la Cartuja for Expo '92**

St John the Baptist by Montañés
in the Convento de Santa Paula

Basílica de la Macarena ❶

Calle Bécquer 1. **Map** 2 D3.
[95 437 01 95. 🚌 C1, C2, 2, 10, 13, 14. ◯ 9:30am–1pm, 5–9pm daily. ● Easter hols. **Treasury**
◯ 9:30am–1pm, 5–8pm daily.

THE BASÍLICA de la Macarena was built in 1949 in the Neo-Baroque style by Gómez Millán as a new home for the much-loved Virgen de la Esperanza Macarena. It butts on to the 13th-century Iglesia de San Gil, where the image was housed until a fire in 1936.

The image of the Virgin, standing above the main altar amid waterfalls of gold and silver, has been attributed to Luisa Roldán (1656–1703), the most talented female artist of the Seville School. The wall-paintings, by Rafael Rodríguez Hernández, date from 1982.

The Virgin's magnificent pro-cessional gowns and jewels are held in the Treasury museum.

Convento de Santa Paula ❷

C/ Santa Paula 11. **Map** 2 E5. [95 453 63 30. 🚌 10, 11. ◯ 10am–12:45pm, 4:30–6pm Tue–Sun. Groups only in the morning. 🖼 📱

FOUNDED IN 1475, Santa Paula is a working convent and home to 40 nuns. The museum consists of two galleries filled with religious artifacts and

paintings. Marmalades and jams, made by the nuns, are sold in a room by the exit. The nave of the convent church has an elaborate wooden roof, dating from 1623. Among the statues in the church are St John the Evangelist and St John the Baptist, both the work of Juan Martínez Montañés.

Iglesia de San Pedro ❸

Plaza San Pedro. **Map** 2 D5. [95 421 68 58. 🚌 10, 11, 12, 24, 27, 32. ◯ 8:30–11:30am, 7–8:30pm Mon–Sat, 9:30am–1:30pm, 7–8:30pm Sun. 📱

DIEGO VELAZQUEZ, the Golden Age painter *(see p28)*, was baptized in this church in 1599. It is built in a typically Sevil-lian mix of architectural styles. Mudéjar elements survive in the lobed brickwork of its tower, which is surmounted by a Baroque *(see p21)* belfry. The principal portal – facing the Plaza de San Pedro – is also Baroque, and was added by Diego de Quesada in 1613.

The poorly lit interior has a Mudéjar wooden ceiling and west door. The vault of one of its chapels is decorated with exquisite geometric patterns of interlacing bricks.

Behind the church, in Calle Doña María Coronel, cakes are sold from a revolving drum in the wall of the 14th-century Convento de Santa Inés. Fronting its church is an arcaded patio, decorated with 17th-century frescoes by Francisco de Herrera.

Modern tilework adorning the front of the Iglesia de San Pedro

Palacio de San Telmo ❹

Avenida de Roma. **Map** 3 C3. [95 503 55 05. 🚌 C3, C4, 5, 34. ◯ by appointment only. 📱 🚫 📱

THIS IMPOSING PALACE, named after the patron saint of navigators, was built in 1682 as a university to train ships' pilots, navigators and high-ranking officers. In 1849 the palace became the residence of the Dukes of Monpensier and until 1893 its vast grounds included what is now the Parque María Luisa. Today it is the presidential headquarters of the Junta de Andalucía (the regional government).

The most striking feature of the Palacio de San Telmo is the

Parque María Luisa ❻

Map 4 D4. 🚌 C1, C2, 30, 31, 33, 34. 📱 **Museo Arqueológico** [95 423 24 01. ◯ 3–8pm Tue, 9am–8pm Wed–Sat, 9am–2pm Sun. 🖼 (free for EU citizens). 🚫 **Museo de Artes y Costumbres Populares**
[95 423 25 76. ◯ as above. 🖼 🚫 📱

PRINCESS MARIA LUISA donated part of the grounds of the Palacio de San Telmo to the city for this park in 1893.

Plaza de España
was built in a theatrical style by Aníbal González.

The Glorieta de Bécquer
is an arbour with sculpted figures depicting the phases of love – a tribute to poet Gustavo Adolfo Bécquer.

exuberant Churrigueresque portal designed by Leonardo de Figueroa, and completed in 1734. Surrounding the Ionic columns are allegorical figures representing the Sciences and Arts. St Telmo, holding a ship and charts, is flanked by the sword-bearing St Ferdinand and St Hermenegildo, with a cross. On the north façade is ranged a row of sculptures of Sevillian celebrities, added by Susillo in 1895. Among them are artists such as Montañés, Murillo and Velázquez.

Opposite is Seville's most famous hotel, the Alfonso XIII, dating from the 1920s. Its centrepiece is a grand patio with a fountain and orange trees. Non-residents are welcome to visit the bar and the restaurant.

Universidad ❺

Calle San Fernando 4. **Map** 3 C3.
📞 95 455 10 00. 🚌 C3, C4, 5, 25, 26, 34. 🕐 8am – 8:30pm Mon – Fri.
⬤ public hols.

THE FORMER Real Fábrica de Tabacos (Royal Tobacco Factory) is now part of Seville University. In the 19th century, three-quarters of Europe's cigars were manufactured here, rolled by 10,000 *cigarreras* (female cigar-makers). It was these hot-blooded *cigarreras* who inspired French author Mérimée to create his famous gypsy heroine, *Carmen*.

Built in 1728–71, the factory complex is the largest building in Spain after El Escorial (*see pp312–13*) near Madrid.

Baroque fountain in one of the patios in the Universidad

The moat and watchtowers are evidence of the importance given to protecting the king's lucrative tobacco monopoly.

Landscaped by Jean Forestier, director of the Bois de Boulogne in Paris, as the leafy setting for the 1929 Ibero-American Exposition. The legacies of this extravaganza are the Plaza de España, decorated with regional scenes on ceramic tiles, and the Plaza de América, both the work of Aníbal González.

On the latter, in the Pabellón Mudéjar, the Museo de Artes y Costumbres Populares displays traditional Andalusian folk arts. The Neo-Renaissance Pabellón de las Bellas Artes houses the provincial Museo Arqueológico. Exhibits devoted to the Roman era include statues and fragments found at Itálica (*see p452*).

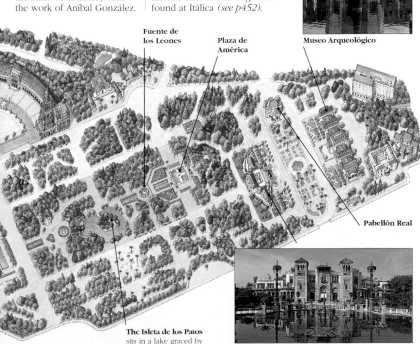

Fuente de los Leones

Plaza de América

Museo Arqueológico

Pabellón Real

The Isleta de los Patos sits in a lake graced by ducks and swans.

Museo de Artes y Costumbres Populares

Decorative tiles at Cerámica Santa Ana, a popular ceramics shop in Triana

Triana 7

Map 3 A2. 🚍 *C3, 40, 43.*

THIS CLOSE-KNIT AREA, named after the Roman Emperor Trajan, was once Seville's gypsy quarter. Triana remains a traditional working-class district, with compact, flower-filled streets and a tangibly independent atmosphere. For centuries it has been famous for its potteries. The best-known of its ceramics shops today is Cerámica Santa Ana at No. 31 Calle San Jorge.

A good way to approach Triana is across the Puente de Isabel II, leading to the Plaza del Altozano. This square has glass-fronted, wrought-iron balconies called *miradores*. Nearby is one of the characteristic streets of the area, the Calle Rodrigo de Triana, with its houses painted in white and ochre. It is named after the Andalusian sailor who was the first to sight the shores of the New World on Columbus's momentous voyage of 1492.

The Iglesia de Santa Ana, founded in the 13th century and splendidly renovated, is Triana's most popular church. In the baptistry is the Gypsy Font, which is believed to pass on the gift of flamenco song to the children of the faithful.

Isla de la Cartuja 8

Map 1 B2. 📞 *95 446 00 89.*
🌐 *www.junta-andalucia.es-cultura*
🚍 *C1, C2.* **Monasterio de Santa María de las Cuevas** ⬜ *Apr–Sep: 10am–9pm Tue–Sat, 10am–3pm Sun; Oct–Mar: 10am–8pm Tue–Sat, 10am–3pm Sun.* 🔲 🔥 **Centro Andaluz de Arte Contemporaneo** 📞 *95 503 70 70.* ⬜ *as above.* 🔲 *(free Tue).* **Isla Mágica** 📞 *902 16 17 16.* ⬜ *Mar & Apr: 11am–7 or 9pm daily; May–Sep: 11am–10pm or midnight daily.* ⬛ *Dec–Feb* 🔲 🔥 🌐 *www.islamagica.es*

THE ISLA DE LA CARTUJA was the site of Expo '92 *(see pp64–5)*. Since then, large-scale redevelopment has been gradually transforming it into a complex of exhibition halls, museums and leisure areas.

The 15th-century Carthusian Monasterio de Santa María de las Cuevas, inhabited by monks until 1836, is at the heart of the area. Columbus stayed and worked here, and his body lay buried in the crypt of its church, the Capilla Santa Ana, between 1507 and 1542. The monastery was restored as a central exhibit for Expo '92.

Nearby, the Museo de Arte Contemporaneo houses works by Andalusian artists, as well as Spanish and international art.

The centrepiece of Expo, the Lago de España, is now part of the Isla Mágica theme park, which opened in 1997. This recreates the journeys and exploits of the explorers who set out from Seville in the 16th century on voyages of discovery to the New World. The Jaguar, a rollercoaster hurtling at 85 km/h (53 mph), is the park's most thrilling ride.

Main entrance of the Carthusian Monasterio de Santa María de las Cuevas, founded in 1400

Seville Street Finder

THE MAP REFERENCES given with the sights described in the Seville section of the guide refer to the maps on the following pages. Map references are also given for Seville hotels (*see pp561–2*) and restaurants (*pp600–1*). The schematic map below shows the area of Seville covered by the *Street Finder*. The symbols used for the sights and other features are listed in the key at the foot of the page.

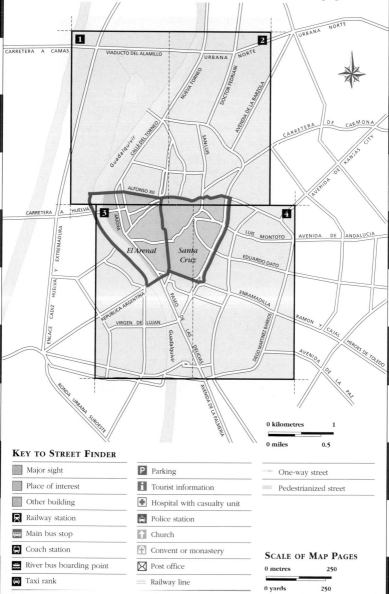

1 CARRETERA A CAMAS — VIADUCTO DEL ALAMILLO — URBANA NORTE

2 URBANA NORTE

3 El Arenal

4 Santa Cruz

0 kilometres 1
0 miles 0.5

KEY TO STREET FINDER

▨ Major sight	🅿 Parking	— One-way street
▨ Place of interest	🛈 Tourist information	▨ Pedestrianized street
▨ Other building	✚ Hospital with casualty unit	
🚉 Railway station	👮 Police station	
🚌 Main bus stop	✝ Church	
🚍 Coach station	✞ Convent or monastery	
🚤 River bus boarding point	⊠ Post office	**SCALE OF MAP PAGES**
🚕 Taxi rank	═ Railway line	0 metres 250
		0 yards 250

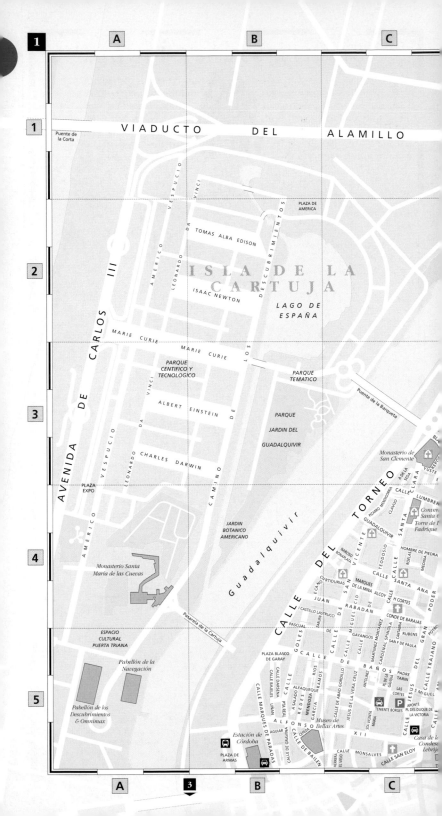

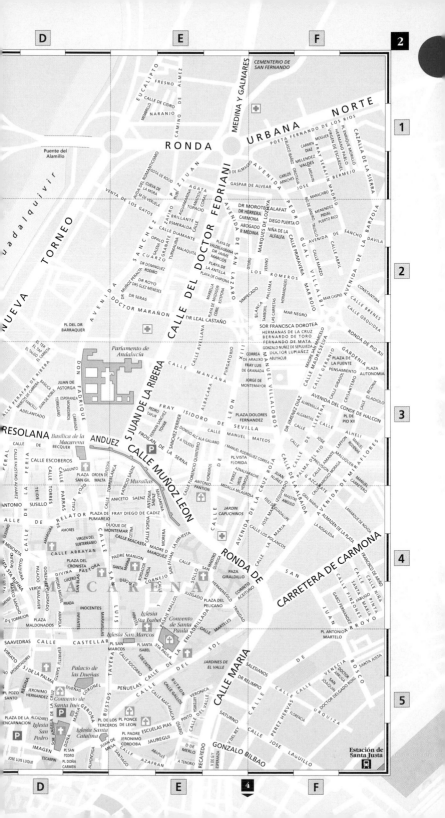

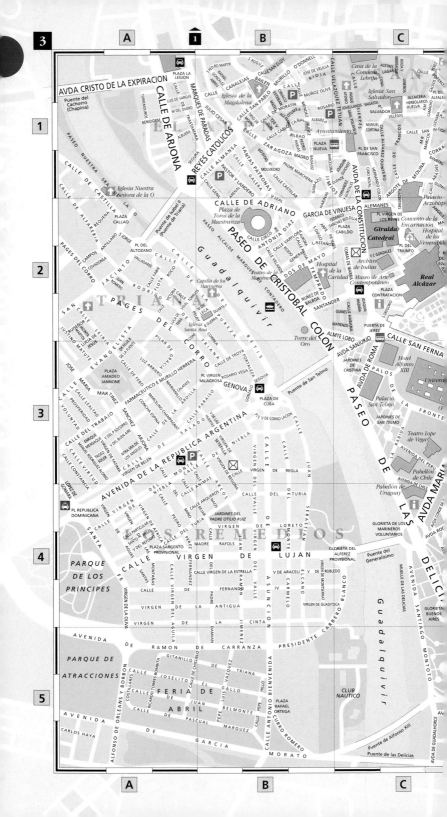

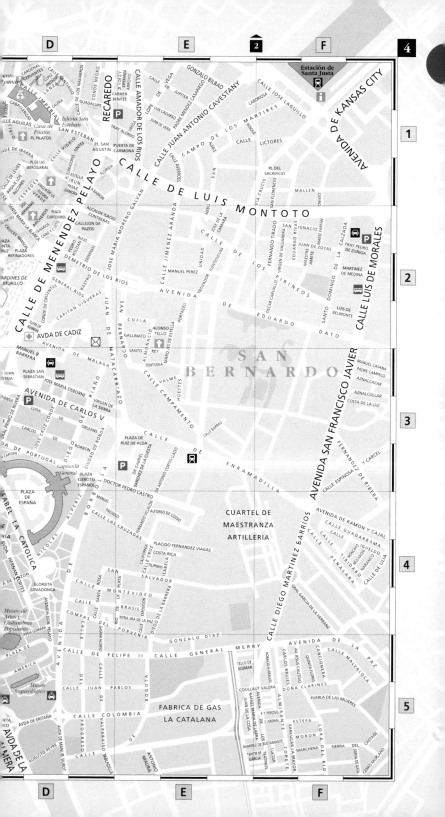

ANDALUSIA

HUELVA · CÁDIZ · MÁLAGA · GIBRALTAR · SEVILLA
CÓRDOBA · GRANADA · JAÉN · ALMERÍA

ANDALUSIA IS WHERE *all Spain's stereotypes meet. Bullfighters, beaches, flamenco, white villages, cave houses, gaudy fiestas, religious processions, tapas and sherry are all here in abundance. But each is part of a larger whole, which includes great art and architecture, nature reserves and an easy-going way of life.*

The eight provinces of Andalusia stretch across Southern Spain from the deserts of Almería to the Portuguese border. One of Spain's longest rivers, the Guadalquivir, bisects the region. Andalusia is linked to the central tableland by a pass, the Desfiladero de Despeñaperros. The highest peaks on the Spanish mainland are in Andalusia's Sierra Nevada.

Successive invaders left their mark on Andalusia. The Romans built cities in this southern province, which they called Baetica, among them Córdoba, its capital, and the well-preserved Itálica near Seville. It was in Andalusia that the Moors lingered longest and left their greatest buildings – Córdoba's Mezquita and the splendid palace of the Alhambra in Granada.

Inevitably, perhaps, the most visited places are the great cities and the busy Costa del Sol, with Gibraltar, a geographical and historical oddity, at its western end. But there are many attractions tucked into other corners of the region. Many of the sights of Huelva province, bordering Portugal, are associated with Christopher Columbus, who set sail from here in 1492. Film directors have put to good use the atmospheric landscapes of Almería's arid interior, which are reminiscent of the Wild West or Arabia. Discreetly concealed among the countless olive groves that cover Jaén province, but not to be missed, are Andalusia's two lovely Renaissance towns, Úbeda and Baeza.

The city of Jaén surrounded by olive groves, seen from the Castillo de Santa Catalina

◁ **Doorway into the *mihrab* (prayer niche) in the Mezquita at Córdoba**

Exploring Andalusia

ANDALUSIA IS SPAIN'S MOST VARIED region. It offers dramatic desert scenery at Tabernas, water sports on the Costa del Sol, skiing in the Sierra Nevada and sherry tasting in Jerez. Of the many nature reserves, the vast, watery Doñana teems with birdlife, while Cazorla is a rugged limestone massif. Granada and Córdoba are unmissable for their Moorish heritage; Úbeda and Baeza are Renaissance gems; and Ronda is one of dozens of superb white towns.

Badajoz, Mérida
N432
24
SIERRA MORENA
N433
Serpa, Beja
Rivera de Huelva
CAZALLA DE LA SIERRA
N630 (E803)
A432
Viar
1
SIERRA DE ARACENA
A452
MEDINA AZAHARA
27
CÓRDOBA
A431
PALMA DEL RÍO
25
Odiel
N435
A499
Guadalquivir
NIV (E5)
ÉCIJA
26
MONTILLA
ITÁLICA
23
A472
HUELVA
2
SEVILLA
22
CARMONA
A49 (E1)
4
MONASTERIO DE LA RÁBIDA
3
PALOS DE LA FRONTERA
Guadaira
OSUNA
21
EL ROCÍO
5
6
A494
PARQUE NACIONAL
ANTEQUERA
SANLÚCAR DE BARRAMEDA
7
A382
18
11
GARGANTA DEL CHORRO
8
ARCOS DE LA FRONTERA
RONDA
13
12
JEREZ DE LA FRONTERA
PUEBLOS BLANCOS
9
CÁDIZ
A390
MEDINA SIDONIA
MARBELLA
16
COSTA DEL
10
ALGECIRAS
14
15
GIBRALTER
TARIFA
COSTA DE LA LUZ
0 kilometres 25
0 miles 25

KEY

- Motorway
- Major road
- Minor road
- Scenic route
- River
- Viewpoint

The smart marina at Sotogrande

GETTING AROUND

Andalusia has a modern motorway network, with the principal NIV (E5) from Madrid following the Guadalquivir valley to Córdoba, Seville and Cádiz. The fast AVE train links Seville and Córdoba with Madrid. Though most other large towns are on the rail network, services may be infrequent. Coaches cover most of the region, but journeys can be slow. A car is essential for exploring remoter areas. The main airports are Málaga, Seville, Jerez and Gibraltar.

SEE ALSO

• *Where to Stay* pp563–7

• *Restaurants and Bars* pp601–5

Singers in festive spirit at a village christening

Ciudad Real

Madrid

ANDÚJAR 42

BAEZA 43 44 ÚBEDA

CAZORLA

PARQUE NATURAL DE CAZORLA 45

VÉLEZ BLANCO 46

41

Murcia

PRIEGO DE CÓRDOBA 30

MONTEFRÍO 31

GRANADA

38 40 39 LACALAHORRA

MOJÁCAR 47

48 TABERNAS

37 36 LAUJAR DE ANDARAX

SIERRA NEVADA

LANJARÓN 34

35 LAS ALPUJARRAS

32 33

NERJA ALMUÑÉCAR

REMOLINOS

49

50

PARQUE NATURAL DE CABO DE GATA

SIGHTS AT A GLANCE

The famed *jamón ibérico* hanging in a bar in Jabugo, Sierra de Aracena

Sierra de Aracena ❶

Huelva. 🚏 *El Repilado*. 🚌 *Aracena*.
ℹ️ *Aracena, 959 12 82 06*. 🛍️ *Sat.*

THIS WILD MOUNTAIN RANGE is one of the most remote and least visited corners of Andalusia. On the hillside above its main town, Aracena, are the ruins of a Moorish fort. The hill is pitted with caverns and in one of these, the **Gruta de las Maravillas**, is a lake in a chamber hung with many stalactites.

The village of **Jabugo** is famed for the tastiest cured ham in Spain, *jamón ibérico*, or *pata negra (see p401)*.

Off the C421 are the giant opencast mines at Minas de Riotinto, where iron, copper and silver have been exploited since Phoenician times. The **Museo Minero** in the village traces the history of the Rio Tinto Company.

🦌 **Gruta de las Maravillas**
Pozo de la Nieve. 📞 *959 12 83 55*.
🕐 *daily*. 📷 🎫
🏛️ **Museo Minero**
Plaza del Museo. 📞 *959 59 00 25*.
🕐 *daily*. 📷 ♿ 🎫

Huelva ❷

Huelva. 🏙️ *140,000*. 🚉 🚌 ℹ️
Avda Alemania 12, 959 25 74 03.
🛍️ *Fri*. 🎉 *Las Columbinas (3 Aug)*.

FOUNDED AS ONUBA by the Phoenicians, Huelva had its grandest days as a Roman port. It was almost wiped out in the great Lisbon earthquake of 1755. It is an industrial city today, sprawling around the quayside on the Río Odiel.

Columbus's departure for the New World *(see p52)* from Palos de la Frontera, across the Río Odiel estuary, is celebrated in the excellent **Museo Provincial**, which also charts the history of the Rio Tinto mines.

Bronze jug, Museo Provincial, Huelva

To the east of the centre, the Barrio Reina Victoria is a bizarre example of English mock-Tudor suburban bungalows built by the Rio Tinto Company for its workers in the early 20th century. South of the town, at Punta del Sebo, the Monumento a Colón, a rather bleak statue of Columbus created by Gertrude Vanderbilt Whitney in 1929, dominates the Odiel estuary.

ENVIRONS: There are three resorts with sandy beaches near Huelva: **Punta Umbria**, on a promontory next to the bird-rich wetlands of the Marismas del Odiel; **Isla Cristina**, which is also an important fishing port and has excellent seafood restaurants; and **Mazagón** with miles of windswept dunes.

The hilly region east of Huelva known as **El Condado** produces several of Andalusia's finest wines, and Bollullos del Condado has the largest wine cooperative in the region. **Niebla**, nearby, has a Roman bridge. The town walls and 12th-century **Castillo de los Guzmanes** are both Moorish.

🏛️ **Museo Provincial**
Alameda Sundheim 13. 📞 *959 25 93 00*. 🕐 *Tue –Sat*. ♿
♣ **Castillo de los Guzmanes**
C/ Campo Castillo, Niebla. 📞 *959 36 22 70*. 🕐 *daily*.

Monasterio de la Rábida ❸

Huelva. 🚌 *from Palos de la Frontera*.
📞 *959 35 04 11*. 🕐 *Tue–Sun*. ♿ 🎫

FOUR KILOMETRES (2 miles) to the north of Palos de la Frontera is the Franciscan **Monasterio de la Rábida**, founded in the 15th century.

In 1491, a dejected Columbus sought refuge here after his plans to sail west to find the East Indies had been rejected by the Catholic Monarchs. Its prior, Juan Pérez, fatefully used his considerable influence as Queen Isabella's confessor to reverse the royal decision.

Inside, frescoes painted by Daniel Vásquez Díaz in 1930 glorify the explorer's life and discoveries. Also worth seeing are the Mudéjar cloisters, the flower-filled gardens and the beamed chapterhouse.

Frescoes depicting the life of Columbus at the Monasterio de la Rábida

Palos de la Frontera ❹

Huelva. 🏠 7,000. 🚉 🚌 Parque Botánico José Celestino Mutis Paraje de la Rábida, 959 53 05 35. 🏛 Sat. 🎎 Santa María de la Rábida (3 &16 Aug).

Columbus put to sea on 3 August 1492 from Palos, the home town of his two captains, the brothers Martín and Vicente Pinzón. Martín's former home, the **Casa Museo de Martín Alonso Pinzón**, is now a small museum of exploration, and his statue stands in the main square.

The 15th-century **Iglesia de San Jorge** has a fine portal, through which Columbus left after hearing Mass before boarding the *Santa María*. The pier is now silted up.

ENVIRONS: In the beautiful white town of **Moguer** are treasures such as the 16th-century hermitage of Nuestra Señora de Montemayor, and the Neo-Classical town hall *(ayuntamiento)*. The **Convento de Santa Clara** and the Monasterio de San Francisco have pretty cloisters.

🏛 **Casa Museo de Martín Alonso Pinzón**
Calle Colón 24. 📞 959 35 01 99. ◯ Mon–Sat.
🏛 **Convento de Santa Clara**
Plaza de las Monjas. 📞 959 37 01 07. ◯ Tue–Sat. ⬤ public hols. 🎎

El Rocío ❺

Huelva. 🏠 1,200. 🚉 🚌 Avda de la Canaliega, 959 44 38 08. 🏛 Tue. 🎎 Romería (May/Jun). 🆆 www.donana.es

Bordering the wetlands of the Parque Nacional de Doñana *(see pp440–41)*, El Rocío is famous for its annual *romería*, which sees almost a million people converge on the village. Many of the pilgrims travel from distant parts of Spain, some on gaudily decorated ox-carts, to visit the **Iglesia de Nuestra Señora del Rocío**. A statue of the Virgin in the church is believed to have performed miraculous healings since 1280. Early on the Monday morning, men from Almonte fight to carry the statue in procession, and the crowd clambers on to the float to touch the image.

Iglesia de Nuestra Señora del Rocío, El Rocío

ANDALUSIA'S FIESTAS

Crowds following the image of the Virgin at El Rocío

Carnival *(Feb/Mar)*, Cádiz. The whole city puts on fancy dress for one of Europe's largest and most colourful carnivals. Groups of singers practise for many months to perform ditties satirizing current fashions, celebrities and politicians.
Romería de la Virgen de la Cabeza *(last Sun in Apr)*, Andújar (Jaén). A mass pilgrimage to a lonely sanctuary in the Sierra Morena.
Día de la Cruz *(first week in May)*, Granada and Córdoba. Neighbourhood groups compete to create the most colourful crosses adorned with flowers on squares and street corners.
Córdoba Patio Fiesta *(mid-May)*. Flower-decked patios in old Córdoba are opened to the public with displays of flamenco.
El Rocío *(May/Jun)*. More than 70 brotherhoods of pilgrims arrive at the village of El Rocío to pay homage to the Virgen del Rocío.
Columbus Festival *(late Jul/early Aug)*, Huelva. This celebration of Columbus's voyage is dedicated to the native music and dance of a different Latin American country every year.
Exaltación al Río Guadalquivir *(mid-Aug)*, Sanlúcar de la Barrameda (Cádiz). Horses are raced on the beach at the mouth of the Río Guadalquivir.

Parque Nacional de Doñana ❻

Doñana national park is ranked among Europe's greatest wetlands. Together with its adjoining protected areas, the park covers in excess of 75,000 hectares (185,000 acres) of marshes and sand dunes. The area used to be a hunting ground *(coto)* belonging to the Dukes of Medina Sidonia. As the land was never suitable for human settlers, wildlife was able to flourish. In 1969, this large area became officially protected. In addition to a wealth of endemic species, thousands of migratory birds stop over in winter when the marshes become flooded again, after months of drought.

Bird-spotting from boat on the Guadalquivir

Shrub Vegetation
Backing the sand dunes is a thick carpet of lavender, rock rose and other low shrubs.

Umbrella Pine
This species of pine tree (Pinus pinea) *thrives in the wide dune belt, putting roots deep into the sand. The trees may get buried beneath the dunes.*

Palacio del Acebrón

El Rocío

La Rocina

H612

El Acebuche

Matalascañas

Palacio de Doñana ●

Laguna de Santa Olay

Coastal Dunes
Softly rounded, white dunes, up to 30 m (100 ft) high, fringe the park's coastal edge. The dunes, ribbed by prevailing winds off the Atlantic, shift constantly.

Monte de Doñana, the wooded area behind the sand dunes, provides shelter for lynx, deer and boar.

The Interior
The number of visitors to the park's interior is strictly controlled to ensure minimal environmental impact. The only way to view the wildlife here is on officially guided day tours.

Key

▢	Marshes
▢	Dunes
•••	National park boundary
•••	Protected area
▬	Road
✢	Viewpoint
ℹ	Tourist information
P	Parking
🚌	Coach stop

Deer
Fallow deer (Dama dama) *and larger red deer* (Cervus elaphus) *roam the park. Stags engage in fierce contests in late summer as they prepare for breeding.*

Wild cattle use the marshes as water holes.

Imperial Eagle
The imperial eagle (Aquila heliaca adalberti) *is one of Doñana's rarest birds.*

José Antonio Valverde

Marisma de Iznalcázar

Marisma Gallega

Río Guadiamar

Río Guadalquivir

Sanlúcar de Barrameda

Fábrica de Hielo

Greater Flamingo
During the winter months, the salty lakes and marshes provide the beautiful, pink greater flamingo (Phoenicopterus ruber) *with crustaceans, its main diet.*

THE LYNX'S LAST REFUGE

The lynx is one of Europe's rarest mammals. In Doñana about 60 pairs of Spanish lynx *(Lynx pardellus)* have found a refuge. They have yellow-brown fur with dark brown spots and pointed ears with black tufts. Research is under way into this shy, nocturnal animal, which tends to stay hidden in scrub. It feeds mainly on rabbits and ducks, but might catch an unguarded fawn.

The elusive lynx, only glimpsed with patience

0 kilometres 5

0 miles 5

Sanlúcar de Barrameda **❼**

Cádiz. 🏠 *62,000.* 🚌 ℹ️ *Calzada del Ejército, 956 36 61 10.* 🚐 *Wed.* 🎪 *Exaltación al Río Guadalquivir and horse races (mid-Aug).*

A FISHING PORT at the mouth of the Río Guadalquivir, Sanlúcar is overlooked by a Moorish **castle**. This was the departure point for Columbus's third voyage in 1498 and also for Magellan's 1519 expedition to circumnavigate the globe.

Sanlúcar is best known for its light, dry manzanilla sherry made by, among other producers, **Bodegas Barbadillo**. Boats from the quay take visitors across the river to the Parque Nacional de Doñana *(see pp440–41)*.

ENVIRONS: Chipiona, along the coast, is a lively little resort town with an excellent beach. The walled town of **Lebrija**, inland, enjoys views over vineyards. Its Iglesia de Santa María de la Oliva is a reconsecrated 12th-century Almohad mosque.

🍷 **Bodegas Barbadillo**
C/ Luis de Eguilaz 11. 📞 *956 38 55 00.* ⏰ *Mon–Fri (by appt).* ♿

Entrance to the Barbadillo bodega in Sanlúcar de Barrameda

Jerez de la Frontera **❽**

Cádiz. 🏠 *250,000.* ✈️ 🚌 🚉 ℹ️ *Plaza del Arenal, 956 35 96 54.* 🚐 *Mon.* 🎪 *Grape Harvest (Sep).*

J EREZ IS THE CAPITAL of sherry production *(see pp402–3)* and many bodegas can be visited. Among the well-known names are **González Byass** and **Pedro Domecq**.

The city is also famous for its **Real Escuela Andaluza de Arte Ecuestre**, a school of equestrian skills. There are public dressage displays on Thursdays. If you visit on another day you may be able to watch the horses being trained.

The **Museo de Relojes**, nearby, has one of the largest clock collections in Europe. On the Plaza de San Juan, the 18th-century **Palacio de Penmartín** houses the Centro Andaluz de Flamenco, where exhibitions give a good introduction to this music and dance tradition *(see pp406–7)*. The partially restored, 11th-century **Alcázar** encompasses a well-preserved mosque, now a church. Just to the north is the **cathedral**, whose most interesting exhibit, *The Sleeping Girl* by Zurbarán, is in the sacristy.

ENVIRONS: The port of **El Puerto de Santa María** exports great quantities of sherry. Here, too, several bodegas can be visited including **Osborne** and **Terry**. The town also has a 13th-century castle and one of the largest and most famous bullrings in Spain.

🐎 **Real Escuela Andaluza de Arte Ecuestre**
Duque de Abrantes. 📞 *956 31 80 08 (by appt).* ⏰ *Mon–Fri.* 📷 ♿
🏛 **Museo de Relojes**
Calle Cervantes 3. 📞 *956 18 21 00.* ⏰ *closed for restoration.* 📷 ♿
🐎 **Palacio de Pemartín**
Plaza de San Juan 1. 📞 *956 34 92 65.* ⏰ *Mon–Fri.* ⬤ *public hols.*
⚓ **Alcázar**
Alameda Vieja. 📞 *956 31 97 98.* ⏰ *daily.* ⬤ *public hols.* 📷 ♿ 🎫
🍷 **Sherry Bodegas**
⏰ *phone for tour times.* 📷
González Byass, C/ Manuel María González 12, Jerez. 📞 *956 35 70 00.*
Pedro Domecq, C/ San Ildefonso 3, Jerez. 📞 *956 15 15 00.* **Sandeman**, C/ Pizarro 10, Jerez. 📞 *956 15 17 00.*
Osborne, C/ de los Moros, Puerto de Santa María. 📞 *956 86 91 00.*
Terry, C/ Toneleros, Puerto de Santa María. 📞 *956 85 77 00.*

Real Escuela Andaluza de Arte Ecuestre, Jerez de la Frontera

Cádiz

**Egyptian mask,
Museo de Cádiz**

JUTTING OUT OF the Bay of Cádiz, and almost entirely surrounded by water, Cádiz lays claim to being Europe's oldest city. Legend names Hercules as its founder, although history credits the Phoenicians with establishing the town of Gadir in 1100 BC. Occupied by the Carthaginians, Romans and Moors in turn, the city also prospered after the Reconquest *(see pp50–51)* on wealth taken from the New World. In 1587 Sir Francis Drake sacked the city in the first of many British attacks in the war for world trade. In 1812 Cádiz briefly became Spain's capital when the nation's first constitution was declared here *(see p59)*.

VISITORS' CHECKLIST

Cádiz. 155,000. Plaza de Sevilla, 902 24 02 02. Plaza de la Hispanidad, 956 21 17 63. Calle Nueva 6, 956 25 86 46; Plaza de San Juan de Dios 11, 956 24 10 01. Mon. Carnival (Feb/Mar). www.cadizayto.es

Exploring Cádiz

The joy of visiting Cádiz is to wander along the waterfront with its well-tended gardens and open squares before exploring the old town, which is full of narrow alleys busy with market and street life.

The pride of the city is its Carnival *(see p439)* – a riotous explosion of festivities, fancy dress, singing and drinking.

⛪ Catedral

Known as the Catedral Nueva (New Cathedral) and built on the site of an older one, this Baroque and Neo-Classical church, with its dome of golden-yellow tiles, is one of Spain's largest. In the crypt is the tomb of composer Manuel de Falla (1876–1946), native of Cádiz. The cathedral's treasures are stored in the Casa de la Contaduría, behind the cathedral.

🏛 Museo de Cádiz

Plaza de Mina. 956 21 22 81. Wed–Sun, Tue (for groups). On the ground floor of this spacious museum there are archaeological exhibits charting the history of Cádiz. Upstairs is one of the largest art galleries in Andalusia, including works by Rubens, Zurbarán and Murillo. On the third floor is a collection of puppets made for village fiestas.

🏛 Torre Tavira

Calle Marqués del Real Tesoro 10. 956 21 29 10. daily. The city's official watchtower in the 18th century has now been converted into a camera obscura, and offers great views.

⛪ Oratorio de San Felipe Neri

This 18th-century church has been a shrine to liberalism since 1812. In that year, as Napoleon tightened his grip on Spain during the War of Independence *(see pp58–9)*, a provisional government assembled here to try to lay the foundations of Spain's first constitutional monarchy. The liberal constitution it declared was bold but ineffectual.

Zurbarán's *Saint Bruno in Ecstasy*, in the Museo de Cádiz

CÁDIZ CATHEDRAL

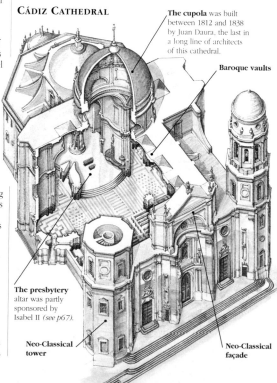

The cupola was built between 1812 and 1838 by Juan Daura, the last in a long line of architects of this cathedral.

Baroque vaults

The presbytery altar was partly sponsored by Isabel II *(see p67)*.

Neo-Classical tower

Neo-Classical façade

Fishing boats at the resort of Zahara de los Atunes on the Costa de la Luz

Costa de la Luz ⓐ

Cádiz. 🚊 Cádiz. 🚌 Cádiz, Tarifa.
ℹ️ Plaza San Antonio, 956 80 70 61.

THE COSTA DE LA LUZ (Coast of Light) between Cádiz and Tarifa, at Spain's southernmost tip, is an unspoiled, windswept stretch of coast characterized by strong, pure light – the source of its name. From the Sierra del Cabrito, to the west of Algeciras, it is often possible to see the outline of Tangier and the parched Moroccan landscape below the purple-tinged Rif mountains across the narrow Strait of Gibraltar.

Tarifa is named after an 8th-century Moorish commander, Tarif ben Maluk, who landed there with his forces during the Moorish conquest *(see pp48–9)*. Later, Tarifa and its 10th-century castle were defended by the legendary hero, Guzmán, during a siege by the Moors in 1292.

Tarifa has since become the windsurfing capital of Europe. The breezes that blow on to this coast also drive the numerous wind turbines visible in the hills above Tarifa.

Off the N340 (E5), at the end of a long, narrow road which strikes out across a wilderness of cacti, sunflowers and lone cork trees, is **Zahara de los Atunes**, a modest holiday resort with a few hotels. **Conil de la Frontera**, to the west, is busier and more built up.

The English admiral Nelson defeated a Spanish and French fleet off **Cabo de Trafalgar** in 1805, but died in the battle.

A Tour Around the Pueblos Blancos ⓑ

INSTEAD OF SETTLING on Andalusia's plains, where they would have fallen prey to bandits, some Andalusians chose to live in fortified hilltop towns and villages. These are known as *pueblos blancos* (white towns) because they are whitewashed in the Moorish tradition *(see p22)*. They are working agricultural towns today, but touring them will reveal a host of references to the past.

Jimena de la Frontera ⑨
Set amid hills, where wild bulls graze among cork and olive trees, this town has a ruined Moorish castle.

Ubrique ②
Nestling at the foot of the Sierra de Ubrique, this *pueblo* is known for its flourishing leather industry.

SEVILLA

CÁDIZ, JEREZ

Arcos de la Frontera ①

A372

Embalse de los Hurones

Charco de los Hurones

CA5221

CA503

La Sauceda

KEY

━━ Tour route

═══ Other roads

TIPS FOR DRIVERS

Tour length: 205 km (127 miles).
Stopping-off points: There are places to stay and eat at all of these pueblos, but Ronda has the widest range of hotels (see p566) and restaurants (see p605). Arcos has a parador (see p563).

Gaucín ⑧
From here there are unsurpassed vistas over the Mediterranean, the Atlantic, the Rock of Gibraltar and across the strait to the Rif mountains of North Africa.

0 kilometres   10

0 miles   5

Arcos de la Frontera ⓫

Cádiz. 🏛 *30,000.* 🚍 🛈 *Plaza del Cabildo, 956 70 22 64.* 🚌 *Fri.*
🎪 *Velada de Nuestra Señora de las Nieves (4–6 Aug).*
Ⓦ www.ayuntamientoarcos.org

ALTHOUGH LEGEND has it that a son of Noah founded Arcos it is more probable that it was the Iberians. It gained the name Arcobriga in the Roman era and, under the Caliphate of Córdoba *(see p48),* became the Moorish stronghold of Medina Arkosh. It is an archetypal white town, with a labyrinthine old quarter.

On the Plaza de España, at the top of the town, are the parador *(see p563)* and the **Iglesia de Santa María de la Asunción**, a Late Gothic-Mudéjar building noted for its choir stalls and altarpiece. The huge, Gothic **Iglesia de San Pedro**, perched on the edge of a cliff formed by the Río Guadalete, is a striking building. Nearby is the **Palacio del Mayorazgo**, which has an ornate Renaissance façade. The **town hall** *(ayuntamiento)* has a fine Mudéjar ceiling.

ENVIRONS: In the 15th-century the Guzmán family was granted the dukedom of **Medina Sidonia**, a white town atop a conical hill, southwest of Arcos de la Frontera. The family grew wealthy from its investments in the Americas and, as a result, Medina Sidonia became one of the most important ducal seats in Spain. The Gothic Iglesia de Santa María la Coronada is the town's finest building. It contains a notable collection of Renaissance religious art.

Iglesia de Santa María de la Asunción in Arcos de la Frontera

🏛 **Palacio del Mayorazgo**
C/ San Pedro 2. ☎ *956 70 30 13 (Casa de Cultura).* ◯ *Mon–Fri.* ♿
🏛 **Ayuntamiento**
Plaza del Cabildo. ☎ *956 70 00 02.* ◯ *by permission.* ⬤ *public hols.*

Zahara de la Sierra ③
Fanning out below a castle ruin, this fine *pueblo blanco* has been declared a national monument.

Grazalema ④
This village in the Sierra de Grazalema has the highest rainfall in Spain.

Ronda la Vieja ⑤
Significant remains of the Roman town of Acinipo, including a theatre, can be visited.

Setenil ⑥
Some of the streets of this unusual white town, which climbs up the sides of a gorge, are covered by rock overhangs. The gorge was carved out of volcanic tufa rock by the Río Trejo.

Ronda ⑦
(see pp446–7)

Street-by-Street: Ronda ⑬

Plate hand-painted in Ronda

O NE OF THE MOST spectacularly located cities in Spain, Ronda sits on a massive rocky outcrop, straddling a precipitous limestone cleft. Because of its impregnable position this town was one of the last Moorish bastions, finally falling to the Christians in 1485. On the south side perches a classic Moorish *pueblo blanco (see pp444–5)* of cobbled alleys, window grilles and dazzling whitewash – most historic sights are in this part of the town. Located in El Mercadillo, the newer town, is one of the oldest bullrings in Spain.

★ Puente Nuevo
An impressive feat of 18th-century civil engineering, the "New Bridge" over the 100-m (330-ft) deep Tajo gorge joins old and new Ronda.

Convento de Santo Domingo was the local headquarters of the Inquisition *(see p264).*

To El Mercadillo, Plaza de Toros, parador *(see p566)* and tourist information

SANTO DOMINGO

CALLE ARMIÑÁN

TENORIO

Casa del Rey Moro
From this 18th-century mansion, built on the foundations of a Moorish palace, 365 steps lead down to the river.

Mirador El Campillo (viewpoint)

PLAZA DEL CAMPILLO

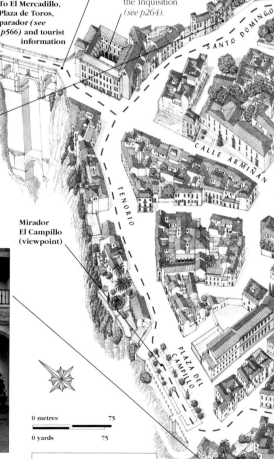

| 0 metres | 75 |
| 0 yards | 75 |

★ Palacio Mondragón
Much of this palace was rebuilt following the Reconquest (see pp50–51), but its arcaded patio is adorned with original Moorish mosaics and plasterwork.

STAR SIGHTS

★ Puente Nuevo

★ Palacio Mondragón

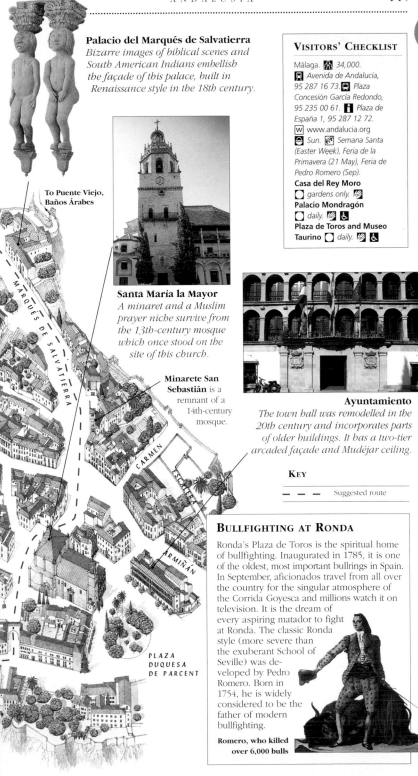

Palacio del Marqués de Salvatierra
Bizarre images of biblical scenes and South American Indians embellish the façade of this palace, built in Renaissance style in the 18th century.

To Puente Viejo, Baños Árabes

Santa María la Mayor
A minaret and a Muslim prayer niche survive from the 13th-century mosque which once stood on the site of this church.

Minarete San Sebastián is a remnant of a 14th-century mosque.

VISITORS' CHECKLIST

Málaga. 🚗 *34,000.*
🚉 *Avenida de Andalucía, 95 287 16 73.* 🚌 *Plaza Concesión García Redondo, 95 235 00 61.* ℹ️ *Plaza de España 1, 95 287 12 72.*
W www.andalucia.org
🗓️ *Sun.* 🎭 *Semana Santa (Easter Week), Feria de la Primavera (21 May), Feria de Pedro Romero (Sep).*
Casa del Rey Moro
⚪ *gardens only.* ♿
Palacio Mondragón
⚪ *daily.* ♿
Plaza de Toros and Museo Taurino ⚪ *daily.* ♿

Ayuntamiento
The town hall was remodelled in the 20th century and incorporates parts of older buildings. It has a two-tier arcaded façade and Mudéjar ceiling.

KEY

– – – Suggested route

BULLFIGHTING AT RONDA

Ronda's Plaza de Toros is the spiritual home of bullfighting. Inaugurated in 1785, it is one of the oldest, most important bullrings in Spain. In September, aficionados travel from all over the country for the singular atmosphere of the Corrida Goyesca and millions watch it on television. It is the dream of every aspiring matador to fight at Ronda. The classic Ronda style (more severe than the exuberant School of Seville) was developed by Pedro Romero. Born in 1754, he is widely considered to be the father of modern bullfighting.

Romero, who killed over 6,000 bulls

Algeciras ⑭

Cádiz. 🏛 180,000. 🚌 ℹ️ Calle
Juan de la Cierva, 956 57 26 36.
🚌 Tue. 🎭 Feria Real (24 Jun–2 Jul).

FROM THE INDUSTRIAL city of
Algeciras, there are spectacular views of Gibraltar, 14 km
(9 miles) away across its bay.
The city is a major fishing port
and Europe's main gateway for
ferries to North Africa, especially Tangier and Spain's
territories of Ceuta and Melilla.

Gibraltar ⑮

British Crown Colony. 🏛 31,500. 🚌
ℹ️ Duke of Kent House, Cathedral
Square, 9567 749 50. 🚌 Wed & Sat.
🎭 Nat Day (10 Sep).
w www.gibraltar.gi

THE HIGH, ROCKY headland of
Gibraltar was signed over
to Britain "in perpetuity" at the
Treaty of Utrecht in 1713 (see
p58). Today, about 4 million
people stream across the
border annually from La Línea
de la Concepción in Spain.

Among the chief sights of
Gibraltar are those testifying to
its strategic military importance
over the centuries. Half way up

St Michael's Cave, which served as
a hospital during World War II

the famous Rock are an 8th-
century Moorish castle, whose
keep is still used as a prison,
and 80 km (50 miles) of **siege
tunnels** housing storerooms
and barracks. **St Michael's
Cave**, which served as a hospital during World War II, is now
used for classical concerts.

The **Apes' Den**, near Europa
Point, Gibraltar's southernmost
tip, is home to the tailless apes.
Legend says that the British will
keep the Rock only as long as
the apes remain there, despite
the machinations of politicans.

A cable car takes visitors to
the **Top of the Rock** at 450 m
(1,475 ft). **Gibraltar Museum**
charts the colony's history.

🎪 **The Keep, Siege Tunnels,
St Michael's Cave, Apes' Den**
Upper Rock Area. ☎ 9567 749 50.
🔲 daily. ● 1 Jan, 25 Dec. 🎫
🏛 **Gibraltar Museum**
18 Bombhouse Lane. ☎ 9567 742
89. 🔲 Mon–Sat. ● public hols. 🎫

The Costa del Sol

THANKS TO ITS AVERAGE of 300 days' sunshine
a year and its varied coastline, the Costa
del Sol, between Gibraltar and Málaga, offers
a full range of beach-based holidays and water
sports. Complementing the sophistication and
luxury of Marbella are many other popular
resorts aimed at the mass market. More than
30 of Europe's finest golf courses lie just inland.

Puerto Banús is Marbella's
ostentatious marina. The
expensive shops, restaurants
and glittering nightlife reflect
the wealth of its clientele.

Estepona's quiet evenings
make it popular with families
with young children. Behind
the big hotels are old squares
shaded by orange trees.

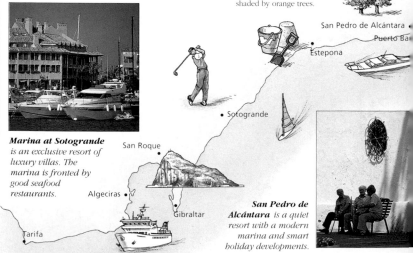

San Pedro de Alcántara

Puerto Ba[

Estepona

Sotogrande

San Roque

San Pedro de
Alcántara is a quiet
resort with a modern
marina and smart
holiday developments.

***Marina at Sotogrande**
is an exclusive resort of
luxury villas. The
marina is fronted by
good seafood
restaurants.*

Algeciras

Gibraltar

Tarifa

Yachts and motorboats in the exclusive marina of Marbella – the summer home of the international jet set

Marbella ⓰

Málaga. 🏘 *150,000.* 🚊 🛈 *Glorieta de la Fontanilla, Paseo Marítimo, 95 277 14 42.* 🚌 *Mon.* 🎭 *San Berna-bé (Jun).* 🌐 *www.marbella2000.com*

MARBELLA IS ONE of Europe's most exclusive holiday resorts, frequented by royalty and film stars. In winter, the major attraction is the golf. Among the delights of the old town, with its spotlessly clean alleys, squares, and smart shops and restaurants, is the **Iglesia de Nuestra Señora de la Encarnación**. The **Museo de Grabado Español Contemporáneo** displays some of Picasso's least-known work. The beaches are named Babaloo, Victor's, Don Carlos, Cabopino and Las Dunas.

🏛 **Museo de Grabado Español Contemporáneo**
C/ Hospital Bazan. 📞 *95 282 50 35.* 🕐 *Sun – Fri.* ● *public hols, Sun in summer.* 🎫

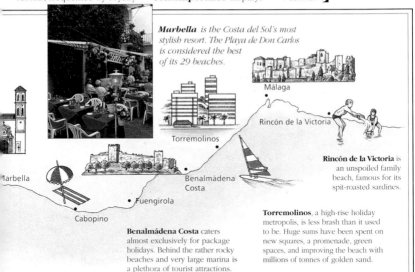

Marbella *is the Costa del Sol's most stylish resort. The Playa de Don Carlos is considered the best of its 29 beaches.*

Málaga

Rincón de la Victoria

Torremolinos

Benalmádena Costa

Marbella

• Fuengirola

Cabopino

Rincón de la Victoria is an unspoiled family beach, famous for its spit-roasted sardines.

Torremolinos, a high-rise holiday metropolis, is less brash than it used to be. Huge sums have been spent on new squares, a promenade, green spaces, and improving the beach with millions of tonnes of golden sand.

Benalmádena Costa caters almost exclusively for package holidays. Behind the rather rocky beaches and very large marina is a plethora of tourist attractions.

Cabopino, on a not-too-crowded stretch of coast, is a wide, sandy nudist beach beside a modern marina.

0 kilometres   10

0 miles   10

Fuengirola *still has an active fishing port – as these boxes of fresh fish suggest – although it is better known today as a package-holiday resort with a chiefly British clientele. It has a spectacular backdrop of steep, ochre mountains.*

The main façade of Málaga's cathedral, consecrated in 1588

Málaga ⑰

Málaga. 🏙 650,000. ✈ 🚉 🚌 ⛴
ℹ Pasaje de Chinitas 4, 95 204
88 04. 🚌 Sun. 🎭 Carnival (Feb/Mar),
Feria (second Sat–third Sun of Aug).
🌐 www.andalucia.org

MÁLAGA, the second largest city in Andalusia, is today a thriving port, just as it was in Phoenician times (when it was known as Malaca), and again under the Romans and then the Moors. It also flourished during the 19th century, when sweet Málaga wine *(see p402)* was one of Europe's most popular drinks – until phylloxera ravaged the area's vineyards in 1876.

The **cathedral** was begun in 1528 by Diego de Siloé, but it is a bizarre mix of styles. The half-built second tower, abandoned in 1765 when funds ran out, gave the cathedral its nickname: La Manquita ("the one-armed one").

Málaga's former Museo de Bellas Artes is being adapted to house a new **Museo Picasso** displaying works by the native artist. The **Casa Natal de Picasso**, where the painter spent his early years, is now the Picasso Foundation.

Málaga's vast **Alcazaba** *(see p49)* was built between the 8th and 11th centuries. There is a partially excavated Roman amphitheatre by its entrance, but the real attraction is the display of Phoenician, Roman and Moorish artifacts in the **Museo Arqueológico**.

On the hill directly behind the Alcazaba are the ruins of the **Castillo de Gibralfaro**, a 14th-century Moorish castle.

ENVIRONS: In the beautiful hills to the north and east of Málaga is the **Parque Natural de los Montes de Málaga**. Wildlife, such as eagles and wild boars, thrive here amid the scent of lavender and wild herbs. Walkers can follow a number of scenic marked trails. Going north on the C345 you can also visit a small preserved winery of the 1840s.

🏛 Museo de Picasso
Calle San Agustín 8. ℹ 95 260 27 31.
● until mid-2003.
♠ Alcazaba and Museo Arqueológico
Calle Alcazabilla. ℹ 95 221 60 05.
○ Wed–Sun.

Garganta del Chorro ⑱

Málaga. 🚉 El Chorro. 🚌 Parque
Ardeles. ℹ Avenida de la Constitución,
Álora, 95 249 83 80.
🌐 www.ayto-alora.org

UP THE FERTILE Guadalhorce valley, beyond the village of El Chorro, is one of the geographical wonders of Andalusia. The Garganta del Chorro is an immense chasm, 180 m (590 ft) deep and in places only 10 m (30 ft) wide, cut by the river through a limestone mountain. Downstream, a hydroelectric plant detracts from the wildness of the place.

The **Camino del Rey** is a catwalk clinging to the rock face which leads to a bridge across the gorge. It is, however, closed to the public.

ENVIRONS: Álora, a classic white town *(see p444)* with a ruined Moorish castle and an 18th-century church, lies 12 km (7 miles) down the valley.

Along the twisting MA441 from Álora is the village of **Carratraca**. In the 19th and early 20th centuries, Europe's highest society travelled here for the healing powers of the sulphurous springs. These days, Carratraca has a faded glory – water still gushes out at 700 litres (155 UK and 185 US gal) a minute and the outdoor baths remain open, but they are little used.

The Garganta del Chorro, rising high above the Guadalhorce river

Weathered limestone formations in El Torcal

El Torcal ⑲

Málaga. 🚊 *Antequera*. 🚌 *Antequera*. 🛈 *Antequera, 95 270 25 05.*

A MASSIVE EXPOSED HUMP of limestone upland, which has been slowly weathered into bizarre rock formations and caves, the Parque Natural del Torcal is very popular with hikers. Footpaths lead from a visitors' centre in the middle. Walks of up to two hours are marked by yellow arrows; longer walks by red.

The park is also a pleasure for natural historians, with fox and weasel populations, and colonies of eagles, hawks and vultures. It also protects rare plants and flowers, among them species of wild orchid.

Antequera ⑳

Málaga. 🏃 *40,000.* 🚊 🚌 🛈 *Pl San Sebastián 7, 95 270 25 05.* 🗓 *Tue.* 🎉 *Ferias (end May & mid-Aug).*

T HIS BUSY MARKET TOWN was strategically important first as Roman Anticaria and later as a Moorish border fortress defending Granada.

Of its many churches, the **Iglesia de Nuestra Señora del Carmen**, with its vast Baroque altarpiece, is not to be missed. At the opposite end of the town is the 19th-century **Plaza de Toros**, with a museum of bullfighting.

The hilltop **castle** was built in the 13th century on the site of a Roman fort. Visitors can walk round the castle walls by approaching through the 16th-century Arco de los Gigantes.

There are excellent views of Antequera from the Torre del Papabellotas on the best-preserved part of the wall.

In the town below, the 18th-century **Palacio de Nájera** is the setting for the Municipal Museum, the star exhibit of which is a splendid Roman bronze statue of a boy.

The massive **dolmens**, just outside the town, are thought to be the burial chambers of tribal leaders and date from around 2500–2000 BC.

ENVIRONS: Laguna de la Fuente de Piedra, north of Antequera, teems with bird life, including huge flocks of flamingoes, which arrive to breed after wintering in West Africa. A road off the N334 leads to a lakeside viewing point. There is a visitors' centre in Fuente de Piedra village. To the east, also off the N334, is **Archidona**, worth a stop to admire its extraordinary, 18th-century, octagonal Plaza

The triumphal, 16th-century Arco de los Gigantes, Antequera

Ochavada built in French style, but which also incorporates traditional Andalusian features.

🎪 **Plaza de Toros**
Carretera de Sevilla. 📞 95 270 81 42. 🗓 *Tue–Sun.* **Museo Taurino** 🗓 *Sat, Sun, public hols.*
🏛 **Palacio de Nájera**
Coso Viejo. 📞 95 270 40 21. 🗓 *Tue–Sun.* ⬤ *public hols.* 📷

Osuna ㉑

Sevilla. 🏃 *17,000.* 🚊 🚌 🛈 *Plaza Mayor, 95 481 57 32.* 🗓 *Mon.* 🎉 *San Alcadio (12 Jan), Virgen de la Consolación (8 Sep).*

Palacio del Marqués de la Gomera, in Osuna, completed in 1770

O SUNA was once a key Roman garrison town. It rose again to prominence in the 16th century under the Dukes of Osuna, who wielded immense power. In the 1530s they founded the **Colegiata de Santa María**, a grand church with a Baroque reredos and paintings by José de Ribera. This was followed in 1548 by the **University**, a rather severe building with a beautiful patio. Some fine mansions, among them the **Palacio del Marqués de la Gomera**, also reflect the town's former glory.

ENVIRONS: To the east lies **Estepa**, whose modern-day fame rests on its biscuits – *polvorones* and *mantecados* (*see p401*). The Iglesia del Carmen has a black and white, Baroque façade.

Tomb of Servilia in the Roman necropolis in Carmona

Carmona ㉒

Sevilla. 🏛 *25,000.* 🚌 ℹ *Arco de la Puerta de Sevilla, 95 419 09 55.* 🚍 *Mon & Thu.* 🎡 *Feria (May), Fiestas Patronales (8–16 Sep).* 🅦 *www. turismo.carmona.org*

CARMONA IS THE FIRST major town east of Seville, its old quarter built on a hill above the suburbs on the plain. Beyond the **Puerta de Sevilla**, a gateway in the Moorish city walls, is a dense cluster of mansions, Mudéjar churches, and winding streets.

The Plaza de San Fernando has a feeling of grandeur which is characterized by the Renaissance façade of the old **Ayuntamiento**. The present town hall, set just off the square, dates from the 18th century; in its courtyard are some Roman mosaics. Close by is the **Iglesia de Santa María la Mayor**. Built in the 15th century over a mosque, whose patio still survives, this is the finest of Carmona's churches.

Dominating the town are the ruins of the **Alcázar del Rey Pedro**, once a palace of Pedro I, known as Pedro the Cruel. Parts of it now form a parador *(see p563).*

Just outside Carmona is the **Necrópolis Romana**, the extensive remains of a Roman burial ground. A site museum displays some of the items found in the graves, including statues, glass and jewellery.

🏛 **Ayuntamiento**
Calle Salvador 2. ☎ *95 414 00 11.* ☐ *Mon–Fri.* ● *public hols.*
🏛 **Necrópolis Romana**
Avenida Jorge Bonsor 9. ☎ *95 414 08 11.* ☐ *Tue–Sun.* ● *Mon & Sun in summer; public hols.*

Itálica ㉓

Sevilla. ☎ *95 599 73 76.* 🚌 *from Seville.* ☐ *Apr–Sep: 8:30am– 8:30pm Tue–Sat, 9am–3pm Sun; Oct–Mar: 9am–5:30pm Tue–Sat, 10am–4pm Sun.* 🎫

ITÁLICA WAS FOUNDED in 206 BC by Scipio Africanus. One of the earliest Roman cities in Hispania *(see pp46–7)*, it grew to become important in the 2nd and 3rd centuries AD. Emperor Hadrian, who was born in the city and reigned from AD 117–138, added marble temples and other grand buildings.

Archaeologists have speculated that the changing course of the Río Guadalquivir may have led to Itálica's later demise during Moorish times.

Roman mosaic from Itálica

Next to the vast but crumbling **amphitheatre** is a display of finds from the site. More treasures are displayed in the Museo Arqueológico in Seville *(see p427).*

The traces of Itálica's streets and the mosaic floors of some villas can be seen. However, little remains of the city's temples or of its baths as most of the stone and marble has been plundered over the centuries.

Some well-preserved Roman baths and a theatre can be seen in **Santiponce**, a village just outside the site.

Sierra Morena ㉔

Sevilla and Córdoba. 🚉 *Estación de Cazalla y Constantina.* 🚌 *Constantina, Cazalla.* ℹ *El Robledo, 95 588 15 97.*

THE SIERRA MORENA, clad in oak and pine woods, runs across the north of the provinces of Sevilla and Córdoba. It forms a natural frontier between Andalusia and the plains of neighbouring Extremadura and La Mancha. Smaller sierras (ranges of hills) within the Sierra Morena chain are also named individually.

Fuente Obejuna, north of Córdoba, was immortalized by Lope de Vega *(see p280)* in his play about an uprising in 1476 against a local overlord. The Iglesia de San Juan Bautista in **Hinojosa del Duque** is a vast church in both Gothic and Renaissance styles. **Belalcázar** is dominated by the huge tower of a ruined 15th-century castle dominates. Storks nest on the church towers of the plateau of **Valle de los Pedroches**, east of Belalcázar.

Cazalla de la Sierra, the main town of the sierra north of Seville, is cosmopolitan, and popular with young *Sevillanos* at weekends. A unique, pungent concoction of cherry liqueur and aniseed, Liquor de Guindas, is produced here.

Constantina, to the east, is more peaceful and has superb views across the countryside.

A cow grazing in the pastures of the Sierra Morena north of Seville

Palma del Río 25

Córdoba. 19,000.
Cardenal Portocarrero, 957 64 43 70. Tue. Ferias (19–21 May & 18–20 Aug). www.interbook.net/ayuntamiento/palmadelrio

THE ROMANS sited a strategic settlement here, on the road between Córdoba and Itálica, almost 2,000 years ago. The remains of the 12th-century city walls are a reminder of the town's frontier days under the Almohads (see p50).

The **Iglesia de la Asunción**, a Baroque church, dates from the 18th century. The **Monasterio de San Francisco** is now a hotel (see p566), and guests can eat dinner in the 15th-century refectory of the Franciscan monks. Palma del Río is the home town of El Cordobés, one of Spain's most famous matadors. His biography, *Or I'll Dress You in Mourning*, paints a vivid picture of life in the town and of the hardship which followed the end of the Civil War.

Bell tower, La Asunción

ENVIRONS: One of the most dramatic silhouettes in Southern Spain breaks the skyline of **Almodóvar del Río**. The Moorish castle – parts of it dating from the 8th century – stands on a hilltop overlooking the whitewashed town and fields of cotton.

⚜ **Castillo de Almodóvar del Río**
957 63 51 16. Sun–Mon.

Écija 26

Sevilla. 38,000. Plaza de España 1, Ayuntamiento 95 590 29 33. Thu. Feria (21–24 Sep). www.ecija.org

ÉCIJA IS NICKNAMED "the frying pan of Andalusia" owing to its famously torrid climate. In the searing heat, the palm trees on the Plaza de España provide blissful shade. An ideal place to sit and observe daily life passing by, this is also a spot for evening strolls.

Écija has 11 Baroque church steeples, many adorned with gleaming *azulejos (see p420)*, and together they make a very impressive sight. The most florid of these is the **Iglesia de Santa María**, which overlooks the Plaza de España. The **Iglesia de San Juan**, with its exquisite, brightly coloured bell tower, is a very close rival.

Of the many mansions along Calle Caballeros, the Baroque **Palacio de Peñaflor** is worth a visit. Its pink marble doorway is topped by twisted columns, while an attractive wrought-iron balcony runs along the whole front façade.

🏛 **Palacio de Peñaflor**
C/ Caballeros 32. 95 483 02 73. daily (courtyard only).

Medina Azahara 27

Córdoba. 957 32 91 30.
Córdoba. 10am–6:30pm Tue–Sat. Sun, Mon.

JUST A FEW kilometres north of Córdoba lies this once glorious palace. Built in the 10th century for Caliph Abd al Rahman III, it is named after his favourite wife, Azahara. He spared no expense, employing more than 15,000 mules,

Detail of wood carving in the main hall of Medina Azahara

4,000 camels and 10,000 workers to bring building materials from as far as North Africa.

The palace is built on three levels and includes a mosque, the caliph's residence and fine gardens (see pp404–405). Marble, ebony, jasper and alabaster once adorned its many halls, and it is believed that shimmering pools of quicksilver added lustre.

Unfortunately, the glory was short-lived. The palace was sacked by Berber invaders in 1010 and over subsequent centuries it was ransacked for its building materials. Now, the ruins give only glimpses of its former splendour – a Moorish main hall, for instance, decorated with marble carvings, still with its fine ceiling of carved wood. The palace is currently being restored.

Trompe l'oeil on the ornate Baroque façade of the Palacio de Peñaflor, Écija

Street-by-Street: Córdoba ㉘

Statue of Maimónides

THE HEART OF CÓRDOBA is the old Jewish quarter, situated to the west of the Mezquita's towering walls. A walk around this area gives the sensation that little has changed since the 10th century when this was one of the greatest cities in the Western world. Wrought ironwork decorates cobbled streets too narrow for cars, where silversmiths create fine jewellery in their workshops. Most of the chief sights are here, while modern city life takes place some blocks north, around the Plaza de Tendillas. To the east of this square is the Plaza de la Corredera, a 17th-century arcaded square with a daily market.

Sinagoga
Hebrew script covers this 14th-century synagogue. Spain's other synagogues are in Toledo, Madrid and Barcelona.

Museo Taurino
A replica of the tomb of the famous torero, Manolete, and the hide of the bull that killed him (see p33) are the star exhibits in this museum of bullfighting.

The Capilla de San Bartolomé,
in Mudéjar style, is decorated with elaborate plasterwork.

★ Alcázar de los Reyes Cristianos
Water terraces and fountains add to the tranquil atmosphere of the gardens belonging to the palace-fortress of the Catholic Monarchs (see pp52–3), built in the 14th century.

KEY

– – – Suggested route

STAR SIGHTS

★ **Alcázar de los Reyes Cristianos**

★ **Mezquita**

The Callejón de las Flores brims with colourful geraniums, which contrast with the whitewashed walls of this alley, leading to a tiny square.

VISITORS' CHECKLIST

Córdoba. 🏠 330,000. 🚉
Glorieta de las Tres Culturas, 957
40 02 02. 🚌 Glorieta de las Tres
Culturas, 957 40 40 40. 🚹
Palacio de Congresos, Calle Torri-
jos 10, 957 47 12 35. 🏪 Tue, Fri
& Sun. 🎭 Semana Santa (Easter
Week), Festival de los Patios (5–11
May), Feria (late May). **Sinagoga**
🕐 Tue–Sun. 🎫 **Museo Taurino**
(closed for refurbishment) 🕐 Tue–
Sun. 🎫 **Alcázar de los Reyes
Cristianos** 🕐 Tue–Sun. 🎫

The Palacio Episcopal now houses the tourist office.

Moorish bronze stag from Medina Azahara, Museo Arqueológico

Exploring Córdoba

Córdoba lies on a sharp bend in the Río Guadalquivir, which is spanned by a Roman bridge linking the 14th-century Torre de la Calahorra and the old town. One of the most atmospheric squares in Andalusia is the Plaza de los Capuchinos. With its haunting stone calvary surrounded by wrought-iron lamps, it is particularly evocative when seen by moonlight.

🏛 Museo de Bellas Artes

Plaza del Potro 1. ☎ 957 47 33 45.
🕐 Tue–Sun.
Exhibits in a former charity hospital include sculptures by local artist Mateo Inurria (1867–1924) and works by Valdés Leal, Zurbarán and Murillo of the Seville School.

🏛 Museo Arqueológico

Plaza Jerónimo Páez 7. ☎ 957 47 40
11. 🕐 Tue–Sun. 🎫
Located in a Renaissance mansion, displays include Roman mosaics, pottery and relief carvings, and impressive finds from the Moorish era.

⚜ Palacio de Viana

Plaza Don Gome 2. ☎ 957 49 67 41.
🕐 Mon–Sat. ● 1–15 June, public
hols. 🎫 📷
Furniture, tapestries, paintings and porcelain are displayed in the 17th-century former home of the Viana family.

🏛 Museo Romero de Torres

Plaza del Potro 1. ☎ 957 49 19 09.
🕐 Tue–Sun. 🎫
Julio Romero de Torres (1874–1930), who was born in this house, captured the soul of Córdoba in his paintings.

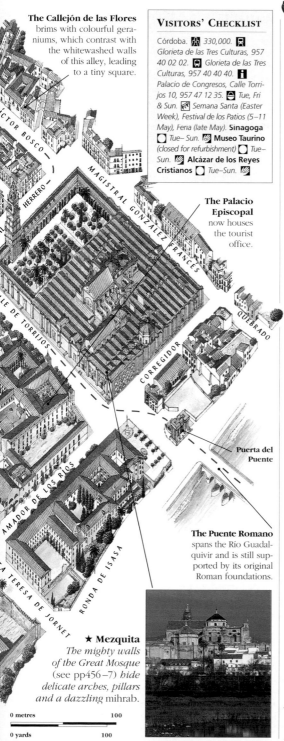

The Puerta del Puente

The Puente Romano spans the Río Guadalquivir and is still supported by its original Roman foundations.

★ Mezquita
The mighty walls of the Great Mosque (see pp456–7) hide delicate arches, pillars and a dazzling mihrab.

0 metres   100

0 yards   100

Córdoba: the Mezquita

ORDOBA'S GREAT MOSQUE, dating back
12 centuries, embodied the power of
Islam on the Iberian Peninsula. Abd al
Rahman I *(see p48)* built the original
mosque between 785 and 787. The
building evolved over the centuries,
blending many architectural forms.
In the 10th century al Hakam II
made some of the most lavish
additions, including the elaborate
mihrab (prayer niche) and the
maqsura (caliph's enclosure).
During the 16th century a
cathedral was built in the heart
of the reconsecrated mosque,
part of which was destroyed.

Patio de los Naranjos
*Orange trees grow in the courtyard
where the faithful washed
before prayer.*

Torre del Alminar
*This bell tower, 93 m (305 ft)
high, is built on the site of
the original minaret. Steep
steps lead to the top for a
fine view of the city.*

**The Puerta del
Perdón** is a Mudéjar-
style entrance gate, built
during Christian rule in
1377. Penitents were
pardoned here.

**Puerta de
San Esteban** is
set in a section of
wall from an earlier
Visigothic church.

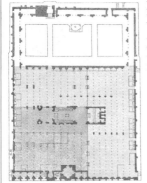

EXPANSION OF THE MEZQUITA

Abd al Rahman I built the
original mosque. Extensions
were added by Abd al Rahman
II, al Hakam II and al Mansur.

KEY TO ADDITIONS

▢	Mosque of Abd al Rahman I
▢	Extension by Abd al Rahman II
▢	Extension by al Hakam II
▢	Extension by al Mansur
▢	Patio de los Naranjos

STAR FEATURES

★ **Arches and Pillars**

★ **Mihrab**

★ **Capilla de
Villaviciosa**

Cathedral

Part of the mosque was destroyed to accommodate the cathedral, started in 1523. Featuring an Italianate dome, it was designed chiefly by members of the Hernán Ruiz family.

VISITORS' CHECKLIST

Calle Torrijos. ▐ 957 47 05 12.
◯ Apr–Jun: 10am–7:30pm; Jul–Oct: 10am–5pm; Nov & Feb: 10am–6pm, Dec & Jan: 10am–5:30pm, Mar: 10am–7pm Mon–Sat. 🅶 🛉 9:30am Mon–Sat; 11am, noon & 1pm Sun & hols.

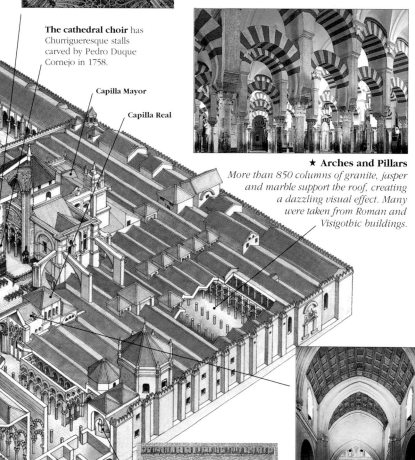

The cathedral choir has Churrigueresque stalls carved by Pedro Duque Cornejo in 1758.

Capilla Mayor

Capilla Real

★ **Arches and Pillars**
More than 850 columns of granite, jasper and marble support the roof, creating a dazzling visual effect. Many were taken from Roman and Visigothic buildings.

★ **Mihrab**
This prayer niche, richly ornamented, held a gilt copy of the Koran. The worn flagstones indicate where pilgrims circled it seven times on their knees.

★ **Capilla de Villaviciosa**
The first Christian chapel was built in the mosque in 1371 by Mudéjar (see p51) craftsmen. Its multi-lobed arches are stunning.

Baroque statuary in the Fuente del Rey at Priego de Córdoba

Montilla ㉙

Córdoba. 🏘 *23,000.* 🚉 🚌 🛈 *Capitan Alonso de Vargas 3, 957 65 24 62.* 🗓 *Fri.* 🎉 *Grape Harvest (late Aug).*

MONTILLA IS THE CENTRE of an important wine region that produces an excellent smooth white fino *(see p402).* Unlike sherry, it is not fortified with alcohol. Several bodegas, including **Alvear** and **Pérez Barquero**, will show visitors around by prior arrangement.

The Mudéjar **Convento de Santa Clara** dates from 1512. The town library is in the **Casa del Inca**, so named because Garcilaso de la Vega, who wrote about the Incas, lived there in the 16th century.

ENVIRONS: Aguilar, 13 km (8 miles) to the south, has the unusual, eight-sided Plaza de San José (built in 1810) and several seigneurial houses.

Baena, 40 km (25 miles) to the west of Montilla, has been famous for its olive oil since Roman times. On the Plaza de la Constitución stands the Casa del Monte, an arcaded mansion dating from the 18th century. During Easter Week thousands of costumed drummers take to the streets.

🍷 **Bodega Alvear**
Avda María Auxiliadora 1. 📞 *957 66 40 14.* 🕐 *Mon–Sat.* 🌙 *public hols.*
🍷 **Bodega Pérez Barquero**
Avda de Andalucía 27. 📞 *957 65 05 00.* 🕐 *Mon–Fri.* 🌙 *public hols.*

Priego de Córdoba ㉚

Córdoba. 🏘 *23,000.* 🚌 🛈 *Calle del Río 33, 957 70 06 25.* 🚌 *Sat.* 🎉 *Feria Real (1–6 Sep).* 🌐 *www.aytopriegodecordoba.es*

PRIEGO DE CÓRDOBA'S claim to be the capital of Cordoban Baroque is borne out by the dazzling work of carvers, ironworkers and gilders in the many houses, and especially churches, built with wealth generated by a prosperous 18th-century silk industry.

A restored Moorish fortress stands in the whitewashed medieval quarter, the **Barrio de la Villa**. Close by is the outstanding **Iglesia de la Asunción**, converted from Gothic to Baroque style by Jerónimo Sánchez de Rueda. Its *pièce de résistance* is the sacristy, created in 1784 by local artist Francisco Javier Pedrajas. The main altar is Plateresque *(see p21).*

At midnight every Saturday the brotherhood of another Baroque church, the **Iglesia de la Aurora**, parades the streets singing songs in praise of the Virgin.

Silk merchants built many of the splendid mansions that follow the curve around the Calle del Río. At the street's end is the Baroque **Fuente del Rey** (The King's Fountain). The 139 spouts splash water into three basins adorned with a riot of statuary.

La Asunción, Priego de Córdoba

ENVIRONS: Zuheros, perched on a crag in the limestone hills northwest of Priego, is one of Andalusia's prettiest villages. **Rute**, to the southwest, is known for its *anís (see p577).*

Alcalá la Real, in the lowlands east of Priego, is overlooked by the hilltop ruins of a castle and a church. There are two handsome Renaissance buildings on its central square: the Fuente de Carlos V and the Palacio Abacia.

Montefrío ㉛

Granada. 🏘 *7,000.* 🚌 🛈 *Plaza España 1, 958 33 60 04.* 🚌 *Mon.* 🎉 *Fiesta patronal (14–18 Aug).*

THE APPROACH to Montefrío from the south offers wonderful views of its tiled rooftops and pretty whitewashed houses running up to a steep crag. This archetypal Andalusian town is topped by the remains of its Moorish fortifications and the 16th-century Gothic **Iglesia de la Villa**, attributed to Diego de Siloé. In the centre of town is the Neo-Classical **Iglesia de la Encarnación**, identifiable by its large dome. The architect Ventura Rodríguez (1717–85) is credited with its design. The town is known for its chorizo.

ENVIRONS: Santa Fé was built by the Catholic Monarchs at the end of the 15th century. Their army camped here while

Barrels of Montilla, the sherry-like wine from the town of the same name

The castle overlooking the resort of Almuñécar on the Costa Tropical

laying siege to Granada, and this was the site of the formal surrender of the Moors in 1492 *(see pp52–3)*. A Moor's severed head, carved in stone, adorns the spire of the parish church.

Sited above a gorge, **Alhama de Granada** was named Al hamma (hot springs) by the Moors. Their baths, close to the spot where the hot water gushes from the ground just outside town, can be seen in the Hotel Balneario.

Loja, on the Río Genil, near Los Infiernos gorge, is known as "the city of water" because of its spring-fed fountains.

Nerja ㉜

Málaga. 🏛 *18,000.* 🚉 🛈 *Calle Puerta del Mar 2, 95 252 15 31.* 🚌 *Tue.* 🎭 *Feria (8–12 Oct).* Ⓦ *www.nerja.net*

THIS WELL-ESTABLISHED resort, built on a cliff above sandy coves, lies at the foot of the beautiful Sierra de Almijara. There are sweeping views up and down the coast from the rocky promontory known as **El Balcón de Europa** (the Balcony of Europe). Along it runs a promenade lined with cafés and restaurants.

East of the town are the **Cuevas de Nerja**, a series of vast caverns which were discovered in 1959. Wall paintings found here are believed to be about 20,000 years old. Only a few of the many cathedral-sized chambers are open to public view. One of these has been converted into an impressive auditorium which has a capacity of several hundred people.

ENVIRONS: In **Vélez-Málaga**, the ruins of the Fortaleza de Belén, a Moorish fortress set dramatically on a rocky outcrop, dominates the medieval Barrio de San Sebastián.

🏛 Cuevas de Nerja
Carretera de las Cuevas de Nerja. █ *95 252 95 20.* ⭕ *daily.* 🅿

Almuñécar ㉝

Granada. 🏛 *21,000.* 🚉 🛈 *Avda Europa, 958 63 11 25.* 🚌 *Fri.* 🎭 *Virgen de la Antigua (15 Aug).* Ⓦ *www.almunecar-ctropical.org*

ALMUÑÉCAR LIES on the Costa Tropical, so named because its climate allows the cultivation of exotic fruit. Just inland, mountains rise to more than 2,000 m (6,560 ft). The Phoenicians founded the first settlement here, called Sexi, and the Romans constructed an aqueduct, the remains of which can be seen today. Almuñécar is now a popular holiday resort.

Above the old town is the **castle**, which was built by the Moors and altered in the 16th century. Below it is the **Parque Ornitológico** (comprising an aviary and botanic gardens) and the ruins of a Roman fish-salting factory. The **Museo Arqueológico** displays a variety of Phoenician artifacts.

ENVIRONS: The ancient white town of **Salobreña** is set amid fields of sugar cane. Narrow streets lead up a hill, first fortified by the Phoenicians, to a restored Arab castle with fine views of the Sierra Nevada *(see p461)*. Modern buildings now line part of Salobreña's beach.

🦜 Parque Ornitológico
Plaza de Abderraman. █ *958 63 11 25.* ⭕ *daily.* 🅿
🏛 Museo Arqueológico
Casco Antiguo. ⭕ *Tue–Sat.* 🅿
🏰 Castillo de Salobreña
Falda del Castillo. █ *958 61 03 14.* ⭕ *Tue–Sun.* 🅿

One of the succession of sandy coves that make up the resort of Nerja

The majestic peaks of the Sierra Nevada towering, in places, to over 3,000 m (9,800 ft) above sea level

Lanjarón ❸

Granada. 🏔 *24,000.* 🚌 🛈 *Plaza de la Constitución 29, 958 71 00 02.* 🗓 *Tue & Fri.* 🎉 *San Juan (24 Jun).*

SCORES OF CLEAR, SNOW-FED springs bubble from the slopes of the Sierra Nevada; their abundance at Lanjarón, on the southern side of this great range of mountains, has given the town a long history as a health spa. From June to October, visitors flock to take the waters for arthritic, dietary and nervous ailments. Bottled water from Lanjarón is sold all over the country.

A major festival begins on the night of 23 June and ends in an uproarious water battle in the early hours of 24 June, the Día de San Juan. Everyone in the streets gets doused.

The town is on the threshold of Las Alpujarras, a scenic upland area of dramatic landscapes, where steep, terraced hillsides and deep-cut valleys conceal remote, whitewashed villages. Roads to and from Lanjarón wind slowly and dizzily around the slopes.

A Tour of Las Alpujarras ❺

THE FERTILE, UPLAND VALLEYS of Las Alpujarras, clothed with chestnut, walnut and poplar trees, lie on the southern slopes of the Sierra Nevada. The architecture of the quaint white villages which cling to the hillsides – compact clusters of irregularly shaped houses with tall chimneys sprouting from flat, grey roofs – is unique in Spain. Local specialities are ham cured in the cold, dry air of Trevélez and brightly coloured, handwoven rugs.

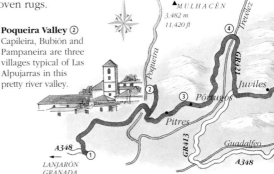

Trevélez ④
Trevélez, in the shadow of Mulhacén, Spain's highest mountain, is famous for its cured ham.

Poqueira Valley ②
Capileira, Bubión and Pampaneira are three villages typical of Las Alpujarras in this pretty river valley.

Orgiva ①
This is the largest town of the region, with a Baroque church in the main street and a lively Thursday market.

Fuente Agria ③
People come to this spring to drink the iron-rich, naturally carbonated waters.

SIERRA
▲ *MULHACÉN*
3,482 m
11,420 ft

GR-421
Juviles
Pórtugos
Pitres
GR413
Guadalfeo
A348

A348
LANJARÓN
GRANADA

SIERRA DE LA

Laujar de Andarax 🞦

Almería. 🚶 2,000. 🚌 🛈 Carretera Laujar–Berja km 1, 950 51 35 48. 🛒 3 & 17 of each month. 🎉 San Vicente (22 Jan), San Marcos (25 Apr), Virgen de la Salud (19 Sep).

L AUJAR, IN THE ARID foothills of the Sierra Nevada looks southwards across the Andarax valley towards the Sierra de Gádor.

Andarax was founded by one of the grandsons of Noah. In the 16th century, Abén Humeya, leader of the greatest Morisco rebellion (see p55), made his base here. The revolt was crushed by Christian troops and Abén Humeya was killed by his own followers. Inside

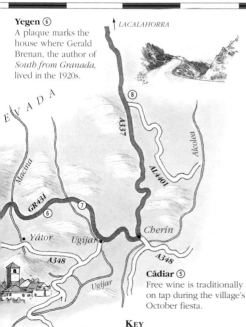

Painting, Iglesia de la Encarnación

Laujar's 17th-century church, **La Encarnación**, is a statue of the Virgin by Alonso Cano. Next to the Baroque **town hall** (ayuntamiento) is a fountain inscribed with some lines written by Francisco Villespesa, a dramatist and poet who was born in Laujar in 1877: "Six fountains has my pueblo/He who drinks their waters/ will never forget them/so heavenly is their taste."

El Nacimiento, a park to the east of Laujar, is a suitable place to have a picnic. You can accompany it with one of the area's hearty red wines. **Ohanes**, above the Andarax valley further to the east, is an attractive hill town of steep streets and whitewashed houses known for its crops of table grapes.

Sierra Nevada 🞨

Granada. 🚌 from Granada. 🛈 Plaza de Andalucía, Cetursa Sierra Nevada, 958 24 91 19.

F OURTEEN PEAKS more than 3,000 m (9,800 ft) high crown the heights of the Sierra Nevada. The snow lingers until July and begins falling again in late autumn. One of Europe's highest roads, the GR411, runs past **Solynieve**, an expanding ski resort at 2,100 m (6,890 ft), and skirts the two highest peaks, **Pico Veleta** at 3,398 m (11,149 ft) and **Mulhacén** at 3,482 m (11,420 ft).

The Sierra's closeness to the Mediterranean and its altitude account for the great diversity of the indigenous flora and fauna found on its slopes – the latter including golden eagles and some rare butterflies.

There are several mountain refuges for the use of serious hikers and climbers.

Yegen ⑥
A plaque marks the house where Gerald Brenan, the author of South from Granada, lived in the 1920s.

LACALAHORRA

Puerto de la Ragua ⑧
This pass, which leads across the mountains to Guadix, is nearly 2,000 m (6,560 ft) high and is often snowbound in winter.

Válor ⑦
Abén Humeya, leader of a rebellion by Moriscos in the 16th century, was born here. A commemorative battle between Moors and Christians is staged each year in mid-September.

Cádiar ⑤
Free wine is traditionally on tap during the village's October fiesta.

KEY

▬	Tour route
═	Other roads
▲	Mountain peak

0 kilometres 5
0 miles 5

TIPS FOR DRIVERS

Tour length: 85 km (56 miles).
Stopping-off points: There are bars and restaurants in Orgiva, Capileira, Bubión (see p602) and Trevélez. Orgiva, Bubión and Trevélez have good hotels (see pp563–7). Orgiva is the last petrol stop before Cádiar.

Granada ⓧ

Stone relief, Museo Arqueológico

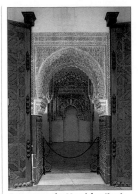

THE GUITARIST ANDRÉS SEGOVIA (1893–1987) described Granada as a "place of dreams, where the Lord put the seed of music in my soul". It was first occupied by the Moors in the 8th century, and its golden period came during the rule of the Nasrid dynasty *(see p51)* from 1238 to 1492, when artisans, merchants, scholars and scientists all contributed to the city's international reputation as a centre for culture. Under Christian rule, following its fall to the Catholic Monarchs in 1492 and the expulsion of the Moors *(see pp52–3)*, the city blossomed in Renaissance splendour. There was a period of decline in the 19th century, but Granada has recently been the subject of renewed interest and efforts are being made to restore parts of it to their past glory.

Entrance to the Moorish *mihrab* in the Palacio de la Madraza

Façade of Granada cathedral

Exploring Granada
The old city centre around the cathedral is a maze of narrow one-way streets. It contains the Alcaicería – a reconstruction of a Moorish bazaar that burned down in 1843. Granada's two main squares are the Plaza Bib-Rambla, near the cathedral, and the Plaza Nueva. From the latter, Cuesta de Gomérez leads up to the city's two principal monuments: the Alhambra and the Generalife. On a hill opposite is the Albaicín district.

Churches well worth a visit are the Iglesia de San Juan de Dios, almost overwhelming in its wealth of Baroque decoration, and the Renaissance Iglesia de San Jerónimo.

🔒 Cathedral
On the orders of the Catholic Monarchs, work on the cathedral began in 1523 to plans in a Gothic style by Enrique de Egas. It continued under the Renaissance maestro, Diego

de Siloé, who also designed the façade and the magnificent, circular Capilla Mayor. Under its dome, windows of 16th-century glass depict Juan del Campo's *The Passion*. The west front was designed by the Baroque artist Alonso Cano, who was born in the city. His grave and many of his works can be seen in the cathedral.

🔒 Capilla Real
The Royal Chapel was built for the Catholic Monarchs between 1506 and 1521 by Enrique de Egas. A magnificent *reja* (grille) by Maestro Bartolomé de Jaén encloses the high altar and the Carrara marble figures of Fernando and Isabel, their daughter Juana la Loca (the Mad) and her husband Felipe el Hermoso (the Fair). Their coffins are in the crypt. In the sacristy there are art treasures, including paintings by Botticelli and Van der Weyden, as well as Isabel's crown, Fernando's sword and their army banners.

🔲 Palacio de la Madraza
Calle Oficios 14. **[** *958 22 34 47 or 958 22 1300.* **[** *Sep–Jul: Mon–Fri.*
Originally an Arab university, this building later became the city hall. The façade dates from the 18th century. Inside is a Moorish hall with a finely decorated *mihrab* (prayer niche).

🔲 Corral del Carbón
Calle Mariana Pineda. **[** *958 22 59 90.* **[** *9am–7pm daily.* **[**
This galleried courtyard, formerly a storehouse and inn for merchants, is a unique relic of the Moorish era. In Christian times it was a venue for theatrical performances; it later became a coal exchange. Today it houses craft shops and the main tourist office.

🔲 Casa de los Tiros
Calle Pavaneras. **[** *958 22 10 72.* **[** *2:30–8pm Mon–Fri.*
This fortress-like palace was built in Mudéjar style in the 16th century. It originally belonged to the family that was awarded the Generalife after the fall of Granada. Among

Grille by Maestro Bartolomé de Jaén enclosing the altar of the Capilla Real

Cupola in the sanctuary of the Monasterio de la Cartuja

their possessions was a sword that had belonged to Boabdil. This is carved on the façade, along with statues of Mercury, Hector, Hercules, Theseus and Jason. The building owes its name to the muskets that project from its battlements: *tiro,* in Spanish, meaning shot.

🏯 Alhambra and Generalife
See pp466–7.

🏯 El Bañuelo
Carrera del Darro 31. ☎ 958 22 59 90. ⏰ Tue–Sat. ● public hols.
These brick-vaulted Arab baths were built in the 11th century. The columns are topped by reused Visigothic and Roman capitals as well as Arab ones.

🏛 Museo Arqueológico
Carrera del Darro 43. ☎ 958 22 56 40. ⏰ daily. ● am Mon & Tue, Sun.

VISITORS' CHECKLIST

Granada. 🏙 250,000. ✈ 12 km (7 miles) southwest of city. 🚊 Avenida de Andalucía, 902 24 02 02. 🚌 Carretera de Jaén, 958 24 71 28. 🛈 Corral del Carbón, C/ Mariana Pineda, 958 24 71 28 🛢 Sat & Sun. 🎉 Semana Santa (Easter Week), Día de la Cruz (3 May), Corpus Christi (May/Jun).

This museum occupies the Casa de Castril, a Renaissance mansion with a Plateresque *(see p21)* portal. It displays Iberian, Phoenician and Roman finds from Granada province.

⛪ Monasterio de la Cartuja
A Christian warrior called El Gran Capitán founded this monastery outside Granada in 1516. There is a dazzling cupola by Antonio Palomino, and an extravagant Churrigueresque *(see p21)* sacristy by Luis de Arévalo and Luis Caballo.

GRANADA CITY CENTRE

Alhambra ⑥
El Bañuelo ⑦
Capilla Real ②
Casa de los Tiros ⑤
Cathedral ①
Corral del Carbón ④
Museo Arqueológico ⑧
Palacio de la Madraza ③

0 metres 250
0 yards 250

KEY

■ See pp464–5
🅿 Parking
🛈 Tourist information
⛪ Church
⛩ Convent or monastery

Street-by-Street: the Albaicín

Ornate plaque on a house in the Albaicín

THIS CORNER OF THE CITY, clinging to the hillside opposite the Alhambra, is where one feels closest to Granada's Moorish ancestry. A fortress was first built here in the 13th century and there were once over 30 mosques. Most of the city's churches were built over their sites. Along the cobbled alleys stand *cármenes*, villas with Moorish decoration and gardens, secluded from the world by their high walls. In the jasmine-scented air of evening, take a walk up to the Mirador de San Nicolás. The view over the maze of rooftops of the Alhambra glowing in the sunset is magical.

Street in the Albaicín
Steep and sinuous, the Albaicín's streets are truly labyrinthine. Many street names start with Cuesta, *meaning slope.*

Real Chancillería
Built in 1530 by the Catholic Monarchs, the Royal Chancery has a beautiful Renaissance façade.

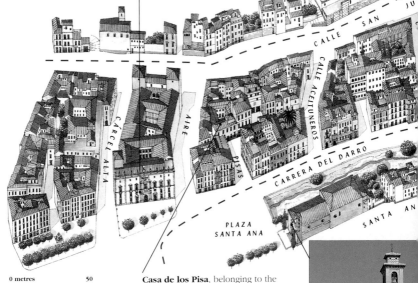

Casa de los Pisa, belonging to the Knights Hospitallers, displays works of art – some depicting St John of God, who died here in 1550.

★ Iglesia de Santa Ana
At the end of the Plaza Nueva stands this 16th-century brick church in Mudéjar style. It has an elegant Plateresque portal and, inside, a coffered ceiling.

| 0 metres | 50 |
| 0 yards | 50 |

STAR SIGHTS

★ Iglesia de Santa Ana

★ Museo Arqueológico

★ El Bañuelo

★ Museo Arqueológico
The ornate Plateresque carvings on the museum's façade include this relief of two shields. They show heraldic devices of the Nasrid kings of Granada, who were defeated by the Catholic Monarchs in 1492 (see pp52–3).

Carrera del Darro
The road along the Río Darro leads past crumbling bridges and the fine façades of ancient buildings, now all restored.

To Mirador de San Nicolás

KEY

– – – Suggested route

DE LOS REYES

PLAZA CONCEPCIÓN

CARNERO

BAÑUELO

CONCEPCIÓN

CALLE ZAFRA

CALLE GLORIA

CARRETERA DEL SANTISIMO

CARRERA DEL DARRO

To Sacromonte

RÍO DARRO

The Convento de Santa Catalina was founded in 1521.

SACROMONTE

Granada's gypsies formerly lived in the caves honey-combing this hillside. In the past, travellers would go there to enjoy spontaneous outbursts of flamenco. Today, virtually all the gypsies have moved away, but touristy flamenco shows of variable quality are still performed here in the evenings (*see pp406–407*). Sitting at the very top of the hill is the Abadía del Sacromonte, a Benedictine monastery. The ashes of St Cecilio, Granada's patron saint, are kept inside.

Gypsies dancing flamenco, 19th century

★ El Bañuelo
Star-shaped openings in the vaults let light into these well-preserved Moorish baths, which were built in the 11th century.

The Alhambra

A MAGICAL USE of space, light, water and decoration characterizes this most sensual piece of architecture. It was built under Ismail I, Yusuf I and Muhammad V, caliphs when the Nasrid dynasty *(see pp50–51)* ruled Granada. Seeking to belie an image of waning power, they created their idea of paradise on Earth. Modest materials were used (plaster, timber and tiles), but they were superbly worked. Although the Alhambra suffered pillage and decay, including an attempt by Napoleon's troops to blow it up, in recent times it has undergone extensive restoration and its delicate craftsmanship still dazzles the eye.

Sala de la Barca

★ Salón de Embajadores

The ceiling of this sumptuous throne room, built from 1334 to 1354, represents the seven heavens of the Muslim cosmos.

★ Patio de Arrayanes

This pool, set amid myrtle hedges and graceful arcades, reflects light into the surrounding halls.

Patio de Machuca

Entrance

Patio del Mexuar

This council chamber, completed in 1365, was where the reigning sultan listened to the petitions of his subjects and held meetings with his ministers.

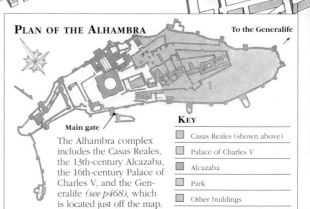

PLAN OF THE ALHAMBRA

To the Generalife

Main gate

The Alhambra complex includes the Casas Reales, the 13th-century Alcazaba, the 16th-century Palace of Charles V, and the Generalife *(see p468)*, which is located just off the map.

KEY

☐ Casas Reales (shown above)
☐ Palace of Charles V
☐ Alcazaba
☐ Park
☐ Other buildings

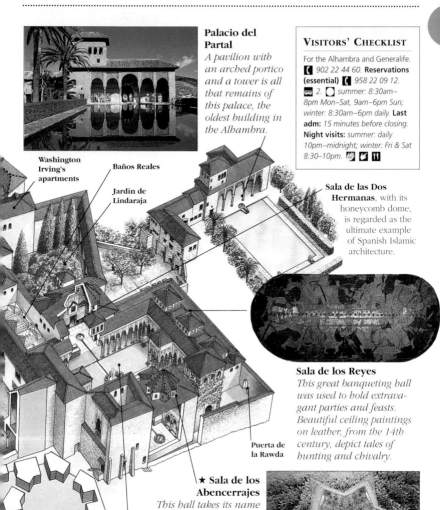

Palacio del Partal

A pavilion with an arched portico and a tower is all that remains of this palace, the oldest building in the Alhambra.

Washington Irving's apartments

Baños Reales

Jardín de Lindaraja

Sala de las Dos Hermanas, with its honeycomb dome, is regarded as the ultimate example of Spanish Islamic architecture.

Sala de los Reyes

This great banqueting hall was used to hold extravagant parties and feasts. Beautiful ceiling paintings on leather, from the 14th century, depict tales of hunting and chivalry.

Puerta de la Rawda

★ Sala de los Abencerrajes

This hall takes its name from a noble family, who were rivals of Boabdil (see pp52–3). According to legend, he had them massacred while they attended a banquet here. The geometrical ceiling pattern was inspired by Pythagoras' theorem.

The Palace of Charles V (1526) houses a collection of Spanish-Islamic art, whose highlight is the Alhambra vase *(see p48).*

★ Patio de los Leones

Built by Muhammad V, this patio is lined with arcades supported by 124 slender marble columns. At its centre, a fountain rests on 12 stocky, marble lions.

STAR FEATURES

★ Salón de Embajadores

★ Patio de Arrayanes

★ Sala de los Abencerrajes

★ Patio de los Leones

Granada: Generalife

FROM THE ALHAMBRA'S northern side, a footpath leads to the Generalife, the country estate of the Nasrid kings. Here, they could escape from palace intrigues and enjoy tranquillity high above the city, a little closer to heaven. The name Generalife, or Yannat al Arif, has various interpretations, perhaps the most pleasing being "the garden of lofty paradise". The gardens, begun in the 13th century, have been modified over the years. They originally contained orchards and pastures. The Generalife provides a magical setting for Granada's annual music and dance festival *(see p37).*

The Patio de la Acequia *is an enclosed oriental garden built round a long central pool. Rows of water jets on either side make graceful arches above it.*

Sala Regia

Jardines Altos (Upper Gardens)

The Escalera del Agua is a staircase with water flowing gently down it.

The Patio de los Cipreses, otherwise known as the Patio de la Sultana, was the secret meeting place for Zoraya, wife of the Sultan Abu-l-Hasan, and her lover, the chief of the Abencerrajes.

Entrance

The Patio de Polo was the courtyard where palace visitors, arriving on horseback, would tether their steeds.

The Patio del Generalife *lies just before the entrance to the Generalife. The walk from the Alhambra to the Generalife gardens passes first through the Jardines Bajos (lower gardens), before crossing this Moorish patio with its characteristically geometric pool.*

The forbidding exterior of the castle above Lacalahorra

Castillo de Lacalahorra 39

Lacalahorra (Granada). (*958 67 70 98*. 🚌 *Guadix*. ○ *Wed.*

GRIM, IMMENSELY THICK walls and stout, cylindrical corner towers protect the castle on a hill above the village of Lacalahorra. Rodrigo de Mendoza, son of Cardinal Mendoza, had the castle built for his bride: the work was carried out between 1509 and 1512 by Italian architects and craftsmen. Inside is an ornate, arcaded Renaissance courtyard over two floors with pillars and a staircase carved from Carrara marble.

Guadix 40

Granada. 🏛 *20,000*. 🚉 🚌 **ℹ** *Carretera de Granada, 958 66 26 65.* 🚋 *Sat.* 🎉 *Fiesta & Feria (31 Aug – 5 Sep).* 🌐 *www.guadixymarquesado.org*

THE TROGLODYTE QUARTER, with 2,000 caves that have been inhabited for centuries, is the town's most remarkable sight. The **Cueva-Museo** shows how people live underground.

The **cathedral** was begun in 1594 by Diego de Siloé and finished, by Gaspar Cayón and Vicente de Acero, between 1701 and 1796. Relics of San Torcuato, who founded Spain's first Christian bishopric, are kept in the cathedral museum.

Near the Moorish **Alcazaba**, dating from the 10th and 11th centuries, is the Mudéjar-style **Iglesia de Santiago**, a church with a fine coffered ceiling. The 16th-century **Palacio de Peñaflor** is being restored.

🏛 **Cueva-Museo Al Fareria**
C/ San Miguel. ○ *Mon–Sat.* 📷

Jaén 41

🏛 *113,000*. 🚉 🚌 **ℹ** *Calle Maestra 13, 953 14 04 55.* 🚌 *Thu.* 🎉 *Nuestra Señora de la Capilla (11 Jun), San Lucas (18 Oct), Romería de Santa Catalina (25 Nov).*

THE MOORS called Jaén *Geen* – meaning "way station of caravans" – because of its strategic site on the road beween Andalusia and Castile. Their hilltop fortress was rebuilt as the **Castillo de Santa Catalina** after it was captured by King Fernando III in 1246. Part of it is now a parador *(see p565).*

Andrés de Vandelvira, who was responsible for many of Úbeda's fine buildings *(see pp472–3)*, designed Jaén's **cathedral** in the 16th century. Later additions include the two 17th-century towers that now flank the west front.

An old mansion, the **Palacio Villardompardo**, houses a museum of arts and crafts, and also gives access to the **Baños Árabes**, the 11th-century baths of Ali, a Moorish chieftain. These have horseshoe arches, ceilings with small, star-shaped windows and two ceramic vats in which bathers once immersed themselves. Tucked away in an alley is the **Capilla de**

San Andrés, a Mudéjar chapel founded in the 16th century by Gutiérrez González who, as treasurer to Pope Leo X, was endowed with extensive privileges. A gilded iron screen by Maestro Bartolomé de Jaén is the highlight of the chapel.

The **Real Monasterio de Santa Clara** was founded in the 13th century and has a lovely cloister dating from the late 16th century. Its church, which has a coffered ceiling, contains a bamboo image of Christ made in Ecuador.

The **Museo Provincial** displays Roman mosaics and sculptures, and Iberian, Greek and Roman ceramics.

Horseshoe arches supporting the dome at the Baños Árabes, Jaén

♠ **Castillo de Santa Catalina**
Carretera al Castillo.
(*953 12 07 33.* ○ *Wed.*
🏛 **Palacio Villardompardo**
Plaza Santa Luisa de Marillac. (*953 23 62 92.* ○ *Tue – Sun.* ● *public hols.* 🌐 *www.promojaen.es*
🏛 **Museo Provincial**
Po de la Estación 27. (*953 25 06 00.* ○ *Tue – Sun.* ● *public hols.*

Whitewashed cave dwellings in the troglodyte quarter of Guadix

Roman bridge spanning the Guadalquivir at Andújar

Andújar ㊷

Jaén. ⌂ *39,000.* 🚌 🚍 ℹ *Pl Santa María. Torre del Reloj, 953 50 49 59.* 🛒 *Tue.* 🎉 *Romería (last Sun of Apr).*

ANDÚJAR IS KNOWN FOR its olive oil and its pottery. It stands on the site of an Iberian town, Iliturgi, which was destroyed in the Punic Wars *(see p46)* by Scipio. The Roman conquerors built the 15-arched bridge spanning the Río Guadalquivir.

In the central square is the Gothic **Iglesia de San Miguel**, with paintings by Alonso Cano. The **Iglesia de Santa María la Mayor** has a Renaissance façade and a Mudéjar tower. Inside it is El Greco's *Christ in*

the Garden of Olives (c.1605). A pilgrimage to the nearby **Santuario de la Virgen de la Cabeza** takes place in April.

ENVIRONS: The mighty fortress of **Baños de la Encina** has 15 towers and ramparts built by Caliph Al Hakam II in AD 967. Further north, the road and railway between Madrid and Andalusia squeeze through a spectacular gorge in the eastern reaches of the Sierra Morena, the **Desfiladero de Despeñaperros**.

Baeza ㊸

See pp474–5.

Úbeda ㊹

Jaén. ⌂ *34,000.* 🚌 ℹ *Palacio Marqués de Contadero, C/ Baja del Marqués 4, 953 75 08 97.* 🛒 *Sun.* 🎉 *San Miguel (28 Sep).*

ÚBEDA IS A SHOWCASE of Renaissance magnificence, thanks to the patronage of some of Spain's most influential men of the 16th century. These included such dignitaries as Francisco de los Cobos, secretary of state, and his great-nephew, Juan Vázquez de Molina, who gave his name to Úbeda's most historic square. Surrounded by elegant palaces and churches, it is undoubtedly the jewel in Úbeda's crown. The old town is contained within city walls that were first raised by the Moors in 852.

Created on the orders of the Bishop of Jaén around 1562, the colossal former **Hospital de Santiago** was designed by Andrés de Vandelvira, who refined the Spanish Renaissance style into its more austere characteristics. The façade is flanked by square towers, one topped with a blue-and-white-tiled spire. Today the building is a conference centre.

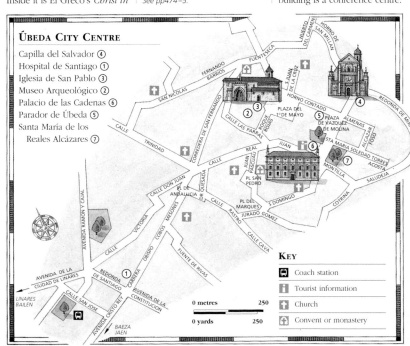

ÚBEDA CITY CENTRE

Capilla del Salvador ④
Hospital de Santiago ①
Iglesia de San Pablo ③
Museo Arqueológico ②
Palacio de las Cadenas ⑥
Parador de Úbeda ⑤
Santa María de los
    Reales Alcázares ⑦

0 metres   250

0 yards   250

KEY

🚌 Coach station

ℹ Tourist information

✝ Church

✛ Convent or monastery

◁ **Fields of poppies and olive groves south of Andújar in the province of Jáen**

Laguna de Valdeazores in the Parque Nacional de Cazorla

Sited in the 15th-century Casa Mudéjar, the **Museo Arqueológico** exhibits artifacts from Neolithic to Moorish times.

The **Iglesia de San Pablo** has a 13th-century apse and a beautiful 16th-century chapel by Vandelvira. It is surmounted by a Plateresque tower that was completed in 1537.

A monument to the poet and mystic St John of the Cross (1549–91) stands in the **Plaza de Vázquez de Molina**. The **Capilla del Salvador**, on the square, was designed by three 16th-century architects – Diego de Siloé, Andrés de Vandelvira and Esteban Jamete – as the personal chapel of Francisco de los Cobos. Behind it stand Cobos' palace, with a Renaissance façade, and the Hospital de los Honrados Viejos (Hospital of the Honoured Elders), looking on to the Plaza de Santa Lucía. From here, the Redonda de Miradores follows the line of the city walls and offers views of the countryside.

Plaza Vázquez de Molina also holds Úbeda's **parador** (*see p567*). Built in the 16th century, but much altered in the 17th, it was the residence of Fernando Ortega Salido, dean of Málaga and chaplain of the Capilla del Salvador.

Úbeda's town hall and tourist office occupy the **Palacio de las Cadenas**, a mansion built ?or Vázquez de Molina by ?ndelvira. It gets its name ?n the iron chains *(cadenas)* ? attached to the columns ?rting the main doorway. ? on the square are the ?of **Santa María de los ?lcázares**, which

dates mainly from the 13th century, and the **Cárcel del Obispo** (Bishop's Jail), where nuns who had been punished by the bishop were confined.

🏛 **Museo Arqueológico**
Casa Mudéjar, Calle Cervantes 6.
█ 953 75 37 02. ○ *Tue–Sun.* ⑤
🏥 **Hospital de Santiago**
Calle Obispo Cubos 2. █ 953 75 08 42. ○ *daily.*

Capilla del Salvador, Úbeda, one of Spain's finest Renaissance churches

Parque Natural de Cazorla ⑮

Jaén. 🚌 *Cazorla.* ℹ *Calle Juan Domingo 2, 953 72 01 15.*

FIRST-TIME VISITORS are amazed by the spectacular scenery of this 214,336-ha (529,409-acre) nature reserve with thickly wooded mountains rising to peaks of 2,000 m (6,500 ft) and varied, abundant wildlife.

Access to the Parque Natural de Cazorla, Segura y Las Villas is via the town of Cazorla. Its imposing Moorish **Castillo de la Yedra** houses a folklore museum. From Cazorla, the road winds upwards beneath the much-photographed remains of the clifftop castle at **La Iruela**. After crossing a pass it drops down to a crossroads (El Empalme del Valle) in the valley of the Río Guadalquivir. Roads lead to the source of the river and to the peaceful modern parador *(see p564)*.

The main road through the park follows the river. The information centre at Torre del Vinagre is 17 km (11 miles) from the crossroads.

ENVIRONS: There is a well-restored Moorish castle at **Segura de la Sierra**, 30 km (19 miles) from the reserve's northern edge. Below it is an unusual rock-hewn bullring.

♙ **Castillo de la Yedra**
█ 953 71 00 39. ○ *Tue–Sun.*
● *17 Sep–1 Nov, 24 & 31 Dec.*
▨ *(free for EU citizens).*

CAZORLA'S WILDLIFE

More than 100 bird species live in this nature reserve, some very rare, such as the golden eagle and the griffon vulture. Cazorla is the only habitat in Spain, apart from the Pyrenees, where the lammergeier lives. Mammals in the park include the otter – active at dawn and dusk – mouflon and wild boar, and a small remaining population of Spanish ibex. The red deer was reintroduced in 1952. Among the flora supported by the limestone geology is the indigenous *Viola cazorlensis*.

Wild boar foraging for roots, insects and small mammals

Street-by-Street: Baeza ⑬

**Coat of arms,
Casa del Pópulo**

NESTLING AMID the olive groves that characterize much of Jaén province, beautiful Baeza is a small town, unusually rich in Renaissance architecture. Called Beatia by the Romans and later the capital of a Moorish fiefdom, Baeza is portrayed as a "royal nest of hawks" on its coat of arms. It was conquered by Fernando III in 1226 – the first town in Andalusia to be definitively won back from the Moors – and was then settled by Castilian knights. An era of medieval splendour followed, reaching a climax in the 16th century, when Andrés de Vandelvira's splendid buildings were erected. In the early 20th century, Antonio Machado, one of his generation's greatest poets, lived here.

★ **Palacio de Jabalquinto**
An Isabelline-style (see p20) façade, flanked by elaborate, rounded buttresses, fronts this splendid Gothic palace.

Antigua Universidad
From 1542 until 1825, this Renaissance and Baroque building was one of Spain's first universities.

Torre de los Aliatares is a 1,000-year-old tower built by the Moors.

Ayuntamiento
Formerly a jail and a courthouse, the town hall is a dignified Plateresque structure (see p21). The coats of arms of Felipe II, Juan de Borja and of the town of Baeza adorn its upper façade.

Casas Consistoriales Bajas

La Alhóndiga, the old corn exchange, has impressive t[...] tier arches run[...] along its front[...]

PLAZA SANTA CRUZ

SAN FELIPE

BEATO ÁVILA

ROMANO

COMPAÑIA

BARBACANA

MERCADERÍAS

PLAZA DE ESPAÑA

To ↑ Úbeda

PASEO DE LA CONSTITUCIÓN

NARVAEZ

PASEO DE TUNDIDORES

BECERRA

GASPAR

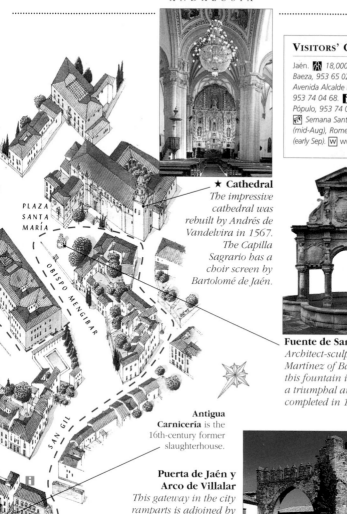

PLAZA
SANTA
MARÍA

OBISPO MENGIBAR

SAN GIL

VISITORS' CHECKLIST

Jaén. 18,000. Linares-Baeza, 953 65 02 02. Avenida Alcalde Puche Pardo, 953 74 04 68. Plaza del Pópulo, 953 74 04 44. Tue. Semana Santa (Easter), Feria (mid-Aug), Romería de la Yedra (early Sep). W www.andalucia.org

★ **Cathedral**
The impressive cathedral was rebuilt by Andrés de Vandelvira in 1567. The Capilla Sagrario has a choir screen by Bartolomé de Jaén.

Fuente de Santa María
Architect-sculptor Ginés Martínez of Baeza designed this fountain in the form of a triumphal arch. It was completed in 1564.

Antigua Carnicería is the 16th-century former slaughterhouse.

Puerta de Jaén y Arco de Villalar
This gateway in the city ramparts is adjoined by an arch erected in 1521 to appease Carlos I (see p54) after a rebellion.

| 0 metres | 75 |
| 0 yards | 75 |

KEY

ℹ️ Tourist information

– – – Suggested route

To Jaén

★ **Plaza del Pópulo**
The Casa del Pópulo, a fine Plateresque palace, now the tourist office, overlooks this square. In its centre is the Fuente de los Leones, a fountain with an Ibero-Roman statue flanked by lions.

STAR SIGHTS

★ **Palacio de Jabalquinto**

★ **Cathedral**

★ **Plaza del Pópulo**

Renaissance castle overlooking the village of Vélez Blanco

Vélez Blanco ⁴⁶

Almería. 🏘 2,400. 🚌 Vélez Rubio. 🛈 Ayuntamiento, Calle Corredera 38, 950 41 50 01. 🚍 Wed. 🎉 Cristo de la Yedra (second Sun of Aug).

Dominating this pleasant village is the mighty **Castillo de Vélez Blanco**. It was built between 1506–13 by the first Marquis de Los Vélez. The Renaissance interiors are now displayed in the Metropolitan Museum in New York, but there is a reconstruction of one of the patios.

Just outside Vélez Blanco, the **Cueva de los Letreros** contains paintings from c.4000 BC. One depicts the Indalo, a figure holding a rainbow and believed to be a deity with magical powers, now adopted as the symbol of Almería.

🛈 **Cueva de los Letreros**
Camino de la Cueva de los Letreros. 🔲 daily.

Mojácar ⁴⁷

Almería. 🏘 5,000. 🚌 🛈 Plaza Nueva, 950 61 50 25. 🚍 Wed, Sun. 🎉 Moors and Christians (second weekend of Jul), San Agustín (28 Aug).

From a distance, Mojácar shimmers like the mirage of a Moorish citadel, its white houses cascading over a lofty ridge, 2 km (1 mile) inland from long, sandy beaches.

Following the Civil War (see pp62–3), the village fell into ruin as most of its inhabitants emigrated, but in the 1960s it was discovered by tourists, which gave rise to a new era of prosperity. The old gateway in the walls still remains, but otherwise the village has been completely rebuilt and holiday complexes have grown up along the nearby beaches. The coast south from Mojácar is among the least built up in Spain, with only small resorts and villages along its length.

Tabernas ⁴⁸

Almería. 🏘 3,000. 🚌 🛈 Ayuntamiento, Plaza del Pueblo 1, 950 36 50 02. 🚍 Wed. 🎉 Virgen de las Angustias (11–15 Aug).

Tabernas is set in Europe's only desert. The town's Moorish fortress dominates the harsh surrounding scenery of cactus-dotted, rugged, eroded hills and dried-out riverbeds, which has provided the setting for many classic spaghetti westerns, such as A Fistful of Dollars. Two film sets can be visited: **Mini-Hollywood** and

Texas Hollywood, 1 km (1 mile) and 4 km (2 miles) from Tabernas respectively.

Not far from town is a solar energy research centre, where hundreds of heliostats follow the course of southern Andalusia's powerful sun.

Environs: Sorbas sits on the edge of the deep chasm of the Río de Aguas. It has two notable buildings: the 16th-century Iglesia de Santa María and a 17th-century mansion said to have been a summer retreat for the Duke of Alba.

Nearby is the karst scenery, honeycombed with hundreds of cave systems, of the **Yesos de Sorbas** nature reserve. Permission to explore them is required from Andalusia's environmental department.

🎬 **Mini-Hollywood**
Carretera N340. 📞 950 36 52 36. 🔲 daily. ● Mon in winter. 🎥

🎬 **Texas Hollywood**
Carretera N340, Tabernas. 📞 950 16 54 58. 🔲 daily. 🎥

Desert landscape around Tabernas, reminiscent of the Wild West

Still from For a Few Dollars More by Sergio Leone

SPAGHETTI WESTERNS

Two Wild West towns lie off the N340 highway west of Tabernas. Here, visitors can re-enact classic film scenes or watch stunt men performing bank hold-ups and saloon brawls. The poblados del oeste were built during the 1960s and early 1970s when low costs and eternal sunshine made Almería the ideal location for spaghetti westerns. Sergio Leone, director of The Good, the Bad and the Ugly, built a ranch here and film-sets sprang up in the desert. Local gypsies played Indians and Mexicans. The deserts and Arizona-style badlands are still used for television commercials and series, and by film directors such as Steven Spielberg.

The 10th-century Alcazaba, which dominates Almería's old town

Almería ㊾

Almería. 🏛 170,000. ☐ ☐
ℹ Parque Nicolás Salmerón, 950 27
43 55. ☐ Tue, Fri & Sat. 🎭 Feria (last
week of Aug).
ⓦ www.almeria-turismo.org

ALMERÍA'S colossal **Alcazaba**, dating from AD 995, is the largest fortress built by the Moors in Spain. The huge structure bears witness to the city's golden age, when it was an important port under the Caliphate of Córdoba (see pp48–9). The Moorish city, known as Al Mariyat (Mirror of the Sea), exported mainly brocade, silk and cotton.

During the Reconquest, the Alcazaba withstood two major sieges before eventually falling to the armies of the Catholic Monarchs (see pp52–3) in 1489. The royal coat of arms can be seen on the Torre del Homenaje, built during their reign. The Alcazaba also has a Mudéjar chapel and gardens.

Adjacent to the Alcazaba is the old fishermen's and gypsy quarter of **La Chanca**, where some families live in caves with brightly painted façades and modern interiors. On Mondays a lively street market is held. Although this district is picturesque, it is also desperately poor and it is unwise to walk around here alone or at night with valuables.

Berber pirates from North Africa often raided Almería. Consequently, the **cathedral** is almost more like a castle than a place of worship, with four towers, thick walls and slit windows. The site was once a mosque. This was turned into a church, but

in 1522 it was destroyed in an earthquake. Work on the present building began in 1524 under the direction of Diego de Siloé, who designed the nave and high altar in Gothic style. The Renaissance façade and the carved walnut choir stalls are by Juan de Orea.

Brightly coloured entrance to a gypsy cave in La Chanca district

Traces of Moorish Almería's most important mosque can be seen in the **Templo San Juan**. The **Plaza Vieja** is an attractive 17th-century arcaded square. On one side is the **town hall** (ayuntamiento), with a cream and pink façade (1899).

ENVIRONS: One of Europe's most important examples of a Copper Age settlement lies at **Los Millares**, near Gádor, 17 km (11 miles) to the north of Almería. As many as 2,000 people may have occupied the site around 2500 BC.

⚜ **Alcazaba**
Calle Almanzor. 🄲 950 27 16 17.
☐ Tue–Sun. ⬤ 1 Jan, 25 Dec.
🈹 (free for EU citizens).
🏠 **Los Millares**
Calle Santa Fé de Mondújar.
🄲 950 23 50 10. ☐ Wed–Sun.

Parque Natural de Cabo de Gata ㊿

Almería. ☐ San José. ℹ Centro de
Visitantes de las Amoladeras,
Carretera–Cabo de Gata km 6, 950
16 04 35.

TOWERING CLIFFS of volcanic rock, sand dunes, salt flats and secluded coves characterize the 29,000-ha (71,700-acre) Parque Natural de Cabo de Gata. Within its confines are a few fishing villages, and the small resort of San José, on a fine sandy bay. A lighthouse stands at the dramatic end of the cabo (cape), which can be reached by road from the village of Cabo de Gata. The park includes a stretch of seabed 2 km (1 mile) wide and the marine flora and fauna protected within it attract scuba-divers and snorkellers.

The dunes and saltpans between the cape and the Playa de San Miguel are a habitat for thorny jujube trees. Thousands of migrating birds stop here, and among the 170 or so bird species recorded are flamingoes, avocets, griffon vultures and Dupont's larks.

ENVIRONS: Set amid citrus trees on the edge of the Sierra de Alhamilla, **Níjar's** fame stems from the pottery and the handwoven jarapas – blankets and rugs – that are made here. The barren plain between Níjar and the sea has been brought under cultivation using vast plastic greenhouses to conserve the scarce water.

The dramatic, dark volcanic rocks at Cabo de Gata, east of Almería

SPAIN'S
ISLANDS

Introducing Spain's Islands

S PAIN'S TWO GROUPS OF ISLANDS lie in separate seas –
the Balearics in the Mediterranean and the Canaries
in the Atlantic, off the African coast. Both are popular
package-tour destinations blessed with warm climates,
good beaches and clear waters. But each has more to
offer than high-rise hotels, fast-food restaurants and
discos. The Balearics have white villages, wooded
hills, caves and prehistoric monuments, while the
extraordinary volcanic landscapes of the Canaries are
unlike any other part of Spain. Four of Spain's national
parks *(see pp26–7)* are in the Canary Islands.

Ibiza (see pp486–8) *is the liveliest
of the Balearic Islands. Ibiza town
and Sant Antoni are the main tourist
centres, offering good nightlife and
excellent beaches.*

*Eivissa
(Ibiza)*

Formentera

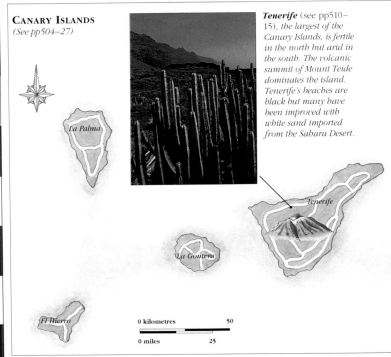

CANARY ISLANDS
(See pp504–27)

La Palma

Tenerife (see pp510–
15), *the largest of the
Canary Islands, is fertile
in the north but arid in
the south. The volcanic
summit of Mount Teide
dominates the island.
Tenerife's beaches are
black but many have
been improved with
white sand imported
from the Sahara Desert.*

Tenerife

La Gomera

El Hierro

0 kilometres   50

0 miles   25

◁ **Vines growing in the volcanic soil of Lanzarote, protected by drystone walls**

In Menorca (see pp498–503) tourism has developed more slowly than in Mallorca and Ibiza, and the island has largely avoided being over-commercialized. Scattered across the countryside are the ruins of unique Bronze Age buildings.

BALEARIC ISLANDS
(See pp482–503)

Menorca

Mallorca

0 kilometres 50

0 miles 25

Mallorca (see pp490–97), best known for its beaches, has caves and other natural features to explore. The most spectacular of the island's historic sights is the great Gothic cathedral in Palma, which rises above the boats moored in the old harbour.

Lanzarote (see pp524–6) is the most attractive of the Canary Islands, even though the landscape is strikingly bare. White houses contrast starkly with black volcanic fields. The most dramatic attraction is Timanfaya National Park, including the Montañas del Fuego.

Lanzarote

Fuerteventura

an Canaria

Gran Canaria (see p518–21) centres on a symmetrical volcanic cone. The capital city of Las Palmas has some interesting museums and monuments. In contrast, the sprawling Maspalomas, on the south coast, is the biggest holiday resort in Spain.

THE BALEARIC ISLANDS

IBIZA · FORMENTERA · MALLORCA · MENORCA

*C*HIC RESORTS *and attractive coves and beaches, combined with a climate which is hot but never uncomfortably so, have made tourism the mainstay of life along the coasts of the Balearic Islands. Inland, there is peace and quiet in abundance, and a great variety of sights to seek out: wooded hills, pretty white villages, monasteries, country churches, caves and prehistoric monuments.*

Standing at a crossroads in the Mediterranean, the Balearic Islands have been plundered or colonized in turn by Phoenicians, Greeks, Carthaginians, Romans, Moors and Turks. In the 13th century Catalan settlers brought their language, a dialect of which is widely spoken today.

The islands can justifiably claim to cater for all tastes: from sun-seekers on package holidays, for whom the larger resorts serve as brash fun factories, to jet-setters and film stars, who head for luxurious but discreet hideaways in the hills. The largest island, where tourism has been established the longest, is Mallorca. A massive Gothic cathedral stands near the waterfront of Palma, the capital. Menorca's green countryside is dotted with prehistoric monuments and its towns full of noble, historic mansions. The coast of Ibiza is notched by innumerable rocky coves. The island's hilly interior is characterized by brilliant white farmhouses and robust churches. On Formentera, small and relatively undeveloped, the pace of life is slow. The islets surrounding the four principal islands are mainly uninhabited; one of them, Cabrera (off Mallorca), is a national park.

through the window of one of Ibiza's traditional, whitewashed farmhouses

massive, heavily buttressed cathedral overlooking Palma de Mallorca's harbour

Exploring the Balearics

THOUGH THE BALEARIC ISLANDS are often associated with high-density, inexpensive package tourism, they offer enough variety to satisfy everyone's tastes. For those unattracted by the bustle of the coastal resorts and their beautiful beaches, the countryside and the old towns of Palma, Ibiza, Maó and Ciutadella are relatively undisturbed. Mallorca is by far the most culturally rich of the Balearics, with its distinguished collection of modern and traditional galleries, and interesting museums. Menorca is strong on Neolithic remains and neo-colonial architecture, while Ibiza is for lovers of clear, painterly light and rustic peasant houses; it also has some of the wildest nightclubs in Europe. Formentera – for many, the most alluring island – has crystal water, white sand, a pure, parched landscape and total tranquillity.

Poblat des Pescadors in the tourist village of Binibeca

Early-morning mist on the waters of Port de Pollença in Menorca

MALLORCA

0 kilometres 25

0 miles 15

GETTING AROUND
Nearly all foreign visitors to the Balearics arrive by plane: Mallorca, Menorca and Ibiza have connections to major European cities as well as Madrid, Barcelona and Valencia. Several airlines fly to most other Spanish cities out of Son Sant Joan airport in Palma. Another way of arriving is by boat from Barcelona, Valencia, Alicante or Dénia. Between the islands there are regular ferry services, run by Transmediterránea and Flebasa. Mallorca is the only island with rail services, which run between Palma and Inca, and between Palma and Sóller. Roads vary from excellent to poor, depending on how far you stray from the tourist trail. The best way to get around the islands is by car, except on Formentera, where the ideal mode of transport is the bicycle.

Sights at a Glance

A peaceful stroll on the sands of Ibiza's Sant Miquel beach

See Also

• *Where to Stay* pp568–9

• *Restaurants and Bars* pp605–607

The rocky coast around the Coves d'Artá in Mallorca

Key

▬▬	Motorway
▬▬	Major road
▬▬	Minor road
▬▬	Scenic route
▬▬	River
☀	Viewpoint

Ibiza

THIS SMALL ISLAND, the nearest of the Balearics to the coast of Spain, was unknown and untouched by tourism until the 1960s, when it suddenly appeared in Europe's holiday brochures along with Benidorm and Torremolinos. There is still a curious, indefinable magic about Ibiza (Eivissa) and the island has not entirely lost its character. The countryside, particularly in the north, is a rural patchwork of groves of almonds, olives and figs, and wooded hills. Ibiza town retains the air of a 1950s Spanish provincial borough. At once package-tour paradise, hippie hideout and glamour hot spot, this is one of the Mediterranean's mythical destinations.

An Ibizan shepherdess

The bustling harbour of the resort of Sant Antoni

Sant Antoni ❶

Baleares. 🏠 15,500. 🚌 ⛴
🛈 Passeig de Ses Fonts, 971 34 33 63. 🎉 Sant Antoni (17 Jan), Sant Bartolomé (24 Aug).
🖥 www.santantoni.net

IBIZA'S SECOND TOWN, Sant Antoni was known by the Romans as Portus Magnus because of its large natural harbour. Formerly a tiny fishing village, it has turned into a sprawling and exuberant resort. Although it was once notoriously over-commercialized, the town has recently undergone a dramatic facelift. Nevertheless, the 14th-century parish church of Sant Antoni is practically marooned in a sea of modern high-rise hotels.

To the north of Sant Antoni, on the road to Cala Salada, is the chapel of **Santa Agnès**, an unusual early Christian temple (not to be confused with the village of the same name). When this catacomb-like chapel was discovered, in 1907, it contained Moorish weapons and fragments of pottery.

Sant Josep ❷

Baleares. 🏠 13,700. 🛈 Carrer Pedro Escanellas 39, 971 80 01 25.
🎉 Sant Josep (19 Mar).

THE VILLAGE of Sant Josep, the administrative centre of southwest Ibiza, lies in the shadow of Ibiza's highest mountain. At 475 m (1,560 ft), Sa Talaiassa offers a panorama of all Ibiza, including the islet of **Es Vedrá**, rising from the

The salt lakes of Ses Salines, a haven for many bird species

sea like a rough-cut pyramid. For the most accessible view of this enormous rock, take the coastal road to the sandy cove of Cala d'Hort where there are a number of good restaurants and a quiet beach.

ENVIRONS: Before tourism, salt was Ibiza's main industry, most of it coming from the salt flats at **Ses Salines** in the southeast corner of the island. Mainland Spain is the chief consumer of this salt, but much goes to the Faroe Islands and Scandinavia for salting fish. It is loaded on to ships at Ibiza's southernmost port, La Canal. Ses Salines is also an important refuge for birds, including the flamingo. **Es Cavallet**, 3 km (2 miles) east, is an unspoiled stretch of soft, white sand.

Ibiza ❸

Baleares. 🏠 32,700. ✈ 🚌 ⛴
🛈 Calle Antonio Riquer 2, Andenes del Puerto, 971 30 19 00. 🏪 Mon-Sat (summer only). 🎉 Fiestas Patronales (1–8 Aug), San Juan Bautista (24 Jun). 🖥 www.visitbalears.com

THE OLD QUARTER of Ibiza (Eivissa), known also as Dalt Vila, or upper town, is a miniature citadel guarding the mouth of the almost circular bay. The **Portal de ses Taules**, a magnificent gateway in the north wall of the 16th-century fortifications, carries the finely carved coat of arms of the kingdom of Aragón, to which the Balearic Islands belonged in the Middle Ages (see p217). Outside the walls is the 16th-century **Església de Santo**

Domingo with its three red-tiled domes. The Baroque interior, with its barrel-vaulted ceiling and frescoed walls, has been restored to its former glory. Works of art by Erwin Bechtold, Barry Flanagan and other artists connected with Ibiza are on display in the **Museu d'Art Contemporani**, just inside the Portal de ses Taules. Crowning the whole Dalt Vila is the **cathedral**, a 13th-century Catalan Gothic building with 18th-century additions. The cathedral's Museo de la Sacristia houses assorted works of art.

Under the Carthaginians, the soil of Ibiza was considered holy. The citizens of Carthage deemed it an honour to be buried in the **Necropolis de Puig d'es Molins**, thought to contain over 4,000 graves. The **Museu de Arqueología** is attached to the site.

The crossroads village of **Jesús**, 3 km (2 miles) north, is

A backstreet in the Sa Penya district of Ibiza town

well worth a visit for its pretty 16th-century church. Originally built as part of a Franciscan monastery, it has a 16th-century altarpiece by Rodrigo de Osona the Younger.

🏛 **Museu d'Art Contemporani**
Ronda Narcés Puget. 【 971 30 27 23. ☐ Mon–Sat. ◯ public hols. 🧖
🏠 **Necropolis de Puig d'es Molins**
Via Romana 31. 【 971 30 17 71. ☐ Tue–Sun. 🧖

Els Amunts ❹

Baleares. 🚌 Sant Miquel. 🛈 Santa Eulària d'es Riu, (971) 33 07 28.

Els amunts is the local name for the uplands of northern Ibiza, which stretch from Sant Antoni on the west coast to Sant Vicenç in the northeast. Though hardly a mountain range – Es Fornás is the highest point, at a mere 450 m

A view across the port towards Ibiza's upper town

(1,480 ft) – the area's inaccessibility has kept it unspoiled. There are few special sights here, apart from the landscape: pine-clad hills sheltering fertile valleys whose rich red soil is planted with olive, almond and fig trees, and the occasional vineyard. Tourist enclaves are also scarce – except for a handful of small resorts, such as Port de Sant Miquel, Portinatx and Sant Vicenç. Inland, villages like Sant Joan and Sant Agnès offer an insight into Ibiza's quiet, rural past.

The architectural highpoints of northern Ibiza are several beautiful white churches, like the one in **Sant Miquel** which, on Thursdays in summer, is host to a display of Ibizan folk dancing. Outside Sant Llorenç is the tranquil, fortified hamlet of **Balàfia**, with flat-roofed houses, tiny whitewashed alleys, and a watchtower that was used as a fortress during raids by the Turks.

IBIZA'S HOTTEST SPOTS

Ibiza's reputation for extraordinary summer nightlife is largely justified. The main action takes place in two areas: the Calle de la Virgen in the old harbour district, with its bars, fashion boutiques and restaurants; and the mega-discos out of town – Ku Prigilege, Pachá, Amnesia and Es Paradis. When the last of these is closing, at about 7am, the wildest club of them all, Space, is only just opening its doors. Ibiza has long been a magnet for the rich and famous. Celebrities seem to have become more elusive of late, but a few well-known faces can often be glimpsed dining in the restaurant Las Dos Lunas, and taking the rays the next day on the beach at Ses Salines.

Nightclubbers enjoying a bubble bath at Amnesia

One of the many beautiful beaches along the unspoiled shores of the island of Formentera

Santa Eulària ❺

Baleares. 🏠 21,100. 🚌 ⛴ ℹ️
*Carrer Mariano Riquer Wallis 4, 971 33
07 28.* 🚌 *Wed.* 🎉 *Es Cana (15 Aug).*

DESPITE CATERING for tourism, the town of Santa Eulària d'es Riu (Santa Eulalia del Río), situated on the island's only river, has managed to hold on to its character far more than many other Spanish resorts.

The 16th-century church, with its pretty covered courtyard, and the surrounding old town, were built on the top of a little hill, the **Puig de Missa**, because this site was more easily defended in times of war than the shore below.

Adjacent to the church is the **Museu Etnològic**, a folk museum, which is housed in an ancient but tastefully adapted Ibizan farmhouse. Included in the exhibits (labelled in Catalan only) are traditional costumes, farming implements, toys and

The domed roof of Santa Eulària's 16th-century church

an olive press. A fascinating collection of old photographs reveals the drastic and irreversible changes Ibiza has suffered over the last 50 years.

🏛️ **Museu Etnològic**
Puig de Missa. 📞 *971 33 28 45.*
⏰ *Mon–Sat.*

Formentera ❻

Baleares. 🏠 6,000. ⛴ *from Ibiza.*
ℹ️ *Calle Calpe, La Savina, 971 32 20
57.* 🌐 *www.illadeFormentera.com*

AN HOUR'S BOAT RIDE from Ibiza harbour will bring you to this largely unspoiled island where the waters are blue and the way of life slow.

From the small port of La Savina, where the boat docks, there are buses to other parts of the island, or you can hire a car, moped or bicycle from one of the shops nearby.

Sant Francesc, Formentera's tiny capital, is situated 3 km (2 miles) from La Savina. Most of the island's amenities are in this town, plus a pretty church (built in 1729), in the main square, and a folk museum.

From Sant Francesc, a bumpy minor road leads for 9 km (6 miles) southwards, ending at Cap de Barbaria, the site of an 18th-century defensive tower and a lighthouse.

Formentera is entirely flat, apart from the small plateau of **La Mola**, which takes up the whole eastern end of the island. From the fishing port of Es Caló the road winds up-

wards past the Restaurante Es Mirador, with its panoramic view of western Formentera, to the village of Nostra Senyora del Pilar on top of the plateau. About 3 km (2 miles) to the east is a lighthouse, Far de la Mola, sited on the highest point of the island. Nearby stands a monument to Jules Verne (1828–1905), who used Formentera for the setting of one of his novels, *Hector Servadac*.

Although there are many purple road signs indicating places of cultural interest on Formentera, most lead only to disappointment. But one sight well worth seeking out is the megalithic sepulchre of **Ca Na Costa** (1800–1600 BC) near Sant Francesc, the only one of its kind in the Balearics. This monument, a circle of upright stone slabs, pre-dates the Carthaginians (*see pp45–6*).

However, the island's great strength is not its history and culture, but its landscape, which has a spare and delicate beauty and some of the Mediterranean's last unspoiled shorelines. The finest beaches are, arguably, Migjorn, Tramuntana, and Cala Saona, all southwest of Sant Francesc. Illetes and Llevant are two beautiful beaches on either side of a long sandy spit in the far north of the island. If the water is calm you can wade through it from the Pas d'es Trocadors (where Illetes and Llevant meet) to the island of **Espalmador** – with its natural springs, superb beaches and lighthouse – which lies between Formentera and Ibiza.

Regional Food: The Balearic Islands

Mayonnaise

Traditional food is being rediscovered in the Balearics. It varies from island to island but reflects the cuisine of Catalonia, with its combinations of sweet and savoury, and nuts and dried fruit. Pork is a main ingredient, and vegetable dishes and soups are also typical fare. Menorca's capital, Maó, lays claim to the invention of mayonnaise, which is often served with succulent fish and shellfish. Mallorca is the home of the savoury *sobrassada (see p493)*, a delicious spicy sausage, and the sweet pastry known as *ensaimada*.

Huevos a la sollerica *are fried eggs served on top of smooth, red* sobrassada *sausage, served with a pea sauce.*

Langosta a la parrilla *partners spiny lobster with the local mayonnaise, which is made with eggs and olive oil.*

Berenjenas rellenas *are aubergines stuffed with onions, herbs and bread. Tomatoes and pork are also often added.*

Tumbet, *made in a brown earthenware* greixera *or casserole, combines layers of peppers and tomato with potato.*

Coca de trampó *is a pizza-style dish, topped with a selection of fresh vegetables, especially onions and peppers.*

Ensaimada *is a spiral-shaped yeast bun from Mallorca, and can be eaten either for breakfast or as a tea-time snack.*

DRINKS

While in Menorca 200 years ago, sailors from the English navy introduced the islanders to the potent drink of gin with lemon. A highly perfumed gin is still made on the island. A large selection of herb and other liqueurs is made in the Balearics, including *palo*, flavoured with crushed almond shells. The Balearics produce few wines. The main wine region, a *denominación de origen (see p576)*, is around Binissalem in Mallorca, and produces mainly light whites and rosés. There are several red Mallorcan wines, which are best drunk young. The most popular Spanish drinks from the mainland, such as *anís*, brandy, beer and sangria *(see p577)*, are available everywhere in the Balearics.

Herb liqueur

Almond liqueur

Gin

Mallorca

MALLORCA IS OFTEN LIKENED TO A CONTINENT rather than simply an island. Its varied nature never fails to astonish, whether you are looking for landscape, culture or just entertainment. No other European island has a wider range of scenery, from the fertile plains of central Mallorca to the almost alpine peaks of the Tramuntana. The island's mild climate and lovely beaches have made it one of Spain's foremost package tour destinations but there is a wealth of culture, too, evident in sights like Palma Cathedral (*see pp496–7*). Mallorca's appeal lies also in its charm as a living, working island: the cereal and fruit crops of the central plains, and the vineyards around Binissalem are vital to the island's economy.

Terraced orange grove in the Sierra Tramuntana

Andratx ❼

Baleares. ∰ *8,500*. 🚊 🚌 *Plaça Miguel Moner 1, 971 62 80 00.* 🚐 *Wed.* 🎉 *San Pedro (29 Jun).* 🌐 *www.balearweb.com*

THIS SMALL TOWN lies amid a valley of almond groves in the shadow of Puig de Galatzó, which rises to 1,026 m (3,366 ft). With its ochre and white shuttered houses and the old watchtowers perched high on a hill above the town, Andratx is a very pretty place.

The road southwest leads down to **Port d'Andratx** 5 km (3 miles) away. Here, in an almost totally enclosed bay, expensive yachts are moored in rows along the harbour and luxury holiday homes pepper the surrounding hillsides. In the past, Port d'Andratx's main role was as the fishing port and harbour for Andratx, but since the early 1960s it has gradually been transformed into an exclusive holiday resort for the rich and famous. When visiting Port d'Andratx, it is a good idea to leave all thoughts of the real Mallorca behind and simply enjoy it for what it is – a chic and affluent resort.

La Granja ❽

Carretera de Esporles Bufar. 📞 *971 61 00 32.* 🏠 ⭕ *daily.* 🎦 🛗

LA GRANJA is a private estate, or *possessió*, near the little country town of Esporles. Formerly a Cistercian convent, it is now the property of the Seguí family, who have opened their largely unspoiled 18th-century house to the public as a kind of living museum of traditional Mallorca. Peacocks roam the gardens, salt cod and hams hang in the kitchen, *The Marriage of Figaro* plays in the ballroom, and the slight air of chaos just adds to the charm of the place.

Bust of Frédéric Chopin at Valldemossa

Valldemossa ❾

Baleares. ∰ *1,650*. 🚊 🚌 *Plaza Cartuja 11, 971 61 21 06.* 🚐 *Sun.* 🎉 *Santa Catalina Tomas (28 Jul), San Bartolomé (24 Aug).* 🌐 *www.valldemossa.com*

THIS PLEASANT mountain town will forever be linked with the name of George Sand, the French novelist who stayed here during the winter of 1838–9 and later wrote unflatteringly of the island in *Un Hiver à Majorque*. Dearer to Mallorcans is the Polish composer Frédéric Chopin (1810–49) who stayed with Sand at the **Real Cartuja de Jesús de Nazaret**. "Chopin's cell", off the monastery's main courtyard, is where a few of his works were written, and still houses the piano on which he composed.

Nearby is a 17th-century pharmacy displaying outlandish medicinal preparations such as "powdered nails of the beast". In the cloisters is an art museum with works by Tàpies, Miró and the Mallorcan artist Juli Ramis (1909–90), and a series of Picasso illustrations, *The Burial of the Count of Orgaz*, inspired by the El Greco painting of the same name (*see p28*).

🏛 **Real Cartuja de Jesús de Nazaret**
Plaça de la Cartuja de Valldemossa.
📞 *971 61 21 06.* ⭕ *daily.* 🎦 🛗

A view across the harbour of Port d'Andratx

Alfàbia ⑩

Carretera de Sóller km 17. 📞 971 61
31 23. 🚌 tour bus from Palma.
⬤ Sat pm & Sun. 📷

VERY FEW *possessións* in
Mallorca are open to the
public, which makes Alfàbia
worth visiting. The house and
garden are an excellent example of a typical Mallorcan
aristocratic estate and exude a
Moorish atmosphere. Very little
remains of the original 14th-
century architecture, so it is
well worth looking out for the
Mudéjar inscription on the ceiling of the entrance hall and the
Hispano-Arabic fountains and
pergola. The garden is a sumptuous 19th-century creation,
making imaginative use of
shade and the play of water.

Sóller ⑪

Baleares. 🏠 11,000. 🚂 🚌 ℹ️
Plaça Constitució 1, 971 63 80 08.
🚌 Sat. 📷 second Sun of May.

SÓLLER IS A LITTLE TOWN grown
fat on the produce of its
olive groves and orchards,
which climb up the slopes of
the Sierra Tramuntana. In the
19th century Sóller traded its
oranges and wine for French
goods, and the town retains a
faintly Gallic, bourgeois feel.

One of Sóller's best-known
features is its delightfully old-
fashioned narrow-gauge railway, complete with quaint
wooden carriages. The town,
whose station is in the Plaça
d'Espanya, lies on a scenic
route between Palma and the
fishing village of Port de Sóller
5 km (3 miles) to the west.

ENVIRONS: From Sóller a road
winds southwards along the
spectacular west coast to **Deià**
(Deyá). This village was once
the home of Robert Graves
(1895–1985), the English poet
and novelist, who came to
live here in 1929. His simple
tombstone can be seen in the
small cemetery. The **Museu
Arqueològic**, curated by the
archaeologist William Waldren,
offers a glimpse into prehistoric
Mallorca. Outside the village
is **Son Marroig**, the estate of
Austrian Archduke Ludwig

Houses and trees crowded together on the hillside of Deià

Salvator (1847–1915), who
documented the Balearics in a
series of books included in a
display of his possessions on
the first floor.

🏛 Museu Arqueològic
Es Clot Deià. 📞 971 63 90 01.
⬤ Fri–Sun. ♿

Statue of La Moreneta at the
Santuario de Lluc

Santuario de
Lluc ⑫

Lluc. 🚌 from Palma. 📞 971 87
15 25. ⬤ daily. 📷 museum only.

HIGH IN THE MOUNTAINS of
the Sierra Tramuntana, in
the remote village of Lluc, is
an institution regarded by
many as the spiritual heart of
Mallorca. The Santuario de
Lluc was built mainly in the
17th and 18th centuries on the
site of an ancient shrine. The
monastery's Baroque church,
with its imposing façade,

contains the stone image of
La Moreneta, the Black Virgin
of Lluc, supposedly found by
a young shepherd boy on a
nearby hilltop in the 13th
century. Along the Camí dels
Misteris, the paved walkway
up to this hilltop, there are
some bronze bas-reliefs by the
Catalan architect and designer
Antoni Gaudí (see pp136–7).
Just off the main Plaça dels
Pelegrins are a café and bar, a
pharmacy and a shop selling
a variety of local handicrafts,
wines and foods. The museum,
situated on the first floor, includes Mallorcan paintings and
medieval manuscripts. The
monastery incorporates a guest
house (see p568).

From Lluc, 13 km (8 miles)
of tortuous road winds through
the hills and descends towards
the coast, ending at the beautiful rocky bay of **Sa Calobra**.
From here, it is just 5 minutes'
walk further up the coast to the
Torrent de Pareis, a deep gorge
opening into the sea.

Sheer cliff face rising out of the
sea at Sa Calobra

The cloisters of the Convent de Santo Domingo in Pollença

Pollença ⓭

Baleares. 🏘 *14,000.* 🚌 ℹ *Calle Juan 23, 971 86 54 67.* 🚌 *Sun.* 🎭 *Sant Antoni (17 Jan).* 🌐 *www.ajpollenca.net*

ALTHOUGH POLLENÇA has become one of Mallorca's most popular tourist spots, it still appears unspoiled. The town, with its ochre-coloured stone houses and winding lanes, is picturesquely sited on the edge of fertile farmland. The Plaça Major, with its bars frequented mainly by locals, has an old-world atmosphere.

Pollença has fine churches, including the elegant 18th-century **Parròquia de Nostra Senyora dels Angels** and the Convent de Santo Domingo, which contains the **Museu Municipal**, with its displays on local archaeology. This convent also holds Pollença's Music Festival in August and early September. A chapel on the top of a hill, **El Calvari**, is

reached either by road or a torturous climb of 365 steps. On the altar there is a Gothic Christ, carved in wood.

ENVIRONS: Alcúdia, 10 km (6 miles) to the east, is surrounded by 14th-century walls pierced by two majestic gateways. Near the town centre is the **Museu Monografico de Pollentia**, which exhibits statues, jewellery and other remains found in the Roman settlement of Pollentia, 2 km (1 mile) south of Alcúdia.

🏛 **Museu Municipal**
Carrer Santo Domingo. 📞 *971 53 66 15.* ⏰ *daily.*
🏛 **Museu Monografico de Pollentia**
Calle San Jaume 30, Alcúdiá. 📞 *971 54 70 04.* ⏰ *Tue–Sun.* 🎫

Palma de Mallorca ⓮

See pp494–7.

Puig de Randa ⓯

8 km (5 miles) northeast of Llucmajor. 🚌 *to Llucmajor, then taxi.* ℹ *El Arenal, 971 44 04 14.*

IN THE MIDDLE of a fertile plain called the *pla* rises a mini-mountain 543 m (1,780 ft) high, the Puig de Randa. It is said that Mallorca's greatest son, the 14th-century theologian and mystic Ramon Llull, came to a hermitage on this mountain to meditate and write his religious treatise, *Ars Magna*. On the way up Puig de Randa there are two small monasteries, the 14th-century Santuari de Sant Honorat and the Santuari de Nostra Senyora de Gràcia. The latter, built on a ledge under an overhanging cliff, contains a 15th-century chapel with fine Valencian tiles inside, and offers an open view of the *pla*.

On the mountain top is the **Santuari de Cura**, built to commemorate Llull's time on the *puig*, and largely devoted to the study of his work. Its central courtyard is built in the typical beige stone of Mallorca. A small museum, housed in a 16th-century former school off the courtyard, contains some of Llull's manuscripts.

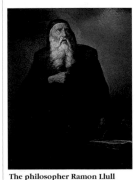

The philosopher Ramon Llull

Capocorb Vell ⓰

14 km (9 miles) south of Llucmajor. 📞 *971 18 01 55.* 🚌 *from El Arenal.* ⏰ *Fri–Wed.* 🎫

MALLORCA is not as rich in megalithic remains as Menorca, but this *talaiotic* village *(see p503)* in the stony flatlands of the southern coast is worth seeing – particularly on a quiet day when you can wander among the stones in peace. The settlement, which dates back to around 1000 BC, originally consisted of five *talaiots* (stone tower-like structures with timbered roofs) and 28 smaller dwellings. Little is known about its inhabitants and the uses for some of the rooms inside the buildings, such as the tiny underground gallery. Too small for living in, this room may have been used to perform magic rituals.

Part of the charm of this place lies in its surroundings among fields of fruit trees and dry stone walls, a setting that somehow complements the ruins. Apart from a snack bar nearby, the site remains mercifully undeveloped.

One of the *talaiots* of Capocorb Vell

Cabrera ⑰

Baleares. 🚢 from Colònia Sant Jordi. 🛈 Carrer Doctor Barraquer 5, Colònia Sant Jordi, 971 65 60 73 (summer); 971 64 91 17 (winter).

FROM THE BEACHES of Es Trenc and Sa Ràpita, on the south coast of Mallorca, Cabrera looms on the horizon. The largest island in an archipelago of the same name, it lies 18 km (11 miles) from the most southerly point of Mallorca. Cabrera is home to several rare plants, reptiles and seabirds, such as Eleonora's falcon. The waters are important for marine life. All this has resulted in it being declared a national park *(see pp26–7)*. For centuries Cabrera was used as a military base and it has a small population. On it stands a 14th-century castle.

A street in Felanitx

Felanitx ⑱

Baleares. 🏠 15,000. 🚍 🛈 Ronda Crucero Balear, 971 58 00 51. 🛒 Sun. 🎉 Sant Joan Pelós (24 Jun).

THIS BUSTLING agricultural town is the birthplace of Renaissance architect Guillem Sagrera (1380–1456) and the 20th-century painter Miquel Barceló. Felanitx is visited mainly for three reasons: the imposing façade of the 13th-century church, the **Esglesia de Sant Miquel**; its *sobrassada de porc negre* (a spiced raw sausage made from the meat of the local black pig) and its lively religious fiestas including Sant Joan Pelós *(see p499)*.

About 5 km (3 miles) southeast is the **Castell de Santueri**, founded by the Moors but rebuilt in the 14th century by the kings of Aragón, who ruled Mallorca. Though a ruin, it is worth the detour for the views to the east and south from its vantage point, 400 m (1,300 ft) above the plain.

Coves del Drac ⑲

1 km (1 mile) south of Porto Cristo. 🚍 from Porto Cristo. 📞 971 82 07 53. 🛈 daily. 🚫 1 Jan, 25 Dec. 🎫

MALLORCA has innumerable caves, ranging from mere holes in the ground to cathedral-like halls. The four vast chambers of the **Coves del Drac** are reached by a steep flight of steps, at the bottom of which is the beautifully lit cave known as "Diana's Bath". Another chamber holds the large underground lake, Martel, which is 39 m (128 ft) below ground level and is 177 m (580 ft) long. Music fills the air of the cave, played from boats plying the lake. Equally dramatic are the two remaining caves, charmingly named "The Theatre of the Fairies" and "The Enchanted City".

ENVIRONS: The **Coves dels Hams** is so called because some of its stalactites are shaped like hooks – *hams* in Mallorcan. The caves are 500 m (1,640 ft) long and contain the "Sea of Venice", an underground lake on which musicians sail in a small boat.

The entrance to the **Coves d'Artá**, near Capdepera, is 40 m (130 ft) above sea level and affords a wonderful view. The caves' main attraction is a stalagmite 22 m (72 ft) high.

🏛 **Coves dels Hams**
11 km (7 miles) from Manacor towards Porto Cristo. 📞 971 82 09 88. 🛈 daily. 🚫 1 Jan, 25 Dec. 🎫

🏛 **Coves d'Artá**
Carretera Canyamel. 📞 971 84 12 93. 🛈 daily. 🚫 1 Jan, 25 Dec. 🎫

The dramatically lit stalactites of the Coves d'Artá

Street-by-Street: Palma ⑭

Forn des Teatre pastry shop

O N AN ISLAND whose name has become synonymous with mass tourism, Palma surprises by its cultural richness. Under the Moors it was already a prosperous town of fountains and cool courtyards. After he had conquered it in 1229, Jaime I wrote, "It seemed to me . . . the most beautiful city we had ever seen". Signs of Palma's past wealth are still evident in the sumptuous churches, grand public buildings and fine private mansions that crowd the old town. The hub of the city is the old-fashioned Passeig des Born, whose cafés invite you to try one of Mallorca's specialities, the *ensaimada*, a spiral of pastry dusted with icing sugar.

The Forn des Teatre is an old pastry shop noted for its *ensaimadas* and *gató* (almond cake).

The Fundació la Caixa, once the Gran Hotel, is now a cultural centre.

PLAÇA REI JOAN CARLES

PASSEIG DES BORN

CARRER UNIO

CARRER FA...

CARRER DE PALAU REIAL

CARRER DE SAN...

CARRER MIRA...

AVINGUDA D'ANTONI MAURA

Palau de l'Almudaina
This once-royal Moorish palace now houses a museum, whose highlights include the chapel of Santa Ana, with its Romanesque portal, and the Gothic tinell *or salon.*

STAR SIGHTS

★ **Cathedral**

★ **Basílica de Sant Francesc**

La Llotja is a beautiful 14th-century exchange with tall windows and delicate tracery.

To Castell de Bellver and Fundació Pilar i Joan Miró

★ **Cathedral**
Built of golden limestone quarried from Santanyi, Palma's huge Gothic cathedral stands in a dramatic location near the waterfront.

Parc de la Mar

KEY

— — — Suggested route

To Estació de RENFE and
Estació de Autobuses

Plaça del Marqués
de Palmer

0 metres   100

0 yards   100

A view along the circular walls of
the Castell de Bellver

★ Basílica de Sant Francesc

*The church and
cloister of St Francis are
in a refined Gothic style
with a Baroque altarpiece
and rose window.*

**The Museu
Diocesà**,
housed in the
Bishop's Palace,
has a collection of
religious artifacts.

Museu de Mallorca

*The museum has displays on
local history, art and
architecture, including this
statue of an ancient warrior.*

Banys Àrabs

*The 10th-century baths,
with their well-preserved
arches, are a remnant of
the Balearic Islands'
Moorish culture.*

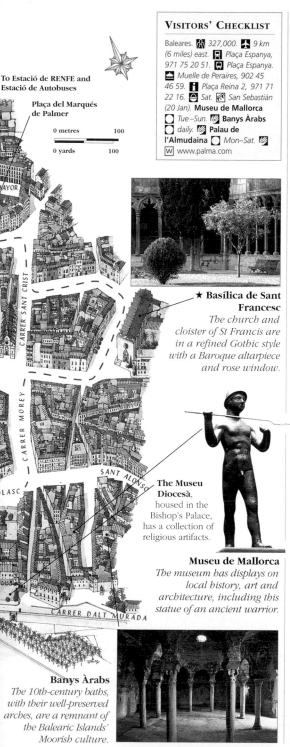

⚓ Castell de Bellver

West side of Palma Bay. 971 73
06 57. daily.
About 2 km (1 mile) from the
city centre, standing 113 m
(370 ft) above sea level, is
Palma's Gothic castle. It was
commissioned by Jaime II
during the short-lived Kingdom of Mallorca (1276–1349)
as a summer residence, but
soon after became a prison,
and remained as such until
1915. The castle, situated on
a wooded hill overlooking
the bay of Palma, is of an
unusual circular design.
    Three of its towers are set
into the main castle wall; the
other is set apart from it, but
linked by a high walkway.
From some angles the castle
looks more decorative than
defensive: witness the cloister
of delicate arches that rings
the central courtyard.

🏛 Fundació Pilar i Joan Miró

Carrer Joan de Saridakis 29. 971 70
14 20. Tue–Sun.
When Joan Miró died in 1982,
his wife took on the task of
converting his former studio
and home into an art centre.
The building – christened
"the Alabaster Fortress" by
the Spanish press – is a
stunning example of modern
architecture designed by
Navarrese architect Rafael
Moneo. It incorporates Miró's
original studio (complete with
unfinished paintings), a
permanent collection of the
painter's work, a shop, a
library and an auditorium.

Palma Cathedral

ACCORDING TO LEGEND, when Jaime I of Aragón was caught in a storm on his way to conquer Mallorca in 1229, he vowed that if God led him to safety he would build a great church in his honour. In the following years the old mosque of Medina Mayurqa was torn down and architect Guillem Sagrera (1380–1456) drew up plans for a new cathedral. In 1587 the last stone was added to the soaring vaults. Over subsequent years the cathedral has been rebuilt, notably early this century when the interior was remodelled by Antoni Gaudí *(see pp136–7)*. Today Palma Cathedral, or Sa Seu, as Mallorcans call it, is one of the most breathtaking buildings in Spain, combining vast scale with typically Gothic elegance *(see p20)*.

Bell Tower
This robust tower was built in 1389 and houses nine bells, the largest of which is known as Aloi, meaning "praise".

Palma Cathedral
One of the best-sited cathedrals anywhere, it is spectacularly poised high on the sea wall, above what was once Palma's harbour.

STAR FEATURES

★ **Great Rose Window**

★ **Baldachino**

19th-century tower

Entrance to cathedral museum

Portal Major

Flying buttresses

Cathedral Museum
One of the highlights of the beautifully displayed collection in the Old Chapterhouse is a 15th-century reliquary of the True Cross which is encrusted with jewels and precious metals.

★ Great Rose Window
The largest of seven rose windows looks down from above the High Altar like a gigantic eye. Built in 1370 with stained glass added in the 16th century, the window has a diameter of over 11 m (36 ft).

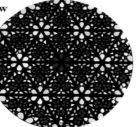

VISITORS' CHECKLIST

Plaça Salmoina. ☎ 971 72 31 30. ◷ Apr–Oct: 10am–5:30pm Mon–Fri; Nov–Mar: 10am–2:30pm Mon–Fri, (10am–1:30pm Sat all year). ● public hols. 🎟 ✝ 9am, 7pm daily; (Oct–Mar 9am, 7pm Sat, Sun). ♿

The Great Organ was built with a Neo-Gothic case in 1795, and restored in 1993 by Gabriel Blancafort.

Capella de la Trinitat
This tiny chapel was built in 1329 as the mausoleum of Jaime II and III of Aragón. It contains their alabaster tombs.

The Capella Reial, or Royal Chapel, was redesigned by Antoni Gaudí between 1904 and 1914.

Bishop's Throne
Built in 1269 and made of Carrara marble, the chair is embedded in a Gothic vaulted niche.

Choir stalls

Portal del Mirador

Nave
The magnificent ceiling, 44 m (144 ft) high, is held up by 14 slender pillars. At over 19 m (62 ft) wide, it is one of the broadest naves in the world.

★ Baldachino
Gaudí's bizarre wrought-iron canopy above the altar incorporates lamps, tapestries and a multicoloured crucifix.

Menorca

MENORCA IS THE BALEARIC ISLAND furthest from the mainland and it is set apart from the rest of the country in many other ways. The coastline of Menorca is, arguably, more unspoiled than in any other part of Spain. Its countryside remains largely green and pleasant with cows roaming the meadows. The old towns of Maó – the island's capital – and Ciutadella are filled with noble, historic buildings and beautiful squares. Menorca also has abundant reminders of its more distant history: the island boasts a spectacular hoard of Bronze Age stone structures, which provide an invaluable insight into its prehistoric past. The Menorcans are often more inclined to drink the locally brewed gin *(ginebra)* than the wine which is favoured elsewhere in Spain.

Fishermen mending their nets in Ciutadella's harbour

The peaceful seafront of Ciutadella at twilight

Ciutadella 20

Baleares. 🏛 *22,300.* 🚌 🛥 🛈 *Plaça de la Catedral 5, 971 38 26 93.* 🚍 *Fri & Sat.* 🎪 *Sant Joan (24 Jun).* 🌐 *www.visitmenorca.org*

THE KEY DATE in the history of Ciutadella is 1558. In that year the Turks, under Barbarossa, entered and decimated the city, consigning 3,495 of its citizens to the slave markets of Constantinople. Of Ciutadella's main public buildings, only the fine Catalan Gothic **Església Catedral de Menorca** managed to survive this fearsome onslaught in more or less its original condition, only later to be stripped of all its paintings, ornaments and other treasures by Republican extremists during the Civil War.

The nearby **Plaça des Born** was built as a parade ground for Moorish troops and from 1558 was gradually rebuilt in Renaissance style. Today it is one of Spain's most impressive squares, containing pleasant cafés and bordered by shady palm trees. At the centre of the Plaça des Born is an obelisk which commemorates the "Any de sa Desgràcia" (Year

The historic Plaça des Born in the centre of Ciutadella

of Misfortune), when the Turks invaded the city. Around the square are the Gothic-style **town hall** *(ajuntament)*, the late 19th-century **Teatre Municipal des Born**, and a series of aristocratic mansions with Italianesque façades, the grandest of which is the early 19th-century **Palau de Torre-Saura**. From the northern end of the square there is a fine view over the small harbour.

If you walk up the Carrer Major des Born past the cathedral, you come to **Ses Voltes**, an alley lined on both sides by whitewashed arches. Turn right along the Carrer des Seminari for the Baroque **Església dels Socors** and the **Museu Diocesà** with its displays of ecclesiastical paraphernalia. In the narrow streets of the old town there are many impressive palaces, but only the early 19th-century **Palau Salort**, on the Carrer Major des Born, is open to the public. The delightful Art Nouveau **market** (1895), its ironwork painted in smart municipal dark green, stands nearby.

The peace of Ciutadella is disturbed every June by the Festa de Sant Joan, an entertaining and spectacular ritual of horsemanship. During the festival the local gin *(ginebra)* is drunk copiously and the city grinds to a halt for a week.

🏛 **Museu Diocesà**
Seminari 5. 📞 *971 48 12 97.* ⭘ *daily.* 🎫
🎪 **Palau Salort**
Carrer Major del Born 9. 📞 *971 38 00 56.* ⭘ *Apr–Oct: Mon–Sat.* 🎫

Ferreries ㉑

Baleares. 🏘 *4,000.* ▣ ▐ *Carrer Sant Bartomeu 55, 971 37 30 03.* ▣ *Tue, Fri, Sat.* 🎪 *Sant Bartomeu (23–5 Aug).*

FERRERIES LIES in between Maó and Ciutadella and sprang up when a road was built to connect the two towns. Today Ferreries is an attractive village of white houses, built against the slope of a hill. The simple church, Sant Bartomeu, dates from 1770.

The bay of **Santa Galdana**, 10 km (6 miles) to the south, is even prettier. You can take a pleasant walk from the beach inland through the fertile river-bed of Barranc d'Algendar.

Courtyard in the Santuari del Toro

Es Mercadal ㉒

Baleares. 🏘 *2,500.* ▣ ▐ *Carrer Major 16, 971 37 50 02.* ▣ *Sun.* 🎪 *Sant Martí (third Sun of Jul).*

ES MERCADAL is a small country town – one of the three, with Alaior and Ferreries, that are strung out along the main road from Maó to Ciutadella.

The town is unremarkable in itself, but within reach of it are three places of interest.

El Toro, 3 km (2 miles) to the east, is Menorca's highest mountain, at 350 m (1,150 ft). It is also the spiritual heart of the island and at its summit is the Santuari del Toro, built in 1670, which is run by nuns.

About 10 km (6 miles) north of Es Mercadal, the fishing village of **Fornells** transforms itself every summer into an outpost of St Tropez. In the harbour, smart yachts jostle with fishing boats, and the local jet-set crowd into the Bar Palma. Fornells' main culinary speciality is the *caldereta de llagosta* (lobster casserole), but the quality varies and prices can be high.

The road-cum-dirt track to the **Cap de Cavalleria**, 13 km (8 miles) north of Es Mercadal, passes through one of the Balearics' finest landscapes. Cavalleria is a rocky promontory, whipped by the tramontana wind from the north. It juts out into a choppy sea which, in winter, looks more like the North Atlantic than the Mediterranean. At the western edge of the peninsula are the remains of Sanitja, a Phoenician village mentioned by Pliny in the 1st century AD. The road leads to a headland, with a lighthouse and cliffs 90 m (295 ft) high, where peregrine falcons, sea eagles and kites ride the wind.

Further west along the coast is a string of fine, unspoiled beaches, though with difficult access: Cala Pregonda, Cala del Pilar and La Vall d'Algaiarens are three of the most beautiful.

Horse rearing in the fiesta of Sant Lluís

THE BALEARIC ISLANDS' FIESTAS

Sant Antoni Abat *(17 Jan)*, Mallorca. This fiesta is celebrated with parades and the blessing of animals all over Mallorca and in Sant Antoni in Ibiza.

Sant Joan *(24 Jun)*, Ciutadella (Menorca). The horse plays a major part in Menorca's festivals. In the streets and squares of Ciutadella on 24 June, the Day of St John the Baptist, elegantly dressed riders put their horses through ritualized medieval manoeuvres. The fiesta reaches a climax when the horses rear up on their hind legs and the jubilant crowds swarm around them trying to hold them up with their hands. Similarly, the annual fiesta in Sant Lluís, which takes place at the end of August, sees many of the locals taking to the streets on horseback.

Sant Joan Pelós *(24 Jun)*, Felanitx (Mallorca). As part of this fiesta, a man is dressed in sheepskins to represent John the Baptist.

Romeria de Sant Marçal *(30 Jun)*, Sa Cabeneta (Mallorca). A feature of this fiesta is a market selling *siurells*, primitive Mallorcan whistles.

Our Lady of the Sea *(16 Jul)*, Formentera. The island's main fiesta honours the Virgen del Carmen, patroness of fishermen, with a flotilla of fishing boats.

A quiet stretch of beach at Santa Galdana

The steep hillside of Maó running up from the harbour

Maó ㉓

Baleares. 🏙 *23,000.* 🚉 🚌 🚢 🛈
Plaça de S'Esplanada 40, 971 36 23 71.
🚍 *Tue, Sat.* 🎉 *Fiestas de Gracia (7–8 Sep), Fiesta de Sant Antoni (17 Jan).*

THE QUIETLY ELEGANT town of Maó has lent its Spanish name, Mahón, to mayonnaise *(see p489)*. It was occupied by the British three times during the 18th century. The legacy of past colonial rule can be seen in sober Georgian town houses, with their dark green shutters and sash windows.

Maó's harbour is one of the finest in the Mediterranean. Taking the street leading from the port to the upper town, the S-shaped Costa de Ses Voltes, you come to the 18th-century **Església del Carme**, a former Carmelite church whose cool white cloister now houses an attractive fruit and vegetable market. Behind the market is Maó's only museum, the **Col·lecció Hernández**

Sanz Hernández Mora, which houses Menorcan art and antiques. The nearby Plaça Constitució is overlooked by the church of Santa Maria, which has a huge organ. Next door is the **town hall** *(ajuntament)* with its Neo-Classical façade, into which is mounted the famous clock donated by Sir Richard Kane (1660–1736), the first British governor of Menorca,

Located at the end of the Carrer Isabel II is the **Església de Sant Francesc**, with an intriguing Romanesque doorway and Baroque façade. The church houses the Museu de Menorca (currently undergoing refurbishment). Two minutes' walk south of here will take you to Maó's main square, the Plaça de S'Esplanada, behind which is the **Ateneu Científic Lliterat Artistic**, a centre of Menorca-related culture and learning. Inside are collections of local ceramics and maps, and a library. It is advisable

to obtain permission before looking around. On the north side of the harbour is a mansion known as **Sant Antoni** or the Golden Farm. As Maó's finest example of Palladian architecture, it has an arched façade, painted plum red, with white arches, in the traditional Menorcan style. The British admiral, Nelson, is thought to have stayed here. The house has a collection of Nelson memorabilia and a fine library but is closed to the public.

🏛 **Col·lecció Hernández Sanz Hernández Mora**
Claustre del Carme 5.
📞 *971 35 05 97.* ◯ *Mon–Sat.*
🏛 **Ateneu Científic Lliterat Artistic**
C/ Rovellada de Dalt 25. 📞 *971 35 21 94.* ◖ *Sun, public hols.*

Cales Coves ㉔

Baleares. 🚍 *Sant Climent, then 25 mins walk.* 📞 *Maó, 971 36 37 90.*

O N EITHER SIDE of a pretty bay can be found Cales Coves – the site of Neolithic dwellings of up to 9 m (30 ft) in length, hollowed out of the rock face. The caves, thought to have been inhabited since prehistoric times, are today occupied by a community of people seeking an alternative lifestyle. Some of the caves have front doors, chimneys and even butane cookers.

About 8 km (5 miles) west, along the coast, lies Binibeca, a tourist village built in a style sympathetic to old Menorca. The jumble of white houses and tiny streets of the Poblat de Pescadors, an imitation fishing village, have the look of the genuine article.

Modern sculpture outside one of the dwellings at Cales Coves

◁ **The clear blue waters of Cala Turqueta in Menorca**

Ancient Menorca

MENORCA IS EXCEPTIONALLY RICH in prehistoric remains – the island has been described as an immense open-air museum. The majority of the sites are the work of the "talaiotic" people who lived between 2000–1000 BC and are named after the *talaiots* or huge stone towers that characterize the Menorcan landscape. There are hundreds of these Bronze Age villages and structures dotted around the island. Usually open to the public and free of charge, these sites provide an invaluable insight into the ancient inhabitants of the Balearics.

Huge *talaiot* amid the settlement of Trepucó

DIFFERENT STRUCTURES

The ancient stone structures scattered around the countryside of Menorca and, to a lesser extent, Mallorca can be placed into three main categories: *taulas, talaiots* and *navetas*.

Taulas *are two slabs of rock, one placed on top of the other, in a "T" formation. Suggestions as to their possible function range from a sacrificial altar to a roof support.*

Talaiots *are circular or square buildings that may have been used as meeting places and dwellings.*

Navetas *are shaped like upturned boats and apparently had a dual role as dwellings and burial quarters. At least ten of these remain in Menorca.*

Spectacular *taula* at Talatí de Dalt, standing 3 m (10 ft) high

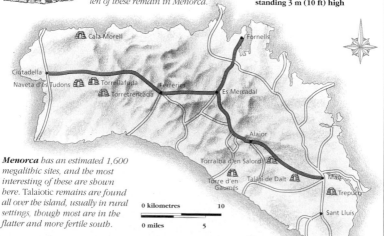

Menorca has an estimated 1,600 megalithic sites, and the most interesting of these are shown here. Talaiotic remains are found all over the island, usually in rural settings, though most are in the flatter and more fertile south.

0 kilometres   10

0 miles   5

THE CANARY ISLANDS

LA PALMA · EL HIERRO · LA GOMERA · TENERIFE
GRAN CANARIA · FUERTEVENTURA · LANZAROTE

POISED ON THE EDGE OF THE TROPICS *west of Morocco, the Canaries enjoy a generous supply of sunshine, pleasantly tempered by the trade winds. Their scenery ranges from lava desert to primeval forest and from sand dunes to volcanic peaks. The old towns on the main islands have colonial centres, full of character.*

Seven islands and half a dozen islets make up the Canary archipelago. They are the tips of hundreds of volcanoes that first erupted from the sea bed 14 million years ago. Teneguía on La Palma last erupted in 1971.

In the 14th and 15th centuries, when navigators discovered the islands and claimed them for Spain, they were inhabited by the Guanches, who practised a stone culture. Sadly, little evidence of them remains.

Today the islands are divided into two provinces. The four western isles, making up the province of Santa Cruz de Tenerife, are all mountainous; Tenerife's colossal dormant volcano, Mount Teide, casts the world's biggest sea-shadow. La Palma, El Hierro and La Gomera, where Columbus stayed on his voyages, are all small, unspoiled islands, not yet developed for mass tourism.

The eastern islands belong to the province of Las Palmas. Forested Gran Canaria is the biggest and its capital, Las Palmas de Gran Canaria, is a colonial town. Lanzarote, by contrast, is flat, with lunar landscapes, while Fuerteventura has long, virgin beaches.

Protected area of sand dunes at Maspalomas, next to the busy Playa del Inglés, Gran Canaria

◁ **La Rambla banana plantation on the north coast of the island of Tenerife**

Exploring the Western Islands

T ENERIFE HAS THE WIDEST RANGE of holiday attractions of any of the Canary Islands. The province of Santa Cruz de Tenerife also includes the three tiny westerly islands of La Palma, La Gomera and El Hierro, which are scarcely developed for tourism and have no large resorts. Gradually, more visitors are discovering these peaceful, green havens. If you enjoy walking, wildlife and mountain scenery, visit one of these hideaways. All three islands have comfortable hotels, including paradors. But compared with Gran Canaria and the eastern islands, there are fewer sandy beaches here, and little organized entertainment or sightseeing.

Las Teresitas artificial beach, Santa Cruz de Tenerife

SIGHTS AT A GLANCE

Candelaria **8**
Los Cristianos **4**
La Gomera **3**
El Hierro **2**
La Laguna **9**
Montes de Anaga **10**
La Orotava **7**
La Palma **1**
Parque Nacional del Teide pp514–15 **5**
Puerto de la Cruz **6**
Santa Cruz de Tenerife **11**

Roque Bonanza on the rocky east coast of El Hierro

KEY

▰▰	Motorway
▬▬	Major road
▭▭	Minor road
▰▰	Scenic route
◠	River
✸	Viewpoint

Terraced hillside, maximizing cultivation in the lush green Valle Gran Rey, in western La Gomera

GETTING AROUND

From mainland Spain there are flights *(see p628)* and ferries *(see p629)* to the Canary Islands. Transport to the small islands is mainly from Tenerife. La Gomera is easily reached by ferry or hydrofoil from Los Cristianos, or by plane from Gran Canaria or Tenerife. Airports on La Palma and El Hierro are served by regular flights from Tenerife's northern airport of Los Rodeos. Unless you take an organized coach trip, a car is essential to see the island scenery. Roads are improving, but great care is needed for mountain driving.

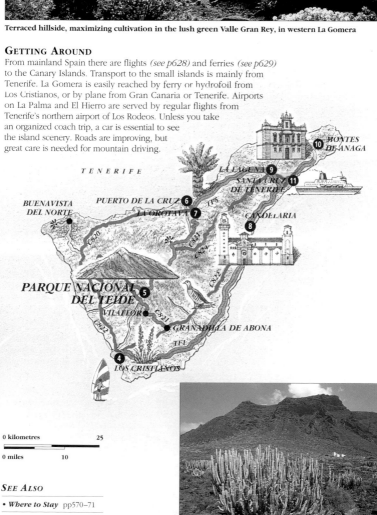

MONTES DE ANAGA

TENERIFE

LA LAGUNA ⑨

SANTA CRUZ DE TENERIFE ⑪

PUERTO DE LA CRUZ ⑥

LA OROTAVA ⑦

BUENAVISTA DEL NORTE

CANDELARIA ⑧

PARQUE NACIONAL DEL TEIDE ⑤

VILAFLOR

GRANADILLA DE ABONA

LOS CRISTIANOS ④

0 kilometres 25

0 miles 10

SEE ALSO

The wild landscape of Punta de Teno in western Tenerife

La Palma **❶**

Santa Cruz de Tenerife. 🏔 *82,400.*
☒ 🚢 *Santa Cruz de la Palma.*
🛈 *Calle O'Daly 22, Santa Cruz de la Palma, 922 41 21 06.*
🅦 *www.la-palmaturismo.com*

REACHING AN ALTITUDE of 2,426 m (7,959 ft) on a land base of less than 706 sq km (280 sq miles), La Palma is the world's steepest island. It lies on the northwestern tip of the archipelago and has a cool, moist climate and lush vegetation. The mountainous interior is covered with forests of pine, laurel and giant fern.

The centre of the island is dominated by **La Caldera de Taburiente**, a volcano's massive crater, more than 8 km (5 miles) wide. National park status *(see pp26–7)* is an indication of its botanical and geological importance. The International Astrophysics Observatory crowns the summit. A couple of roads traverse

The Parque Nacional de la Caldera de Taburiente, La Palma

La Palma's dizzy heights, offering spectacular views of the craters of La Cumbrecita and Roque de los Muchachos.

Santa Cruz de la Palma, the island's main town and port, is an elegant place of old houses with balconies, some fine churches and several 16th-century buildings. In the cobbled street behind the seafront, Calle O'Daly (named after an Irish banana trader), are the Iglesia El Salvador, boasting a Mudéjar coffered ceiling, and the town hall *(ayuntamiento)*, which is housed in a cardinal's palace. A full-sized cement replica of the *Santa María*, Columbus's flagship, stands at the end of the Plaza Alameda.

The tortuous mountain road southwest of Santa Cruz winds over Las Cumbres mountains via Breña Alta to **El Paso** in the centre of the island. A relatively sizeable community, the village is known for its silk production and hand-rolled cigars.

Pastel façades and delicate wooden balconies in Santa Cruz, La Palma

Among the almond terraces and vineyards of southern La Palma, solidified lava from the Teneguia volcano is a reminder of its recent activity *(see p527)*.

Craters on El Hierro, Spain's most western territory

El Hierro **❷**

Santa Cruz de Tenerife. 🏔 *8,000.*
☒ 🚢 *Puerto de la Estaca.* 🛈 *Calle Doctor Quintero Magdaleno 4, Valverde, 922 55 03 02.*
🅦 *www.el-hierro.org*

DUE TO A DEARTH of sandy beaches, El Hierro has escaped tourist invasions. Instead it has caught the attentions of naturalists. Its hilly landscape and unusual fauna and flora are part of its appeal. El Hierro is the smallest of the Canaries, and the furthest west; consequently it is the last place in Spain where the sun sets.

Valverde, the island's capital; stands inland at 600 m (2,000 ft) above sea level. Canary pines and peculiarly twisted

LA GOMERA'S WHISTLE LANGUAGE

The problems of communication posed by La Gomera's rugged terrain produced an unusual language, known as El Silbo. This system of piercing whistles probably developed because its sounds carry across the great distances from one valley to the next. Its origins are mysterious, but it was allegedly invented by the Guanches *(see p523)*. Few young Gomerans have any use for El Silbo today, and the language would probably be dead if it were not for the demonstrations of it still held for interested visitors at the parador, and in the restaurant at Las Rosas.

El Silbo practised on La Gomera

juniper trees cover El Hierro's mountainous interior, best seen from the many footpaths and scenic viewpoints along the roads. A ridge of woodland, curving east-west across the island, marks the edge of a volcano. The crater forms a fertile depression known as El Golfo.

In the far west is the **Ermita de los Reyes**, a place of pilgrimage and the starting point of the island's biggest fiesta, held in July every four years.

The turquoise seas off the south coast are popular with skin-divers, who base themselves in the small fishing village of **La Restinga**.

La Gomera ❸

Santa Cruz de Tenerife. ⚏ 17,150.
✈ ⛴ 🛈 Calle Real 4, San Sebastián de la Gomera, 922 14 15 12.
🌐 www.gomera-island.com

LA GOMERA is the most accessible of the smaller western islands, only 40 minutes by hydrofoil from Los Cristianos on Tenerife (90 minutes by ferry), or by plane from Tenerife or Gran Canaria. Many come to La Gomera for a day only, taking a coach trip. Others hire a car and explore on their own: a scenic but exhausting drive for a single day as the terrain is intensely buckled, and the central plateau is deeply scored by dramatic ravines. Driving across these gorges involves negotiating countless dizzying hairpin bends.

The best way to enjoy the island is to stay awhile and

Terraced hillsides in the fertile Valle Gran Rey, La Gomera

explore it at leisure, preferably doing some walking. On a fine day, La Gomera's scenery is glorious. Rock pinnacles jut above steep slopes studded with ferns while terraced hillsides glow with palms and flowering creepers. The best section, the **Parque Nacional de Garajonay**, is a UNESCO World Heritage Site.

San Sebastián, La Gomera's main town and ferry terminal, is situated on the east coast, a scattering of white buildings around a small beach. Among its sights are some places associated with Columbus (see pp54–5), who topped up

his water supplies here before setting out on his adventurous voyages. A well in the customs house bears the grand words "With this water America was baptized". According to legend he also prayed in the Iglesia de la Asunción, and stayed at a local house.

Beyond the arid hills to the south lies **Playa de Santiago**, the island's only real resort, which has a grey pebble beach. **Valle Gran Rey**, in the far west, is a fertile valley of palms and staircase terraces. These days it is colonized by foreigners attempting alternative lifestyles. In the north, tiny roads weave a tortuous course around several pretty villages, plunging at intervals to small, stony beaches. **Las Rosas** is a popular stop-off for coach parties, who can enjoy the visitors' centre and a restaurant with a panoramic view.

The road towards the coast from Las Rosas leads through the town of **Vallehermoso**, dwarfed by the huge **Roque de Cano**, which is an impressive mass of solidified lava. Just off the north coast stands **Los Órganos**, a fascinating rock formation of crystallized basalt columns resembling the pipes of an organ.

Juniper trees on El Hierro, twisted and bent by the wind

Tenerife

I N THE LANGUAGE of its aboriginal Guanche inhabitants, Tenerife means "Snowy Mountain", a tribute to its most striking geographical feature, the dormant volcano of Mount Teide, Spain's highest peak. The largest of the Canary Islands, Tenerife is a roughly triangular landmass rising steeply on all sides towards the cloud-capped summit that divides it into two distinct climatic zones: damp and lushly vegetated in the north, sunny and arid in the south. Tenerife offers a more varied range of attractions than any of the other Canary Islands, including its spectacular volcanic scenery, water sports and a vibrant atmosphere after dark. Its beaches, however, have unenticing black sand and are rather poor for swimming. The main resorts are crowded with high-rise hotels and apartments, offering nightlife but little peace and quiet.

Bananas in northern Tenerife

Los Cristianos ❹

Santa Cruz de Tenerife. 🏠 29,800.
🚌 🚢 🛈 Calle General Franco, 922
75 71 37. 🚢 Sun. 🎭 Fiesta del
Carmen (first Sun of Sep).

T HE OLD FISHING VILLAGE of Los Cristianos, on Tenerife's south coast, has grown into a town spreading out along the foot of barren hills. Ferries and hydrofoils make regular trips from its little port to La Gomera and El Hierro (see pp508–9).

To the north lies the modern expanse of **Playa de las Américas**, Tenerife's largest development. It offers visitors a cheerful, relaxed, undemanding cocktail of sun and fun.

A brief sortie inland leads to the much older town of **Adeje** and to the **Barranco del Infierno**, a wild gorge with an attractive waterfall (two hours' walk from Adeje).

Along the coast to the east, the **Costa del Silencio** is a pleasant contrast to most of

the other large resorts, with its bungalow developments surrounding fishing villages. Los Abrigos has lively fish restaurants lining its harbour.

Further east, **El Médano** shelters below an ancient volcanic cone. Its two beaches are popular with windsurfers.

Parque Nacional del Teide ❺

See pp514–15.

Puerto de la Cruz ❻

Santa Cruz de Tenerife. 🏠 24,000.
🚌 🛈 Plaza Europa, 922 38 60 00.
🚢 Sat. 🎭 Carnival (Feb–Mar), Fiesta del Carmen (second Sun of Jul).

P UERTO DE LA CRUZ, the oldest resort in the Canaries, first sprang to prominence in 1706, when a volcanic eruption obliterated Tenerife's principal port of Garachico. Puerto de

la Cruz took its place, later becoming popular with genteel English convalescents. The town's older buildings give it much of its present character.

The beautiful Lago Martiánez lido, designed by the Lanzarote architect César Manrique (see p524), compensates for a lack of good beaches with its sea water pools, palms and fountains. Other attractions include the tropical gardens of **Loro Parque**, where visitors can also see parrots and dolphins.

Outside town, the **Bananera El Guanche** plantation has an exhibition on bananas and other tropical crops. **Icod de los Vinos**, a short drive west, attracts crowds for its spectacular ancient dragon tree.

🌿 **Loro Parque**
C/ Bencomo, Punta Brava.
📞 922 37 38 41. ⭕ daily. 🖼️ ♿
🌿 **Bananera El Guanche**
Carretera Botánico, La Orotava.
📞 922 33 18 53. ⭕ daily. 🖼️ ♿

THE DRAGON TREE

The Canary Islands have many unusual plants, but the dragon tree (Dracaena draco) is one of the strangest. This primitive creature looks a little like a giant cactus, with swollen branches that sprout multiple tufts of spiky leaves. When cut, the trunk exudes a reddish sap once believed to have magical and medicinal properties. Dragon trees form no annual rings, so their age is a mystery. Some are thought to be hundreds of years old. The most venerable surviving specimen can be seen at Icod de los Vinos.

The landscaped Lago Martiánez lido, Puerto de la Cruz

La Orotava ❼

Santa Cruz de Tenerife. 🏘 *37,800.*
🚌 ℹ *Carrera del Escultor Estevez 2,
922 32 30 41.* 🎭 *Carnival (Feb/Mar),
Corpus Christi (May/Jun).*

A SHORT distance from Puerto
de la Cruz, in the fertile
hills above the Orotava valley,
La Orotava makes a popular
excursion. The old part of this
historic town clusters around
the large **Iglesia de Nuestra
Señora de la Concepción**.
This domed Baroque building
with twin towers was built in
the late 18th century to replace
an earlier church that was destroyed in earthquakes at the
beginning of that century.

In the surrounding streets
and squares are numerous
old churches, convents and
grand houses with elaborately
carved wooden balconies.
The **Casas de los Balcones**
and **Casa del Turista** both
have pretty interior courtyards
that are open to the public.

**Nuestra Señora de la Candelaria,
patron saint of the Canary Islands**

Candelaria ❽

Santa Cruz de Tenerife. 🏘 *13,300.*
🚌 ℹ *Plaza del Cit, 922 50 04 15.*
🚌 *Sat, Sun.* 🎭 *Nuestra Señora de
la Candelaria (14–15 Aug).*

T HIS COASTAL TOWN is famous
for its shrine to **Nuestra
Señora de la Candelaria**, the
Canary Islands' patron saint,
whose image is surrounded
by flowers and candles in a
modern church in the main
square. This gaudy Virgin,
supposedly washed ashore in

Statue of a Guanche chief on the seafront of Candelaria

pagan times, was venerated
before Christianity reached
the island. In 1826 a tidal wave
returned her to the sea, but a
replica draws pilgrims to worship here every August. Outside, stone effigies of Guanche
chiefs line the sea wall.

La Laguna ❾

Santa Cruz de Tenerife. 🏘 *128,000.*
🚌 ℹ *C/ Obispo Rey Redondo 1, 922
63 11 94.* 🚌 *daily.* 🎭 *San Benito
(15 Jul).* 🌐 *www.historiaviva.org*

A BUSTLING university town
and former island capital,
La Laguna is the second largest
settlement on Tenerife.

In its old quarter, best explored on foot, there are many
atmospheric squares, historic
buildings and good museums.
Most of the sights lie between
the bell-towered **Iglesia de
Nuestra Señora de la Con-
cepción** (1502), and the Plaza
del Adelantado, on which
stand the town hall, a convent
(with a traditional balcony)
and the **Palacio de Nava**.

Montes de Anaga ❿

Santa Cruz de Tenerife. 🚌 *Santa Cruz
de Tenerife, La Laguna.*

T HE RUGGED MOUNTAINS north
of Santa Cruz are kept
green and lush by a cool, wet
climate. They abound with a
wide variety of interesting
birds and plants, including
cacti, laurels and tree heathers.
Walking the mountain trails is
very popular, and maps showing many of the best paths
are readily available from the
tourist office. A steep road
with marker posts climbs up
from the village of San Andrés
by the beautiful but artificial
beach of Las Teresitas. On
clear days there are marvellous
vistas along the paths, especially from the viewpoints of
Pico del Inglés and Bailadero.

Winding down through the
laurel forests of Monte de las
Mercedes and the colourful
valley of Tejina you reach
Tacoronte with its interesting
churches, an ethnographic
museum and a bodega, where
you can sample local wines.

THE CANARY ISLANDS' FIESTAS

Carnival *(Feb/Mar)*, Santa Cruz de Tenerife. One of Europe's biggest carnivals, this grand street party is a lavish spectacle of extravagant costumes and Latin American dance music to rival that of Rio de Janeiro. For years under the Franco regime, Carnival was suppressed for its irreverent frivolity. It begins with the election of a queen of the festivities and builds up to a climax on Shrove Tuesday when there is a large procession. The "funeral" of an enormous mock sardine takes place on Ash Wednesday. Carnival is also celebrated on the islands of Lanzarote and Gran Canaria.

Revellers in Carnival outfits on Tenerife

Corpus Christi *(May/Jun)*, La Orotava (Tenerife). The streets of the town are filled with flower carpets in striking patterns, while the Plaza del Ayuntamiento is covered in copies of works of art, formed from coloured volcanic sands.
Descent of the Virgin of the Snows *(Jul, every five years: 2005, 2010)* Santa Cruz de La Palma.
Romería de la Virgen de la Candelaria *(15 Aug)*, Candelaria (Tenerife). Pilgrims come here in their thousands to venerate the Canary Islands' patroness.
Fiesta del Charco *(7–11 Sep)*, San Nicolás de Tolentino (Gran Canaria). People leap into a large saltwater pond to catch mullet.

Large ships moored at the busy port of Santa Cruz de Tenerife

Santa Cruz de Tenerife ⓫

Santa Cruz de Tenerife. 🏛 *213,000.*
🚌 ✈ 🚢 *Plaza de España 1, 922 23 95 92.* 🚪 *Sun.* 🎉 *Carnival (Feb/Mar), Día de la Cruz (3 May).*
🆆 *www.cabtfe.es*

TENERIFE'S CAPITAL city is an important regional port, with a deep-water harbour suitable for large ships. Its most attractive beach, **Las Teresitas**, lies 8 km (5 miles) to the north. Completely artificial, it was created by importing millions of tonnes of golden Saharan sand and building a protective reef just offshore. Shaded by palms, backed by mountains and so far devoid of concrete hotel developments, the result improves on anything nature has bestowed on Tenerife.

Santa Cruz can boast many handsome historic buildings. The hub of the town is around the **Plaza de España**, situated near the harbour. Just off it is the Calle de Castillo, the main shopping street. Its two most noteworthy churches are the **Iglesia de Nuestra Señora de la Concepción**, with parts dating from 1500, and Baroque **Iglesia de San Francisco**.

Particularly interesting is the **Museo de la Naturaleza y el Hombre**, in the Palacio Insular, where Guanche mummies grin in glass cases. Inside the museum you can also see the cannon which is alleged to have removed the arm of the British admiral Nelson during an unsuccessful raid on the city in the late 18th century.

Other attractions include the **Museo de Bellas Artes** which features old masters as well as modern works. Many of its paintings focus on local events and landscapes. Contemporary sculptures adorn the **Parque Municipal García Sanabria**, a pleasant park with shady paths, laid out in 1926.

In the morning, visit the **Mercado de Nuestra Señora de África**, which combines a bazaar with a food market. Outside stalls sell domestic goods; those inside offer an eclectic mix of live chickens, spices and cut flowers. Santa Cruz is especially worth a visit during its flamboyant carnival.

🏛 **Museo de la Naturaleza y el Hombre**
Calle Fuentes Morales. 📞 *922 20 93 20.* 🕐 *Tue–Sun.* 🎫 👥
🏛 **Museo de Bellas Artes**
Calle José Murphy 12. 📞 *922 24 43 58.* 🕐 *Mon–Fri.*

The artificial beach of Las Teresitas in Santa Cruz

Regional Food: The Canary Islands

Although sometimes hard to find, there is a regional cuisine in the Canaries. It combines elements of Guanche cooking with ingredients originally from other continents, such as sweetcorn and bananas. A climate of eternal spring provides a wealth of other fruit and vegetables. The sea supplies many colourful fish, like the purple and yellow *vieja* or bass which is eaten with *mojo*, a sauce that varies in its ingredients and colour depending on whether coriander (cilantro) or paprika is used. Many dishes are served with wrinkled *papas arrugadas* (jacket potatoes cooked in heavily salted water). *Gofio* is a Guanche corn-meal that is made into porridge and bread and used to thicken stews. Desserts include *bien-mesabe*, a sweet cream of almonds, egg yolk and cinnamon.

Sweetcorn

Sancocho, *parboiled fish best made with* sama, *a type of bass, is often served with sweet and plain potatoes.*

Sama frita con mojo verde *is fried fish served with a sauce blended from garlic, coriander (cilantro) and vinegar.*

Potaje de berros, *a thick soup, contains watercress, pork ribs, corn on the cob, potatoes, beans (garbanzos) and cumin.*

Conejo al salmorejo, *an appetizing stew made with rabbit and tomato, is best eaten with* papas arrugadas.

Arroz con verduras *is a colourful mixture of rice with chopped peppers, sweetcorn and tomatoes.*

Puchero *is the local saffron-flavoured stew, made with chorizo sausage, beans, chick-peas and potatoes.*

Canary bananas *are the sweet La Gomera variety, small and aromatic. They are made into fritters and tarts; or served with rice and eggs, or meat sauce. Other fruits available are guava, mango and papaya.*

DRINKS

In the early 17th century the Canary Islands were renowned for their amber-coloured Malvasía wine, which is rich, sweet and highly alcoholic. The best of it is made on Lanzarote. Less potent red and white wines are produced in the Tacoronte-Acentejo region of Tenerife. The Canary Islands also offer a selection of locally made spirits, most notable of which is the excellent white and dark rum *(ron)*. Other drinks include liqueurs flavoured with coffee, orange or bananas, and a rough *coñac* (brandy).

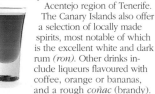

Dark Canary rum

Parque Nacional del Teide ❺

TOWERING OVER TENERIFE, Mount Teide, surrounded by a wild volcanic landscape, is an awesome sight. Millions of years ago a much larger adjacent cone exploded, leaving behind the devastation of Las Cañadas, a 16-km (10-mile) wide crater, and the smaller volcano, Teide, on its northern edge. Today volcanic material forms a wilderness of weathered, mineral-tinted rocks, ash beds and lava streams. A single road crosses the plateau of Las Cañadas, passing a parador, cable car station, and visitors' centre. Follow the marked paths to see the best of this unique, protected area.

Volcanic Landscapes
The eight-minute cable car ride leaves you 160 m (525 ft) short of Teide's summit. A path through volcanic rubble gives unforgettable views.

Pico del Teide, which is still volcanically active, is Spain's highest summit.

Pico Viejo, a volcanic cone also known as Montaña Chahorra, last erupted in the 18th century.

PICO DEL TEID

3,718 m

PICO VIEJO

3,414 m

CHÍO

Mirador de Chío

C823

LLANO DE UCANCA

Mirador de Boca Tauce

VILAFLOR

ROQUES DE GARCÍA

Mirador de La Ruleta

C821   Mirad de Uc

0 kilometres   2

0 miles   1

KEY

═══ Road

──── Track

- - - Footpath

Los Roques de García
These flamboyantly shaped lava rocks near the parador are some of the most photographed in the whole park. The rocks of Los Azulejos, nearby, glitter blue-green because of the copper deposits within them.

WILD FLOWERS

The inhospitable badlands of Las Cañadas are inhabited by some rare and beautiful plants. Many of these are unique to the Canary Islands. Most striking is the tall *Echium wildprettii*, a kind of viper's bugloss, whose red spires reach 2 m (6 ft) in early summer. Other common plants include Teide broom, the distinctive Californian poppy, and a unique species of violet. The best time of year for flower-spotting is May to June. Displays housed in the visitors' centre will help identify them. Don't take any plants away with you: all vegetation within the park is strictly protected and must not be uprooted or picked.

La Caldera de Las Cañadas

A rim of fractured crags forms a pie-crust edge to the sides of this enormous caldera – a wide volcanic crater (see p527). Now collapsed and intensely eroded, the perimeter of the caldera measures 45 km (28 miles).

At El Portillo Visitors' Centre, a video film and exhibition chart the origins of the park.

SANTA CRUZ DE TENERIFE

P i El Portillo

Refugio de Altavista

C827

Mirador de San José

Mirador del Tabonal Negro

LAS CAÑADAS

rador de ñadas del de

Las Cañadas

The flat expanses of the seven cañadas (small sandy plateaux) were created by the collapse of ancient craters. Several colourful plants have managed to colonize this dusty, barren wasteland.

Parador

The recently refurbished Parador de Cañadas del Teide (see p571) is set in the midst of the surreal scenery, and makes an excellent base for those who want to explore the park thoroughly.

Canary mustard *(Sisymbrium bourgaenum)*

Teide wallflower *(Erysium scoparium)*

Teide violet *(Viola cheiranthifolia)*

Teide viper's bugloss *(Echium wildprettii)*

Exploring the Eastern Islands

THE EASTERN PROVINCE of the Canary Islands – Las Palmas – comprises the islands of Gran Canaria, Lanzarote and Fuerteventura. All feature unusual and spectacular scenery, plenty of sunshine and excellent sandy beaches, but each has a very different atmosphere. Gran Canaria boasts the only really large town, Las Palmas de Gran Canaria, which is also the administrative centre for the eastern islands. It also offers the biggest resort, Maspalomas, with its Playa del Inglés, which has a package holiday feel. As a contrast, the white beaches of Fuerteventura have been left fairly undeveloped and it is still possible to find privacy among their sand dunes. Lanzarote has fine beaches, too, while its interior is dominated by a volcanic landscape which makes for great excursions.

Corralejo's beach, in the north of Fuerteventura

The marina at Puerto Rico, in southern Gran Canaria

GETTING AROUND

Most people travel from mainland Spain to the eastern islands by air *(see p628)*. The alternative is a long sea crossing from Cádiz *(see p629)*. There are flights between all the islands, mainly from Gran Canaria. There are also regular inter-island ferries. Taxis and public transport are fine within resorts, but expensive over long distances. Cars can be hired on all the islands, usually at airports or ferry terminals. The main roads are well-surfaced and fast on the flatter sections, though traffic in Gran Canaria can be heavy in places. A four-wheel drive Jeep is advisable to reach some remoter beaches.

0 kilometres   25

0 miles   10

SIGHTS AT A GLANCE

Agaete **15**
Arrecife **27**
Betancuria **20**
Caleta de Fustes **21**
Corralejo **23**
Costa Teguise **28**
Haría **30**
Jameos del Agua **31**
Maspalomas **14**
Las Palmas de
  Gran Canaria **17**
Parque Nacional de
  Timanfaya **25**

Península de Jandía **19**
Playa Blanca **24**
Puerto del Carmen **26**
Puerto de Mogán **12**
Puerto del Rosario **22**
Puerto Rico **13**
Tafira **16**
Teguise **29**

Tour
Cruz de Tejeda **18**

*ISLA DE
ALEGRANZA*

*ISLA
GRACIOSA*

JAMEOS DEL AGUA
HARÍA **30** **31**

TEGUISE **29**
PARQUE NACIONAL
DE TIMANFAYA **25**
28 COSTA
TEGUISE
YAIZA
26 **27**
ARRECIFE
PURTO DEL CARMEN

LANZAROTE

PLAYA BLANCA **24**

CORRALEJO **23**

LA OLIVA

FUERTEVENTURA

TINDAYA

600
22 PUERTO DEL
ROSARIO
610

BETANCURIA **20**
ANTIGUA
CALETA DE FUSTES **21**
PAJARA
TUINEJE

GRAN TARAJAL

TARAJALEJO

NÍNSULA DE JANDÍA

KEY

▬▬	Motorway
▬▬	Major road
▬▬	Minor road
▬▬	Scenic route
≈	River
☼	Viewpoint

SEE ALSO

- *Where to Stay* pp570–71

- *Restaurants and Bars*
  pp608–609

Volcanoes of Montañas de Fuego in Parque Nacional de Timanfaya, Lanzarote

Gran Canaria

Farmer and donkey

GRAN CANARIA IS THE MOST POPULAR of the Canary Islands, with over 3 million holiday-makers visiting it each year. The island offers a surprising range of scenery, climate, resorts and attractions within its compact bounds. Winding roads follow the steep, ruggedly beautiful terrain which rises to a symmetrical cone at the centre of the island. Las Palmas, Gran Canaria's capital and port, is the largest city in the Canaries, and Maspalomas/Playa del Inglés, in the south, is one of the biggest resorts in Spain. Both tourist meccas are packed with high-rise hotels and villa complexes, but not far away there is some marvellous scenery to discover.

Holiday-makers on the golden sands of Puerto Rico beach

Puerto de Mogán ⑫

Las Palmas. 🏘 *1,500.* 🛈 *Avenida Tomás Roca Bosch, 928 56 91 00.* 🚍 *Fri.* 🎪 *Virgen del Carmen (Jul).*

SITUATED AT THE END of the verdant valley of Mogán, this is one of Gran Canaria's most appealing and successful developments - an idyll to many visitors after the brash concrete of Playa del Inglés. Based around a small fishing port, it consists of a village-like complex of pretty, white, creeper-covered houses and a similarly designed hotel built around a marina. Boutiques, bars and restaurants add an ambience without any of the accompanying rowdiness.

The sandy beach, sheltered between the cliffs, is scarcely big enough for all visitors; a car is recommended to reach more facilities at Maspalomas. Ferries provide a leisurely way to get to nearby resorts.

Sun worshippers in Puerto Rico

Puerto Rico ⑬

Las Palmas. 🏘 *1,800.* 🛈 *Avenida de Mogán, 928 56 00 29.* 🎪 *María de Auxiliadora (May).*

THE BARREN CLIFFS west of Maspalomas now sprout apartment complexes at every turn. Puerto Rico is an over-developed resort, but has one of the more attractive beaches on the island, a firm crescent of imported sand supplemented by lidos and excellent water sports facilities. It is a great place to learn sailing, diving and windsurfing, or just to lie back, relax and soak up the ultraviolet – Puerto Rico enjoys the best sunshine record in the whole of Spain.

Maspalomas ⑭

Las Palmas. 🏘 *38,700.* ✈ 🛈 *Avda de España, 928 76 25 91.* 🚍 *Wed & Sat.* 🎪 *San Bartolomé (24 Aug).* 🖳 *www.maspalomas-web.org*

WHEN THE FAST motorway from Las Palmas airport first tips you into this bewildering mega-resort, it seems like a homogeneous blur, but gradually three separate communities emerge. **San Agustín**, the furthest east, is sedate compared with the others. It has a series of beaches of dark sand, attractively sheltered by low cliffs and landscaped promenades, and a casino.

The next exit off the coastal highway leads to **Playa del Inglés**, the largest and liveliest resort, a triangle of land jutting into a huge belt of golden sand. Developed from the end of the 1950s, the area is built up with giant blocks of flats linked by a maze of roads. Many hotels lack sea views, though most have spacious grounds with swimming pools. At night the area pulsates with

Floral arches decorating a street of apartments in Puerto de Mogán

bright disco lights and flashing neon. There are more than 300 restaurants and over 50 discos in this resort alone.

West of Playa del Inglés the beach undulates into the **Dunas de Maspalomas**. A relieving contrast to the hectic surrounding resorts, these dunes form a nature reserve protected from further development. The western edge of the dunes (marked by a lighthouse) is occupied by a cluster of luxury hotels. Just behind the dunes lies a golf course encircled by bungalow estates.

Everything is laid on for the package holiday: water sports, excursions, fast food. Relief from beach fatigue comes with go-karts, camel safaris and funfairs. Best of these include **Palmitos Park**, with exotic birds in subtropical gardens; and **Sioux City**, a funpacked Western theme park.

Palmitos Park
Barranco de los Palmitos. ☎ 928 14 12 76. ◯ daily.

Sioux City
Cañón del Águila. ☎ 928 76 25 73. ◯ Tue–Sun.

Agaete ⓯

Las Palmas. 5,800. Calle Antonio de Armas 1, 928 89 80 02. Fiesta de la Rama (4 Aug).

THE CLOUDIER northern side of the island is far greener and lusher than the arid south, and banana plantations take up most of the coastal slopes. Agaete, on the northwest coast, a pretty scatter of white houses around a striking rocky bay,

The rocky shore and steep cliffs of the northeast coast near Agaete

is growing into a small resort. Every August, Agaete holds the Fiesta de la Rama, a Guanche *(see p523)* rain-making ritual which dates from long before the arrival of the Spanish. An animated procession of villagers bearing green branches heads from the hills above the town down to the coast and into the sea. The villagers beat the water to summon the rain.

Sights in Agaete include the little **Ermita de las Nieves**, containing a fine 16th-century Flemish triptych and model sailing ships, and the **Huerto de las Flores**, a botanical garden. Ask for the key to the garden at the town hall, which is located on the same street.

ENVIRONS: A brief detour inland up along the Barranco de Agaete takes you through a fertile valley of papaya, mango and citrus trees. North of Agaete are the towns of Guía and Gáldar. Though there is little to see here, both parish churches do contain examples of the religious statuary of the celebrated 18th-century sculptor, José Luján Pérez.

Nearby, towards the north coast, lies the **Cenobio de Valerón**. One of the most dramatic of the local Guanche sights, this cliff-face is pockmarked with nearly 300 caves beneath a basalt arch. These are believed to have been hideaways for Guanche priestesses, communal grainstores and refuges from attack.

Huerto de las Flores
Calle Huertas. ◯ daily.

Miles of wind-sculptured sand: the dunes at Maspalomas

Tafira ⑯

Las Palmas. 🏠 23,000. 🅿
ℹ Jardín Canario, 928 35 36 04.
🎭 San Francisco (Oct).

THE HILLS SOUTHWEST of Las Palmas have long been desirable residential locations. A colonial air still wafts around Tafira's patrician villas. The **Jardín Canario**, a botanical garden founded in 1952, is the main reason for a visit. Plants from all of the Canary Islands can be studied in their own, re-created habitats.

Near La Atalaya lies one of Gran Canaria's most impressive natural sights – the **Caldera de la Bandama**. This is a volcanic crater 1,000 m (3,300 ft) wide, best seen from the Mirador de Bandama where you gaze down into the green depression about 200 m (660 ft) deep. Some of the inhabited caves in the **Barranco de Guayadeque**, a valley of red rocks to the south, were dug in the late 15th century. A few of them have electricity.

🌺 **Jardín Canario**
Carretera de Dragonal, Tafira.
📞 928 35 36 04. ⏱ daily.
W www.step.es/jardcan

Las Palmas de Gran Canaria ⑰

Las Palmas. 🏠 355,000. ✈ ⛴
ℹ Parque de Santa Catalina, 928 21 96 00. 🎭 Carnival (Feb/Mar).

LAS PALMAS IS THE LARGEST city in the Canary Islands. A bustling seaport and industrial city, it sees 1,000 ships docking

Palm trees in a natural setting in the Jardín Canario, Tafira

each month. Las Palmas has faded somewhat from the days when wealthy convalescents flocked here in winter and glamorous liners called in on transatlantic voyages. But it remains a vibrant place to visit.

Las Palmas is a sprawling city built around an isthmus and its layout can be confusing. The modern commercial shipping area, Puerto de la Luz, takes up the eastern side of the isthmus, which leads to the former island of La Isleta, a sailors' and military quarter. On the other side of the isthmus is the crowded **Playa de las Canteras**, a 3-km (2-mile) long stretch of golden beach. The promenade behind has been built up with bars, restaurants and hotels.

Bronze dog at Plaza Santa Ana

The town centre stretches along the coast from the isthmus. For a pleasant scenic tour, begin in the **Parque Santa Catalina**, near the port. This is a popular, shady square of

cafés and newspaper kiosks. In the leafy residential quarter of Ciudad Jardín are the Parque Doramas and the traditional casino hotel of Santa Catalina.

The **Pueblo Canario** is a tourist enclave where visitors can watch folk dancing, and browse in the craft shops and the small art gallery. All this can be viewed from above by walking uphill towards the Altavista district and the Paseo Cornisa.

At the end of town is the Barrio Vegueta, an atmospheric quarter which dates back to the Spanish conquest. At its heart stands the **Catedral de Santa Ana**, begun in 1500. The adjacent **Museo Diocesano de Arte Sacro** contains works of religious art. The square in front is guarded by Canarian dogs in bronze.

Nearby, the **Casa de Colón** is a 15th-century governor's residence where Columbus stayed. A museum dedicated to his voyages displays charts, models and diary extracts.

Early history can be seen in the **Museo Canario**, which contains Guanche mummies, skulls, pottery and jewellery.

🏛 **Museo Diocesano de Arte Sacro**
Calle Espíritu Santo 20. 📞 928 31 49 89. ⏱ Mon–Sat. 🔴 public hols. 🈺
🏛 **Casa de Colón**
Calle Colón. 📞 928 31 23 84. ⏱ daily.
🏛 **Museo Canario**
Calle Doctor Verneau 2. 📞 928 33 68 00. ⏱ daily. 🈺

The Casa de Colón museum, Las Palmas, dedicated to Columbus

Tour of Cruz de Tejeda ⑱

GRAN CANARIA'S mountainous interior makes for an ideal day tour, from any part of the island. Choose a fine day or the views may be obscured. The route from Maspalomas leads through dry ravines of bare rock and cacti, becoming more fertile with altitude. Roads near the central highlands snake steeply through shattered, tawny crags, past caves and pretty villages to panoramic viewpoints from which you can see Mount Teide *(see pp514–15)* on Tenerife. On the north side, the slopes are much lusher, growing citrus fruits and eucalyptus trees.

White farmhouses en route to Teror

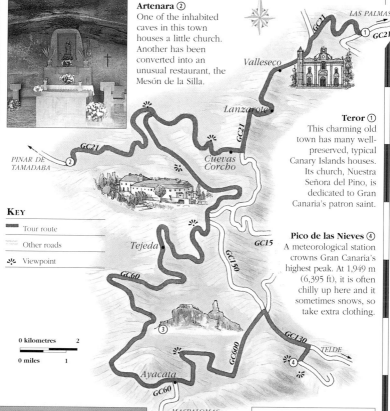

Artenara ②
One of the inhabited caves in this town houses a little church. Another has been converted into an unusual restaurant, the Mesón de la Silla.

PINAR DE TAMADABA

KEY

Tour route

Other roads

☆ Viewpoint

0 kilometres 2

0 miles 1

Valleseco

Lanzarote

Cuevas Corcho

Tejeda

GC21 GC15 GC150 GC60 GC600 GC130

Ayacata GC60

↓MASPALOMAS

Teror ①
This charming old town has many well-preserved, typical Canary Islands houses. Its church, Nuestra Señora del Pino, is dedicated to Gran Canaria's patron saint.

Pico de las Nieves ④
A meteorological station crowns Gran Canaria's highest peak. At 1,949 m (6,395 ft), it is often chilly up here and it sometimes snows, so take extra clothing.

TELDE

Roque Nublo ③
This 60-m (195-ft) high jagged spike of basalt tops a 1,700-m (5,578-ft) peak. Together with nearby Roque Bentayga, it was sacred to the Guanches. It's a stiff climb to the summit.

TIPS FOR DRIVERS

Length: 35–45 km (22–28 miles).
Stopping-off points: the Mesón de la Silla cave-restaurant in Artenara is a popular lunch spot.
Note: roads can be narrow with few passing places; sudden patches of cloud or mist may loom without warning.

Fuerteventura

LYING JUST 100 KM (60 MILES) off the Atlantic coast of Morocco, leaf-shaped Fuerteventura is continually battered by coastal winds. It is the second largest of the Canary Islands after Tenerife, and the most sparsely populated: its 30,000 inhabitants are outnumbered by goats. The island used to be densely wooded, but European settlers cut down the timber for shipbuilding; the dry climate and the goats have since reduced the vegetation to parched scrub. It is so dry that water has to be shipped over from the mainland. The only significant revenue is tourism, but the tourist industry is still in its infancy compared with the other main islands. However, visitors are increasing in number as thousands of sun-worshippers flock to more than 150 splendid beaches. The island is popular with water sports fans and naturists.

A herd of goats near the airport on Fuerteventura

Península de Jandía ⓵⑨

Las Palmas. ✈ Costa Calma, Morro Jable. ⛴ (jetfoil) from Gran Canaria. ℹ Centro Comercial, Jandía Beach Local 88, 928 54 07 76.

EXCELLENT BEACHES of pale sand fringe the elongated Jandía peninsula in the south of Fuerteventura. A string of *urbanizaciones* (apartment complexes) now takes up much of the peninsula's sheltered east coast (Sotavento).

Costa Calma, a burgeoning cluster of modern complexes, offers the most interesting beaches with long stretches of fine sand interrupted by low cliffs and coves. **Morro Jable**, a fishing village now swamped by new developments, lies at the southern end of a vast, glittering strand. Beyond Morro Jable, the access road dwindles away into a potholed track leading towards the lonely lighthouse at Punta de Jandía.

Expanses of deserted sand, accessible only by four-wheel drive vehicle, line the westerly, windward coast (Barlovento) – too exposed for all but the hardiest beach lovers. Some of the island's best subtropical marine life can be found in this area, however, making it popular with skin divers.

During World War II, Jandía belonged to a German entrepreneur. It was out of bounds to locals and acquired its own mystique. Even today, rumours of spies, submarines and secret Nazi bases still circulate.

Betancuria ⓶⓪

Las Palmas. 🏛 735. 🚌 ℹ Calle Amador Rodríguez 6, 928 87 80 92. 🎉 San Buenaventura (14 Jul).

INLAND, rugged peaks of extinct volcanoes, separated by wide plains, present a scene of austere grandeur. Scattered, stark villages and obsolete windmills occupy the lowlands which are occasionally fertile enough to nurture a few crops or palm trees. Beyond, devoid of vegetation, the hills form stark outlines. From a distance they appear brown and grey, but close up the rocks glow with an astonishing range of mauves, pinks and ochres. The richness of colour in this interior wilderness is at its

The gilded interior of the Iglesia Santa María in Betancuria

most striking at sunset, when a leisurely drive can reveal some breathtaking scenes.

Betancuria, built on a small volcano in the centre of the island, is named after Jean de Béthencourt, Fuerteventura's 15th-century conqueror, who moved his capital inland to thwart pirates. Nestling in the mountains, this peaceful oasis is now the island's prettiest village. The **Iglesia de Santa María** contains gilded altars, decorated beams and sacred relics. Ask for the key at the caretaker's house nearby. The **Museo Arqueológico** houses many local artifacts.

ENVIRONS: To the south, the village of **Pájara** boasts a 17th-century church with a curiously decorated doorway. Its design of serpents and strange beasts is believed to be of Aztec influence. Inside, the twin aisles both contain statues: one of a radiant Madonna and Child in white and silver, the other a Virgen de los Dolores in black.

La Oliva, to the north, was the site of the Spanish military headquarters until the 19th century. The Casa de los Coroneles (House of the Colonels) is a faded yellow mansion with a grand façade and hundreds of windows. Inside it has coffered ceilings. The fortified church and the arts centre displaying works of Canary Islands artists are also worth a visit.

🏛 **Museo Arqueológico**
Calle Roberto Roldán. 📞 928 87 82 41. 🕐 Tue–Sun. 🚫 ♿

Caleta de Fustes 21

Las Palmas. 🏃 785. 🚌 🛈 *Calle dos Avenidas 10, El Castillo, 928 16 32 86.* 🚢 *Sat.* 🎭 *Día del Carmen (16 Jul).*

Sᴏᴜᴛʜ ᴏғ Puerto del Rosario, about halfway down the eastern coast of the island, lies Caleta de Fustes. This attractive and tasteful group of low-rise, self-catering holiday centres surrounds a horseshoe bay of soft, gently shelving sand. The largest complex, El Castillo, takes its name from an 18th-century watchtower situated by the harbour.

There are many water sports facilities, including diving and windsurfing schools, as well as the Pueblo Majorero, an attractive "village" of shops and restaurants around a central plaza near the beach. These features make Caleta de Fustes one of Fuerteventura's most relaxed and pleasant resorts, popular with all nationalities.

Fishing boats on a beach on the Isla de Lobos, near Corralejo

Puerto del Rosario 22

Las Palmas. 🏃 28,200. ✈ 🚌 🚢 🛈 *Avenida de la Constitución 5, 928 53 08 44* 🎭 *El Rosario (7 Oct).*

Fᴜᴇʀᴛᴇᴠᴇɴᴛᴜʀᴀ's commercial and administrative capital was founded in 1797. It was originally known as Puerto de Cabras (Goats' Harbour), after a nearby gorge that was once used for watering goats, but was rechristened to smarten up its image in 1957. As Puerto del Rosario is the only large port on Fuerteventura, it is the base for inter-island ferries and a busy fishing industry. The town is also enlivened by the presence of the Spanish Foreign Legion, which occupies large barracks here.

Corralejo 23

Las Palmas. 🏃 5,700. 🚢 🛈 *Plaza Pública, 928 86 62 35.* 🚢 *Mon, Tue, Thu, Fri.* 🎭 *Día del Carmen (16 Jul).*

Tʜɪs ᴍᴜᴄʜ-ᴇxᴘᴀɴᴅᴇᴅ fishing village is now (together with the Jandía peninsula) one of the island's two most important resorts. Its main attraction is a belt of glorious sand dunes stretching to the south, resembling the Sahara in places, and protected as a nature reserve. This designation arrived too late, however, to prevent the construction of two obtrusive hotels right on the beach.

The rest of the resort, mostly consisting of apartments, spills out haphazardly from the town centre. The port area is lively, with busy fish restaurants and an efficient ferry service to Lanzarote, 40 minutes away.

Offshore is the tiny Isla de los Lobos, named after the once abundant monk seals (*lobos marinos*). Today, scuba divers, snorkellers, sport fishers and surfers claim the clear waters. Glass-bottomed cruise boats take less adventurous excursionists to the island for barbecues and swimming trips.

Tʜᴇ Gᴜᴀɴᴄʜᴇs

When Europeans first arrived in the Canary Islands in the late 14th century, they discovered a tall, white-skinned race, who lived in caves and later in small settlements around the edges of barren lava fields. Guanche was the name of one tribe on Tenerife, but it came to be used as the European name for all the indigenous tribes on the islands, and it is the one that has remained. The origins of the Guanches are still unclear, but it is probable that they arrived on the islands in the 1st or 2nd century BC from Berber North Africa. Within 100 years of European arrival the Guanches had been subdued and virtually exterminated by the ruthless conquistadors. Very few traces of their culture remain today.

Reminders of the Guanches can be seen in many places in the Canaries. Specimens of their mummified dead, as well as baskets and stone and bone artifacts, are on display in several museums and there are statues of chiefs in Candelaria (see p511) on Tenerife.

Guanche bowl for preparing *gofio* (see p513)

A Guanche basket

Lanzarote

THE EASTERNMOST and fourth largest of the Canary Islands is virtually treeless and relies on desalination plants for some of its water. Yet many visitors consider Lanzarote the most attractive of all the islands for the vivid shapes and contrasting colours of its volcanic landscapes. Despite low rainfall, carefully tended crops flourish in its black volcanic soil. Locals pride themselves on the way their island has been preserved from the worst effects of tourism; there are no garish billboards, overhead cables or high-rise buildings. Its present-day image owes much to the artist César Manrique. Touring the spectacular volcanic Timanfaya National Park is a favourite trip.

Wind turbines harnessing Lanzarote's winds for power

Playa Blanca ㉔

Las Palmas. 🏘 *4,000.* 🚌 ⛴
ℹ *Calle El Varadero 2, 928 51 90 18.* 🎉 *Nuestra Señora del Carmen (Jul).*

THE FISHING VILLAGE origins of this resort are readily apparent around its harbour. Although it has expanded in recent years, Playa Blanca

Las Coloradas beach near Playa Blanca in southern Lanzarote

remains an agreeably family-oriented place with some character. It has plenty of cafés and restaurants, shops and bars, and several large hotels. However, the buildings are well dispersed and the resort is rarely noisy at night. Visitors converge here not for nightlife or contrived entertainment, but for relaxing beach holidays. There are one or two good stretches of sand near to the town, but the most enticing lie hidden around the rocky

headlands to the east, where the clear, warm sea laps into rocky coves, and clothes seem superfluous. **Playa Papagayo** is the best known of these, but a diligent search will probably gain you one all to yourself. A four-wheel drive vehicle is advisable to negotiate the narrow, unsurfaced roads which lead to these beaches.

Parque Nacional de Timanfaya ㉕

Las Palmas Yaiza. ℹ *Icona, 928 84 02 38.* 🚌 *from Arrecife.* ⭕ *daily.* 🎫 ⓦ *www.mma.es*

FROM 1730–36, a series of volcanic eruptions took place on Lanzarote. Eleven villages were buried in lava, which eventually spread over 200 sq km (77 sq miles) of Lanzarote's most fertile land. Miraculously, no one was killed, though many islanders subsequently emigrated.

Today, the volcanoes that once devastated Lanzarote provide one of its most lucrative and enigmatic attractions, aptly known as the **Montañas del Fuego** (Fire Mountains). They are part of the Parque Nacional de Timanfaya, established in 1974 to protect a fascinating and important geological record. The entrance to the park lies just north of the small village of Yaiza. Here you can pause and take a 15-minute camel ride up the volcanic slopes for wonderful views across the park. Afterwards, you pay the entrance fee and drive through haunting scenery of dark, barren lava cinders

CÉSAR MANRIQUE (1920–92)

Local hero César Manrique trained as a painter, and spent time in mainland Spain and New York before returning to Lanzarote in 1968. He campaigned for traditional and environmentally friendly development on the island for the remaining part of his life, setting strict building height limits and colour requirements. Dozens of tourist sites throughout the Canaries benefited from his talents and enthusiasm.

César Manrique in 1992

Camel rides from Yaiza across the Montañas de Fuego

topped by brooding red-black volcano cones. Finally, you will reach **Islote de Hilario**. You can park at El Diablo panoramic restaurant. From here, buses take visitors for exhilarating hour-long tours of the desolate, lunar-like landscapes.

Afterwards, back at Islote de Hilario, guides will provide graphic demonstrations that this volcano is not extinct but only dormant: brushwood pushed into a crevice bursts instantly into a ball of flame, while water poured into a sunken pipe shoots out in a scorching jet of steam.

The road from Yaiza to the coast leads to the **Salinas de Janubio** where salt is extracted from an old volcano crater. Nearby are the boiling springs of **Los Hervideros** and further north, at **El Golfo**, an eerie emerald-coloured lagoon.

Puerto del Carmen ㉖

Las Palmas. 🏘 13,700. 🚌 🚢 🚹
Avenida de la Playa, 928 51 53 37.
📅 Nuestra Señora del Carmen (Jul).
W www.turismolanzarote.com

MORE THAN 60 PER CENT of Lanzarote's tourists stay in this resort, which stretches several kilometres along the seafront. The coastal road carves its way through a solid slab of holiday infrastructure: car hire offices, banks, bureaux de change, shops, bars, restaurants and discos. Behind the roadside arcades lie countless villas, apartments and hotels.

Though dense, the buildings are pleasantly designed and unoppressive. All have easy access to a long golden beach, Playa Blanca, which in places

is very wide. Another beach nearby is Playa de los Pocillos. The original village lies west of the port, away from the hustle and bustle of the resort.

Fishing boat in Arrecife port

Arrecife ㉗

Las Palmas. 🏘 42,200. ✈ 🚌 🚹
Blas Cabrera Felipe, 928 81 17 62. 🚢
Sat. 📅 San Ginés (25 Aug).

ARRECIFE, with its modern buildings and lively streets, is the commercial and administrative centre of the

island. Despite its modern trappings, the capital retains much of its old charm, with palm-lined promenades, a fine beach and two small forts. Only the 18th-century **Castillo de San José**, now a museum of contemporary art, is open to the public. The fort was renovated by César Manrique, and one of his paintings is on display here. An historic house, **La casa de los Arroyo**, is noted for its scientific library and is open to the public.

⚓ **La Casa de los Arroyo**
Arrecife. 🎟 928 80 17 29.
☐ Mon–Fri.
⚓ **Castillo de San José**
Puerto de Naos. 🎟 928 81 23 21.
☐ daily. ● 1 Jan, 24 Dec.

Costa Teguise ㉘

10 km (6 miles) north of Arrecife.
🚌 🚹 Avda Islas Canarias 11–12,
928 82 72 92.

THIS RESORT, largely financed by a mining conglomerate, has transformed the arid, low-lying terrain north of Arrecife into an extensive cluster of timeshare accommodation, leisure clubs and luxury hotels. The contrast between old town Teguise, Lanzarote's former capital, and the exclusive, new Costa Teguise is striking. Fake greenery and suburban lamps line boulevards amid barren ashlands. White villas line a series of small sandy beaches. The high level of investment has succeeded in attracting jet-set clientele. King Juan Carlos also has a villa here.

Umbrellas on the beach, Puerto del Carmen

Iglesia de San Miguel on the main square in Teguise

Teguise 29

Las Palmas. 11,500. *Plaza General Franco 1, 928 84 50 72. Sun. Dia del Carmen (16 Jul), Las Nieves (5 Aug).*

TEGUISE, the island's capital until 1852, is a well-kept, old-fashioned town with wide, cobbled streets and patrician houses grouped around the **Iglesia de San Miguel**. The best time to visit is on a Sunday, when there is a lively handicrafts market and folk dancing. Just outside Teguise, the castle of Santa Bárbara contains the **Museo del Emigrante Canario**, which tells the story of Canarian emigrants to South America.

ENVIRONS: To see more of inland Lanzarote, follow the central road south of Teguise, through the strange farmland of **La Geria**. Black volcanic ash has been scooped into protective, crescent-shaped pits which trap moisture to enable vines and other crops to flourish. **Mozaga**, one of the main villages in the area, is a major centre of wine production. On the roadside near Mozaga is the *Monumento al Campesino*, Manrique's *(see p524)* striking modern sculpture dedicated to Lanzarote's farmers.

Halfway between Teguise and Arrecife is the **Fundación César Manrique**. The fascinating former home of the artist incorporates five lava caves. It contains some of his own work and his collection of contemporary art.

🏛 Museo del Emigrante Canario
Montaña de Guanapay. 928 84 50 74. daily.
🏛 Fundación César Manrique
Taro de Tahíche. 928 84 31 38. daily.

Haría 30

Las Palmas. 4,000. *Plaza de la Constitución 1, 928 83 52 51. San Juan (24 Jun).*

PALM TREES and white, cube-shaped houses distinguish this picturesque village. It acts as a gateway to excursions round the northern tip of the island. The road to the north gives memorable views over exposed cliffs, and the 609-m (2,000-ft) high Monte Corona.

ENVIRONS: From Manrique's **Mirador del Río** you can see La Graciosa and the northernmost of the Canary Islands, Alegranza. **Orzola** is a delightful fishing village providing fish lunches as well as boat trips to La Graciosa. To the south are the Mala prickly pear plantations, where cochineal (crimson dye) is extracted from the insects which feed on the plants. Nearby is the **Jardín de Cactus**, a well-stocked cactus garden, which has a smart restaurant, again designed by Manrique.

🎥 Mirador del Río
Haría. 928 17 35 36. daily.
🌵 Jardín de Cactus
Guatiza. 928 52 93 97. daily.

Landscaped pool on top of the caves of Jameos del Agua

Jameos del Agua 31

Las Palmas. 928 84 80 20. daily.

AN ERUPTION of the Monte Corona volcano formed the Jameos del Agua lava caves on Lanzarote's northeast coast. In 1965–8, these were landscaped by César Manrique into an imaginative subterranean complex containing a restaurant, nightclub, a swimming pool edged by palm trees, and gardens of oleander and cacti. Steps lead to a shallow seawater lagoon where a rare species of blind white crab, unique to Lanzarote, glows softly in the dim light. An exhibition on volcanology and Canarian flora and fauna also deserves a look. Folk-dancing evenings are regularly held in this unusual setting.

ENVIRONS: Another popular attraction is the nearby **Cueva de los Verdes**, a tube of solidfed lava stretching 6 km (4 miles) underground. Guided tours of the caves are available.

🎥 Cueva de los Verdes
Haría. 928 17 32 20. daily.

Volcanic ash swept into crescent-shaped pits for farming, La Geria

Volcanic Islands

THE VOLCANIC ACTIVITY which formed the Canary Islands has created a variety of scenery, from distinctive lava formations to enormous volcanoes crowned by huge, gaping craters. The islands are all at different stages in their evolution. Tenerife, Lanzarote, El Hierro and La Palma are still volcanically active; dramatic displays of flames and steam can be seen in Lanzarote's Montañas de Fuego *(see p524)*. The last eruption was on La Palma in 1971.

Origin of the Islands
The Canaries are situated above faults in the earth's crust, which is always thinner under the oceans than under the continents. When magma (molten rock) rises through these cracks volcanoes are formed.

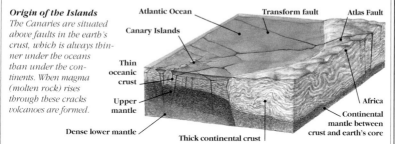

Atlantic Ocean   Transform fault   Atlas Fault

Canary Islands

Thin oceanic crust

Upper mantle

Dense lower mantle

Thick continental crust

Africa

Continental mantle between crust and earth's core

EVOLUTION OF THE CANARY ISLANDS

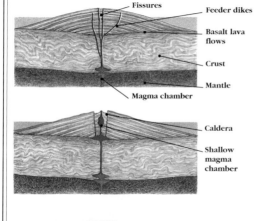

Fissures

Feeder dikes

Basalt lava flows

Crust

Mantle

Magma chamber

Caldera

Shallow magma chamber

Sea level

Exposed solidified magma chamber

1 *Lanzarote, El Hierro and La Palma* are wide, gently sloping shield volcanoes standing on the sea floor. All of them are composed of basalt formed by a hot, dense magma. The flexible crust is pressed down by the weight of the islands.

2 *An explosive eruption* can empty the magma chamber, leaving the roof unsupported. This collapses under the weight of the volcano above to form a depression, or caldera, such as Las Cañadas on Tenerife. There are thick lava flows during this stage of the island's evolution.

3 *If eruptions cease* a volcano will be eroded by the action of the sea, and by wind and rain. Gran Canaria's main volcano is in the early stages of erosion, while the volcano on Fuerteventura has already been deeply eroded, exposing chambers of solidified magma.

Rope lava near La Restinga, El Hierro

Pico Viejo crater, next to Mount Teide, Tenerife *(see p514)*

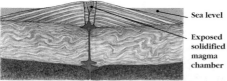

TRAVELLERS' NEEDS

WHERE TO STAY

MEDIEVAL CASTLES turned into luxury hotels and mansions converted into youth hostels typify the variety of places to stay in Spain. The tourists who sustain Spain's economy have almost 10,000 establishments to choose from, offering around one million beds. Suites in once-royal palaces are at the top of the scale. Then there are luxury beach hotels on the

Logo for a luxury five-star hotel

Costa del Sol and in the Balearic and the Canary Islands. Visitors can also stay on remote farms, or in villas and old houses let for self-catering. For budget travel there are pensions, family-run *casas rurales* and guest houses, camp sites, and refuges with stunning views for mountaineers. Some of the best hotels in all these categories and in every style and price range are listed on pages 536–71.

Hotel de la Reconquista, Oviedo, an 18th-century mansion *(see p539)*

HOTEL GRADING AND FACILITIES

ALL OF SPAIN'S hotels are classified into categories and awarded stars by the country's regional tourist authorities. Hotels (indicated by an H on a blue plaque near the hotel door) are awarded from one to five stars. Hostals (Hs) and pensions (P) offer fewer comforts but are correspondingly cheaper than hotels.

Spain's star-rating system reflects the number and range of facilities available – whether the hotel has air conditioning, for instance, or a lift – rather than the quality of service.

Most hotels have restaurants that are open to non-residents. Although hotel-residencias (HR) and hostal-residencias (HsR) do not have dining rooms, some serve breakfast. Among Spain's largest hotel chains are **Grupo Sol Meliá**, **Grupo Riu** and **NH**. Many large tour operators book rooms in Spain's best hotels.

PARADORS

PARADORS are government-run hotels, classified from three to five stars. Spain's first parador opened in the Sierra de Gredos in 1928 *(see p556)*; there is now a wide network of them on the mainland and the islands. They are located close together so that there is never more than a day's drive to the nearest one. The best are in former royal hunting lodges, monasteries, castles and other monuments; some modern paradors have been purpose-built, often in spectacular scenery or in towns of historic interest *(see pp534–5)*.

A parador is not necessarily the best hotel in town, but it can be counted on to

deliver a predictably high level of comfort. The bedrooms are usually spacious and comfortable, and are furnished in a way that varies little from parador to parador.

If you plan to tour in high season or to stay in the smaller paradors, it is wise to reserve a room. The paradors may be booked through the **Central de Reservas** in Madrid or through their London agent, **Keytel International**.

PRICES

SPANISH LAW requires all hotel managements to display their prices behind reception and in every room. As a rule, the higher a hotel's star-rating, the more you pay. Rates for a double room can be as little as 18 euros a night for a cheap one-star hostal; a five-star hotel will cost more than 180 euros a night, but a room price higher than 240 euros a night is exceptional.

Prices usually vary according to room, region and season. A suite or a very spacious room, or one with a view, a balcony or other special feature, may cost more than average. Rural and suburban hotels are generally less expensive than those in the city centre. All the prices given on pages 536–71 are based on mid-season or high-season rates. High season

Jaén's parador, a modern extension of the medieval castle *(see p5*

◁ **Madrileños** enjoying afternoon sunshine, drinks and conversation in the Plaza Mayor

generally covers July and August, but in some areas it runs from April to October and in the Canary Islands the winter is high season.

Many of Spain's city hotels charge especially inflated rates for their rooms during major fiestas, such as the April Fair in Seville *(see p413)*, Los Sanfermines in Pamplona *(see p128)*, Carnival in Santa Cruz de Tenerife and Easter Week *(see p34)* in many places.

Most hotels quote prices per room and meal prices per person without including VAT *(IVA)*, which is currently 7 per cent in most of Spain, but 5 per cent in the Canary Islands.

The glass-domed foyer of the Palace Hotel, Madrid *(see p553)*

BOOKING AND CHECK-IN

OFF-SEASON IN RURAL or small towns you are unlikely to need to book ahead; but if you plan to travel in high season or want to stay in a particular hotel, you should reserve a room by phone, e-mail or through a travel agent. You will need to reserve if you want a special room: one with a double bed (twin beds are the norm); on the ground floor; away from a noisy main road; or a room with a view.

The resort hotels often close from autumn to spring. Before you travel, it is always advisable to check that your preferred hotels will be open at that time of year.

You will not normally be asked for a deposit when you book a hotel room. However, deposit of 20–25 per cent

may be requested if you book during a peak period or for a stay of more than a few nights. Send it by credit card or giro in Spain and by credit card or banker's draft from outside the country. If you have to cancel, do so at least a week before the booking date or you may lose all or some of the deposit.

Most hotels will honour a booking only until 8pm unless business is poor. If you are delayed, call the hotel to assure them you are coming and to tell them when to expect you.

When you check in you will be asked for your passport or identity card to comply with Spanish police regulations. It will normally be returned to you promptly as soon as your details have been copied.

You are expected to check out of your room by noon on the last day of your stay, or to pay for another night.

PAYING

HOTELS THAT ACCEPT credit cards are listed on pages 536–71. In some large, busy hotels you may be asked to sign a blank credit card pay slip on arrival. Under Spanish law it is fraudulent to ask you to do this; you should refuse.

Eurocheques are accepted in some hotels, but personal cheques are not accepted in Spanish hotels, even if backed by a cheque guarantee card or drawn on a Spanish bank. Many people pay cash and in some cheap hotels this may be the only payment accepted.

Around 1.5–2 euros is the usual tip for all hotel staff.

The pretty beach of Meliá Salinas Hotel, Lanzarote *(see p571)*

CASAS RURALES

THE OWNERS OF some country houses (*casas rurales*) accept a few visitors, usually in high season. They are most numerous in Asturias, Navarra, Aragón and Catalonia (where they are called *cases de pagès*). They are becoming common in Galicia and Cantabria (where they are called *casonas*), and in Andalusia.

Casas rurales range in style from stately manor houses to small, isolated farms. Some offer bed and breakfast; some an evening meal or full board. Most are self-catering.

Do not expect hotel service or a long list of facilities in a *casa rural*. You may, however, be given a friendly welcome and good home cooking, all at a very affordable price.

You can book accommodation in *casas rurales* directly or through various regional associations, such as **RAAR** in Andalusia, **Rutastur** in Asturias, **TVR** in Aragón, and **Turisverd** in Catalonia.

El Nacimiento, Turre, a charming Andalusian *casa rural* (see p567)

SELF-CATERING

Villas and holiday flats let by the week are plentiful along the Spanish coasts. In scenic areas of the countryside there are many *casas rurales* (farm and village houses) for rent by the day. To obtain information about the *casas rurales*, contact their regional organizations *(see p531)*. They also take bookings. **The Individual Traveller's Spain** is a UK organization that acts as an agent for owners of holiday houses and flats in Spain, as does **Hometours International Inc.** in the US. Other organizations and owners of holiday homes advertise in the travel sections of UK Sunday newspapers. Tour operators offer a range of self-catering accommodation.

The prices for self-catering accommodation vary according to the location, the property and the season. A four-person villa with a pool can cost under 240 euros for a week if it is inland and 960 euros a week or more if it is on the coast.

An apartment hotel is a new type of accommodation; in Andalusia it is called a *villa turística*. Half hotel, half holiday flats, it gives guests a choice between self-catering (all rooms have a kitchen) or eating in the hotel restaurant. Holiday villages are similar, often catering for specialist interests. One example is the village of Ainsa in the mountain sports region of Aragón *(see p547)*, which offers a mix of camping and hostel accommodation, with restaurants and bars.

Typical holiday villas in Lanzarote's Puerto del Carmen, the Canary Islands

YOUTH HOSTELS AND MOUNTAIN REFUGES

To use the network of *albergues juveniles* (youth hostels) in Spain you need to show a YHA (Youth Hostel Association) card from your country or an international card, which you can buy from any hostel. Prices per person for bed and breakfast are lower than hotel prices.

Youth hostels can be booked directly or through the **Red Española de Albergues Juveniles** (Spanish Network of Youth Hostels). Despite the name, there is no age limit.

Mountaineers heading for the more remote areas may use the *refugios* (refuges). These are shelters with a dormitory, cooking facilities and heating. Some are huts with about six bunks; others are mountain houses with up to 50 beds.

The *refugios* are marked on large-scale maps of mountain areas and national parks. They are administered by the regional mountaineering

associations and usually owned by clubs. The **Federación Española de Montañismo** and the local tourist offices will supply their addresses.

La Oliva monastery, Navarra *(see p126)*, welcomes paying guests

MONASTERIES AND CONVENTS

If you have a taste for peace and austerity you may enjoy a night in one of Spain's 150 religious houses where guests are welcome. Most belong to the Benedictine and the Cistercian orders. Room prices are inexpensive. They are not hotels, however; you have to book ahead by writing or by phone; and few have private telephones or television. The guests may be asked to tidy their rooms, observe the same strict mealtimes as the monks or nuns and to help with the washing up. Some convents admit only women and some monasteries only men.

Youth hostel in rustic style on the edge of Cazorla nature reserve, Jaén

CAMP SITES

T HERE ARE more than 1,200 camp sites scattered across Spain. Most of them are on the coasts, but there are also some outside the major cities and in the most popular areas of countryside. Most sites have electricity and running water; some also have launderettes, playgrounds, restaurants, shops, a swimming pool and other amenities.

It is sensible to carry a camping carnet with you. This can be used instead of a passport to check in at sites and it covers you for third-party insurance. Carnets are issued in the UK by the AA, RAC and **The Camping and Caravanning Club**.

Every year, the *Guía Oficial de Campings* is published by Turespaña. Information about camp sites is available from the **Federación Española de Empresarios de Campings y Ciudades de Vacaciones** (Spanish Camp Site and Holiday Camp Federation), which also takes bookings. In Spain, camping is only permitted on official sites.

DISABLED TRAVELLERS

H OTEL MANAGERS will advise on access for people in wheelchairs, and the staff will help, but few hotels are well equipped for disabled guests, although some of the youth hostels are. **Servi-COCEMFE** (the Confederación Coordinadora Estatal de Minusválidos Físicos de España) runs a hotel in Madrid for disabled people's groups. Servi-COCEMFE and Viajes 2000 *(see p613)* advise on hotels for guests with special needs. A UK charity, Holiday Care Service, produces a fact sheet on Spain. **IHD** (International Help for the Disabled), which is based in France, will arrange transport, hotels and other help for visitors to the Costa del Sol and Mallorca.

Sign for a camp site

View from the Cabina Verónica mountain refuge, Picos de Europa

FURTHER INFORMATION

E VERY SPRING, Turespaña publishes the *Guía Oficial de Hoteles*, which is sold in Spanish bookshops and news-stands and can be consulted in Spanish tourist offices. It lists every pension, hostal and hotel in Spain and gives their star-rating, their prices and a resumé of their facilities.

Each *comunidad autónoma* distributes a list of the hotels and other accommodation in its area via the tourist offices.

DIRECTORY

HOTEL CHAINS

Grupo Riu
℡ 971 49 08 21.
FAX 971 74 38 98.
W www.riuhotels.com

Grupo Sol-Meliá
℡ 902 14 44 44.
FAX 91 579 13 92.
W www.solmelia.com

NH-Hoteles
℡ 91 451 97 18.
FAX 91 442 44 02.
W www.nh-hoteles.es

PARADORS

Central de Reservas
Calle Requena 3,
28013 Madrid.
℡ 91 516 66 66.
FAX 91 516 66 57.
W www.parador.es

Keytel International
402 Edgware Road,
London W2 1ED.
℡ 020 7616 0300 in UK.
FAX 020 7616 0317 in UK.

SELF-CATERING AND BED AND BREAKFAST

Asociacion Gallega de Turismo Rural
Recinto Ferial, Apdo 26,
Silleda 36540 Pontevedra.
℡ 986 58 00 50.
FAX 986 58 01 62.

Hometours International Inc.
PO Box 11503, Knoxville,
TN 3739, USA.
℡ 865 690 8484.

The Individual Traveller's Spain
Bignor, Pulborough,
West Sussex RH20 1QD.
℡ 01798 869485 in UK.

RAAR
Apartado (de Correos)
2035, 04080 Almería.
℡ 950 26 50 18.
FAX 950 27 04 31.
W www.raar.es

Rutastur
C/ Marques de Canillejas
12, Bajo, 33500 Llanes
(Asturias).
℡ 902 10 70 70.
FAX 98 540 25 41.

Turisverd
Plaça Sant Josep Oriol 4,
08002 Barcelona.
℡ 93 412 69 84.
FAX 93 412 50 16.

TVR
C/ Porches de Galicia 4,
22002 Huesca.
℡ 974 29 41 41.
FAX 974 29 41 29

YOUTH HOSTELS

Red Española de Albergues Juveniles
Gran Via 10, 28004 Madrid.
℡ 91 580 42 16.
FAX 91 402 21 94.

MOUNTAIN REFUGES

Federación de Montañismo
C/ Floridablanca 75,
08015 Barcelona.
℡ 93 426 42 67.
FAX 93 426 33 87.

CAMPING

The Camping and Caravanning Club
℡ 02476 422024 in UK.

Federación de Empresarios de Campings
C/ San Bernardo 97–99,
28015 Madrid.
℡ 91 448 12 34.
W www.vayacamping.net

DISABLED TRAVELLERS

SATH
347 Fifth Ave.
New York, NY 10016
℡ 212 447 7284.
W www.sath.org

Servi-COCEMFE
C/ Luis Cabrera 63,
28002 Madrid.
℡ 91 744 36 00.
FAX 91 413 19 96.

FURTHER INFORMATION

Spanish Tourist Office
23 Manchester Square,
London W1M 5AP.
℡ 020 7486 8077.
FAX 020 7486 8034.
W www.tourspain.es

Spain's Best: Paradors

PARADOR IS AN OLD SPANISH WORD for a lodging place for travellers of respectable rank. In the late 1920s a national network of state-run hotels called paradors was established. Many of the nearly 90 paradors are converted castles, palaces or monasteries, although some have been purpose-built in strategic tourist locations. They are generally well signposted and the prices are comparable with other luxury hotels. All offer a high degree of comfort and service, and have restaurants which offer regional cuisine.

Hotel de los Reyes Católicos, one of the sights of Santiago de Compostela (see p86), may be the world's oldest hotel. It was founded as a hospital in 1499 (see p537).

Hotel de los Reyes Católicos

Parador de León

Parador de León is housed in the Hostal San Marcos, one of Spain's finest Renaissance buildings (see p21). The main hall has a magnificent coffered ceiling (see p556).

Parador de Guadalupe is a 16th-century former hospice for pilgrims. It stands beside a famous monastery in Extremadura (see p560).

Parador de Arcos de la Frontera is situated in one of the archetypal pueblos blancos (white towns). Its wide, semicircular terrace offers panoramic views of the Moorish castle, the Guadalete river and the rolling farmland beyond (see p563).

Parador de Guadalupe

Parador de Granada

Parador de Arcos de la Frontera

Parador de Granada is a captivating 15th-century convent built in the beautiful gardens of the Alhambra at the instruction of the Catholic Monarchs. Antique Spanish furniture fills the halls and rooms of this atmospheric parador, and an old roofless chapel forms a patio. Advance booking is essential (see p565

Parador de Sigüenza, *a massive hilltop castle enclosing a large courtyard, was formerly a Visigothic, then a Moorish, fortress. It is approached from the historic town below by a steep cobbled street* (see p559).

Parador de Viella is set in the spectacular Vall d'Arán and surrounded by high peaks. There is ample opportunity for outdoor activity, from skiing to hunting and fishing *(see p547)*.

Parador de Viella

Parador de Sigüenza

Parador de Alcañiz

Parador de Cuenca

Parador de Alcañiz *is located in a castle-monastery built by the Knights of Calatrava in the 12th century. Despite its imposing size, the parador has only 12 rooms. The cloister is now a peaceful garden* (see p548).

0 kilometres	200
0 miles	100

Parador de Cuenca is housed in the converted 16th-century convent of San Pablo. It enjoys magnificent views of the attractive old town *(see p558)*.

Parador de Cañadas del Teide is a recently refurbished parador situated in the Mount Teide National Park (see pp514–15) on Tenerife. From its terraces there are views of the volcanic landscape (see p571).

THE CANARY ISLANDS

Choosing a Hotel

THE HOTELS in this guide have been selected across a wide price range for excellent facilities and location. Many also have a highly recommended restaurant. The chart lists hotels by region, starting in the north; colour-coded thumb tabs indicate the regions covered on each page. For more details on restaurants see pages 578–609.

	CREDIT CARDS	NUMBER OF ROOMS	PRIVATE PARKING	SWIMMING POOL	GARDEN OR TERRACE
GALICIA					
ALFOZ: *Pazo Galea.* €€ Castro de Ouro, 27776 (Lugo). **(** & **FAX** *982 55 83 23.* A 19th-century *pazo* (Galician manor house) with a splendid garden. The bedrooms are simple and modern. The owners, a Galician family, operate an original fulling mill and a flour mill as a tourist attraction. **■** TV		5	■		■
BAIONA: *Villa Sol.* €€ C/ Palos de la Frontera 12, 36300 (Pontevedra). **(** *986 35 56 91.* **FAX** *986 35 67 02.* A family-run hotel in an old country house decorated with antiques. Children are not admitted during the high season. ● *until Oct 2002.* **■**	MC V	6	■		■
BAIONA: *Parador de Baiona.* W www.parador.es €€€€€ Carretera de Baiona, 36300 (Pontevedra). **(** *986 35 50 00.* **FAX** *986 35 50 76.* This parador, built in the style of an old manor house or *pazo*, is located within the walls of Monterreal castle. **■** TV	AE DC MC V	122	■	●	■
BRIÓN: *Hotel Casa Rosalía.* @ romanulloa@interbook.net €€ Calle Soigrexia, Los Ángeles, 15280 (A Coruña). **(** *981 88 75 80.* **FAX** *981 88 75 57.* A country house hotel, stone-built and surrounding a cloister. It offers simple accommodation 25 km (16 miles) from the coast and Santiago de Compostela. The hotel contains a popular restaurant. **■** TV	DC MC V	30		●	■
CAMBADOS: *Parador de Cambados.* W www.parador.es €€€ Paseo de Cervantes, 36633 (Pontevedra). **(** *986 54 22 50.* **FAX** *986 54 20 68.* This parador, on an estuary of the Rías Baixas, occupies a handsome *pazo* built round a large courtyard garden where drinks are served. Galician specialities and local wines are served in the restaurant. **■** TV	AE DC MC V	63	■		■
CERVO: *Pousada O'Almacén.* €€ Carretera de Sargadelos 2, 27891 (Lugo). **(** *982 55 78 36.* **FAX** *982 55 78 94.* A restored 18th-century building, once a food store for neighbouring hamlets. The best bedrooms look on to the Río Xunco. **■** TV	AE DC MC V	7			■
CORNIDE: *Casa Grande de Cornide.* @ casagcornide@teleline.es €€€ Calo, Teo, 15886 (A Coruña). **(** *981 80 55 99.* **FAX** *981 80 57 51.* A welcoming small bed and breakfast hotel in a renovated house near Santiago de Compostela. It has a library and a garden with two traditional *hórreos* (granaries) and an 18th-century dovecote. **■** TV	AE DC MC V	10	■	●	■
A CORUÑA: *Ciudad de La Coruña.* €€€ Paseo de Adormideras, 15002. **(** *981 21 21 00.* **FAX** *981 22 46 10.* A hotel with views over A Coruña bay, and a beach nearby. It has spacious, modern bedrooms and gym and spa facilities. **■** TV ▤	AE DC MC V	131	■	●	■
A ESTRADA: *Pazo de Leira Herminia.* €€ Calle Carballeira 6, Nigoi, 36684 (Pontevedra). **(** & **FAX** *986 57 32 00.* . A quiet, cosy hotel offering bed and breakfast in a restored, stone-built country house near the source of the Río Liñares. It is a convenient base for visits to the Rías Baixas. **■**		4	■	●	■
FERROL: *Parador de Ferrol.* W www.parador.es €€€€ C/ Almirante Fernández Martín, 15401 (A Coruña). **(** *981 35 67 20.* **FAX** *981 35 67 21.* This spacious parador in the town centre is surrounded by gardens. It is decorated with nautical memorabilia of Ferrol's seafaring past. The bedroom windows look out over the harbour. **■** TV	AE DC MC V	38	■		
A GUARDA: *Convento de San Benito.* €€ Plaza de San Benito, 36780 (Pontevedra). **(** *986 61 11 66.* **FAX** *986 61 15 17.* A converted 16th-century convent in which the nuns' cells have been transformed into bedrooms for the guests. They surround a small cloister with a palm tree and a stone fountain. **■** TV	AE DC MC V	24			■

<table>
<tr><td>

Price categories for a standard double room per night, with tax, breakfast and service included:

€ under 50 euros
€€ 50–75 euros
€€€ 75–100 euros
€€€€ 100–125 euros
€€€€€ over 125 euros

</td><td>

CREDIT CARDS
Indicates which credit cards are accepted: *AE* American Express; *DC* Diners Club; *MC* Master Card/Access; *V* Visa
PARKING
Parking provided by the hotel in a private car park or a private garage on the hotel site or very close by. Some hotels charge for use of private parking facilities.
SWIMMING POOL
Hotel pool outdoors unless otherwise stated.
GARDEN
Hotel with garden, courtyard or terrace, often providing tables for eating outdoors.

</td></tr>
</table>

	CREDIT CARDS	NUMBER OF ROOMS	PRIVATE PARKING	SWIMMING POOL	GARDEN OR TERRACE
NEDA: *Pazo da Merced.* @ pazomerced@arrakis.es €€€ Pazo da Merced, 15510 (A Coruña). (981 38 29 00. FAX 981 38 01 04. A restored, 17th-century stone manor house with its own chapel, at the head of the Ría de Ferrol. ⊟ TV &	AE DC MC V	8	■	●	■
POBRA DE TRIVES: *Casa Grande de Trives.* w www.casagrandetrives.com €€ Calle Marqués de Trives 17, 32780 (Ourense). (& FAX 988 33 20 66. A *pousada* (small hotel) in an 18th-century stone manor, with a coat of arms on its central tower. Antiques and old paintings decorate the cosy interior. There is a chapel with a magnificent reredos. ⊟ TV	AE DC MC V	9	■		■
PONTEVEDRA: *Parador de Pontevedra.* w www.parador.es €€€€ Calle Barón 19, 36002. (986 85 58 00. FAX 986 85 21 95. An elegant parador in a stately manor in the old town. The decor incorporates antiques, gilt mirrors, chandeliers and tapestries. ⊟ TV ▤	AE DC MC V	47	■		■
RIBEIRA: *Fonteclara.* €€ C/ Sta Marina de Ribeira 6, 36685 (Pontevedra). (986 57 32 09. FAX 981 36 49 99. An old Galician country house of great character, peacefully located in the valley of the Río Ulloa. Visitors are offered bed and breakfast, and a sitting room with an open fireplace. ⊟ &	V	8	■	●	■
SANTIAGO DE COMPOSTELA: *Hesperia Compostela.* €€€€€ C/ Horreo 1, (A Coruña). (981 58 57 00. FAX 981 58 52 90. A hotel in the centre of town which has recently been renovated. The building itself is very old, and the interior is decorated in a 'classic' style to reflect the exterior architecture. A restaurant is available. ⊟ TV	AE DC MC V	99			
SANTIAGO DE COMPOSTELA: *Parador Reyes Católicos.* €€€€€ Praza do Obradoiro 1, 15705 (A Coruña). (981 58 22 00. w www.parador.es. Built under the Catholic Monarchs for poor pilgrims, this 16th-century parador is one of the world's grandest hotels (*see p86*). It is built round four arcaded patios with fountains. ⊟ TV & ▤	AE DC MC V	136	■		■
O SAVIÑAO: *Torre de Vilariño.* € Calle Fión 47, 27548 (Lugo). (& FAX 982 45 22 60. A 17th-century inn converted into a hotel offering bed and breakfast, mainly to tourists following the so-called "Route of the Romanesque". The owners serve food and wine they make themselves. ⊟ TV	DC V	9	■	●	■
SISÁN-CAMBADOS: *Pazo Carrasqueira.* @ p.carrasqueira@eresmas.net €€€ Calle Carrasqueira, 36638 (Pontevedra). (& FAX 986 71 00 32. A guest house in a rural mansion, with a carved granite staircase and cosy bedrooms on the top floor. Fish, seafood, and Albariño wine (produced on the estate) are served in the dining room. ⊟ TV	AE MC V	9	■		■
A TOXA: *Gran Hotel de La Toja.* @ info@latojagranhotel.com €€€€€ O Grove, 36991 (Pontevedra). (986 73 00 25. FAX 986 73 00 26. This mansion, built at the end of the 19th century on an island planted with palm and pine trees, is reached from the mainland by an iron bridge. The hotel has a ballroom and a health and fitness centre. ⊟ TV	AE DC MC V	197	■	●	■
TUI: *Parador de Tui.* w www.parador.es €€€ Avenida de Portugal, 36700 (Pontevedra). (986 60 03 09. FAX 986 60 21 63. The public and guest rooms have superb views over the town of Tui and across the Río Miño, which forms the frontier with Portugal. The menu includes eels and oysters. ⊟ TV	AE DC MC V	30	■	●	■
VERÍN: *Parador de Verín.* w www.parador.es €€€ Monterrei, 32600 (Ourense). (988 41 00 75. FAX 988 41 20 17. Verín's parador is on a hilltop, surrounded by lawns and trees, with views across a valley to the medieval castle of Monterrei. Vineyards in the valley supply wines for the hotel restaurant. ⊟ TV	AE DC MC V	23	■	●	■

For key to symbols see back flap

Price categories for a standard double room per night, with tax, breakfast and service included:
- € under 50 euros
- €€ 50–75 euros
- €€€ 75–100 euros
- €€€€ 100–125 euros
- €€€€€ over 125 euros

CREDIT CARDS
Indicates which credit cards are accepted: *AE* American Express; *DC* Diners Club; *MC* Master Card/Access; *V* Visa
PARKING
Parking provided by the hotel in a private car park or a private garage on the hotel site or very close by. Some hotels charge for use of private parking facilities.
SWIMMING POOL
Hotel pool outdoors unless otherwise stated.
GARDEN
Hotel with garden, courtyard or terrace, often providing tables for eating outdoors.

	CREDIT CARDS	NUMBER OF ROOMS	PRIVATE PARKING	SWIMMING POOL	GARDEN OR TERRACE
VILAGARCÍA DE AROUSA: *Pazo O'Rial.* W www.pazorial.com €€€ Calle El Rial 1, 36600 (Pontevedra). 986 50 70 11. FAX 986 50 16 76. Tiled floors and stone walls preserve the character of this picturesque old manor; cushions and fine fabrics give comfort. 📶 TV	AE DC MC V	60	■	●	■
VILLALBA: *Parador de Villalba.* W www.parador.es €€€€ Valeriano Valdesuso, 27800 (Lugo). 982 51 00 11. FAX 982 51 00 90. Six rooms of this hotel are found in a medieval octagonal tower, with access to the other rooms through a glass tunnel. 📶 TV	AE DC MC V	48	■		■
VILLALONGA: *Pazo El Revel.* €€€ Camino de la Iglesia 15, 36990 (Pontevedra). 986 74 30 00. FAX 986 74 33 90. A 17th-century manor house, its façade overgrown with creepers. It has peaceful formal gardens and a colonnaded terrace. 📶 TV	V	22	■	●	■
ASTURIAS AND CANTABRIA					
CANGAS DE ONÍS: *Aultre Naray.* W www.aultrenaray.com €€€ Peruyes, 33547 (Asturias). 98 584 08 08. FAX 98 584 08 48. There are mountain views from this country house hotel in one of Northern Spain's least-known corners. Every bedroom is different. 📶 TV	AE DC MC V	10	■		■
CASTROPOL: *Palacete Peñalba.* €€€ C/ El Cotarelo, Figueras, 33794 (Asturias). 98 563 61 25. FAX 98 563 62 47. This hotel in an Art Nouveau mansion built in 1912 by a Gaudí acolyte has oval balconies, curved staircases and its original furniture. 📶 TV	AE DC MC V	12	■		■
COLOMBRES: *La Casona de Villanueva.* @ casonavillanueva@inicia.es €€ Villanueva, Ribadedeva, 33590 (Asturias). 98 541 25 90. FAX 98 541 25 14. An 18th-century village house, carefully restored in the traditional style, with a peaceful atmosphere. 📶	MC V	8	■		■
COLOMBRES: *Mirador de La Franca.* @ lafranca@hotelmirador.com €€€ Playa de La Franca, La Franca, 33590 (Asturias). 98 541 21 45. FAX 98 541 21 53. There are magnificent views from the lounge and restaurant of this hotel in a rocky cove set back from La Franca beach. The waters of the bay are safe for water sports and underwater fishing. 📶 TV	AE DC MC V	61	■		■
COMILLAS: *Casal del Castro.* €€ Calle San Jerónimo, 39520 (Cantabria). 942 72 00 36. FAX 942 72 00 61. A large, 17th-century house decorated and furnished with antiques. It is on the edge of the town, not far from excellent beaches. 📶 TV	MC V	45	■		■
COSGAYA: *Hotel del Oso.* @ hoteldeloso@mundivia.es €€ Ctra Potes–Fuente Dé, 39539 (Cantabria). 942 73 30 18. FAX 942 73 30 36. Surrounded by the mountains of the eastern Picos de Europa, this is a comfortable hotel, very popular with foreign tourists. 📶 TV 🍴	DC MC V	51	■	●	■
ESCALANTE: *San Román de Escalante.* W www.relaischateaux.fr €€€€€ Km2 Ctra Escalante–Castillo, 39795 (Cantabria). 942 67 77 45. FAX 942 67 76 43. A hotel in an exquisitely decorated 17th-century house overlooking trees and meadows. Beside it is a Romanesque chapel. 📶 ▤ TV ♿	AE DC MC V	16	■	●	■
FUENTE DÉ: *Parador de Fuente Dé.* W www.parador.es €€€ Fuente Dé, 39588 (Cantabria). 942 73 66 51. FAX 942 73 66 54. This modern building at the foot of the Picos de Europa cable car has pleasant bedrooms and long galleries with huge windows. It is an ideal base for fishing or walking in the mountains. 📶 TV ♿ ▤	AE DC MC V	78	■		■
GIJÓN: *La Casona de Jovellanos.* @ hotel-lacasona@jazzfree.com €€ Plaza de Jovellanos 1, 33201 (Asturias). 98 534 20 24. FAX 98 535 61 51. A small hotel in an 18th-century building overlooking a little square in the old part of the city, and near the San Lorenzo beach. 📶 TV	AE MC V	13			

GIJÓN: *Parador Molino Viejo.* ⓦ www.parador.es   €€€€   AE DC MC V   40
Parque de Isabel la Católica, 33203 (Asturias). 【 *98 537 05 11.* 🗛 *98 537 02 33.*
A parador in a corner of one of Spain's prettiest parks, in a converted
windmill of a type common in Gijón from the 15th to the 18th century. The
old watercourse is preserved in the grounds. 🛏 ▤ TV

LIÉRGANES: *Posada del Sauce.* @ grupocastlar@mundivia.es   €€€   AE MC V   50
C/ José Antonio, 39722 (Cantabria). 【 *942 52 80 23.* 🗛 *942 52 81 17.*
This is an imposing 19th-century mountain house in a beautiful village. It
has a covered swimming pool, but the bedrooms are rather small. 🛏 TV

LLANES: *Gran Hotel Paraiso.* @ ampudia@jazzfree.com   €€€   AE DC MC V   18
Calle Pidal 2, 33500 (Asturias). 【 *98 540 19 71.* 🗛 *98 540 25 90.*
White marble floors, antique furniture and a grand piano in the lounge
contribute to the kitsch atmosphere of this hotel. It overlooks one of the
town's busiest streets, so book a parking space in advance. 🛏 TV

LLANES: *La Posada de Babel.* @ laposadadebabel@retemail.es   €€€   AE DC MC V   11
La Pereda, 33509 (Asturias). 【 *98 540 25 25.* 🗛 *98 540 26 22.*
The spectacular Picos de Europa towers above this small, family-run hotel.
It is partly modern, but has huge, traditional fireplaces and one bedroom is
a converted *hórreo* (old grain store). ● *15 Dec–15 Feb.* 🛏 TV

OVIEDO: *Hotel de la Reconquista.* ⓦ www.hoteldelareconquista.com   €€€€€   AE DC MC V   142
Calle Gil de Jaz 16, 33004 (Asturias). 【 *98 524 11 00.* 🗛 *98 524 11 66.*
A magnificent 18th-century building with a massive stone coat of arms
above the main entrance. The public rooms are arranged around several
arcaded and balconied courtyards. 🛏 ▤ TV

PECHÓN: *Don Pablo.* @ donpablo@donpablohotel.com   €€   MC V   30
Afueras, 39594 (Cantabria). 【 *942 71 95 00.* 🗛 *942 71 95 23.*
Three houses joined together look like an old ancestral mansion. The hotel
is close to the sea and is family-run, with cosy rooms and a warm
atmosphere. The two pretty attic bedrooms are popular. 🛏 TV

POTES: *El Jisu.*   €€   MC V   9
Ctra Potes–Camaleño, 39587 (Cantabria). 【 *942 73 30 38.* 🗛 *942 73 03 15.*
A chalet hotel in the Liébana Valley, with views of the Picos de Europa.
The cosy sitting rooms are decorated with antiques. 🛏 TV

PRAVIA: *Casa del Busto.*   €€€   AE DC MC V   28
Plaza del Rey Don Silo 1, 33120 (Asturias). 【 *98 582 27 71.* 🗛 *98 582 27 72.*
In a beautiful town, and close to a beach, is this hotel in a 16th-century
house. It is tastefully furnished with period pieces. The bedrooms overlook
a central patio where meals can be served. 🛏 TV

QUIJAS: *Hostería de Quijas.* @ quijas@teleline.es   €€   AE DC MC V   19
Calle Barrio Vinueva, 39590 (Cantabria). 【 *942 82 08 33.* 🗛 *942 83 80 50.*
An 18th-century stone-built mansion on the Santander–Oviedo road, near
Torrelavega. It has broad eaves, bay windows, timbered ceilings and a
magnificent garden. ● *Dec & Jan.* 🛏 TV

QUIJAS: *Posada de la Torre de Quijas.*   €€   AE DC MC V   20
Calle Barrio Vinueva 76, 39590 (Cantabria). 【 *942 82 06 45.* 🗛 *942 83 82 55.*
This hotel is in a restored, 19th-century stone house with wooden bay
windows. It is decorated with farming implements, which give it a rustic
atmosphere. The hotel is on a main road. 🛏 TV

RIBADESELLA: *Gran Hotel del Sella.* @ granhoteldelsella@hotmail.com   €€€€   AE DC MC V   82
Calle Ricardo Cangas 17, 33560 (Asturias). 【 *98 586 01 50.* 🗛 *98 585 74 49.*
The former summer palace of the Marquis of Argüelles now has a new
wing and is a family-run hotel. It is outside town, on the beach, and has a
pool, tennis courts and vast gardens. ● *Oct–Apr.* 🛏 TV ♿

SALAS: *Castillo de Valdés-Salas.*   €€   DC V   12
Plaza de la Campa, 33860 (Asturias). 【 *98 583 22 22.* 🗛 *98 583 22 99.*
A 16th-century restored castle converted into a simple hotel retaining much
of the character of the original building. The local tourist information desk
is in the hotel reception. 🛏 TV

SANTANDER: *Las Brisas.* @ abrisas@cantabria.org   €€€   AE DC MC V   13
Travesía de los Castros 14, 39005 (Cantabria). 【 *942 27 50 11.* 🗛 *942 28 11 73.*
A homely hotel in a 19th-century white villa close to the popular Sardinero
beach. Breakfast can be served on a seaside terrace. ● *Dec–Feb.* 🛏 TV

For key to symbols see back flap

	CREDIT CARDS	NUMBER OF ROOMS	PRIVATE PARKING	SWIMMING POOL	GARDEN OR TERRACE

Price categories for a standard double room per night, with tax, breakfast and service included:

€ under 50 euros
€€ 50–75 euros
€€€ 75–100 euros
€€€€ 100–125 euros
€€€€€ over 125 euros

CREDIT CARDS
Indicates which credit cards are accepted: *AE* American Express; *DC* Diners Club; *MC* Master Card/Access; *V* Visa
PARKING
Parking provided by the hotel in a private car park or a private garage on the hotel site or very close by. Some hotels charge for use of private parking facilities.
SWIMMING POOL
Hotel pool outdoors unless otherwise stated.
GARDEN
Hotel with garden, courtyard or terrace, often providing tables for eating outdoors.

	Credit Cards	Number of Rooms	Private Parking	Swimming Pool	Garden or Terrace
SANTANDER: *Hotel Real.* @ realsantander@husa.es €€€€€ Paseo Pérez Galdós 28, 39005 (Cantabria). 942 27 25 50. FAX 942 27 45 73. An elegant, formal hotel, visible on the city's highest hill. It was built late in the 19th century for nobility accompanying the royal family on holiday. The balconies give views over the bay. 🔒 ▤ TV ♿	AE DC MC V	123	■		■
SANTILLANA DEL MAR: *Posada de Santa Juliana.* € Calle Carrera 19, 39330 (Cantabria). 942 84 01 06. FAX 942 84 01 70. A small guest house located unpromisingly over a souvenir shop, but with charming attic rooms. Guests may eat in a bar across the street. 🔒 TV	AE DC MC V	6			
SANTILLANA DEL MAR: *Altamira.* @ info@hotelaltamira.com €€ Calle Cantón 1, 39330 (Cantabria). 942 81 80 25. FAX 942 81 80 36. A town-centre hotel in a restored 16th-century palace. The old wooden staircase leads to bedrooms with beams and polished floors. 🔒 TV	AE DC MC V	32			■
SANTILLANA DEL MAR: *Parador Gil Blas.* W www.parador.es €€€€ Plaza Ramón Pelayo 11, 39330 (Cantabria). 942 81 80 00. FAX 942 81 83 91. This stone mansion, begun in the 15th century, has a pretty patio. Bare walls and tiled floors enhance the medieval atmosphere. 🔒 TV ♿	AE DC MC V	54	■		■
SAN VICENTE DE TORANZO: *Posada del Pas.* €€ Ctra N623 Burgos–Santander, 39699 (Cantabria). 942 59 44 11. FAX 942 59 43 86. An 18th-century stone mountain house in a green valley on the Santander–Burgos road accommodates this popular hotel. 🔒 TV	AE DC MC V	32	■	●	■
SOLARES: *Hosteria Palacio los Marqueses de Valbuena.* €€ Calle General Mola 6, 39710 (Cantabria). 942 52 28 66. FAX 942 52 21 76. A medieval monastery with an imposing façade and a chapel. The public rooms are spacious and the bedrooms comfortable. 🔒 TV	AE DC MC V	27	■		■
TARAMUNDI: *La Rectoral.* @ larectoral@infonegocio.com €€€€ Taramundi, 33775 (Asturias). 98 564 67 67. FAX 98 564 67 77. A former priest's house deep in the Asturian countryside has been tastefully converted into a quiet and atmospheric hotel. The ample bedrooms all have views of the surrounding mountains. 🔒 ▤ TV	AE DC MC V	18	■		■

BASQUE COUNTRY, NAVARRA AND LA RIOJA

	Credit Cards	Number of Rooms	Private Parking	Swimming Pool	Garden or Terrace
ANGUIANO: *Abadía de Valvanera.* @ hosval@fer.es € Monasterio de Valvanera, 26323 (La Rioja). 941 37 70 44. FAX 941 37 71 94. Queen Isabel I stayed in this Benedictine monastery in 1482. The surroundings are beautiful, the rooms simple, and the food good. 🔒	AE DC MC V	29	■		■
ARGOMÁNIZ: *Parador de Argómaniz.* @ argomaniz@parador.es €€€ Carretera NI, 01192 (Álava). 945 29 32 00. FAX 945 29 32 87. Kings have lodged in this 17th-century stone palace. Its location on the slopes of Mount Zabalgaña is peaceful, with good views. 🔒 TV	AE DC MC V	53	■		■
AXPE-ATXONDO: *Mendi Goikoa.* @ mendigoikoa@terra.es €€€ Calle Barrio de San Juan 33, 48292 (Vizcaya). 94 682 08 33. FAX 94 682 11 36. Twin stone houses built in the 18th century have been converted into a pleasant hotel in the peaceful heart of the Valle de Atxondo. 🔒	DC MC V	12	■		
BAKIO: *Hostería del Señorío de Bizkaia.* @ hostbizkaia@hosteriasreales.com €€€ Calle José María Cirarda 4, 48130 (Vizcaya). & FAX 94 619 47 25. A stone building with wooden balconies houses this hotel. In summer concerts are held in the garden. Bakios beach is nearby. 🔒 TV	AE DC MC V	16	■		■
BILBAO (BILBO): *Iturrienea.* €€ Calle Santa María 14, 48007 (Vizcaya). 94 416 15 00. FAX 94 415 89 29. This venerable old hotel has recently undergone quite a transformation and now boasts huge rooms with modern decor. 🔒 TV	DC MC V	21			

BILBAO (BILBO): *Conde Duque.* @ reservas@condeduque.com €€€€
Paseo Campo Volantín 22, 48007 (Vizcaya). [94 445 60 00. FAX 94 445 60 66.
This establishment has an intriguing selling point: it has rooms which are claimed to be specially designed with women in mind.
Cards: AE DC MC V — *Rooms:* 67

BILBAO (BILBO): *De Deusto.* www.nh-hoteles.es €€€€
Calle Francisco Macia 9, 48014 (Vizcaya). [94 476 00 06. FAX 94 476 21 99.
This pleasant hotel has gained a good reputation for itself since it opened in 1992. Very handy for the Guggenheim.
Cards: AE DC MC V — *Rooms:* 70

BILBAO (BILBO): *Gran Hotel Ercilla.* @ ercilla@hotelercilla.es €€€€€
Calle Ercilla 37–9, 48011 (Vizcaya). [94 470 57 00. FAX 94 443 93 35.
Bilbao's largest hotel is centrally located, comfortable, welcoming and bustling with life. It has a very good restaurant.
Cards: AE DC MC V — *Rooms:* 345

DONAMARIA: *Donamaria'ko Benta.* @ donamariako@jet.es €€
Barrio Ventas 4, 31750 (Navarra). [948 45 07 08.
This is a small, family-run hotel in a stone-built Pyrenean mountain house, with the five bedrooms in an annexe. The proprietors create a pleasant atmosphere and serve excellent food in the restaurant.
Cards: V — *Rooms:* 5

ELIZONDO: *Casa Urruska.* €
Barrio de Bearzun, 31700 (Navarra). [& FAX 948 45 21 06.
This isolated stone farmhouse at the head of a pretty valley is a family house offering beds and a breakfast of good fresh farm food.
Cards: MC V — *Rooms:* 5

EZCARAY: *Albergue de La Real Fábrica.* €
Carretera de Santo Domingo, 20280 (La Rioja). [941 35 44 74. FAX 941 35 41 44.
This hotel, which occupies a restored textile mill in a small town, is an economical place for a quiet night after hill walking.
Cards: AE DC MC V — *Rooms:* 36

FITERO: *Gustavo Adolfo Bécquer.* @ balneario@fitero.com €€
C/ Extramuros, Baños de Fitero, 31593 (Navarra). [948 77 61 00. FAX 948 77 62 25.
One of two hotels on the site of the Roman baths – this hotel has a thermal spring in the basement. Bathing, massage and many treatments are available. The hotel also has extensive sports facilities
Cards: V — *Rooms:* 194

HARO: *Los Agustinos.* @ hagustinos@hagustinos.tsai.com €€€€
Calle San Agustín 2, 26200 (La Rioja). [941 31 13 08. FAX 941 30 31 48.
A lounge in a vast, arched chamber hung with tapestries is one of the highlights of this hotel in a former Augustinian monastery. Another is the magnificent central patio in the old cloister.
Cards: AE DC MC V — *Rooms:* 62

HONDARRIBIA (FUENTERRABÍA): *Pampinot.* €€€€
Calle Nagusia 5, 20280 (Guipúzcoa). [943 64 06 00. FAX 943 64 51 28.
An atmosphere of warmth is achieved by the team of women who run this hotel in a 16th-century mansion in old Hondarribia.
Cards: AE DC MC V — *Rooms:* 8

HONDARRIBIA (FUENTERRABÍA): *Parador de Hondarribia.* €€€€
Plaza de Armas 14, 20280 (Guipúzcoa). [943 64 55 00. www.parador.es
This is an elegant parador in the restored fortress that occupies the highest point of this historic town. Weapons and other memorabilia of its colourful history adorn the walls.
Cards: AE DC MC V — *Rooms:* 36

LAGUARDIA: *Posada Mayor de Migueloa.* www.mayordemigueloa.com €€€
Calle Mayor de Migueloa 20, 01300 (Álava). [945 62 11 75. FAX 945 62 10 22.
This beautiful mansion can be found in the pedestrianized old town of Laguardia. It was built in 1640 and still features its original granite walls, beams and tiled floors.
Cards: AE MC V — *Rooms:* 8

LECUMBERRI: *Ayestarán.* €
Calle Aralar 22, 31870 (Navarra). [& FAX 948 50 41 27.
Part of this family-run hotel, on both sides of the Pamplona–San Sebastián road, was built in the 1920s. The service is extraordinarily friendly.
Cards: MC V — *Rooms:* 91

LOGROÑO: *Herencia Rioja.* www.nh-hoteles.es €€€€
Calle Marqués de Murrieta 14, 26005 (La Rioja). [941 21 02 22. FAX 941 21 02 06.
A modern hotel near Logroño's historic quarter. It has comfortable cheerful bedrooms and a restaurant serving haute cuisine.
Cards: AE DC MC V — *Rooms:* 83

MUNDAKA: *El Puerto.* @ hotelpuerto@euskalnet.net €€
Calle Portu Kalea 1, 48360 (Vizcaya). [94 687 67 25. FAX 94 687 67 26.
A fisherman's house with two floors converted into a simple, cosy hotel. The windows give quite stunning views over the sea.
Cards: DC MC V — *Rooms:* 11

For key to symbols see back flap

<table>
<tr><td colspan="2">

Price categories for a standard double room per night, with tax, breakfast and service included:

€ under 50 euros
€€ 50–75 euros
€€€ 75–100 euros
€€€€ 100–125 euros
€€€€€ over 125 euros

</td><td colspan="5">

CREDIT CARDS
Indicates which credit cards are accepted: *AE* American Express; *DC* Diners Club; *MC* Master Card/Access; *V* Visa
PARKING
Parking provided by the hotel in a private car park or a private garage on the hotel site or very close by. Some hotels charge for use of private parking facilities.
SWIMMING POOL
Hotel pool outdoors unless otherwise stated.
GARDEN
Hotel with garden, courtyard or terrace, often providing tables for eating outdoors.

</td></tr>
</table>

	CREDIT CARDS	NUMBER OF ROOMS	PRIVATE PARKING	SWIMMING POOL	GARDEN OR TERRACE
MUNDAKA: *Atalaya.* @ reservas@hotel-atalaya-mundaka.com €€€ Paseo de Txorrokopunta 2, 48360 (Vizcaya). (94 617 70 00. FAX 94 687 68 99. Next to the fishing port, at the mouth of a sea inlet, is this hotel built at the beginning of the 20th century. It has a clean and well-kept air, small but pleasant bedrooms, large window galleries and a garden. ⊟ TV	AE DC MC V	11	▪		▪
OLITE: *Casa Zanito.* €€ Rua Mayor 16, 31390 (Navarra). (948 74 00 02. FAX 948 71 20 87. An unpretentious family-run restaurant-with-rooms in a narrow street in the lovely old centre of a historic town. ⊟ ▤ TV	AE DC MC V	16			
OLITE: *Parador de Olite.* Ⓦ www.parador.es €€€€ Plaza de los Teobaldos 2, 31390 (Navarra). (948 74 00 00. FAX 948 74 02 01. Occupying part of the 15th-century castle and palace of Carlos III, king of Navarra, this parador has some modern bedrooms. There are some pricier but atmosphreric rooms in the old part of the castle. ⊟ ▤ TV ᕕ	AE DC MC V	43			▪
PAMPLONA (IRUÑA): *Tres Reyes.* @ hotel3reys@abc.ibernet.com €€€€€ Jardines de la Taconera, 31001 (Navarra). (948 22 66 00. FAX 948 22 29 30. A large modern building between the old and new towns on the edge of the Taconera gardens. The bedrooms have balconies. The services range from a gym and a sauna to hairdressing and valeting. ⊟ ▤ TV ᕕ	AE DC MC V	160	▪	●	▪
PUENTE LA REINA: *Mesón del Peregrino.* @ elperegrino@teleline.es €€€ Ctra Pamplona–Logroño, 31100 (Navarra). (948 34 00 75. FAX 948 34 11 90. A tasteful roadside restaurant-with-rooms in an old stone house near the junction of the two main pilgrim routes to Santiago. ⊟ ▤ TV	MC V	14	▪	●	▪
RONCESVALLES (ORREAGA): *La Posada.* € Carretera de Francia, 31650 (Navarra). (& FAX 948 76 02 25.5. In 1612 this historic inn opened to cater for pilgrims to Santiago de Compostela. Its austere bedrooms with tiled floors are still cheap. ⊟	MC V	18	▪		
SAN SEBASTIÁN (DONOSTIA): *La Galería.* Ⓦ www.hotellagaleria.com €€€ Infanta Cristina 1–3, 20008 (Guipúzcoa). (943 21 60 77. FAX 943 21 12 98. A new hotel on Ondarreta beach in a building that dates from the end of the 19th century. It has two charming attic rooms. ⊟ TV	MC V	23	▪		
SAN SEBASTIÁN (DONOSTIA): *Monte Igueldo.* @ hotel@monteigueldo.com €€€€ Paseo del Faro 134, 20008 (Guipúzcoa). (943 21 02 11. FAX 943 21 50 28. Superbly located on Monte Igueldo, this hotel has panoramic views across the city and the bay. It has a rooftop swimming pool. ⊟ TV	AE DC MC V	125	▪	●	▪
SAN SEBASTIÁN (DONOSTIA): *Niza.* @ niza@adegi.es €€€€ Calle Zubieta 56, 20007 (Guipúzcoa). (943 42 66 63. FAX 943 44 12 51. A seafront hotel in Belle Époque style on La Concha beach, with sunny bedrooms and a café terrace overlooking the beach. ⊟ TV	AE DC MC V	41	▪		▪
SAN SEBASTIÁN (DONOSTIA): *De Londres y de Inglaterra.* €€€€€ Calle Zubieta 2, 20007 (Guipúzcoa). (943 44 07 70. FAX 943 44 04 91. A 19th-century palace in a privileged situation on La Concha beach, which was transformed into a hotel in 1902. ⊟ ▤ TV ᕕ	AE DC MC	148	▪		
SAN SEBASTIÁN (DONOSTIA): *María Cristina.* €€€€€ C/ Oquendo 1, 20004 (Guipúzcoa). (943 43 76 00. FAX 943 43 76 76. A luxurious, well-sited hotel built in 1912 and decorated in Belle Époque style. It is the venue of the annual San Sebastián film festival. ⊟ ▤ TV	AE DC MC V	136	▪		▪
SANTO DOMINGO DE LA CALZADA: *Parador de Santo Domingo.* €€€€ Plaza del Santo 3, 26250 (La Rioja). (941 34 03 00. FAX 941 34 03 25. Ⓦ www.parador.es A hospital founded in the 12th century for pilgrims to Santiago de Compostela has been converted into this parador. It has an imposing lounge divided by arches, and a beautiful carved ceiling. ⊟ ▤ TV ᕕ �ᐧ	AE DC MC V	61	▪		

VITORIA (GASTEIZ): *General Álava.* @ hga@hga.info   €€€€   AE DC MC V   114
Avenida Gasteiz 79, 01009 (Álava). 📞 945 22 22 00. FAX 945 24 83 95.
A modern hotel with comfortable bedrooms in the new town near the
Palacio de Congresos. The restaurant serves regional dishes. 🛏 ▤ ♿

YESA: *Hospedería de Leyre.* W www.monasterio-de-leyre.com   €€   AE DC MC V   29
Monasterio de Leyre, 31410 (Navarra). 📞 948 88 41 00. FAX 948 88 41 37.
This hotel occupies part of an 11th-century monastery, spectacularly
located beneath crags in a beautiful landscape. The rooms are plain and
clean and the hotel has a good restaurant. 🛏 ▤

ZARAUTZ: *Karlos Arguiñano.* @ hotel-ka@teleline.es   €€€€   AE DC MC V   12
Calle Mendilauta 13, 20800 (Guipúzcoa). 📞 943 13 00 00. FAX 943 13 34 50.
An elegant hotel in a stone tower-cum-mansion, with views of the sea. It is
owned by a TV chef and has an excellent restaurant. 🛏 TV

BARCELONA

OLD TOWN: *Hostal d'Avinyo.* Map 5 B2. W www.hostalavinyo.com   €   MC V   28
Avinyo 42, 08002. 📞 93 318 79 45. FAX 93 318 68 93.
This renovated, central hotel near the Port Vell, La Ramblas and Picasso
Museum is good value for money. 🛏

OLD TOWN: *Lloret.* Map 5 A1.   €€   MC V   56
Rambla de Canaletas 125, 08002. 📞 93 317 33 66. FAX 93 301 92 83.
There are views of the city from the foyer of this popular hotel near the
Plaça de Catalunya – but streetside bedrooms can be noisy. 🛏 ▤ TV

OLD TOWN: *Rembrandt.* Map 5 A2.   €€   24
Carrer de Portaferrissa 23, 08002. 📞 & FAX 93 318 10 11.
A clean, homely hotel in the Barri Gòtic, popular with students. A tiled
courtyard is a sitting area. Some bedrooms share bathrooms. 🛏

OLD TOWN: *Toledano.* Map 5 A1. W www.hoteltoledano.com   €€   AE DC MC V   28
Ramblas 138, 08002. 📞 93 301 08 72. FAX 93 412 31 42.
A small hotel near the Plaça de Catalunya, with a lounge overlooking the
Ramblas. The rooms are basic and can be noisy. 🛏 TV ♿

OLD TOWN: *España.* Map 2 F3. W www.hotelespanya.com   €€€   AE DC MC V   84
Carrer de Sant Pau 9–11, 08001. 📞 93 318 17 58. FAX 93 317 11 34.
Domènech i Montaner, the outstanding Modernista architect, designed
the lower floor of this hotel. The bedrooms are all modern. 🛏 ▤ ♿

OLD TOWN: *Jardí.* Map 5 A2. @ hoteljardi@retemail.es   €€€   AE DC MC V   40
Plaça Sant Josep Oriol 1, 08002. 📞 93 301 59 00. FAX 93 342 57 33.
A popular hotel overlooking a leafy square. Some bedrooms have been
renovated and have good views; the others are cheaper. 🛏 ▤ TV

OLD TOWN: *Atlantis.* Map 2 F1. @ hotelatlantis@retemail.es   €€€€   AE DC MC V   42
Carrer de Pelai 20, 08001. 📞 93 318 90 12. FAX 93 412 09 14.
This modern, inexpensive hotel is centrally located near the Plaça de
Catalunya. The bedrooms have a range of facilities. 🛏 ▤ TV ♿

OLD TOWN: *Gaudí.* Map 2 F3. W www.hotelgaudi.es   €€€€   AE DC MC V   73
Carrer Nou de la Rambla 12, 08001. 📞 93 317 90 32. FAX 93 412 26 36.
A pleasant hotel in a street adjoining the Rambla de Catalunya, near Gaudí's
Palau Güell, with comfortable, well-equipped rooms. 🛏 ▤ TV ♿ 🍴

OLD TOWN: *Mesón Castilla.* Map 2 F1.   €€€€   AE DC MC V   57
Carrer de Valdonzella 5, 08001. 📞 93 318 21 82. FAX 93 412 40 20.
A comfortable hotel, if a little old-fashioned, in a building with a
Modernista façade near the Casa de la Caritat arts centre. 🛏 ▤ TV ♿

OLD TOWN: *Oriente.* Map 2 F3. @ hoteloriente@husa.es   €€€€   AE DC MC V   142
Ramblas 45–7, 08002. 📞 93 302 25 58. FAX 93 412 38 19.
A former Franciscan friary makes a romantic setting for the Oriente. The
cloister has been converted into a ballroom. Some bedrooms have
balconies overlooking the Ramblas. 🛏 TV 🍴

OLD TOWN: *San Agustín.* Map 2 F3. @ hotelsa@hotelsa.com   €€€€   AE DC MC V   75
Plaça de Sant Agustí 3, 08001. 📞 93 318 16 58. FAX 93 317 29 28.
An attractive hotel with a pleasant first-floor lounge and bar looking across
a square. Some bedrooms have Catalan furniture. 🛏 ▤ TV ♿

Price categories for a standard double room per night, with tax, breakfast and service included:

€ under 50 euros
€€ 50–75 euros
€€€ 75–100 euros
€€€€ 100–125 euros
€€€€€ over 125 euros

CREDIT CARDS
Indicates which credit cards are accepted: *AE* American Express; *DC* Diners Club; *MC* Master Card/Access; *V* Visa
PARKING
Parking provided by the hotel in a private car park or a private garage on the hotel site or very close by. Some hotels charge for use of private parking facilities.
SWIMMING POOL
Hotel pool outdoors unless otherwise stated.
GARDEN
Hotel with garden, courtyard or terrace, often providing tables for eating outdoors.

	CREDIT CARDS	NUMBER OF ROOMS	PRIVATE PARKING	SWIMMING POOL	GARDEN OR TERRACE
OLD TOWN: *Arts.* Map 6 E4. w www.harts.es €€€€€ Carrer de la Marina 19–21, 08005. (93 221 10 00. FAX 93 221 10 70. A modern, super-luxurious beachside hotel in one of Spain's tallest towers. It has a huge swimming pool and a fitness centre. ⊟ ▤ TV & ▯	AE DC MC V	482	■	●	■
OLD TOWN: *Colón.* Map 5 B2. w www.hotelcolon.es €€€€€ Avinguda de la Catedral 7, 08002. (93 301 14 04. FAX 93 317 29 15. From the Colón's front windows guests can watch the *sardana*, the traditional Catalan folk dance, performed in the Plaça de la Catedral, opposite, on Sunday mornings. ⊟ ▤ TV ▯	AE DC MC V	147			■
OLD TOWN: *Le Meridien.* Map 5 A1. €€€€€ Rambla dels Estudis 111, 08002. (93 318 62 00. @ meridien@meridienbarcelona.com An elegant hotel on the Ramblas, popular with rock and film stars; the Rolling Stones on tour once booked the whole hotel. It has an enormous presidential suite and a business centre. ⊟ ▤ TV & ▯	AE DC MC V	208			
OLD TOWN: *Nouvel.* Map 5 A1. €€€€€ Carrer de Santa Anna 18–20, 08002. (93 301 82 74. FAX 93 301 83 70. In a quiet street off the Ramblas, near the Plaça de Catalunya, this well- kept, old-style hotel is tastefully decorated and furnished. ⊟ ▤ TV	MC V	71			
OLD TOWN: *Park.* Map 5 C3. @ parkhotel@parkhotelbarcelona.com €€€€€ Avda Marquès de l'Argentera 11, 08003. (93 319 60 00. FAX 93 319 45 19. A rare gem of 1950s architecture, restored in 1990. Comfortable and intimate with fascinating views over rooftops and the port. ⊟ ▤ TV &	AE DC MC V	91			
OLD TOWN: *Rivoli Ramblas.* Map 5 A1. @ reservas@rivolihotels.com €€€€€ Rambla dels Estudis 128, 08002. (93 302 66 43. FAX 93 318 87 60. An elegant hotel on the Ramblas decorated in contemporary style, with spacious bedrooms and city views from a roof terrace. ⊟ ▤ TV & ▯	AE DC MC V	129	■		■
EIXAMPLE: *Felipe II.* Map 3 C4. w www.lasguias.com € Carrer de Mallorca 329, 08037. (93 458 77 58. FAX 93 207 21 04. A basic, clean hotel in an old apartment block in the Eixample, with a particularly fine antique lift. Some bedrooms share bathrooms. ⊟ TV		11			
EIXAMPLE: *Gran Vía.* Map 3 A5. @ hgranvia@nnhotels.es €€€€ Avda Gran Vía de les Corts Catalanes 642, 08007. (93 318 19 00. FAX 93 318 99 97. A hotel in a late 19th-century building with an ageing grandeur, north of the Plaça de Catalunya adjoining the Passeig de Gràcia. ⊟ ▤ TV &	AE DC MC V	55			■
EIXAMPLE: *Catalunya Plaza.* Map 5 A1. @ catalunya@city-hotels.es €€€€€ Plaça de Catalunya 7, 08002. (93 317 71 71. FAX 93 317 78 55. A city-centre hotel popular with business people. The 19th-century building has large sitting rooms decorated with frescoes. ⊟ ▤ TV & ▯	AE DC MC V	46			
EIXAMPLE: *Clarís.* Map 3 B4. @ claris@derbyhotels.es €€€€€ Carrer Pau Clarís 150, 08009. (93 487 62 62. FAX 93 215 79 70. Located within the walls of an historic palace off the Passeig de Gràcia, this hotel has a recently remodelled interior. ⊟ ▤ TV & ▯	AE DC MC V	120	■	●	■
EIXAMPLE: *Condes de Barcelona.* Map 3 A4. €€€€€ Passeig de Gràcia 73–5, 08008. (93 467 47 80. w www.condesdebarcelona.com This Modernista hotel has an impressive pentagonal lobby with a marble floor, illuminated by a skylight. Book in advance. ⊟ ▤ TV & ▯	AE DC MC V	183	■	●	■
EIXAMPLE: *Ducs de Bergara.* Map 5 A1. w www.hoteles-catalonia.es €€€€€ Carrer de Bergara 11, 08002. (93 301 51 51. FAX 93 317 34 42. A luxury hotel in an exquisite Modernista building, with its original halls and stairways, near the Plaça de la Catedral. It has spacious, well-furnished bedrooms and modern public rooms. ⊟ ▤ TV & ▯	AE DC MC V	150		●	■

EIXAMPLE: *Gran Hotel Calderón*. **Map 3 A5.**　€€€€€　AE DC MC V | 253
Rambla de Catalunya 26, 08007. 【 93 301 00 00. FAX 93 412 41 93.
A modern hotel near the Plaça de Catalunya, with spacious, comfortable rooms, indoor and rooftop pools, and a good restaurant. 🛏 📋 TV 🚻

EIXAMPLE: *Majestic*. **Map 3 A4.** W www.hotelmajestic.es　€€€€€　AE DC MC V | 303
Passeig de Gràcia 68, 08008. 【 93 488 17 17. FAX 93 488 18 80.
A hotel in Neo-Classical style in a very chic street (adjoining the Carrer de Valencia). The bedrooms are well equipped and soundproofed. 🛏 📋 TV 🚻 🍴

EIXAMPLE: *Regente*. **Map 3 A4.** W www.hccwap.com　€€€€€　AE DC MC V | 79
Rambla de Catalunya 76, 08008. 【 93 487 59 89. FAX 93 487 32 27.
A hotel in a Modernista building, with magnificent stained-glass decoration and a small, rooftop pool overlooking Montjuïc. 🛏 📋 TV 🚻

EIXAMPLE: *Ritz*. **Map 3 B5.** W www.ritzbcn.com　€€€€€　AE DC MC V | 122
Avda Gran Vía de les Corts Catalanes 668, 08010. 【 93 318 52 00. FAX 93 318 01 48.
The most elegant of Barcelona's grand hotels, near the Plaça de Catalunya. The large, luxurious bedrooms are decorated in classic style. 🛏 📋 TV 🚻 🍴

FURTHER AFIELD (NORTHWEST): *Gran Derby*. W www.derbyhotels.es €€€€€　AE DC MC V | 40
Loreto 28, 08029. 【 93 322 20 62. FAX 93 419 68 20.
Attractive suites are the only accommodation offered here. There is no restaurant; guests may dine in the Hotel Derby over the road. 🛏 📋 TV

FURTHER AFIELD (WEST): *Princesa Sofía Intercontinental*　€€€€€　AE DC MC V | 500
Plaça de Pius XII 4, 08028. 【 93 508 10 00. FAX 93 508 10 01. @ barcelona@interconti.com
A vast, luxury hotel decorated in marble, wood and bronze, with a restaurant and bar. There is a function room for reunions and meetings. 🛏 📋 TV 🚻

CATALONIA

ALBONS: *Albons Hotel*. W www.hotelalbous.com　€€€€　AE DC MC V | 32
Ctra Figueres–La Bisbal, 17136 (Girona). 【 972 78 85 00. FAX 972 78 86 58.
An ultramodern, original hotel in the heart of the Empordà region. The bathrooms are spectacular and the cooking is excellent. Activities include swimming, gliding and horse riding. ● 16 Dec–17Feb. 🛏 📋 TV 🚻 🍴

ANDORRA LA VELLA: *Andorra Park Hotel*.　€€€€€　AE DC MC V | 40
Les Canals 24 (Andorra). 【 00-376 82 09 79. W www.andorraparkhotel.com
One of Andorra's most luxurious hotels, the Andorra Park is modern and built into a steep, wooded hillside. It has a library, a swimming pool hewn out of rock, and is beside a department store. 🛏 TV 🍴

ARTIES: *Parador Don Gaspar de Portolà*.　€€€€　AE DC MC V | 57
Ctra a Baqueira-Beret, 25599 (Lleida). 【 973 64 08 01. FAX 973 64 10 01.
A modern, warm, comfortable parador, near the Vall d'Arán ski resorts, ideal for après-ski rest. Beside it is a medieval chapel. 🛏 TV 🚻 🍴

AVINYONET DE PUIGVENTÓS: *Mas Pau*. W www.maspau.com　€€€　AE DC MC V | 20
Ctra Figueres–Olot, 17742 (Girona). 【 972 54 61 54. FAX 972 54 63 26.
A beautiful hotel in a 17th-century house, surrounded by wooded farmland. The bedrooms and suites give on to a garden. ● 7 Jan–15 Mar. 🛏 📋 TV 🚻 🍴

BAQUEIRA-BERET: *Royal Tanau*. W www.solmelia.com　€€€€€　AE DC MC V | 30
Carretera de Beret, 25598 (Lleida). 【 973 64 44 46. FAX 973 64 43 44.
A luxurious hotel in the Tanau skiing area, with a ski lift to the pistes. It has full après-ski facilities. ● Apr–Jun, Sep–Nov. 🛏 TV 🚻 🍴

BEGUR (BAGUR): *Aigua Blava*. W www.aiguablava.com　€€€€€　AE MC V | 88
Platja de Fornells, 17255 (Girona). 【 972 62 20 58. FAX 972 62 21 12.
A charming hotel on a small beach in an attractive spot on the Costa Brava, from which there are marvellous sea views. ● Nov–mid-Feb. 🛏 📋 TV

BOLVIR DE CERDANYA: *Torre del Remei*. W www.torredelremei.com €€€€€　AE DC MC V | 11
Camí Reial, 17539 (Girona). 【 972 14 01 82. FAX 972 14 04 49.
An Art Nouveau mansion with a large garden has become a refined hotel full of comforts, such as video players in bedrooms. 🛏 📋 TV 🍴

CADAQUÉS: *Misty*.　€€　DC MC V | 11
Carretera Nova Port, Lligat, 17488 (Girona). 【 972 25 89 62. FAX 972 15 90 90.
Three houses and a swimming pool surrounded by gardens make up this appealing hotel, one of the most unusual on the Costa Brava. ● Jan. 🛏 TV

Price categories for a standard double room per night, with tax, breakfast and service included:

€ under 50 euros
€€ 50–75 euros
€€€ 75–100 euros
€€€€ 100–125 euros
€€€€€ over 125 euros

CREDIT CARDS
Indicates which credit cards are accepted: *AE* American Express; *DC* Diners Club; *MC* Master Card/Access; *V* Visa
PARKING
Parking provided by the hotel in a private car park or a private garage on the hotel site or very close by. Some hotels charge for use of private parking facilities.
SWIMMING POOL
Hotel pool outdoors unless otherwise stated.
GARDEN
Hotel with garden, courtyard or terrace, often providing tables for eating outdoors.

	CREDIT CARDS	NUMBER OF ROOMS	PRIVATE PARKING	SWIMMING POOL	GARDEN OR TERRACE
CASTELLDEFELS: *Gran Hotel Rey Don Jaime.* €€€€€ Avenida del Hotel 22, 08860 (Barcelona). 93 665 13 00. www.grup-sateras.com This hotel is in traditional Mediterranean style with arches and white-washed walls. It is on a hilltop giving views over the coast.	AE DC MC V	234	■	●	■
CASTELLÓ D'EMPÚRIES: *Allioli.* €€ Urbanització Castell Nou, 17486 (Girona). 972 25 03 00. FAX 972 25 03 00. A 17th-century Catalan farmhouse with considerable character, just off the main Rosas–Figueres road. The restaurant is a popular place for Sunday lunch among the local people.	AE DC MC V	42	■		■
L'ESPLUGA DE FRANCOLÍ: *Hostal del Senglar.* www.hostaldelsenglar.com €€ Pl de Montserrat Canals 1, 43440 (Tarragona). 977 87 01 21. FAX 977 87 01 27. A whitewashed hotel over three floors with a garden. A delicious menu of dishes traditional to the area is served in the restaurant.	AE DC MC V	40	■		■
L'ESPLUGA DE FRANCOLÍ: *Masía del Cadet.* masiadelcadet@yahoo.es €€ Les Masies de Poblet, 43449 (Tarragona). & FAX 977 87 08 69. An inexpensive hotel near the monastery of Poblet in a tastefully renovated, 15th-century house. The bedrooms are austere and quiet. ● *Nov–early Dec.*	AE DC MC V	12	■		■
LA GARRIGA: *Blancafort.* www.balnearioblancafort.com €€€€ Carrer Banys 59, 08530 (Barcelona). 93 871 46 00. FAX 93 871 57 50. A 19th-century hotel in a relaxing spa town near Barcelona. There are simple bedrooms and games facilities in the lounges. (The hotel is being refurbished in 2002 but will remain open.)	MC V	56	■	●	■
LA GARRIGA: *La Garriga.* www.termes.com €€€€€ Carrer Banys 23, 08530 (Barcelona). 93 871 70 86. FAX 93 871 78 87. Affluent people from Barcelona have been visiting this spa town for its waters since 1876. Children under 12 years old are not admitted.	AE MC V	22	■	●	■
GRANOLLERS: *Fonda Europa.* €€€ Carrer Anselm Clavé 1, 08400 (Barcelona). 93 870 03 12. FAX 93 870 79 01 This small hotel has been an inn for travellers since 1714. The rooms are on the second floor and are decorated in Art Deco style.	AE DC MC V	7			
LLORET DE MAR: *Santa Marta.* www.hstamarta.com €€€€€ Platja Santa Cristina, 17310 (Girona). 972 36 49 04. FAX 972 36 92 80. A modern hotel with sporting facilities in its grounds. It is in a pine wood that extends to a quiet cove. ● *15 Dec–mid-Feb.*	AE DC MC V	78	■	●	■
MONTSENY: *San Bernat.* www.husa.es €€€€ Finca El Cot, 08460 (Barcelona). 93 847 30 11. FAX 93 847 32 20. A big country house in the Sierra de Montseny, with a façade cloaked in greenery. There are beautiful grounds with lawns and a pond.	MC V	20	■	●	■
PERAMOLA: *Can Boix.* hotel@canboix.com €€€€ Afueras, 25790 (Lleida). 973 47 02 66. FAX 973 47 02 81. Run by a family of distinguished restaurateurs, this simple, good-value hotel is convenient for walking in the Pyrenean foothills. ● *mid-Jan–mid-Feb, 1 Nov–mid-Nov.*	AE DC MC V	41	■	●	■
S'AGARÓ: *Hostal de la Gavina.* www.lagavina.com €€€€€ Plaça de la Rosaleda, 17248 (Girona). 972 32 11 00. FAX 972 32 15 73. An elegant beach mansion in Mediterranean style with an exclusive feel. It is set in its own estate, with beautiful gardens. ● *mid-Oct–Easter.*	AE DC MC V	74	■	●	■
SANTA CRISTINA D'ARO: *Mas Torrellas.* €€ Carretera Sta Cristina-Platja d'Aro, 17246 (Girona). 972 83 75 26. FAX 972 83 75 27. An 18th-century country house hotel. Its most comfortable bedroom is in a distinctive yellow tower, built at a later date. ● *Nov–Feb.*	AE DC MC V	17	■	●	■

SANT SADURNÍ DE NOVA: *Sol i Vi.* ⓦ www.solivi.com €€
Ctra Sant Sadurní–Villafranca, 08739 (Barcelona). 🅒 93 899 32 04. FAX 93 899 34 35.
Three generations of the host family cater to the needs of guests staying at this charming house surrounded by vineyards. The rooms are light, airy and rustic in style. ● *two weeks in Jan.* 🏨 🍽 TV

| | AE DC MC V | 25 | | | |

LA SEU D'URGELL: *Parador de La Seu d'Urgell.* ⓦ www.parador.es €€€€
Carrer Sant Domènec 6, 25700 (Lleida). 🅒 973 35 20 00. FAX 973 35 23 09.
Only the cloister, now the lounge, remains of a convent that occupied this site close to the 12th-century cathedral of La Seu. The dining room and indoor swimming pool have glass ceilings. 🏨 🍽 TV 🔗 🍴

| | AE DC MC V | 80 | | | |

LA SEU D'URGELL: *El Castell.* ⓦ www.hotelcastell.com €€€€€
Carretera N260 km 229, 25700 (Lleida). 🅒 973 35 07 04. FAX 973 35 15 74.
This sumptuous hotel is a low, modern building beneath the medieval castle of Seu d'Urgell. There are impressive views across the mountains of El Cadí and the ski slopes of Andorra are nearby. 🏨 🍽 TV 🍴

| | AE DC MC V | 38 | | | |

SITGES: *La Santa María.* €€
Passeig Ribera 52, 08870 (Barcelona). 🅒 93 894 09 99. FAX 93 894 78 71.
A cheery modern hotel hidden behind an older frontage of five floors. The restaurant has tables on the seafront. ● *Dec–Feb.* 🏨 🍽 TV 🔗 🍴

| | AE DC MC V | 53 | | | |

SITGES: *Capri Veracruz.* €€€
Avinguda de Sofía 13–15, 08870 (Barcelona). 🅒 93 811 02 67. FAX 93 894 51 88.
Built in the 1950s near the beach, in one of the quieter parts of Sitges, this hotel has simple bedrooms and a family atmosphere. 🏨 🍽 TV 🔗

| | AE DC MC V | 69 | | | |

SITGES: *San Sebastián Playa.* ⓦ www.solmelia.com €€€€€
Carrer Port Alegre 53, 08870 (Barcelona). 🅒 93 894 86 76. FAX 93 894 04 30.
This hotel on the beach near the old part of the town has very attentive staff and comfortable bedrooms, a restaurant and a meeting room. 🏨 🍽 TV 🔗

| | AE DC MC V | 51 | | | |

TAVÉRNOLES: *El Banús.* ⓦ www.elbanus.com €€€€€
El Banús, 08519 (Barcelona). 🅒 93 812 26 91. FAX 93 888 70 12.
A small, partly 15th-century farmhouse, furnished with Banús family heirlooms, offering three apartments. Minimum stay is two nights. ● *Nov–Mar.* 🏨

| | AE MC V | 3 | | | |

TARRAGONA: *Lauria.* ⓦ www.hlauria.es €€
Rambla Nova 20, 43004. 🅒 977 23 67 12. FAX 977 23 67 00.
A modern, functional hotel in the town centre and close to the sea, with an elegant entrance under balustraded stone stairs. 🏨 🍽 TV

| | AE DC MC V | 72 | | | |

TORRENT: *Mas de Torrent.* €€€€€
Afueras, 17123 (Girona). 🅒 972 30 32 92. FAX 972 30 32 93.
A superbly converted, 18th-century country house in large, terraced gardens. It has magnificent views. 🏨 🍽 TV 🔗 🍴

| | AE DC MC V | 39 | | | |

TORTOSA: *Parador Castillo de La Zuda.* ⓦ www.parador.es €€€€
Castillo de la Zuda, 43500 (Tarragona). 🅒 977 44 44 50. FAX 977 44 44 58.
A medieval castle built by the Moors makes a magnificent hilltop parador with views of the town and the Río Ebro valley. 🏨 🍽 TV 🍴

| | AE DC MC V | 72 | | | |

TREDÒS: *Hotel de Tredòs.* ⓦ www.hoteltredos.com €€€
Carretera a Baqueira-Beret, 25598 (Lleida). 🅒 973 64 40 14. FAX 973 64 43 00.
Skiers and mountain walkers find this hotel in the Vall d'Arán good value. It is built of stone and slate in the local style. ● *Oct, Nov, May, Jun.* 🏨 🍽 TV 🔗 🍴

| | MC V | 43 | | | |

VIELHA (VIELLA): *Parador Valle de Arán.* ⓦ www.parador.es €€€
Carretera Pont de Suert, 25530 (Lleida). 🅒 973 64 01 00. FAX 973 64 11 00.
This modern parador has a semicircular lounge dominated by a large window from which there are magnificent mountain views. 🏨 🍽 TV 🔗 🍴

| | AE DC MC V | 118 | | | |

VILADRAU: *Hostal de la Glòria.* @ hostalgloria@infomail.lacaixa.es €€
Carrer Torreventosa 12, 17406 (Girona). 🅒 93 884 90 34. FAX 93 884 94 65.
A hotel with a family atmosphere in a traditional Catalan house above the Sierra de Montseny. Full of copper pots and brass lamps.
● *Christmas period.* 🏨 TV

| | DC MC V | 23 | | | |

VILANOVA I LA GELTRÚ: *César.* @ hotelcesar@terra.es €€
Carrer Isaac Peral 4–8, 08800 (Barcelona). 🅒 93 815 11 25. FAX 93 815 67 19.
This hotel, near the Ribes Roges beach, is owned by two sisters who pay great attention to detail, from the furniture and the fabrics in the bedrooms to the well-known restaurant. 🏨 🍽 TV 🔗

| | AE DC MC V | 36 | | | |

| Price categories for a standard double room per night, with tax, breakfast and service included:
€ under 50 euros
€€ 50–75 euros
€€€ 75–100 euros
€€€€ 100–125 euros
€€€€€ over 125 euros | **CREDIT CARDS** Indicates which credit cards are accepted: *AE* American Express; *DC* Diners Club; *MC* Master Card/Access; *V* Visa
PARKING Parking provided by the hotel in a private car park or a private garage on the hotel site or very close by. Some hotels charge for use of private parking facilities.
SWIMMING POOL Hotel pool outdoors unless otherwise stated.
GARDEN Hotel with garden, courtyard or terrace, often providing tables for eating outdoors. | | CREDIT CARDS | NUMBER OF ROOMS | PRIVATE PARKING | SWIMMING POOL | GARDEN OR TERRACE |

ARAGÓN

AINSA: *Casa Cambra.* Ⓦ www.morillodetou.com   €
Morillo de Tou, Ctra Barbastro–Ainsa km 45, 22395 (Huesca). **📞** & **FAX** 974 50 07 93.
The hotel is one of three in a formerly abandoned Pyrenean village, rebuilt as a holiday complex with a large camp site, restaurants and bars. 🛏 🍴
Credit Cards: MC V — *Rooms:* 17 — Private Parking ■ — Swimming Pool ● — Garden ■

ALBARRACÍN: *Arabia.* Ⓦ www.montesuniversales.com   €€
Calle Bernardo Zapater 2, 44100 (Teruel). **📞** 978 71 02 12. **FAX** 978 71 02 37.
A restored 17th-century convent in a picturesque town. Some bedrooms have views of Albarracín's rooftops and its surrounding hills. 🛏 📺
Credit Cards: MC V — *Rooms:* 21 — Private Parking ■ — Garden ■

ALBARRACÍN: *Casa de Santiago.*   €€
Calle Subida a las Torres 11, 44100 (Teruel). **📞** 978 70 03 16.
Albarracín's most beautiful hotel, in a restored mansion near the Plaz Mayor. The interior features custom-made furniture. ● mid-Feb–Mar. 🛏 🍴
Credit Cards: MC V — *Rooms:* 9

ALBARRACÍN: *Albarracín.* Ⓦ www.gargallohoteles.com   €€€
Calle Azagra, 44100 (Teruel). **📞** 978 71 00 11 **FAX** 978 71 00 36.
A 16th-century Gothic mansion in a stepped street of medieval houses. The views from the windows are stunning. 🛏 📺 🍴
Credit Cards: AE DC MC V — *Rooms:* 43 — Garden ■

ALCAÑIZ: *Parador de Alcañiz.* @ alcañiz@parador.es.   €€€€€
Castillo de Calatravos, 44600 (Teruel). **📞** 978 83 04 00. **FAX** 978 83 03 66.
This 12th-century monastery-castle once belonged to the Knights of Calatrava. Its decor is a modern interpretation of medieval castle style. 🛏 🍽 📺 ♿
Credit Cards: AE DC MC V — *Rooms:* 37 — Garden ■

ALQUÉZAR: *Villa de Alquézar.*   €
Pedro Arnal Cavero 12, 22145 (Huesca). **📞** & **FAX** 974 31 84 16.
An old house in a medieval village, near the Sierra de Guara nature reserve. Some rooms have mountain views. ● 15 days in Feb. 🛏 🍽 📺 ♿
Credit Cards: AE MC V — *Rooms:* 31 — Garden ■

BENASQUE: *Ciria.* Ⓦ www.hotelciria.com   €€€
Avenida de los Tilos, 22440 (Huesca). **📞** 974 55 16 12. **FAX** 974 55 16 86.
An efficient, friendly family runs this Pyrenean hotel. It has four cosy attic suites and two luxurious 'Royal' suites with hydro massage baths. There are bicycles for hire. The restaurant, *El Fogueril*, is the best in the area. 🛏 📺 🍴
Credit Cards: MC V — *Rooms:* 44 — Garden ■

BIELSA: *Parador de Bielsa.* Ⓦ www.parador.es   €€€€
Valle de Pineta de Bielsa, 22350 (Huesca). **📞** 974 50 10 11. **FAX** 974 50 11 88.
A parador beautifully located in wooded country on the edge of Ordesa National Park. It is warm and inviting inside. ● 6 Jan–15 Feb. 🛏 🍽 📺 ♿ 🍴
Credit Cards: AE DC MC V — *Rooms:* 39 — Garden ■

CANFRANC-ESTACIÓN: *Santa Cristina de Somport.* Ⓦ www.santacristina.com €€
Ctra de Francia N330, 22880 (Huesca). **📞** 974 37 33 00. **FAX** 974 37 33 10.
This hotel is near the Somport Pass, which is on one of the main pilgrim routes from France to Santiago de Compostela. In summer, the hotel arranges guided mountain walks. ● mid-Oct–Dec. 🛏 📺
Credit Cards: AE DC MC V — *Rooms:* 58 — Garden ■

FUENTESPALDA: *Torre del Visco.* @ torredelvisco@mixmail.com   €€€€€
Carretera de Valderrobres 15, 44587 (Teruel). **📞** 978 76 90 15. **FAX** 978 76 90 16.
A 15th-century farmhouse in a remote river valley. Room prices include breakfast and dinner based on vegetables from the farm. ● 8–18 Jan. 🛏
Credit Cards: MC V — *Rooms:* 14 — Private Parking ■ — Garden ■

HUESCA: *Pedro I de Aragón.*   €€€€€
Calle del Parque 34, 22003. **📞** 974 22 03 00. **FAX** 974 22 00 94.
A stylish modern hotel in the city centre, bristling with facilities. The bedrooms are soundproofed and ten have private terraces. 🛏 🍽 📺 🍴
Credit Cards: AE DC MC V — *Rooms:* 130 — Private Parking ■ — Swimming Pool ● — Garden ■

JACA: *Conde Aznar.* Ⓦ www.jaca.com   €€
Paseo de la Constitución 3, 22700 (Huesca). **📞** 974 36 10 50. **FAX** 974 36 07 97.
A simple, hospitable, good-value hotel in an old urban mansion on a classy avenue. It has a good restaurant serving local dishes. 🛏 📺 🍴
Credit Cards: AE MC V — *Rooms:* 24 — Garden ■

JACA: *Gran Hotel.* @ gh@inturmark.es   €€€ | AE DC MC V | 165
Paseo de la Constitución 1, 22700 (Huesca). **(** *974 36 09 00.* FAX *974 36 40 61.*
A modern hotel, centrally located next to a park, within reach of the ski
slopes around Somport Pass. ● *Apr, May & Nov.* 🚗 TV

MORA DE RUBIELOS: *Jaime I.*   €€ | AE DC MC V | 35
Plaza de la Villa, 44400 (Teruel). **(** & FAX *978 80 00 67.*
A handsome stone building with wooden balconies and simple rooms in a
town full of mansions on the edge of the Maestrazgo region. 🚗 TV ❚❚

NUÉVALOS: *Monasterio de Piedra.* W www.monasteriopiedra.com   €€€ | AE DC MC V | 61
Monasterio de Piedra, 50210 (Zaragoza). **(** *976 84 90 11.* FAX *976 84 90 54.*
Beside a nature reserve is this former Cistercian monastery, now a hotel.
Among its original details are alabaster windowpanes. 🚗 TV ❚❚

SALLENT DE GÁLLEGO: *Villa de Sallent.* W www.valledepena.com   €€ | AE DC MC V | 81
Urbanización El Formigal, 22640 (Huesca). **(** *974 49 02 23.* FAX *974 49 01 50.*
At the foot of the pistes of Formigal ski resort, this family-run hotel is
welcoming at dusk. It has open fires and warm bedrooms. 🚗 TV ♿ ❚❚

SALLENT DE GÁLLEGO: *Almud.* W www.hotelalmud.com   €€€ | AE DC MC V | 10
Espadilla 11, 22640 (Huesca). **(** & FAX *974 48 85 40.*
A charming, homely hotel in the Pyrenees. All rooms are decorated with
antiques. The bar is in the former stables in the cellar. 🚗 TV

SOS DEL REY CATÓLICO: *Parador de Sos del Rey Católico.*   €€€€ | AE DC MC V | 65
Arquitecto Sainz de Vicuna 1, 50680 (Zaragoza). **(** *948 88 80 11.* FAX *948 88 81 00.*
The parador, at one end of the medieval wall, blends with the town's
historic architecture and has fine country views. ● *7 Jan–21 Feb,*
public hols. 🚗 TV ♿

TERUEL: *Parador de Teruel.* W www.parador.es   €€€ | AE DC MC V | 60
Ctra a Zaragoza, 44080. **(** *978 60 18 00.* FAX *978 60 86 12.*
This parador is in leafy surroundings a little outside the city, set back from
a main road. It has a pleasant, covered terrace-bar. 🚗 TV ♿ ❚❚

TERUEL: *Reina Cristina.*   €€€€ | AE DC MC V | 81
Paseo del Ovalo 1, 44001. **(** *978 60 68 60.* FAX *978 60 53 63.*
The Reina Cristina is a modern, city-centre hotel, in easy reach of the main
monuments. Some of the bedrooms have terraces. 🚗 ☰ TV ♿

VILLANÚA: *Faus Hütte.*   €€ | AE DC MC V | 12
Ctra de Francia, 22870 (Huesca). **(** *974 37 81 36.* FAX *974 37 81 98.*
This hotel deep in the Pyrenees is owned by a mountain guide. It is a good
base for skiing, hill-walking and other mountain activities. It is also on the
pilgrim's route to Santiago de Compostela. 🚗 TV ❚❚

ZARAGOZA: *Hesperia Zaragoza.* W www.hoteles-hesperia.es   €€€ | AE DC MC V | 86
Conde de Aranda 48, 50003. **(** *976 28 45 00.* FAX *976 28 27 17.*
This hotel, not far from the city centre, is comfortable and popular with
business travellers. 🚗 ☰ TV ♿ ❚❚

ZARAGOZA: *Tibur.*   €€€ | AE DC MC V | 50
Plaza de la Seo 2 & 3, 50001. **(** *976 20 20 00.* FAX *976 20 20 02.*
The Tibur is conveniently located in the old heart of the city, with views of
the Basílica del Pilar. The bedrooms are well equipped. 🚗 ☰ TV ♿ ❚❚

ZARAGOZA: *Gran Hotel.* @ nhgranhotel@nh-hoteles.es   €€€€ | AE DC MC V | 134
Calle Joaquín Costa 5, 50001. **(** *976 22 19 01.* FAX *976 23 67 13.*
Zaragoza's city-centre grand hotel was opened in 1929 by Alfonso XIII. It
has colonnades and a magnificent domed salon. 🚗 ☰ TV ❚❚

VALENCIA AND MURCIA

ÁGUILAS: *Carlos III.* W www.hotelcarlosiii.com   €€€ | AE DC MC V | 32
Calle Rey Carlos III 22, 30880 (Murcia). **(** *968 41 16 50.* FAX *968 41 16 58.*
A modern town-centre hotel near the beach in a small Murcian resort. The
restaurant serves fish, seafood and other local dishes. 🚗 ☰ TV

ALICANTE (ALACANT): *Les Moges Palace.*   € | DC MC V | 18
San Agustín 4, 03002. **(** *965 21 50 46.* FAX *965 14 71 89*
Overlooking Alicante's Baroque town hall, this family-run pension offers
good value and individually decorated rooms with period furnishings.
There is one room with a sauna and jacuzzi at a higher rate. 🚗 ☰ TV

<table>
<tr><td>

Price categories for a standard double room per night, with tax, breakfast and service included:

€ under 50 euros
€€ 50–75 euros
€€€ 75–100 euros
€€€€ 100–125 euros
€€€€€ over 125 euros

</td><td>

CREDIT CARDS
Indicates which credit cards are accepted: *AE* American Express; *DC* Diners Club; *MC* Master Card/Access; *V* Visa
PARKING
Parking provided by the hotel in a private car park or a private garage on the hotel site or very close by. Some hotels charge for use of private parking facilities.
SWIMMING POOL
Hotel pool outdoors unless otherwise stated.
GARDEN
Hotel with garden, courtyard or terrace, often providing tables for eating outdoors.

</td></tr>
</table>

	CREDIT CARDS	NUMBER OF ROOMS	PRIVATE PARKING	SWIMMING POOL	GARDEN OR TERRACE
ALICANTE (ALACANT): *Sidi San Juan.* w www.hotelsidi.es €€€€€ La Doblada 8, Cabo las Huertas, 03540. (965 16 13 00. FAX 965 16 33 46. A luxury hotel outside Alicante, with access to a beach through gardens The bedrooms have sea views and there is a health farm. ⊟ ≡ TV & ⊪	AE DC MC V	176	■	●	■
ARCHENA: *Termas.* @ reservas@balneario-archena-sa.es €€€ Ctra Balneario, 30600 (Murcia). (968 67 01 00. FAX 968 68 80 11. Inside, this spa hotel is decorated in a glorious Mudéjar style, with ornate plasterwork, domes and Moorish arches. Tunnels in the basement are heated by water gushing from the ground. ⊟ ≡ TV & ⊪	AE MC V	71	■	●	■
BOCAIRENT: *L'Estació de Bocairent.* €€ Parque de la Estación, 46880 (Valencia). (962 90 52 11. FAX 962 90 54 23. A small, comfortable hotel set up by the regional tourist board in an old railway station on the edge of a fascinating medieval town. ⊟ ≡ TV & ⊪	DC MC V	14			■
CALP: *Venta la Chata.* € Carretera de Valencia km 172, 03710 (Alicante). (& FAX 965 83 03 08. An old coaching inn on the main road between Alicante and Valencia. The bedrooms are simple, mixing old and new furniture, and some have terraces looking out on a pretty garden. ⊟ TV	DC MC V	17	■		■
CARTAGENA: *Los Habaneros.* w www.hotelhabaneros.com € Calle San Diego 60, 30202 (Murcia). (968 50 52 50. FAX 968 50 91 04. Located on the edge of the old part of town, this hotel offers comfort at an affordable price. It also has a popular restaurant. ⊟ ≡ TV	AE DC MC V	63	■		
CASTELL DE CASTELLS: *Pensión Castells.* @ castells@darburn.com €€ Calle San Vicente 18, 03793 (Alicante). (& FAX 96 551 82 54. An old house in an inland village not far from the Costa Blanca. All the rooms are given a loving touch. The British owners offer bed and breakfast, and they take guests walking in the surrounding hills. ● *Jul–Aug.* ⊟	MC V	4			■
CHULILLA: *Balneario de Chulilla.* €€€ Afueras, 46167 (Valencia). (96 165 70 13. FAX 96 165 70 31. This spa hotel is an inexpensive place to stop while exploring the woods and hills of inland Valencia. It has all the facilities for a rest-cure, including a sauna, a gym, tennis courts and a jacuzzi. ● *late Dec–Feb.* ⊟ ≡ TV & ⊪	V	85		●	■
DENIA: *Rosa.* €€€ Las Marinas, 03700 (Alicante). (96 578 15 73. FAX 96 642 47 74. A modern white villa close to the beach. It was built and is run by a Parisian expatriate who works hard to please his guests. Comfortable rooms have sun-trapping, Florentine-style balconies. ⊟ ≡ TV &	MC V	35	■	●	■
ELX: *Huerto del Cura.* w www.huertodelcura.com €€€€ Porta de la Morera 14, 03203 (Alicante). (96 661 00 11. FAX 96 542 19 10. A secluded hotel in Europe's largest palm tree wood, surrounded by landscaped grounds. The bedrooms are all in Mediterranean-style bungalows. The restaurant is highly regarded. ⊟ ≡ TV & ⊪	AE DC MC V	86	■	●	■
FORCALL: *Palau dels Ossets.* €€€ Plaza Mayor 16, 12310 (Castellón). (964 17 75 24. FAX 964 17 75 56. A tastefully renovated 16th-century mansion on the main square of a quiet village at the heart of El Maestrat. It has wooden beams, tiled floors and well-equipped bedrooms. ⊟ ≡ TV & ⊪	MC V	20	■		■
FORTUNA: *Balneario.* w www.leana.es €€ Calle Balneario, 30630 (Murcia). (968 68 50 11. FAX 968 68 50 87. This hotel has the atmosphere of a former grand hotel. It has Art Nouveau doors and a grand staircase. The two swimming pools are naturally heated, and there is a mini-golf course. ⊟ ≡ TV & ⊪	AE MC V	164	■	●	■

La Manga del Mar Menor: *Regency Hyatt.* €€€€€
La Manga Club Resort, 30385 (Murcia). **(** 968 33 12 34. **w** www.lamanga.hyatt.com.
A luxurious hotel, part of an exclusive resort complex built in the style of a
Spanish village. It is surrounded by palm and olive groves, and has 3 golf
courses, 18 tennis courts and 4 swimming pools. 🚗 🍽 TV ♿ 👤

AE DC MC V	192	▦	⬤	▦

Moraira: *Swiss Hotel Moraira.* €€€€€
Calle Haya 175, 03724 (Alicante). **(** 96 574 71 04. **FAX** 96 574 70 74.
On an estate of holiday villas close to the coast is this exclusive hotel. The
bedrooms are spacious with sunny terraces. ⬤ *Jan–mid-Feb.* 🚗 🍽 TV

| AE DC MC V | 25 | ▦ | ⬤ | ▦ |

Moratalla: *Cenajo.* **w** www.barcelo.com €€
Embalse del Cenajo, 30440 (Murcia). **(** 968 72 10 11. **FAX** 968 72 06 45.
At night, silence descends on this creamy-yellow hotel beside the Cenajo
dam, in a part of rural Murcia where few foreign tourists stray. Horse riding
is one of many activities available. 🚗 TV 🍽 ♿ 👤

| AE DC MC V | 70 | ▦ | ⬤ | ▦ |

Morella: *Cardenal Ram.* **@** hotelcardenalram@ctv.es €€
Cuesta Suñer 1, 12300 (Castellón). **(** 964 17 30 85. **FAX** 964 17 32 18.
A renovated, 16th-century mansion with stone arches and beamed ceilings,
overlooking the main porticoed street of a historic town. 🚗 TV 👤

| MC V | 19 | ▦ | | |

Murcia: *Conde de Floridablanca.* **w** www.hoteles-catalonia.es €€€€
Princesa 18, 30002. **(** 968 21 46 26. **FAX** 968 21 32 15.
A comfortable, good-value hotel across the river from the city centre,
furnished with antiques and decorated with stained glass. 🚗 🍽 TV ♿

| AE DC MC V | 82 | ▦ | | |

Murcia: *Arco de San Juan.* **w** www.arcosanjuan.com €€€€€
Plaza de Ceballos 10, 30003. **(** 968 21 04 55. **FAX** 968 22 08 09.
The restoration of this hotel near the cathedral has won awards. The decor
combines contemporary materials with antiques. 🚗 🍽 TV ♿ 👤

| AE DC MC V | 96 | ▦ | | |

Penáguila: *Mas de Pau.* €€
Ctra Alcoi Penáguila km 9, 03815 (Alicante). **(** 96 551 31 11. **FAX** 96 551 31 09.
A 19th-century house in a landscape of almond and olive trees near Alcoi.
It has small bedrooms, some overlooking the Sierra Aitana. 🚗 TV 👤

| AE DC MC V | 18 | ▦ | ⬤ | |

Peñíscola: *Benedicto XIII.* **@** benexiii@arrabis.es €€€
Urbanización Las Atalayas, 12598 (Castellón). **(** 964 48 08 01. **FAX** 964 48 95 23.
A white villa in a quiet private estate on a hillside above Peñíscola. Its
terraces and arched windows give views of the town. ⬤ *Oct–Mar.* 🚗 🍽 TV 👤

| AE DC MC V | 30 | ▦ | ⬤ | ▦ |

Peñíscola: *Hostería del Mar.* **w** www.hosteriadelmar.net €€€€€
Avenida Papa Luna 18, 12598 (Castellón). **(** 964 48 06 00. **FAX** 964 48 13 63.
Many of the rooms in this modern beach hotel have sea views. Animated
medieval banquets are a house speciality. 🚗 🍽 TV 👤

| AE DC MC V | 86 | ▦ | ⬤ | ▦ |

Puzol: *Monte Picayo.* **w** www.hrsl.com €€€€€
Autopista A7, exit Puzol, 46530 (Valencia). **(** 96 142 01 00. **FAX** 96 142 21 68.
A luxury hotel close to the Valencia bypass but surrounded by gardens,
with its own casino and bullring. Some of the bedrooms have a private
garden and swimming pool. 🚗 🍽 TV 👤

| AE DC MC V | 83 | ▦ | ⬤ | ▦ |

El Saler: *Parador de El Saler.* **w** www.parador.es €€€€€
Avda de los Pinares 151, 46012 (Valencia). **(** 96 161 11 86. **FAX** 96 162 70 16.
A modern parador, peacefully situated beside the sea near L'Albufera and
surrounded by a renowned golf course. 🚗 🍽 TV ♿ 👤

| AE DC MC V | 58 | ▦ | ⬤ | ▦ |

Valencia: *Ad Hoc.* **@** adhoc@nexo.net €€€€
Calle Boix 4, 46003. **(** 96 391 91 40. **FAX** 96 391 36 67.
A chic hotel in a renovated, soundproofed, 19th-century building in the
historic quarter of the city, near the Río Turia gardens. 🚗 🍽 TV ♿ 👤

| AE DC MC V | 28 | ▦ | | |

Valencia: *Inglés.* **w** www.solmelia.es €€€€
Calle Marqués de Dos Aguas 6, 46002. **(** 96 351 64 26. **FAX** 96 394 02 51.
This convenient city-centre hotel is in the old palace of the Dukes of
Cardona, next to the National Ceramics Museum. All the bedrooms look on
to the street. The restaurant serves Valencian cuisine. 🚗 🍽 TV ♿ 👤

| AE DC MC V | 63 | ▦ | | |

Valencia: *Reina Victoria.* **w** www.husa.es €€€€€
Calle Barcas 4, 46002. **(** 96 352 04 87. **FAX** 96 352 27 21.
In the city centre, near the Plaza del Ayuntamiento, this elegant hotel, built
in the late 19th century, has modern bedrooms. 🚗 🍽 TV 👤

| AE DC MC V | 97 | ▦ | | |

For key to symbols see back flap

<table>
<tr><td colspan="2">

Price categories for a standard double room per night, with tax, breakfast and service included:

€ under 50 euros
€€ 50–75 euros
€€€ 75–100 euros
€€€€ 100–125 euros
€€€€€ over 125 euros

CREDIT CARDS
Indicates which credit cards are accepted: *AE* American Express; *DC* Diners Club; *MC* Master Card/Access; *V* Visa
PARKING
Parking provided by the hotel in a private car park or a private garage on the hotel site or very close by. Some hotels charge for use of private parking facilities.
SWIMMING POOL
Hotel pool outdoors unless otherwise stated.
GARDEN
Hotel with garden, courtyard or terrace, often providing tables for eating outdoors.

</td></tr>
</table>

	CREDIT CARDS	NUMBER OF ROOMS	PRIVATE PARKING	SWIMMING POOL	GARDEN OR TERRACE
LA VILA JOIOSA (VILLAJOYOSA): *El Montiboli.* w www.servigroup.es €€€€€ Partida El Montiboli, 03570 (Alicante). (96 589 02 50. FAX 96 589 38 57. This hotel is perched on a low cliff outside the town, and looks down on a secluded beach. 🛏 📋 📺 ♿ 🍴	AE DC MC V	58	■	●	■
XÀBIA (JÁVEA): *Solymar.* €€€ Montañar 1, Avda del Mediterraneo 83, 03730 (Alicante). (96 646 19 19. FAX 96 646 19 07. This small hotel has simple, but perfectly pleasant bedrooms, some of which have balconies with sea views. 🛏 📋 📺 ♿	AE DC MC V	38			■
XÀBIA (JÁVEA): *Parador de Jávea.* w www.parador.es €€€€ Avda Mediterráneo 7, 03730 (Alicante). (96 579 02 00. FAX 96 579 03 08. A parador in the middle of Arenales beach. The dining room looks across the terrace to splendid gardens, and the bedroom balconies have sea views. There are water sports facilities nearby. 🛏 📋 📺 ♿ 🍴	AE DC MC V	70	■	●	■

MADRID

	CREDIT CARDS	NUMBER OF ROOMS	PRIVATE PARKING	SWIMMING POOL	GARDEN OR TERRACE
OLD MADRID: *Hostal Buenos Aires.* **Map 1 D1.** €€ Gran Vía 61, 28013. (91 542 01 02. FAX 91 542 28 69. A simple, economical hotel, conveniently located on the busy Gran Vía. The public rooms are pleasantly decorated. Each of the bedrooms has its own balcony or small terrace. 🛏 📋 📺	DC MC V	25			
OLD MADRID: *Inglés.* **Map 5 A1.** €€€€ Calle de Echegaray 8, 28014. (91 429 65 51. FAX 91 420 24 23. A good-value, family-run hotel with its own garage. The bedrooms facing the street are sunny but the back rooms are quieter. 🛏 📺	AE DC MC V	58	■		
OLD MADRID: *Arosa.* **Map 2 F2.** w www.bestwesterncom €€€€€ Calle de la Salud 21, 28013. (91 532 16 00. FAX 91 531 31 27. This centrally located hotel off the Gran Vía and the Puerta del Sol is popular with international and business visitors to Madrid. All the bedrooms are comfortable and well soundproofed. 🛏 📋 📺	AE DC MC V	134	■		
OLD MADRID: *Carlos V.* **Map 2 E3.** w www.hotelcarlosv.com €€€€€ Calle Maestro Vitoria 5, 28013. (91 531 41 00. FAX 91 531 37 61. A city-centre hotel in a pedestrian street beside the Puerta del Sol, run by a family. There are interconnecting bedrooms, family rooms,rooms with balconies and top-floor rooms with sizeable sun terraces. 🛏 📋 📺	AE DC MC V	67			
OLD MADRID: *Gaudí.* **Map 2 E2.** w www.hoteles-catalonia.es €€€€€ Gran Vía 9, 28013. (91 531 22 22. FAX 91 531 54 69. This centrally located hotel in a Modernista style includes Gaudí decor details in the rooms. The five suites on the top floor are recommended, with Jacuzzis and great views. 🛏 📋 📺 ♿ 🍴	AE DC MC V	185		●	
OLD MADRID: *Tryp Gran Vía.* **Map 2 F2.** w www.solmelia.com €€€€€ Gran Vía 25, 28013. (91 522 11 21. FAX 91 521 24 24. A chain hotel in one of the city's busiest streets. Some of the furniture is in the style of the 1960s and 1970s. 🛏 📋 📺	AE DC MC V	174			
OLD MADRID: *Tryp Rex.* **Map 2 E2.** w www.solmelia.com €€€€€ Gran Vía 43, 28013. (91 547 48 00. FAX 91 547 12 38. A chain hotel in an old building between the Plaza del Callao and the Plaza de España, close to a large public car park. It has spacious public rooms and well-equipped bedrooms, each with its own safe. 🛏 📋 📺	AE DC MC V	144			
BOURBON MADRID: *Mora.* **Map 5 C2.** €€ Paseo del Prado 32, 28014. (91 420 15 69. FAX 91 420 05 64. A 1930s hotel with an attractive entrance. Its rooms and facilities are functional, but its prices are low and it is centrally located. 🛏 📋 📺	AE DC MC V	61			

Bourbon Madrid: *Santander.* **Map 5 A1.** €€ · MC V · 35
Calle de Echegaray 1, 28014. 91 429 46 44. FAX 91 369 10 78.
This small, friendly family hotel offering neat, comfortable, simple rooms has been popular with travellers since it opened in the 1920s.

Bourbon Madrid: *Palace.* **Map 5 B1.** www.luxurycollection.com €€€€€ · AE DC MC V · 465
Plaza de las Cortes 7, 28014. 91 360 80 00. FAX 91 360 81 00.
This gracious Belle Époque hotel with a glass dome and a colonnade, has accommodated statesmen and the spy, Mata Hari. The bedrooms are elegant and the service welcoming and efficient.

Bourbon Madrid: *Ritz.* **Map 5 C1.** www.ritz.es €€€€€ · AE DC MC V · 158
Plaza de la Lealtad 5, 28014. 91 521 28 57. FAX 91 532 87 76.
Inaugurated in 1910 as a hotel for aristocrats, the Ritz is still one of Spain's most elegant hotels (*see p274*). It has an ornate, circular foyer and a terrace garden, and offers musical teas and brunches.

Bourbon Madrid: *Suecia.* **Map 3 B5.** www.hotelsuecia.com €€€€€ · AE DC MC V · 128
Calle Marqués de Casa Riera 4, 28014. 91 531 69 00. FAX 91 521 71 41.
Centrally located near the Puerta del Sol, the Suecia has a small, seventh-floor terrace for relaxing and sunbathing.

Bourbon Madrid: *Suite Prado.* **Map 5 A1.** www.suiteprado.com €€€€€ · AE DC MC V · 18
Manuel Fernández y González 10, 28014. 91 420 23 18. FAX 91 420 05 59.
A stylish apartment hotel of luxurious suites a short distance from the Prado and the Museo Thyssen-Bornemisza.

Bourbon Madrid: *Tryp Reina Victoria.* **Map 5 A1.** €€€€€ · AE DC MC V · 201
Plaza Santa Ana 14, 28012. 91 531 45 00. FAX 91 522 03 07. www.solmelia.com
Ernest Hemingway once lodged in this historic hotel, a graceful edifice and a traditional haunt of bullfighting aficionados.

Bourbon Madrid: *Villa Real.* **Map 5 B1.** www.derbyhotels.es €€€€€ · AE DC MC V · 115
Plaza de las Cortes 10, 28014. 91 420 37 67. FAX 91 420 25 47.
Located close to the Prado, this stylish hotel is housed in an early 19th-century building.

Bourbon Madrid: *Wellington.* **Map 4 F4.** €€€€€ · AE DC MC V · 288
Calle de Velázquez 8, 28001. 91 575 44 00. www.hotel-wellington.com
A stylish hotel built in the early 1950s close to the Parque del Retiro. It is a meeting place for people interested in bullfighting.

Further Afield (East): *Colón.* www.fiesta-hotels.com €€€€€ · AE DC MC V · 359
Calle Doctor Esquerdo 119, 28007. 91 573 59 00. FAX 91 573 08 09.
A comfortable hotel is located in a tower block between the Parque del Retiro and the Parque de Roma. It has a gym and business facilities.

Further Afield (East): *NH Alcalá.* www.nh-hoteles.com €€€€€ · AE DC MC V · 146
Calle de Alcalá 66, 28009. 91 435 10 60. FAX 91 435 11 05.
A hotel with a friendly atmosphere across the street from the Parque del Retiro. The back bedrooms overlook a pretty garden.

Further Afield (North): *Hostal Sil.* **Map 3 A4.** €€ · MC V · 20
Calle Fuencarral 95, 28004. 91 448 89 72. FAX 91 447 48 29.
In a lively part of town, this is a comfortable, convenient hotel with quality bedroom and bathroom furnishings, but low prices.

Further Afield (North): *Mónaco.* **Map 3 B4.** €€€ · AE DC MC V · 34
Calle Barbieri 5, 28004. 91 522 46 30. FAX 91 521 16 01.
The decor of this hotel, formerly Madrid's most famous high-class brothel, is unashamedly kitsch. The bedrooms still have some of their original decadent features.

Further Afield (North): *Castellana Intercontinental.* €€€€€ · AE DC MC V · 313
Paseo de la Castellana 49, 28046. 91 310 02 00. www.interconti.com
This hotel in Madrid's commercial centre is a favourite with business travellers. Guests can choose between two restaurants.

Further Afield (North): *Miguel Ángel.* €€€€€ · AE DC MC V · 271
Calle Miguel Ángel 31, 28010. 91 442 81 99. www.occidental-hoteles.com
Beside the Paseo de la Castellana, the Miguel Ángel combines modern comfort with classic style. One of its two fine restaurants holds dinner dances until 3am.

For key to symbols see back flap

Price categories for a standard double room per night, with tax, breakfast and service included: € under 50 euros €€ 50–75 euros €€€ 75–100 euros €€€€ 100–125 euros €€€€€ over 125 euros **Credit Cards** Indicates which credit cards are accepted: *AE* American Express; *DC* Diners Club; *MC* Master Card/Access; *V* Visa **Parking** Parking provided by the hotel in a private car park or a private garage on the hotel site or very close by. Some hotels charge for use of private parking facilities. **Swimming Pool** Hotel pool outdoors unless otherwise stated. **Garden** Hotel with garden, courtyard or terrace, often providing tables for eating outdoors.	**CREDIT CARDS**	**NUMBER OF ROOMS**	**PRIVATE PARKING**	**SWIMMING POOL**	**GARDEN OR TERRACE**

FURTHER AFIELD (NORTH): *Santo Mauro.* Ⓦ www.ac-hoteles.com €€€€€
Calle Zurbano 36, 28010. **℡** 91 319 69 00. **FAX** 91 308 54 77.
This palace, built in 1894 in one of Madrid's most elegant streets, has housed embassies. It has a swimming pool beneath a vaulted basement ceiling, and a restaurant occupies the former library. 🛏 🖥 📺

AE DC MC V | 37

FURTHER AFIELD (NORTH): *Villamagna.* **Map 3 D2.** €€€€€
Paseo de la Castellana 22, 28046. **℡** 91 587 12 34. Ⓦ www.madrid.hyatt.com
The Villamagna combines 18th-century decor with modern luxury, and is ringed by gardens. It is popular with business people. 🛏 🖥 📺 ♿

AE DC MC V | 182

FURTHER AFIELD (NORTHEAST): *Conde de Orgaz.* €€€€€
Avenida Moscatelar 24, 28043. **℡** 91 388 40 99. Ⓦ www.zenithhoteles.com
A modern hotel, with big, comfortable bedrooms, near to the airport and the Campo de las Naciones Exhibition Centre. 🛏 🖥 📺 ♿

AE DC MC V | 91

FURTHER AFIELD (NORTHEAST): *NH Príncipe de Vergara.* €€€€€
Calle Príncipe de Vergara 92, 28006. **℡** 91 563 26 95. Ⓦ www.nh-hoteles.com
Part of a chain of well-appointed hotels, the Príncipe de Vergara serves good breakfasts and is reasonable value for money. 🛏 🖥 📺

AE DC MC V | 173

FURTHER AFIELD (NORTHWEST): *Tirol.* Ⓦ www.hotel-tirol.com €€€€€
Calle de Marqués de Urquijo 4, 28008. **℡** 91 548 19 00. **FAX** 91 541 39 58.
A good-value hotel, conveniently located off the Plaza de España and near the student district. The bedrooms are spacious and clean. 🛏 🖥 📺

MC V | 95

FURTHER AFIELD (NORTHWEST): *Tryp Monte Real.* €€€€€
Calle Arroyo Fresno 17, 28035. **℡** 91 316 21 40. Ⓦ www.solmelia.com
Situated in a residential area near the Puerta de Hierro golf course, this imposing modern hotel has a peaceful atmosphere. Its balconies overlook the swimming pool and gardens. 🛏 🖥 📺

AE DC MC V | 80

FURTHER AFIELD (SOUTHEAST): *Agumar.* **Map 6 F4.** €€€€€
Paseo de Reina Cristina 7, 28014. **℡** 91 552 69 00. Ⓦ www.h-santos.es
A stylish hotel near the big museums, with its own collection of good paintings and carpets from the Real Fábrica de Tapices. 🛏 🖥 📺

AE DC MC V | 245

FURTHER AFIELD (SOUTHWEST): *Reyes Católicos.* **Map 1 C5.** €€€€€
Calle del Ángel 18, 28005. **℡** 91 365 86 00. **FAX** 91 365 98 67.
This modern, central hotel is popular and always very busy. Children are made welcome. The bedroom windows are double-glazed for sound-proofing. There are views of the city from the roof terrace. 🛏 🖥 📺

AE DC MC V | 38

MADRID PROVINCE

ALAMEDA DEL VALLE: *La Posada de Alameda.* €€€
Calle Grande 34, 28749. **℡** 91 869 13 37. Ⓦ www.laposadadealameda.com
A sensitively restored farmhouse in the tranquil Lozoya valley, about an hour's drive from Madrid. All the bedrooms are well equipped and some have views of the countryside. Two are in converted silos. 🛏 📺

MC V | 22

CHINCHÓN: *Parador de Chinchón.* Ⓦ www.parador.es €€€€€
Avenida del Generalísimo 1, 28370. **℡** 91 894 08 36. **FAX** 91 894 09 08.
This converted 17th-century monastery has immensely thick walls and is built round an airy green courtyard. Delightful details to look out for include azulejos (*see p420*), frescoes and antiques. 🛏 🖥 📺

AE DC MC V | 38

RASCAFRÍA: *Santa María de El Paular.* Ⓦ www.sierranorte.com €€€€€
Carretera C604 km 25,600, 28740. **℡** 91 869 10 11. **FAX** 91 869 10 06.
This hotel occupies part of a Benedictine monastery in a peaceful corner of the Guadarrama mountains. A mesón (bar-restaurant) offers an informal alternative to the dining room. ⬤ Jan. 🛏 📺

AE DC MC V | 44

SAN LORENZO DE EL ESCORIAL: *El Botánico.* €€€€
Calle Timoteo Padros 16, 28200. █ *91 890 78 79.* FAX *91 890 81 58.*
This 17th–18th-century stone palace was converted into a hotel in 1996. Its
quiet location offers good views of El Escoril monastery and it is situated
opposite the golf course. 🔲 📋 TV 🔲

	20		
AE			
DC			
MC			
V			

TORREJÓN DE ARDOZ: *La Casa Grande.* w www.lacasagrande.es €€€€€
Calle Madrid 2, 28850. █ *91 675 39 00.* FAX *91 675 06 91.*
This luxurious hotel in a 16th-century house is decorated with antiques
which once belonged to the Russian royal family. Catherine the Great is
said to have slept in the bed now in the main suite. 🔲 📋 TV

	8		
AE			
DC			
MC			
V			

CASTILLA Y LEÓN

AGUILAR DE CAMPOO: *Posada de Santa María la Real.* €€
Avenida Cervera, 34800 (Palencia). █ *979 12 20 00.* FAX *979 12 56 80.*
Part of the Institute of Romanesque Studies is in this monastery; the hotel
entrance is at the back and not signposted. The bedrooms are small and
plain, with garden views. The atmosphere is friendly. ● *mid-Jan–1 Feb.* 🔲 TV

	18		
MC			
V			

LA ALBERCA: *Las Batuecas.* @ lasbatuecas@teleline.es €€€
Avda de las Batuecas 6, 37624 (Salamanca). █ *923 41 51 88.* FAX *923 41 50 55.*
On the edge of a pretty village, deep in a green valley, this hotel is a base
for touring the Sierra de Francia. It is a stone and wood building with a
first-floor covered terrace. ● *10 Jan–1 Feb.* 🔲 📋 TV

	38		
MC			
V			

ASTORGA: *Gaudí.* w www.mundicamino.com €€
Plaza Eduardo de Castro 6, 24700 (León). █ *987 61 56 54.* FAX *987 61 50 40.*
This stylish hotel is on the same square as Gaudí's Modernista Bishop's
Palace. The bedrooms overlook the palace and the cathedral. 🔲 TV ♿

	35		
AE			
DC			
MC			
V			

ÁVILA: *Hostería de Bracamonte.* €€
Calle Bracamonte 6, 05001. █ *920 25 12 80.* FAX *920 25 38 38*
A charming, traditionally Castilian hotel with exposed beams and tiled
floors. It is in a quiet location, close to the cathedral and the town walls.
The bedrooms are attractively decorated. 🔲 TV

	24		
MC			
V			

ÁVILA: *Palacio Valderrábanos.* w www.palaciovalderrabanos.com €€€€
Plaza de la Catedral 9, 05001. █ *920 21 10 23.* FAX *920 25 16 91.*
A spacious, sedate hotel in a stately 15th-century mansion beside the
cathedral. There is a suite in the watchtower. 🔲 📋 TV

	73		
AE			
DC			
MC			
V			

ÁVILA: *Parador de Ávila.* w www.parador.es €€€€
C/ Marqués de Canales de Chozas 2, 05001. █ *920 21 13 40.* FAX *920 22 61 66.*
A parador in a 15th-century mansion next to Ávila's walls. From some
rooms guests can watch storks nest on a gateway in spring. 🔲 📋 TV

	61		
AE			
DC			
MC			
V			

BENAVENTE: *Parador de Benavente.* w www.parador.es €€€€€
Paseo de Ramón y Cajal, 49600 (Zamora). █ *980 63 03 00.* FAX *980 63 03 03.*
Only the Tower of the Snail remained of Benavente castle in the wake of
Napoleon's troops. As part of the parador, it now accommodates an
extraordinary lounge with a Mudéjar ceiling from a church. 🔲 📋 TV ♿

	30		
AE			
DC			
MC			
V			

EL BURGO DE OSMA: *Virrey II.* w www.virreypalafox.com €€€€
Calle Mayor 4, 42300 (Soria). █ *975 34 13 11.* FAX *975 34 08 55.*
A lavish hotel near the old town. It is very comfortable, spotlessly clean
and has efficient, friendly staff and a good restaurant. 🔲 TV ♿

	52		
AE			
DC			
MC			
V			

BURGOS: *Mesón del Cid.* @ mesondelcid@terra.es €€€€
Plaza de Santa María 8, 09003. █ *947 20 87 15.* FAX *947 26 94 60.*
This stylish hotel, across a little square from the cathedral, is dedicated to
the conquering medieval hero, El Cid. 🔲 📋 TV

	50		
AE			
DC			
MC			
V			

BURGOS: *Landa Palace.* w www.landapalace.es €€€€€
Carretera Madrid–Irún km 235, 09001. █ *947 25 77 77.* FAX *947 26 46 76.*
An extravagant hotel on the city outskirts. The authentic-looking stone
vaults roofing the dining room and the pool are 1960s, not Gothic; but the
medieval tower was transported from a nearby village. 🔲 📋 TV ♿

	36	●	
MC			
V			

CASTRILLO DE LOS POLVAZARES: *Cuca la Vaina.* €€
Calle El Jardín, 24718 (León). █ & FAX *987 69 10 78.*
A quiet, charming hotel occupying a renovated, stylishly decorated stone
house in a well-preserved village in the Maragato region. 🔲 TV

	7		
MC			
V			

<table>
<tr><td>

Price categories for a standard double room per night, with tax, breakfast and service included:

€ under 50 euros
€€ 50–75 euros
€€€ 75–100 euros
€€€€ 100–125 euros
€€€€€ over 125 euros

</td><td>

CREDIT CARDS
Indicates which credit cards are accepted: *AE* American Express; *DC* Diners Club; *MC* Master Card/Access; *V* Visa
PARKING
Parking provided by the hotel in a private car park or a private garage on the hotel site or very close by. Some hotels charge for use of private parking facilities.
SWIMMING POOL
Hotel pool outdoors unless otherwise stated.
GARDEN
Hotel with garden, courtyard or terrace, often providing tables for eating outdoors.

</td></tr>
</table>

	CREDIT CARDS	NUMBER OF ROOMS	PRIVATE PARKING	SWIMMING POOL	GARDEN OR TERRACE
CIUDAD RODRIGO: *Parador de Ciudad Rodrigo.* W www.parador.es €€€€ Plaza del Castillo 1, 37500 (Salamanca). 923 46 01 50. FAX 923 46 04 04. This, the first parador to be installed in a historic building, preserves some of the atmosphere of a 12th-century castle. The prize suite has a circular bedroom with a domed roof. 🛏 ▤ TV	AE DC MC V	35	■		■
COLLADO HERMOSO: *Molino de Río Viejo.* €€€ Carretera N110, km172, 40170 (Segovia). 921 40 30 63. FAX 921 40 30 51. A cosy hotel in an old mill among poplars beside the Río Viejo is a good base for exploring the countryside of Segovia province. There are horses available for riding enthusiasts. Booking is essential. 🛏	MC V	6	■		■
COVARRUBIAS: *Arlanza.* W www.ctv.es/users/arlanza €€ Calle Mayor 11, 09346 (Burgos). 947 40 64 41. FAX 947 40 63 59. Overlooking a cobbled square in a medieval village., this hotel offers simple accommodation in an old building with black beams and a handsome staircase. Mountain food is served, including wild boar. ● *mid-Dec–1 Mar.* 🛏 TV	AE DC MC V	38			■
HOYOS DEL ESPINO: *El Milano Real.* W www.elmilanoreal.com €€€ Calle Toleo, 05634 (Ávila). 920 34 91 08. FAX 920 34 91 56. A personal touch, a relaxed atmosphere and silent nights make El Milano Real a good holiday hotel. Excursions on horseback are organized along packhorse tracks in the picturesque Sierra de Gredos. 🛏 TV	AE DC MC V	21	■		■
LEÓN: *Alfonso V.* W www.iova-sa.com €€€€€ Avenida Padre Isla 1, 24002. 987 22 09 00. FAX 987 22 12 44. Inside, this comfortable hotel in the city centre is contemporary in style. An extravagant, curvaceous staircase giving some interesting perspectives is its most impressive feature. 🛏 ▤ TV	AE DC MC V	62	■		
LEÓN: *Parador de San Marcos.* W www.parador.es €€€€€ Plaza de San Marcos 7, 24001. 987 23 73 00. FAX 987 23 34 58. This parador is in the Hostal San Marcos, a former convent and one of Spain's loveliest Renaissance buildings. It has a magnificent hall with a coffered ceiling and luxurious old and modern bedrooms. 🛏 TV &	AE DC MC V	230	■		
NAVARREDONDA DE GREDOS: *Parador de Gredos.* W www.parador.es €€€€ Carretera Barraco-Bejar, km 43, 05635 (Ávila). 920 34 80 48. FAX 920 34 82 05. Inaugurated in 1928 by Alfonso XIII, this was the first parador in Spain. Its setting is a beautiful pine wood in the Sierra de Gredos. It is restful and a good base for exploring the surrounding mountains. 🛏 TV &	AE DC MC V	76	■		■
PEDRAZA DE LA SIERRA: *La Posada de Don Mariano.* €€€ Calle Mayor 14, 40172 (Segovia). & FAX 921 50 98 86. It is hard to nominate the best hotel in this lovely village. Don Mariano and El Hotel de la Villa are the work of the same decorator. Every room looks like something out of a decor magazine. 🛏 TV	AE DC MC V	18	■		
PEDRAZA DE LA SIERRA: *El Hotel de la Villa.* W www.estancias.com €€€€ Calle Calzada 5, 40172 (Segovia). 921 50 86 51. FAX 921 50 86 53. No two bedrooms in this charming hotel are alike. All are exquisitely decorated with floral wallpapers and furnished with antiques. 🛏 ▤ TV	AE DC MC V	26	■		
PONFERRADA: *El Temple.* W www.hosteleriaelon.com €€ Avenida de Portugal 2, 24400 (León). 987 41 00 58. FAX 987 42 35 25. El Temple's façade is a replica of the town's Templar castle. The decor evokes the Middle Ages with antiques and stone walls. 🛏 ▤ TV &	AE DC MC V	112	■		■
SALAMANCA: *Gran Hotel.* W www.helcom.es €€€€€ Plaza Poeta Iglesias 3, 37001. & FAX 923 21 35 00. A hotel with spacious, quiet bedrooms near the spectacular Plaza Mayor, popular with bullfighters and their entourages. 🛏 ▤ TV	AE DC MC V	136	■		

SALAMANCA: *Las Torres.* W www.mmteam.interbook.net €€€€€ — AE DC MC V — 44
Plaza Mayor 26, 37002. 923 21 21 00. FAX 923 21 21 01.
The restaurant of this hotel overlooks Salamanca's magnificent Plaza Mayor. Guests can take advantage of many extras, from a rapid clothes valeting service to complementary toiletries. 🛏 🗐 TV ♿

SALAMANCA: *Rector.* W www.terra.es €€€€€ — AE DC MC V — 13
Paseo del Rector Esperabé 10, 37008. 923 21 84 82. FAX 923 21 40 08.
The façade looks old but the hotel was built in the 1940s by an architect who specialized in reproducing old styles. Inside, leather sofas and stained glass suggest restrained elegance. 🛏 🗐 TV

SANTA MARÍA DE MAVE: *Hostería El Convento.* W www.turpalencia.com €€ — AE DC MC V — 25
Santa María de Mave, 34492 (Palencia). 979 12 36 11. FAX 979 12 54 92.
Just off the N661 south of Aguilar is this family-run hotel in a former convent in pretty countryside. Several public areas have decorative stonework. Traditional Castilian food is served in the restaurant. 🛏

SANTO DOMINGO DE SILOS: *Tres Coronas de Silos.* €€€ — AE DC MC V — 16
Plaza Mayor 6, 09610 (Burgos). 947 39 00 47. FAX 947 39 00 65.
A modest inn in an 18th-century mansion dominating the village square, with an arched doorway and a proud coat of arms. Bare stone walls and seasoned wood lend atmosphere to the interior. 🛏 TV

SEGOVIA: *Los Linajes.* W www.estancias.com €€€ — AE DC MC V — 53
Calle Doctor Velasco 9, 40003. 921 46 04 75. FAX 921 46 04 79.
Hidden behind an ancient half-timbered, red-brick façade is a modern hotel which steps down the hillside beside the city walls in eight levels. The higher your room level, the better the view. 🛏 🗐 TV ♿

SEGOVIA: *Infanta Isabel.* W www.hotelinfantaisabel.com €€€€ — AE DC MC V — 27
Plaza Mayor, 40001. 921 46 13 00. FAX 921 46 22 17.
A modern hotel in *fin de siècle* style, complemented by traditional Segovian decor. The bedrooms are cosy. 🛏 🗐 TV

SEGOVIA: *Parador de Segovia.* W www.parador.es €€€€€ — AE DC MC V — 113
Carretera de Valladolid, 40003. 921 44 37 37. FAX 921 43 73 62.
This luxury parador has been strategically sited just outside Segovia so that guests can enjoy magnificent views of the city while sunbathing in the gardens. Facilities include a gym and an indoor pool. 🛏 🗐 TV ♿

SIGUERUELO: *Posada de Sigueruelo.* W www.situral.com €€€ — MC V — 6
Calle Badén 40, 40590 (Segovia). & FAX 921 50 81 35.
Breakfast and dinner are included in the room price of this rural house. The owners organize riding, cycling, walking and canoeing. 🛏

SOLOSANCHO: *Sancho de Estrada.* @ hotellesmayoral@hotellesmayoral.com €€€ — DC MC V — 12
Castillo de Villaviciosa, 05130 (Ávila). & FAX 920 29 10 82.
The medieval castle of Villaviciosa, built to defend the Roman roads over the Sierra de Gredos, has been restored. There are coats of arms and other medieval touches in the very small bedrooms. ● *mid-Jan–7 Feb.* 🛏 TV

SORIA: *Valonsadero.* €€€ — AE MC V — 8
Carretera de Burgos km 359, 42005. 975 18 00 06. FAX 975 18 01 01.
This cosy mountainside hotel is a tranquil retreat, located just 5 km (3 miles) outside Soria. Walking and riding can be enjoyed here. 🛏 🗐 TV ♿

SORIA: *Parador de Soria.* W www.parador.es €€€€ — AE DC MC V — 34
Parque del Castillo, 42005. 975 24 08 00. FAX 975 24 08 03.
The image and examples of the work of the Spanish poet, Antonio Machado, decorate the walls of this parador in a hilltop park. It over-looks the wooded Duero valley. 🛏 🗐 TV

VALLADOLID: *Lasa.* @ hotellasa@cempresarial.com €€€ — AE DC MC V — 62
Calle Acera de Recoletos 21, 47004. 983 39 02 55. FAX 983 30 25 61.
A renovated, 19th-century apartment block in the city centre. The bedrooms are double-glazed to reduce street noise. 🛏 🗐 TV

VILLAFRANCA DEL BIERZO: *Parador de Villafranca.* €€€€ — AE DC MC V — 39
Avenida de Calvo Sotelo, 24500 (León). 987 54 01 75. W www.parador.es
This rural parador has well-kept gardens and an attractive dining room. The town was founded by French pilgrims and is traditionally a stop on the pilgrimage route to Santiago de Compostela. 🛏 TV

For key to symbols see back flap

Price categories for a standard double room per night, with tax, breakfast and service included:	**CREDIT CARDS** Indicates which credit cards are accepted: *AE* American Express; *DC* Diners Club; *MC* Master Card/Access; *V* Visa		
€ under 50 euros	**PARKING** Parking provided by the hotel in a private car park or a private garage on the hotel site or very close by. Some hotels charge for use of private parking facilities.		
€€ 50–75 euros	**SWIMMING POOL** Hotel pool outdoors unless otherwise stated.		
€€€ 75–100 euros	**GARDEN**		
€€€€ 100–125 euros	Hotel with garden, courtyard or terrace, often providing		
€€€€€ over 125 euros	tables for eating outdoors.		

		CREDIT CARDS	NUMBER OF ROOMS	PRIVATE PARKING	SWIMMING POOL	GARDEN OR TERRACE
ZAMORA: *Hostería Real de Zamora.* @ hostzamora@wanadoo.es €€ Cuesta de Pizarro 7, 49027. 【 & FAX *980 53 45 45.* The Inquisition once occupied this 16th-century mansion beside the city wall and near the Río Duero. Now it is a good-value hotel with a pretty courtyard at its centre. Basque cooking is served. 🔒 TV		AE DC MC V	18			▪
ZAMORA: *Parador de Zamora.* W www.parador.es €€€€€ Plaza de Viriato 5, 49001. 【 *980 51 44 97.* FAX *980 53 00 63.* A city-centre parador in a Renaissance mansion. From a magnificent courtyard bordered by carved stone pillars, stone stairs lead to a sunny gallery furnished with antiques and pot plants. 🔒 ▤ TV ♿		AE DC MC V	52	▪	●	▪

CASTILLA-LA MANCHA

		CREDIT CARDS	NUMBER OF ROOMS	PRIVATE PARKING	SWIMMING POOL	GARDEN OR TERRACE
ALARCÓN: *Parador de Alarcón.* W www.parador.es €€€€€ Avda Amigos de los Castillos 3, 16213 (Cuenca). 【 *969 33 03 15.* FAX *969 33 03 03.* A medieval fortress stunningly located above the Júcar valley. The lounge and dining room are vaulted chambers with thick walls. 🔒 ▤ TV		AE DC MC V	13	▪		▪
ALBACETE: *Los Llanos.* W www.solmelia.com €€€€ Avenida de España 9, 02002. 【 *967 22 37 50.* FAX *967 23 46 07.* A modern hotel overlooking a verdant park. It has a gym, a hair salon and a giant video screen in the TV room. 🔒 ▤ TV		AE DC MC V	102			
ALBACETE: *Parador de Albacete.* W www.parador.es €€€€ Carretera N301 km 251, 02000. 【 *967 24 53 21.* FAX *967 24 32 71.* A purpose-built parador with shady terraces and a pool, decorated with ox yokes and other rural implements. 🔒 ▤ TV		AE DC MC V	70	▪	●	▪
ALMAGRO: *Almagro.* W www.confortelalmagro.com €€€ Carretera de Bolaños, 13270 (Ciudad Real). 【 *926 86 00 11.* FAX *926 86 06 18.* This chain hotel in the new town is a brick building with two floors and a balcony. It offers business services and bicycles for hire. 🔒 ▤ TV ♿		AE MC V	50			
ALMAGRO: *Parador de Almagro.* W www.parador.es €€€€€ Ronda de San Francisco 31, 13270 (Ciudad Real). 【 *926 86 01 00.* FAX *926 86 01 50.* One of Spain's most charming paradors is in a 16th-century convent. Most bedrooms look on to one of 14 courtyards. A lace maker works in one courtyard, keeping the town's tradition alive. 🔒 ▤ TV ♿		AE DC MC V	54	▪	●	▪
AYNA: *Felipe II.* W www.paralelo40.org €€ Avenida Manuel Carrera 9, 02125 (Albacete). 【 & FAX *967 29 50 83.* The semicircular layout of this modern, family-run hotel in the mountains of Albacete allows every bedroom to have a balcony giving a panoramic view of the town and the valley. 🔒 TV		AE DC MC V	42	▪	●	▪
BALLESTEROS DE CALATRAVA: *Palacio de la Serna.* €€€€€ Calle Cervantes 18, 13432 (Ciudad Real). 【 *926 84 22 08.* W www.palaciodelaserna.com An 18th-century farm on the plains of La Mancha, in a mix of Castilian and modern styles. It is quiet and comfortable. There are excursions on horse-back and on mountain bikes into the nearby hills. ● *2nd week of Jan.* 🔒 ▤ TV ♿		AE DC MC V	19	▪	▪	▪
BETETA: *Los Tilos.* @ lostilos@faec.org € Extrarradio, 16870 (Cuenca). 【 *969 31 80 98.* FAX *969 31 82 99.* This traditional whitewashed country house, near a mineral spring in the beautiful Serranía de Cuenca, offers basic, affordable rooms. It is popular with ramblers and nature lovers. ● *mid-Jan–1 Mar.* 🔒 TV		AE DC MC V	24			▪
CUENCA: *Posada de San José.* W www.posadasanjose.com €€ Calle Julián Romero 4, 16001. 【 *969 21 13 00.* FAX *969 23 03 65.* An original, charming hotel run by a Canadian-Spanish couple in an historic building in the old part of town. It is curiously labyrinthine, and lovingly decorated with antiques and frescoes. 🔒		AE DC MC V	30			▪

CUENCA: *La Cueva del Fraile.* W www.hotelcuevadelfraile.com €€€€
Carretera Cuenca–Buenache km 7, 16001. ℂ 969 21 15 71. FAX 969 25 60 47.
In a green valley outside Cuenca, this hotel is built around a white patio. It
has tennis courts and bicycles for hire. ● 2 Jan–6 Feb.

AE	60
DC	
MC	
V	

CUENCA: *Leonor de Aquitania.* W www.hotelleonordeaquitania.com €€€€
Calle San Pedro 58–60, 16001. ℂ 969 23 10 00. FAX 969 23 10 04.
Hunting trophies are displayed in the lobby of this hotel in the old part of
town. The bedrooms are welcoming and cosy, and some have views of the
gorge of the Río Huécar.

AE	46
DC	
MC	
V	

CUENCA: *Parador de Cuenca.* W www.parador.es €€€€€
Paseo Hoz del Huécar, 16001. ℂ 969 23 23 20. FAX 969 23 25 34.
The 16th-century convent of San Pablo, on the opposite side of the Río
Huécar from the city, is an elegant parador. Cuenca's famous old hanging
houses (*see p.367*) can be seen from the bedrooms.

AE	63
DC	
MC	
V	

GUADALAJARA: *España.* €€
Calle Teniente Figueroa 3, 19001. ℂ 949 21 13 03. FAX 949 21 13 05.
A family-run hotel in a 19th-century mansion in the centre of the city. The
modernized interior is lightened by touches of originality, such as a mural
on the staircase. The staff can advise on sightseeing.

AE	40
DC	
MC	
V	

MANZANARES: *Parador de Manzanares.* W www.parador.es €€€€
Ctra Madrid–Cádiz km 174, 13200 (Ciudad Real). ℂ 926 61 04 00. FAX 926 61 09 35.
In one of the main cities of La Mancha's principal wine region, this parador
is a base for exploring Don Quixote country.

AE	50
DC	
MC	
V	

OROPESA: *Parador de Oropesa.* W www.parador.es €€€€
Plaza del Palacio 1, 45560 (Toledo). ℂ 925 43 00 00. FAX 925 43 07 77.
The Sierra de Gredos forms a backdrop to this medieval fortress rising
above a plain of olive groves and vineyards. It has plenty of modern
comforts, including a Jacuzzi in one bedroom.

AE	48
DC	
MC	
V	

OSSA DE MONTIEL: *Albamanjón.* W www.albamanjon.com €€€
Laguna de San Pedro 16, 02611 (Albacete). ℂ 926 69 90 48. FAX 926 69 91 20.
This modern complex features a mix of local and Andalusian styles and is
the best hotel beside the Lagunas de Ruidera, La Mancha's string of
attractive turquoise lakes. It is beautifully decorated with tiles and
climbing plants.

AE	8
MC	
V	

PASTRANA: *Hospedería Real de Pastrana.* W www.hosteriasreales.com €€
Convento del Carmen, 19100 (Guadalajara). ℂ & FAX 949 37 10 60.
A hotel in a wing of the Monasterio del Carmen, founded by St Teresa of
Ávila, with simple, quiet rooms. On one side is the valley of the Río Tajo
and on the other the picturesque town of Pastrana.

AE	27
DC	
MC	
V	

PUERTO LÁPICE: *Aprisco de Puerto Lápice.* €
Carretera Madrid–Cádiz km 134, 13650 (Ciudad Real). ℂ & FAX 926 57 61 50.
An economical overnight stop next to a popular, often crowded restaurant
on the Madrid–Andalusia road. The lounge has rustic decor and is crammed
with ornaments, including a boar's head.

MC	17
V	

SIGÜENZA: *El Molino de Alcuneza.* W www.molinodealcuneza.com €€€€
Ctra de Alboreca km 0.5, 19264 (Guadalajara). ℂ 949 39 15 01. FAX 949 34 70 04.
This cosy former mill in the Alcarria has exquisitely decorated rooms.
Dinner includes fresh produce from the kitchen garden.

AE	11
DC	
MC	
V	

SIGÜENZA: *Parador de Sigüenza.* W www.parador.es €€€€
Plaza del Castillo, 19250 (Guadalajara). ℂ 949 39 01 00. FAX 949 39 13 64.
Sigüenza's massive castle overlooks the town from a hilltop. Its former VIP
guests include the Catholic Monarchs (*see pp52–3*). It is furnished in regal
style and the bedrooms surround a courtyard.

AE	81
DC	
MC	
V	

TALAVERA DE LA REINA: *Beatriz.* €€€
Avenida de Madrid 1, 45600 (Toledo). ℂ 925 80 76 00. FAX 925 81 58 08.
A modern hotel on the town's edge, on the road from Madrid. In the cellar
is an anti-nuclear refuge built by the owner.

AE	164
DC	
MC	
V	

TOLEDO: *La Almazara.* W www.hotelalmazara €€
Carretera Toledo–Argés, 45080. ℂ 925 22 38 66. FAX 925 25 05 62.
This 16th-century country house hotel is high on a wooded hilltop outside
Toledo, and has a magnificent view. Obliging and informal staff
compensate for simple bedrooms and limited facilities.

AE	28
DC	
MC	
V	

Price categories for a standard double room per night, with tax, breakfast and service included:

€ under 50 euros
€€ 50–75 euros
€€€ 75–100 euros
€€€€ 100–125 euros
€€€€€ over 125 euros

CREDIT CARDS
Indicates which credit cards are accepted: *AE* American Express; *DC* Diners Club; *MC* Master Card/Access; *V* Visa
PARKING
Parking provided by the hotel in a private car park or a private garage on the hotel site or very close by. Some hotels charge for use of private parking facilities.
SWIMMING POOL
Hotel pool outdoors unless otherwise stated.
GARDEN
Hotel with garden, courtyard or terrace, often providing tables for eating outdoors.

	CREDIT CARDS	NUMBER OF ROOMS	PRIVATE PARKING	SWIMMING POOL	GARDEN OR TERRACE
TOLEDO: *Hostal del Cardenal.* w www.cardenal.asernet.es €€€€ Paseo de Recaredo 24, 45004. 〔 925 22 49 00. FAX 925 22 29 91. Now an historic hotel by the city walls, this 18th-century mansion was formerly the residence of the archbishop of Toledo. It has splendid, sculpted ceilings and pretty brick courtyards. 🛏 🗏 TV	AE DC MC V	27			■
TOLEDO: *Pintor El Greco.* w www.hotelpintorelgreco.com €€€€ Calle Alamillos del Tránsito 13, 45002. 〔 925 21 42 50. FAX 925 21 58 19. A 17th-century house in Toledo's former Jewish quarter has been discreetly extended behind the original façade and patio. Wrought iron and traditional ceramics add character to the hotel. 🛏 🗏 TV 🕭	AE DC MC V	33			
TOLEDO: *Parador de Toledo.* w www.parador.es €€€€€ Cerro del Emperador, 45002. 〔 925 22 18 50. FAX 925 22 51 66. There is a spectacular view of Toledo from the terrace of this parador on the brow of a hill overlooking the city. The hotel is popular with sightseers and photographers, so book in advance. 🛏 🗏 TV	AE DC MC V	76		●	■
TRAGACETE: *Hostal El Gamo.* € Plaza de los Caídos 2, 16150 (Cuenca). 〔 969 28 90 08. FAX 969 28 92 28. A good-value hostal and hotel in a peaceful village among hills and woods in the Serranía de Cuenca, near the Río Cuervo's source. 🛏	MC V	75			
VALDEPEÑAS: *Meliá El Hidalgo.* w www.solmelia.com €€€€ Ctra Madrid–Cádiz km 194, 13300 (Ciudad Real). 〔 926 31 30 88. FAX 926 31 33 36. A roadside motel built in the 1960s in a landscape of vineyards. The bright rooms each have direct access to the swimming pool. 🛏 🗏 TV 🕭	AE DC MC V	54	■	●	■

EXTREMADURA

	CREDIT CARDS	NUMBER OF ROOMS	PRIVATE PARKING	SWIMMING POOL	GARDEN OR TERRACE
ALMENDRAL: *Rocamador.* w www.rocamador.com €€€€ Carretera Badajoz–Huelva, 06800 (Badajoz). 〔 924 48 90 00. FAX 924 48 90 01. There is a special atmosphere at this former monastery, which has been carefully restored as a hotel. Thought has gone into the details to ensure that guests have a comfortable stay. 🛏 TV	AE DC MC V	26	■	●	■
BADAJOZ: *Río.* @ hotelrio@hotelrio.net €€€€ Avenida Adolfo Díaz Ambrona 13, 06006. 〔 924 27 26 00. FAX 924 27 38 74. A comfortable, modern hotel in the city centre. As well as all the standard facilities it has a bingo hall and a solarium. 🛏 🗏 TV	AE DC MC V	101	■	●	■
CÁCERES: *Parador de Cáceres.* w www.parador.es €€€€ Calle Ancha 6, 10003. 〔 927 21 17 59. FAX 927 21 17 29. A small parador in the converted 14th-century Palace of Torreorgaz. Inside it is a labyrinth of stairs, doors, patios and corridors. 🛏 🗏 TV	AE DC MC V	31	■		
CÁCERES: *Meliá Cáceres.* w www.solmelia.com €€€€€ Plaza de San Juan 11, 10003. 〔 927 21 58 00. FAX 927 21 40 70. This 16th-century mansion beside the city walls has been renovated by a hotel chain. Some of the bedrooms have vaulted ceilings. 🛏 🗏 TV	AE DC MC V	86			
GUADALUPE: *Hospedería del Real Monasterio.* €€ Plaza de Juan Carlos I, 10140 (Cáceres). 〔 927 36 70 00. w www.monasterioguadalupe.com The *hospedería* is part of the 16th-century Franciscan monastery which dominates Guadalupe. Many of the rooms which surround the stone courtyard were originally monks' cells. ● mid-Jan–mid-Feb. 🛏 🗏	MC V	47			■
GUADALUPE: *Parador de Guadalupe.* w www.parador.es €€€€ C/ Marqués de la Romana 12, 10140 (Cáceres). 〔 927 36 70 75. FAX 927 36 70 76. A pilgrim's hospice in the 16th century, this parador has a central court-yard planted with citrus trees. The rooms in the modern annexe are spacious, but those in the old building are more popular. 🛏 🗏 TV	AE DC MC V	41	■	●	■

JARANDILLA DE LA VERA: *Parador de Jarandilla.* W www.parador.es €€€€
Avenida de García Prieto 1, 10450 (Cáceres). 927 56 01 17. FAX 927 56 00 88.
This imposing 15th-century castle, where the Emperor Carlos V stayed for a
year, has been modernized without losing its medieval feel. It has rose
gardens, a tennis court and a children's play area.

	AE	53
	DC	
	MC	
	V	

JEREZ DE LOS CABALLEROS: *Los Templarios.* €€
Carretera de Villanueva, 06380 (Badajoz). 924 73 16 36. FAX 924 75 03 38.
A modern hotel named after the Knights Templar who played an important
part in the history of the area. All the bedrooms have views over the valley.
A wide terrace surrounds the pool.

	AE	49
	DC	
	MC	
	V	

LOSAR DE LA VERA: *Antigua Casa del Heno.* €
Finca Valdepimienta, 10460 (Cáceres). & FAX 927 19 80 77.
A simple old stone farmhouse surrounded by oak trees and meadows. It
offers bed and breakfast, and is most popular in the spring when the cherry
trees come into blossom. ● 10th Jan–10th Feb.

	MC	7
	V	

LOSAR DE LA VERA: *Hostería Fontivieja.* W www.geocities.com/fontivieja €€
Calle Mártires 11, 10460 (Cáceres). & FAX 927 57 01 08.
A small, family-run hotel in a peaceful olive grove outside the town. Two
bedrooms have terraces with views of the countryside.

	AE	20
	MC	
	V	

MALPARTIDA DE PLASENCIA: *Cañada Real.* W www.hotelcreal.es €€€
Ctra Comarcal 511, 10680 (Cáceres). 927 45 94 07. FAX 927 45 94 34.
This modern hotel is in easy striking distance of Plasencia and the nature
reserve. The bedrooms are comfortable and spacious.

	AE	61
	DC	
	MC	
	V	

MÉRIDA: *Parador de Mérida.* W www.parador.es €€€€
Plaza de la Constitución 3, 06800 (Badajoz). 924 31 38 00. FAX 924 31 92 08.
A converted 17th-century Baroque convent on a shady square. Roman
columns, inscriptions in Arabic and Visigothic capitals have been preserved.
The lounge is in a former chapel.

	AE	82
	DC	
	MC	
	V	

MÉRIDA: *Velada Mérida.* W www.veladahoteles.com €€€€
Avenida Princesa Sofia, 06800 (Mérida). 924 31 51 10. FAX 924 31 15 52.
Conveniently located near the cultural centre of Mérida, the Velada Mérida
has good transport links to the rest of the city. The restaurant offers
traditional Méridan dishes, served on a terrace during the summer months.

	AE	99
	DC	
	MC	
	V	

MÉRIDA: *Tryp Medea.* W www.solmelia.com €€€€€
Avenida de Portugal, 06800 (Badajoz). 924 37 24 00. FAX 924 37 30 20.
The semicircular shape of this modern hotel near the ancient Roman bridge
suggests an amphitheatre. The hotel has two swimming pools (one
indoors), a gym, a sauna and a squash court.

	AE	126
	DC	
	MC	
	V	

PLASENCIA: *Alfonso VIII.* W www.hotelalfonsoviii.com €€€€€
Avenida Alfonso VIII 32, 10600 (Cáceres). 927 41 02 50. FAX 927 41 80 42.
A modern hotel, centrally located near the Parque de la Isla (where there is
a swimming pool), with very attentive staff.

	AE	55
	DC	
	MC	
	V	

TRUJILLO: *Mesón La Cadena.* €
Plaza Mayor 8, 10200 (Cáceres). 927 32 14 63. FAX 927 32 31 16.
This restaurant-with-rooms in an attractive granite house on the main
square offers a cheaper alternative to the parador. The bedrooms,
decorated with textiles made locally, are on the third floor.

	AE	8
	MC	
	V	

TRUJILLO: *Parador de Trujillo.* W www.parador.es €€€€
Calle Santa Beatriz de Silva 1, 10200 (Cáceres). 927 32 13 50. FAX 927 32 13 66.
This charming parador, built in the 1980s, incorporates parts of a 16th-
century convent, including the former cloister. The parador is within
walking distance of Trujillo's sights, but away from its noise.

	AE	46
	DC	
	MC	
	V	

ZAFRA: *Huerta Honda.* W www.hotelhuertahonda.com €€€
Avenida López Asme 30, 06300 (Badajoz). 924 55 41 00. FAX 924 55 25 04.
Many regular guests feel this hotel offers accommodation as good as the
parador next door. The restaurant is also good value.

	AE	48
	MC	
	V	

ZAFRA: *Parador de Zafra.* W www.parador.es €€€€
Pl del Corazón de María 7, 06300 (Badajoz). 924 55 45 40. FAX 924 55 10 18.
This castle, with its round towers, was built in the 15th century on the ruins
of a Moorish fortress. A beautiful staircase leads from the court-yard, with
an arcaded gallery, to the bedrooms.

	AE	45
	DC	
	MC	
	V	

For key to symbols see back flap

Price categories for a standard double room per night, with tax, breakfast and service included:

€ under 50 euros
€€ 50–75 euros
€€€ 75–100 euros
€€€€ 100–125 euros
€€€€€ over 125 euros

CREDIT CARDS
Indicates which credit cards are accepted: *AE* American Express; *DC* Diners Club; *MC* Master Card/Access; *V* Visa
PARKING
Parking provided by the hotel in a private car park or a private garage on the hotel site or very close by. Some hotels charge for use of private parking facilities.
SWIMMING POOL
Hotel pool outdoors unless otherwise stated.
GARDEN
Hotel with garden, courtyard or terrace, often providing tables for eating outdoors.

	CREDIT CARDS	NUMBER OF ROOMS	PRIVATE PARKING	SWIMMING POOL	GARDEN OR TERRACE

SEVILLE

EL ARENAL: *La Rábida.* **Map 3 B1.** @ hotel-rabida@sol.com   €€
Calle Castelar 24, 41007. (95 422 09 60. FAX 95 422 43 75.
This hotel in one of several old palaces in residential streets near the cathedral has a few modern bedrooms. Its beautiful public rooms are built round two courtyards, one with a stained-glass roof. 🛏 📋 TV

	CREDIT CARDS	NUMBER OF ROOMS	PRIVATE PARKING	SWIMMING POOL	GARDEN OR TERRACE
	AE DC MC V	87			▣

EL ARENAL: *Simón.* **Map 3 B2.** @ hotel-simon@yet.es   €€
Calle García de Vinuesa 19, 41001. (95 422 66 60. FAX 95 456 22 41.
A central hotel in an 18th-century mansion built round a pretty patio planted with ferns. The bedrooms vary in size and quality. Some have balconies overlooking the street. 🛏

	AE DC MC V	30			▣

EL ARENAL: *Taberna del Alabardero.* **Map 3 B1.**   €€€€
Calle Zaragoza 20, 41001. (95 456 06 37. W www.tabernaalabardero.com
This is an exquisite restaurant-with-rooms, occupying a 19th-century mansion. The house is built raound a central courtyard which is illuminated by a stained-glass roof. There are particularly cosy bedrooms on the top floor. 🛏 📋 TV

	AE DC MC V	7	▣		

EL ARENAL: *Las Casas de los Mercaderes.* **Map 3 C1.**   €€€€€
Calle Álvarez Quintero 9–13, 41004. (95 422 12 98. FAX 95 422 98 84.
Although it is surrounded by the city's star sights, this hotel's regulars are business people. Behind a Sevillian mansion façade is a remodelled interior. 🛏 📋 TV

	AE DC MC V	47			

SANTA CRUZ: *Murillo.* **Map 6 E4.** @ murillo@nexo.es   €€€
Calle Lope de Rueda 7 & 9, 41004. (95 421 60 95. FAX 95 421 96 16.
A pleasant, reasonably priced hotel in an old building off Plaza Alfaro, a short walk from the cathedral. Book well ahead for Holy Week and the April Fair. The management also let apartments nearby. 🛏 📋

	AE DC MC V	57			

SANTA CRUZ: *Las Casas de la Judería.* **Map 3 D2.**   €€€€€
Callejón de las Dos Hermanas 7, 41004. (95 441 51 50. W www.casasypalacios.com
Less a hotel, more a labyrinth of suites, some with a private terrace. This is a peaceful place to rest, away from the city rush. 🛏 📋 TV

	AE DC MC V	95	▣		▣

SANTA CRUZ: *Hotel Virgen de los Reyes.* **Map 3 C2.**   €€€€€
Calle Luis Montoto 129–131, 41007. (95 457 66 10. W www.andalunet.com/virgenreyes
This modern hotel is located in the liveliest area of Seville and good views of city life can be had from the balconies of the bedrooms. Quiet patio with traditional Seville tiling. 🛏 📋 TV 🍴

	AE DC MC V	80	▣		

FURTHER AFIELD (LA MACARENA): *Patio de la Cartuja.* **Map 1 C4.**   €€€
Calle Lumbreras 8 & 10, 41002. (95 490 02 00. FAX 95 490 20 56.
A group of old houses has been converted into this hotel in La Macarena. It offers apartments of excellent quality at very competitive prices and a tranquil atmosphere in a busy city. 🛏 📋 TV

	AE MC V	57	▣		▣

FURTHER AFIELD (LA MACARENA): *Baco.* **Map 2 E5.**   €€€€
Plaza Ponce de León 15, 41003. (95 456 50 50. FAX 95 456 36 54.
An old house has been transformed into a modern hotel in Sevillian style. A spiral staircase ascends from reception; the quieter back bedrooms overlook patios with tiles and potted plants. 🛏 📋 TV

	AE DC MC V	25			

FURTHER AFIELD (LA MACARENA): *San Gil.* **Map 2 D4.**   €€€€
Calle Parras 28, 41002. (95 490 68 11. FAX 95 490 69 39. @ hsangil@arrakis.es
This beautiful mansion, built in the early 20th-century, is classed as one of Seville's 100 most important buildings. It has spacious, beautifully furnished rooms and a peaceful garden with palm trees and an old cypress. 🛏 📋 TV &

	AE DC MC V	60	▣	●	▣

FURTHER AFIELD (PARQUE MARÍA LUISA): *Alfonso XIII.* **Map 3** C3. €€€€€
Calle San Fernando 2, 41004. 【 95 491 70 00. ☑ www.westin.com
Elegance and appropriately formal service are assured in Seville's grand
hotel, built in Neo-Mudéjar style. Inside there are chandeliers and statuary;
outdoors there are palm trees. 🛏 ▤ TV ♿
AE DC MC V — 146

FURTHER AFIELD (SOUTH): *Ciudad de Sevilla.* **Map 4** D5. €€€€€
Avenida Manuel Siurot 25, 41013. 【 95 423 05 05. ☑ www.ac-hoteles.com
Behind its old façade, this hotel, away from the centre, is modern. It has
large, light rooms and a rooftop swimming pool. 🛏 ▤ TV ♿
AE DC MC V — 94

ANDALUSIA

ALCALÁ DE GUADAIRA: *Hotel Oromana.* ☑ www.hoteloromana.com €€€
Avenida de Portugal, 41500 (Sevilla). 【 & FAX 95 568 64 00.
On the edge of town, within easy reach of Seville, the Oromana is shaded
by pines. It is run by a team of women who are happy to cater for families
with children and for the disabled. 🛏 ▤ TV
MC V — 30

ALMERÍA: *Torreluz IV.* ☑ www.amtorreluz.com €€€€
Plaza Flores 5, 04001. 【 950 23 49 99. FAX 950 23 47 09.
A smart, city-centre hotel with a spiral staircase and a rooftop pool. The
Torreluzs II and III, sister hotels nearby, are cheaper. 🛏 ▤ TV ♿
AE DC MC V — 102

ARACENA: *Sierra de Aracena.* @ hotelsierradearacena@wanadoo.es €
Gran Vía 21, 21200 (Huelva). 【 959 12 61 75. FAX 959 12 62 18.
This quiet hotel is in the centre of the attractive town of Aracena. The
rooms at the back overlook the town's castle. 🛏 ▤ TV ♿
AE DC MC V — 42

ARACENA: *Finca Buen Vino.* ☑ www.buenvino.com €€€€€
Los Marines, 21293 (Huelva). 【 959 12 40 34. FAX 959 50 10 29.
A stylish modern villa on a hilltop at the heart of a wooded nature reserve.
This is a private home open to guests and it has an informal atmosphere.
Cordon bleu cooking is served by candlelight. 🛏
AE DC — 4

ARCOS DE LA FRONTERA: *Cortijo Faín.* €€€
Carretera de Algar km 3, 11630 (Cádiz). 【 & FAX 956 23 13 96.
This 17th-century farmhouse stands majestically on an estate of olive trees.
The rooms are furnished with antiques and some have old brass bedsteads.
A swimming pool is hidden among the olive trees. 🛏 ▤
AE DC MC V — 11

ARCOS DE LA FRONTERA: *Parador de Arcos de la Frontera.* €€€€
Plaza del Cabildo, 11630 (Cádiz). 【 956 70 05 00. ☑ www.parador.es
A fine mansion, formerly a magistrate's house, on the main square. Its
terrace overhangs a precipice and has spectacular views. 🛏 ▤ TV
AE DC MC V — 24

AYAMONTE: *Riu Canela.* ☑ www.riu-hotels.com €€€€€
Playa de Isla Canela, 21470 (Huelva). 【 959 47 71 24. FAX 959 47 71 70.
With its three pools, one for children, the beachside Riu Palace is more a
summer holiday centre than a hotel. The hotel is on Isla Canela near the
Portuguese border, close to the Algarve. 🛏 ▤ TV ♿
AE DC MC V — 349

BAEZA: *Hospedería Fuentenueva.* @ fuentenueva@mx4.redeste.es €€
Paseo Arca del Agua s/n, 23440 (Jaén). 【 953 74 31 00. FAX 953 74 32 00.
This Renaissance town has an unusual hotel in a converted women's
prison, run by a cooperative of five young hoteliers. 🛏 ▤ TV
AE DC MC V — 12

BENAOJÁN: *Molino del Santo.* ☑ www.andalucia.com/molino €€€
Calle Barriada Estación s/n, 29370 (Málaga). 【 95 216 71 51. FAX 95 216 73 27.
This converted water mill in the hills near Ronda is a relaxing sun trap with
an attractive swimming pool. The British owners are a mine of tourist
information. They keep mountain bikes for guests to rent. 🛏
AE DC MC V — 17

BUBIÓN: *Villa Turística de Bubión.* ☑ www.ctv.es/alpujarr €€€
Calle Barrio Alto, 18412 (Granada). 【 958 76 31 11. FAX 958 76 31 36.
This mini-village is in the distinct building style of the Alpujarras, with flat
roofs and tall chimneys. You can cook in your kitchen or eat in the
informal restaurant. Horse riding and hikes are arranged. 🛏 ▤ ♿
AE DC MC V — 43

CARMONA: *Parador de Carmona.* ☑ www.parador.es €€€€
Calle Alcázar, 41410 (Sevilla). 【 95 414 10 10. FAX 95 414 17 12.
This clifftop parador was built as a fortress by the Moors and became the
palace of the Christian King, Pedro the Cruel. 🛏 ▤ TV ♿
AE DC MC V — 63

Price categories for a standard double room per night, with tax, breakfast and service included: € under 50 euros €€ 50–75 euros €€€ 75–100 euros €€€€ 100–125 euros €€€€€ over 125 euros	**CREDIT CARDS** Indicates which credit cards are accepted: *AE* American Express; *DC* Diners Club; *MC* Master Card/Access; *V* Visa **PARKING** Parking provided by the hotel in a private car park or a private garage on the hotel site or very close by. Some hotels charge for use of private parking facilities. **SWIMMING POOL** Hotel pool outdoors unless otherwise stated. **GARDEN** Hotel with garden, courtyard or terrace, often providing tables for eating outdoors.	CREDIT CARDS / NUMBER OF ROOMS / PRIVATE PARKING / SWIMMING POOL / GARDEN OR TERRACE

Hotel	Credit Cards	Number of Rooms	Private Parking	Swimming Pool	Garden or Terrace
CARMONA: *Casa de Carmona*. W www.casadecarmona.com €€€€€ Plaza de Lasso 1, 41410 (Sevilla). 📞 95 414 33 00. FAX 95 419 01 89. This 16th-century converted palace, decorated in a blend of modern and period styles, has featured in design magazines. Historic Carmona is a good base for exploring Seville province. 🛏 📺 🔧	AE DC MC V	32	■	●	■
CASTELLAR DE LA FRONTERA: *Casa Convento La Almoraima*. €€€€ Finca La Almoraima, 11350 (Cádiz). 📞 956 69 30 02. W www.la-almoraima.com One of Europe's largest country estates (now in public ownership) surrounds this hotel. The house was built by the dukes of Medinaceli in the 17th century and used by them as a hunting lodge. 🛏 📺	AE DC MC V	17	■	●	■
CASTILLEJA DE LA CUESTA: *Hacienda de San Ygnacio*. €€€€ Calle Real 190, 41950 (Sevilla). 📞 95 416 04 30. FAX 95 416 14 37. @ signacio@arrakis.es A 17th-century Andalusian farmhouse built round a patio planted with palms. The dining room was once an olive oil mill. 🛏 📺	AE DC MC V	18	■	●	■
CAZALLA DE LA SIERRA: *Las Navezuelas*. @ navezuela@arrakis.es € Apartado 14, 41370 (Sevilla). 📞 95 488 47 64. FAX 95 448 45 94. The rooms in this charming, family-run farmhouse are furnished with handworked fabrics. Staying here gives visitors a rare opportunity to experience living in an authentic Andalusian *cortijo* (farmstead). 🛏	MC V	10		●	■
CAZALLA DE LA SIERRA: *Hospedería La Cartuja*. W www.skill.es/cartuja €€€ Carretera Cazalla–Constantina km 25, 41370 (Sevilla). 📞 95 488 45 16. FAX 95 488 47 07. An old monastery has been eccentrically rehabilitated by its crusading owner as a refuge for artists. The walls are hung with their paintings. 🛏 📺	AE MC V	12	■	●	■
CAZORLA: *Molino de la Farraga*. W www.molinofarraga.com €€ Apartado 1, 23470 (Jaén). 📞 & FAX 953 72 12 49. A 200-year-old mill, recently renovated, near the Plaza Santa María, is a relaxing stop. An annexe can be rented as a self-catering apartment. 🛏		7			■
CAZORLA: *Parador de Cazorla*. W www.parador.es €€€ Cazorla 23470 (Jaén). 📞 953 72 70 75. FAX 953 72 70 77. The forests and mountains of the Sierra de Cazorla, a major Andalusian nature reserve, are the superb setting for this modern parador. 🛏 📺	AE DC MC V	34	■	●	■
CÓRDOBA: *Maestre*. W www.hotelmaestre.com € Calle Romero Barros 4-6, 14003. 📞 957 47 24 10. FAX 957 47 53 95. Near the Mezquita in the centre of Córdoba, this is a simple, very economically priced hotel with basic modern amenities. 🛏 📺 🔧	AE DC MC V	26	■		■
CÓRDOBA: *Alfaros*. W www.maciahoteles.com €€€€ Calle Alfaros 18, 14001. 📞 957 49 19 20. FAX 957 49 22 10. In a busy street, but soundproofed against traffic noise, Alfaros has three attractive courtyards in Neo-Mudéjar style. 🛏 📺 🔧	AE DC MC V	133	■	●	■
CÓRDOBA: *Occidental*. W www.occidental-hoteles.com €€€€ Calle Poeta Alonso Bonilla 7, 14012. 📞 957 76 74 76. FAX 957 40 04 39. This is a modern hotel in a residential suburb in the north of the city, with coffered ceilings and smart brass lanterns. 🛏 📺 🔧	AE DC MC V	153	■	●	■
DÚRCAL: *Cortijo la Solana*. € La Solana Alta 3, Apartado de Correos 43, 18650 (Granada). 📞 & FAX 958 78 05 75. A country house with extensive grounds in a little-known valley in the mountains of Granada, offering bed and breakfast only.		3			■
GIBRALTAR: *The Rock*. W www.rockhotelgibraltar.com €€€€€ 3 Europa Road. 📞 956 77 30 00. FAX 956 77 35 13. Trading on old-fashioned colonial style and service, Gibraltar's first five-star hotel is elevated above the town and harbour and has views across the bay. Many celebrities have stayed here. 🛏 📺	AE DC MC V	104	■	●	■

GRANADA: *Hotel Navas.* €€€
C/ Navas 22–24, 18009. **(** 958 22 59 59. **FAX** 958 22 75 23.
The Hotel Navas is set within a pedestrian area of Granada, along a street which is thronging with tapas bars. A very modern hotel, the building having been constructed in 1993. 🛏 📖 📺 🕭

| | AE DC MC V | 40 | | | |

GRANADA: *América.* @ hamerica@moebius.es €€€€
Calle Real de la Alhambra 53, 18009. **(** 958 22 74 71. **FAX** 958 22 74 70.
This cosy, affordable, family-run hotel beside the Alhambra is on the same street as Granada's parador. In summer, home cooking is served in a plant-filled courtyard. Always book well in advance. ● *Dec–Feb.* 🛏 📖

| | AE DC MC V | 17 | | | ▣ |

GRANADA: *Alhambra Palace.* Ⓦ www.h-alhambrapalace.com €€€€€
Calle Peña Partida 2 & 4, 18009. **(** 958 22 14 68. **FAX** 958 22 64 04.
A gloriously kitsch mock-Moorish building on the same hill as the Alhambra. A superb terrace has views of old Granada. 🛏 📖 📺 🕭

| | AE DC MC V | 126 | ▣ | | ▣ |

GRANADA: *Parador de Granada.* Ⓦ www.parador.es €€€€€
Calle Real de la Alhambra, 18009. **(** 958 22 14 40. **FAX** 958 22 22 64.
This elegant parador in the gardens of the Alhambra was a convent. For a room in such a spot you must book months ahead. 🛏 📖 📺 🕭

| | AE DC MC V | 36 | ▣ | | ▣ |

JAÉN: *Parador de Jaén.* Ⓦ www.parador.es €€€€
Carretera Sta Catalina, 23001. **(** 953 23 00 00. **FAX** 953 23 09 30.
From this castle-parador above Jaén there are spectacular views of the Sierra Morena. With its dimly lit corridors, small arched windows, huge doors and suits of armour, it retains a medieval atmosphere. 🛏 📖 📺

| | AE DC MC V | 45 | | ● | ▣ |

LOJA: *La Bobadilla.* Ⓦ www.la-bobadilla.com €€€€€
Finca La Bobadilla, 18300 (Granada). **(** 958 32 18 61. **FAX** 958 32 18 10.
Looking rather like a labyrinthine Andalusian village, surrounded by its own estate, this is one of the most luxurious hotels in Europe. Guests can take part in a wide range of sports and activities. 🛏 📖 📺

| | AE DC MC V | 62 | | ● | ▣ |

MÁLAGA: *Don Curro.* Ⓦ www.infonegocio.com/doncurro €€€
Calle Sancha de Lara 7, 29015. **(** 95 222 72 00. **FAX** 95 221 59 46.
The exterior may not be attractive, but inside, this hotel is charming and comfortable, with a friendly, welcoming atmosphere. 🛏 📖 📺

| | AE DC MC V | 118 | ▣ | | |

MARBELLA: *El Fuerte.* Ⓦ www.fuertehoteles.com €€€€€
Avenida El Fuerte, 29600 (Málaga). **(** 95 286 15 00. **FAX** 95 282 44 11.
El Fuerte was the first hotel built in Marbella and it is still one of the best. Some rooms have mountain views and others look out to sea. The hotel has a heated, glassed-in pool and a health centre. 🛏 📖 📺

| | AE DC MC V | 263 | ▣ | ● | ▣ |

MARBELLA: *Marbella Club Hotel.* Ⓦ www.marbellaclub.com €€€€€
Blvr Príncipe von Hohenlohe, 29600 (Málaga). **(** 95 282 22 11. **FAX** 95 282 98 84.
An exclusive, low-level, beachside complex between Marbella and Puerto Banús. There are two pools, one indoors, and subtropical gardens with a choice of places to eat and relax. 🛏 📖 📺

| | AE DC MC V | 137 | ▣ | ● | ▣ |

MAZAGÓN: *Parador de Mazagón.* Ⓦ www.parador.es €€€€€
San Juan del Pto a Matalascañas km 30, 21130. **(** 959 53 63 00. **FAX** 959 53 62 28.
A modern parador on the Huelva coast, between a large, sandy beach and a pine forest. It is in a good location for visiting the wildlife reserve of Doñana National Park nearby. 🛏 📖 📺 🕭

| | AE DC MC V | 43 | ▣ | ● | ▣ |

MIJAS: *Club Puerta del Sol.* Ⓦ www.clubpuertodelsol.galeon.com €€€
Ctra Fuengirola–Mijas km 4, 29650 (Málaga). **(** 95 248 64 00. **FAX** 95 248 54 62.
An elegant, low, U-shaped hotel on a foothill of the Sierra de Mijas. From its gardens, pool and terraces there is an impressive view of Fuengirola and the coast. It has tennis courts and a gym. 🛏 📖 📺 🕭

| | AE DC MC V | 130 | ▣ | ● | ▣ |

MOJÁCAR: *Parador de Mojácar.* Ⓦ www.parador.es €€€€
Avda Mediterraneo, 04638 (Almería). **(** 950 47 82 50. **FAX** 950 47 81 83.
The architecture of this purpose-built parador on the dry, sunny coast of Almería echoes that of the dazzling white cube houses in nearby Mojácar. There are facilities for water sports. 🛏 📖 📺

| | AE DC MC V | 98 | ▣ | ● | ▣ |

NERJA: *Hostal Avalón.* €€
Calle Punta Lara, 29780 (Málaga). **(** & **FAX** 95 252 06 98.
This small hotel above the coast road just outside Nerja has a friendly atmosphere, pleasant, clean bedrooms – all but one with views of the sea – and an informal lounge with comfortable sofas. 🛏

| | MC V | 8 | | ● | ▣ |

	CREDIT CARDS	NUMBER OF ROOMS	PRIVATE PARKING	SWIMMING POOL	GARDEN OR TERRACE

Price categories for a standard double room per night, with tax, breakfast and service included:

€ under 50 euros
€€ 50–75 euros
€€€ 75–100 euros
€€€€ 100–125 euros
€€€€€ over 125 euros

CREDIT CARDS
Indicates which credit cards are accepted: *AE* American Express; *DC* Diners Club; *MC* Master Card/Access; *V* Visa
PARKING
Parking provided by the hotel in a private car park or a private garage on the hotel site or very close by. Some hotels charge for use of private parking facilities.
SWIMMING POOL
Hotel pool outdoors unless otherwise stated.
GARDEN
Hotel with garden, courtyard or terrace, often providing tables for eating outdoors.

OJÉN: *Refugio de Juanar.* @ juanar@spde.es €€€
Sierra Blanca, 29610 (Málaga). 95 288 10 00. FAX 95 288 10 01.
A hunting lodge has been converted into this tranquil, cosy hotel. It is in the Sierras de Ojén, the wooded hills behind Marbella, a region of wildlife interest. The restaurant specializes in regional gastronomy.
AE DC MC V — 26 — ● —

ORGIVA: *Taray.* www.rusticblue.com/za119htm €€€
Ctra Tablate–Albuñol km 18.5, 18000 (Granada). 958 78 45 25. FAX 958 78 45 31.
A hotel in a garden of lawns and olive and orange trees. The bedrooms are large enough to be small apartments. The hotel is in good walking country and horse riding is organized.
AE DC MC V — 27 — ● —

PALMA DEL RÍO: *Hospedería de San Francisco.* www.lascasas.zoom.es €€€
Avenida Pío XII 35, 14700 (Córdoba). & FAX 957 71 01 83.
Built in the 15th century as a Franciscan monastery, this hotel has some bedrooms in former monks' cells. They have hand-painted basins and bedcovers woven by nuns. Meals are served in the cloister.
MC V — 21 — — —

PECHINA: *Balneario de Sierra Albamilla.* www.gratisweb.com/sierraalhamilla €€
Pechina, 04259 (Almería). 950 31 74 13. FAX 950 16 02 57.
This spa hotel in peaceful hills has been restored to its 18th-century glory. There are Roman baths in the basement and, nearby, a naturally heated swimming pool.
AE DC MC V — 18 — ● —

PINOS GENIL: *La Bella María.* €€€
Ctra Sierra Nevada km 8.2, 18191 (Granada). 958 48 87 46. FAX 958 48 87 26.
A modern, family-run hotel just outside Granada, which is well placed for visiting the city or the Sierra Nevada. The rooms are comfortable and airy. Some are large enough for a family of four.
AE DC MC V — 24 — — —

PRADO DEL REY: *Cortijo Huerta Dorotea.* €€
Ctra Vilamartín–Ubrique km 11, 11660 (Cádiz). 956 72 42 91. FAX 956 72 42 89.
On a hill surrounded by olive trees, near the white town of Prado del Rey, is this new hotel, run by a cooperative. Guests can choose rooms or log cabins. Riding is one leisure activity available.
AE MC V — 25 — ● —

EL PUERTO DE SANTA MARÍA: *Monasterio San Miguel.* €€€€€
Calle Larga 27, 11500 (Cádiz). 956 54 04 40. www.jale.com/monasterio
An elegant, rather luxurious hotel, well placed for visits to Cádiz and Jerez de la Frontera. It has a faintly monastic atmosphere, recalling the former function of this Baroque building.
AE DC MC V — 150 — ● —

EL ROCÍO: *Hotel Toruño.* @ h.toruño@autovia.com €€
Plaza Acebuchal 22, 21750 (Huelva). 959 44 23 23. FAX 959 44 23 38.
Occupying a house designed in typical Andalucian style, this modern hotel has a traditional patio surrounded by arches.
AE DC MC V — 30 — — —

RONDA: *Husa Reina Victoria.* www.husa.es €€€€
Calle Jerez 25, 29400 (Málaga). 95 287 12 40. FAX 95 287 10 75.
The Reina Victoria, perched on a cliff edge, has spectacular views. It was Ronda's grand hotel until the parador was built.
AE DC MC V — 90 — ● —

RONDA: *Parador de Ronda.* www.parador.es €€€€€
Plaza España, 29400 (Málaga). 95 287 75 00. FAX 95 287 81 88.
Edging up to Ronda's famous cliff, yet close to the town centre, this modern, purpose-built parador has stunning views over the gorge, especially from the top-floor suites.
AE DC MC V — 78 — ● —

SAN JOSÉ: *Cortijo los Pinos de Alborani* €€€
Cortijo los Pinos de Alborani, 04550 (Almería). 950 35 31 88. FAX 950 35 37 07.
A brand new hotel located in a traditional Andalusian cortijo, which combines the lush greenery of Parque Natural de Sierra Nevada and the sparse landscape of the Almeria desert.
AE DC MC V — 8 — — —

SANLÚCAR DE BARRAMEDA: *Los Helechos.* €€
Plaza Madre de Dios 9, 11540 (Cádiz). ◖ 956 36 13 49. ☎ 956 36 96 50.
Decorated with tiles and pot plants, Los Helechos is a stylish, relaxing
hideaway. Visits to Doñana National Park are arranged. 🛏 ▤ TV
AE DC MC V — 56

SANLÚCAR LA MAYOR: *Hacienda de Benazuza.* @ rvasbenazuza@jet.es €€€€€
Virgen de las Nieves, 41800 (Sevilla). ◖ 95 570 33 44. ☎ 95 570 34 10.
Parts of this old hilltop house are said to be 1,000 years old. It is now a
luxury hotel, furnished in traditional Andalusian style. 🛏 ▤ TV 🔧
AE DC MC V — 44

SAN ROQUE: *Hotel Casa Señorial la Solana.* €€€
Ctra Cádiz–Málaga N340, 11360 (Cádiz). ◖ & ☎ 956 78 02 36.
A useful stop en route to or from the Tangier ferry, this is a pleasant small
hotel in a 200-year-old house set back from the motorway in its own small
estate. The 12 rooms and 6 suites are all different. 🛏 TV
AE DC MC V — 18

SIERRA NEVADA: *Santa Cruz.* @ santacruz@eh.etursa.es €€€
Ctra Sierra Nevada, 18196 (Granada). ◖ 958 48 48 00. ☎ 958 48 48 06.
From the windows and balconies of this high-altitude hotel guests can
contemplate the snowy peaks of the lovely Sierra Nevada. Open fires make
the modern building cosy in winter. 🛏 TV
AE DC MC V — 91

TARIFA: *Hurricane.* ◫ www.hotelhurricane.com €€€€
Carretera N340, 11380 (Cádiz). ◖ 956 68 49 19. ☎ 956 68 03 29.
Tarifa is a mecca for windsurfers and the Hurricane is a temple to the sport
and to physical fitness. It is an imaginative, open-plan building in
subtropical gardens. There are views across the sea to Africa. 🛏
AE DC MC V — 33

TORREMOLINOS: *Hotel Miami.* €€€
Calle Aladino 14, 29620 (Málaga). ◖ 95 238 52 55.
The Miami, between Torremolinos and Málaga, gives welcome respite from
the Costa del Sol's modern developments. It has whitewashed walls, tiles,
iron grilles, balconies and plant pots. 🛏
AE MC V — 26

TREVÉLEZ: *Mesón La Fragua.* €
Calle San Antonio 4, 18417 (Granada). ◖ 958 85 86 26. ☎ 958 85 86 14.
This *mesón* (inn) is in what claims to be the highest village in Spain. There
are great views of the valley from the rooftop terrace. The rooms vary
considerably in size and character. 🛏 TV
MC V — 14

TURRE: *El Nacimiento.* €
Cortijo El Nacimiento, 04639 (Almería). ◖ 950 52 80 90.
This remote and lovely old house is run by a friendly couple. They offer
bed and breakfast, serving organic produce from their farm. 🛏
5

TURRE: *Finca Listonero.* €€€
Cortijo Grande, 04639 (Almería). ◖ & ☎ 950 47 90 94. 94.
This restored farmhouse is in the country near Mojácar. The breakfasts are
generous; home-grown vegetables are served at meals. 🛏 ▤ 🔧
V — 5

ÚBEDA: *Palacio de La Rambla.* €€€
Plaza del Marqués 1, 23400 (Jaén). ◖ 953 75 01 96. ☎ 953 75 02 67.
A 17th-century mansion run by its aristocratic owner as a small, central,
exclusive hotel. The rooms, furnished with heirlooms, enclose a patio
thought to be by the Renaissance architect, Vandelvira. 🛏 ▤ TV 🔧
AE DC MC V — 8

ÚBEDA: *Parador de Úbeda.* ◫ www.@parador.es €€€
Plaza Vázquez de Molina 1, 23400 (Jaén). ◖ 953 75 03 45. ☎ 953 75 12 59.
Presiding over Úbeda's monumental central square, this parador is in a
former 16th-century aristocratic residence. Blue and white tiles adorn the
façade and the house surrounds a pretty courtyard. 🛏 ▤ TV
AE DC MC V — 36

ZUHEROS: *Zuhayra.* €
Calle Mirador 10, 14870 (Córdoba). ◖ 957 69 46 93. ☎ 957 69 47 02.
The principal charm of this simple hotel is its location in a white town on
the edge of a range of high hills. The building imitates the style of the
noble mansion it replaced. Silence reigns at night. 🛏 ▤ TV 🔧
AE DC MC V — 18

THE BALEARIC ISLANDS

FORMENTERA, ES PUJOLS: *Sa Volta.* €€€
Calle Miramar 94, 07871. ◖ 971 32 81 25. ☎ 971 32 82 28.
An inexpensive, family-run hotel in a modern block, three floors high, within
walking distance of the beach in one of Formentera's main resorts. 🛏 TV
AE DC MC V — 18

Price categories for a standard double room per night, with tax, breakfast and service included:

€   under 50 euros
€€   50–75 euros
€€€   75–100 euros
€€€€   100–125 euros
€€€€€   over 125 euros

CREDIT CARDS
Indicates which credit cards are accepted: *AE* American Express; *DC* Diners Club; *MC* Master Card/Access; *V* Visa

PARKING
Parking provided by the hotel in a private car park or a private garage on the hotel site or very close by. Some hotels charge for use of private parking facilities.

SWIMMING POOL
Hotel pool outdoors unless otherwise stated.

GARDEN
Hotel with garden, courtyard or terrace, often providing tables for eating outdoors.

	CREDIT CARDS	NUMBER OF ROOMS	PRIVATE PARKING	SWIMMING POOL	GARDEN OR TERRACE
IBIZA (EIVISSA), IBIZA TOWN: *Hostal La Marina.* @ hmarina@eresmas.com €€ Calle Barcelona 7, 07800. ☎ 971 31 01 72. FAX 971 31 48 94. An old hotel, modernized inside but with much of its 1862 decoration. Airy front bedrooms overlook the harbour. Ù	AE MC V	24			■
IBIZA (EIVISSA), IBIZA TOWN: *El Palacio.* €€€€€ Calle de la Conquista 2, 07800. ☎ 971 30 14 78. FAX 971 39 15 81. A themed hotel in the old town, with Marilyn Monroe penthouse suites and public rooms hung with movie memorabilia. ● *Nov–Apr.* 🅿 ▤ TV	AE DC MC V	7			■
IBIZA (EIVISSA), SANT ANTONI: *Pikes.* @ pikes@ctv.es €€€€€ Camino Sa Vorera, 07820. § 971 34 22 22. ` 971 34 23 12. A chic hotel in a tastefully restored mansion on a hill planted with pines. Celebrities sometimes stay here. 🅿 ▤	AE DC MC V	20	■	●	
IBIZA (EIVISSA), SANT MIQUEL: *Hacienda Na Xamena.* €€€€€ Apto 423, Urb Na Xamena, 07815. ☎ 971 33 45 00. FAX 971 33 46 06. There are stunning views from the bedrooms of this modern clifftop hotel built above a pretty, rocky cove, and from the elegant sun terrace round the swimming pool. ● *Nov–Apr.* 🅿 ▤ TV	AE DC MC V	59	■	●	
IBIZA (EIVISSA), SANTA EULÀRIA D'ES RIU: *Les Terrasses.* €€€€€ Apto 1235, Carretera de Santa Eulària, 07600 ☎ 971 33 26 43. FAX 971 33 89 78. A country house decorated simply but beautifully in Ibizan style, painted white, blue and yellow. Each room is individually decorated. There are quiet corners inside and out to sit and read or relax. ● *Nov–Jan.* 🅿 ▤	MC V	8	■	●	■
MALLORCA, ANDRATX: *Villa Italia.* €€€€€ Camino Sant Carles 13, Port d'Andratx, 07157. ☎ 971 67 40 11. FAX 971 67 33 50. A pink, Florentine-style villa built in the 1920s by an eccentric Italian millionaire for his lover. Inside there are stucco ceilings, marble floors and columns with Roman capitals. ● *mid-Nov–mid-Feb.* 🅿 ▤ TV	AE MC V	16		●	■
MALLORCA, BANYALBUFAR: *Sa Baronía.* €€ Calle Sa Baronia 16, 07191. ☎ & FAX 971 61 81 46. A family-run hotel built as a modern extension to a 17th-century baronial tower. It is in a small village on the island's unspoilt northwest coast. All the bedrooms have terraces with sea views. ● *Nov–Apr.* 🅿	V	39	■		■
MALLORCA, BINISSALEM: *Scott's Hotel.* W www.scottshotel.com €€€€€ Plaza de la Inglesia 12, 07350. ☎ 971 87 01 00. FAX 971 87 02 67. A meticulously restored 18th-century townhouse, whose comforts include handmade beds, a Jacuzzi, library, writing room, bar, and evening snacks. 🅿 ▤	MC V	17	■		■
MALLORCA, DEIÀ: *La Residencia.* @ reservas@hotel-lasresidencia.com €€€€€ Finca Son Canals, 07179. ☎ 971 63 90 11. FAX 971 63 93 70. Two magnificently restored, 16th-century manors on the outskirts of Deià have been made into an elegant hotel. Most bedrooms have four-poster beds and all have traditional Spanish furniture. 🅿 ▤	AE DC MC V	63	■	●	■
MALLORCA, LLUC: *Santuari de Lluc.* @ info@lluc.net € Santuari de Lluc, 07315. ☎ 971 87 15 25. FAX 971 51 70 96. The Santuari de Lluc, high in the Tramuntana mountains, is accessible by car (and by bus in summer). The simple bedrooms are in the monastery buildings. 🅿 ♿	MC V	89	■		■
MALLORCA, PALMA DE MALLORCA: *Born.* @ hotel-born@hotmail.com €€€ Calle Sant Jaume 3, 07012. ☎ 971 71 29 42. FAX 971 71 86 18. The Marquis of Ferrandell's town mansion, built in the 16th century and restored in the 18th, makes a splendid hotel. It has a typical Mallorcan courtyard with palms and a grand staircase. 🅿 ▤ TV	AE DC MC V	30			■

MALLORCA, POLLENÇA: *Illa d'Or.* W www.fehm.es €€€
Paseo de Colón 265, 07470. (971 86 51 00. FAX 971 86 42 13.
Built in the 1930s for elite northern Europeans to summer on the island, the
hotel retains its original furniture and atmosphere. Facilities include a
sauna, a jacuzzi and tennis courts. 🔒 ▤ TV

| | AE DC V | 120 | | | |

MALLORCA, POLLENÇA: *Formentor.* W www.fehm.es €€€€€
Playa de Formentor, 07470. (971 89 91 00. FAX 971 86 42 13.
The visitors' book of this luxury hotel in a beautiful spot on the island's
northwest tip is signed by writers, opera singers, film stars, and the Dalai
Lama. There is a health complex. ● *Oct–Apr.* 🔒 ▤ TV

| | AE DC MC V | 127 | | | |

MALLORCA, RANDA: *Es Recó de Randa.* W www.fehm.es €€€€
Font 13, 07629. (971 66 09 97. FAX 971 66 25 58.
A restaurant-with-rooms in an old stone house in a quiet village at the foot
of the Puig de Randa mountain. There are views of the village and the
mountains from some of the bedroom windows. 🔒 ▤ TV

| | AE MC V | 14 | | | |

MALLORCA, SES SALINES: *Es Turó.* W www.globalred.com €€€€
Ses Salines, 07640. (971 64 95 31. FAX 971 64 95 48.
Rural calm, tasteful comfort and timeless Mallorcan life are combined in this
hotel, converted from an old farmhouse. The hotel contains a small
museum of local life and is surrounded by olive and almond orchards.
● *Dec–Feb.* 🔒 TV 🏊

| | DC MC V | 12 | | | |

MALLORCA, SÓLLER: *Ca N'Aí.* W www.canai.com €€€€€
Camí de Son Salas 501, 07100. (971 63 24 94. FAX 971 63 18 99.
This hotel has been converted from an old Mallorcan house built into the
side of Sóller valley and is covered with orange and palm trees. Inside,
the decor is refined. The service has a personal touch and the cooking is
excellent. ● *Nov–Feb.* 🔒 ▤

| | AE DC MC V | 13 | | | |

MALLORCA, VALLDEMOSSA: *Vistamar.* @ info@vistamarhotel.es €€€€€
Ctra de Valldemossa–Andratx, 07170. (971 61 23 00. FAX 971 61 25 83.
This is a peaceful clifftop hotel situated in a villa that was built early in
the 20th century. The bedrooms are furnished with antiques and
overlook the villa's courtyard. Chopin and George Sand made the nearby
monastery famous. 🔒 ▤ TV

| | AE DC MC V | 19 | | | |

MENORCA, CIUTADELLA: *Hostal Ciutadella.* €
Calle San Eloy 10, 07760. (& FAX 971 38 34 62.
Just a few minutes' walk from the Plaça des Borne, this simple, modern
hotel offers good-value, no-frills accommodation. The rooms are plainly
furnished and spotless. Simple meals are served in the bar. 🔒

| | DC MC V | 17 | | | |

MENORCA, CIUTADELLA: *Patricia.* @ hotel@hesperia-patricia.com €€€€
Paseo San Nicolás 90–92, 07760. (971 38 55 11. FAX 971 48 11 20.
A modern, cream-coloured chain hotel with white bay windows on one of
the town's main avenues, near the harbour. 🔒 ▤ TV

| | AE DC MC V | 44 | | | |

MENORCA, MAÓ: *Del Almirante.* €€
Carretera de Es Castell, 07780. (971 36 27 00. FAX 971 36 27 04.
Built in the 18th century in classic Georgian style, this house became the
home of Admiral Lord Collingwood, a friend of Admiral Nelson. The hotel
has a new wing built round the swimming pool. ● *Nov–Apr.* 🔒 🏊

| | MC V | 36 | | | |

MENORCA, MAÓ: *Capri.* @ rtm@rtmhotels.com €€€
Calle San Esteban 8, 07703. (971 36 14 00. FAX 971 36 73 46.
This is a central hotel in a modern block, five floors high, close to shops,
the harbour and the beach. Most bedrooms have a terrace. 🔒 ▤ TV

| | AE DC MC V | 75 | | | |

MENORCA, MAÓ: *Catalonia Mirador des Port.* €€€
Calle Dalt Vilanova 1, 07701. (971 36 00 16. FAX 971 36 73 46.
This modern, comfortable hotel is located at the western end of town and
has a view across the harbour. Many bedrooms have shuttered terraces,
which are ideal for warm summer evenings. There is a chic designer bar
downstairs. 🔒 ▤ TV

| | AE DC MC V | 69 | | | |

MENORCA, MAÓ: *Port Mahón.* @ portmahon@sethotels.com €€€€
Fort de L'Eau 13, 07701. (971 36 26 00. FAX 971 35 10 50.
Housed in an attractive red and white colonial-style building, this hotel
looks over Maó harbour. Its grounds include wide terraces and a curving
swimming pool surrounded by lawns. 🔒 ▤ TV 🏊

| | AE DC MC V | 82 | | | |

THE CANARY ISLANDS

	CREDIT CARDS	NUMBER OF ROOMS	PRIVATE PARKING	SWIMMING POOL	GARDEN OR TERRACE
FUERTEVENTURA, ANTIGUA: *Barcelo Club El Castillo.* €€ Caleta de Fuste, 36610. ☎ 928 16 31 00. FAX 928 16 30 42. @ ecastillo@barcelo.com The attractive apartments in this village-style complex have direct access to a beach curving round a gentle bay, and to a central plaza of shops, cafés and restaurants. A popular location for water sports. ▦ ♿	DC MC V	384	▦	●	▦
FUERTEVENTURA, CORRALEJO: *Riu Palace Tres Islas.* €€€€€ Grandes Playas, 35660. ☎ 928 53 57 00. FAX 928 53 58 58. w www.riuhotels.com All the bedrooms of this spacious hotel have balconies facing the sea. There are two huge pools set among gardens. ▦ ▤ TV ♿	AE MC V	365	▦	●	▦
FUERTEVENTURA, COSTA CALMA: *Riu Fuerteventura Playa.* €€€€ Urb Cañada del Río, Poligono C1, 35627. ☎ 928 54 73 44. w www.riuhotels.com The two wings of this hotel curve round gardens and swimming pools. It is situated in a secluded spot with direct access to the beach. All the bedrooms are large, and most come with balconies overlooking the sea. ▦ ▤ TV ♿	AE DC MC V	300	▦	●	▦
LA GOMERA, PLAYA DE SANTIAGO: *Jardín Tecina.* €€€€€ Lomada de Tecina, 38811. ☎ 922 14 58 50. FAX 922 14 58 51. Its many facilities make this complex in the hills behind the Playa de Santiago virtually a self-contained resort. A cliffside lift takes guests down to the beach club. ▦ ▤ TV ♿	AE DC MC V	434	▦	●	▦
LA GOMERA, SAN SEBASTIÁN: *Parador de San Sebastián.* €€€€€ San Sebastián de La Gomera, 38800. ☎ 922 87 11 00. w www.parador.es On a clifftop above La Gomera's main town and port, this parador is in traditional style, with pitched ceilings. The bedrooms have dark wood fittings and tiled bathrooms. There are tropical gardens. ▦ ▤ TV	AE DC MC V	58	▦	●	▦
GRAN CANARIA, AGAETE: *Princesa Guayarmina.* €€ Los Berrazales, 35480. ☎ 928 89 80 09. FAX 928 89 85 25. A small, plain hotel in the mountains. The simply furnished rooms overlook a tropical valley. It is excellent value and has friendly staff. ▦	AE MC V	33	▦	●	▦
GRAN CANARIA, MASPALOMAS: *Riu Maspalomas Oasis.* €€€€€ Playa de Maspalomas 3, 35106. ☎ 928 14 14 48. FAX 928 14 11 92. w www.riuhotels.com In a prime, palm-shaded spot by the dunes is this quiet, secluded hotel. The guests are stylishly accommodated in split-level suites with spacious bedrooms. The staff are efficient and pleasant. ▦ ▤ TV	AE DC MC V	342	▦	●	▦
GRAN CANARIA, LAS PALMAS: *NH Imperial Playa.* €€€€€ Calle Ferreras 1, 35008. ☎ 928 46 88 54. FAX 928 46 94 42. w www.nh-hoteles.es A smart, comfortable business hotel in a modern block overlooking Las Canteras beach, close to the port and shops. ▦ ▤ TV	AE DC MC V	142			
GRAN CANARIA, LAS PALMAS: *Santa Catalina.* €€€€€ Calle León y Castillo 227, 35005. ☎ 928 24 30 40. FAX 928 24 27 64. A long-established hotel in a large park. It is a traditional building of the Canary Islands, with carved wooden balconies and a colonial atmosphere. There is an opulent casino and a well-equipped spa centre. ▦ ▤ TV	AE DC MC V	200	▦	●	▦
GRAN CANARIA, PLAYA DEL INGLÉS: *Parque Tropical.* €€€€€ Avenida de Italia 1, 35100. ☎ 928 77 40 12. FAX 928 76 81 37. An attractive hotel in local style with comfortable rooms, direct access to the seafront and good sports facilities. Book ahead. ▦ TV	AE DC MC V	235		●	▦
GRAN CANARIA, PUERTO DE MOGÁN: *Club de Mar.* €€€ Puerto de Mogán, 35138. ☎ 928 56 50 66. FAX 928 56 54 38. w www.clubdemar.com Pretty buildings with rooms and apartments ranged round a small bay with a sandy beach, marina and scuba-diving centre. ▦ ▤ TV ♿	AE MC V	56		●	▦

EL HIERRO, FRONTERA: *Punta Grande.* €€ — 4
Las Puntas, 38911. **[** & **FAX** 922 55 90 81.
Guests are charmed to find themselves in the world's smallest hotel, as listed in *The Guinness Book of Records.*

EL HIERRO, VALVERDE: *Parador El Hierro.* W www.parador.es €€€€ — AE DC MC V — 47
Valverde, 38910. **[** 922 55 80 36. **FAX** 922 55 80 86.
Black cliffs are the backdrop for this modern, pantiled hotel on an isolated beach. A good base for a walking holiday.

LANZAROTE, ARRECIFE: *Lancelot.* @ hlancelot@terra.es €€ — AE DC MC V — 113
Avenida Mancomunidad 9, 35500. **[** 928 80 50 99. **FAX** 928 80 50 39.
This stylish new hotel is located beside a beach of soft, pale sand that has coral reefs lying just offshore. There are good restaurants in both the hotel and the town.

LANZAROTE, COSTA TEGUISE: *Meliá Salinas.* W www.solmelia.com €€€€€ — AE DC MC V — 310
Urbanización Costa Teguise, 35509. **[** 928 59 00 40. **FAX** 928 59 03 90.
A vast atrium with central water gardens and ornamental plants is the focus of this modern hotel in the northern area of Costa Teguise. An art museum highlights the island's heritage.

LANZAROTE, PUERTO DEL CARMEN: *Los Fariones.* €€€€ — AE DC MC V — 247
Calle Roque del Este 1, 35510. **[** 928 51 01 75. **FAX** 928 51 02 02. W www.infolanz.es
A secluded hotel on an attractive beach. It is relaxing and comfortable, with spacious bedrooms and a good range of facilities.

LANZAROTE, YAIZA: *Lanzarote Princess.* @ lanpr@h10.es €€€ — AE DC MC V — 410
Calle Maciot, Playa Blanca 35570. **[** 928 51 71 08. **FAX** 928 51 70 11.
A resort hotel that is popular with families. It is cool and light, with split-level areas ornamented with water gardens. There is a large swimming pool.

LA PALMA, BARLOVENTO: *La Palma Romántica.* €€€ — MC V — 41
Calle Las Llanadas, 38726. **[** 922 18 62 21. W www.hotellapalmaromantica.com
Nestling into a hillside high above the sea is this light, airy hotel with spacious rooms. It has an indoor pool, a sauna and a solarium.

TENERIFE, ARONA: *Estefanía.* @ info@hotel-estefania.com €€€€€ — AE DC MC V — 35
Carretera de Arona, 38660. **[** 922 72 93 22. **FAX** 922 75 95 33.
A hotel in the hills behind the Playa de las Américas, with luxurious bedrooms and a cool, stylish decor.

TENERIFE, LA OROTAVA: *Parador de Cañadas del Teide.* €€€€ — AE DC MC V — 37
Apto de Correos 15, Cañadas del Teide, 38300. **[** 922 38 64 15. W www.parador.es
There are views of Mount Teide from this modern parador, which looks like an Alpine chalet. It is inside the national park.

TENERIFE, PLAYA DE LAS AMÉRICAS: *Jardín Tropical.* €€€€€ — AE DC MC V — 432
Urbanización San Eugenio, 38660. **[** 922 74 60 00. **FAX** 922 74 60 60.
Situated right in the heart of the resort, with access to the seafront, this is an imaginative hotel with turrets and tiled patios. There are seven function rooms.

TENERIFE, PUERTO DE LA CRUZ: *Monopol.* @ monopol@interbook.net €€€€ — AE DC MC V — 94
Calle Quintana 15, 38400. **[** 922 38 46 11. **FAX** 922 37 03 10.
An old-style, family-run hotel with a plant-filled patio with wooden balustrades. The bedrooms are modern and spacious.

TENERIFE, PUERTO DE LA CRUZ: *Botánico.* €€€€€ — AE DC MC V — 252
Calle Richard J Yeoward, 38400. **[** 922 38 14 00. W www.hotelbotanico.com
The sea is some distance away from this restful hotel near the Botanic Gardens, but it offers excellent leisure facilities, including golf, tennis, a sauna, a jacuzzi and a gymnasium.

TENERIFE, SANTA CRUZ DE TENERIFE: *Náutico.* @ nautico@a-caledonia.com €€€ — AE DC MC V — 40
C/ Profesor Peraza de Ayala 13, 38001. **[** 922 24 70 66. **FAX** 922 24 72 76.
A small, modern block behind the port, close to a bus stop for Las Teresitas beach. The small café serves a good Spanish breakfast.

TENERIFE, VILAFLOR: *Alta Montaña.* € — AE DC MC V — 10
Calle Morro del Cano 1, 38613. **[** 922 70 90 00. **FAX** 922 70 92 93.
A small, homely hotel with spectacular views. It is run by a friendly Belgian couple, who serve organic food in their restaurant.

RESTAURANTS AND BARS

ONE OF THE JOYS of eating out in Spain is the sheer sociability of the Spanish. Family and friends, often with children in tow, can be seen eating out from early in the day until after midnight.

Spanish food has a regional bias. Traditional restaurants originated as taverns and tapas bars serving dishes based on local produce. Spain also has

Wall tile advertising a Barcelona restaurant

its fair share of top-quality gourmet restaurants, notably in the Basque Country.

The restaurants listed on pages 578–609 have been selected for their food and conviviality. Pages 574–7 illustrate some of the best tapas and drinks; and each of the book's five regional sections includes features on the area's unique food and wines.

Bodegas are bars that specialize in wines and do not serve food

RESTAURANTS AND BARS

THE CHEAPEST and quickest places to eat are the bars and cafés that serve tapas. Some bars, however, especially *pubs* (late-opening bars for socializing) serve no food.

Family-run *bar-restaurantes*, *ventas*, *posadas*, *mesones* and *fondas* – all old words for the different types of inn – serve inexpensive, sit-down meals. *Chiringuitos* are beachside bars. They open only during the summer season.

Spain's top restaurants tend to be clustered in the Basque Country, Galicia, Barcelona, Catalonia and Madrid.

Most restaurants close one day a week, some for lunch or dinner only, and most for an annual holiday. They also close on some public holidays. The main closing times of the restaurants on pages 578–609 are listed at the end of each entry. Always check these opening times, however, when phoning to book a table.

EATING HOURS IN SPAIN

THE SPANISH often have two breakfasts *(desayunos)*. The first is a light meal of biscuits or toast with olive oil or butter and jam and *café con leche* (milky coffee). A more substantial breakfast may follow between 10 and 11am, perhaps in a café. This may consist of a savoury snack, such as a *bocadillo* (sandwich) with sausage, ham or cheese, or a thick slice of *tortilla de patatas* (potato omelette). Fruit juice, coffee or beer are the usual accompaniments.

Decoration, Barcelona bar

From about 1pm people will stop in the bars for a beer or a *copa* (glass) of wine with tapas. By 2pm those who can will have arrived home from work for *la comida* (lunch), which is the main meal of the day. Others will choose to have lunch in a restaurant.

The cafés, *salones de té* (tea rooms) and *pastelerías* (pastry shops) fill up by about 5:30 or

6pm for *la merienda* (tea) of sandwiches, pastries or cakes, with coffee, tea or juice. Snacks like *churros* (fried batter sticks) can also be bought from stalls.

By 7pm, bars are crowded with people having tapas with sherry, wine or beer. In Spain *la cena* (dinner or supper), begins at about 10pm. Restaurants sometimes begin their evening service earlier for tourists. In summer, however, Spanish families and groups of friends often do not sit down to eat until as late as midnight. At weekend lunch times, especially in summer, you may find that restaurants are filled by large and noisy family gatherings.

HOW TO DRESS

A JACKET AND TIE are rarely required, but the Spanish dress smartly, especially for city restaurants. Day dress is casual in beach resorts, but shorts are frowned on in the evenings.

The parador restaurant in Pedraza de la Sierra, Segovia *(see p595)*

Pavement tables outside a cafeteria, in Cadaqués on the Costa Brava

READING THE MENU

A SIDE FROM TAPAS, perhaps the cheapest eating options in Spanish restaurants are the fixed-price *platos combinados* (meat or fish with vegetables and, usually, chips) and the *menú del día*. A *plato combinado* is only offered by cheaper establishments. Most restaurants – but not all – offer an inexpensive, fixed-price *menú del día*, normally of three courses, but with little choice. Some gourmet restaurants offer a *menú de degustación* consisting of a choice of six or seven of the head chef's special dishes.

The Spanish word for menu is *la carta*. It starts with *sopas* (soups), *ensaladas* (salads), *entremeses* (hors d'oeuvres), *huevos y tortillas* (eggs and omelettes) and *verduras y legumbres* (vegetable dishes).

Main courses are *pescados y mariscos* (fish and shellfish) and *carnes y aves* (meat and poultry). Daily specials are chalked on a board or clipped to menus. Paella and other rice dishes may be served as the first course. A useful rule is to follow rice with meat, or start with *serrano* ham or salad and then follow with a paella.

Desserts are called *postres* in Spanish. All restaurants offer fresh fruit (the usual dessert in Spain) but otherwise the range of *postres* is generally poor. The better restaurants offer a limited choice, perhaps *natillas* (custard) and *flan* (crème caramel). Gourmet restaurants have more creative choices.

Vegetarians are rather poorly catered for in Spain, but in big cities such as Madrid there are a handful of vegetarian restaurants. Most menus have a vegetable or egg dish.

All eating places welcome children and will serve small portions if requested.

Las Torres de Ávila *(see p185)*, a distinctive Barcelona bar

WINE CHOICES

D RY FINO WINES are perfect with shellfish, *serrano* ham, olives, soups and most first courses. Main courses are commonly accompanied by wines originating from Ribera del Duero, Rioja, Navarra or Penedès. A typical bar might serve wines from Valdepeñas or the local vineyards. Oloroso wines *(see p577)* are often ordered as a *digestif*.

SMOKING

I N FINE RESTAURANTS customers are offered *puros* (cigars) with their coffee and brandy. Many people in Spain smoke and very few restaurants have non-smoking areas or tables.

PRICES AND PAYING

I F YOU ORDER from *la carta* in a restaurant, your bill can soar way above the price of the *menú del día*, especially if you order pricey items, such as fresh seafood, fish or *ibérico* ham *(see p438)*. If there is an expensive fish such as sole or swordfish on the menu at a bargain price, it may be frozen. Sea bass and other popular fish and shellfish, such as large prawns, lobster and crab, are priced by weight as a rule.

La cuenta (the bill) includes service charges and perhaps a small cover charge. Prices on menus do not include 7 per cent VAT *(IVA)*, which is usually added when the bill is totalled. The Spanish hardly ever tip restaurant waiters more than 5 per cent, often just rounding up the bill.

Cheques are rarely used in Spain. Traveller's cheques are usually accepted but you may be given a poor rate of exchange. The major credit cards and international direct debit cards are now accepted in most restaurants. However, do not expect to pay by credit card in smaller eating or drinking places like tapas bars, cafés, village *mesones*, roadside *ventas*, *pubs* or bodegas.

WHEELCHAIR ACCESS

S INCE RESTAURANTS are rarely designed for wheelchairs, phone in advance (or ask the hotel staff to call) to check on access to tables and toilets.

Early 20th-century decor in a Madrid bar

Choosing Tapas

TAPAS, SOMETIMES CALLED PINCHOS, are small snacks that originated in Andalusia in the 19th century to accompany sherry. Stemming from a bartender's practice of covering a glass with a saucer or *tapa* (cover) to keep out flies, the custom progressed to a chunk of cheese, or a few olives, being placed on a platter to accompany a drink. Once free of charge, tapas usually have to be paid for nowadays. Choose from a range of appetizing varieties, from cold meats or cheeses to elaborately prepared hot dishes of seafood, meat or vegetables.

Dry fino sherry

Fritura de pescado *is a mixture of fried fish and seafood served with lemon. It includes red mullet, squid and baby hake or other available fresh fish.*

Albondigas *(meatballs) are a hearty tapa and may be served with a zesty tomato sauce.*

Jamón serrano, *salt-cured ham dried in mountain (serrano) air, can be served unadorned in chunks (tacos) or in thin slices (lonchas). This basic tapas dish is often accompanied by bread.*

Gambas a la plancha *is a simple but flavourful dish of whole grilled unpeeled prawns.*

Tortilla a la española *is the ubiquitous thick Spanish omelette, a tasty dish of onion and potato, bound together with seasoned egg. It is served in wedges or small squares.*

Mejillones a la marinera *is a dish of mussels cooked in a tasty sauce of sautéed onion and garlic, white wine, olive oil, lemon juice and parsley.*

Almendras fritas *(fried salted almonds) are a common snack, since almond trees grow in many parts of Spain. Pistachios (pistachos), salted peanuts (cacahuetes) and sunflower seeds (pipas) can also be ordered to accompany a drink.*

Pollo al ajillo, *a widely available tapa, consists of small pieces of chicken (often wings or legs) browned in oil and then gently simmered in an appetizing garlic-flavoured sauce.*

Banderillas *are canapés skewered on toothpicks. Popular ingredients include marinated fish and vegetables, hard-boiled egg, prawns, gherkin, and olives. The entire canapé should be eaten at once, to blend the flavours together*

Ensaladilla rusa (*Russian salad*) *is cold dish of tuna, prawns, potatoes, carrots and peas coated with mayonnaise. It may be topped with peppers or egg.*

Chorizo, *a popular sausage that is flavoured with garlic and paprika, is usually eaten cold; but some kinds are fried and served hot.*

Patatas bravas *is a piquant dish of potatoes fried in oil and coated in a spicy tomato sauce flavoured with onion, garlic, white wine, parsley and red chilli peppers. The bite-sized morsels are both delicious and filling.*

Olives *are common tapas, and come in several varieties. Gordals are fat Seville olives. Manzanillas may be pitted and stuffed with anchovies, almonds or pimientos. Some olives are marinated in herbs and oil or vinegar.*

Salpicón de mariscos *is a luxurious cold salad consisting of an assortment of fresh seafood, including lobster, crab and prawn, with chopped tomatoes. The salad is coated in a zesty vinaigrette flavoured with onion and red peppers.*

Calamares fritos *are squid rings which have been dusted with flour before being deep fried in olive or vegetable oil. They are served garnished with a slice of lemon.*

Ensalada de pimientos rojos *is a colourful cold salad of roasted red peppers and tomatoes. The juices from the roasting are combined with olive oil and vinegar to make a delicious sauce for the salad.*

Queso manchego, *sheep's cheese from La Mancha (see p321), is Spain's most popular cheese. It comes served with bread in either a mild, semisoft form (semicurado) or, when left to age, a tangy mature form (curado).*

TAPAS BARS

Even a small village will have at least one bar where the locals go to enjoy drinks, tapas and conversation with friends. On Sundays and holidays, the favourite places are packed with whole families enjoying the fare. In larger towns it is customary to move from bar to bar, sampling the specialities of each. A tapa is a single serving, whereas a *ración* serves two or three. *Bocadillos*, sandwiches filled with the same ingredients as tapas, can also be ordered. Tapas are generally eaten standing at the bar rather than sitting at a table, for which a surcharge is usually made.

Friends gathered for conversation and a selection of tapas in a local bar

What to Drink in Spain

SPAIN IS ONE OF THE WORLD'S largest wine-producing countries and many fine wines are made here, particularly reds in La Rioja and sherry in Andalusia. Many other beverages – both alcoholic and nonalcoholic – are served in bars and cafés, which provide an important focus for life in Spain. Spaniards are also great coffee drinkers. In the summer months a tempting range of cooling drinks is on offer, in addition to beer, which is always available. Brandy and a variety of liqueurs, such as *anís*, are drunk as apéritifs and *digestifs*, as is chilled pale gold fino sherry.

Customers enjoying a drink at a terrace café in Seville

A plate of *churros* (batter sticks)

Hot chocolate

Café con leche

Camomile   **Lime flower**

HOT DRINKS

CAFE CON LECHE is a large half-and-half measure of milk and coffee; *café cortado* is an espresso with a splash of milk; *café solo* is a black coffee. Hot chocolate is also popular and is often served with *churros* (batter sticks). Herbal teas include *manzanilla* (camomile) and *tila* (lime flower).

COLD DRINKS

IN MOST SPANISH TOWNS and cities it is safe to drink the tap water, but people generally prefer to buy bottled mineral water, either still *(sin gas)* or sparkling *(con gas)*. Besides soft drinks, a variety of other thirst-quenching summer beverages is available, including *horchata (see p243),* a sweet, milky drink made from ground *chufas* (earth almonds). Another popular refreshing drink is *leche merengada* (iced milk with sweet meringue floating in it). *Gaseosa*, fizzy lemonade, can be drunk either on its own or as a mixer, usually with wine. *Zumo de naranja natural* (freshly squeezed orange juice) is an excellent thirst quencher.

Sparkling and still mineral water

Horchata*, made from *chufas

SPANISH WINE

Wine has been produced in Spain since pre-Roman times and there is a great variety on offer today, including famous types such as Rioja. The key standard for the industry is the *Denominación de Origen* (DO) classification, a guarantee of a wine's origin and quality. *Vino de la Tierra* is a classification of wines below that of DO in which over 60 per cent of the grapes come from a specified region. *Vino de Mesa*, the lowest category, covers basic unclassified wines. For more detailed information on Spain's principal wine producing regions, refer to the following pages: Northern Spain *(see pp74–5)*, Eastern Spain *(see pp192–3)*, Central Spain *(see pp322–3)*, and Southern Spain *(see pp402–3)*.

Penedès white wine   **Rioja red wine**   **Sparkling wine *(cava)***

SPIRITS AND LIQUEURS

S PANISH BRANDY, which comes mainly
from the sherry bodegas in Jerez,
is known as *coñac*. Most bodegas
produce at least three different labels
and price ranges. Magno is a good
middle-shelf brandy; top-shelf labels
are Lepanto and Larios. *Anís*, which
is flavoured with aniseed, is a popular
liqueur. *Pacharán*, made from sloes,
is sweet and also tastes of aniseed.
Licor 43 is a vanilla liqueur. Ponche
is brandy that has been aged and
flavoured with herbs.

Anís   **Pacharán**   **Licor 43**   **Ponche**

BEER

M OST SPANISH BEER *(cerveza)*
is bottled lager, although
you can sometimes find it on
draught. Popular
brands include San
Miguel, Cruzcampo
Mahou and Águila.
To order a glass of
beer in a bar ask for
una caña. Alcohol-
free lager *(cerveza
sin alcohol)* is also
available in most
bars in Spain.

Bottled beers

SHERRY

S HERRY IS PRODUCED in bodegas in
Jerez de la Frontera (Andalusia)
and in nearby towns Sanlúcar de
Barrameda and El Puerto de Santa
María *(see pp402–3)*. Although
not officially called sherry, similar
kinds of wine are pro-
duced in Montilla near
Córdoba. Pale fino is
dry and light and excel-
lent as an apéritif. Amber
amontillado (aged fino)
has a strong, earthy
taste while oloroso is
full-bodied and ruddy.

Two brands of fino sherry

**Red wine
and
lemonade**

MIXED DRINKS

S ANGRIA IS A refreshing mixture of red wine, *gaseosa*
(lemonade) and other ingredients including chopped fruit
and sugar. Wine diluted with
lemonade is called *vino con gaseosa*.
Another favourite drink is *Agua de
Valencia*, a refreshing blend of *cava*
(sparkling wine) and orange juice. Young
people will often order the popular
cubalibres, cola with rum or gin.

Sangria

Cubalibre   **Vino con
gaseosa**

HOW TO READ A WINE LABEL

If you know what to look for, the
label will provide a key to the wine's
flavour and quality. It will bear the
name of the wine and its producer or
bodega *(see p619)*, its vintage if there
is one, and show its *Denominación
de Origen* (DO) if applicable. Wines
labelled *cosecha* are recent vintages
and the least expensive, while *crianza*
and *reserva* wines are aged a minimum
of two or three years – part of that
time in oak casks – and therefore more
expensive. Table wine *(Vino de Mesa)*
may be *tinto* (red), *blanco* (white) or
rosado (rosé). *Cava* is a sparkling wine
made by the *méthode champenoise* in
specified areas of origin.

Brand name   **Company's crest**

**Capacity of
the bottle**

**Estate-bottled
rather than
cooperative**

**The wine's
*Denominación
de Origen***

75 cl.   13% Alc.

MARQUÉS DE MURRIETA
Embotellado por: BODEGAS MARQUÉS DE MURRIETA, S.A. - YGAY

Vinos de Rioja

YGAY

(LOGROÑO)

EMBOTELLADOR Nº 53 LO

**RESERVA
COSECHA 1970**

The vintage   **Symbol for region**

Choosing a Restaurant

THE RESTAURANTS in this guide have been selected across a wide range of price categories for their good value, exceptional food and interesting location. This chart lists the restaurants by region, starting with Galicia. Use the colour-coded thumb tabs, which indicate the regions covered on each page, to guide you to the relevant section of the chart.

		CREDIT CARDS	TAPAS BAR	FIXED-PRICE MENU	GOOD WINE LIST	OUTDOOR TABLES

GALICIA

BAIONA: *Moscón.* €€
Calle Alférez Barreiro 2 (Pontevedra). ☎ 986 35 50 08.
Galician cuisine including a tasty fish *caldeirada* (casserole) spiced with paprika. The harbour view makes for a pleasant dining experience. 🗐 🕭
Credit cards: AÉ DC MC V. Good Wine List.

BETANZOS: *La Casilla.* €
Avenida de Madrid 90 (A Coruña). ☎ 981 77 01 61.
This old stone house by the roadside is famous throughout Spain for its omelettes. You can admire the garden from the terrace. ● *Mon.* 🕭
Credit cards: DC MC V. Fixed-Price Menu. Good Wine List. Outdoor Tables.

BUEU: *A Centoleira.* €€€
Playa de Beluso 28 (Pontevedra). ☎ 986 32 08 96.
Choose your own lobster from the aquarium or try the hake with clams accompanied by a good Albariño wine. ● *Mon & Oct.* 🗐
Credit cards: AE DC MC V. Tapas Bar. Fixed-Price Menu. Good Wine List. Outdoor Tables.

A CORUÑA: *La Penela.* €€
Plaza de María Pita 12. ☎ 981 20 92 00.
Simple, unpretentious dining both indoors and out. The roast veal, Spanish omelette, and Galician-style monkfish are specialities. ● *Sun.* 🗐
Credit cards: AE DC MC V. Good Wine List. Outdoor Tables.

A CORUÑA: *Casa Pardo.* €€€
Calle Novoa Santos 15. ☎ 981 28 00 21.
This tavern by the fishing port is renowned for its monkfish. The blackberry crème caramel is also popular. ● *Sun, last 2 weeks Jun.* 🗐
Credit cards: AE DC MC V. Fixed-Price Menu. Good Wine List.

O GROVE: *Crisol.* €€€
Calle Hospital 10–12 (Pontevedra). ☎ 986 73 00 29.
A variety of seafood and shellfish dishes are served here, using first-class ingredients. The dining room overlooks the sea. ● *Mon.* 🗐
Credit cards: AE MC V. Fixed-Price Menu. Good Wine List.

A GUARDA: *Anduriña.* €€€
Calle Calvo Sotelo 58 (Pontevedra). ☎ 986 61 11 08.
Watch the fishing boats bring in their catch as you enjoy fresh hake, turbot or a fish casserole in this port-side restaurant. 🗐 🕭
Credit cards: AE DC MC V. Tapas Bar. Fixed-Price Menu. Good Wine List. Outdoor Tables.

LUGO: *Alberto.* €€
Calle Cruz 4. ☎ 982 22 83 10.
Award-winning chef Alberto García's delicacies include beef entrecôte served in a green turnip sauce and sea bass with baby eels. ● *Sun.* 🗐
Credit cards: AE DC MC V. Tapas Bar. Fixed-Price Menu. Good Wine List.

LUGO: *Verruga.* €€€
Calle Cruz 12. ☎ 982 22 98 55.
This restaurant offers a wide variety of seafood from its own hatchery. Try the red peppers stuffed with crab meat and the delicious home-made *filloas* (crêpes) prepared in different ways. ● *Mon.* 🗐 🕭
Credit cards: AE DC MC V. Tapas Bar. Fixed-Price Menu. Good Wine List.

OURENSE: *Pingallo.* €
Rúa San Miguel 6. ☎ 988 22 00 57.
Wholesome home cooking, with Galicia's trademark dish of *lacón con grelos* (turnip greens with ham). Try the cutlets of beef or kid. ● *Wed D.*
Credit cards: AE MC V. Tapas Bar. Fixed-Price Menu. Good Wine List. Outdoor Tables.

OURENSE: *San Miguel.* €€€
Rúa San Miguel 12–14. ☎ 988 22 12 45.
Innovative Galician cuisine specializing in seafood dishes. Try the sea bass in crayfish sauce or the fresh oysters and cockles. 🗐 🕭
Credit cards: AE DC MC V. Tapas Bar. Fixed-Price Menu. Good Wine List.

PADRÓN: *Casa Ramallo.* €€
Calle Castro 5, Rois (A Coruña). ☎ 981 80 41 80.
Home-grown vegetables and hearty fish casseroles are served in this rustic house. The xobiña guisada is a tasty casserole of sardines with potatoes and tomatoes. The home-made desserts are delicious. ● *Mon.* 🗐
Credit cards: AE V. Good Wine List.

Price categories for a three-course evening meal for one, including a half-bottle of house wine, tax and service:

€ under 20 euros
€€ 20–30 euros
€€€ 30–40 euros
€€€€ over 40 euros

TAPAS BAR
In addition to the main dining room, there is a bar serving tapas (see pp574–5) and raciones (larger portions).
FIXED-PRICE MENU
A good-value, fixed-price menu is offered at lunch or dinner, or both, usually with three courses.
GOOD WINE LIST
Denotes a wide range of good wines, or a more specialized selection of local wines.
OUTDOOR TABLES
Facilities for eating outdoors, on a terrace, or in a garden or courtyard, often with a good view.

	CREDIT CARDS	TAPAS BAR	FIXED-PRICE MENU	GOOD WINE LIST	OUTDOOR TABLES

PONTEVEDRA: *Doña Antonia.* €€
Calle Soportales, Plaza de la Herrería 9 primer piso. ☎ 986 84 72 74.
Contemporary European cuisine in a refined setting overlooking the lovely Plaza de la Herrería. The lukewarm monkfish salad and the nougat ice-cream with hazelnuts and pistachios are favourites. ● Sun. ▤
MC V — Good Wine List

SAN SALVADOR DE POYO: *Casa Solla.* €€€
Avenida Sineiro 5 (Pontevedra). ☎ 986 87 28 84.
Specialities of this elegant restaurant, housed in a lovely old *pazo* (manor house), include lobster salad with tomato vinaigrette and sea bass served on a bed of leeks. ● Mon, Thu D, Sun D, 25 Dec. ▤ &
AE DC MC V — Good Wine List, Outdoor Tables

SANTIAGO DE COMPOSTELA: *Moncho Vilas.* €€€
Avenida de Villagarcía 21 (A Coruña). ☎ 981 59 83 87.
Exemplary Galician dishes are served at this restaurant. The fish and seafood, such as clams, scallops and spiny lobster, are ultra-fresh, and the meat and *empanadas* excellent. A separate bar serves tapas. ▤
AE DC MC V — Tapas Bar, Fixed-Price Menu, Good Wine List

SANTIAGO DE COMPOSTELA: *Toñi Vicente.* €€€€
Avenida Rosalía de Castro 24 (A Coruña). ☎ 981 59 41 00.
Worshippers of Galician haute cuisine flock faithfully to Toñi's culinary temple. The marinated sea bass salad and the hake cooked in a shell of potato are just two of her creations. ● Sun, 2 weeks Jan, 2 weeks Aug. ▤ &
AE DC MC V — Fixed-Price Menu, Good Wine List

SANXENXO: *La Taberna de Rotilio.* €€€€
Avenida del Puerto (Pontevedra). ☎ 986 72 02 00.
Located in the cellar of the hotel, this smart restaurant has gained fame for its innovative approach to Galician cuisine. The chef's creations include a monkfish *caldeirada*, an all-time favourite. ● Mon & mid Dec–mid Jan. ▤
AE DC MC V — Fixed-Price Menu, Good Wine List

VEDRA: *Roberto.* €€€
San Julián de Sales (A Coruña). ☎ 981 51 17 69.
With an emphasis on fish and vegetables, Roberto Crespo uses home-grown produce to create interesting dishes such as sea bass with turnip greens. In the garden is a 300-year-old magnolia tree. ● Sun D, Mon & Jan. &
DC MC V — Fixed-Price Menu, Good Wine List, Outdoor Tables

VERÍN: *Gallego.* €€
Carretera N525, Albarellos de Monterrei (Ourense). ☎ 988 41 82 02.
Enjoy traditional Galician recipes, including a wide variety of seafood and shellfish, in this bright dining room with views of the countryside. ▤ &
AE DC MC V — Tapas Bar, Fixed-Price Menu, Good Wine List, Outdoor Tables

VIGO: *El Castillo.* €€€
Parque del Castro (Pontevedra). ☎ 986 42 11 11.
There is a stunning view of Vigo and the ria from this elegant hilltop restaurant which specializes in grilled fish and meat. ● Mon. ▤
AE DC MC V — Fixed-Price Menu, Good Wine List

VILAGARCÍA DE AROUSA: *El Lagar.* €€
Pazo Sobrán, Villajuan de Arosa (Pontevedra). ☎ 986 50 09 09.
Situated in a large 11th-century *pazo* (manor house), this building is reputedly older than the cathedral of Santiago de Compostela. Informal dining with good regional cooking. (Reservations obligatory.) ● Sun D. &
AE MC V — Tapas Bar, Fixed-Price Menu

VILAGARCÍA DE AROUSA: *Chocolate.* €€€
Avenida de Cambados 151 (Pontevedra). ☎ 986 50 11 99.
Manolo Cores, a local personality and master of the grill, offers a balanced selection of seafood and meat. He is proud to tell you that his wife's savoury sweetcorn and cockle pies are unbeatable. ● Sun D. ▤
AE DC MC V — Good Wine List

VILLAFRAMIL: *La Villa.* €€
Carretera Oviedo–A Coruña (Lugo). ☎ 982 12 30 01.
This charming 300-year-old village house has been artfully restored and specializes in traditional regional food. The hake served with caviar and the tender Galician veal are recommended. &
AE DC MC V — Fixed-Price Menu, Good Wine List, Outdoor Tables

Price categories for a three-course evening meal for one, including a half-bottle of house wine, tax and service:

€ under 20 euros
€€ 20–30 euros
€€€ 30–40 euros
€€€€ over 40 euros

TAPAS BAR
In addition to the main dining room, there is a bar serving tapas (see pp574–5) and raciones (larger portions).
FIXED-PRICE MENU
A good-value, fixed-price menu is offered at lunch or dinner, or both, usually with three courses.
GOOD WINE LIST
Denotes a wide range of good wines, or a more specialized selection of local wines.
OUTDOOR TABLES
Facilities for eating outdoors, on a terrace, or in a garden or courtyard, often with a good view.

	CREDIT CARDS	TAPAS BAR	FIXED-PRICE MENU	GOOD WINE LIST	OUTDOOR TABLES

ASTURIAS AND CANTABRIA

AVILÉS: *Real Balneario de Salinas.* €€€
Calle Juan Sitges 3, Salinas (Asturias). (98 551 86 13.
This lovely restaurant in the seaside resort of Salinas is owned by a prestigious Avilés restaurateur. The emphasis of the seasonal menu is on seafood, and the baby eels are the house speciality. ● Jan. ▤ ♿
AE DC MC V

CANGAS DE ONÍS: *La Cabaña.* €€
Calle Susierra 34 (Asturias). (98 594 00 84.
A popular grillroom with a wood fire where suckling pig and baby lamb are roasted to perfection. Finish with cheese or apple pie.
● Wed D, Thu & Feb. ▤ ♿
AE DC MC V

CASTAÑEDA: *Hostería de Castañeda.* €€
Calle Villabañez (Cantabria). (942 59 81 13.
After seeing the nearby caves at Puente Viesgo, relax in the converted stables of this 17th-century farmhouse. Tuck into the wild boar stew with fine herbs or the sirloin steak with mushrooms. ▤
AE DC MC V

CASTRO URDIALES: *Mesón del Marinero.* €€€€
Calle Correría 23 (Cantabria). (942 86 00 05.
This listed historic building houses a stylish seafood restaurant. The portions are generous and its proximity to the fishing port is evident in the freshness of the produce. Excellent wine list.
AE DC MC V

CASTROPOL: *El Risón de Peñamar.* €€
Calle del Puerto (Asturias). (98 563 50 65.
Delightful rustic house with a terrace by the banks of the Eo ria where you can savour authentic Asturian cuisine. ● Mon & Nov. ♿
AE DC MC V

COMILLAS: *El Capricho de Gaudí.* €€€
Barrio de Sobrellano (Cantabria). (942 72 03 65.
Antoni Gaudí's whimsical architectural wonder provides a unique setting for this sophisticated restaurant. The salmon in anchovy cream and the turbot with garlic sprouts are recommended. ● Mon (winter) & mid Jan–mid Feb. ▤ ♿
AE DC MC V

COSGAYA: *Mesón del Oso.* €€
Carretera Potes–Fuente Dé (Cantabria). (942 73 30 18.
Delightful country hotel and restaurant by the Río Deva with views of the Picos de Europa. The veal steaks and *cocido lebaniego* – a rich stew with chickpeas (garbanzos) and pork – are local specialities. ● Jan–mid Feb.
MC V

CUDILLERO: *Mariño.* €€€
Playa de la Concha de Artedo (Asturias). (98 559 01 86.
The fish casseroles, *calderadas*, are this restaurant's speciality. A typical dish is *curadillo* (a member of the shark family). ● Feb. ♿
AE DC MC V

ESCALANTE: *San Román de Escalante.* €€€€
Carretera Escalante–Castillo (Cantabria). (942 67 77 28.
This lovely old mountain house, set in gardens with a 12th-century chapel, is the elegant setting for French-style cuisine. ● mid Dec–mid Jan. ▤ ♿
AE DC MC V

LAREDO: *Risco.* €€€€
Calle la Arenosa 2 (Cantabria). (942 60 50 30.
Book a table by one of the large panoramic windows with wonderful views of the bay and savour a hake stew with potatoes and clams in *salsa verde* (a garlic and parsley sauce), or cod prepared with fried red peppers.
AE DC MC V

LASTRES: *El Cafetín.* €€
Calle Matemático Pedrayes (Asturias). (98 585 00 85.
Fresh sea produce is served with regional specialities such as *pote asturiano* (stew made with white beans and sausage meat), on advance request. ● Wed.
AE DC MC V

Luarca: *Villa Blanca.* €€
Avenida de Galicia 25–27 (Asturias). ☎ 98 564 10 79.
Try your hand at pouring cider in the rustic bar and then enjoy the *pitu de aldea* (chicken served with peas and small potatoes). ● Mon. 目 ㅎ

	AE	●	■		■
	DC				
	MC				
	V				

Oviedo: *El Raitán.* €€
Plaza de Trascorrales 6 (Asturias). ☎ 98 521 42 18.
Discover the variety of Asturian cuisine with the nine-course lunch time *menú de degustación*, served by waiters in regional costume. ● Sun D. 目

	AE	●	■	●	
	DC				
	MC				
	V				

Potes: *Martín.* €
Calle Roscabao, Urbanización Ivana (Cantabria). ☎ 942 73 02 33.
Authentic regional cooking including the hearty *cocido lebaniego* – a stew with chickpeas (garbanzos) and pork – and peppers stuffed with local Treviso cheese.There are great views of the countryside. ● Jan. ㅎ

	AE	●	■	●	■
	MC				
	V				

Prendes: *Casa Gerardo.* €€€
Carretera N632 (Asturias). ☎ 98 588 77 97.
This delightful restaurant reputedly serves the best *fabada* – a rich stew with white beans and black/blood sausage. ● Sun–Thu D, Jan. 目 ㅎ

	AE	●	■	●	
	DC				
	MC				
	V				

Puente Arce: *El Molino.* €€€€
Carretera Nacional (Cantabria). ☎ 942 57 50 55.
Aesthetically and gastronomically, this has to be the finest dining experience in the area. Housed in a converted mill, it offers sophisticated Cantabrian cuisine, with romantic views of the river. ● Mon in winter. ㅎ

	AE			●	■
	DC				
	MC				
	V				

Ramales de la Victoria: *Río Asón.* €€€€
Calle Barón de Adzaneta 17 (Cantabria). ☎ 942 64 61 57.
Off the beaten tourist track hides one of Cantabria's best restaurants. The salmon is caught in the nearby Río Asón, and the seasonal menu will delight even the most sophisticated of palates. ● Mon & Jan. 目 ㅎ

	AE			●	
	DC				
	MC				
	V				

Reinosa: *Vejo.* €€
Avenida de Cantabria 83 (Cantabria). ☎ 942 75 17 00.
Tender veal is this modern restaurant's speciality. The sirloin with foie gras and truffles is delectable, and the Cantabrian cheese board will give you an idea why this region is renowned for its dairy products.

	AE	●	■	●	■
	DC				
	MC				
	V				

Santander: *Bodega del Riojano.* €€
Calle Río de la Pila 5 (Cantabria). ☎ 942 21 67 50.
This colourful bodega is as famous for its decorative wine barrels, painted by Spanish artists, as it is for its delicious food. The stuffed red peppers are said to be "the best in the world". Good selection of tapas. ● Mon (winter). 目

	AE	●	■	●	
	DC				
	MC				
	V				

Santander: *Zacarías.* €€
Calle Hernán Cortés 38 (Cantabria). ☎ 942 21 23 33.
Featuring authentic Cantabrian dishes, this popular restaurant and lively tapas bar will give you a complete taste of regional specialities. 目 ㅎ

	AE	●	■	●	
	DC				
	MC				
	V				

Taramundi: *El Mazo.* €€
Cuesta de la Rectoral (Asturias). ☎ 98 564 67 60.
This old rectory house offers simple, home cooking in an enchanting rural setting. Sirloin steak with local Cabrales blue cheese is one dish. ● Wed. 目

	AE	■		●	■
	DC				
	MC				
	V				

BASQUE COUNTRY, NAVARRA AND LA RIOJA

Aoiz: *Beti Jai.* €€
Calle Santa Agueda 2 (Navarra). ☎ 948 33 60 52.
Old town house in the main square with views of the river, serving authentic Navarrese cuisine. The sheep's tripe (*menudicos*), pig's trotters and the home-made sponge cake are local specialities. 目

| | MC | ● | ■ | ● | ■ |
| | V | | | | |

Azpeitia: *Kiruri Jatetxea.* €€
Barrio de Loiola 23 (Guipúzcoa). ☎ 943 81 56 08.
Enjoy the Guridi family's traditional Basque dishes such as *txangurro* (spider crab baked and served in the shell) or *lubina al txacoli* (sea bass cooked in the local white wine). 目 ㅎ

	AE	●	■	●	■
	DC				
	MC				
	V				

Bilbao (Bilbo): *Zortziko.* €€€€
Calle Alameda Mazarredo 17 (Vizcaya). ☎ 94 423 97 43.
Contemporary haute cuisine served in a beautiful and elegant building, declared a historic monument. The menu is seasonal and the creative Basque elaborations are sublime. ● Sun. 目

	AE	●	■	●	
	DC				
	MC				
	V				

For key to symbols see back flap

Price categories for a three-course evening meal for one, including a half-bottle of house wine, tax and service:

€ under 20 euros
€€ 20–30 euros
€€€ 30–40 euros
€€€€ over 40 euros

TAPAS BAR
In addition to the main dining room, there is a bar serving tapas *(see pp574–5)* and *raciones* (larger portions).

FIXED-PRICE MENU
A good-value, fixed-price menu is offered at lunch or dinner, or both, usually with three courses.

GOOD WINE LIST
Denotes a wide range of good wines, or a more specialized selection of local wines.

OUTDOOR TABLES
Facilities for eating outdoors, on a terrace, or in a garden or courtyard, often with a good view.

	CREDIT CARDS	TAPAS BAR	FIXED-PRICE MENU	GOOD WINE LIST	OUTDOOR TABLES
CINTRUÉNIGO: *Maher.* €€€€ Calle Ribera 19 (Navarra). 948 81 11 50. Innovative cuisine is impeccably presented in this basement restaurant. Asparagus pudding, rice with hare, and suckling lamb ribs in a delicious mushroom sauce are all house specialities. ● *Sun D, Mon.* ▤	AE DC MC V	●	■	●	
EGÜES: *Mesón Egües.* €€€ Carretera de Aoiz (Navarra). 948 33 00 81. Enjoy excellent meat and fish in this cosy restaurant with a rustic atmosphere. Specialities include turbot and chargrilled steaks, and delicious fresh foie gras. Good home-made desserts. ● *Mon.* ▤ &	AE DC MC V			●	
ELORRIO: *Nico.* €€€ Plaza Arbol de Guernika 4 (Vizcaya). 946 82 04 69. This old Vizcayan house with wooden beams and rustic decor is a popular eating spot serving simple yet tasty cooking. ● *Aug.*	AE MC V		■		
ESTELLA (LIZARRA): *Navarra.* €€ Calle Gustavo de Maeztu 16, Los Llanos (Navarra). 948 55 10 69. Traditional regional cuisine is served in this grand house, with tiles depicting Navarra's former kings. The *blanca de navarra* (a lemon and honey ice-cream, served with fresh cream and nuts) is superb. ● *Mon.* ▤	AE MC V	●	■	●	■
EZCARAY: *Echaurren.* €€€ Calle Héroes del Alcázar 2 (La Rioja). 941 35 40 47. One of La Rioja's emblematic restaurants, run by the delightful Paniego family. The region's superlative vegetables are cooked to perfection and there is a great variety of Rioja and Albariño wines. ● *Sun D, Nov.* ▤ &	AE DC MC V		■	●	
GALDÁCANO: *Aretxondo.* €€€€ Calle Elexalde 20 (Vizcaya). 944 56 76 71. One of the region's best restaurants, this is a veritable showcase of sophisticated Basque cooking, and well worth the drive of 10 km (6 miles) from Bilbao. Reservations are advised. ● *Mon.* ▤ &	AE MC V		■	●	
GETARIA: *Elkano.* €€€€ Calle Herrerita 2 (Guipúzcoa). 943 14 06 14. Pedro Arregui is famous for his grilled fish dishes. The squid served with its own ink and the turbot are both excellent. The best Basque brand of *txacoli* wine – Txomín Echaniz – is also available here. ● *Sun D, Mon (winter).* ▤ &	AE DC MC V			●	
HARO: *Terete.* €€ Calle Lucrecia Arana 17 (La Rioja). 941 31 00 23. This ancient wood-burning oven has been roasting lamb since 1877. Sit at the long wooden tables and savour the Riojan specialities, accompanied by a bottle of house wine. ● *Mon.* ▤ &	MC V		■	●	
HONDARRIBIA (FUENTERRABÍA): *Sebastián.* €€€ Calle Mayor 9–11 (Guipúzcoa). 943 64 01 67. A 16th-century house in the historic part of town serving Basque-French cuisine. Game dishes are available in season. ● *Sun D, Mon, Feb & Nov.* &	AE DC MC V		■	●	
KORTEZUBI: *Lezika.* €€€ Barrio Basondo 8, Santimamiñe (Vizcaya). 946 25 29 75. Close to the Santimamiñe caves is this delightful 18th-century country house serving traditional Basque cuisine, such as hake in *salsa verde*, and red beans with ham and sausage. Good selection of wines. ● *Sun–Wed D.* ▤ &	AE DC MC V	●	■	●	■
LAGUARDIA: *Posada Mayor de Migueloa.* €€€ Calle Mayor de Migueloa 20 (Álava). 945 62 11 75. The elegant and beautifully restored 17th-century palace of Viana now houses one of La Rioja's best restaurants. The roast lamb and the Riojan potatoes (*a la riojana*) are just two of the specialities. ● *Xmas–late Jan.* ▤ &	AE DC MC V	●	■	●	■

LASARTE: *Martín Berasategui.* €€€€
Calle Loidi 4 (Guipúzcoa). **[** 943 36 64 71.
One of the area's leading restaurants, in a converted farmhouse. The cold
potato soup with smoked bacon is just one of Martín's creations. He will
also design a menu to fit your budget. ● *Sun D, Mon, Tue, Sat L.* ▤ &
AE DC MC V

LEKEITIO: *Mesón Arropain.* €€€
Carretera de Marquina, Arropain, Ispaster (Vizcaya). **[** 94 684 03 13.
A rustic farmhouse with an emphasis on seafood. Grilled turbot, baked
crayfish and spider crab are all specialities. The home-made *cuajada* (a
curd pudding) is typical of the region. ● *Wed & mid Dec–mid Jan.* &
AE DC MC V

LOGROÑO: *El Cachetero.* €€€
Calle Laurel 3 (La Rioja). **[** 941 22 84 63.
Home-style local cuisine is served in this cosy restaurant. The vegetable
dishes are excellent, and it is also a good place to try roast kid. Desserts
include *arroz con leche* (rice pudding). ● *Sun & 1–15 Aug.* ▤ &
DC MC V

OIARTZUN: *Zuberoa.* €€€€
Calle Iturriotz Auzoa 8 (Guipúzcoa). **[** 943 49 12 28.
One of Spain's best restaurants, Zuberoa is set in a 600-year-old farm-house,
where the Arbelaitz brothers maintain a high level of culinary artistry.The
foie gras with chickpea (garbanzo) sauce is a classic. ● *Mon & Sun D.* ▤ &
AE DC MC V

PAMPLONA (IRUÑA): *Alhambra.* €€€
Calle Bergamín 7 (Navarra). **[** 948 24 50 07.
Typical Navarrese cooking is served in this welcoming restaurant. The
artichokes, the truffle and vegetable purée and the mushroom risotto are all
delicious appetizers. Good selection of local wines. ● *Sun.* ▤ &
AE DC MC V

PAMPLONA (IRUÑA): *Europa.* €€€
Calle Espoz y Mina 11 Olave (Navarra). **[** 948 22 18 00.
Located in the old part of the city near the cathedral, this first-floor restaurant
offers a range of traditional Navarrese dishes. One of their specialities is
menestre de verdura (vegetable stew). ● *Sun.* &
AE MC V

PASAI DONIBANE: *Casa Cámara.* €€
Pasajes de San Juan 79 (Guipúzcoa). **[** 943 52 36 99.
Choose your own live lobster from the aquarium or try the baked spider
crab as you admire panoramic sea views. ● *Mon & Sun D.* &
MC V

PUENTE LA REINA: *Mesón el Peregrino.* €€€
Carretera Pamplona-Logroño (Navarra). § 948 34 00 75.
This charming country inn provides a peaceful setting to enjoy refined,
regional cuisine. Savour veal cheeks in an onion sauce and finish off with a
white chocolate mousse. ● *Mon.* ▤
DC MC V

SAN SEBASTIÁN (DONOSTIA): *Akelaré.* €€€€
Paseo Padre Orcolaga 56, Barrio de Igueldo (Guipúzcoa). **[** 943 21 20 52.
A Spanish gastronomic temple with spectacular views of rolling hills which
plunge into the sea. To savour the chef's star dishes, try the seven-course
menú de degustación. Smart dress. ● *Mon, Sun D; Feb & early Oct.* ▤ &
AE DC MC V

SAN SEBASTIÁN (DONOSTIA): *Arzak.* €€€€
Calle Alto del Miracruz 21 (Guipúzcoa). **[** 943 27 84 65.
According to many gourmets, this is Spain's best restaurant. Master chef Juan
Mari Arzak's international reputation for innovative Basque cuisine, rewarded
with three Michelin stars, is well deserved. ● *Sun D, Mon; late June & Nov.* ▤ &
AE DC MC V

TAFALLA: *Túbal.* €€€
Plaza de Navarra 6 (Navarra). **[** 948 70 08 52.
This historic building has 18 balconies overlooking the square. Try the crêpes
filled with borage, a traditional Navarrese vegetable. ● *Sun D, Mon.* ▤ &
AE DC MC V

VIANA: *Borgia.* €€€€
Calle Serapio Urra (Navarra). **[** 948 64 57 81.
A small restaurant in the historic part of town with an interesting seasonal
menu. The artichokes with foie gras served on a bed of watercress and the
lamb marinated in herbs with a gin sauce are specialities. ● *Sun & Aug.*
AE DC MC V

VITORIA (GASTEIZ): *Dos Hermanas.* €€€
Madre Vedruna 10 (Álava). **[** 945 13 29 34.
Classic regional cooking with a seasonal menu. The tuna served on a bed
of peppers and the oxtail stew are both delicious. ● *Sun.* ▤ &
AE DC MC V

For key to symbols see back flap

<table>
<tr><td>

Price categories for a three-course evening meal for one, including a half-bottle of house wine, tax and service:

€ under 20 euros
€€ 20–30 euros
€€€ 30–40 euros
€€€€ over 40 euros

</td><td>

TAPAS BAR
In addition to the main dining room, there is a bar serving tapas *(see pp574–5)* and *raciones* (larger portions).
FIXED-PRICE MENU
A good-value, fixed-price menu is offered at lunch or dinner, or both, usually with three courses.
GOOD WINE LIST
Denotes a wide range of good wines, or a more specialized selection of local wines.
OUTDOOR TABLES
Facilities for eating outdoors, on a terrace, or in a garden or courtyard, often with a good view.

</td></tr>
</table>

	CREDIT CARDS	TAPAS BAR	FIXED-PRICE MENU	GOOD WINE LIST	OUTDOOR TABLES

VITORIA (GASTEIZ): *Ikea.*   €€€€
Portal de Castilla 27 (Álava). ☏ 945 14 47 47.
José Ramón Berriozabal masterfully combines traditional Basque cuisine with a French influence. The hake fillet in *salsa verde* is a classic dish. The foie gras terrine and the Bresse pigeon are both exquisite. ● Mon. ▤
(Credit cards: AE DC MC V; Fixed-Price Menu; Good Wine List)

BARCELONA

OLD TOWN: *Agut.* Map 5 A3.   €
Carrer Gignàs 16. ☏ 93 315 17 09.
Painters used to exchange their artwork for a hearty, honest Catalan meal here. Nowadays the specialities include an aubergine (eggplant) terrine and succulent blood red steaks from Girona. ● Sun D, Mon; Aug. ▤ ♿
(Credit cards: MC V; Fixed-Price Menu; Good Wine List)

OLD TOWN: *Can Culleretes.* Map 5 A2.   €
Carrer Quintana 5. ☏ 93 317 30 22.
The city's oldest restaurant, established in 1786, serves traditional dishes like *pica pica de pescado* (a seafood medley). ● Sun D, Mon, 3 weeks of Jul. ▤ ♿
(Credit cards: MC V; Fixed-Price Menu; Good Wine List)

OLD TOWN: *Egipte.* Map 2 F2.   €
Ramblas 79. ☏ 93 317 74 80.
This lively place, once a monks' residence, serves Mediterranean specialities, and salt cod prepared in ten different ways. ▤ ♿
(Credit cards: AE DC MC V; Fixed-Price Menu; Good Wine List)

OLD TOWN: *Fonda Senyor Parellada.* Map 5 B3.   €
Carrer de la Argentería 37. ☏ 93 310 50 94.
With old chandeliers and candlesticks on the tables, this atmospheric restaurant is a great choice for authentic Catalan cuisine. ▤ ♿
(Credit cards: AE DC MC V; Good Wine List)

OLD TOWN: *Les Quinze Nits.* Map 5 A3.   €
Plaça Reial 6. ☏ 93 317 30 75.
Conveniently located, this attractive restaurant draws a young crowd and offers good Catalan dishes at reasonable prices. ● 24 Dec D & 25 Dec. ▤ ♿
(Credit cards: AE DC MC V; Fixed-Price Menu; Good Wine List; Outdoor Tables)

OLD TOWN: *Romesco.* Map 2 F3.   €
Carrer de Sant Pau 28. ☏ 93 318 93 81.
A popular spot just off the Ramblas with home-style cooking, a lively atmosphere and unbeatable prices. The house speciality is *frijoles* (a Cuban dish of rice, black beans, fried banana and eggs). ● Sun & Aug.
(Tapas Bar; Fixed-Price Menu)

OLD TOWN: *Amaya.* Map 5 A1.   €€
Ramblas 20–24. ☏ 93 302 10 37.
This classic, popular Basque-Catalan restaurant offers a good selection of tapas at the bar and half portions of many dishes that appear on the encyclopedic menu. Fantastic wine list. ▤ ♿
(Credit cards: AE DC MC V; Tapas Bar; Fixed-Price Menu; Good Wine List; Outdoor Tables)

OLD TOWN: *Café de l'Acadèmia.* Map 2 F3.   €€
Carrer de l'Edó 1. ☏ 93 315 00 26.
This attractive restaurant gives a new interpretation to traditional Catalan cuisine. Modern details and paintings combine well with stone walls.
● Sat, Sun, public hols. ▤ ♿
(Credit cards: AE DC MC V; Fixed-Price Menu; Outdoor Tables)

OLD TOWN: *Cal Pep.* Map 5 B3.   €€
Plaça de les Olles 8. ☏ 93 310 79 61.
According to some seafood fanatics, Pep's *pescado frito* (fried fish) is the best in the world! Other recommended dishes include clams with ham, fried baby squid, and crayfish. ● Mon L, Sun, public hols, Easter, Aug, 24, 25 & 26 Dec. ▤
(Credit cards: AE DC MC V; Tapas Bar)

OLD TOWN: *Estevet.* Map 2 F1.   €€
Carrer de Valldonzella 46. ☏ 93 302 41 86.
Traditional, welcoming restaurant decorated with original ceramic tiles and paintings from grateful customers. Be guided by the ebullient owner for the starters. ● Sun, public hols. ▤ ♿
(Credit cards: AE DC MC; Fixed-Price Menu; Good Wine List)

OLD TOWN: *Can Majó*. **Map 5 B5.** €€€ | AE DC MC V
Carrer de l'Almirall Aixada 23. 93 221 54 55.
This renowned seafood restaurant in Barceloneta serves great rice dishes such as a peeled shellfish paella and *suquet* (a delicious hot fish and potato stew). Extensive wine list. ● *Sun D & Mon.* 目 ৬

OLD TOWN: *Reial Club Marítim de Barcelona*. **Map 5 A4.** €€€ | AE DC MC V
Moll d'Espanya. 93 221 62 56.
Nautical club restaurant with spectacular views of the port. The elaborate cuisine includes aubergine (eggplant) terrine with goat's cheese, and gilthead with apples and a cider sauce. ● *Sun D, 24 & 25 Dec.* 目 ৬

OLD TOWN: *Set Portes*. **Map 5 B3.** €€€ | AE DC MC V
Passeig de Isabel II 14. 93 319 29 50.
This lavishly decorated restaurant is reminiscent of an elegant Parisian café. Specialities include 11 different types of paella, and delicious home-made cannelloni. Efficient service and a good wine list. 目

OLD TOWN: *Talaia Mar*. **Map 6 E5.** €€€€ | AE DC MC V
Anexo Torre Mapfre, Carrer de la Marina 16. 93 221 90 90.
This stunning, sleek, circular restaurant, with views of the marina, offers extremely good food. The menu varies with the season. You can order half portions (*pica pica*) of most dishes. 目 ৬

EIXAMPLE: *Amaltea*. **Map 3 A5.** € | MC V
Carrer de la Diputacion 164. 93 454 86 13.
This vegetarian restaurant is a good lunchtime choice (it shuts at 10pm). Simple but innovative dishes are made with the best seasonal ingredients. 目 ৬

EIXAMPLE: *El Tragaluz*. **Map 3 A3.** €€€ | AE DC MC V
Passeig Concepció 5. 93 487 06 21.
Two different dining concepts are offered here: a sushi bar in front, and contemporary Mediterranean cuisine behind. The ground floor bar serves cocktails. The restaurant's logo is by graphic designer Javier Mariscal. 目 ৬

EIXAMPLE: *La Venta*. €€€ | AE DC MC V
Plaça Doctor Andreu. 93 212 64 55.
At the foot of Tibidabo is this attractive restaurant. The glass-covered terraces are open in summer and provide great views of the city. A range of regional dishes are served, made with the best seasonal ingredients. ● *Sun.* 目 ৬

EIXAMPLE: *Roig Robí*. **Map 3 A2.** €€€€ | AE DC MC V
Carrer de Séneca 20. 93 218 92 22 or 93 217 97 38.
Intimate restaurant offering authentic Catalan cuisine, with a lovely interior courtyard for summer. The terrines, fresh salads and any of the rice or seafood dishes are bound to please. ● *Sat L, Sun & public hols.* 目 ৬

FURTHER AFIELD (NORTHWEST): *Chicoa*. €€ | AE MC V
Carrer d'Aribau 73. 93 453 11 23.
A haven for lovers of salt cod, with more than ten different preparations of the celebrated *bacallà*. As well as many other seafood and meat dishes, there is a good Penedès rosé house wine. ● *Sun, Mon D & Aug, public hols.* 目 ৬

FURTHER AFIELD (NORTHWEST): *Tiro Mimet*. €€ | AE MC V
Carrer de Sant Marius 22. 93 211 77 66.
The cuisine here can best be described as Catalan-French. Hot and cold duck livers are served as well as a wide variety of mushrooms, and game in season. Good selection of Catalan wines and *cavas*. ● *Sun & Aug.* 目

FURTHER AFIELD (NORTHWEST): *Giardinetto Notte*. **Map 3 A2.** €€€ | AE DC MC V
Carrer Granada del Penedès 22. 93 218 75 36.
Mediterranean and Italian dishes are served in this romantic setting. Try the home-made pasta with a bottle of Catalan wine. ● *Sat L, Sun, public hols, Aug.* 目

FURTHER AFIELD (NORTHWEST): *La Balsa*. €€€ | AE DC MC V
Carrer de Infanta Isabel 4. 93 211 50 48.
There are great views from the terrace. The Catalan cuisine includes an excellent goose liver as a starter. ● *Mon L, Sun, 25 & 26 Dec, Easter, Aug L.*

FURTHER AFIELD (NORTHWEST): *Botafumeiro*. **Map 3 A2.** €€€€ | AE DC MC V
Carrer Gran de Gràcia 81. 93 218 42 30.
Fine-quality seafood and Galician specialities are served in this stylish restaurant. The shellfish dishes are served in generous portions and the desserts are mouthwatering. Extensive wine list. ● *3 weeks in Aug.* 目 ৬

For key to symbols see back flap

Price categories for a three-course evening meal for one, including a half-bottle of house wine, tax and service:

€ under 20 euros
€€ 20–30 euros
€€€ 30–40 euros
€€€€ over 40 euros

TAPAS BAR
In addition to the main dining room, there is a bar serving tapas (see pp574–5) and raciones (larger portions).

FIXED-PRICE MENU
A good-value, fixed-price menu is offered at lunch or dinner, or both, usually with three courses.

GOOD WINE LIST
Denotes a wide range of good wines, or a more specialized selection of local wines.

OUTDOOR TABLES
Facilities for eating outdoors, on a terrace, or in a garden or courtyard, often with a good view.

	CREDIT CARDS	TAPAS BAR	FIXED-PRICE MENU	GOOD WINE LIST	OUTDOOR TABLES
FURTHER AFIELD (NORTHWEST): *Jaume de Provença.* €€€€ Carrer de Provença 88. 93 430 00 29. The chef's original and creative Catalan cuisine has established his restaurant as among the city's finest. Despite the business-like decor the food is excellent and the service attentive. ● Sun D, Mon, Aug. 目 ⑤	AE DC MC V		■	●	
FURTHER AFIELD (WEST): *Peixerot.* **Map 1 B1.** €€€ Torre Catalunya, Carrera de Tarragona 177. 93 424 69 69. First-class seafood predominates on the menu of this comfortable, modern restaurant. Great rice dishes and shellfish. ● Sat D, Sun, Aug. 目	AE DC MC V			●	
FURTHER AFIELD (WEST): *Neichel.* €€€€ Beltrán i Rózpide 1–5. 93 203 84 08. European haute cuisine with Catalan touches is served in one of the city's most prestigious establishments. It has an excellent selection of cheese and over 350 wine labels. ● Sun, Mon, Aug, public hols. 目	AE DC MC V		■	●	

CATALONIA

	CREDIT CARDS	TAPAS BAR	FIXED-PRICE MENU	GOOD WINE LIST	OUTDOOR TABLES
ALTAFULLA: *Faristol.* €€ Carrer de Sant Martí 5 (Tarragona). 977 65 00 77. Wine was once made in this delightful 18th-century house, which is today still decorated with antiques. To finish off your meal try the super chocolate mousse. ● Oct–May: Mon–Thu; Jun–15 Sep: L.	DC MC V			●	■
ANDORRA LA VELLA: *Borda Estevet.* €€ Carretera de la Comella 2 (Andorra). 376 86 40 26. This old country house, decorated in rustic style, was until recently used for the traditional practice of drying tobacco from the nearby fields. Ask for the meat *a la "llosa"* (brought to you on a hot slate). ● 1 Jan. 目 ⑤	AE MC V			●	■
ARENYS DE MAR: *Hispania.* €€€€ Carrer Real 54, Carretera NII (Barcelona). 93 791 04 57. Authentic Catalan cuisine which has won accolades from near and far. The classic clam *suquet*, similar to a fricassee, and the *crema catalana* (a rich caramel custard) are both delicious. ● Sun D, Tue, Oct, Easter. 目 ⑤	AE DC MC V			●	
ARTIES: *Casa Irene.* €€€ Hotel Valarties, Calle Mayor 3 (Lleida). 973 64 43 64. Located in a picturesque village, this restaurant offers wonderful, French-influenced food and three *menús de degustación*. ● Tue L, Mon, Nov. 目 ⑤	AE DC MC V		■	●	■
BERGA: *Sala.* €€€ Passeig de la Pau 27 (Barcelona). 93 821 11 85. Classic Catalan dishes are offered here, many of which feature mushrooms. Game is available in season. ● Sun D, Mon. 目	AE DC MC V			●	
BOLVIR DE CERDANYA: *Torre del Remei.* €€€€ Camí Reial (Girona). 972 14 01 82. This stunning palace surrounded by gardens has been impeccably restored and now houses an elegant restaurant and hotel. The chef will delight you with his gourmet dishes and superb wine selection. 目 ⑤	AE DC MC V		■	●	■
CALAFELL PLAYA: *Giorgio.* €€ Carrer Ángel Guimerá 4 (Tarragona). 977 69 11 59. Delicious Italian food with home-made pasta, bread and desserts, served on a terrace overlooking the sea. The lasagne is legendary but be sure to reserve as there are only ten tables. ○ Fri, Sat, Sun, public hols; daily in summer.			■	●	■
CAMBRILS: *Joan Gatell-Casa Gatell.* €€€€ Passeig Miramar 26, Cambrils Port (Tarragona). 977 36 00 57. Seafood is the speciality here. The rice dishes, shellfish and lobster casserole are all first class. ● Sun D, Mon, mid Dec–mid Jan, 1–15 May. 目	AE DC MC V		■	●	■

CASTELL-PLATJA D'ARO: *Cal Rei.* €€
Barri de Crota 3 (Girona). (972 81 79 25.
Lovely 14th-century *masía* (farmhouse), decorated in keeping with the
period, serving innovative cuisine of the Empordà region. The oven-baked
codfish is one example. ● *Mon D, Tue, Nov.* 目 &

	AE		▨	●	▨
	DC				
	MC				
	V				

FIGUERES: *Emporda.* €€€€€
Hotel Emporda, Carretera NII (Girona). (972 50 05 62.
Gourmets congregate here to enjoy Jaime Subiro's legendary cuisine. The
fresh broad (fava) beans with mint and the salt cod with a garlic mousseline
are both exquisite. Delightful terrace for dining in the summer. 目 &

	AE		▨	●	▨
	DC				
	MC				
	V				

GIRONA: *El Celler de Can Roca.* €€€€€
Carretera Taialá 40. (972 22 21 57.
The capital's best restaurant – try Juan Roca's lamb stuffed with
sweetbreads (offal) and cinnamon. ● *Sun, Mon, 1–15 Jul, 25 Dec.* 目 &

	AE		▨	●	
	DC				
	MC				
	V				

LLEIDA: *Forn del Nastasi.* €€€
Carrer Salmerón 10. (973 23 45 10.
Excellent regional cuisine including chargrilled vegetables (*escalivada*) and
snails *a la llauna* (baked in the oven). ● *Sun D, Mon, early Aug.* 目 &

	AE		▨	●	
	DC				
	MC				
	V				

LLORET DE MAR: *El Trull.* €€€
Ronda Europa, Cala Canyelles (Girona). (972 36 49 28.
Rustic dining room with marine motifs where you can choose your lobster
from the aquarium and then watch it sizzle on the open grill. The *arrosat*
(noodles prepared with seafood) is also a good choice. ● *24 Dec.* 目 &

	AE		▨	●	▨
	DC				
	MC				
	V				

MARTINET: *Boix.* €€€
Carretera N260 km 264 (Lleida). (973 51 50 50.
A famous Catalan restaurant, located on the banks of the Río Segre, serving
roast leg of lamb so tender you can eat it with a spoon! 目 &

	AE		▨	●	▨
	DC				
	MC				
	V				

PERALADA: *Castell de Peralada.* €€€
Casino Castell de Peralada, Carrer San Joan (Girona). (972 53 81 25.
Dine in the unique medieval setting of this castle turned casino and try
dishes of the Empordà region and the castle's own house wine. 目

	AE		▨	●	▨
	MC				
	V				

REUS: *El Pa Torrat.* €€
Avinguda Reus 24, Castellvell del Camp (Tarragona). (977 85 52 12.
Regional home cooking with dishes such as roast rabbit with *allioli* (garlic
mayonnaise) and *calamares.* ● *Sun D, Mon D, Tue, late Aug, 22 Dec–6 Jan.* 目 &

	AE		▨	●	
	MC				
	V				

ROSES: *El Bulli.* €€€€
Cala Montjoi (Girona). (972 15 04 57.
Considered by many to be one of Spain's best restaurants and perhaps one
of Europe's most beautiful, El Bulli is a must on any gourmet's itinerary.
Expensive, but definitely worth the treat. ● *30 Sep–beg Apr.*

	AE		▨	●	
	DC				
	MC				
	V				

SANT CARLES DE LA RÀPITA: *Miami Can Pons.* €€€
Avinguda Constitució 37 (Tarragona). (977 74 05 51.
Good-quality Catalan cooking is served here by the Pons family. The *suquet*
and the *crema catalana* are just two of the specialities. ● *3 weeks in Jan.* 目

	AE		▨	●	
	DC				
	MC				
	V				

SANT CELONI: *El Racó de Can Fabes.* €€€€
Carrer de Sant Joan 6 (Barcelona). (93 867 28 51.
Santi Santamaría is considered one of Spain's best chefs and this country
restaurant is a gastronomic paradise. The seasonal menu combines many
types of fresh regional produce. ● *Sun D, Mon, 2.weeks in Feb.* 目 &

	AE		▨	●	
	DC				
	MC				
	V				

SANT FELIÚ DE GUIXOLS: *Can Toni.* €€
Carrer Garrofers 54 (Girona). (972 32 10 26.
Enjoy traditional cooking of the Empordà region here. Many dishes include
mushrooms when in season (September–March). ● *Mon.* 目 &

	DC	●	▨	●	
	MC				
	V				

SANT FELIÚ DE GUIXOLS: *Eldorado Petit.* €€€€
Rambla de Vidal 23 (Girona). (972 32 18 18.
First-class ingredients make for superb Mediterranean cuisine at this
restaurant, including meat and fish carpaccios. ● *Wed in winter.* 目 &

	AE			●	
	DC				
	MC				
	V				

SANT SADURNI D'ANOIA: *El Mirador de les Caves.* €€€
Carretera Sant Sadurni–Ordal km 4, Subirats (Barcelona). (93 899 31 78.
The duck with a foie gras and truffle sauce is one of the superb dishes
served here. ● *Sun D, Mon D, 8–23-Aug, 23 Dec–7 Jan.* 目 &

	AE		▨	●	
	DC				
	MC				
	V				

Price categories for a three-course evening meal for one, including a half-bottle of house wine, tax and service:

€ under 20 euros
€€ 20–30 euros
€€€ 30–40 euros
€€€€ over 40 euros

TAPAS BAR
In addition to the main dining room, there is a bar serving tapas (see pp574–5) and raciones (larger portions).
FIXED-PRICE MENU
A good-value, fixed-price menu is offered at lunch or dinner, or both, usually with three courses.
GOOD WINE LIST
Denotes a wide range of good wines, or a more specialized selection of local wines.
OUTDOOR TABLES
Facilities for eating outdoors, on a terrace, or in a garden or courtyard, often with a good view.

	CREDIT CARDS	TAPAS BAR	FIXED-PRICE MENU	GOOD WINE LIST	OUTDOOR TABLES
LA SEU D'URGELL: *El Castell.* €€€€ Carretera N260 km 229 (Lleida). ☎ 973 35 07 04. At the foot of Seu d'Urgell castle, surrounded by beautiful countryside, lies this idyllic hotel-restaurant serving modern Catalan cuisine. The wine list will delight even sophisticated wine lovers. 🍴 ♿	AE DC MC V			●	■
SITGES: *EL Velero.* €€€ Passeig de la Ribera 38 (Barcelona). ☎ 93 894 20 51. Creations here include sole fillets on a bed of mushrooms and crab sauce. ● Sun, Mon in winter; 23 Dec–7 Jan; Mon, Tue in Summer. 🍴 ♿	AE DC MC V		■	●	
TARRAGONA: *El Merlot.* €€€ Carrer Caballers 6. ☎ 977 22 06 52. Situated in the old part of town, this restaurant serves Mediterranean cuisine, based on first-class local produce. Specialities include game dishes (available in season) and home-made desserts. ● Mon L, Sun. 🍴	AE DC MC V		■	●	■
VALLS: *Masía Bou.* €€€€ Carretera Lleida km 21.5 (Tarragona). ☎ 977 60 04 27. Many interesting dishes are on the menu. The speciality is *calçotadas* (onions charred over embers, served with *romesco* sauce). ● Tue in summer. 🍴 ♿	AE MC V		■	●	■
VIC: *Floriac.* €€ Carretera Manresa–Vic N 141 km 39.5, Collsuspina (Barcelona). ☎ 93 743 02 25. A 16th-century *masía* (farmhouse) surrounded by woods, serving regional fare. The game dishes, available in winter, are excellent. ● 2 weeks in Feb, 2 weeks in Jul.	AE DC MC V		■	●	■
VILAFRANCA DEL PENEDÈS: *Cal Ton.* €€€ Calle Casal 8 (Barcelona). ☎ 93 890 37 41. Creative Mediterranean cooking using local ingredients is featured here. The wines and service match the good food. ● Sun D, public hols D, Mon. 🍴	AE DC MC V			●	
ARAGÓN					
AINSA: *Bodegas del Sobrarbe.* €€ Plaza Mayor 2 (Huesca). ☎ 974 50 02 37. Get a taste of medieval history in the vaulted wine cellar of this 11th-century house. Typical Pyrenean dishes include game and *ternasco* (tender suckling lamb roasted on a wood fire). ● Jan–Feb.	AE DC MC V		■	●	■
ALCAÑIZ: *Meseguer.* €€ Avenida del Maestrazgo 9 (Teruel). ☎ 978 83 10 02. Popular for its updated home-cooking at reasonable prices, the menu includes a delicious vegetable stew (*menestra*) and white beans with partridge. Good local wines. ● Sun, mid–late Sep. 🍴 ♿	DC MC V		■	●	
BARBASTRO: *Flor.* €€ Calle Goya 3 (Huesca). ☎ 974 31 10 56. Seasonal menu with fresh produce from the Vero valley and an excellent wine cellar. The rissotto with wild mushrooms and Aragon cheeses (*arroces salteados con setas y quesos aragoneses fundidos*) is recommended. 🍴 ♿	AE DC MC V		■		
BIESCAS: *Casa Ruba.* €€ Calle Esperanza 18–20 (Huesca). ☎ 974 48 50 01. The Ruba family has been serving traditional Aragonese dishes here since 1884. This delightful mountain hotel offers game dishes in season and delicious mushroom and vegetable savoury pies. ● mid-Oct–mid-Nov. 🍴 ♿	AE MC V	●	■	●	■
BORJA: *La Bóveda del Mercado.* €€ Plaza del Mercado 4 (Zaragoza). ☎ 976 86 82 51. Carefully restored 16th-century wine cellar where you can enjoy original dishes using Jewish and Arab recipes as a base. One example is the *delicias de sartén* (fried pastry with aniseed and cinnamon). ● Mon & Feb & public hols.	MC V		■	●	

CANTAVIEJA: *Buj.*   €€
Avenida del Maestrazgo 6 (Teruel). 964 18 50 33.
A simple, family-run restaurant by the roadside. The stuffed potatoes and
mushroom soup are always on the menu due to popular demand. Game
dishes are available in season. Open lunch times only. ● Feb. &

CARIÑENA: *La Rebotica.*   €€   MC
Calle San José 3 (Zaragoza). 976 62 05 56.   V
Try any of the 58 varieties of local Cariñena wine available in this
converted village pharmacy. Most of the recipes are elaborated with wine.
● Mon, Sun–Fri D, 3 weeks in Aug, 1 week after Easter. ▤ &

ESQUEDAS: *Venta del Sotón.*   €€   AE
Carretera Tarragona–San Sebastián km 227 (Huesca). 974 27 02 41.   DC
This wayside inn is one of Aragón's leading restaurants, with a creative cuisine   MC
including local specialities and grilled dishes. ● Sun D, Mon, 15 Jan–15 Feb. ▤ & V

HUESCA: *Las Torres.*   €€€   AE
Calle María Auxiliadora 3. 974 22 82 13.   DC
The Abadía brothers offer an interesting seasonal menu with innovative   MC
flourishes. The crispy grouper served on a bed of pig's trotters, with a   V
raisin and pine nut sauce, should give you an idea.
● Sun, Easter, 15–30 Aug. ▤ &

LA IGLESUELA DEL CID: *Casa Amada.*   €   MC
Calle Fuente Nueva 10 (Teruel). 964 44 33 73.   V
Regional cooking, a simple setting and affordable prices ensure a steady
crowd. Try the walnut crème caramel. ● Sun D in winter, 24 & 25 Dec. ▤ &

JACA: *La Cocina Aragonesa.*   €€€   AE
Calle Cervantes 5 (Huesca). 974 36 10 50.   MC
One of the best restaurants in the area, serving elaborate regional cuisine. V
In winter, the partridge stuffed with foie gras or the wild boar meatballs
can be enjoyed around the fireplace. ● Wed. ▤

NUÉVALOS: *Conventual.*   €   AE
Hotel Monasterio de Piedra (Zaragoza). 976 84 90 11.   DC
Typical Aragonese cuisine is offered in this 12th-century monastery set in a MC
beautiful nature reserve. ▤ &   V

RUBIELOS DE MORA: *Portal del Carmen.*   €€   DC
Calle Glorieta 2 (Teruel). 978 80 41 53.   MC
A former Carmelite monastery with a delightful cloister, specializing in regional   V
food and wine. The salmon and trout are from the nearby fish farms and the
tocinillo de cielo (an egg yolk dessert) is heavenly. ● Thu, 5–25 May. ▤ &

SENEGÜÉ: *Casbas.*   €   AE
Carretera a Biescas (Huesca). 974 48 01 49.   DC
A restaurant with a large wood fire where skiers and hikers congregate for   MC
a hearty meal. The typical mountain dessert of aged wine with sliced   V
peaches is a very popular choice. ● Sep. ▤ &

TERUEL: *La Menta.*   €€   AE
Calle Bartolomé Esteban 10. 978 60 75 32.   DC
One of the best restaurants in the area, offering an original menu with   MC
Basque and Catalan influences. The delicious *pastel ruso* is a traditional   V
Aragón cake. ● Sun, mid–late Jan, mid–late Jul. ▤ &

UNCASTILLO: *Casa Sierra.*   €€   MC
Calle Mediavilla 71 (Zaragoza). 976 67 94 81.   V
Simple yet tasty regional dishes, such as dried white beans with olive oil,
and breadcrumbs with grapes. ○ Sat, Sun, public hols (Jul–15 Sep: daily). ▤ &

ZARAGOZA: *La Rinconada de Lorenzo.*   €€   AE
Calle la Salle 3. 976 55 51 08.   DC
Typical Aragonese cuisine is served here, such as *migas con jamón* (bread-   MC
crumbs with ham) and *ternasco al horno* (roast lamb). Desserts include   V
higos con nueces (figs with nuts). ● Sun D & Mon in Jul & Aug, Easter. ▤ &

ZARAGOZA: *Gayarre.*   €€€   AE
Carretera del Aeropuerto 370. 976 34 43 86.   DC
Lovely house with a pretty garden, just outside the city. The menu is seasonal   MC
with an emphasis on regional vegetables, such as borage, which are used   V
in a variety of salads. Good service and wine list. ● Sun D & Mon. ▤ &

For key to symbols see back flap

<table>
<tr><td>

Price categories for a three-course evening meal for one, including a half-bottle of house wine, tax and service:

€ under 20 euros
€€ 20–30 euros
€€€ 30–40 euros
€€€€ over 40 euros

</td><td>

TAPAS BAR
In addition to the main dining room, there is a bar serving tapas *(see pp574–5)* and *raciones* (larger portions).
FIXED-PRICE MENU
A good-value, fixed-price menu is offered at lunch or dinner, or both, usually with three courses.
GOOD WINE LIST
Denotes a wide range of good wines, or a more specialized selection of local wines.
OUTDOOR TABLES
Facilities for eating outdoors, on a terrace, or in a garden or courtyard, often with a good view.

</td></tr>
</table>

	Credit Cards	Tapas Bar	Fixed-Price Menu	Good Wine List	Outdoor Tables

ZARAGOZA: *La Venta del Cachirulo.* €€€
Autovía de Logroño km 1.5 (Zaragoza). ⏺ 976 46 01 46.
A large, elegantly decorated Aragonese house. The beef cutlet is brought to you on a bed of glowing salt embers allowing you to grill it to perfection. There is a wide variety of vegetable dishes. ⏺ *Sun D & 1–15 Aug.* 🍴 ♿
Credit Cards: AE, DC, MC, V · Fixed-Price Menu · Good Wine List

VALENCIA AND MURCIA

ALICANTE (ALACANT): *Dársena.* €€€
Marina Deportiva, Muelle 6, Puerto. ⏺ 96 520 75 89.
With 150 different rice dishes on the menu, you might find it hard to choose. The generous portions are served in individual paella pans. ⏺ *Sun D.* 🍴 ♿
Credit Cards: AE, DC, MC, V · Tapas Bar · Fixed-Price Menu · Good Wine List

ALICANTE (ALACANT): *Nou Manolín.* €€€
Villegas 3. ⏺ 96 520 03 68.
In the heart of the historic centre, this atmospheric restaurant is located in the house where local author, Gabriel Miró, was born. Try one of the rice dishes or the fish cooked in salt *(dorada a la sal)*. 🍴 ♿
Credit Cards: AE, DC, MC, V · Good Wine List

ALTEA: *Raco de Toni.* €€
Calle de la Mar 127 (Alicante). ⏺ 96 584 17 63.
Regional food including rice dishes and locally caught fish is served in this simple, cosy restaurant. The rice with salt cod and vegetables and the anchovies stuffed with peppers are two of the specialities. ⏺ *Nov.* 🍴 ♿
Credit Cards: AE, DC, MC, V · Tapas Bar · Fixed-Price Menu · Good Wine List

BENIDORM: *El Molino.* €€
Carretera Alicante–Valencia km 123 (Alicante). ⏺ 96 585 71 81.
Thousands of wine bottles decorate this restaurant, where chef Dmitri serves traditional fare including *nayuscas* (grilled crêpes filled with ham and caviar). ⏺ *Mon.* 🍴
Credit Cards: AE, MC, V · Good Wine List · Outdoor Tables

BENIDORM: *La Palmera-Casa Paco Nadal.* €€
Avenida Severo Ochoa, Rincón de Loix (Alicante). ⏺ 96 585 32 82.
Agreeable place just outside Benidorm offering regional specialities. The rice with monkfish and clams is especially good. ⏺ *Mon, 24 Dec–8 Jan.* 🍴
Credit Cards: AE, DC, MC, V · Good Wine List · Outdoor Tables

BENIMANTELL: *L'Obrer.* €
Carretera de Alcoi 27 (Alicante). ⏺ 96 588 50 88.
A rustic-style restaurant, decorated with locally made ceramics. Enjoy such delicious home-made desserts as almond cake with chocolate. ⏺ *Fri & Jul.* 🍴 ♿
Credit Cards: AE, DC, MC, V · Tapas Bar · Fixed-Price Menu · Good Wine List

BENIMANTELL: *Venta la Montaña.* €
Carretera de Alcoi 9, Benimantell (Alicante). ⏺ 96 588 51 41.
A picturesque mountain inn decorated with antique farming implements where wholesome dishes, such as the typical *olleta de trigo* (a broth made with pork, vegetables and wheat), are served. ⏺ *Mon, D daily in winter.* 🍴 ♿
Credit Cards: MC, V · Tapas Bar · Fixed-Price Menu · Good Wine List · Outdoor Tables

BENISSANÓ: *Levante.* €
Calle Virgen del Fundamento 27 (Valencia). ⏺ 96 278 07 21.
You can't leave Valencia without trying the excellent paellas here, cooked over a wood fire. One of the region's largest and best wine cellars is also at your disposal. Open lunch times only. ⏺ *Tue & mid Jul–early Aug.* 🍴
Credit Cards: AE, MC, V · Fixed-Price Menu · Good Wine List

BUÑOL: *Venta L'Home.* €€
Autovía NIII Madrid–Valencia, Ventamina exit (Valencia). ⏺ 96 250 35 15.
A 17th-century coaching inn now housing a delightful restaurant decorated with rustic touches. Great Valencian cuisine such as rabbit with honey or lamb with olives. Good local wines. 🍴 ♿
Credit Cards: AE, DC, MC, V · Tapas Bar · Fixed-Price Menu · Good Wine List · Outdoor Tables

CASTELLÓ DE LA PLANA: *La Tasca del Puerto.* €€€
Avenida del Puerto 13, El Grao (Castellón). ⏺ 964 28 44 81.
Specialities include rice dishes, *fideuà* (noodles) and *calderetas* (fish casseroles). There are good views of the harbour and sea. ⏺ *Sun D, Mon.* 🍴 ♿
Credit Cards: AE, DC, MC, V · Fixed-Price Menu · Good Wine List

COCENTAINA: *L'Escaleta.* €€€
Subida Estación Norte 205 (Alicante). 96 559 21 00.
This basement restaurant, tastefully decorated with tiles and old brass items, serves imaginative dishes such as millefeuille of pumpkin. Excellent desserts – try the traditional *arroz y tallaetes.* ● *Sun D, Mon.*
AE DC MC V

CULLERA: *Casa Salvador.* €€
L'Estany de Cullera (Valencia). 96 172 01 36.
Sited on a pretty inlet of a lake (*estany*), this restaurant in two cottages serves 30 different rice dishes and fish specialities. Some of the fish are caught in the lake and the vegetables are home-grown.
AE DC MC V

ELX: *Mesón El Granaíno.* €€
Calle José María Buch 40 (Alicante). 96 546 01 47.
The bar is very popular, offering more than 100 different tapas. The dining room, decorated in traditional Andalusian style, serves regional and southern dishes. The wine cellar contains over 5,000 bottles. ● *Sun, 2 weeks in Aug.*
AE DC MC V

FORCALL: *Mesón de la Vila.* €
Plaza Mayor 8 (Castellón). 964 17 11 25.
Enjoy affordable regional dishes in the vaulted basement of this 15th-century building, which was once the town hall. Try the rabbit, served with either truffles or white snails from the region. ○ *Mon & late Oct.*
AE DC MC V

GANDIA: *Gamba.* €€€€
Carretera Nazaret–Oliva, Gandía-Playa (Valencia). 96 284 13 10.
Although you can't see the sea from here, the fish and shellfish are fresh from the fishermen's nets. The set menu (*menú dirigido*) offers shellfish and a rice or noodle dish. Open lunch times only. ● *L (except Sun) in summer & Nov.*
AE DC MC V

MORAIRA: *Girasol.* €€€€
Carretera Moraira–Calpe km 1.5 (Alicante). 96 574 43 73.
Joachim Koerper's innovative Mediterranean cuisine has won over gourmets throughout Europe and is perfectly complemented by the refined decoration of this seaside villa. ● *Winter· Mon, Nov.*
AE DC MC V

MORELLA: *Casa Roque.* €€
Cuesta San Juan 1 (Castellón). 964 16 03 36.
Diners come from near and far to savour Roque Gutiérrez's lamb stuffed with truffles. Or try the duck with red wine and bitter orange essence, and the mushrooms served with truffles. ● *Sun D, Mon (except Jul & Aug), mid–end Oct.*
AE DC MC V

MURCIA: *Morales.* €€
Avda de la Constitución. 968 23 10 26.
In this central restaurant you can opt for a great variety of dishes, such as a tart of *turrón* (almond paste). ● *Sat D, Sun, 15–31 Aug.*
AE DC MC V

MURCIA: *Hispano.* €€€
Calle Arquitecto Cerdán 7. 968 21 61 52.
Regional cooking, including *caldero marinero del Mar Menor* (a typical seafood casserole). The vegetable paella and the gilthead cooked in salt are also delicious. Good selection of regional wines. ● *Jul–Aug: Sun.*
AE DC MC V

ORIHUELA: *Casa Corro.* €
Palmeral de San Antón (Alicante). 96 530 29 63.
A popular family-run establishment serving dishes such as *arroz con costra* (baked rice with crust) and stew with meatballs. ● *Mon D, 15 Aug–1 Sep.*
DC MC V

ORIHUELA: *Cabo Roig.* €€
Urbanización Cabo Roig, Playas de Orihuela (Alicante). 96 676 02 90.
Perched on top of the cliff with magnificent views of the Costa Blanca, Cabo Roig offers a great variety of seafood and rice dishes. The ancient watchtower houses a collection of over 20,000 bottles of wine.
AE DC MC V

POLOP DE LA MARINA: *Ca l'Angeles.* €
Calle Gabriel Miró 12 (Alicante). 96 587 02 26.
Eat in one of three dining rooms, with wooden beams and rustic decor. Dishes include roast baby kid with almonds. ● *Tue & Jul.*
MC V

SANTA POLA: *Batiste.* €€
Avenida Pérez Ojeda 6, Playa de Poniente (Alicante). 96 541 14 85.
Reasonably priced seafood and shellfish as well as delicious rices, such as *arroz a banda* (fish risotto), feature at this classic restaurant. The sea bass in puff pastry is also a speciality. ● *19 Mar D, 6 Sep L, 24 Dec D.*
AE DC MC V

For key to symbols see back flap

	CREDIT CARDS	TAPAS BAR	FIXED-PRICE MENU	GOOD WINE LIST	OUTDOOR TABLES

Price categories for a three-course evening meal for one, including a half-bottle of house wine, tax and service:

€ under 20 euros
€€ 20–30 euros
€€€ 30–40 euros
€€€€ over 40 euros

TAPAS BAR
In addition to the main dining room, there is a bar serving tapas (*see pp574–5*) and *raciones* (larger portions).
FIXED-PRICE MENU
A good-value, fixed-price menu is offered at lunch or dinner, or both, usually with three courses.
GOOD WINE LIST
Denotes a wide range of good wines, or a more specialized selection of local wines.
OUTDOOR TABLES
Facilities for eating outdoors, on a terrace, or in a garden or courtyard, often with a good view.

VALENCIA: *La Rosa.* €€
Paseo del Neptuno 70. (96 371 20 76.
Typical beachside restaurant with around 30 different rice dishes and a good assortment of fresh fish and shellfish. ● weekends & end Jun–Sep. 目 &
AE DC MC V — Good Wine List ●, Outdoor Tables ■

VALENCIA: *Albacar.* €€€€
Calle Sorní 35. (96 395 10 05.
Enjoy innovative cuisine in attractive surroundings. Try the lukewarm salad of fish with tarragon vinaigrette, and finish with the excellent ravioli with piña colada and rum. ● Sat L, Sun, public hols, Easter, Aug–mid Sep. 目 &
AE MC V — Good Wine List ●

VINARÒS: *El Langostino de Oro.* €€
Calle San Francisco 31. (964 45 12 04.
Carefully selected seafood menu, including seafood *suquet*. The rice dishes and the *fideus rosetjats* (specially prepared noodles) are also very popular, and the date tart excellent. ● Mon, mid-Sep–mid-Oct. 目 &
AE DC MC V — Fixed-Price Menu ■

MADRID

OLD MADRID: *Malacatín.* Map 2 E5. €
Calle de la Ruda 5. (91 365 52 41.
This old bar has a one-item menu: *cocido madrileño*. It must be ordered the day before. Price includes wine and dessert. ● Sun & Aug. 目
V — Tapas Bar ●, Fixed-Price Menu ■

OLD MADRID: *El Estragón.* Map 1 C4. €
Plaza de la Paja 10. (91 365 89 82.
Located off a quiet square near the Palacio Real, this popular vegetarian restaurant is pleasantly decorated. The menu changes regularly and offers a variety of dishes including delicious gazpacho. 目 & ground floor only.
Tapas Bar ●, Fixed-Price Menu ■

OLD MADRID: *Casa Ciriaco.* Map 1 C4. €€
Calle Mayor 84. (91 548 06 20.
A traditional tavern near the Royal Palace, renowned for its *gallina en pepitoria* (a chicken stew with egg and saffron). ● Wed & Aug. 目 &
DC MC V — Tapas Bar ●, Fixed-Price Menu ■, Good Wine List ●

OLD MADRID: *Casa Patas.* Map 5 A2. €€
Calle Cañizares 10. (91 369 04 96.
Known for its flamenco shows in the evening, Casa Patas is also an original place to eat in the heart of Old Madrid. Well-stocked tapas bar and unbeatable fixed-price menu. ● Sun. 目 &
AE DC MC V — Tapas Bar ●, Fixed-Price Menu ■

OLD MADRID: *Taberna Bilbao.* Map 1 C4. €€
Calle Costanilla de San Andres 8. (91 365 61 25.
A Basque tavern serving home-made specialities such as *bacalao* (codfish) cooked in a range of styles. The baby squid (*chipirones*) are also excellent, prepared in their own ink. ● Mon. 目 &
MC V — Tapas Bar ●

OLD MADRID: *Botín.* Map 2 E4. €€€
Calle de Cuchilleros 17. (91 366 42 17.
Reputedly the oldest restaurant in the world, dating back to 1725. The original wood-burning oven is still used to cook the traditional Castilian roast lamb and suckling pig. Reasonable fixed-price menu. 目
AE DC MC V — Fixed-Price Menu ■, Good Wine List ●

OLD MADRID: *Casa Lucio.* Map 2 D5. €€€
Calle Cava Baja 35. (91 365 32 52.
This historic tavern serves Castilian specialities. The fried eggs with potatoes are exquisite and the rice pudding renowned. ● Sat L & Aug. 目
AE DC MC V — Tapas Bar ●, Good Wine List ●

OLD MADRID: *Lhardy.* Map 2 F3. €€€€
Carrera de San Jerónimo 8. (91 521 33 85.
Established in 1839 and conserving its true character with chandeliers, mirrors and dark wood-panelled walls, this restaurant serves what is arguably the most classic *cocido madrileño*. ● Sun D & Aug. 目
AE DC MC V — Tapas Bar ●, Fixed-Price Menu ■, Good Wine List ●

BOURBON MADRID: *Champagnería Gala*. **Map 5 B2.**   €
Calle Moratín 22. **〔** *91 429 25 62.*
Admire the indoor patio and chandeliers and enjoy a generous set menu
with Catalan specialities at an unbelievably reasonable price. 📗

BOURBON MADRID: *Pimiento Verde*. **Map 4 E4.**   €€
Calle Lagasca 46. **〔** *91 576 41 35.*
Typical Basque cuisine is served in a restaurant decorated in cider-house
style including excellent meat and fish dishes. The adjoining lively tavern
serves excellent tapas. ⬤ *Sun.* 📗
AE MC V

BOURBON MADRID: *Al Mounia*. **Map 4 D4.**   €€€
Calle de Recoletos 5. **〔** *91 435 08 28.*
Madrid's finest Moroccan restaurant serving authentic couscous and *tajine*
(lamb stew). If you have room, there is the rich house dessert.
⬤ *Sun, Mon, Easter & Aug.* 📗
AE DC MC

BOURBON MADRID: *Teatriz*. **Map 4 E3.**   €€€
Calle Hermosilla 15. **〔** *91 577 53 79.*
A restaurant in the stalls of an old theatre, with a cocktail bar on the stage.
Italian-inspired food, such as a salmon and sole *carpaccio.* 📗 ♿
AE DC MC V

BOURBON MADRID: *Alkalde*. **Map 4 E3.**   €€€€
Calle Jorge Juan 10. **〔** *91 576 33 59.*
Call in for Basque specialities in the dining room or at the lively tapas
bar. The spider crab soup, the *chipirones* (small squid cooked in its ink)
and the clams in a white wine, onion and garlic sauce are all good.
⬤ *Jul & Aug: Sat & Sun.* 📗
AE DC MC V

BOURBON MADRID: *El Amparo*. **Map 4 E4.**   €€€€
Callejón de Puigcerdá 8. **〔** *91 431 64 56.*
New Basque Cuisine in what many consider to be Madrid's nicest setting,
with a skylight that lets you gaze up at the stars. The tuna mousse with
lobster and parsley oil is just one creation. ⬤ *Sat L, Sun, public hols, Aug.* 📗
AE MC V

BOURBON MADRID: *Paradis*. **Map 5 B1.**   €€€€
Calle Marqués de Cubas 14. **〔** *91 429 73 03.*
Part of a successful Catalan chain, offering high-quality Mediterranean
cuisine. The grilled vegetables and the rice dishes make delicious starters.
They can be followed by any of the fresh fish. ⬤ *Sat L, Sun, public hols.* 📗 ♿
AE DC MC V

BOURBON MADRID: *Viridiana*. **Map 6 D1.**   €€€€
Calle Juan de Mena 14. **〔** *91 523 44 78.*
Innovative Spanish cuisine complemented by an encyclopedic wine list is
offered in this restaurant decorated with stills from Luis Buñuel's film
Viridiana. The creative menu changes frequently. ⬤ *Sun & Aug.* 📗
AE MC V

FURTHER AFIELD (EAST): *La Taberna de la Daniela*.   €€
Calle General Pardiñas 21. **〔** *91 575 23 29.*
A short but well-chosen menu is offered at this restaurant. The only thing
served at lunch times is *cocido madrileño*, or you can choose from a wide
range of tapas at the bar. Good home-made desserts. 📗
AE MC V

FURTHER AFIELD (NORTHWEST): *Baden*.   €€
Calle General Rodrigo 17. **〔** *91 553 87 96.*
A lively tapas bar and a cosy restaurant are combined at Baden, which is
located in a students' area of the city. The meat and fresh fish are a hearty,
good choice and the pizzas are the best in Madrid. 📗
AE DC MC V

FURTHER AFIELD (NORTH): *Casa Ricardo*.   €€
Calle Fernando El Católico 31. **〔** *91 447 61 19.*
This typical Spanish bar offers good, home-style dishes. The oxtail soup is
delicious as are the baby squid prepared in their own ink. ⬤ *Sun D.* 📗 ♿
DC MC V

FURTHER AFIELD (NORTH): *La Barraca*. **Map 3 A5.**   €€
Calle de la Reina 29. **〔** *91 532 71 54.*
Over ten different Valencia-style rice dishes and paellas are on offer here,
made with first-class ingredients. Good home-made desserts. 📗
AE DC

FURTHER AFIELD (NORTH): *El Puchero*. **Map 3 A2.**   €€
Calle de Larra 13. **〔** *91 445 05 77.*
Popular, unfussy restaurant offering hearty, home-style cooking. The baby
broad (fava) beans with ham, the roast suckling pig and the game stews
are legendary, as are the cantankerous waitresses. ⬤ *Sun & Aug.* 📗
AE MC V

	CREDIT CARDS	TAPAS BAR	FIXED-PRICE MENU	GOOD WINE LIST	OUTDOOR TABLES

Price categories for a three-course evening meal for one, including a half-bottle of house wine, tax and service:

€ under 20 euros
€€ 20–30 euros
€€€ 30–40 euros
€€€€ over 40 euros

TAPAS BAR
In addition to the main dining room, there is a bar serving tapas *(see pp574–5)* and *raciones* (larger portions).
FIXED-PRICE MENU
A good-value, fixed-price menu is offered at lunch or dinner, or both, usually with three courses.
GOOD WINE LIST
Denotes a wide range of good wines, or a more specialized selection of local wines.
OUTDOOR TABLES
Facilities for eating outdoors, on a terrace, or in a garden or courtyard, often with a good view.

FURTHER AFIELD (NORTH): *Goizeko Kabi.*   €€€€
Calle Comandante Zorita 37. ◖ *91 533 01 85.*
Traditional Basque cuisine served in a refined setting. Excellent fresh produce and seafood are the basis of the chef's creations. Good wine list and delectable desserts. ● *Sat L, Jul & Aug.* 目 ♿

AE DC MC V — Good Wine List

FURTHER AFIELD (NORTH): *Jockey.* Map 4 D2.   €€€€
Calle Amador de los Ríos 6. ◖ *91 319 10 03.*
Among Madrid's top five restaurants, frequented by gourmets and celebrities, Jockey offers a seasonal menu. Excellent poultry and game dishes and a superb wine list. Smart dress. ● *Sat L, Sun, public hols, Aug.* 目 ♿

AE DC MC V — Good Wine List

FURTHER AFIELD (NORTH): *Zalacain.*   €€€€
Calle Álvarez de Baena 4. ◖ *91 561 48 40.*
Considered Madrid's finest restaurant, Zalacain lives up to its reputation with a luxurious setting, attentive service and, above all, delicious Basque-oriented cuisine. Smart dress. ● *Sat L, Sun, Easter, Aug, public hols.* 目 ♿

AE DC MC V — Good Wine List

FURTHER AFIELD (NORTHEAST): *Sacha.*   €€€
Calle Juan Hurtado de Mendoza 11, Entrada Posterior. ◖ *91 345 59 52.*
Decorated like a cosy bistro, this restaurant serves specialities such as partridge with rice and mushrooms. ● *Sun, Aug & public hols.* 目 ♿

AE DC MC V — Good Wine List, Outdoor Tables

FURTHER AFIELD (NORTHEAST): *Cabo Mayor.*   €€€€
Calle Juan Ramón Jiménez 37. ◖ *91 350 87 76.*
One of Madrid's finest seafood restaurants with Cantabrian-Navarrese cuisine. Try the delicious fresh pasta and prawn (shrimp) salad or monkfish and mushrooms. Excellent wines and desserts. ● *Sat L, Sun & public hols.* 目

AE DC MC V — Fixed-Price Menu, Good Wine List, Outdoor Tables

FURTHER AFIELD (NORTHEAST): *El Olivo.*   €€€€
Calle General Gallegos 1. ◖ *91 359 15 35.*
Top of the line Mediterranean cuisine, with olive oil as the underlying culinary theme. The owner will advise you on which of the 40 different olive oils will best accompany your meal. ● *Sun, Mon, public hols, late Aug.* 目

AE DC MC V — Fixed-Price Menu, Good Wine List

MADRID PROVINCE

ARANJUEZ: *Casa Pablo.*   €€€
Calle Almíbar 42. ◖ *91 891 14 51.*
A centrally located tavern offering solid home cooking. Try the pheasant with grapes or the fresh asparagus and strawberries. ● *Aug.* 目 ♿

AE MC V — Tapas Bar, Fixed-Price Menu, Good Wine List

CHINCHÓN: *Mesón de la Virreina.*   €€
Plaza Mayor 28. ◖ *91 894 00 15.*
Traditional Castilian food, including sopa castellana – a garlic soup with chickpeas *(garbanzos)* is prepared in this 16th-century building. 目 ♿

AE DC MC V — Tapas Bar, Fixed-Price Menu

MORALZARZAL: *El Cenador de Salvador.*   €€€€
Avenida de España 30. ◖ *91 857 77 22.*
Many gourmets make the trek from Madrid to Moralzarzal just for the pleasure of dining in this lovely chalet. The exquisite seasonal cooking is bound to delight even the most refined taste buds. ● *Sun D, Mon.* 目 ♿

AE DC MC V — Fixed-Price Menu, Good Wine List, Outdoor Tables

PATONES DE ARRIBA: *El Poleo.*   €€€
Travesía del Arroyo 1–3. ◖ *91 843 21 01.*
This picturesque town with slate-oofed houses boasts a wonderful restaurant offering Navarrese-style cuisine. ◗ *Fri–Sun & public hols.* 目

AE DC MC V — Tapas Bar, Good Wine List, Outdoor Tables

SAN LORENZO DE EL ESCORIAL: *Taberna La Cueva.*   €€
Calle San Antón 4. ◖ *91 890 15 16.*
Juan de Villanueva, architect of the Prado, designed this 18th-century inn whose specialities include the *huevos a la cueva* (fried eggs and ham served in a nest of straw potatoes). ● *Mon.*

MC V — Tapas Bar, Fixed-Price Menu, Good Wine List

Castilla y León

Aranda de Duero: *Mesón La Villa.* €€€
Plaza Mayor 3 (Burgos). 947 50 10 25.
High-quality regional cooking with a great variety of Castilian dishes –
pickled partridge, sweetbreads (offal) with mushrooms, and *menestra de
verduras* (vegetable stew). Impressive selection of local wines. ● *Mon.*
AE DC MC V

Arévalo: *Asador La Cubas.* €€
Calle Figones 9 (Ávila). 920 30 01 25.
This converted wine cellar with clay casks set into the walls offers delicious
suckling lamb and pig roasted in the wood-burning oven, and tasty regional
desserts such as sweet custard fritters (*leche frita*). ● *Sun–Fri D & late Jun.*
AE DC MC V

Astorga: *La Peseta.* €
Plaza de San Bartolomé 3 (León). 987 61 72 75.
A family-run restaurant with a tradition for hearty, healthy cooking. Try the
pork and bean stew accompanied by local Bierzo wine. ● *Sun D, late Oct.*
AE MC V

Ávila: *Mesón del Rastro.* €€
Plaza del Rastro 1. 920 21 12 18.
Authentic regional dishes are offered in this truly Castilian restaurant
nestled in the city wall. The *Judías de El Barco de Ávila* (dried white beans
served in a thick sauce with chorizo) is an all-time favourite.
AE DC MC V

Burgos: *Casa Ojeda.* €€€
Calle Vitoria 5. 947 20 90 52.
The city's most traditional restaurant serving classic dishes such as roast
suckling lamb, and *morcilla* (a black/blood sausage) with red peppers. There
is an extensive choice of Ribera del Duero and La Rioja wines. ● *Sun D.*
AE DC MC V

Covarrubias: *El Galín.* €
Plaza de Doña Urraca 4 (Burgos). 947 40 65 52.
The Galín is a simple, busy restaurant in the main square, preparing
succulent baby lamb and other hearty regional dishes such as *olla podrida*
(a thick, bean-based broth). Good tapas bar. ● *Tue & Sep.*
AE DC MC V

El Burgo de Osma: *Virrey Palafox.* €€€
Calle Universidad 7, El Burgo de Osma (Soria). 975 34 02 22.
This restaurant, near the village centre, is popular during February and March,
when it offers a 'pig-killing' menu – all the meat products of a pig, killed
that morning, are eaten by customers th... ● *Jun D.*
AE DC MC V

Frómista: *Hostería de Los Palmeros.* €€
Plaza San Telmo 4 (Palencia). 979 81 00 67.
This ancient inn on the Road to Santiago has been agreeably restored. The
menu offers good Castilian dishes including baby pigeon casserole and
tocinillo de cielo (sweet candied egg yolks) for dessert. ● *Mon D & Tue.*
AE DC MC V

La Granja de San Ildefonso: *Hilaria.* €€
Carretera Madrid-Valladolid km 124 (Segovia). 921 47 02 92.
The owners of this family-run restaurant still use an original recipe for their
white bean stew. Good roast suckling lamb and pig. ● *Mon.*
AE MC V

León: *Mesón Leonés del Racimo de Oro.* €€
Calle Caño Vadillo 2. 987 25 75 75.
Traditional cooking in the stables of a 17th-century inn. In winter there are
game dishes and stews, such as the *cocido leonés* (a hearty broth of chickpeas
(garbanzos), potatoes, bacon, blood sausage and cabbage). ● *Sun D & Tue D.*
AE DC MC

Palencia: *Casa Damián.* €€
Calle Ignacio Martínez de Azcoitia 9. 979 74 46 28.
A reliable restaurant with provincial specialities including a fresh *menestra
de verduras* and delicious *buñuelos* (sweet fritters). ● *Mon, Sun D & Aug.*
AE DC MC V

Pedraza de la Sierra: *Hostería Pintor Zuloaga.* €€
Calle Matadero 1 (Segovia). 921 50 98 35.
Located in a former Inquisition house, this restaurant serves traditional
Castilian fare such as roast pork and lamb, and hearty stews. ● *Tue.*
AE DC MC V

Ponferrada: *Azul-Montearenas.* €€
Carretera NVI Madrid–A Coruña km 380 (León). 987 41 70 12.
Simple, home-style cooking is prepared in this restaurant with mountain
views. Try the chard filled with shrimp and monkfish. ● *Sun D.*
AE DC MC V

Price categories for a three-course evening meal for one, including a half-bottle of house wine, tax and service:

€ under 20 euros
€€ 20–30 euros
€€€ 30–40 euros
€€€€ over 40 euros

TAPAS BAR
In addition to the main dining room, there is a bar serving tapas *(see pp574–5)* and *raciones* (larger portions).
FIXED-PRICE MENU
A good-value, fixed-price menu is offered at lunch or dinner, or both, usually with three courses.
GOOD WINE LIST
Denotes a wide range of good wines, or a more specialized selection of local wines.
OUTDOOR TABLES
Facilities for eating outdoors, on a terrace, or in a garden or courtyard, often with a good view.

	CREDIT CARDS	TAPAS BAR	FIXED-PRICE MENU	GOOD WINE LIST	OUTDOOR TABLES
QUINTANA DE RANEROS: *Bodega El Cercao.* €€ Calle de la Bodega 4, Finca El Cercao (León). (987 28 01 28. This huge 17th-century wine cellar is one long maze of underground passages and rustic dining rooms. Enjoy any of the traditional dishes, such as *morcilla* (blood sausage) with locally grown red Bierzo peppers.	AE DC MC V	●	■	●	■
SALAMANCA: *Río de la Plata.* €€€ Plaza del Peso 1. (923 21 90 05. A tiny, popular restaurant next to the Plaza Mayor, serving a great variety of fresh fish and Castilian dishes, all of superb quality. ● *Mon & Jul.* ▤	AE MC V	●	■		
SANTA MARÍA DE MAVE: *Hostería El Convento.* €€ Santa María de Mave (Palencia). (979 12 36 11. This ancient Benedictine monastery on the banks of the Río Pisuerga now houses an inn serving traditional Castilian fare, including lamb roasted in a wood-burning oven and *sopa castellana* (a rich garlic soup). &	AE DC MC V	●	■	●	■
SANTO DOMINGO DE SILOS: *Casa Emeterio.* €€ Hotel Tres Coronas de Silos, Plaza Mayor 6 (Burgos). (947 39 00 47. After admiring the monastery you can relax in the rustic dining room of this large, 18th-century house and enjoy good, regional cooking. &	AE DC MC V	●	■	●	
SEGOVIA: *Mesón de Cándido.* €€€ Plaza del Azoguejo 5. (921 42 81 03. Don't leave town without visiting Mesón de Cándido, *the* place to eat in Segovia. The restaurant has good views of the Roman aqueduct and serves local specialities such as roast lamb and suckling pig. ▤ &	AE DC MC V	●			■
SEPÚLVEDA: *Cristóbal.* €€ Calle Conde de Sepúlveda 9 (Segovia). (921 54 01 00. Enjoy impressive views of the Duratón gorges as you dine on hearty stews and, reputedly, the best roast lamb in the region. ● *Tue, early Sep & late Dec.* ▤	AE DC MC V	●	■	●	
TORDESILLAS: *El Torreón.* €€€ Calle Burgos Portugal 11 (Valladolid). (983 77 01 23. Specializing in first-class grilled meats, El Torreón has a reproduction of the Convento de Santa Clara's beautiful ceiling. Book ahead. ● *Sun & late Sep.* ▤	AE DC MC V			●	
TORRECABALLEROS: *El Rancho de la Aldegüela.* €€ Plaza Marques de Lozoya 3 (Segovia). (921 40 10 46. A country house with rustic decor serving regional specialities such as *revuelto de morcilla* (scrambled eggs with blood sausage). ● *Oct–Jun: Mon–Thu D.* ▤	AE DC MC V	●		●	■
VALLADOLID: *La Fragua.* €€€ Paseo de Zorilla 10. (983 33 87 85. The rich garlic soup, lamb casserole in white wine and spring vegetables, and the veal stew are all proof that this is a truly Castilian restaurant. Fish is a speciality too. Great tapas bar. ● *Sun D & Aug.* ▤ &	AE DC MC V	●		●	
VILLAFRANCA DEL BIERZO: *La Charola.* € Carretera NVI Madrid–A Coruña km 406 (León). (987 54 00 95. A family-run restaurant by the side of the road, serving generous portions of regional dishes. Simple, reliable and inexpensive. ▤ &	AE DC MC V	●	■	●	
ZAMORA: *Pizarro.* €€ Cuesta de Pizarro 7. (980 53 45 45. Once used as an Inquisition palace, this 16th-century building serves regional and Basque specialities such as sole with anchovy sauce.	AE DC MC V		■	●	
ZAMORA: *Rey Sancho II.* €€ Parque de la Marina Española (Zamora). (980 52 60 54. This restaurant overlooks the park, in the modern centre of town. The menu offers regional dishes such as *arroz a la zamorana* (Zamoran rice). ▤	AE DC MC V		■		■

CASTILLA-LA MANCHA

ALBACETE: *Nuestro Bar.* €€ Calle Alcalde Conangla 102. **(** *967 24 33 73.* The dining room serves regional dishes and a *menú de degustación* which includes specialities of La Mancha such as *gazpacho manchego* (a rich game stew thickened with biscuits). The restaurant also has a great tapas bar. ● *Sun D & Jul.* ▤	AE DC MC V	●	▥	●	▥
ALMAGRO: *El Corregidor.* €€ Calle Jerónimo Ceballos 2 (Ciudad Real). **(** *926 86 06 48.* This delightful old house, with many dining rooms and a central patio, is one of Castilla-La Mancha's prettiest restaurants. Creative, regional cuisine including the town's speciality, pickled aubergines (eggplant). ● *Sep–Jun: Mon; Aug.* ▤	AE DC MC V	●	▥	●	▥
ALMANSA: *Mesón de Picelín.* €€€ Calle Norias 10 (Albacete). **(** *967 34 00 07.* Considered by many to be one of the region's best restaurants. You can try authentic regional dishes including their famous *gazpacho manchego* made with chicken, rabbit and partridge. ● *Sun D, Mon, Aug.* ▤ ♿	AE DC MC V	●	▥	●	
BETETA: *Hotel Los Tilos.* €€ Extrarradio (Cuenca). **(** *969 31 80 98.* A simple, unfussy hotel restaurant serving typical mountain dishes, such as onion soup, venison stew and *morteruelo* (a mixed game pâté). ♿	AE DC MC V	●	▥		
BRIHUEGA: *Asador El Tolmo.* €€ Avenida de la Constitución 26 (Guadalajara). **(** *949 28 04 76.* The traditional Castilian decor is in keeping with the cuisine, which includes roast kid, beans with partridge and home-made desserts. ▤ ♿	MC V	●	●		
CIUDAD REAL: *Gran Mesón.* €€ Ronda de Ciruela 34. **(** *926 22 72 39.* Ample set menu with regional specialities such as *gachas* (gruel), *pisto* (a vegetable mix), suckling pig and local cheese and wines. ● *Sun D.* ▤ ♿	AE MC V		▥	●	
CUENCA: *Marlo.* €€€ Calle Colón 41. **(** *969 21 11 73.* Fish and shellfish feature predominantly on the modern menu here, and there are also good meat dishes. Try the stuffed partridge. ▤	AE MC V	●	▥	●	
CUENCA: *Mesón Casas Colgadas.* €€€ Calle Canónigos. **(** *969 22 35 09.* Dine above the gorge in one of Cuenca's famous hanging houses. Unbeatable views combined with great regional cuisine. ● *Mon D.* ▤	AE DC MC V	●	▥	●	
GUADALAJARA: *Minaya.* €€ Calle Mayor 23. **(** *949 21 22 53.* A wonderful 16th-century palace with period furniture. The short seasonal menu has an emphasis on grilled meats and roast kid. ● *Sun.* ▤	AE DC MC V	●	▥	●	
GUADALAJARA: *Amparito Roca.* €€€ Calle Toledo 19. **(** *949 21 46 39.* This pleasantly decorated house offers traditional Spanish cuisine with innovative touches. The venison sirloin served in a mushroom sauce and the scrambled eggs with potato and salmon are examples. ● *Sun & Aug.* ▤ ♿	AE MC V		▥	●	▥
JADRAQUE: *El Castillo.* €€ Carretera de Soria km 46 (Guadalajara). **(** *949 89 02 54.* After visiting the castle, stop here for delicious roast kid or any of the other classic Castilian dishes prepared in this typical *mesón* (inn). ▤	AE DC MC V	●	▥	●	▥
MANZANARES: *Mesón Sancho.* € Calle Jesús del Perdón 26 (Ciudad Real). **(** *926 61 10 16.* This simple, down-to-earth restaurant serves typical, robust dishes such as garlic soup, *duelos y quebrantos* (scrambled eggs with pork) and rabbit *a la manchega* (in a sauce), washed down with local wine. ▤ ♿	AE DC MC V	●	▥	●	
LAS PEDROÑERAS: *Las Rejas.* €€€€ Avenida de Brasil (Cuenca). **(** *967 16 10 89.* Spain's garlic capital also has a first-class restaurant with an appetizing seasonal menu and an unforgettable garlic soup. Many dishes feature regional produce. Try the fresh *manchego* cheese salad. ● *Mon & late Jul.* ▤ ♿	AE DC MC V		▥	●	

<table>
<tr><td>

Price categories for a three-course evening meal for one, including a half-bottle of house wine, tax and service:

€ under 20 euros
€€ 20–30 euros
€€€ 30–40 euros
€€€€ over 40 euros

</td><td>

TAPAS BAR
In addition to the main dining room, there is a bar serving tapas (see pp574–5) and raciones (larger portions).
FIXED-PRICE MENU
A good-value, fixed-price menu is offered at lunch or dinner, or both, usually with three courses.
GOOD WINE LIST
Denotes a wide range of good wines, or a more specialized selection of local wines.
OUTDOOR TABLES
Facilities for eating outdoors, on a terrace, or in a garden or courtyard, often with a good view.

</td></tr>
</table>

	CREDIT CARDS	TAPAS BAR	FIXED-PRICE MENU	GOOD WINE LIST	OUTDOOR TABLES

PUERTO LÁPICE: *Venta del Quijote.* €€
Calle Molino 4 (Ciudad Real). 926 57 61 10.
Set in the heart of Don Quixote territory, this legendary inn evokes Cervantes' masterpiece. Sit around the pebbled courtyard and enjoy any of the Manchegan specialities. 🔲 &

| AE DC MC V | | ■ | ● | ■ |

SIGÜENZA: *El Motor.* €€€
Avenida Juan Carlos I, 2 (Guadalajara). 949 39 08 27.
As well as the typical roast suckling pig and lamb you can also try the fried breadcrumbs (*migas*) or the garlic soup (*sopa castellana*). 🔲 &

| AE MC V | ● | ■ | ● | ■ |

TALAVERA DE LA REINA: *Antonio.* €
Avenida de Portugal 8 (Toledo). 925 80 40 17.
A bar serving good-quality tapas at reasonable prices, and a dining room offering great regional food, make this a popular place. ● Sun D, 1–15 Jul. 🔲 &

| AE DC MC V | ● | ■ | ● | |

TOLEDO: *Hostal del Cardenal.* €€
Paseo de Recaredo 24. 925 22 08 62.
Once the summer residence of Cardinal Lorenzana, this 18th-century palace retains its beautiful garden, enclosed by the city walls. It serves garlic soup, suckling pig and the famous Toledo *mazapán* (marzipan). 🔲

| AE DC MC V | | ■ | ● | ■ |

TOLEDO: *La Lumbre.* €€
Calle Real de Arrabal 3. 925 22 03 73.
A lovely old house with wooden beams, next to the Puerta de Bisagra. The meat dishes, such as roast suckling pig and lamb, are especially good, and there is delicious *manchego* cheesecake for dessert. ● Sun & Jul. 🔲

| AE DC MC V | | ■ | ● | |

TOLEDO: *Adolfo.* €€€
Calle de Granada 6. 925 22 73 21.
Set in the heart of Toledo's Jewish quarter, the Adolfo, with its tiles, columns, antiques and a wonderful 15th-century Mudéjar coffered ceiling, serves game in winter and fresh trout from the Río Tajo. ● Sun D & late Jul. 🔲 &

| AE DC MC V | ● | ■ | ● | |

TRAGACETE: *El Gamo.* €
Plaza Fuente del Pino 2 (Cuenca). 969 28 90 08.
This mountain inn has a simple, family-run restaurant where you can try home-style cooking, such as venison stew and *morteruelo*. &

| MC V | ● | ■ | | ■ |

VALDEPEÑAS: *Baviera.* €
Calle 6 de Junio 44 (Ciudad Real). 926 32 40 84.
A centrally located restaurant serving authentic cuisine of La Mancha. The *galianos* (a typical dish made with game) and the mountain rabbit with garlic are two specialities. Good selection of Valdepeñas wines. ● Tue & late Aug. 🔲

| AE DC MC V | ● | ■ | ● | |

VILLALBA DE LA SIERRA: *Nelia.* €€
Ruta de la Ciudad Encantada km 21 (Cuenca). 969 28 10 21.
A wood and stone restaurant on the banks of the Río Júcar. The wild boar meatballs, the marinated venison and the vegetables in puff pastry are all superb. Good Valdepeñas wines. ● Wed & mid Jan–mid Feb. 🔲 &

| AE MC V | ● | ■ | ● | ■ |

EXTREMADURA

ALMENDRALEJO: *Nando.* €
Calle Ricardo Romero 12 (Badajoz). 924 66 12 71.
The dining room serves generous portions of rice with rabbit, *judiones* (locally grown beans prepared with pig's knuckle or partridge) and fresh fish. Good tapas bar for trying local specialities. ● Sun D. 🔲

| AE MC V | ● | ■ | | |

BADAJOZ: *Aldebarán.* €€€
Avenida de Elvas, Urbanización Guadiana. 924 27 42 61.
One of Badajoz province's finer restaurants. Creations include the pickled Iberian pork salad and pigeon in wine sauce. ● Sun. 🔲 &

| AE DC MC V | | ■ | ● | |

CÁCERES: *El Figón de Eustaquio.* €€ AE DC MC V
Plaza de San Juan 14. [927 24 81 94.
Simple restaurant in the historic part of town where you can sample
genuine Extremaduran cooking such as trout *a la extremeña* (stuffed with
ham) and the house soup of tomato with poached egg. 🍴 &

CÁCERES: *Atrio.* €€€ DC MC V
Avenida de España 30. [927 24 29 28.
Innovative, contemporary cuisine offset by elegant decor in Cáceres' most
sophisticated restaurant. The tender venison fillets served with muscat
grapes and pears is just one of the chef's creative combinations. ● *Sun D.* &

GUADALUPE: *Hospedería del Real Monasterio.* € MC V
Plaza de Juan Carlos I (Cáceres). [927 36 70 00.
Owned by the Franciscan order, this restaurant offers simple regional
cooking. The tomato soup, the roast kid and the *migas extremeñas*
(breadcrumbs with pork) are all recommended. ● *mid Jan–mid Feb.* 🍴

GUADALUPE: *Mesón El Cordero.* €€ AE DC MC V
Calle Alfonso Onceno 27 (Cáceres). [927 36 71 31.
Regional specialities are served in the cosy wood-panelled dining room.
Enjoy the fresh vegetable *menestra* (stew) or the partridge casserole as you
admire the view of the mountains. ● *Mon & Feb.* 🍴

JARANDILLA DE LA VERA: *Cueva de Puta Parió.* € AE DC MC V
Calle Francisco Pizarro 8 (Cáceres). [927 56 03 92.
A lively and popular tavern with good regional dishes including tomato soup
and lamb casserole, and locally produced house wine. ● *Mon & late Sep.* 🍴

JEREZ DE LOS CABALLEROS: *La Ermita.* € MC V
Calle Doctor Benítez 9 (Badajoz). [924 73 14 76.
This 17th-century chapel converted into a wine cellar now houses a
restaurant serving local dishes. Sample the partridge stew or the typical
revuelto de espárragos, made with scrambled eggs and asparagus tips. &

LOSAR DE LA VERA: *Carlos V.* € AE DC MC V
Avenida de Extremadura 45 (Cáceres). [927 57 06 36.
Home cooking and lovely views of the mountains and the Tiétar valley.
The *revuelto con criadillas de tierra* (scrambled eggs with white truffles),
the roast kid and the steaks are all specialities. ● *Mon, mid-Oct–Nov.* 🍴 &

MÉRIDA: *Nicolás.* €€ AE DC MC V
Calle Félix Valverde Lillo 13 (Badajoz). [924 31 96 10.
You might want to visit the small brick wine cellar for an apéritif before
tucking into the regional specialities such as the delicious lamb with plums
or the pork sirloin with peppers. Pretty garden and terrace. ● *Sun D.* 🍴

MÉRIDA: *Parador de Mérida.* €€€ AE DC MC V
Plaza de la Constitución 3 (Badajoz). [924 31 38 00.
This lovely old convent now houses a parador and a restaurant well worth
a visit. Savour regional specialities such as Extremaduran cheeses, cold
meats, and the *caldereta de cordero* (lamb casserole). 🍴 &

MÉRIDA: *Rufino.* €€€ AE DC MC V
Plaza Santa Clara 2 (Badajoz). [924 31 20 01.
Typical Extremaduran cuisine is produced to a high standard at this
restaurant. Classic dishes on the menu include *revuelto con criadillas de
tierra* (scrambled eggs with white truffles). ● *Sun, 1–15 Sep.* 🍴 &

PLASENCIA: *Alfonso VIII.* €€€ AE DC MC V
Avenida Alfonso VIII 32 (Cáceres). [927 41 02 50.
Creative cuisine, relying heavily on local produce and updated traditional
recipes. Try the kid stew or the Iberian ham. 🍴 &

PLASENCIA: *El Rincón Extremeño.* €€€ AE DC MC V
Calle Vidrieras 8 (Cáceres). [927 41 11 50.
Traditional Plasencian dishes, including frogs in *salsa verde*, lizard (in
season) and more "usual" fare such as suckling pig. Be sure to try the
raspberry, cheese and honey dessert called *Tío Pichu.* 🍴 &

PUEBLA DE LA REINA: *Mesón La Jara-Casa Andrés.* € MC V
Calle Luis Chamizo 14 (Badajoz). [924 36 00 05.
This charming mesón has become a sanctuary of authentic regional food.
Those with stamina can try the 14-course meal. 🍴

	CREDIT CARDS	TAPAS BAR	FIXED-PRICE MENU	GOOD WINE LIST	OUTDOOR TABLES

Price categories for a three-course evening meal for one, including a half-bottle of house wine, tax and service:

€ under 20 euros
€€ 20–30 euros
€€€ 30–40 euros
€€€€ over 40 euros

TAPAS BAR
In addition to the main dining room, there is a bar serving tapas (see pp574–5) and raciones (larger portions).
FIXED-PRICE MENU
A good-value, fixed-price menu is offered at lunch or dinner, or both, usually with three courses.
GOOD WINE LIST
Denotes a wide range of good wines, or a more specialized selection of local wines.
OUTDOOR TABLES
Facilities for eating outdoors, on a terrace, or in a garden or courtyard, often with a good view.

Restaurant	Price	Credit Cards	Tapas Bar	Fixed-Price Menu	Good Wine List	Outdoor Tables
TRUJILLO: *Mesón La Troya.*	€	MC V	●	■	●	■
TRUJILLO: *Pizarro.*	€€	MC V		■	●	
ZAFRA: *Barbacana.*	€€€	AE DC MC V		■	●	
EL ARENAL: *Bodegón Torre del Oro.* Map 3 B2.	€€	AE DC MC V	●	■	●	■
EL ARENAL: *El Burladero.* Map 3 B1.	€€€	AE DC MC V	●	■	●	
EL ARENAL: *Enrique Becerra.* Map 3 B1.	€€€	AE DC MC V	●		●	
EL ARENAL: *La Isla.* Map 3 B2.	€€€	AE DC MC V	●		●	■
SANTA CRUZ: *Las Meninas.* Map 3 D1.	€	AE V	●	■		
SANTA CRUZ: *Casa Robles.* Map 3 C1.	€€	AE DC MC V	●	■	●	
SANTA CRUZ: *Corral del Agua.* Map 3 C2.	€€	AE DC MC V		■	●	■
SANTA CRUZ: *Mesón de la Infanta.* Map 3 B2.	€€	MC V	●		●	

TRUJILLO: *Mesón La Troya.*
Plaza Mayor 10 (Cáceres). **(** *927 32 13 64.*
A typical *mesón* dating back to the 16th century, serving regional food in hearty portions. The *migas* (breadcrumbs) with pork, the dried white beans in sauce, and the lamb in its own juice are all recommended. ☰

TRUJILLO: *Pizarro.*
Plaza Mayor 13 (Cáceres). **(** *927 32 02 55.*
The decor in this restaurant has changed little since it opened before the Civil War. Enjoy traditional dishes such as tomato soup with figs and grapes, and chicken stuffed with truffles. ● *Tue.* ☰

ZAFRA: *Barbacana.*
Hotel Huerta Honda, Avenida López Asme 30 (Badajoz). **(** *924 55 41 00.*
This 16th-century house, finely decorated with antiques, provides a lovely backdrop for good regional and Basque cuisine, including roast suckling lamb with rosemary and fillet of hake with clams. ● *Sun D.* ☰

SEVILLE

EL ARENAL: *Bodegón Torre del Oro.* **Map 3 B2.**
Postigo del Carbon 15. **(** *95 422 08 80.*
This combined bar and dining room specializes in *raciones*. Try the *garbanzos con espinacas* (chickpeas/garbanzos with spinach), *puntillitas* (tiny grilled cuttlefish) or the *punta de solomillo* (fillet tip). &

EL ARENAL: *El Burladero.* **Map 3 B1.**
Hotel Colón, Calle Canalejas 1. **(** *95 422 29 00.*
Decorated with bullfighting memorabilia, this restaurant offers caviar and filet mignon as well as local dishes such as *puchero* (meat-in-a-pot). ☰ &

EL ARENAL: *Enrique Becerra.* **Map 3 B1.**
Calle Gamazo 2. **(** *95 421 30 49.*
This plush restaurant-bar attracts well-heeled customers for apéritifs and meals. Besides a fine selection of fish and meat dishes, the daily specials feature Andalusian home-style cooking. ● *Sun.* ☰

EL ARENAL: *La Isla.* **Map 3 B2.**
Calle Arfe 25. **(** *95 421 26 31.* FAX *95 456 22 19.*
An attractive, centrally located restaurant featuring superb seafood: turbot, bream and delicacies such as *percebes* (sea barnacles). ● *Aug.* ☰

SANTA CRUZ: *Las Meninas.* **Map 3 D1.**
Calle Santo Tomás 3. **(** *95 422 62 26.*
Hearty food and good prices make this a popular place. Excellent local dishes, such as braised bull's tail or *potage* of chickpeas/garbanzos and cod. ☰

SANTA CRUZ: *Casa Robles.* **Map 3 C1.**
Calle Álvarez Quintero 58. **(** *95 456 32 72.*
Right in the heart of Seville, this lively place has three small dining rooms. Fish is a speciality – fried, baked or with rice – and there is an excellent choice of fresh shellfish. Good meat dishes and tapas. ☰

SANTA CRUZ: *Corral del Agua.* **Map 3 C2.**
Callejón del Agua 6. **(** *95 422 48 41.*
Dine on the cool patio in a lee of the Reales Alcázares gardens. The menu emphasizes seasonal specialities, carefully prepared and served. ● *Sun.*

SANTA CRUZ: *Mesón de la Infanta.* **Map 3 B2.**
Calle Dos de Mayo 26. **(** *95 456 15 54.*
Set in a restored historic building in the heart of the lively El Arenal district, this restaurant offers an excellent choice of traditional dishes. ● *Tue.* ☰ &

Santa Cruz: *Hostería del Laurel.* **Map** 3 C2. €€€
Plaza de los Venerables 5. 95 422 02 95.
Rustic decoration, with wooden barrels and colourful wall tiles. Try local
specialities: *serrano* ham and *tortilla de patatas* (potato omelette).

Santa Cruz: *La Albahaca.* **Map** 3 D2. €€€
Plaza de Santa Cruz 12. 95 422 07 14. www.andalunet.com/la-albahaca
This 1920s mansion furnished with 17th-century antiques makes a fine
setting in which to enjoy good Basque-influenced food. Sun.

Santa Cruz: *Egaña Oriza.* **Map** 3 C3. €€€€
Calle San Fernando 41. 95 422 72 11. FAX 95 450 27 27. oriza@yet.es
Tucked against the walls of the Alcázar gardens is this stylish place. Fish is a
speciality, and both the meat dishes and desserts are superb. Sat am, Sun.

Further Afield (West): *Río Grande.* **Map** 3 B3. €€
Calle Betis. 95 427 83 71. FAX 95 427 86 46.
Terrific location, where you can enjoy the gazpacho or the *rabo de toro*
(braised bull's tail) on a terrace overlooking the Guadalquivir.

Further Afield (West): *Ox's.* **Map** 3 C3. €€€
Calle Betis 61. 95 427 62 75. FAX 95 427 84 65.
A small and intimate *asador* (grill room) specializing in grilled meats. Clams
with artichokes and *angulas* (tiny baby eels) are specialities. Mon.

ANDALUSIA

Aljaraque: *Las Candelas.* €€
Avenida de Huelva (Huelva). 959 31 84 33.
An attractive restaurant with a rustic dining room serving fine local seafood
and excellent meat dishes. Sun.

Almería: *Rincón de Juan Pedro.* €
Calle Federico Castro 2. 950 23 58 19.
Andalusian meat and seafood specialities, and local dishes such as *trigo a
la cortijera* (a stew with wheat berries, meat and sausage). Mon.

Almería: *Bellavista.* €€€
Urbanizacion Bellavista Llanos del Alquián. 950 29 71 56.
This restaurant offers top-quality fish and shellfish prepared in various
ways. It is also a good place to try baby kid. Sun D, Mon, mid-Oct–Dec.

Almería: *Club de Mar.* €€€€
Playa de la Almadravilla 1. 950 23 50 48. restclubmar@larural.es
Enjoy fresh fish and shellfish right on the seafront. The *bullabesa* (Spanish
bouillabaisse) and *fritura* (mixed fried fish) are specialities.

Almuñécar: *El Bodegón.* €
Avenida del Mediterraneo 51, 18690. 958 63 33 44. FAX 958 63 43 04.
The food at this beachfront eatery is a mixture of typical Andalucian cuisine
and international fare. A pianist helps to enhance the friendly atmosphere.

Antequera: *La Espuela.* €€
Paseo de Maria Cristina, Plaza de Toros (Málaga). 952 70 34 24.
Uniquely situated in a bullring, this restaurant prepares Andalusian dishes
including the town speciality, *porra* (a thick gazpacho).

Baeza: *Juanito.* €€
Avenida Arca del Aguan (Jaén). 953 74 00 40. FAX 953 74 23 24.
Right in the heart of the olive belt, Juanito offers a selection of olive oils to
accompany your meal. Specialities include spinach casserole. Mon D, Sun.

Baeza: *Andrés de Vandelvira.* €€€
Calle San Francisco 14 (Jaén). 953 74 81 72. FAX 953 74 81 72.
Located in a 16th-century monastery built by Andrés de Vandelvira,
Jaén's Renaissance architect, this restaurant serves typical regional food:
cardos (cardoons, a type of artichoke) in a cream sauce, and partridge
salad. Mon.

Bailén: *Zodíaco.* hzodiaco@ocijaen.com €€
Carretera Madrid–Cádiz km 294 (Jaén). 953 67 10 58. FAX 953 67 19 06.
Cold soups are on the menu in summer, such as *ajo blanco* (white garlic)
with almonds. Other specialities include the *revuelto* (scrambled eggs with
ham, asparagus, prawns/shrimp and elvers) and partridge.

For key to symbols see back flap

						CREDIT CARDS	TAPAS BAR	FIXED-PRICE MENU	GOOD WINE LIST	OUTDOOR TABLES

Price categories for a three-course evening meal for one, including a half-bottle of house wine, tax and service:

€ under 20 euros
€€ 20–30 euros
€€€ 30–40 euros
€€€€ over 40 euros

TAPAS BAR
In addition to the main dining room, there is a bar serving tapas *(see pp574–5)* and *raciones* (larger portions).
FIXED-PRICE MENU
A good-value, fixed-price menu is offered at lunch or dinner, or both, usually with three courses.
GOOD WINE LIST
Denotes a wide range of good wines, or a more specialized selection of local wines.
OUTDOOR TABLES
Facilities for eating outdoors, on a terrace, or in a garden or courtyard, often with a good view.

Entry	Price	Credit Cards	Tapas Bar	Fixed-Price Menu	Good Wine List	Outdoor Tables
LOS BARRIOS: *Mesón El Copo.* Autovía Cádiz–Malaga, Salida 111/112, Palmones (Cádiz). ☎ 956 67 77 10. Dine on superb seafood, from fried anchovies to lobster and sea bass. Order a few shellfish dishes *para picar* (to share as a starter) and follow with the *dorada al horno* (bream casserole with potatoes). ● Sun. ▤	€€€	AE DC MC V	●	■	●	
BUBIÓN: *Villa Turística de Bubión.* Calle Barrio Alto (Granada). ☎ 958 76 31 11. This restaurant in the Alpujarras serves typical mountain food such as *plato alpujarreño* (potatoes with egg, sausage, ham and pork loin). ▤ ♿	€	AE DC MC V		■	■	■
CÁDIZ: *Ventorillo del Chato.* Carretera Cádiz–San Fernando km 684. ☎ 956 25 00 25. This old rustic inn offers seafood, venison and a stew of the day such as *berza* (vegetable and sausage) or *menudo* (tripe). ● Sun. ▤ ♿	€€€	AE DC MC V			●	
CÁDIZ: *El Faro.* Calle San Félix 15. ☎ 956 21 10 68. FAX 956 21 21 88. Classic restaurant with a warm atmosphere. The menu, a superb blend of modern and traditional dishes, changes daily but always features local seafood, as in the *tortillitas de camarones* (fritters of tiny shrimps). ▤ ♿	€€€	AE DC MC V	●		●	
CÁDIZ: *El Aljibe.* Calle Plocia 25. ☎ 956 26 66 56. Noted for its good quality ingredients and imaginative combination of classic and modern cooking. Try the clams in parsley and garlic sauce. ▤ ♿	€€	AE DC MC V	●		●	■
CÓRDOBA: *Federación de Peñas.* Calle Conde y Luque 8. ☎ 957 47 54 27. FAX 957 47 21 00. Inexpensive local food. Try the *rabo de toro* (braised bull's tail), a house speciality, or the *cardos* (cardoons) with clams. ♿	€	AE DC MC V		■	■	■
CÓRDOBA: *Almudaina.* Jardines de los Santos Mártires 1. ☎ 957 47 43 42. FAX 957 48 34 94. Once the palace of Bishop Leopold of Austria, this mansion serves typical dishes from the Sierra Morena, including venison and boar. ▤	€€	AE DC MC V		■		
CÓRDOBA: *El Churrasco.* Calle Romero 16. ☎ 957 29 08 19. FAX 957 29 40 81. The speciality here is charcoal-grilled meat, but vegetable dishes such as *salmorejo* (a thick tomato soup served with crisp wafers of aubergine/eggplant) are also good. Sip an apéritif in the nearby wine cellars. ● Aug. ▤	€€	AE DC MC V	●		●	
CÓRDOBA: *Taberna Pepe de la Judería.* Calle Romero 1. ☎ 957 20 07 44. FAX 957 42 20 63. Sit in the dining rooms festooned with photos of notable customers and try the gazpacho or the *flamenquín* (fried rolls of veal and ham). ▤	€€€	AE DC MC V	●	■	●	■
CÓRDOBA: *El Blasón.* Calle José Zorilla 11 (Córdoba). ☎ 957 48 06 25. The ground-floor café in this charming old house, situated near Córdoba's main shopping area, is an ideal place for light meals. ▤	€€€	AE DC MC V	●	■	●	■
CÓRDOBA: *Caballo Rojo.* @ caballorojo@teleline.es Calle Cardenal Herrero 28 (Córdoba). ☎ 957 47 53 75. FAX 957 47 47 42. A lovely restaurant offering traditional dishes, including many adapted from Moorish and Sephardic recipes. Enjoy lamb with honey or *Sefardí* salad of wild mushrooms, asparagus, roasted peppers and salt cod. ▤ ♿	€€€	AE DC MC V	●	■	●	■
ESTEPONA: *La Alborada.* Puerto Deportivo de Estepona (Málaga). ☎ 95 280 20 47. This quayside eatery serves excellent paella and other rice dishes, such as *arroz a la banda* (fish risotto). ● Wed & weekdays in winter. ♿	€€	AE DC MC V			●	■

FUENGIROLA: *Portofino.* €€
Edificio Perla 1, Paseo Marítimo 29 (Málaga). [952 47 06 43. FAX 952 66 56 15.
This seafront restaurant is popular for its friendly service and good Italian food,
such as the fish and shellfish brochette. ● *mid-Jul–mid-Sep L, Mon, early Jul.* ▤ &

AE
DC
MC
V

GRANADA: *Don Giovanni.* €
Avenida de Cádiz Zaidin 65. [958 81 87 51.
It is hard to beat Don Giovanni's prices for oven-baked pizzas and the
wide variety of pastas, meat dishes and salads. ● *Wed & 1 wk in Aug.* ▤ &

AE
DC
MC
V

GRANADA: *Carmen de San Miguel.* €€
Plaza Torres Bermejas 3. [958 22 67 23. FAX 958 53 51 98.
The specialities at this restaurant include the seafood salad and a dessert
made with almonds and strawberries. Views of the Albaicín. ● *Sun.* ▤

AE
DC
MC
V

GRANADA: *Casa Bienvenido.* €€
Calle San José 1, Monachil. [& FAX 958 50 05 03.
Home-style cooking, using vegetables and meat grown on the farm. The
daily specials include lentils with rice and sausages. ● *Mon.* ▤ &

AE
DC
MC
V

GRANADA: *Chikito.* €€
Plaza Campillo 9. [958 22 33 64. FAX 958 22 37 55.
Built on the site of a café where Lorca and his contemporaries used to
meet, Chikito serves broad (fava) beans with ham and Sacromonte omelette
as specialities. Try the *piononos* (anise-scented cake). ● *Wed.* ▤ &

AE
DC
MC
V

GRANADA: *Mirador de Morayma.* €€
Calle Pianista García Carillo 2. [958 22 82 90. FAX 958 22 81 25.
Situated in the Albaicín with views of the Alhambra, this restaurant
specializes in typical dishes of Granada, such as *remojón* (a salad of
oranges and codfish) and *choto albaicinero* (kid fried with garlic). ▤

AE
MC
V

GRANADA: *Velázquez.* €€
Calle Emilio Orozco 1. [958 28 01 09. FAX 958 28 79 66.
The ambience here is warm and the food imaginative, with modern
interpretations of such Moorish dishes as *bstella* (a meat pastry with pine
nuts and almonds), and savoury almond cream soup. ● *Sun & Aug.* ▤ &

AE
DC
MC
V

GRANADA: *Ruta del Veleta.* €€€
Carretera Sierra Nevada 50, Cenes de la Vega. [958 48 61 34. FAX 958 48 62 93.
The decoration, with typical Alpujarran textiles and ceramic jugs, goes well
with the traditional cuisine – roast baby kid and good seafood. ▤

AE
DC
MC
V

HUELVA: *El Estero.* €
Avenida Martín Alonso Pinzón 13. [959 25 65 72. FAX 959 28 27 11.
A good, centrally located restaurant, serving local fare. Enjoy *chocos con
habas* (cuttlefish and beans) or sole stuffed with oysters. ▤

AE
DC
MC
V

ISLA CRISTINA: *Casa Rufino.* €€
Avenida de la Playa (Huelva). [959 33 08 10. FAX 959 34 34 70.
A popular beachside place whose *el tonteo* menu (for four) comprises eight
different fish in sauces, including angler fish in raisin sauce. ● *Nov.* &

AE
DC
MC
V

JABUGO: *Mesón Sánchez Romero Carvajal.* €€
Carretera San Juan del Puerto (Huelva). [959 12 10 71. FAX 959 12 12 66.
Fine Jabugo hams are made here and the adjoining bar-restaurant is a good
place to sample them. Besides dishes featuring ham and sausage, try the
fresh *ibérico* pork dishes, such as *presa de paletilla al mesón.* ▤ &

AE
MC
V

JAÉN: *Casa Vicente.* €€
Calle Francisco Martín Mora 1. [953 23 28 16.
Vicente serves typical dishes from Jaén – lamb stew, spinach casserole,
artichokes in sauce – in a classic setting with a central patio. ▤

DC
MC
V

JEREZ DE LA FRONTERA: *La Mesa Redonda.* €€
Calle Manuel de la Quintana 3 (Cádiz). [& FAX 956 34 00 69.
A charming restaurant, where the dedication to fine cooking is very much in
evidence. Try the *mojama* (cured tuna) as a starter. ● *Sun & public hols.* ▤ &

AE
DC
MC
V

JEREZ DE LA FRONTERA: *Gaitán.* €€€
Calle Gaitán 3 (Cádiz). [956 34 58 59.
Gaitán's innovative chef combines Basque and Andalusian influences to
create dishes such as hake confit with roasted vegetables and laurel, and
breast of chicken with foie gras and pine nuts. ▤

AE
DC
MC
V

For key to symbols see back flap

Price categories for a three-course evening meal for one, including a half-bottle of house wine, tax and service:

€ under 20 euros
€€ 20–30 euros
€€€ 30–40 euros
€€€€ over 40 euros

TAPAS BAR
In addition to the main dining room, there is a bar serving tapas *(see pp574–5)* and *raciones* (larger portions).
FIXED-PRICE MENU
A good-value, fixed-price menu is offered at lunch or dinner, or both, usually with three courses.
GOOD WINE LIST
Denotes a wide range of good wines, or a more specialized selection of local wines.
OUTDOOR TABLES
Facilities for eating outdoors, on a terrace, or in a garden or courtyard, often with a good view.

	Credit Cards	Tapas Bar	Fixed-Price Menu	Good Wine List	Outdoor Tables
LOJA: *La Finca.* €€€€ Hotel La Bobadilla, Autovía Granada–Sevilla (Granada). 🕻 958 32 18 61. Worth a detour off the *autovía*, this exceptional restaurant is a place for fine dining. The chef makes creative use of fresh vegetables, capon and pork grown on the farm, game (in season) and seafood. 🍴	AE DC MC V		■	●	■
MÁLAGA: *Marisquería Santa Paula.* €€ Avenida de los Guindos, Barriada Santa Paula. 🕻 95 223 65 57. 📠 952 23 94 45. One of Málaga's traditional seafood bars, Santa Paula serves a great *fritura* (mixed fish fry) and *mariscada* (selection of shellfish). 🍴 ♿	AE DC MC V	●		●	■
MÁLAGA: *Mesón Astorga.* €€ Calle Gerona 11. 🕻 95 234 68 32. 📠 95 234 25 63. Flair using Málaga's superb local produce makes this restaurant popular. Try the fried aubergine (eggplant) drizzled with molasses, or the salad of fresh tuna with sherry vinegar dressing. Lively tapas bar. ⬤ *Sun.* 🍴 ♿	AE DC MC V	●		●	■
MANILVA: *Macues.* €€ Puerto Deportivo de la Duquesa Local 13 (Málaga). 🕻 95 289 03 95. At this restaurant, with its covered terrace overlooking the yacht harbour, your fish will be brought round for inspection before it is cooked. Fish baked in salt is a speciality, and the meat is good too. ⬤ *Mon & Feb.* 🍴 ♿	AE DC MC V			●	■
MARBELLA: *Santiago.* €€€ Paseo Marítimo 5 (Málaga). 🕻 95 277 43 39. 📠 95 282 45 03. This is probably the best place for seafood on the Costa del Sol. On any day, there might be 40 to 50 fish and shellfish dishes, including paella, and good meat dishes such as pig and suckling lamb. ⬤ *Nov.* 🍴 ♿	AE DC MC V	●	■	●	■
MARBELLA: *Toni Dalli.* €€€ El Oasis, Carretera de Cádiz km 176 (Málaga). 🕻 95 277 00 35. This lovely white palace flanked by palms, right on the beach, makes for a great night out. The Italian-influenced food includes home-made pastas, meat and fish. Live music is sometimes provided by Toni himself. ♿	AE DC MC V		■		■
MARBELLA: *Triana.* €€€ Calle Gloria 11 (Málaga). 🕻 95 277 99 62. An intimate restaurant, right in the centre of Marbella's old town, specializing in Valencia-style rice dishes. Apart from paella, there is *caldoso con langosta* (soupy rice with lobster). ⬤ *Mon.* 🍴	AE DC MC V			●	
MARBELLA: *La Hacienda.* €€€€ Urbanización Hacienda Las Chapas, Ctra Cádiz km 193 (Málaga). 🕻 95 283 12 67. Set in a gracious villa, the restaurant has gardens with sea views. The food – Andalusian with French touches – includes specialities such as guinea fowl with raisin sauce, and game in season. ⬤ *mid Nov–mid Dec.* ♿	AE DC MC V		■	●	■
MARBELLA: *La Meridiana.* €€€€ Camino de la Cruz (Málaga). 🕻 95 277 76 25. 📠 95 282 60 24. Situated in Marbella's rarefied heights, La Meridiana has a canopied garden room and adjoining patio bar. The menu features dishes such as swordfish *carpaccio*, artichokes with foie gras, and game in season. ⬤ *Jan.* 🍴	AE DC MC V	●	■	●	■
MIJAS: *El Castillo.* €€ Plaza de la Constitución, Pasaje de los Pescadores 2 (Málaga). 🕻 95 248 53 48. This rustic-style restaurant serves up both typically Andalucian and international dishes. A flamenco show makes for a lively atmosphere on certain nights of the week. ⬤ *Fri.*	AE DC MC V			●	■
MOTRIL: *Tropical.* €€€ Avenida Rodríguez Acosta 23 (Granada). 🕻 & 📠 95 860 04 50. Both seafood, such as bass with *ajo verde* (green garlic), and meat, such as *choto a la brasa* (roast baby kid), are specialities here. ⬤ *Sun.* 🍴	AE DC MC V		■	●	

PALMA DEL RÍO: *Hospedería de San Francisco.* €€
Avenida Pío XII 35 (Córdoba). 957 71 01 83.
Dine in the cloisters of this out-of-the-way former monastery. The ever-changing menu features superb Basque specialities. ▤
MC V

EL PUERTO DE SANTA MARÍA: *El Faro del Puerto.* €€€
Carretera de Rota km 0.5 (Cádiz). 956 87 09 52. FAX 956 54 04 66.
The menu here offers refined interpretations of modern dishes. Not to be missed are the desserts, especially the oloroso sherry ice-cream. ▤ ᵫ
AE DC MC V

EL PUERTO DE SANTA MARÍA: *Las Bóvedas.* €€€
Monasterio de San Miguel, Calle Larga 27 (Cádiz). 956 54 04 40.
Dine in style under the vaulted brick ceilings of a former monastery. Fish and shellfish are specialities, as is the dessert *tocino de cielo* ("heavenly bacon"), made from egg yolks by nuns. ▤ ᵫ
AE DC MC V

LA RÁBIDA: *Hostería de la Rábida.* €€
Paraje de la Rábida (Huelva). 959 35 03 12.
This restaurant, beside the 14th-century monastery where Christopher Columbus once stayed, has good meat and seafood specialities. ▤
AE DC MC V

RONDA: *Pedro Romero.* €€
Calle Virgen de la Paz 18 (Málaga). 95 287 11 10. FAX 95 287 10 61.
Facing Ronda's graceful bullring, this restaurant serves well-prepared country food. Try the rabbit with thyme or the braised bull's tail. ▤ ᵫ
AE DC MC V

SAN FERNANDO: *Venta Vargas.* €€
Avenida Puente Zuazo (Cádiz). 956 88 16 22.
This popular small town eatery has lots of flamenco atmosphere. Order *raciones* of classics such as *aliñadas* (potato salad). ● *Mon.* ▤ ᵫ
AE DC MC V

SAN ROQUE: *Los Remos en Villa Victoria.* €€€
Ctra San Roque–La Línea 351 km 2.8, Gibraltar Campamento (Cádiz). 956 69 84 12.
Housed in a restored mansion with Mediterranean decor, this restaurant serves exquisite dishes, with a focus on first-rate seafood. A sampling menu includes shrimp fritters and sea nettles. ● *Sun.* ▤
AE DC MC V

SANLÚCAR DE BARRAMEDA: *Casa Bigote.* €€€
Bajo de Guía (Cádiz). 956 36 26 96. FAX 956 36 87 21.
At the mouth of the Río Guadalquivir, this typical sailors' *taberna* is the place to sample *langostinos de Sanlúcar* (large, sweet, striped prawns) and fresh fish from the day's catch, such as baby eels. ● *Sun.* ▤ ᵫ
AE DC MC V

SANLÚCAR LA MAYOR: *La Alquería.* €€€€
Hacienda de Benazuza, Virgen de las Nieves (Sevilla). 95 570 33 44.
The chef at this beautiful country hacienda offers a choice of innovative and simple dishes, all based on quality produce. ● *mid Jul–Sep.* ▤
AE DC MC V

TORREMOLINOS: *Bar Restaurante Casa Juan.* €€
Calle Mar 14, La Carihuela (Málaga). 95 238 41 06. FAX 95 238 55 27.
A popular beachfront restaurant offering favourites such as fish baked in salt and *fritura malagueña* (mixed fish fry). ● *Mon & Dec–mid-Jan.* ▤ ᵫ
AE DC MC V

TORREMOLINOS: *Frutos.* €€€
Urbanización Los Álamos, Carretera a Cádiz km 228 (Málaga). 95 238 14 50.
The *grande dame* of Costa del Sol restaurants, serving superb meat and fish. Enjoy suckling pig and follow with *arroz con leche* (rice pudding). ▤
AE DC MC V

VERA: *Terraza Carmona.* €€
Calle Manuel Giménez 1 (Almería). 950 39 07 60. FAX 950 39 13 14.
The specialities here are excellent seafood, and unusual regional dishes such as *gurullos con conejo* (pasta with rabbit). ● *Mon.* ▤ ᵫ
AE DC MC V

THE BALEARIC ISLANDS

FORMENTERA, ES PUJOLS: *Sa Palmera.* €€
Playa Es Pujols. 971 32 83 56.
Freshly caught seafood is served at this seafront restaurant. Try the mixed fish paella or the shellfish casserole (*zarzuela de mariscos*). ● *Nov–Feb.* ᵫ
AE MC V

IBIZA (EIVISSA), IBIZA TOWN: *Ca'n Alfredo.* €€
Paseo Vara de Rey 16. 971 31 12 74.
Regional cuisine is served in this popular establishment. Choose from numerous rice dishes or the *borrida de ratjada* (ray stew). ● *Mon.* ▤ ᵫ
AE DC MC V

For key to symbols see back flap

Price categories for a three-course evening meal for one, including a half-bottle of house wine, tax and service:
€ under 20 euros
€€ 20–30 euros
€€€ 30–40 euros
€€€€ over 40 euros

TAPAS BAR
In addition to the main dining room, there is a bar serving tapas (see pp574–5) and raciones (larger portions).
FIXED-PRICE MENU
A good-value, fixed-price menu is offered at lunch or dinner, or both, usually with three courses.
GOOD WINE LIST
Denotes a wide range of good wines, or a more specialized selection of local wines.
OUTDOOR TABLES
Facilities for eating outdoors, on a terrace, or in a garden or courtyard, often with a good view.

	CREDIT CARDS	TAPAS BAR	FIXED-PRICE MENU	GOOD WINE LIST	OUTDOOR TABLES
IBIZA (EIVISSA), SANTA EULÀRIA D'ES RIU: *Doña Margarita.* €€€ Puerto Deportivo. 971 33 22 00. A port-side restaurant offering fresh fish, perfectly prepared, and a delicious yogurt mousse with raspberry sauce as dessert. ● Mon, Dec & Jan. &	AE DC MC V			●	■
IBIZA (EIVISSA), SANTA GERTRUDIS: *Ca'n Pau.* €€€ Carretera de Sant Miquel. 971 19 70 07. Rustic Ibizan *masía* (farmhouse) serving good Catalan and Mediterranean cuisine. Tender roast kid, quail with cabbage, and rabbit are a few of the specialities, and there is a good selection of Catalan wines. ● Mon, Tue L. &	AE MC V			●	■
IBIZA (EIVISSA), IBIZA TOWN: *El Cigarral.* €€€ Calle Fray Vicente Nicolás 9. 971 31 12 46. A family-run restaurant where the menu changes according to what is fresh in the market. Delicious grilled steaks and fish, complemented by one of the largest selections of wines in Ibiza. ● Sun. 目 &	AE DC MC V			●	
IBIZA (EIVISSA), SANT ANTONI: *Sa Capella.* €€€ Carretera Can Germà km 1. 971 34 00 57. Housed in a former chapel, this restaurant offers an international menu, including good fish and steaks. Open for dinner only. ● Nov–Mar. &	MC V			●	■
IBIZA (EIVISSA), SANT JOSEP: *Cana Joana.* €€€ Carretera Ibiza–Sant Josep km 10. 971 80 01 58; 971 80 03 12. One of the island's most interesting gastronomic offers. The seasonal menu, with Catalan and Mediterranean influences, includes dishes such as potatoes served with a sea urchin sauce. ● Nov–Jan; Jun–Oct: D, Feb–May: Sun D, Mon. &	AE MC V			●	■
MALLORCA, ALCÚDIA: *Mesón Los Patos.* €€ Carretera Sa Pobla–Alcúdia. 971 89 02 65. An agreeably decorated family restaurant with a garden and a children's playground. Simple and traditional Mallorcan dishes, including *arroz brut* (a soupy rice served with meat). ● Tue & mid Jan–Feb. 目 &	AE DC MC V	●	■		
MALLORCA, CALA D'OR: *Port Petit.* €€€ Avenida Cala Llonga. 971 64 30 39. Enjoy creative Mediterranean cuisine overlooking the marina. The prawn (shrimp) *carpaccio* with garlic mousse, and grilled sea bass with ravioli are classics, as is the rich chocolate fondue. Open for dinner only. ● Nov–Apr.	AE DC MC V		■	●	
MALLORCA, CALA RATJADA: *Ses Rotges.* €€€€ Calle Rafael Blanes 21. 971 56 31 08. This lovely old stone mansion, surrounded by palm trees and azaleas, is an ideal setting for sophisticated dining on French cuisine prepared using local produce. Good local wines. ● Nov–Mar. &	AE DC MC V		■	●	■
MALLORCA, DEIÀ: *Bens d'Avall.* €€€€ Urbanización Costa Deià. 971 63 23 81. This cliff-top restaurant offers wonderful views of the coastline. Traditional, regional recipes are given modern touches, creating dishes such as prawn (shrimp) *carpaccio* with pesto and Parmesan. ● Sun D, Mon; Nov–Mar. &	AE DC MC V		■	●	■
MALLORCA, DEIÀ: *El Olivo.* €€€€ Hotel la Residencia, Finca Son Canals. 971 63 93 92. One of the island's best restaurants, with delightful decoration and views of the mountains. Delicious *nouvelle cuisine* incorporating Mediterranean influences, with dishes such as lamb baked with mustard croustade. 目 &	AE DC MC V		■	●	
MALLORCA, INCA: *Celler Ca'n Amer.* €€ Calle Pau 39. 971 50 12 61. This wonderful old wine cellar is now home to one of the island's most authentic regional dishes, *sopa mallorquina*, made with bread and braised vegetables. ● Sun; May–Sep: Sat–Sun. 目	AE MC V			●	

MALLORCA, PAGUERA: *La Gran Tortuga.* €€€
Aldea Cala Fornells 1. 971 68 60 23.
There is a great sea view from the terrace, where you can try home-made
foie gras or hake stuffed with smoked salmon in a spinach sauce. The
atmosphere is agreeable and the service efficient. ● *Dec–Jan: Mon.*

| | AE DC MC V | | | ● | ■ |

MALLORCA, PALMA DE MALLORCA: *Ca'n Carlos.* €€
Calle del Agua 5. 971 71 38 69.
Old Balearic recipes have been revived, providing diners with an authentic
version of the islands' food. The oven-roasted suckling lamb and the hake
with cabbage are just two examples. ● *Sun & public hols.* ▤

| | AE MC V | | | ● | |

MALLORCA, PALMA DE MALLORCA: *Porto Pí.* €€€€
Calle Garita 25. 971 40 00 87.
This elegant old house, surrounded by gardens, is an ideal spot to savour
creative Mediterranean cuisine using first-class ingredients. ● *Sun.* ▤

| | AE DC MC V | | ■ | ● | ■ |

MALLORCA, POLLENÇA: *Celler Ca Vostra.* €€
Carretera Alcúdia–Port de Pollença. 971 86 55 46.
This former wine bar is still decorated with wine barrels. Typical local food,
with fresh fish and *escudella* (a vegetable stew). ● *Tue.* ▤ ⑤

| | MC V | | ■ | ● | |

MALLORCA, PORT D'ANDRATX: *Layn.* €€
Calle Almirante Riera Alemany 19. 971 67 18 55.
This restaurant has its own fishing boat to ensure the freshest of sea fare.
There are also meat specialities including roast suckling pig and beef with
cabbage. Views of the sea from the terrace. ● *Mon, Dec–mid-Jan.*

| | AE DC MC V | | ■ | | ● |

MALLORCA, PORT D'ANDRATX: *Miramar.* €€
Avenida Mateo Bosch 22. 971 67 16 17.
A family-run restaurant with views of the marina, offering good seafood
and impeccable service. Specialities include *arroz negro* (black rice, made
with squid's ink) and shrimps in rock salt. ● *mid-Dec–mid-Jan.*

| | AE DC MC V | | ■ | ● | ■ |

MALLORCA, SÓLLER: *El Guía.* €€€
Calle Castañer 2. 971 63 02 27.
People come from near and far for El Guía's artichokes stuffed with spinach.
Good, tasty, home cooking at excellent prices. ● *Nov–Apr D: Mon.* ▤ ⑤

| | AE DC MC V | | ■ | ● | |

MALLORCA, SON SERVERA: *S'Era de Pula.* €€€
Carretera Son Servera–Capdepera. 971 56 79 40.
A rustic Mallorcan country house in a peaceful spot with mountain views.
The interesting mix of continental and local cuisine features dishes such as
cod with crystallized garlic. ● *Mon & Jan.* ▤ ⑤

| | AE DC MC V | ● | ■ | ● | ■ |

MENORCA, CIUTADELLA: *Club Nautico Ca's Quintu.* €€
Cami Baex 8, Puerto. 971 38 10 02.
This centrally located restaurant serves traditional Menorcan food, with an
emphasis on fresh fish. Try the house speciality, *caldera de langosta*
(lobster casserole) or *caldera de mariscos* (the shellfish version).

| | AE MC V | ● | ■ | | ■ |

MENORCA, CIUTADELLA: *Casa Manolo.* €€€€
Calle Marina 117. 971 38 00 03.
A lively restaurant in the harbour with a delightful terrace overlooking the
marina. Regional seafood dishes including a selection of grilled Menorcan
fish, rice with seafood, and lobster casserole. ● *Nov–Apr.* ▤ ⑤

| | AE DC MC V | | | ● | ■ |

MENORCA, FORNELLS: *Es Cranc.* €€€
Calle Escoles 31. 971 37 64 42.
This establishment deserves the reputation it has throughout the island for
the freshness and preparation of its seafood. The lobster *caldereta* and the
succulent grilled shrimp are two examples. ● *Wed & Dec–Feb.* ▤ ⑤

| | MC V | | ■ | ● | |

MENORCA, MAÓ: *Jágaro.* €€
Moll de Levant 334. 971 36 23 90.
Enjoy an excellent view of the harbour from this restaurant where seafood
dishes predominate in the summer and hearty stews in the winter. The potato
pie and almond pie are popular choices for desserts. ● *Feb, Sun D & Mon D.* ▤ ⑤

| | AE DC MC V | | ■ | ● | ■ |

MENORCA, ES MERCADAL: *Ca'n Aguedet.* €€
Calle Lepanto 23–30. 971 37 53 91.
Authentic Menorcan dishes such as rabbit with figs, cuttlefish with shrimp
and pine nuts, and *arroz de tierra* (a rice and meat dish dating back to
Moorish times). Try a wine from the proprietor's own vineyard. ▤

| | AE DC MC V | | ■ | ● | |

Price categories for a three-course evening meal for one, including a half-bottle of house wine, tax and service:
€ under 20 euros
€€ 20–30 euros
€€€ 30–40 euros
€€€€ over 40 euros

TAPAS BAR
In addition to the main dining room, there is a bar serving tapas (see pp574–5) and raciones (larger portions).
FIXED-PRICE MENU
A good-value, fixed-price menu is offered at lunch or dinner, or both, usually with three courses.
GOOD WINE LIST
Denotes a wide range of good wines, or a more specialized selection of local wines.
OUTDOOR TABLES
Facilities for eating outdoors, on a terrace, or in a garden or courtyard, often with a good view.

THE CANARY ISLANDS

	CREDIT CARDS	TAPAS BAR	FIXED-PRICE MENU	GOOD WINE LIST	OUTDOOR TABLES
FUERTEVENTURA, PUERTO DEL ROSARIO: *Benjamín.* €€ Calle León y Castillo 139. 928 85 17 48. Innovative Canary Islands cooking relying exclusively on local produce. The potatoes with *mojo* (a spicy sauce), the goat's cheese, and sorbet made from prickly pear fruit are all recommended. ● Sun & public hols.	MC V		■	●	
FUERTEVENTURA, PUERTO DEL ROSARIO: *La Casa del Jamón.* €€ La Asomada. 928 53 00 64. Decorated like a traditional Spanish mesón, this family-run restaurant offers a mix of Basque and regional dishes including roast kid and a tasty variety of cheeses and Iberian cold meats. ● Mon, Sun D. 🔊	DC MC V		■	●	
LA GOMERA, SAN SEBASTIÁN DE LA GOMERA: *Casa del Mar.* € Avenida Fred Olsen 2. 922 87 12 19. Simple seafood dishes are served in this family-style restaurant close to the harbour. You can have fish in a stew, in a paella or grilled. ● Sun.	AE DC MC V	●			
GRAN CANARIA, CRUZ DE TEJEDA: *El Refugio.* €€ Cruz de Tejeda. 928 66 65 13. This rustic hotel-restaurant dominates the lovely central mountains. Try the traditional Canary Island cuisine such as roast kid (*cabrito asado*), or the vegetable broth (*potaje canario*).	AE MC V	●	■	●	■
GRAN CANARIA, MASPALOMAS: *Orangerie.* €€€€ Hotel Palm Beach, Avenida Oasis. 928 14 08 06. A lush, tropical setting where you can dine on creative, upmarket cuisine either indoors or out. Open for dinner only. ● Thu, Sun, Jun & Jul. 🔊	AE DC MC V		■		
GRAN CANARIA, LAS PALMAS: *Mesón La Cuadra.* €€ Calle General Mas de Gaminde 32. 928 24 33 80. Choose from either the tempting variety of tapas at the bar, or the truly "home-grown" menu. The proprietor's own farm produces the tender suckling lamb, the goat's cheese and the milk curd dessert. ● Mon. 🔊 🔊	AE DC MC V	●	■		
GRAN CANARIA, LAS PALMAS: *Casa Carmelo.* €€ Paseo de las Canteras 2. 928 46 90 56. The sleek first-floor dining room gives a grandstand view of Las Palmas' superb seafront, which is particularly beautiful at night. The emphasis here is on chargrilled meat and fresh local fish. 🔊	AE DC MC V		■	●	
GRAN CANARIA, PLAYA DEL INGLÉS: *Tenderete II.* €€ Avenida Tirajana 5. 928 76 14 60. Typical Canary Islands cooking with an emphasis on fresh seafood. The fish prepared in rock salt and the *potaje de berros* (watercress broth) are house specialities. Try the locally grown *manga*, similar to mango. ● Sun. 🔊 🔊	AE DC MC V	●		●	■
GRAN CANARIA, SANTA BRÍGIDA: *Las Grutas de Artiles.* €€ Las Meleguinas. 928 64 05 75. A restaurant set in caves, offering authentic Canary Islands specialities and grilled meat. The gardens and swimming pool are ideal for children.	AE DC MC V	●	■	●	■
GRAN CANARIA, VEGA DE SAN MATEO: *Museo Cho-Zacarías.* € Avenida de Tinamar. 928 66 06 27. Old farmers' cottages provide a unique setting for this restaurant. The traditional menu features cherne (a local fish) served in a coriander (cilantro) sauce, and watercress broth. Open lunch times only. ● Mon.	AE DC MC V			●	■
EL HIERRO, LA RESTINGA: *Casa Juan.* € Calle Juan Gutiérrez Monteverde 23. 922 55 71 02. Local families flock to this inexpensive, no frills restaurant. Delicious fresh fish such as *vieja* and *cherne*, accompanied by a *mojo* sauce. ● Wed.	MC V	●			

LANZAROTE, ARRECIFE: *Castillo de San José.* €€
Castillo de San José. 928 81 23 21.
A converted 16th-century fortress, now housing a contemporary art gallery
and restaurant. Enjoy international and regional specialities as you admire
the art on the walls and the views of the harbour. 🗐
AE MC V

LANZAROTE, ARRECIFE: *Colón.* €€€
Cuidad Jardín, Playa del Cable. 928 80 56 49.
Decorated in nautical style, this restaurant serves international and regional
cuisine. The menu includes fresh duck foie gras and fish dishes of the
highest quality. Excellent wine list. 🗐 &
AE DC MC V

LANZAROTE, COSTA TEGUISE: *Mesón La Jordana.* €€
Centro Comercial de Lanzarote, Lanzarote Bay. 928 59 03 28.
A popular and attractive spot where you can sample local fare given a
French touch. Try the fresh *cherne* or the roast kid. ● *Sun & Sep.* 🗐 &
AE MC V

LANZAROTE, YAIZA: *Casa Salvador.* €€
Avenida Playa Blanca. 928 51 70 25.
Located right on the beach, this establishment serves freshly caught fish
and shellfish, as well as good grilled steaks and paellas.
DC MC V

LANZAROTE, YAIZA: *La Era.* €€
Calle El Barranco 3. 928 83 00 16.
La Era is set in one of the few old country houses to survive the island's
volcanic eruptions of 1730 to 1736. Enjoy regional specialities such as lamb,
kid or lentil stew in one of the pretty, rustic dining rooms. &
AE DC MC V

LA PALMA, SANTA CRUZ DE LA PALMA: *Chipi Chipi.* €
Calle Juan Mayor 42. 922 41 10 24.
Just 6 km (4 miles) out of town, this restaurant, with a pretty patio,
specializes in grilled meats and local dishes such as chickpea (garbanzo)
soup. Good selection of island wines. ● *Wed, Sun & Oct–mid-Nov.* &
AE DC MC V

TENERIFE, COSTA ADEJE: *El Patio.* €€€€
Hotel Jardín Tropical, Urbanización San Eugenio. 922 74 60 00.
An enchanting setting for a special evening out. The lovely, flower-filled
patio is ideal for balmy summer nights. Imaginative, modern dishes are
created using local produce. Open for dinner only. Reservations obligatory.
AE DC MC V

TENERIFE, ARONA: *Los Corales.* €€
Carretera General del Norte 130, Junto Úrsula. 922 77 19 19.
Genuine Canary Islands food with creative flourishes and wonderful views
of the valley. The meat or fish carpaccio and the traditional *conejo en
salmorejo* (rabbit terrine) are recommended. ● *Mon.* &
AE DC MC V

TENERIFE, PUERTO DE LA CRUZ: *Régulo.* €€
Calle Pérez Zamora 16. 922 38 45 06.
A charming old building dating from the 16th century close to the centre of
town and the old port, with an agreeable patio. The menu is noted for its
fresh, locally caught fish and Argentinian roast lamb. ● *Sun, Jul.* 🗐 &
AE DC MC V

TENERIFE, PUERTO DE LA CRUZ: *Magnolia "Felipe el Payés".* €€€
Avenida Marqués de Villanueva del Prado. 922 38 56 14.
Assured Catalan cooking, including the traditional *pan con tomate* (bread
with tomato) and *suquet* (fish stew), served in a flamboyant modern dining
room or in the gardens. ● *Tue.* 🗐 &
AE DC MC V

TENERIFE, SANTA CRUZ DE TENERIFE: *Café del Príncipe.* €
Plaza del Príncipe de Asturias. 922 27 88 10.
Sample any of the good local dishes in this pretty restaurant which
overlooks the square in the centre of town. ● *Mon.* &
MC V

TENERIFE, SANTA CRUZ DE TENERIFE: *El Coto de Antonio.* €€€
Calle General Goded 13. 922 27 21 05.
Excellent regional food is served in this simple restaurant near the bullring.
The black potato salad, with salt cod, peppers and olive oil, and the *vieja*
in a coriander (cilantro) sauce are favourites. ● *Sun & Aug.* 🗐 &
AE DC MC V

TENERIFE, TEGUESTE: *El Drago.* €€€
Urbanización San Gonzálo 1. 922 54 30 01.
This delightful 18th-century farmhouse provides a rustic setting for Canary
Islands cooking including watercress broth, *puchero* (vegetable and meat
broth) and fish casserole. ● *Mon, Tue–Thu & Sun D, mid-Aug.* &
AE DC MC V

For key to symbols see back flap

SURVIVAL
GUIDE

PRACTICAL INFORMATION

S PAIN has finally begun to market itself beyond the attractions of its coastline, and now has a solid tourist information infrastructure. There are national tourist offices in every large city, and regional offices in the smaller towns. All offer help with finding accommodation, restaurants and activities in their area. August is Spain's main holiday month.

Old street signs

Many businesses close for the whole month and roads are very busy at the beginning and end of this period. At any time of year, try to find out in advance if your visit coincides with local fiestas, because although these are attractions, they often entail widespread closures. It is a good idea to plan leisurely lunches, as most of Spain stops from 2pm to 5pm.

ERRESERBATUA

BIZKAIKO FORU ALDUNDIA

RESERVADO DIPUTACION FORAL DE BIZKAIA

A bilingual Basque/Castilian reserved parking sign

LANGUAGE

T HE MAIN LANGUAGE of Spain, *Castellano* (Castilian), is spoken by almost everyone. There are three main regional languages: Catalan, spoken in Catalonia, *Gallego* (Galician) in Galicia and *Euskera* (Basque) in the Basque Country. Variants of Catalan are spoken in the Valencia region and also in the Balearic Islands.

People who speak English are often employed in places that deal with tourists.

MANNERS

T HE SPANISH greet and say goodbye to strangers at bus stops and in lifts, shops and other public places. They often talk to people they do not know. People shake hands when introduced and whenever they meet. Women usually kiss on both cheeks when they meet, and friends and family members may kiss or embrace briefly.

VISAS AND PASSPORTS

V ISAS ARE NOT required for citizens of EU countries, Iceland or Norway.

A list of entry requirements, which is available from Spanish embassies, specifies 35 other countries, including New Zealand, Canada, the USA and Australia, whose nationals do not need to apply for a visa if visiting Spain for less than 90 days. Thereafter they may apply to the *Gobierno Civil* (a local government office) for an extension. You need proof of employment or of sufficient funds to support yourself during a long stay. Visitors from other countries must obtain a visa before travelling.

If you intend to stay for a long time in Spain, you should contact your nearest Spanish embassy several months in advance about your needs.

British visitors should note that a Visitor's Passport is no longer available. A full passport must be obtained.

TAX-FREE GOODS AND CUSTOMS INFORMATION

N ON-EU RESIDENTS can reclaim *IVA* (VAT) on single items worth over 90 euros bought in shops displaying a "Tax-free for Tourists" sign. (Food, drink, tobacco, cars, motor-bikes and medicines are exempt.) You pay the full price and ask the sales assistant for a *formulario* (tax exemption form). On leaving Spain, you ask customs to stamp your *formulario* (this must be within six months of the purchase). You receive the refund by mail or on your credit card account.

Banco Exterior branches at Barcelona, Madrid, Málaga, Mallorca, Oviedo, Santander and Seville airports will give refunds on *formularios* stamped by customs.

TOURIST INFORMATION

A LL MAJOR CITIES and towns have *oficinas de turismo*. They will provide town plans, lists of hotels and restaurants, information about the locality and details of activities and events for tourists.

There is a **Spanish National Tourist Office** in several large cities abroad.

OPENING HOURS

M OST MONUMENTS and museums close on Mondays. On other days they generally open from 10am to 2pm, close from 2pm to 5pm, and, in some cases, reopen from 5pm to 8pm. Churches may follow these opening hours or only be opened for services. Admission is charged for most museums and monuments.

In smaller towns it is common for churches, castles and other sights to be kept permanently locked. The key, available to visitors on request, will be lodged with a caretaker in a neighbouring house, in the town hall, or perhaps with the owners of the local bar.

 OFICINA DE TURISMO *i*

Spanish tourist office sign with distinctive "i" logo

 The old town of Ibiza enclosed by its 16th-century walls, seen from the harbour

Students enjoy reduced admission fees to many museums and galleries

FACILITIES FOR THE DISABLED

SPAIN'S NATIONAL association for the disabled, the Confederación Coordinadora Estatal de Minusválidos Físicos de España (COCEMFE), has a tour company, Servi-COCEMFE *(see p533)*, which publishes guides to facilities in Spain and will help plan a holiday to individual requirements.

Tourist offices and the social services departments of town halls can provide information on local conditions and facilities. A travel agency, **Viajes 2000**, specializes in holidays for disabled people. RADAR and Holiday Care Service in the UK *(see p533)* offer limited information on facilities for the disabled in Spanish resorts.

COCEMFE sign for disabled access

SPANISH TIME

IN WINTER, Spain is one hour ahead of Greenwich Mean Time (GMT) and in summer an hour ahead of British Summer Time (BST). The Canary Islands are on GMT in winter and an hour ahead in summer. Spain uses the 24-hour clock, so 1pm = 13:00.

La madrugada is the small hours. *Mañana* (morning) lasts until the late Spanish lunch time at about 2pm and *mediodía* (midday) from about 1–4pm. *La tarde* is the afternoon and evening.

STUDENT INFORMATION

HOLDERS OF THE International Student Identity Card (ISIC) are entitled to benefits, such as discounts on travel and reduced entrance charges to museums and galleries. Information is available from all national student organizations and, in Spain, from the local government-run **Centros de Información Juvenil (CIJ)** in large towns. **Turismo y Viajes Educativos (TIVE)** specializes in student travel.

ELECTRICAL ADAPTORS

SPAIN'S ELECTRICITY supply is 220 volts, but the 125-volt system still operates in some old buildings. Plugs for both have two round pins. A three-tier standard travel converter enables you to use appliances from abroad on both supplies. Heating appliances should be used only on 220 volts.

CONVERSION CHART

Imperial to metric
1 inch = 2.54 centimetres
1 foot = 30 centimetres
1 mile = 1.6 kilometres
1 ounce = 28 grams
1 pound = 454 grams
1 pint = 0.6 litre
1 gallon = 4.6 litres

Metric to imperial
1 millimetre = 0.04 inch
1 centimetre = 0.4 inch
1 metre = 3 feet 3 inches
1 kilometre = 0.6 mile
1 gram = 0.04 ounce
1 kilogram = 2.2 pounds
1 litre = 1.8 pints

DIRECTORY

EMBASSIES

United Kingdom
Calle de Fernando El Santo 16,
28010 Madrid.
[91 700 82 00.
W www.ukinspain.com

United States
Calle de Serrano 75, 28006 Madrid.
[91 577 40 00.
W www.embusa.es

SPANISH TOURIST OFFICES

Australia
Level 24, St Martin's Tower, 31
Market St, Sydney NSW 2000.
[29 261 2433.

Barcelona
Palau Robert, Paseo de Gracia 107,
08008 Barcelona.
[93 238 40 00.
W www.gencat.es/probert

Madrid
Calle Duque de Medinaceli 2,
28014 Madrid.
[91 429 49 51.

Seville
Avenida de la Constitución 21b,
41004 Seville.
[95 422 14 04.
W www.andalucia.org

United Kingdom
22/23 Manchester Square,
London W1M 5AP.
[020 7486 8077.
W www.tourspain.es

United States
666 Fifth Ave,
New York NY 10103.
[(212) 265 8822.
W www.okspain.org

DISABLED

Viajes 2000
Paseo de la Castellana 228–230,
28046 Madrid.
[91 323 10 29.
W www.viajes2000.com

YOUTH/STUDENT

CIJ
Gran Via 10, 28013 Madrid.
[91 580 42 42.
W www.comadrid.es/infojoven

TIVE
Calle Fernando el Católico 88,
28015 Madrid.
[91 543 74 12.
W www.comadrid.es

Personal Security and Health

IN SPAIN, AS IN MOST EUROPEAN countries, rural areas are generally safe, but certain parts of cities are subject to petty crime. Carry cards and money in a belt and never leave anything visible in your car when you park it.

If you are unwell, Spanish pharmacists are qualified to advise and sometimes to prescribe. Emergency phone numbers vary from region to region. The most important ones are given on the opposite page. If you lose your documents, contact your consulate or the local police.

Spanish pharmacy sign

IN AN EMERGENCY

ONLY THE *Policía Nacional* operate a nationwide emergency phone number. Call it even if you need some other service and they will assist you in getting help. Telephone directories list local emergency numbers under *Servicios de Urgencia,* and they appear on tourist maps and leaflets.

For emergency medical treatment call the Cruz Roja (Red Cross), look under *Ambulancias* in the phone book, or go to a hospital casualty department *(Urgencias).*

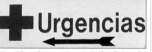

Sign identifying a Cruz Roja (Red Cross) emergency treatment centre

MEDICAL TREATMENT

ALL EU NATIONALS are entitled to Spanish social security cover. To claim, you must obtain Form E111 from the UK Department of Health or from a post office before you travel. You give this form to anyone who treats you, so you may need several photocopies. It comes with a booklet, *Health Advice for Travellers,* which explains exactly what health care you are entitled to and where and how to claim. You may have to pay and reclaim the money later.

Not all treatments are covered by Form E111 and some are costly, so arrange for medical cover before travelling.

If you want private medical care in Spain, ask at a tourist office, or at your embassy or hotel for the name and number of a doctor. If necessary, ask for one who speaks English.

PHARMACIES

SPANISH PHARMACISTS have wide responsibilities. They can advise and, in some cases, prescribe without consulting a doctor. In a non-emergency a *farmacéutico* is a good person to see first. It is easy to find one who speaks English.

The *farmacia* sign is a green or red illuminated cross. Those open at night in a town are listed in the windows of all the local pharmacies. Do not confuse them with *perfumerías,* which sell toiletries only.

PERSONAL SECURITY

VIOLENT CRIME is rare in Spain but visitors should avoid walking alone in poorly lit areas. Wear a bag or camera across your body, not on your shoulder. Men occasionally make complimentary remarks *(piropos)* to women in public, particularly in the street. This is an old custom and not intended to be intimidating.

SPANISH POLICE

THERE ARE ESSENTIALLY three types of police in Spain. The *Guardia Civil* (National Guard) mainly police rural areas. Their uniform is olive green but there are local and regional variations. They impose fines for traffic offences.

The *Policía Nacional,* who wear a blue uniform, operate in towns with a population of more than 30,000. The *Policía Nacional* have been replaced with a regional force, the *Ertzaintza,* in the Basque country, and with the *Mossos d'Esquadra* in Catalonia. These can be distinguished by their respective red and blue berets.

The *Policía Local,* also called *Policía Municipal* or *Guardia Urbana,* dress in blue. They operate independently in each town and also have a separate branch for city traffic control.

All three services will direct you to the relevant authority in the event of an incident requiring police help.

Guardia Civil   **Policía Nacional**   **Policía Local**

DIRECTORY

EMERGENCY NUMBERS

Emergency: all services
📞 112 *(in most important cities).*

Policía
📞 091 Nacional *(nationwide).*

**Fire Brigade
(Bomberos)**
📞 080 *(in most major cities).*

**Ambulance:
(Red Cross, Cruz Roja)**
📞 91 522 22 22. *(This Madrid
number is now the national
number for the Red Cross.)*

*For other cities' emergency services,
consult the local phone directory.*

Patrol car of the Policía Nacional, Spain's main urban police force

Policía Local patrol car, mainly seen in small towns

Cruz Roja (Red Cross) ambulance

The emergency number on the side of fire engines varies regionally

LEGAL ASSISTANCE

SOME INSURANCE POLICIES cover
legal costs, for instance
after an accident. If you are
not covered, telephone your
nearest consulate.

You can also contact the
Colegio de Abogados (lawyers'
association) of the nearest
town or city, which can advise
you where to obtain legal advice or representation locally.

If you need an interpreter,
consult the *Páginas Amarillas
(Yellow Pages)* telephone directory for the region under
Traductores or *Intérpretes.*
Both *Traductores Oficiales*
and *Traductores Jurados* are
qualified to translate legal or
official documents.

PERSONAL PROPERTY

HOLIDAY INSURANCE is there
to protect you financially
from the loss or theft of your
property, but it is always best
to take obvious precautions
against loss and theft.

If you have to carry large
sums of money with you, take
traveller's cheques and, if you
have two credit cards, do not
carry them together. Never
leave a bag or handbag un-
attended anywhere and do
not put down a purse or handbag on the tabletop in a café.

The moment you discover a
loss or theft, report it to the
local police station. To claim
insurance you must do this
immediately, as many com-
panies give you 24 hours only.
Ask the police for a *denuncia*

(written statement), which you
need to make a claim. If your
passport was one of the items
stolen, or if you lose it, report
it to your consulate.

PUBLIC CONVENIENCES

PUBLIC PAY-TOILETS are rare in
Spain. Department stores
are often good places to try,
as are bars and restaurants
where you are a customer. On
motorways, there are toilets
at service stations. You may
have to ask for a key *(la
llave)*, not only at the service
stations but also in some bars
in country areas. It is best to
bring your own tissues, too.
The term generally used for
toilets in Spain is *los servicios.*

OUTDOOR HAZARDS

SPAIN is prey every summer
to forest fires fanned by
winds and fuelled by bone-
dry vegetation. Be sensitive to
fire hazards and use car ash-
trays. Broken glass can start a
fire so be careful to take your
empty bottles away with you.

The sign *coto de caza* in
woodland areas identifies a
hunting reserve where you
must follow the country codes.
Toro bravo means "fighting
bull" – do not approach. A
camino particular sign indicates a private driveway.

If you are climbing or hill-
walking go properly equipped
and let someone know when
you expect to return.

Banking and Local Currency

Y OU MAY ENTER SPAIN with any amount of money, but if you intend to export more than 6,000 euros, you should declare it. Traveller's cheques may be exchanged at banks, *cajas de cambio* (foreign currency exchanges), some hotels and some shops. Banks generally offer the best exchange rates. The cheapest exchange may be offered on your credit or direct debit card, which you can use in cash dispensers (automated teller machines, ATMs) displaying the appropriate sign.

cajero 24 horas

24-hour cash dispenser

BANKING HOURS

S PANISH BANKS are beginning to extend their opening hours, but expect extended hours only at large central branches in the big cities.

Generally, banks are open from 8am to 2pm during the week. Some open until 1pm on Saturdays. Most close on Saturdays in August; in some areas they also close on Saturdays from May to September.

Bureau de change

CHANGING MONEY

M OST BANKS have a foreign exchange desk with the sign *Cambio* or *Extranjero*. Always take your passport as ID to effect any transaction.

You can draw up to 300 euros on major credit cards at a bank. If you bank with **Barclays** or **Lloyds TSB**, it is possible to cash a cheque in the usual way at one of their branches in Spain.

Bureaux de change, with the sign *Caja de Cambio* or "Change", invariably charge higher rates of commission than banks, but they are often open after hours. They are commonly found in the tourist areas of Spanish towns and cities.

Cajas de Ahorro (savings banks) also exchange money. They open from 8:30am to 2pm on weekdays and also on Thursday afternoons from 4:30pm to 7:45pm.

CHEQUES AND CARDS

T RAVELLER'S CHEQUES can be purchased at American Express, Thomas Cook or your bank. All are accepted in Spain. If you exchange AmEx cheques at an AmEx office, commission is not charged. You can purchase cheques in euros from any bank.

Banks require 24 hours' notice to cash cheques larger than 3,000 euros. If you draw more than 600 euros on travellers' cheques, you may be asked to show the purchase certificate.

The most widely accepted card in Spain is the **Visa** card. **Mastercard** (Access)/Euro-card and **American Express** are also useful currency. The major banks will allow cash withdrawals on credit cards.

When you pay for goods or services with a card, cashiers will usually pass your card through a reading machine. Sometimes, however, you will be asked to punch your PIN into a small keypad attached to the machine.

Credit card reader with PIN keypad

CASH DISPENSERS

I F YOUR CARD is linked to your home bank account, you can use it with your PIN to withdraw money from cash dispensers. These are widespread and nearly all take Visa or Mastercard (Access) cards.

When you enter your PIN, instructions are displayed in English, French, German and Spanish. These days, many dispensers are inside buildings and to gain access you will have to run your card through a door-entry system.

Cards with Cirrus and Maestro logos can also be widely used to withdraw money from cash machines.

DIRECTORY

FOREIGN BANKS

Barclays Bank
Plaza de Colón 1, 28046 Madrid.
[91 336 10 00.

Lloyds TSB Bank
Calle Serrano 90,
28006 Madrid.
[91 520 99 00.

LOST CARDS AND TRAVELLER'S CHEQUES

American Express
[00 44 1273 696933 (toll free reversed charge call to UK).

Diners Club
[00 44 1252 513500 (toll free reversed charge call to UK).

Mastercard (Access)
[91 362 62 00 (Spain).

Visa
[900 99 11 24 (Spain).

THE EURO

INTRODUCTION OF the single European currency, the euro, has taken place in 12 of the 15 member states of the EU. Austria, Belgium, Finland, France, Germany, Greece, Ireland, Italy, Luxembourg, The Netherlands, Portugal and Spain chose to join the new currency; the UK, Denmark and Sweden stayed out, with an option to review the decision. The euro was introduced on 1 January 1999, but only for banking purposes. Notes and coins came into circulation on 1 January 2002. A transition period has seen euros and local currency, such as the Spanish peseta, used simultaneously, with national currency phased out after 28 February 2002. Euro notes and coins can be used in the participating states.

Bank Notes

Euro bank notes have seven denominations. The 5-euro note (grey in colour) is the smallest, followed by the 10-euro note (pink), 20-euro note (blue), 50-euro note (orange), 100-euro note (green), 200-euro note (yellow) and 500-euro note (purple). All notes show the 12 stars of the European Union.

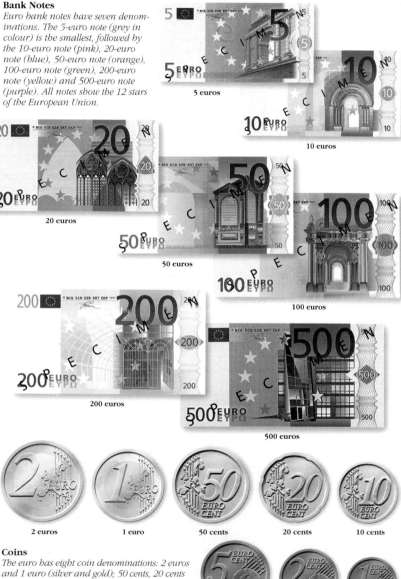

5 euros

10 euros

20 euros

50 euros

100 euros

200 euros

500 euros

2 euros   1 euro   50 cents   20 cents   10 cents

Coins

The euro has eight coin denominations: 2 euros and 1 euro (silver and gold); 50 cents, 20 cents and 10 cents (gold); and 5 cents, 2 cents and 1 cent (bronze). The reverse (number) side of euros are the same in all euro zone countries, but the front is different in each state.

5 cents

2 cents

1 cent

Shopping

SHOPPING IN SPAIN is a pleasurable activity, particularly if you approach it in a leisurely way, punctuating it with frequent breaks for coffee. In small, family-run shops especially, people will go out of their way to fulfil your smallest request. Markets sell the freshest of produce and quality wines can be found at almost any grocer. Leatherwork is still highly regarded among Spain's many traditional crafts. Spanish design has come to the forefront in both fashion and decor. Below is a size conversion chart for clothes and shoes, and suggestions to help you make the most of shopping in Spain.

A drinking vessel or glass *porrón*

Fresh produce in a market in Pollença (Mallorca)

OPENING HOURS

SHOPS USUALLY open at 10am, close at 2pm and reopen from 5pm to 8pm. Bakeries and bars generally open earlier, at around 8am. Hypermarkets and department stores stay open over lunchtime.

Rural markets are held in the morning only. In some regions Sunday trading is just limited to the bakeries, *pastelerías* and newspaper kiosks, but in many holiday resorts shops open on Sunday.

PAYING

CASH AND CREDIT CARDS are the usual methods of payment in Spain. Cheques are rarely accepted. Visitors can reclaim the *IVA* (VAT) charged on all purchases except food, drink, motor vehicles and medicines *(see p612)*. Money-changing and currency are explained on pages 616–17.

LARGER SHOPS

THE HIPERMERCADOS are sited outside towns and can usually be found by following signs to the *centro comercial*. The best known are Alcampo, Carrefour and Hipercor.

Spain's leading department store is El Corte Inglés. It has branches in all cities and most of the larger regional towns.

Major seasonal sales are advertised by the word *Rebajas* displayed in shop windows.

SPECIALIST SHOPS

SPECIALIST SHOPS often represent generations of family business. *Panaderías* (also called *hornos*) are bakeries selling bread, *bollos* (sweet buns) and rolls. Cakes and pastries are sold in *pastelerías;* many sell chocolates, as well. You buy fresh meat from a *carnicería*, but for the best cold meats go to a *charcutería*, which also sells cheese. *Charcuterías* are often found in or near markets. *Pescaderías* sell fish and shellfish, although the best fish is often sold on market stalls.

For fruit and vegetables, a *frutería* or *verdulería* will have better produce, because they stock only what is in season.

Hardware stores are called *ferreterías*. *Librerías* are in fact bookshops, not libraries, and *papelerías* are stationers.

Fans are still in daily use as well as being costume accessories

Anything you buy as a *regalo* (gift) will be gift-wrapped on request. When you buy flowers from a *floristería*, the assistant will expect to arrange them.

MARKETS

EVERY LARGE TOWN has a daily market *(mercado)*, open from 9am to 2pm, and from 5pm to 8pm. Small towns have one or more market days a week.

Markets usually have the best fresh produce, but they sell all types of food, including *frutos secos* (dried fruits) and seasonal produce, such as mushrooms, soft fruit and game. There are also usually other types of goods on sale, such as flowers, hardware and clothes.

Antiques and flea markets *(rastros)* are held everywhere in Spain, but the largest is in Madrid *(see p292)*.

Display of hand-painted ceramics in Toledo

REGIONAL PRODUCTS

SPANISH REGIONAL specialities are often better value when bought where they are made. Each region produces its own type of sausage. In Burgos, for example, *morcilla* (blood sausage) is made and a red chorizo comes from Guijuelo, Extremadura. Andalusia is renowned for olives and olive oil and Galicia for its cheeses.

Seasonal delicacies include *rovellons* (huge golden mushrooms) in Catalonia and tiny fiery peppers, *pimientos de Padrón,* in Galicia.

Some crafts originated with the Moors, such as Toledo's filigree metalwork and the *azulejos* (ceramic tiles) of Andalusia. Paterna and Manises near Valencia, and Talavera de la Reina in Castilla-La Mancha are towns well known for their ceramics.

Lace from the villages of the Sierra de Gata in Extremadura and Galicia's Costa da Morte is prized. Carved fiddles and clogs are Cantabrian crafts. Spanish crafts, such as guitars, fans and flamenco shoes, are sold in major cities.

Basketware is sold in all parts of Spain

WINE AND OTHER BEVERAGES

WINE IS SOLD in grocers and supermarkets, but only specialist dealers do justice to Spain's many vine-growing areas. Local wines can be bought by the litre at a town or village shop (bodega); they can also be bought directly from the vineyard (also called bodegas), but you have to make an appointment to visit.

Spain's most famous vine-growing regions are La Rioja and Navarra *(see pp74–5);* Penedés, where *cava* (sparkling wine) is produced *(see pp192–3);* Valdepeñas *(see pp322–3);* Ribera del Duero *(see pp322–3);* and Jerez, the sherry region *(see pp402–3).*

Among the many Spanish liqueurs are *Pacharán (see p577),* made from sloes, and *licor de bellota,* from acorns.

A range of olives, some flavoured with herbs, on a market stall

HOUSEHOLD AND KITCHEN GOODS

DEPARTMENT STORES have a good selection of household goods, but the *ferreterías* (small hardware shops) often have the more authentic selection. Traditional pottery, such as red clay *cazuelas* (dishes) that can be used in the oven and on the hob are cheap. Paella pans have always been made of iron or enamel, but now come in stainless steel or with non-stick finishes. Table linen is often good value on market stalls. Spanish lighting design is widely admired and sold in *Tienda de Illuminacion.* Wrought-iron goods, such as candlesticks, are always popular.

CLOTHING AND SHOES

THE LARGER CITIES naturally offer the widest selection of clothes shops, but Spanish designer labels can be found even in the smaller towns.

If you wish to purchase an item which needs altering, it is still usual for shops to offer the services of a seamstress for a very modest fee. Most can be persuaded to return your item within two days.

Leather shoes and accessories can be inexpensive and there is a wide range in terms of quality and price. It is the practice in mid-range shops for customers to choose from the selection in the window and give the sales assistant the code number indicated and your *talla* (size). If you want an all-leather shoe, look for *cuero,* the hide label mark. Leather clothes are also good quality and well designed.

SIZE CHART

Women's dresses, coats and skirts

Spanish	40	42	44	46	48	50	52 (size)
British/Australian	8	10	12	14	16	18	20 (size)
British	32	34	36	38	40	42	44 (inches)
Australian	86	91	95	100	105	110	120 (cm)

Women's shoes

Spanish	37	38	39	40	41	42
British	3	4	5	6	7	8
Australian	5	6	7	8	9	10

Men's suits

Spanish	44	46	48	50	52	54	56	58 (size)
British	34	36	38	40	42	44	46	48 (inches)
Australian	87	92	97	102	107	112	117	122 (cm)

Men's shirts (collar size)

Spanish	36	38	39	41	42	43	44	45 (cm)
British	14	15	15½	16	16½	17	17½	18 (inches)
Australian	36	38	39	41	42	43	44	45 (cm)

Men's shoes

Spanish	39	40	41	42	43	44	45	46
British	6	7	7½	8	9	10	11	12
Australian	6	7	7½	8	9	10	11	12

Communications

TELEFONICA, THE SPANISH telecommunications company, has improved its service since it was digitized in 1995, and the state monopoly was removed in 1998. Public telephones are easy to find and most operate with a card or coins, but international calls have a high charge.

The postal service, Correos, is identified by a crown insignia in red or white on a yellow background. Registered post and telegrams can be sent from all Correos offices *(see pp622–3)*. They sell stamps as well, but most people buy them from state-run *estancos* (tobacconists). There are no public phones in Correos offices.

Logo of the Spanish telecom system

USING A COIN AND CARD TELEPHONE

1 Lift the receiver, and wait for the dialling tone and for the display to show *Inserte monedas o tarjeta.*

2 Insert either coins *(monedas)*, using the button on the top right if there is one, or a card *(tarjeta).*

3 Key in the number firmly, but not too fast – Spanish phones require a pause between each digit.

4 As you press the digits, the number you are dialling will appear on the display. You will also be able to see how much money or how many units are left. The display will indicate when you need to deposit more coins.

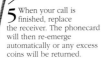

5 When your call is finished, replace the receiver. The phonecard will then re-emerge automatically or any excess coins will be returned.

Spanish phonecard

TELEPHONING IN SPAIN

AS WELL AS PUBLIC telephone boxes *(cabinas)*, there are nearly always payphones in Spanish bars. Both types take coins. Generally, there will be a high minimum connection charge, especially for international calls, so make sure that you have plenty of change at the ready.

Phonecards are far more convenient and can be bought at newsstands and *estancos.* Some phones are equipped with multilingual electronic instruction displays.

There are public telephone offices called *locutorios* where you can make a call and pay for it afterwards. They are usually quieter than phone booths and you do not need coins. Telefónica run the official ones, which are the cheapest type; private ones, often located in shops, are pricier.

There are four charge bands for international calls: European Union countries; non-European Union countries and Northwest Africa; North and South America; and the rest of the world. With the exception of local calls, using the telephone system can be expensive, especially from a hotel, which may add a

USEFUL SPANISH DIALLING CODES

- Whether you are making a call from within a province or a city, or making a call from one province to another, it is necessary (since 1998) to include the area code. Area codes are listed in the A-K phone book or obtained from directory enquiries.
- To make an international call, dial 00, then dial the country code, the area code and the number.
- Country codes are: UK 44; Eire 353; France 33; USA and Canada 1; Australia 61; New Zealand 64. It may be necessary to omit the initial digit of the destination's area code.

- For operator/directory service, dial 1003.
- For international directories, dial 025.
- To make a reversed-charge (collect) call within the EU, dial 900 99 00 followed by the country code; to the USA or Canada, dial 900 99 00 followed by 11 or 15 respectively. Numbers for other countries can be found in the front of the A-K telephone directory under *Modalidades del Servicio Internacional.*
- To report technical faults, dial 1002.
- For the speaking clock dial 093, for the weather 094, for a wake-up call 096.

surcharge. A call from a *cabina* or a *locutorio* costs 35 per cent more than one made from a private phone in someone's home. Reversed-charge (collect) calls made to European Union countries may be dialled directly, but most other reversed-charge calls must be made through the operator.

The Spanish dialling code system works on a provincial basis, with each area code prefixed by the number 9. For example, Barcelona is 93. Since 1998, this code always has to be included, even if you are phoning within a city or province.

When calling Spain from abroad, first dial the international code for Spain (34) followed by the areacode. So, to call Barcelona, you dial 34 93.

Spanish daily papers

Spanish magazines

available on payment of a subscription for a station decoder.

Most foreign films shown on Spanish television (and in cinemas) are dubbed and subtitled films are listed as *V.O. (versión original).*

Several satellite channels, such as CNN, Eurosport and Cinemanía, can be received throughout Spain.

The state radio station, Radio Nacional de España has four stations plus the World Service. News programmes are on R1, classical music on R2, pop music on R3 and news on R5. Local stations also rebroadcast the BBC World Service. They are: Onda Cero Radio in Marbella and Tenerife; Radio Maspalomas in Gran Canaria; and Sunshine Capital Radio in Palma de Mallorca.

Logo of Radio Nacional de España

widely read of the Spanish newspapers, in descending number of sales, are *El País, El Mundo, ABC, La Razon, Diario 16* and *La Vanguardia* (in Catalonia). *El Mundo* is feature led and aimed at a younger market than the other three, which cover international news in more depth. Weekly listings magazines for arts and events are published in Barcelona *(see p184)*, Madrid *(see p306)* and Seville. They are the *Guía del Ocio* in Barcelona and Madrid, and *El Giraldillo* in Seville. Several other cities also have listings magazines.

Local newspapers in Spanish, such as *Levante* in Valencia and *La Gaceta de Canarias* in the Canary Islands, are a useful source of information on local and regional events.

Foreign-language periodicals are published by expatriates in Madrid and in the country's main tourist areas. Examples in English include *Sur* on the Costa del Sol, the *Costa Blanca News* and the *Mallorca Daily Bulletin.* One of the longest-running magazines is *Lookout.* Published in Fuengirola, it features in-depth reports covering all aspects of life in Spain.

NEWSPAPERS AND MAGAZINES

NEWSAGENTS and kiosks in town centres often stock periodicals in English. The newspapers available on publication day are the *International Herald Tribune,* the *Financial Times* and the *Guardian International.* Other English-language and European titles are on sale, but usually not until a day after they have been published.

The European newspaper and popular weekly news magazines such as *Time, Newsweek* and *The Economist* are readily available throughout the country. The most

Public payphone booth, easily visible in a city street

TELEVISION AND RADIO

TELEVISION ESPAÑOLA, Spain's state television company, broadcasts two channels which are called TVE1 and TVE2.

Several of the *comunidades (see pp622–3)* have their own publicly owned television channels which broadcast in the language of the region.

There are three national independent television stations: Antena 3, Tele-5 (Telecinco) and Canal+ (Canal Plus). Some Canal+ programmes are only

A *prensa* (press) sign identifies a newsstand

POSTAL SERVICE

CORREOS, the postal service in Spain, is rather slow. Mail sent to an address in the city where it is posted can take as long as three to four days

Shops with this sign sell stamps

to arrive, while a national delivery may take more than a week. Send any urgent or important post by *urgente* (express) or *certificado* (registered) mail. To be sure of fast delivery it is wise to use a private courier.

Post can be registered and telegrams sent from all Correos offices. However, it is much easier to buy stamps for letters and post-cards from an *estanco* (tobacconist). Postal rates fall into four price bands: the EU; the rest of Europe; the US; and the rest of the world. Parcels have to be weighed and stamped at Correos offices and must be securely tied with string.

The main Correos offices open 8am–9pm from Monday to Friday and 9am–7pm on Saturday. Branches in the suburbs and small towns and villages open 9am–2pm from Monday to Friday and 9am–1pm on Saturday.

SPAIN'S LOTTERIES

Lottery fever is greater in Spain than in any other European country. The Lotería Nacional runs prize draws most Saturdays, plus a few special ones, the *extraordinarios*, of which the biggest is El Gordo ("the Fat One") at Christmas *(see p39)*. It is common to buy a *décimo* (one-tenth of a number), rather than a full ticket. Punters can also try their luck with the ONCE lottery, which has draws daily, the twice-weekly Lotería Primitiva, and the Bono-loto, with four draws a week.

ONCE lottery booth

LETTERS AND FAXES

LETTERS POSTED at a central post office usually arrive more quickly than if posted in a postbox *(buzón)*.

Postboxes in cities are yellow pillar boxes; in towns and villages they are small, wall-mounted postboxes. Poste restante letters should be addressed care of the *Lista de Correos* and the town. You can collect them from main offices. To send and receive money by post ask for a *giro internacional*.

When dealing with businesses in Spain, it is best to phone or fax. The post tends to be used only as a last resort. There are fax facilities in some *locutorios (see p620)* and in hotels and many private shops. Look for a *telefax* sign.

Spanish postbox

LOCAL GOVERNMENT

SPAIN is one of Europe's most decentralized states. Many powers have been devolved to the 17 regions, *comunidades autónomas,* which have their own elected parliaments. These regions have varying degrees of independence from Madrid, with the Basques and Catalans enjoying the most autonomy. The *comunidades* provide some services – such as the promotion of tourism – which were once carried out by central government.

The country is subdivided into 50 provinces, each with its *diputación* (council). The affairs of each of the Balearic and Canary islands are run by an island council.

Every town, or group of villages, is administered by an *ayuntamiento* (town council – the word also means town hall) which is supervised by an elected *alcalde* (mayor) and a team of councillors.

Spanish stamps

ADDRESSES

IN SPANISH ADDRESSES the house number follows the name of the street. The floor of a block of flats comes after a hyphen. Therefore 4-2° means a flat on the second floor of number four. All postcodes have five digits, the first two being the province number.

Murcia's town hall (*ayuntamiento* or *casa consistorial*)

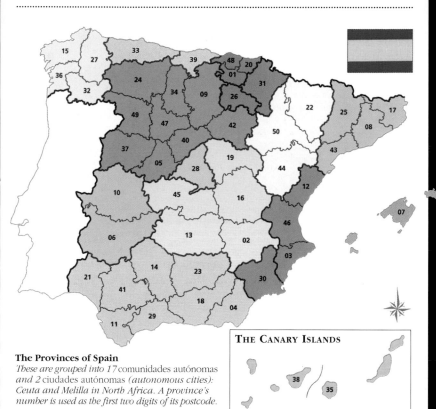

The Provinces of Spain

*These are grouped into 17 comunidades autónomas
and 2 ciudades autónomas (autonomous cities):
Ceuta and Melilla in North Africa. A province's
number is used as the first two digits of its postcode.*

THE CANARY ISLANDS

THE COMUNIDADES OF SPAIN AND THEIR PROVINCES

NORTHERN SPAIN

Galicia
15 A Coruña
27 Lugo
32 Ourense
36 Pontevedra

Asturias   **Cantabria**
33 Asturias
39 Cantabria

Basque   **Navarra**   **La Rioja**
Country
Basque Country (Euskadi)
01 Álava
20 Guipúzcoa
48 Vizcaya
*Comunidad Foral
de Navarra*
31 Navarra
La Rioja
26 La Rioja

EASTERN SPAIN

Catalonia
08 Barcelona
17 Girona
25 Lleida
43 Tarragona

Aragón
22 Huesca
44 Teruel
50 Zaragoza

Valencia   **Murcia**
Comunidad Valenciana
03 Alicante
12 Castellón
46 Valencia
Murcia
30 Murcia

CENTRAL SPAIN

Madrid
28 Comunidad de Madrid

Castilla-La Mancha
02 Albacete
13 Ciudad Real
16 Cuenca
19 Guadalajara
45 Toledo

Extremadura
06 Badajoz
10 Cáceres

Castilla y León
05 Ávila
09 Burgos
24 León
34 Palencia
37 Salamanca
40 Segovia
42 Soria
47 Valladolid
49 Zamora

SOUTHERN SPAIN

Andalusia
04 Almería
11 Cádiz
14 Córdoba
18 Granada
21 Huelva
23 Jaén
29 Málaga
41 Sevilla

SPAIN'S ISLANDS

The Balearic Islands (Islas Baleares)
07 Baleares

The Canary Islands (Islas Canarias)
35 Las Palmas
38 Santa Cruz de Tenerife

Sports and Outdoor Activities

SPAIN IS ONE OF EUROPE'S most geographically diverse
countries. Its mountain ranges, woodlands and deltas
are all fertile ground for scenic tours and sports holidays
as alternatives to a break on the beach. It also has a full
calendar of seasonal and annual events and activities
(see pp36–9). Tourist offices will provide lists of leisure
and sporting activities in their region. These pages give an
idea of the range of activities there is to choose from.

**A game of golf on a course on
Ibiza in the Balearic Islands**

SPECIALIST HOLIDAYS

ALL SPANISH tourist offices
provide details of special
interest holidays. Cookery,
wine and painting holidays,
and tours led by professional
historians and archaeologists,
are increasingly popular. There
is a wide choice for nature
lovers and photographers,
particularly in Spain's many
national parks.

Information about courses in
Spanish language and culture
is provided by **Canning
House** in London and by the
Instituto Cervantes.

GOLF AND TENNIS

SPAIN NOW HAS an abundance
of golf courses, some with
activities for non-golfers. The
**Real Federación Española
de Golf** will give locations and
more detailed information.

In most tourist areas there
are tennis courts for hire by
the hour and some hotels have
tennis courts for their guests
(see pp536–71). Travel agents
arrange tennis holidays for enthusiasts. For more information
contact the **Real Federación
Española de Tenis**.

WALKING, CYCLING AND
HORSE RIDING

MANY tour operators now
specialize in outdoor
holidays. The **Federación
Hípica Española** and Spanish
tourist offices have information
on horse riding and pony
trekking in most regions.

The road to Santiago de
Compostela *(see pp78–9)* is
Spain's most famous walk
and some national parks *(see
pp26–7)* have spectacular
routes for mountain-walking.
Picturesque minor roads in
many regions of Spain are
excellent for cycle-touring.

**Walking along the Río Cares in
the Picos de Europa in Asturias**

MOUNTAIN SPORTS

SPAIN'S MOST POPULAR resorts
for downhill skiing are in
the Vall d'Aran in Catalonia
(see pp200–201), and in the
Sierra Nevada, near Granada
(see p461). Downhill skiing is
often possible in the Sierra de
Guadarrama north of Madrid,
and there is cross-country skiing in other mountain areas.

Every region of this mountainous country has a climbing
association. The **Federación
Española de Montañismo**
will supply details. This
national organization has information about climbing and
many other mountain sports.

AIR SPORTS

A PRIVATE pilot's licence is
valid in Spain for up to six
months. The **Federación
Nacional de Deportes
Aéreos** will send information
about Spanish airfields and
clubs where visitors can
practise flying *(vuelo)*, gliding
(vuelo sin motor) and para-
chuting *(salto en paracaídas)*.

The organization also gives
information on places where
tourists can go ballooning
(volar en globo), hang-gliding
(ala delta) and paragliding
(parapente). Parts of Castilla y
León and Castilla-La Mancha
are recognized internationally
as excellent venues for hang-
gliding, and the Valle de
Abdalajís, north of Málaga, is
well known for paragliding.

Paragliding above the Vall d'Aran in the eastern Pyrenees

White water rafting in the Spanish Pyrenees

WATER SPORTS

THERE IS WHITE WATER RAFTING and canoeing on rivers in Catalonia, Aragón and many other regions of Spain. Sort, a village in the Catalonian Pyrenees, is one of Europe's prime river sports resorts.

Boating, sailing and wind-surfing are very popular. The tourist offices at the coastal resorts of the mainland and in the islands give information about local hire of boats and sailboards. Experienced wind-surfers head for Tarifa *(see p444)*, whose windswept location has made it one of Europe's windsurfing capitals.

Sailing information is held by the **Real Federación Española de Vela**.

Beaches, marinas and ports that meet strict European standards of cleanliness and safety are permitted to fly a *bandera azul* (blue flag).

Windsurfing off Fuerteventura in the Canary Islands

NATURISM

CONTACT THE **Asociacion Naturista de Almeria y Murcia**, or coastal tourist offices for nudist beaches.

Fly-fishing in the rivers of Castilla y León, famous for their trout

FIELD SPORTS

IF YOU WANT TO HUNT or shoot in Spain you must first apply for a licence and be properly insured. To obtain a licence you apply to the *comunidad* (regional government) of the area where you want to hunt. The fees tend to be high.

Permits for river or sea fish-ing for any length of period from one day to one year, and for fishing competitions, are issued by the *comunidades*. The **Federación Española de Caza** (for hunting) and the **Federación Española de Pesca** (for fishing) give infor-mation on where each different field sport is permitted, the dates of open seasons, and advise on licences. Travel agents and hotels specializing in hunting and fishing trips will obtain licences for clients.

TRAVEL INFORMATION

S PAIN HAS AN INCREASINGLY EFFICIENT transport system. All the major cities have airports and flights from all over the globe arrive at those of Madrid and Barcelona. Both the road and rail networks were greatly improved during the 1980s and in the run-up to Expo and the Olympics in 1992 *(see p65)*. Intercity rail services are efficient, but coaches are a faster and more frequent option between smaller towns. In much of rural Spain, however, public transport is limited and a car is the most practical solution for getting about. Ferries connect mainland Spain with the UK, North Africa and the Balearic and Canary islands.

✈ aeropuerto

Sign for an airport

Shopping at Barcelona's El Prat airport

ARRIVING BY AIR

S PAIN IS SERVED by most international airlines. **Iberia**, the national airline, has scheduled flights daily into Madrid and Barcelona from all west European capitals (but just four times a week from Dublin), and once or twice weekly from most east European capitals.

British Airways offers scheduled flights to Spain. It serves Madrid and Barcelona daily from London Heathrow and London Gatwick; also Madrid from Manchester, and Barcelona from Birmingham. Two budget airlines, **Easyjet** and Go, fly to Spain out of Luton and Stansted airports.

Of the US airlines serving Spain, **Delta Airlines** flies to both Madrid and Barcelona, **American Airlines** flies to Madrid. Iberia has a comprehensive service from the USA, as well as direct flights to many destinations in Spain from Toronto and Montreal.

BARAJAS AIRPORT, MADRID

Madrid's airport is 13 km (8 miles) from the city centre. The international terminal is Terminal 1. Iberia flights to the EU countries of Germany, Austria, Belgium, France, Holland, Italy, Luxembourg and Portugal use Terminal 2. Domestic flights are served from Terminals 2 and 3. It takes only 12 minutes by metro to reach the central station of Nuevos Ministerios, where numerous airlines have set up check-in facilites. Taxis are also available and a shuttle bus runs every 12 minutes to the city centre.

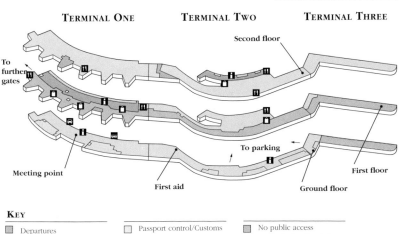

TERMINAL ONE   **TERMINAL TWO**   **TERMINAL THREE**

Second floor

To further gates

To parking

Meeting point

First aid

First floor

Ground floor

KEY

■ Departures	□ Passport control/Customs	■ No public access
□ Arrivals	□ Public access	■ Restricted access
■ Check-in	□ Ticket sales	

INTERNATIONAL AIRPORTS

THE MOST REGULAR international services operate from Madrid and Barcelona. The busiest international airports for scheduled and charter flights in Spain are marked on the map on pages 10–11.

Palma de Mallorca, Tenerife Sur, Las Palmas de Gran Canaria, Málaga, Lanzarote, Ibiza, Alicante, Fuerteventura and Menorca handle large amounts of holiday traffic. The first four are especially busy – Palma topped 19 million passengers in 1999. Most is seasonal traffic, mainly from north European countries, and at peak summer holiday time these airports can get crowded. Details of public transport to and from Spain's most important airports are given on page 628.

All the Balearic and Canary islands have international air ports, except Hierro and La Gomera which have domestic

Iberia plane on the tarmac of Seville airport

ones. Melilla and Ceuta are also served by domestic flights only.

AIR FARES

AIR FARES for flights to Spain vary through the year, depending on demand. They are generally highest during the summer months. Special deals, particularly for weekend city breaks, are often offered in the winter and may include a number of nights at a hotel. Look out for Iberia's "Bravo"

air fares, and for **Go** for competitive deals. Christmas and Easter flights are almost always booked up well in advance.

Charter flights from the UK serve airports such as Alicante, Málaga and Girona near beach resorts. These can be very cheap, but less reliable, and often fly at unsociable hours. Make sure your agent is ABTA bonded before booking. Local car hire companies may offer good deals at resort airports, but read rental terms carefully.

EL PRAT AIRPORT, BARCELONA

Barcelona's airport is 12 km (7 miles) from the city centre. Terminal A handles international arrivals and foreign airlines' departures. Terminals B and C are for departures on Spanish airlines and arrivals from European Union countries. Trains to the Plaça de Catalunya in the city centre leave every 30 minutes. For intercity rail connections, get off at Barcelona-Sants station. There is also a shuttle bus, the Aerobús, running every 15 minutes, which will also leave you in Plaça de Catalunya.

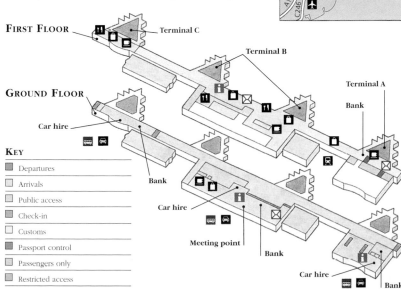

FIRST FLOOR

Terminal C

Terminal B

Terminal A

GROUND FLOOR

Bank

Car hire

KEY

Departures

Arrivals

Public access

Check-in

Customs

Passport control

Passengers only

Restricted access

Bank

Car hire

Meeting point

Bank

Car hire

Bank

Insignia of Spain's national airline

DOMESTIC FLIGHTS

MOST OF Spain's domestic flights have traditionally been operated by **Iberia**. In recent years, however, this monopoly has been broken to encourage competition. The two main alternative carriers are **Air Europa** and **Spanair**.

The most frequent shuttle service is the Puente Aéreo, run between Barcelona and Madrid by Iberia. It flies every 15 minutes at peak business times, hourly at other times. A self-ticketing machine allows passengers to buy tickets up to 15 minutes before a flight departs. When a flight is full, waiting passengers are always offered a seat on the next available shuttle. The flight usually takes 50 minutes.

Air-Nostrum, Air Europa and Spanair services between Madrid and the regional capitals are not as frequent as the Puente Aéreo, but their prices are usually slightly lower. They operate in a similar way to Apex tickets:

the earlier the booking is made, the greater the discount. The cheapest ticket, which must be booked a week in advance, can save up to one-third of the full price. Flights to the provincial cities usually operate in the morning and evening. They can be expensive, costing as much as 120 euros for a one-way trip. Pressure from the intercity rail services may eventually result in lower air fares.

Self-ticketing machine

Flights to the Balearic and Canary islands, and island-hopping flights between them, are operated by an Iberia-affiliated company: **Binter**. Travel agencies often offer a variety of special deals on internal flights, which may include one night or more in a hotel. It is worth shopping around. These deals are advertised in the Spanish press.

Some flights from domestic airports are billed as international flights but they do not go directly to foreign destinations. Instead, they stop en route at major cities like Madrid or Barcelona.

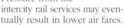

The departures concourse in Seville Airport

AIRPORT	ℂ INFORMATION	DISTANCE TO CITY CENTRE	PUBLIC TRANSPORT TIME TO CITY CENTRE
Alicante	96 691 94 00	13 km (8 miles)	Bus: 20 mins
Barcelona	93 298 38 38	12 km (7 miles)	Rail: 20 mins Bus: 25 mins
Bilbao	94 486 96 64	10 km (6 miles)	Bus: 30 mins
Madrid	91 305 83 43	13 km (8 miles)	Bus: 30 mins
Málaga	95 204 88 38	10 km (6 miles)	Rail: 15 mins Bus: 20 mins
Palma de Mallorca	971 78 90 00	9 km (6 miles)	Bus: 30 mins
Las Palmas de Gran Canaria	928 57 90 00	20 km (12 miles)	Bus: 30 mins
Santiago de Compostela	981 54 75 00	10 km (6 miles)	Bus: 30 mins
Seville	95 444 90 00	10 km (6 miles)	Rail: 15 mins Bus: 30 mins
Tenerife Sur – Reina Sofía	922 75 90 00	64 km (40 miles) to Santa Cruz	Bus: 60 mins
Valencia	96 370 95 00	9 km (5 miles)	Rail: 20 mins Bus: 30 mins

ARRIVING BY SEA

Ferries connect the Spanish mainland to the Balearic and Canary islands, to North Africa and to the UK. All the important routes are served by car ferries. It is always wise to make an advance booking, especially in summer.

Two routes link Spain with the UK. **Brittany Ferries** sails between Plymouth in the UK and Santander in Cantabria; and **P&O European Ferries** sails from Portsmouth into Santurce harbour, near Bilbao in the Basque Country. The crossings take over 24 hours. Each ship has cabins, chairs to sleep on, a restaurant, cafés and a cinema. Discos are sometimes held on board.

FERRIES TO THE ISLANDS

Frequent crossings run from Barcelona and Valencia on the mainland to the three main Balearic islands. The crossings, on **Trasmediterránea** ferries, take about eight hours. The same company also operates frequent inter-island services; and small operators take day-trippers (passengers only) from Ibiza to Formentera. Storms are rare in this part of the Mediterranean and crossings are, therefore, usually calm and comfortable.

Trasmediterránea operates a weekly service from Cádiz in Andalusia to the main ports of the Canary Islands – Las Palmas de Gran Canaria and Santa Cruz de Tenerife. Crossings normally take 39 hours.

Ferry in port at Los Cristianos (Tenerife) in the Canary Islands

Car ferries link the islands with each other. Trasmediterránea also runs passengers-only services between the islands of Gran Canaria, Tenerife and Fuerteventura, and between Tenerife and La Gomera.

The ferries to Spain's islands have cabins, cafés, restaurants, bars, shops, cinemas, pools and sunbathing decks for the summer. They are also fitted with lifts and other facilities for people with special needs, and they even have kennels. A variety of entertainment, such as films and discos, is provided on the long crossing from the mainland to the Canary Islands.

Ferries logo

FERRIES TO AFRICA

Trasmediterranea operates ferries daily to the Spanish territories in North Africa: from Málaga and Almería to Melilla, and from Algeciras to Ceuta. Ferries also cross to Tangier in Morocco from Algeciras.

Trasmediterránea car ferry to the Balearic Islands in Barcelona harbour

Travelling by Train

Logo of the Spanish national railways

THE SPANISH STATE RAILWAY, **RENFE** *(Red Nacional de Ferrocarriles Españolas),* operates a service that is continually improving, particularly between cities. The fastest intercity services are called the TALGO and the AVE – their names are acronyms for the high-speed, luxury trains that run on these routes. *Largo recorrido* (long-distance) and *regionales y cercanías* (regional and local) trains are notoriously slow, many stopping at every station. They are much cheaper than the high-speed trains but can take hours longer.

ARRIVING BY TRAIN

THERE ARE SEVERAL routes to Spain from France. The main western route runs from Paris through Hendaye in the Pyrenees to San Sebastián. The eastern route from Paris runs via Cerbère and Port Bou to Barcelona. The trains from London, Brussels, Amsterdam, Geneva, Zurich and Milan all reach Barcelona via Cerbère. At Cerbère there are connections with the TALGO and the *largo recorrido* (long-distance) services to Valencia, Málaga, Seville and Madrid, and other major destinations. If you book a sleeper on the TALGO from Paris, you travel to your destination without having to change trains.

EXPLORING BY TRAIN

SPAIN OFFERS many options for train travellers. In the last ten years, the TALGO high-speed services have belied Spain's reputation for inefficiency and it is now possible to travel the long distances between the main cities extremely quickly. Ticket prices compare very favourably with the cost of high-speed train fares in many other countries in Europe. AVE is the efficient high-speed rail service between Madrid and Seville via Córdoba. The full journey normally takes two and a half hours.

The *largo recorrido* (long-distance) trains are so much slower you usually need to travel overnight. You can

AVE high-speed trains at Estación de Santa Justa in Seville

choose between a *cochecama* (compartment with two *camas* or beds) or a *litera*, one of six seats in a compartment which converts into a bunk bed. You reserve these when booking and pay a supplement. You should book at least a month in advance, but bear in mind that it is difficult to change a ticket you have paid for.

Regionales y cercanías (the regional and local services) are frequent and very cheap. You buy the tickets from machines on the station.

Some cities have more than one station. In Madrid the major stations for regional and long-distance trains are Atocha, Chamartín and Norte. The AVE runs from Atocha, the TALGO from all three. Sants and Francia are Barcelona's two principal stations. In Seville Santa Justa is the only station for regional and international services.

Logo for a high-speed rail service

FARES

SPANISH RAILWAYS offer a 10 per cent discount on specified days to encourage people to travel. They are called *días azules* (blue days) and are indicated in the timetables in blue.

Fares for rail travel in Spain are structured according to the speed and quality of the service. Tickets for the TALGO and AVE are most expensive.

Interrail tickets for people under 26, and Eurodomino tickets for people over 26, are available from major travel agencies in Europe and from RENFE ticket offices in Spain. Always take proof of your identity when booking.

Holidays on Spain's two luxury trains *(see p631)* are expensive but offer high standards of comfort.

REGIONAL RAILWAYS

THREE OF THE *comunidades autónomas* have regional rail companies. Catalonia and Valencia each has its own *Ferrocarrils de la Generalitat:*

SPAIN'S PRINCIPAL **RENFE** NETWORK

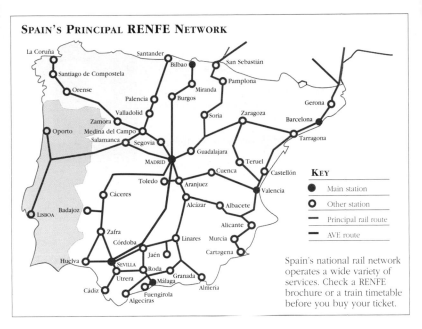

KEY

● Main station

○ Other station

— Principal rail route

— AVE route

Spain's national rail network operates a wide variety of services. Check a RENFE brochure or a train timetable before you buy your ticket.

respectively the **FGC** and the **FGV**; and the Basque Country has the **ET** *(Eusko Trenbideak).*

Tickets for two special trains, similar to the Orient Express, can be obtained from travel agents. Tickets for *Al Andalus Expres,* which tours Andalusia, including Seville and Granada, can also be bought through RENFE. While **FEVE** *(Ferro-carriles de Vía Estrecha)* run *El Transcantábrico,* which travels Spain's north coast between San Sebastián and Santiago de Compostela. Passengers travel in style in 14 period carriages built between 1900–30 and since restored.

The regional tourist offices publicize unusual rail services, such as the narrow-gauge lines to Inca and Sóller in Mallorca.

BOOKING TICKETS

TALGO, AVE and any other tickets for *largo recorrido* travel by train may be booked and bought at any of the major railway stations from the *taquilla* (ticket office). They are also sold by all travel agents in Spain, who will charge a commission. RENFE tickets are sometimes sold by travel agents in other countries. Telephone reservations may be made directly to all RENFE

Ticket machine for local and regional lines

ticket offices using a credit card number. A booking may be made or a special pass purchased as long as 59 days ahead of travel.

Tickets for local and regional services are purchased from the station *taquilla.* In larger stations they can be bought from ticket machines but these only accept coins. Tickets for *cercanías* (local services) cannot be reserved. For a one-way journey ask for *ida* and for a return ask for *ida y vuelta.*

TIMETABLES

RENFE TIMETABLES change in May and October each year. They are not very easy to obtain outside Spain, but your travel agent will be able to provide the correct times of trains for your journey. In Spain timetables are available from RENFE offices. Most come in the form of leaflets and are broken down into the various types of journey: intercity, *largo recorrido* and *regionales. Cercanías* timetables are posted on boards at local railway stations.

Atocha, one of Madrid's largest mainline railway stations

Travelling by Road

Spain's fastest roads are its *autopistas*. They are normally dual carriageways and are subsidized by *peajes* (tolls). *Autovías* are similar but have no tolls. The *carretera nacional* is the countrywide network of main roads or highways with the prefix N. Smaller minor roads are generally less well kept but are often a more leisurely and enjoyable way to see rural areas of Spain. These pages tell you how to use the roads, tolls and parking meters, how to buy petrol, and explain important driving regulations.

Sign for national highway N110

Cambio de sentido (slip road) 300 m (330 yd) ahead

ARRIVING BY CAR

Many people drive to Spain via the French motorways. The most direct routes across the Pyrenees, using the motorways, pass through Hendaye on the western flank and Port Bou in the east. Other, rather more tortuous routes may be used, from Toulouse through the Vall d'Aran, for instance. From the UK there are car ferries from Plymouth to Santander and from Portsmouth to Bilbao in northern Spain *(see p629)*.

WHAT TO TAKE

A green card and a bail bond from a motor insurance company are needed in order to extend your comprehensive cover to Spain. The RAC, the AA and Europ Assistance have sound rescue and recovery policies with European cover.

Spanish law requires you to carry with you at all times your vehicle's registration document, a valid insurance certificate and your driving licence. You must always be able to show a passport or a national identity card as ID. You must also display a sticker with the car's country of registration on the rear of the vehicle.

The headlights of right-hand drive vehicles will have to be adjusted or deflected. This is done with stickers that can be bought at ferry ports and on ferries. You risk on-the-spot fines if you do not carry a red warning triangle, spare light bulbs and a first-aid kit.

In winter you should carry chains if you intend to drive in mountain areas. In summer, it is a good idea to take drinking water with you if you are travelling in a remote area.

BUYING PETROL

In Spain *gasolina* (petrol) and *gasóleo* (diesel) are priced by the litre. *Gasolina sin plomo* (unleaded petrol) is available everywhere. All cost more at the *autopista* service stations. Self-service stations, where you fill up yourself, are common. You must wait for service if there are attendants. They will ask *¿cuánto?* (how much?); you should reply *lleno* (fill the tank) or specify an amount in euros: *dos euros por favor.* Small stations do not all accept credit cards. If you use your credit card to pay at a motorway service station you will be asked to show your passport or ID. Modern pumps sometimes operate by credit card. You run your card through the machine, press the buttons to indicate the amount of petrol you want in pesetas, and then serve yourself.

RULES OF THE ROAD

Most traffic regulations and warnings to motorists are represented on signs by easily recognized symbols. But Spain has a few road rules and signs that may be unfamiliar to some drivers from other countries.

To turn left at a busy junction or across oncoming traffic you may have to turn right first and cross a main road, often by way of traffic lights, a bridge or an under-pass. If you are going the wrong way on a motorway or a main road with a solid white line, you are allowed to turn round where you see a sign for a *cambio de sentido*.

At any crossing you must give way to the right unless a sign indicates otherwise. It is compulsory always to wear seat belts if they are fitted in front and rear seats. Oncoming drivers may flash their headlights at you to mean "you go"; "danger"; "your lights are on unnecessarily"; or (most often) "speed trap ahead".

Speed limit 50 km/h (31 mph)

Pedestrian crossing sign

A filling station run by a leading chain with branches throughout Spain

Speed Limits and Fines

Speed limits on the roads in Spain for cars without trailers are as follows:
• 120 km/h (75 mph) on *autopistas* (toll motorways).
• 100 km/h (62 mph) on *autovías* (non-toll motorways).
• 90 km/h (56 mph) on *carreteras nacionales* (main roads) and *carreteras comarcales* (secondary roads).
• 50 km/h (31 mph) in built-up areas.

Speeding fines are imposed on the spot at the rate of six euros for every kilometre per hour over the limit. Fines for other traffic offences (such as turning the wrong way into a one-way street) depend on the severity of the offence and the whim of a police officer.

Tests for drink-driving and fines for drivers over the blood alcohol legal limit, which is 30 mg per millilitre, are now imposed frequently throughout the country.

Blue *autopista* (motorway) sign for motorists approaching the A6

Motorways

Spain has more than 2,000 km (1,240 miles) of *autopistas*, and many more are planned. They are toll roads and they are rather expensive to use. The long-distance tolls are calculated per kilometre and the rate varies from region to region. Among the busiest and most expensive are the A7 along the south coast to Alicante and the A68 Bilbao-Zaragoza *autopista*.

There are service stations every 40 km (25 miles) or so along the *autopistas,* marked by a blue and white parking sign (P) or a sign indicating the services available. About 1 km (550 yd) from a service station, a sign indicates the distance to the next one and lists its services. Most have fuel, toilets, a shop for maps,

Driving through the Sierra Nevada along one of Europe's highest roads

coffee and snacks, and a café which serves full meals.

Emergency telephones occur every 2 km (1.25 miles) along the *autopistas*.

Using Autopista Tolls

If you are travelling a long distance on the *autopista* you pick up a ticket from a toll booth *(peaje)* as you drive on to it and give it up at a booth as you exit. Your toll will be calculated according to the distance you have covered. Over some short stretches of motorways near to cities a fixed price is charged. Tolls can be paid either in cash or by credit card.

You must join one of three channels at the *peaje* leading to different booths. Do not drive into *telepago,* a credit system for which you need a chip on your windscreen. *Automático* has machines for you to pay by credit card or with exactly the right coins. In *manual* an attendant in the booth takes your ticket and your money.

The *peaje manual* channel, with attendant

PEAJE TOLL

Autopista toll booths ahead

Other Roads

Carreteras nacionales, Spain's main roads, have black and white signs and are designated N *(Nacional)* plus a number. Those with Roman numerals (NIII) start at the Puerta del Sol, Madrid. The distance from the Kilometre Zero mark in the Puerta del Sol *(see p262)* appears on kilometre markers. Those with ordinary numbers (N6) have kilometre markers giving the distance from the provincial capital. Some *carreteras nacionales* are dual carriageways, but most are single-lane roads and can be slow. They tend to be least busy at lunch time, from 2–5pm, when many lorry drivers stop for lunch.

Autovías are new roads built in recent years to motorway standard to replace N roads. They have blue signs similar to *autopista* signs. Because they have no tolls they are busier than *autopistas*.

Carreteras comarcales, secondary roads, have a number preceded by a letter C. Other minor roads have numbers preceded by letters representing the name of the province such as the LE 1313 in Lleida. On any road in winter, watch out for signs indicating whether a mountain pass ahead is open *(abierto)* or closed *(cerrado)*.

CAR HIRE

AS WELL AS the international car hire companies, a few Spanish companies, such as **Atesa**, operate nationwide. You can probably negotiate the best deal with an international company from home. There are also fly-drive and other package deals, including car hire. Fly-drive, an option for two or more travellers, can be arranged by travel agents.

There are car hire desks at airports and offices in the large towns. Alternatively, if you wish to hire a car locally for, say, a week or less, you can arrange it with a local travel agent. A car for hire is called a *coche de alquiler*.

For chauffeur-driven cars in Spain, **Avis** offer deals from major cities. Car-hire prices and conditions vary according to the region and locality.

Some of the leading car-hire companies operating in Spain

MAPS

FOLD-OUT ROAD MAPS can be obtained at airports, on the ferries and from tourist offices. The Spanish Ministry of Transport publishes a comprehensive road map in book form, the *Mapa Oficial de Carreteras*. Campsa, the oil company, publishes the *Guía Campsa*, a road map and restaurant guide in one book. Michelin publishes a useful series of maps (440–448, with orange covers) at a scale of 1:400,000 (1 cm:4 km), which covers Spain in eight sections, including the islands. They are sold at bookshops and petrol stations all over Spain.

A series of more detailed maps at 1:200,000 for cycling, walking and other specialist uses is published by Plaza y Janés. Military maps at scales of 1:50,000 and 1:100,000 are available from **Stanfords Travel Bookshop** in London and from specialist bookshops

City taxis with their logo and official numbers

and some local bookshops in Spain. Tourist offices in towns and cities usually have a give-away street map of the town showing the principal sights.

There are detailed street maps of central Barcelona on pages 176–81, of Madrid on pages 298–303 and of Seville on pages 430–33 of this guide.

PARKING

THE HOURS for which drivers have to pay for parking in Spain are 8am until 2pm and 4pm until 8pm on Mondays to Saturdays.

As a rule, you may not park where the pavement edge is painted yellow or where a no parking sign is displayed. Occasionally there is a no parking sign on both sides of a city street, one saying "1–15" and the other "16–30". This means that you can park on one side of the street only for the fortnight indicated on the sign.

In the cities, non-metered, on-street parking is generally hard to find, but there are blue pay and display parking spaces. To use them you buy a ticket from the machine and display it on the inside of your windscreen. The cost varies, but averages about 1–2 euros per hour. You can usually park at the same spot for up to two hours. The penalties for infringements vary from town to town.

Major cities have many large underground car parks. You collect a ticket when you enter, retain it, and pay the attendant as you drive out.

A parking ticket machine

TAXIS

THERE IS NO CENTRAL system for taxis in Spain. Every city and/or region has its own design and tariffs for its taxis. All will display a green light if they are free. Most taxis are metered and at the start of the journey a minimum fee will be shown on the meter. In smaller villages the taxi service may well be run by a resident driving an unmetered private car. Ask at the hotel reception or in a nearby shop for the name and number of a local driver. It is best to negotiate a price for the trip before you set off.

In the cities there are taxi ranks at the airports, the railway and bus stations and usually in the main shopping areas. Tips of about 1 euro will be acceptable.

ROAD CONDITIONS AND WEATHER FORECASTS

TO HEAR RECORDED road and traffic information call the national toll-free number for **Información de Tráfico de Carreteras**. This service is in Spanish only. Ask your hotel receptionist to call for you if you need a translation. The RAC offers route-planning services tailored to individual requirements, which may include current road conditions. The weather information service, **Teletiempo**, gives forecasts for the regions and provinces, as well as the national and international weather. It also gives information on maritime and mountain conditions.

No parking at any time of day

ARRIVING BY COACH

O FTEN THE CHEAPEST WAY TO reach and travel around Spain is by coach. **Eurolines** operates routes throughout Europe and runs daily services to Madrid and Barcelona.

Coaches from the UK depart from London Victoria Coach Station. Tickets may be bought from National Express offices or travel agents, or a credit card booking may be made by phone. The journey to both cities takes about 24 hours.

TRAVELLING AROUND SPAIN BY COACH

T HERE IS NO Spanish national coach company, but private regional companies operate routes around the country. The largest coach tour company, **Autocares Juliá**, which acts as an agent for Eurolines in Spain, offers itineraries, coach holidays and sightseeing trips nationwide. Other coach companies operate in particular regions – Alsina Graells, for instance, covers most of the south and east of Spain. Tickets and information for long-distance travel are available at all main coach stations and

Alsina Graells, a regional coach service

from travel agents but they cannot always be booked in advance. In Madrid there are several coach stations. The biggest of them are **Estación Sur**, which serves the whole of Spain; **Intercambiador des Autobuses**, for terminals in the north; and **Terminal Auto Res**, serving Valencia, Extremadura and Andalusia.

CYCLING

Cycling is popular in Spain and there are bicycles for hire in most tourist spots but there are few cycle lanes, even in towns. Bicycles may be carried on *cercanías* trains after 2pm on Fridays until the last train on Sunday night, on any *regional* train

Cycle touring, a popular holiday activity

with a goods compartment, and on all long-distance overnight trains. If you need to take your bicycle long-distance at other times, you should check it in an hour before the train departs. You may have to send it as luggage and pay a baggage charge based on its weight. It might not travel with you so you will have to collect it when it arrives.

LOCAL BUSES

L OCAL BUS routes and timetables are posted at bus terminuses and stops. You pay on the bus or buy strips of ten tickets called *billetes bonobus* from *estancos* (tobacconists).

Indicators for Seville's circular bus routes

General Index

U

Acknowledgments

DORLING KINDERSLEY would like to thank the following people whose contributions and assistance made preparation of this book possible.

MAIN CONTRIBUTORS
JOHN ARDAGH is a journalist and writer, and the author of several books on modern Europe.

DAVID BAIRD, resident in Andalusia from 1971 to 1995, is the author of *Inside Andalusia*.

VICKY HAYWARD, a writer, journalist and editor, lives in Madrid, and has travelled extensively in Spain.

ADAM HOPKINS is an indefatigable travel writer and author of *Spanish Journeys: A Portrait of Spain*.

LINDSAY HUNT has travelled widely and has contributed to several Eyewitness Travel Guides.

NICK INMAN writes regularly on Spain for books and magazines.

PAUL RICHARDSON is the author of *Not Part of the Package*, a book on Ibiza, where he lives.

MARTIN SYMINGTON is a regular contributor to the *Daily Telegraph*. He also worked on the *Eyewitness Travel Guide to Great Britain*.

NIGEL TISDALL, contributor to the *Eyewitness Travel Guide to France*, is the author of the *Insight Pocket Guide to Seville*.

ROGER WILLIAMS has contributed to Insight Guides on Barcelona and Catalonia, and was the series contributor to the *Eyewitness Travel Guide to Provence*.

ADDITIONAL CONTRIBUTORS
Mary Jane Aladren, Pepita Aris, Emma Dent Coad, Rebecca Doulton, Harry Eyres, Josefina Fernández, Anne Hersh, Nick Rider, Mercedes Ruiz Ochoa, David Stone, Clara Villanueva, Christopher Woodward, Patricia Wright.

ADDITIONAL ILLUSTRATIONS
Arcana Studio, Richard Bonson, Louise Boulton, Martine Collings, Brian Craker, Jared Gilbey (Kevin Jones Associates), Paul Guest, Steven Gyapay, Claire Littlejohn.

ADDITIONAL PHOTOGRAPHY
Tina Chambers, Geoff Dann, Phillip Dowell, Mike Dunning, Neil Fletcher, Steve Gorton, Frank Greenaway, Derek Hall, Colin Keates, Alan Keohane, Dave King, D Murray, Cyril Laubsouer, Stephen Oliver, J Selves, Mathew Ward.

CARTOGRAPHY
Lovell Johns Ltd (Oxford), ERA-Maptec Ltd.

DESIGN AND EDITORIAL ASSISTANCE
Sam Atkinson, Pilar Ayerbe, Rosemary Bailey, Vicky Barber, Teresa Barea, Cristina Barrallo, Jill Benjamin, Chris Branfield, Daniel Brett, Gretta Britton, Lola Carbonell, Peter Casterton, Elspeth Collier, Carey Combe, Jonathan Cox, Martin Cropper, Linda Doyle, Elena González, Des Hemsley, Tim Hollis, Michael Lake, Erika Lang, Rebecca Lister, Sarah Martin, Jane Oliver, Simon Oon, Mike Osborn, Malcolm Parchment, Anna Pirie, Zoë Ross, Anna Streiffert, Helen Townsend, Andy Wilkinson, Robert Zonenblick.

PROOFREADER
Stewart J Wild.

INDEXER
Hilary Bird.

SPECIAL ASSISTANCE
DORLING KINDERSLEY would like to thank the regional and local tourist offices, *ayuntamientos*, shops, hotels, restaurants and other organizations in Spain for their invaluable help. Particular thanks also to Dr Giray Ablay (University of Bristol); María Eugenia Alonso and María Dolores Delgado Peña (Museo Thyssen-Bornemisza); Ramón Álvarez (Consejería de Educación y Cultura, Castilla y León); Señor Ballesteros (Santiago de Compostela Tourist Office); Carmen Brieva, Javier Campos and Luis Esteruelas (Spanish Embassy, London); Javier Caballero Arranz; Fernando Cañada López; The Club Taurino of London; Consejería de Turismo, Castilla-La Mancha; Consejería de Turismo and Consejería de Cultura, Junta de Extremadura; Mònica Colomer and Montse Planas (Barcelona Tourist Office); María José Docal and Carmen Cardona (Patronato de Turismo, Lanzarote); Edilesa; Klaus Ehrlich; Juan Fernández, Lola Moreno and others at El País-Aguilar; Belén Galán (Centro de Arte Reina Sofía); Amparo Garrido, Adolfo Díaz-Cáceres (Albacete Tourist Office); Professor Nigel Glendinning (Queen Mary and Westfield College, University of London); Pedro Hernández; Insituto de Cervantes, London; Victor Jolín (SOTUR); Joaquim Juan Cabanilles (Servicio de Investigación Prehistórica, Valencia); Richard Kelly; Mark Little (*Lookout* Magazine); Carmen López de Tejada and Inma Felipe (Spanish National Tourist Office, London); Caterine López and Ana Roig Mundi (ITVA); Julia López de la Torre (Patrimonio Nacional, Madrid); Lovell Johns Ltd (Oxford); Josefina Maestre (Ministerio de Agricultura, Pesca y Alimentación); Juan Malavia García and Antonio Abarca (Cuenca Tourist Office); Mario (Promoción Turismo, Tenerife); Janet Mendel; Javier Morata (Acanto Arquitectura y Urbanismo. Madrid); Juan Carlos Murillo; Sonia Ortega and Bettina Krücken (Spain Gourmetour); Royal Society for the Protection of Birds (UK); Alícia Ribas Sos; Katusa Salazar-Sandoval (Fomento de Turismo, Ibiza); María Ángeles Sánchez and Marcos; Ana Sarrieri (Departamento de Comercio, Consumo y Turismo, Gobierno Vasco); Klaas Schenk; María José Sevilla (Foods From Spain); The Sherry Institute of Spain (London); Anna Skidmore (Fomento de Turismo, Mallorca); Philip Sweeney; Rupert Thomas; Mercedes Trujillo and Antonio Cruz Caballero (Patronato de Turismo, Gran Canaria); Gerardo Uarte (Gobierno de Navarra); Fermín Unzue (Dirección General de Turismo, Cantabria); Puri Villanueva.

ARTWORK REFERENCE

Sr Joan Bassegoda, Catedral Gaudí (Barcelona); José Luis Mosquera Muller (Mérida); Jorge Palazón, Paisajes Españoles (Madrid).

PHOTOGRAPHY PERMISSIONS

THE PUBLISHER would like to thank the following for their kind assistance and permission to photograph at their establishments:© Patrimonio Nacional, Madrid; Palacio de la Almudaina, Palma de Mallorca; El Escorial, Madrid; La Granja de San Ildefonso; Convento de Santa Clara, Tordesillas; Las Huelgas Reales, Burgos; Palacio Real, Madrid; Monasterio de las Descalzas; Bananera "El Guanche S.L."; Museo Arqueológico de Tenerife-OACIMC del Excmo, Cavildo Insular de Tenerife; Asociación de Encajeras de Acebo-Cáceres; Museo de Arte Abstracto Español, Cuenca; Fundación Juan March; Pepita Alia Lagartera; Museo Naval de Madrid; © Catedral de Zamora; Museo de Burgos; Claustro San Juan de Duero, Museo Numantino, Soria; San Telmo Museoa Donostia-San Sebastián; Hotel de la Reconquista, Oviedo; Catedral de Jaca; Museo de Cera, Barcelona; Museu D'Història de la Ciutat, Barcelona; © Capitol Catedral de Lleida; Jardí Botànic Marimurtra, Estació Internacional de Biologia Mediterrània, Girona; Museo Arqueológico Sagunto (Teatro Romano-Castillo); Museo Municipal y Ermita de San Antonio de la Florida, Madrid. Also all the other churches, museums, hotels, restaurants, shops, galleries and sights too numerous to thank individually.

PICTURE CREDITS

Key: t=top; tl=top left; tlc=top left centre; tc=top centre; trc=top right centre; tr=top right; cla=centre left above; ca=centre above; cra=centre right above; cl=centre left; c=centre; cr=centre right; clb=centre left below; crb=centre right below; cb=centre below; bl=bottom left; br=bottom right; b=bottom; bc=bottom centre; bcl=bottom centre left; bcr=bottom centre right; (d)=detail.

Every effort has been made to trace the copyright holders. Dorling Kindersley apologizes for any unintentional omissions and would be pleased, in such cases, to add an acknowledgment in future editions.

Works of art have been published with the permission of the following copyright holders: *Dona i Ocell* Joan Miró © ADAGP, Paris & DACS, London 172tl; *Guernica* Pablo Ruiz Picasso 1937 © DACS 1996 289cb; *Morning* George Kolbe © DACS 1996; *Peine de los Vientos* Eduardo Chillida 118b; Various works by Joaquín Sorolla © DACS 1996 295t; *Rainy Taxi* Salvador Dalí © DEMART PRO ARTE BV/DACS 1996 205tr; *Tapestry of the Foundation* Joan Miró 1975 © ADAGP, Paris & DACS, London; *Three Gypsy Boys* © Joan Rebull 1976 140bl.

The publisher would like to thank the following individuals, companies and picture libraries for their kind permission to reproduce their photographs: ACE PHOTO AGENCY: Bob Masters 22b; Mauritius 19t;

Bill Wassman 306b; AISA ARCHIVO ICONOGRÁFICO, BARCELONA: 18t, 32bl, 42l, 44ca, 44cb, 45bl, 45br, 46cra, 46cb, 47tl, 48cla, 48bl(d), 50bl, 50br, 50 cla, 50–51, 51cl, 51cra, 51bl, 52bl, 57br, 61tr, 63tl, 63b, 264t, 293b, 337bl, 405bl, 405br, 406cl, 465 br; Biblioteca Nacional, Madrid *Felipe V* Luis Meléndez 67bl; Catedral de Sevilla *Ignacio de Loyola* Alonso Vázquez 120bl(d); *Camilo José Cela* Álvaro Delgado 1916 © DACS 1996 31br (d); *La Tertulia del Pombo* José Gutiérrez Solana 1920 © DACS 1996 289t; Museo de América, Madrid *Vista de Sevilla* Alonso Sánchez Coello 54cb; Museo de Bellas Artes, Seville *Sancho Panza y El Rucio* Moreno Carbonero 56ca; Museo de Bellas Artes, Valencia *Ecce Homo* Juan de Juanes 242lb; Museo Frankfurt *La Armada* 55tl; Museo de Historia de México *Hernán Cortés* S.E. Colane 54bl(d); Museo Histórico Militar, San Sebastián *Guerra Carlista* 59br(d); Museo Lázaro Galdiano, Madrid *Lope de Vega* Caxes 280tr; Museo Nacional del Teatro *Poster for "Yerma"* (FG Lorca) Juan Antonio Morales y José Caballero © DACS 1996 31tr; Museo del Prado, Madrid *La Rendición de Breda* Diego Velázquez 57cb, *El Tres de Mayo de 1808 en Madrid* Francisco de Goya y Lucientes 58-59(d), *La Reina María Luisa* María Francisco de Goya 58cla, *Carlos IV* Francisco de Goya 67bc, *Los Borrachos* Diego de Velázquez 282t, *Saturno devorando a un hijo* Francisco de Goya 284tr, *El Descendimiento* Van der Weyden 285b; Real Academia de Bellas Artes de San Fernando, Madrid *El Sueño del Caballero* Antonio de Pereda 56–57(d); AKG, London: 63cr; ALLSPORT: Stephen Munday 38cr; AQUILA: Adrian Hoskins 200cla, 200clb; Mike Lane 325clb; James Pearce 195bl; ARCAID: Paul Raftery 116bl; ARXIU MAS: 32bl, 33bl, 47crb, 52tl, 53cl, 53br(d); Museo del Prado, Madrid *Felipe II* Sánchez Coello 66br(d); Patrimonio Nacional 55cl, 55b(d).

JAUME BALANYA: 1634crb.

BIOFOTOS: Heather Angel 76cla, 76bl; BRIDGEMAN ART LIBRARY: *St Dominic enthroned as Abbot* Bartolomé Bermejo 284tl; Index/Museo del Prado, Madrid *Auto-da-fé in the Plaza Mayor* Francisco Rizi 264c; Musée des Beaux Artes, Berne *Colossus of Rhodes* Salvador Dalí 1954 DEMART PRO ARTE BV/DACS 1996 29tr; Museo del Prado, Madrid *Charles IV and his Family* Francisco de Goya y Lucientes 29cb, *The Adoration of the Shepherds* El Greco 282tc, *The Annunciation* Fra Angelico 282cb, *The Clothed Maja* Francisco de Goya y Lucientes 283t, *The Naked Maja* Francisco de Goya y Lucientes 283ca, *The Three Graces* Peter Paul Rubens 283cb, *The Martydom of St Philip* José de Ribera 283b; Museo Picasso, Barcelona *Las Meninas, Infanta Margarita* Pablo Ruiz Picasso 1957 © DACS 1996 28tl; *Children On the Beach* Joaquin y Bastida Sorolla © DACS 1996 285t; Phoenix Galleries, London *Rooftops, Fortna Luxt, Majorca* Frederick Gore 8-9; MICHAEL BUSSELLE: 197r, 199b, 200t.

CENTRO DE ARTE REINA SOFÍA: *Bertsolaris* Zubiaurre © DACS 1996 121cb, *Paisaje de Cadaqués* Salvador Dalí 1923 © DEMART PRO ARTE

BV/DACS 1996 288cb, *Accidente* Ponce de León 288b, *Toki-Egin (Homenaje a San Juan de la Cruz)* Eduardo Chillida 1952 © DACS 2002 289bl; Cephas: Mick Rock 25bl, 38t, 74t, 192tr, 192cl, 193tr, 322tr, 402tr, 403br, 403cr; Roy Stedall 403tr; Cocomfe: 613b; Bruce Coleman: Eric Crichton 194tr; José Luis González Grande 195tr; Werner Layer 325tl; Andy Purcell 27ca; Hans Reinhard 76crb; Norbert Schwirtz 195tl; Colin Varndell 195crb; Dee Conway: 407cl, 407cr; Sylvia Cordaiy Photo Library: Chris North 34tl; Joe Cornish: 24ca, 328, 346b, 354tr; Giancarlo Costa: 33bc; Cover: Genin Andrada 36b, 39b; Angel Bocalandro 624tl; Austin Catalan 64bl; Juan Echeverria 27cra, 37br, 521bl; Pepe Franco 182c; Quim Llenas 121ca, 305tl; Matías Nieto 39c; José R Platón 624tr; F J Rodríguez 121bl.

J D Dallet: 65tr,440tl, 575br.

Edex: 47bl, 387b; Edilesa: 334b; El Deseo: Pedro Almodóvar 295b; Paco Elvira: 26crb; EMI: Hispavox 358b; Equipo 28: 407t; ET Archive: 48br; Europa Press: 19c, 64tl, 65ca; Mary Evans Picture Library: 9t, 52cla, 59bl, 69t, 133r, 187t, 255r, 264bl, 317, 397r, 447b, 479, 529r, 611r; Explorer 406t; Eye Ubiquitous: James Davis Travel Photography 17t, 208br.

Firo Foto: 153c; 509t; Fototeca: IFEMA: Philipe Imbault 304br; Fundación César Manrique: 524br; Fundación Colección Thyssen-Bornemisza: *Madonna of Humility* Fra Angelico 173t, *La Virgen del Árbol* Petrus Christus 278tr, *Harlequin with a mirror* Pablo Ruiz Picasso 1923 © DACS 1996 278c, *Hotel Room* © Edward Hopper 1931 2/6bl, *Portrait of Baron H H H Thyssen Bornemisza* © Lucian Freud 1981–82 278br, *Venus y Cupido* Peter Paul Rubens (after 1629) 279tl, *Saint Jerome in the Wilderness* Tiziano c.1575 279tr, *Santa Casilda* Francisco de Zurbarán 1640–1645 279c, *Autumn Landscape in Oldenburg* Karl Schmidt-Rottluff 1907 © DACS 1996 279b; Fundació Joan Miró, Barcelona: *Flama en L'espai i dona nua* Joan Miró 1932 © ADAGP, Paris and DACS, London 1996 168t.

Godo Foto: 210b, 211t, 215t, 239b, 245t, 315bl; Ronald Grant Archive: *For a Few Dollars More* © United Artists 476b. © FMGB Guggenheim Bilbao Museoa: London 1999. Erica Barahona Ede. All rights reserved. Partial or total reproduction is prohibited 116t, 116br, 117t, 117b.

Robert Harding Picture Library: 15t, 137tr, 156ca, 168b, 169b, 239t, 293t, 487br; Julia Bayne 186–187; Nigel Blythe 15b, 145c; Bob Cousins 22clb; Robert Frerck 439tr; James Strachan 270tl; María Victoria Hernández: 509b; Hulton Deutsch Collection: 62b, 373br.

Iberdiapo: Triangle 500–501; The Image Bank, London: Andra Pistolesi 170; Mark Romanelli 136bl; Mathew Weinreb 157b; Images Colour Library: 629b; A.G.E Fotostock 24tr, 25tr, 26cra, 26ca, 26br, 32tr, 33ca, 36c, 38cl, 118b, 164, 183t, 183c, 201br, 223ca, 223br, 304t, 307c, 325cla, 331

tr, 403cl, 406br, 442b, 473t, 507t, 533tr, 625c, 625b; Horizon International 32-33, 136cb; Incafo: J A Fernández & C De Noriega 71bl, 121br; Juan Carlos Muñoz 378b, 473b; A Ortega 26bl; Index: 30tl, 44c, 44b, 45c, 45cb, 46tl, 49b, 50cra, 52br (d), 55tr, *Los Moriscos suplicando al rey Felipe III* 57c, 60–61, 61b, 63 cl, *Carlos I* 66tc, 66 bl, 67br, 467ca; Bridgeman, London 54cra; CCJ 19b; X Correa 44tl; *Garrote Vil* José Gutiérrez Solana 1931 © DACS 1996 61clb(d); Galería del Ateneo, Madrid *Lucio Anneo Seneca* Villodas 46cla (d); Galeria Illustres Catalonia, Barcelona *Joan Prim I Prats* J Cusachs 59ca(d); Image *José Zorilla* 31bl; Instituto Valencia de Don Juan, Madrid *Carlos V* Simón Bening 55crb; Iranzo 52cra; Mithra 48clb, 54br (d), 60tl; Museo de América, Madrid *Indio Yumbo y Frutas Tropicales* 55cra; Museo Lázaro Galdiano, Madrid *Lope de Vega* Anonymous 30c, *Félix Lope de Vega* Francisco Pacheco 56br(d); Museo Municipal, Madrid *Fiesta en la Plaza Mayor de Madrid* Juan de la Corte 57tl; Museo del Prado, Madrid *Ascensión de un globo Montgolfier en Madrid* Antonio Carnicero 58cra(d), *José Moreño Conde de Floridablanca* Francisco de Goya 58br(d), *Flota del Rey Carlos III de España* A Joli 59tl(d); National Maritime Museum, Greenwich *Batalla de Trafalgar* Chalmers 58cb; A Noé 52cb; Palacio del Senado, Madrid *Alfonso X "El Sabio"* Matías Moreno 30b(d), *Rendición de Granada* Francisco Pradilla 52–53(d); Patrimonio Nacional 47br; Private Collection, Madrid *Pedro Calderón de la Barca* Antonio de Pereda 57bl(d); Real Academia de Bellas Artes de San Fernando, Madrid *San Diego de Alcalá dando de comer a los pobres* Bartolomé Esteban Murillo 57ca(d), *Fernando VII* Francisco de Goya 67tl(d), *Isabel II* 67tr, *José Maria de Pereda* Francisco Goya 22tl; Tovy 65cb; Nick Inman: 194bc, 243tr, 612t, 615cb, 622tr, 631b; Institut Turístic Valencià: 235br.

César Justel: 335b.

Anthony King: 281t.

L'Estartit Tourist Board: 207c; Life File Photographic: 207c; Tony Abbott 324cla; Xavier Catalan 137cb; Emma Lee 137cra, 402tl, 635tr; Neil Lukas: 440cb, 440b.

Magnum: S Franklin 64cb; Jean Gaumy 64br, 65tl; Imagen MAS, Leon: 337tr; John Miller: 196l, 478–479, 481cb, 505r, 514b, 519b, 524t, 525b; Museo Arqueológico De Villena: 44–45; Museu Nacional D'art De Catalunya: Museu d'Art Modern *El Tombant del Loing* Alfred Sisley 151t; Museo Nacional Del Prado: *El Jardín de las Delicias* 282b; Museu Arqueològic De Barcelona: 167c; Museu Picasso Barcelona: *Auto Retrato* Pablo Ruiz Picasso 1899–1900 © DACS 1996 148b; *Las Meninas* Pablo Ruiz Picasso 1957 © DAC S 1996 149b.

Naturpress: Oriol Alamany 27bl; J L Calvo & J R Montero 325crb; José Luis Grande 441b; Walter Kwaternik 26clb, 27bc, 324cra, 325cra; Francisco Márquez 441cb, 398bl; Aurelio Martín 27br, Sebastián Martín 325bc; José A Martínez 76tr,

Toledo *El Entierro del Conde de Orgaz* El Greco 28ca; *Portrait II* Joan Miró 1938 © ADAGP, Paris and DACS, London 1996 288t; Monasterio Santa Maria, Barcelona *Virgen con Niño* Ferrer Bassa 28clb(d); Museo de Bellas Artes, Cádiz *San Bruno en Éxtasis* Zurbarán 443tr; Museo Casa Gredo, Toledo *Carlos II* Miranda Correño 66tr(d); Museo del Ejército, Madrid *Isabel II* Madrazo 58tl; Museo Municipal de Bellas Artes, Tenerife *Retrato de Boabdil o Abu Abdala* 53tr(d); Museo Nacional de Escultura, Valladolid *Natividad* Berruguete 349tr; Museo Naval, Madrid *Desembarco de Colón* José Garnelo 53tl; Museo Naval Laminas, Madrid *Carabelas de Colón* Monleón 53bl(d); Museo del Prado, Madrid *El Salvador* José de Ribera 28crb, *Las Meninas o Familia de Felipe V* Diego Velázquez 28–29, *Felipe III* Pedro A Vidal 56bl, *Felipe V* 58bl, Guernica Pablo Ruiz Picasso 1937 © DACS 1996, 62–63, *Felipe IV* Diego Velázquez 66bc(d), *Bodegón* Zurbarán 284b, *David Vencedor de Goliat* Caravaggio 285c; Palacio Moncloa *Interior de la Catedral de Santiago* Villaamil Pérez 78–79; *Mujer en Azul* Pablo Ruiz Picasso 1901 © DACS 1996 288ca; Private Colection, Palma *Oleo Sobre Lienzo* Joan Miró 1932 © ADAGP, Paris and DACS, London 29ca; Real Academia de Bellas Artes de San Fernando *Fray Pedro Machado* Zurbarán 271tr.

PANOS PICTURES: Adrian Evans 64–65; JOSÉ M PÉREZ DE AYALA: 26cr, 440tr, 440ca, 441t, 441ca; THE PHOTOGRAPHERS LIBRARY: 499tr; PICTURES COLOUR LIBRARY: 18b, 26tr, 158-159, 248b, 398cl; PRISMA 60ca, 61crb, 62ca, 62cb, 63tr, 93t, 136br, 229c, 240t, 307t, 435, 492br, 508cl, 515clb, 515cb, 515crb, 515bl, 519t, 527bl, 527br; *Franco* Aguiar 67tr; *El ingenioso hidalgo Don Quixote de la Mancha* 1605 Ricardo Balaca 377br; Diputación de Madrid *Francisco Bahamonde Franco* Enrique Segura 62tl; Domènech & Azpiliqueta 114t; Albert Heras 182b; Marcel Jaquet 507b, 517b; Hans Lohr 459b; *Los Niños de la Concha* Bartolomé Esteban Murillo 29bl(d); Museo de Arte Moderno, Barcelona *Pío Baroja* Ramón Casas 60cb(d); Museo de Bellas Artes, Bilbao *Condesa Mathieu de Noailles* Ignacio Zuloaga y Zubaleta © DACS 1996 114b; Museo de Bellas Artes, Zaragoza *Príncipe de Viana* José Moreno Carbonero 126b (d); Mateu 185c; Palacio del Senado, Madrid *Alfonso XIII* Aquino © DACS 1996 67cr; Patrimonio Nacional Palacio de Riofrío,

Segovia: 60br; *Auto Retrato* Pablo Ruiz Picasso 1907 © Succession Picasso DACS 1996 61ca; Marta Povo 626t; Real Academia de Bellas Artes de San Fernando, Madrid *Las Bodas de Camacho* José Moreno Carbonero 31tl(d), *Procession of the Flagellants* Francisco de Goya 264br(d); *Emilio Castelar* Joaquin Sorolla © DACS 1996 60bl. REX FEATURES: Sipa Press 205cb; © ROYAL MUSUEM OF SCOTLAND: Michel Zabé 43t.

MARÍA ÁNGELES SÁNCHEZ: 34tr, 35b, 39t, 75t, 94cl, 14l, 280tl, 294b, 369c, 387tr, 508t, 508cr, 508b, 512c, 523t; SCIENCE PHOTO LIBRARY: Geospace 10l; 6 TOROS 6: 33cb; SPANISH TOURIST BOARD: 245c; SPECTRUM COLOUR LIBRARY: 132–133, 136tr, 528–529; STOCKPHOTOS, Madrid: Marcelo Brodsky 36t; Campillo 625t; Heinz Hebeisen 37bl; Mikael Helsing 624b, 314tl; David Hornback 17b; Javier Sánchez 314tl; Werner Otto Reisefotografie 629t; JAMES STRACHAN: 281b, 292t, 292c, 294t; TONY STONE WORLDWIDE: Doug Armand 16b; Jon Bradley 304bl; Robert Everts 422ca.

VISIONS OF ANDALUCÍA: Michelle Chaplow 406–407; J D Dallet 379tr; VU: Christina García Rodero 2–3, 16c, 34b, 35c, 35t, 128cl, 246–247, 350l, 413cr.

CHARLIE WAITE: 470–471; WERNER FORMAN ARCHIVE: Museo de Arte Hispanomusulmán 48t; Museum of Catalan Art, Barcelona 326tl; National Maritime Museum, Greenwich 48cr; ALAN WILLIAMS: 74b; PETER WILSON: 254–255, 272, 444b, 445c, 451t, 457t; WORLD PICTURES: 305c, 488t. ZEFA: 1.

Front endpaper: All special photography except JOE CORNISH cbl; JOHN MILLER tr; SPECTRUM COLOUR LIBRARY ca; PETER WILSON cbr.

JACKET
Front - DK PICTURE LIBRARY: Max Alexander cr; GETTY IMAGES: Michelle Chaplow c; Shaun Egan bl; Robert Everts main image. Back - CORBIS: Bob Krist t; GETTY IMAGES b. Spine - GETTY IMAGES: Robert Everts.

All other images © Dorling Kindersley. For further information see www.DKimages.com

Phrase Book

IN AN EMERGENCY

Help!	¡Socorro!	soh-**koh**-roh
Stop!	¡Pare!	**pah**-reh
Call a doctor!	¡Llame a un médico!	yah-meh ah oon meh-dee-koh
Call an ambulance!	¡Llame a una ambulancia!	yah-meh ah oonah ahm-boo-**lahn**-thee-ah
Call the police!	¡Llame a la policía!	yah-meh ah lah poh-lee-**thee**-ah
Call the fire brigade!	¡Llame a los bomberos!	yah-meh ah lohs bohm-**beh**-rohs
Where is the nearest telephone?	¿Dónde está el teléfono más próximo?	dohn-deh ehs-**tah** ehl teh-**leh**-foh-noh mahs prohx-ee-moh
Where is the nearest hospital?	¿Dónde está el hospital más próximo?	dohn-deh ehs-**tah** ehl ohs-pee-**tahl** mahs prohx-ee-moh

COMMUNICATION ESSENTIALS

Yes	Sí	see
No	No	noh
Please	Por favor	pohr fah-**vohr**
Thank you	Gracias	**grah**-thee-ahs
Excuse me	Perdone	pehr-**doh**-neh
Hello	Hola	**oh**-lah
Goodbye	Adiós	ah-dee-**ohs**
Goodnight	Buenas noches	**bweh**-nahs **noh**-chehs
Morning	La mañana	lah mah-**nyah**-nah
Afternoon	La tarde	lah **tahr**-deh
Evening	La tarde	lah **tahr**-deh
Yesterday	Ayer	ah-**yehr**
Today	Hoy	oy
Tomorrow	Mañana	mah-**nya**-nah
Here	Aquí	ah-**kee**
There	Allí	ah-**yee**
What?	¿Qué?	keh
When?	¿Cuándo?	**kwahn**-doh
Why?	¿Por qué?	pohr-**keh**
Where?	¿Dónde?	**dohn**-deh

USEFUL PHRASES

How are you?	¿Cómo está usted?	**koh**-moh ehs-**tah** oos-**tehd**
Very well, thank you.	Muy bien, gracias.	mwee bee-**ehn grah**-thee-ahs
Pleased to meet you.	Encantado de conocerle.	ehn-kahn-**tah**-doh deh koh-noh-**thehr**-leh
See you soon.	Hasta pronto.	ahs-tah **prohn**-toh
That's fine.	Está bien.	ehs-**tah** bee-**ehn**
Where is/are ...?	¿Dónde está/están ...?	**dohn**-deh ehs-**tah**/ehs-**tahn**
How far is it to ...?	¿Cuántos metros/ kilómetros hay de aquí a ...?	**kwahn**-tohs meh-trohs/kee-**loh**-meh-trohs eye deh ah-**kee** ah
Which way to ...?	¿Por dónde se va a ...?	pohr **dohn**-deh seh bah ah
Do you speak English?	¿Habla inglés?	**ah**-blah een-**glehs**
I don't understand	No comprendo	noh kohm-**prehn**-doh
Could you speak more slowly please?	¿Puede hablar más despacio por favor?	pweh-deh ah-**blahr** mahs dehs-pah-thee-oh pohr fah-**vohr**
I'm sorry.	Lo siento.	loh see-**ehn**-toh

USEFUL WORDS

big	grande	**grahn**-deh
small	pequeño	peh-**keh**-nyoh
hot	caliente	kah-lee-**ehn**-teh
cold	frío	**free**-oh
good	bueno	**bweh**-noh
bad	malo	**mah**-loh
enough	bastante	bahs-**tahn**-teh
well	bien	bee-**ehn**
open	abierto	ah-bee-**ehr**-toh
closed	cerrado	thehr-**rah**-doh
left	izquierda	eeth-key-**ehr**-dah
right	derecha	deh-**reh**-chah
straight on	todo recto	toh-doh **rehk**-toh
near	cerca	**thehr**-kah
far	lejos	**leh**-hohs
up	arriba	ah-**ree**-bah
down	abajo	ah-**bah**-hoh

early	temprano	tehm-**prah**-noh
late	tarde	**tahr**-deh
entrance	entrada	ehn-**trah**-dah
exit	salida	sah-**lee**-dah
toilet	lavabos, servicios	lah-**vah**-bohs, sehr-**bee**-thee-ohs
more	más	mahs
less	menos	**meh**-nohs

SHOPPING

How much does this cost?	¿Cuánto cuesta esto?	**kwahn**-toh **kwehs**-tah ehs-toh
I would like ...	Me gustaría ...	meh goos-ta-**ree**-ah
Do you have?	¿Tienen?	tee-**yeh**-nehn
I'm just looking, thank you.	Sólo estoy mirando, gracias.	soh-loh ehs-**toy** mee-**rahn**-doh **grah**-thee-ahs
Do you take credit cards?	¿Aceptan tarjetas de crédito?	ah-**thehp**-tahn tahr-**heh**-tahs deh **kreh**-dee-toh
What time do you open?	¿A qué hora abren?	ah keh oh-rah **ah**-brehn
What time do you close?	¿A qué hora cierran?	ah keh oh-rah thee-**ehr**-rahn
This one.	Éste	**ehs**-teh
That one.	Ése	**eh**-seh
expensive	caro	**kahr**-oh
cheap	barato	bah-**rah**-toh
size, clothes	talla	**tah**-yah
size, shoes	número	**noo**-mehr-oh
white	blanco	**blahn**-koh
black	negro	**neh**-groh
red	rojo	**roh**-hoh
yellow	amarillo	ah-mah-**ree**-yoh
green	verde	**behr**-deh
blue	azul	ah-**thool**
antiques shop	la tienda de antigüedades	lah tee-**ehn**-dah deh ahn-tee-gweh-**dah**-dehs
bakery	la panadería	lah pah-nah-deh-**ree**-ah
bank	el banco	ehl **bahn**-koh
book shop	la librería	lah lee-breh-**ree**-ah
butcher's	la carnicería	lah kahr-nee-theh-**ree**-ah
cake shop	la pastelería	lah pahs-teh-leh-**ree**-ah
chemist's	la farmacia	lah fahr-**mah**-thee-ah
fishmonger's	la pescadería	lah pehs-kah-deh-**ree**-ah
greengrocer's grocer's	la frutería la tienda de comestibles	lah froo-teh-**ree**-ah lah tee-**yehn**-dah deh koh-mehs-**tee**-blehs
hairdresser's	la peluquería	lah peh-loo-keh-**ree**-ah
market	el mercado	ehl mehr-**kah**-doh
newsagent's	el kiosko de prensa	ehl kee-**ohs**-koh deh **prehn**-sah
post office	la oficina de correos	lah oh-fee-**thee**-nah deh kohr-**reh**-ohs
shoe shop	la zapatería	lah thah-pah-teh-**ree**-ah
supermarket	el supermercado	ehl soo-pehr-mehr-**kah**-doh
tobacconist	el estanco	ehl ehs-**tahn**-koh
travel agency	la agencia de viajes	lah ah-**hehn**-thee-ah deh bee-**ah**-hehs

SIGHTSEEING

art gallery	el museo de arte	ehl moo-**seh**-oh deh **ahr**-teh
cathedral	la catedral	lah kah-teh-**drahl**
church	la iglesia la basílica	lah ee-**gleh**-see-ah lah bah-**see**-lee-kah
garden	el jardín	ehl hahr-**deen**
library	la biblioteca	lah bee-blee-oh-**teh**-kah
museum	el museo	ehl moo-**seh**-oh
tourist information office	la oficina de turismo	lah oh-fee-**thee**-nah deh too-**rees**-moh
town hall	el ayuntamiento	ehl ah-yoon-tah-mee-**ehn**-toh
closed for holiday	cerrado por vacaciones	thehr-**rah**-doh pohr bah-kah-thee-**oh**-nehs
bus station	la estación de autobuses	lah ehs-tah-thee-**ohn** deh owtoh-**boo**-sehs
railway station	la estación de trenes	lah ehs-tah-thee-**ohn** deh **treh**-nehs

STAYING IN A HOTEL

Do you have a vacant room?	¿Tienen una habitación libre?	tee-**eh**-nehn oo-nah ah-bee-tah-thee-**ohn lee**-breh
double room	habitación doble	ah-bee-tah-thee-**ohn doh**-bleh
with double bed	con cama de matrimonio	kohn kah-mah deh mah-tree-**moh**-nee-oh
twin room	habitación con dos camas	ah-bee-tah-thee-**ohn** kohn dohs **kah**-mahs
single room	habitación individual	ah-bee-tah-thee-**ohn** een-dee-vee-doo-**ahl**
room with a bath	habitación con baño	ah-bee-tah-thee-**ohn** kohn bah-nyoh
shower	ducha	**doo**-chah
porter	el botones	ehl boh-**toh**-nehs
key	la llave	lah **yah**-veh
I have a reservation.	Tengo una habitación reservada.	tehn-goh **oo**-na ah-bee-tah-thee-**ohn** reh-sehr-**bah**-dah

EATING OUT

Have you got a table for . . .?	¿Tienen mesa para . . .?	tee-**eh**-nehn meh-sah pah-**rah**
I want to reserve a table.	Quiero reservar una mesa.	kee-eh-roh reh-sehr-**bahr** oo-nah **meh**-sah
The bill please.	La cuenta por favor.	lah **kwehn**-tah pohr fah-**vohr**
I am a vegetarian	Soy vegetariano/a	soy beh-heh-tah-ree-**ah**-no/na
waitress/	camarera/	kah-mah-**reh**-rah
waiter	camarero	kah-mah-**reh**-roh
menu	la carta	lah **kahr**-tah
fixed-price menu	menú del día	meh-**noo** dehl **dee**-ah
wine list	la carta de vinos	lah **kahr**-tah deh **bee**-nohs
glass	un vaso	oon **bah**-soh
bottle	una botella	oo-nah boh-**teh**-yah
knife	un cuchillo	oon koo-**chee**-yoh
fork	un tenedor	oon teh-neh-**dohr**
spoon	una cuchara	oo-nah koo-**chah**-rah
breakfast	el desayuno	ehl deh-sah-**yoo**-noh
lunch	la comida/ el almuerzo	lah koh-**mee**-dah/ ehl ahl-**mwehr**-thoh
dinner	la cena	lah **theh**-nah
main course	el primer plato	ehl pree-**mehr plah**-toh
starters	los entremeses	lohs ehn-treh-**meh**-sehs
dish of the day	el plato del día	ehl **plah**-toh dehl **dee**-ah
coffee	el café	ehl kah-**feh**
rare	poco hecho	**poh**-koh **eh**-choh
medium	medio hecho	**meh**-dee-oh **eh**-choh
well done	muy hecho	mwee **eh**-choh

MENU DECODER

al horno	ahl **ohr**-noh	baked
asado	ah-**sah**-doh	roast
el aceite	ah-**thee-eh**-teh	oil
las aceitunas	ah-theh-**toon**-ahs	olives
el agua mineral	ah-gwa mee-neh-**rahl**	mineral water
sin gas/con gas	seen gas/kohn gas	still/sparkling
el ajo	**ah**-hoh	garlic
el arroz	ahr-**rohth**	rice
el azúcar	ah-**thoo**-kahr	sugar
la carne	**kahr**-neh	meat
la cebolla	theh-**boh**-yah	onion
la cerveza	thehr-**beh**-thah	beer
el cerdo	**therh**-doh	pork
el chocolate	choh-koh-**lah**-teh	chocolate
el chorizo	choh-**ree**-thoh	red sausage
el cordero	kohr-**deh**-roh	lamb
el fiambre	fee-**ahm**-breh	cold meat
frito	**free**-toh	fried
la fruta	**froo**-tah	fruit
los frutos secos	froo-tohs **seh**-kohs	nuts
las gambas	**gahm**-bahs	prawns
el helado	eh-**lah**-doh	ice cream
el huevo	oo-**eh**-voh	egg
el jamón serrano	hah-**mohn** sehr-**rah**-noh	cured ham

el jerez	heh-**rehz**	sherry
la langosta	lahn-**gohs**-tah	lobster
la leche	**leh**-cheh	milk
el limón	lee-**mohn**	lemon
la limonada	lee-moh-**nah**-dah	lemonade
la mantequilla	mahn-teh-**kee**-yah	butter
la manzana	mahn-**thah**-nah	apple
los mariscos	mah-**rees**-kohs	seafood
la menestra	meh-**nehs**-trah	vegetable stew
la naranja	nah-**rahn**-hah	orange
el pan	**pahn**	bread
el pastel	pahs-**tehl**	cake
las patatas	pah-**tah**-tahs	potatoes
el pescado	pehs-**kah**-doh	fish
la pimienta	pee-mee-**yehn**-tah	pepper
el plátano	**plah**-tah-noh	banana
el pollo	**poh**-yoh	chicken
el postre	**pohs**-treh	dessert
el queso	**keh**-soh	cheese
la sal	sahl	salt
las salchichas	sahl-**chee**-chahs	sausages
la salsa	**sahl**-sah	sauce
seco	**seh**-koh	dry
el solomillo	soh-loh-**mee**-yoh	sirloin
la sopa	**soh**-pah	soup
la tarta	**tahr**-tah	pie/cake
el té	teh	tea
la ternera	tehr-**neh**-rah	beef
las tostadas	tohs-**tah**-dahs	toast
el vinagre	bee-**nah**-greh	vinegar
el vino blanco	**bee**-noh **blahn**-koh	white wine
el vino rosado	**bee**-noh roh-**sah**-doh	rosé wine
el vino tinto	**bee**-noh **teen**-toh	red wine

NUMBERS

0	cero	**theh**-roh
1	uno	**oo**-noh
2	dos	dohs
3	tres	trehs
4	cuatro	**kwa**-troh
5	cinco	**theen**-koh
6	seis	says
7	siete	**see**-eh-teh
8	ocho	**oh**-choh
9	nueve	**nweh**-veh
10	diez	dee-**ehth**
11	once	**ohn**-theh
12	doce	**doh**-theh
13	trece	**treh**-theh
14	catorce	kah-**tohr**-theh
15	quince	**keen**-theh
16	dieciséis	dee-eh-thee-**seh-ees**
17	diecisiete	dee-eh-thee-see-**eh**-teh
18	dieciocho	dee-eh-thee-**oh**-choh
19	diecinueve	dee-eh-thee-**nweh**-veh
20	veinte	**beh**-een-teh
21	veintiuno	beh-een-tee-**oo**-noh
22	veintidós	beh-een-tee-**dohs**
30	treinta	**treh**-een-tah
31	treinta y uno	treh-een-tah ee **oo**-noh
40	cuarenta	kwah-**rehn**-tah
50	cincuenta	theen-**kwehn**-tah
60	sesenta	seh-**sehn**-tah
70	setenta	seh-**tehn**-tah
80	ochenta	oh-**chehn**-tah
90	noventa	noh-**vehn**-tah
100	cien	thee-**ehn**
101	ciento uno	thee-**ehn**-toh **oo**-noh
102	ciento dos	thee-**ehn**-toh dohs
200	doscientos	dohs-thee-**ehn**-tohs
500	quinientos	khee-nee-**ehn**-tohs
700	setecientos	seh-teh-thee-**ehn**-tohs
900	novecientos	noh-veh-thee-**ehn** tohs
1,000	mil	meel
1,001	mil uno	meel **oo**-noh

TIME

one minute	un minuto	oon mee-**noo**-toh
one hour	una hora	**oo**-na **oh**-rah
half an hour	media hora	**meh**-dee-a **oh**-rah
Monday	lunes	**loo**-nehs
Tuesday	martes	**mahr**-tehs
Wednesday	miércoles	mee-**ehr**-koh-lehs
Thursday	jueves	hoo-**weh**-vehs
Friday	viernes	bee-**ehr**-nehs
Saturday	sábado	**sah**-bah-doh
Sunday	domingo	doh-**meen**-goh

Barcelona Transport Map

The metro is the quickest way of getting around Barcelona. It runs from 5am–11pm Mon–Thu; 5am–1am Fri and Sat; and 6:30am–12pm Sun. In the stations the lines are identified by number and colour; platform signs display the name of the last station on the line. You can buy a one-journey ticket (*billete*) or a discounted, ten-trip *tarjeta*: the T-1, which is valid for the metro only; or the T-2, which is valid for the metro and the buses. Tickets for the interconnecting FF CC suburban rail network, which runs from the city centre out to the airport and to Barcelona's environs, and for the funiculars, must be purchased separately.

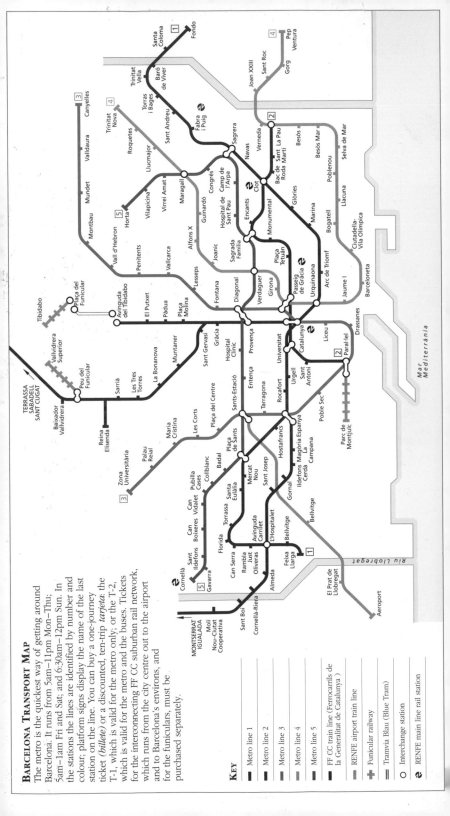

Key

▬▬	Metro line 1
▬▬	Metro line 2
▬▬	Metro line 3
▬▬	Metro line 4
▬▬	Metro line 5
▬▬	FF CC train line (Ferrocarrils de la Generalitat de Catalunya)
▬▬	RENFE airport train line
✛✛	Funicular railway
‖‖	Tramvia Blau (Blue Tram)
○	Interchange station
🚄	RENFE main line rail station